10th Conference on Lexical and Computational Semantics (*SEM 2021)

Held online due to COVID-19

Bangkok, Thailand
5 – 6 August 2021

ISBN: 978-1-7138-3388-8

Printed from e-media with permission by:

Curran Associates, Inc.
57 Morehouse Lane
Red Hook, NY 12571

CURRAN ASSOCIATES INC. proceedings .com

Some format issues inherent in the e-media version may also appear in this print version.

Association for Computational Linguistics
209 N. Eighth Street
Stroudsburg, Pennsylvania 18360

Phone: 1-570-476-8006
Fax: 1-570-476-0860

acl@aclweb.org

Additional copies of this publication are available from:

Curran Associates, Inc.
57 Morehouse Lane
Red Hook, NY 12571 USA
Phone: 845-758-0400
Fax: 845-758-2633
Email: curran@proceedings.com
Web: www.proceedings.com

* SEM 2021

The 10th Conference on Lexical and Computational Semantics

Proceedings of the Conference

August 5 - 6, 2021
Bangkok, Thailand (online)

Message from the General Chair and the Program Chairs

Welcome to ***SEM 2021**, the Joint Conference on Lexical and Computational Semantics! The conference celebrates a small jubilee, with its **10th** edition, and we are pleased to present this volume containing the accepted long and short papers.

*SEM 2021 was held as a virtual conference following ACL-IJCNLP 2021, on August 5-6, 2021, due to the exceptional circumstances imposed by the COVID-19 pandemic.

Since its first edition in 2012, *SEM has become a major venue to present recent advances in all areas of lexical and computational semantics, including semantic representations, semantic processing, multilingual semantics, and others. *SEM is sponsored by SIGLEX, the ACL Special Interest Group on the Lexicon.

*SEM 2021 received 78 submissions in 10 areas:

- Theoretical and formal semantics
- Sentiment analysis and argument mining
- Semantics in NLP applications
- Semantic composition and sentence-level semantics
- Resources and evaluation
- Psycholinguistics, cognitive linguistics and semantic processing
- Multilinguality
- Lexical semantics and word representations
- Commonsense reasoning and natural language understanding

We compiled an exciting program across all these areas. This year saw a particularly strong batch of submissions; finally, **30** papers were accepted – **21** long papers and **9** short papers.

The submitted papers were carefully evaluated by a program committee led by 20 area chairs, who coordinated a panel of 174 reviewers. Each submission was reviewed by three reviewers, who were encouraged to discuss any divergence in evaluations. The papers in each area were subsequently assessed by the area chairs, who added meta-reviews to explain their accept/reject suggestions. The final selection was made by the program co-chairs after an independent check of all the reviews, meta-reviews, and discussions with the area chairs. The reviewers' recommendations were also used to shortlist a set of papers nominated for the Best Paper Award.

We are also very excited to have two excellent keynote speakers: **Diyi Yang** (Georgia Institute of Technology) discussing the inclusion of social factors into natural language processing models, and **Felix Hill** (DeepMind) talking about learning embodied language.

We are deeply thankful to all area chairs and reviewers for their invaluable help in the selection of the program, for their readiness in engaging in thoughtful discussions about individual papers, and for providing valuable feedback to the authors. We are grateful to our Publicity chair, Yashar Mehdad (Facebook AI), who set up and regularly updated *SEM's website and publicized it through social media. We thank the Publication Chair, Mark-Christoph Müller (HITS), for his help with the compilation of the proceedings, and the ACL-IJCNLP 2021 workshop organizers for all the valuable help and support with organisational aspects of the conference. Finally, we thank all our authors and presenters for making *SEM 2021 such an exciting event. We hope you will find the content of these proceedings as well as the program of *SEM 2021 enjoyable, interesting and inspirational!

Vivi Nastase and **Ivan Vulić**, Program Co-Chairs

Lun-Wei Ku, General Chair

*SEM 2021 Organizing Committee

General Chair

Lun-Wei Ku, Academia Sinica

Program Chairs

Vivi Nastase, University of Zürich

Ivan Vulić, University of Cambridge & PolyAI

Publicity Chair

Yashar Mehdad, Facebook AI

Publication Chair

Mark-Christoph Müller, Heidelberg Institute for Theoretical Studies

Area Chairs

Lexical semantics and word representations

Goran Glavaš, University of Mannheim
Ryohei Sasano, Nagoya University

Semantic composition and sentence representations

Raffaella Bernardi, University of Trento
Daniel Hershcovich, University of Copenhagen

Discourse, dialogue, and generation

Asad B. Sayeed, University of Gothenburg
Thang Vu, University of Stuttgart

Multilinguality

Johannes Bjerva, Aalborg University
Edoardo Maria Ponti, Mila Quebec AI Institute & McGill University

Psycholinguistics and semantic processing

Cecilia Ovesdotter Alm, Rochester Institute of Technology
Emily Prud'hommeaux, Boston College

Resources and evaluation

Nitin Madnani, ETS
Alla Rozovskaya, CUNY

Theoretical and formal semantics

Kilian Evang, University of Düsseldorf

Commonsense reasoning and natural language understanding

Antoine Bosselut, Stanford University

Eunsol Choi, University of Texas at Austin

Sentiment analysis and argument mining

Philipp Cimiano, University of Bielefeld

Thamar Solorio, University of Houston

Semantics in NLP applications

Valerio Basile, University of Turin

Ivan Habernal, TU Darmstadt

Els Lefever, Ghent University

Program Committee

Amine Abdaoui, Mostafa Hany Mohamed Anwar Abdou, Rodrigo Agerri, Pooja Aggarwal, Ameeta Agrawal, Alan Akbik, Marianna Apidianaki, Ron Artstein, Ehsaneddin Asgari, Giosuè Baggio, Sivaji Bandyopadhyay, Forrest Sheng Bao, Francesco Barbieri, Jeremy Barnes, Pierpaolo Basile, Roberto Basili, Gábor Berend, Sabine Bergler, Jean-Philippe Bernardy, Eduardo Blanco, Michael Bloodgood, marianna bolognesi, Johan Bos, Chloé Braud, Paul Buitelaar, Aoife Cahill, Erik Cambria, Giuseppe Castellucci, Hande Celikkanat, Tuhin Chakrabarty, Franklin Chang, Stergios Chatzikyriakidis, Aditi Chaudhary, Muhao Chen, Emmanuele Chersoni, Christos Christodoulopoulos, Oana Cocarascu, Robin Cooper, Bonaventura Coppola, Danilo Croce, Walter Daelemans, Marco Del Tredici, Rodolfo Delmonte, Gaël Dias, Haibo Ding, Lucia Donatelli, Jakub Dotlacil, Katrin Erk, Arash Eshghi, Luis Espinosa Anke, Mariano Felice, Stella Frank, Diego Frassinelli, Jonathan Ginzburg, Voula Giouli, Max Glockner, Dagmar Gromann, Kristina Gulordava, Binod Gyawali, Udo Hahn, Christian Hardmeier, Bradley Hauer, Yoshihiko Hayashi, Pedram Hosseini, Xinyu Hua, Patrick Huber, Julie Hunter, Jena D. Hwang, Nancy Ide, Kokil Jaidka, Salud María Jiménez Zafra, Hiroshi Kanayama, Jenna Kanerva, Mladen Karan, Omid Kashefi, Roman Klinger, Thomas Kober, Elena Kochkina, Grzegorz Kondrak, Alexander König, Germán Kruszewski, Dan Lassiter, Anne Lauscher, Alessandro Lenci, Haoran Li, Xiang Lorraine Li, Robert Litschko, Yang Liu, Wei Lu, Emma Manning, Alda Mari, Edison Marrese-Taylor, Eugenio Martínez-Cámara, Jonathan May, Sahisnu Mazumder, John P. McCrae, Nick McKenna, Julian Michael, Rada Mihalcea, Tristan Miller, Koji Mineshima, Amita Misra, Richard Moot, Gaku Morio, Larry Moss, Philippe Muller, Nona Naderi, Preslav Nakov, Diarmuid Ó Séaghdha, Robert Östling, Alexis Palmer, Debjit Paul, Paolo Pedinotti, Maxime Peyrard, Sandro Pezzelle, Jonas Pfeiffer, Nghia The Pham, Manfred Pinkal, Barbara Plank, Adam Poliak, Maja Popović, Christopher Potts, Matthew Purver, Alessandro Raganato, Carlos Ramisch, Michael Regan, Christian Retoré, German Rigau, Gil Rocha, Irene Russo, Farig Sadeque, Mehrnoosh Sadrzadeh, Marina Santini, Bianca Scarlini, Yves Scherrer, David Schlangen, Dominik Schlechtweg, Sabine Schulte im Walde, Weiyan Shi, Vered Shwartz, Luca Soldaini, Xingyi Song, Vivek Srikumar, Kevin Stowe, Sara Stymne, Yoshihiko Suhara, Aarne Talman, Alexandros Tantos, Andon Tchechmedjiev, Gaurav Singh Tomar, Samia Touileb, Rocco Tripodi, Sowmya Vajjala, Tim Van de Cruys, Rossella Varvara, Raúl Vázquez, Noortje Venhuizen, Yannick Versley, Serena Villata, Aline Villavicencio, Veronika Vincze, Ekaterina Vylomova, Jin Wang, Charles Welch, Matthijs Westera, Genta Indra Winata, Grégoire Winterstein, Shijie Wu, Peng Xu, Dong Yu, Roberto Zamparelli, Alessandra Zarcone, Torsten Zesch, Shuai Zhang.

Invited Talk: Why Do Embodied Language Learning?

Felix Hill
Deep Mind

Abstract: In this talk, I'll give some good reasons to study language learning and processing in the context of an embodied or situated agent. Learning in an embodied context is fundamentally different from other ML settings. Working out how to perceive and move in addition to understanding and using language can be a substantial additional burden for the learner. However, I will show that it can also bring important benefits. The embodied learner sees the world from an egocentric perspective, is necessarily located at a specific place at a given time, exerts some control over the learning data it encounters, and confronts face-on the relationship between language and the physical world. These factors place strong constraints on the learner's experience, which can in turn lead to more human-like learning outcomes. Our findings suggest that embodied learning may play an important role in convincingly replicating human linguistic intuitions and behaviours in a machine.

Bio: Felix Hill is a Research Scientist at DeepMind, and leads a team focusing on grounded language learning and processing. He has a Masters degree in pure mathematics from the University of Oxford, and a Masters in Psycholinguistics and PhD in Computer Science from the University of Cambridge. His graduate studies focused on representation-learning in neural network models of language, on which he worked with many great collaborators including Ivan Vulić, Douwe Kiela, Yoshua Bengio, Kyunghyun Cho and Jason Weston. At DeepMind, he has focused on developing better learning, meta-learning, reasoning, memory systems and generalization in agents that explore and interact with simulated environments.

Invited Talk: Seven Social Factors in Natural Language Processing: Theory and Practice

Diyi Yang
Georgia Institute of Technology

Abstract: Recently, natural language processing (NLP) has had increasing success and produced extensive industrial applications. Despite being sufficient to enable these applications, current NLP systems often ignore the social part of language, e.g., who says it, in what context, for what goals. In this talk, we take a closer look at social factors in language via a new theory taxonomy, and its interplay with computational methods via two lines of work. The first one studies what makes language persuasive by introducing a semi-supervised method to leverage hierarchical structures in text to recognize persuasion strategies in good-faith requests. The second part demonstrates how various structures in conversations can be utilized to generate better summaries for everyday interaction. We conclude by discussing several open-ended questions towards how to build socially aware language technologies, with the hope of getting closer to the goal of human-like language understanding.

Bio: Diyi Yang is an assistant professor in the School of Interactive Computing at Georgia Tech. She is broadly interested in Computational Social Science, and Natural Language Processing. Diyi received her PhD from the Language Technologies Institute at Carnegie Mellon University. Her work has been published at leading NLP/HCI conferences, and also resulted in multiple award nominations from EMNLP, ICWSM, SIGCHI and CSCW. She is named as a Forbes 30 under 30 in Science, a recipient of IEEE AI 10 to Watch, and has received faculty research awards from Amazon, Facebook, JPMorgan Chase, and Salesforce.

Table of Contents

Conference Program

Semantics in NLP

Did the Cat Drink the Coffee? Challenging Transformers with Generalized Event Knowledge
Paolo Pedinotti, Giulia Rambelli, Emmanuele Chersoni, Enrico Santus, Alessandro Lenci and Philippe Blache

Can Transformer Language Models Predict Psychometric Properties?
Antonio Laverghetta Jr., Animesh Nighojkar, Jamshidbek Mirzakhalov and John Licato

Semantic shift in social networks
Bill Noble, Asad Sayeed, Raquel Fernández and Staffan Larsson

A Study on Using Semantic Word Associations to Predict the Success of a Novel
Syeda Jannatus Saba, Biddut Sarker Bijoy, Henry Gorelick, Sabir Ismail, Md Saiful Islam and Mohammad Ruhul Amin

Recovering Lexically and Semantically Reused Texts
Ansel MacLaughlin, Shaobin Xu and David A. Smith

NLU and Inference

Generating Hypothetical Events for Abductive Inference
Debjit Paul and Anette Frank

NeuralLog: Natural Language Inference with Joint Neural and Logical Reasoning
Zeming Chen, Qiyue Gao and Lawrence S. Moss

Teach the Rules, Provide the Facts: Targeted Relational-knowledge Enhancement for Textual Inference
Ohad Rozen, Shmuel Amar, Vered Shwartz and Ido Dagan

ParsFEVER: a Dataset for Farsi Fact Extraction and Verification
Majid Zarharan, Mahsa Ghaderan, Amin Pourdabiri, Zahra Sayedi, Behrouz Minaei-Bidgoli, Sauleh Eetemadi and Mohammad Taher Pilehvar

BiQuAD: Towards QA based on deeper text understanding
Frank Grimm and Philipp Cimiano

Word Usage

Lexical Semantics

Did the Cat Drink the Coffee? Challenging Transformers with Generalized Event Knowledge

Paolo Pedinotti
University of Pisa
paolo.pedinotti@phd.unipi.it

Giulia Rambelli
University of Pisa - Aix-Marseille University
giulia.rambelli@phd.unipi.it

Emmanuele Chersoni
The Hong Kong Polytechnic University
emmanuelechersoni@gmail.com

Enrico Santus
Bayer Pharmaceuticals
esantus@gmail.com

Alessandro Lenci
University of Pisa
alessandro.lenci@unipi.it

Philippe Blache
Aix-Marseille University
blache@lpl-aix.fr

Abstract

Prior research has explored the ability of computational models to predict a word semantic fit with a given predicate. While much work has been devoted to modeling the typicality relation between verbs and arguments in isolation, in this paper we take a broader perspective by assessing whether and to what extent computational approaches have access to the information about the typicality of entire events and situations described in language (*Generalized Event Knowledge*).

Given the recent success of Transformers Language Models (TLMs), we decided to test them on a benchmark for the *dynamic estimation of thematic fit*. The evaluation of these models was performed in comparison with SDM, a framework specifically designed to integrate events in sentence meaning representations, and we conducted a detailed error analysis to investigate which factors affect their behavior. Our results show that TLMs can reach performances that are comparable to those achieved by SDM. However, additional analysis consistently suggests that TLMs do not capture important aspects of event knowledge, and their predictions often depend on surface linguistic features, such as frequent words, collocations and syntactic patterns, thereby showing sub-optimal generalization abilities.

1 Introduction

People can discriminate between typical (e.g., *A cop arrested a thief*) and atypical events (e.g., *A thief arrested a cop*) and exploit this ability in online sentence processing to anticipate the upcoming linguistic input. Brains have been claimed to be "prediction machines" (Clark, 2013) and psycholinguistic research has shown that a crucial ingredient of such predictive ability is the knowledge about events and their typical participants stored in human semantic memory, also referred to as **Generalized Event Knowledge** (GEK) by McRae and Matsuki (2009). To make an example, if we were asked to think about things that are played with a guitar, we would quickly and more or less unanimously think of words such as *song*, *piece* or *riff*.

Computational models of predicate-argument typicality, generally referred to as *thematic fit* in the psycholinguistic literature (McRae et al., 1998), extract typical arguments from parsed corpora. However, GEK is not just storing relations between words: The fact that this knowledge is generalized – that is, it is based on an abstract representation of what is typical – allows us to easily classify new argument combinations as typical or atypical. Furthermore, psycholinguistic studies (Bicknell et al., 2010; Matsuki et al., 2011) have shown that humans are able to combine and dynamically update their expectations during sentence processing: for example, their expectations given the sequence *The barber cut the* _ differ from the ones given *The lumberjack cut the* _, since the integration of knowledge "cued" by the agent argument with the verb will lead to the activation of different event scenarios. In Distributional Semantics, sophisticated models of the GEK have been proposed to make predictions on upcoming arguments by integrating the cues coming from the verb and the previously-realized arguments in the sentence (Lenci, 2011; Chersoni et al., 2019). Since such knowledge is acquired from both first-hand and linguistic experience (McRae and Matsuki, 2009), an important assumption of this literature is that, at least for its "linguistic subset", the GEK can be modeled with distributional information extracted

Proceedings of the 10th Conference on Lexical and Computational Semantics, pages 1–11
August 5–6, 2021, Bangkok, Thailand (online) ©2021 Association for Computational Linguistics

from corpora (Chersoni et al., 2017, 2021).

Language Models are trained to make predictions given a context, and thus, they can also be viewed as models of GEK. This approach is promising if one considers the success of recent Transformer-based Language Models (henceforth TLMs), which are trained on huge corpora and contain a massive number of parameters. Even if these models receive extensive training and have been shown to capture linguistic properties (Jawahar et al., 2019; Goldberg, 2019), it is not obvious whether they acquire the aspects of GEK that have been modeled explicitly in previous approaches. To the best of our knowledge, Transformers have never been tested on dynamic thematic fit modeling, nor their performance has been compared with traditional distributional models. Our current work is addressing this issue.

Contributions:

1. we propose a methodology to adapt TLMs to the dynamic estimation of thematic fit, using a dataset that contains several types of argument combinations differing for their typicality;

2. we present a comprehensive evaluation of various TLMs on this task, performed by comparing them to a strong distributional baseline;

3. we conduct further analysis aimed at identifying the potential limitations of TLMs as models of GEK.

Our results are relevant for researchers interested in assessing the linguistic abilities of TLMs, as well as those working on applications involving TLMs, such as text generation.

2 Related Work

In its classical form, the thematic fit estimation task consists in comparing a candidate argument or *filler* (e.g., *wine*) with the typical fillers of a given verb role (e.g., agent, patient, etc.), either in the form of exemplars previously attested in a corpus (Erk, 2007; Vandekerckhove et al., 2009; Erk et al., 2010) or in the form of a vector-based prototype (Baroni and Lenci, 2010; Sayeed and Demberg, 2014; Sayeed et al., 2015; Greenberg et al., 2015a,b; Sayeed et al., 2016; Santus et al., 2017; Chersoni et al., 2020). Additionally, recent studies explored the use of masked language modeling with BERT for scoring the candidate arguments (Metheniti et al., 2020). Performance in the thematic fit task is typically measured with the correlation between the output scores of the model and human-elicited typicality judgments for verb-argument pairs (McRae et al., 1998; Ferretti et al., 2001; Padó, 2007; Zhang et al., 2019; Marton and Sayeed, 2021).

In the simplest and most common version of this task, the typicality of verb argument-pairs is evaluated in isolation. Thematic fit is instead a *dynamic concept*: The expectations for an argument in a given verb role do not depend just on the verb, but also on the compositional combination with the other arguments in the sentence (Bicknell et al., 2010). To check the ability of computational models to account for the compositional update of argument expectations, Lenci (2011) framed the problem as a binary classification task: A system is presented a sentence pair, with one sentence expressing a typical real-world situation (*The journalist is checking the report*) and the other sentence expressing a plausible but less typical one (*The mechanic is checking the report*), and the task is to assign a higher thematic fit/typicality score to the former. Notice that the two sentences differ only for one argument, and that the "atypical" one might, however, be a common filler with respect to the verb target role (e.g., *report* is a typical patient for *check*, it is just less plausible in combination with *mechanic* as an agent).

Several models have tried to tackle the "dynamic" version of the thematic fit task, either based on classical distributional spaces (Chersoni et al., 2016, 2019) or on more sophisticated neural network architectures (Tilk et al., 2016; Hong et al., 2018). On the evaluation side, those works made use of the experimental materials of the study by Lenci (2011), which are, however, limited to agent-verb-patient triples. The recently-introduced DTFit dataset (Vassallo et al., 2018) is, in comparison, larger in size and provides more variety of fillers and roles (including instruments, locations and time). Other studies introduced larger datasets, but focused on more specific notions of event plausibility (e.g. the plausibility depending on the physical properties of the participants) (Wang et al., 2018; Porada et al., 2019; Ko et al., 2019).

3 Experimental Settings

3.1 Dataset

The **DTFit** (Vassallo et al., 2018) dataset has been specifically designed for the evaluation of dynamic thematic fit. [1] The dataset contains pairs of tuples that differ only for one element, which can be either a typical or atypical filler of a given role in the event described by the tuple (cf. Table 1). The dataset includes tuples of different lengths, and the typicality of a given argument depends on its interaction with all the other elements. For each tuple, the authors collected typicality judgments by asking English native speakers how common was the event described. Scores range from 1 (very atypical) to 7 (very typical). The dataset mainly targets knowledge about professions, but also other typical everyday situations (e.g., what a dog typically eats, what a grandmother typically does).

The authors created several datasets, which differ with respect to the semantic role of the candidate filler. For our experiments, we selected the datasets created by the authors for the following relations: $\{$**Instrument**, **Time**, **Location**$\}_{\text{DTFit}}$. Additionally, from the original dataset containing agent-verb-patient triples, we derived two datasets, that we named $\textbf{Agent}_{\text{DTFit}}$ and $\textbf{Patient}_{\text{DTFit}}$. In $\textbf{Agent}_{\text{DTFit}}$, the tuples forming a pair differ with respect to the typicality of the agent. In $\textbf{Patient}_{\text{DTFit}}$, they differ for the typicality of the patient. We thus get a total of five datasets, each of which covers a different semantic relation. The latter two datasets have the same properties of the others, but they put stronger emphasis on the dynamic nature of thematic fit, as the atypical filler is still a typical complement of the verb alone. Conversely, the atypical candidate fillers in the other datasets are appropriate fillers of the role, but, in most cases, they do not relate to the other elements of the tuple. Therefore, $\textbf{Agent}_{\text{DTFit}}$ and $\textbf{Patient}_{\text{DTFit}}$ are more challenging for computational models, as the typicality of a filler can only be determined through the composition of the verb with another argument. Accordingly, models have to update their predictions by accurately taking into account the whole context.

For each tuple in DTFit, the task for our models is to predict the upcoming argument on the basis of the previous ones. Models were evaluated in terms of Spearman correlation between the human ratings and the models' scores. Moreover, we performed a second evaluation for $\textbf{Agent}_{\text{DTFit}}$ and $\textbf{Patient}_{\text{DTFit}}$, consisting of measuring the accuracy of each system in assigning a higher thematic fit score to typical tuples. To the best of our knowledge, the only attempts to test computational models on this dataset have been done by the authors of the original paper and by Chersoni et al. (2019). In both works, distributional prototype models of thematic fit have been used.

[1] All the datasets used for the experiments described in this paper can be found at the link: `https://github.com/giuliarambelli/transformers_thematic_fit`.

Role	Tuple	Typical	Atypical
Agent	_ mix paint	painter	cook
Patient	tailor sew _	dress	wound
Instrument	cook clean fish _	knife	sponge
Time	cat chase bird _	hunting	marriage
Location	sailor mop deck _	boat	theatre

Table 1: Examples of tuples from DTFit.

3.2 Models

In our experiments, we compared the performance of TLMs with the Structured Distributional Model (SDM), which has been recently shown to be an efficient model for the dynamic estimation of thematic fit (Chersoni et al., 2019).

3.2.1 Structured Distributional Model

The **Structured Distributional Model** (SDM) proposed by Chersoni et al. (2019) combines word embeddings and formal semantics to specifically represent GEK and the dynamic construction of sentence meaning. Like traditional distributional models of thematic fit, it builds a prototype representation for a given role (e.g., the typical patient of *sing*) from its typical fillers, but its novelty is that the fillers are retrieved from an external resource called *Distributional Event Graph* (henceforth, *DEG*). *DEG* represents GEK as a graph automatically built from parsed corpora, where the nodes are words associated to a numeric vector, and the edges are labeled with syntactic relations and weighted using statistic association measures. Thus, given a lexical cue w, it is possible to identify the events in which w takes part and to retrieve words related to w on both the paradigmatic and the syntagmatic axis.

The formal structure at the basis of SDM consists of two semantic structures: the *linguistic condition* (LC), a context-independent tier of meaning that represents the lexical items in a sentence, and the *active context* (AC), which accumulates contextual information activated by lexical items. The crucial aspect of SDM is that it associates a vector representation to these formal structures: $\vec{LC}$ is the sum of the embeddings of the lexical items of a sentence; $\vec{AC}$, for each syntactic slot, is represented as the centroid vector built out of the role vectors $\vec{r_1}, ..., \vec{r_n}$ available in AC, corresponding to the syntactic associates of the lexical items that have been already processed.

In our implementation of SDM, the DEG was constructed by extracting syntactic relations from a concatenation of the ukWaC corpus (Baroni et al., 2009), a dump of Wikipedia 2018 and the British National Corpus (Leech, 1992). The final graph contains words with a minimum frequency of 300 and events with a minimum frequency of 30. We used as lexical embeddings the publicly-available FastText vectors extracted from Wikipedia.[2] For our experiments, we built a semantic representation for each tuple in the dataset, like in Chersoni et al. (2019). We used the information in LC and AC to assign a typicality score to each candidate filler of a role in the dataset. The scoring function for a given role filler is the following:

$$\frac{cos(\vec{f}, \vec{LC}(sent)) + cos(\vec{f}, \vec{AC}(sent))}{2} \quad (1)$$

where $\vec{f}$ is the embedding of the candidate filler; $\vec{LC}(sent)$ is a vector obtained from the sum of the embeddings of the verb and of the argument other than f; $\vec{AC}$ stands for the updated expectation prototype for the role filled by f. In other words, we quantify the typicality of an argument given a tuple as the average of i.) the cosine similarity between the argument embedding and the additive combination of the other argument vectors ($\vec{LC}$), and ii.) the cosine similarity between the argument embedding and the prototype vector representing the active context ($\vec{AC}$). In the cases where $\vec{AC}$ cannot be derived (because DEG does not store syntactic relations involving the context words), we take only the cosine between $\vec{f}$ and $\vec{LC}(sent)$ as the final score.

3.2.2 Transformer-based Language Models

We experimented with four TLMs to test how different architectures, training objectives, and sizes of the training corpus affect performance.[3]

BERT (Devlin et al., 2019) consists of a series of stacked Transformer encoders. It was trained using both a masked language modeling objective (i.e., predicting a masked word from its left- and right-context), and a next sentence prediction objective (i.e., whether a sentence follows another sentence or not), on a combination of the BooksCorpus and English Wikipedia (13GB in total). The model uses WordPiece vocabulary. To test if the model size can affect BERT performance, we used both the `base` (Number of layers=12, Hidden size=768) and the `large` (L=24, H=1024) versions.

RoBERTa (Liu et al., 2019), which we used in the `large` version, is based on the same architecture as BERT, but it was trained on a much larger corpus (160GB) and without the next sentence prediction objective. In our experiments, we used the large version (L=24, H=1024).

In contrast with the bidirectional nature of BERT and RoBERTa, **GPT2** (Radford et al., 2019) is a uni-directional LM, which means that the training objective is to predict the next word, given all of the previous ones. It was trained on WebText, for a total of 8 million documents of data (40 GB). We employed the `medium` version of GPT2 (L=24, H=1024). We chose GPT2-medium since its dimensions are comparable to those of BERT and RoBERTa large. Moreover, both RoBERTa and GPT2 make use of a Byte-Pair Encoding tokenizer.

For our investigation, we designed the experiment as follows. First, we derived simple sentences from the tuples by adding definite articles to the words, [CLS] at the beginning of the input and a period to signal the end of the sentence (e.g., `[CLS] The tailor sewed the dress.`). Then, we masked the candidate filler (*dress* in the example) and we computed the probability distribution of the entire model's vocabulary for that position. The model typicality score is the probability assigned to the candidate filler, when the candidate filler is included in the model's vocabulary. In case a word to be scored is not included in the vocabularies of all the models that we used, we decided to disregard its tuple and the respective typical/atypical counterpart. For this reason, the final results only take in consideration a subset of the original datasets, which varies from model to model. Additionally, we computed a baseline for each Transformer model, where the model is prevented from attending to the other tokens in the sequence when making predictions.

[2] `https://fasttext.cc/docs/en/english-vectors.html`

[3] For all experiments involving TLMs, we use pre-trained models available in the HuggingFace's Python library Transformers (Wolf et al., 2019).

	Coverage	SDM	BERT-base(line)	BERT-large	ROBERTA-large	GPT-2 medium
Agent$_{\text{DTFit}}$	105/134	0.58	0.46 (0.1)	0.53	**0.64**	-
Patient$_{\text{DTFit}}$	323/402	0.62	0.59 (0.06)	**0.64**	**0.64**	0.63
Instrument$_{\text{DTFit}}$	31/100	**0.58**	0.52 (0.08)	0.53	0.5	0.5
Time$_{\text{DTFit}}$	89/100	0.58	0.63 (0.06)	0.64	**0.66**	**0.66**
Location$_{\text{DTFit}}$	115/150	0.65	0.72 (0.06)	0.71	0.73	**0.74**

Table 2: Spearman Correlation for the DTFit datasets.

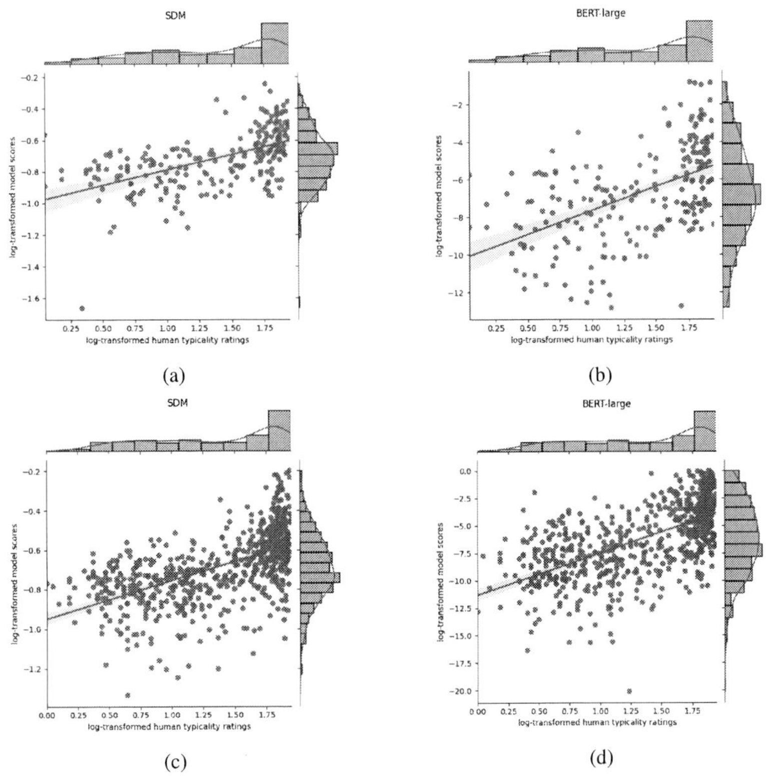

Figure 1: Correlation of elicited judgments and model-derived scores for **Agent**$_{\text{DTFit}}$ (a-b) and **Patient**$_{\text{DTFit}}$ (c-d) datasets.

4 Results and Analysis

In this section, we provide the results of the experiments on the DTFit datasets. Since the models cover different portions of the original tuples, we performed the evaluation over the common pairs.

Table 2 reports the correlation scores for all the five datasets.[4] Values in brackets refer to the Spearman correlation obtained by the baseline. As the baseline scores are very similar across models, we reported the results only for BERT-base.

At a glance, we observe that both SDM and TLMS obtain quite strong correlations, going from 0.46 to a maximum of 0.74 across datasets and models. Specifically, we notice that TLMS tend to reach higher performances compared to the distributional approach. However, a marginally significant improvement of the correlations over SDM is obtained only for **Location**$_{\text{DTFit}}$ ($p < 0.05$ for Locations, $p < 0.1$ for the other roles).[5] This result is interesting, considering that SDM is trained on a really small corpus compared to TLMS (for instance, RoBERTa is trained on 160 GB of text). Another remark is that even if TLMS differ for architecture, training objective and data, BERT-large, RoBERTa and GPT-2 tend to achieve very similar performances, while correlation scores are lower for BERT-base.

As there is no significant difference between

[4]We do not computed GPT-2 scores for **Agent**$_{\text{DTFit}}$, as the model cannot make predictions based on context because the candidate filler occurs at the beginning of the sentence.

[5]The p-value was computed with Fisher's r-to-z transformation, one-tailed test.

SDM and TLMs results, we plotted an example of the relationship between the human ratings and the model-derived scores to provide a better picture of the models' predictions. For visualization purposes, we applied a logarithmic transformation to the scores. For **Agent**$_{\text{DTFit}}$, we observe that SDM and BERT-large have a different trend. In the former (see Figure 1a), the majority of the points follow a roughly linear relationship, and there is a small variation around the regression line (with few outliers). On the contrary, BERT-large scores show more variance (Figure 1b). This trend is confirmed (even if it is less evident) for **Patient**$_{\text{DTFit}}$, where both SDM (Figure 1c) and BERT-large (Figure 1d) have a large amount of variance, and quite a few outliers. To verify these observations, we compared the sum of the BERT-large residuals with that of SDM (we first normalized the models' scores with min-max scaling in order to make them comparable). For both subsets, the sum of residuals is higher for BERT-large than SDM, which is especially the case for **Agent**$_{\text{DTFit}}$ (31.43 versus 17.85; 67.04 versus 63.47 for **Patient**$_{\text{DTFit}}$).

Finally, we also performed a *binary classification task* for **Agent**$_{\text{DTFit}}$ and **Patient**$_{\text{DTFit}}$. In this case, we evaluated models on their ability to assign a higher score to the filler in the typical condition. As shown in Table 3 (left columns), the accuracy values are always high and the TLMs scores are comparable with the SDM ones.

	DTFit		**Wang2018**	
	Agent	Patient	Agent	Patient
SDM	**.89**	**.91**	.65	.66
BERT-base	.77	.85	.76	.63
BERT-large	.83	.89	**.77**	.65
ROBERTA-large	**.89**	**.91**	.76	**.73**
GPT-2 medium	-	.90	-	.64

Table 3: Accuracy in the binary classification task for DTFit (agent and patient roles) and Wang2018 datasets.

5 Do Transformers Really Encode GEK?

The above results *prima facie* suggest that TLMs are able to model the dynamic interaction between the sentence elements to compute the typicality value of a candidate filler. However, analyzing the errors of the TLMs can be revealing of how they make their predictions.

Table 4 presents some of the **Patient**$_{\text{DTFit}}$ pairs where BERT-base prefers the atypical filler. In all these cases, BERT simply seems to rely on frequent verb objects, without composing and integrating the verb expectations with information from other elements of the context (the agent in this case), which is a key aspect of human GEK and is reflected in the typicality judgments. However, we cannot make any claims about the event knowledge of TLMs from these examples alone, as only in some cases (such as *The cat drank the* ***coffee***) the atypical tuples evoke events unlikely to take place in the real world (i.e., it may happen frequently that *a chemist pours the juice*, even if this is not a typical action for a chemist). To better understand if this can lead TLMS to make really implausible predictions, we carried out an additional experiment where we tested the models on a diagnostic dataset controlled for the frequency of the association between the verb and the filler. In this experiment, we also tried to address the question of whether TLMs rely more heavily on the local context when making predictions.

Furthermore, TLMs' natural preference for what is more frequent could help them in the typicality task, as a typical event is often a frequent one. Their good performance could be due to the fact that they memorize frequent sequences during training. Therefore we tested TLMs on a different dataset, in which atypical but physically plausible events (e.g., *The cloth erased the cream*) are distinguished from atypical and implausible ones (e.g., *The cloth erased the house*). Frequency effects on performance should be alleviated in this setting, as both types of events in the dataset are atypical and, hence, rare. This task requires fine-grained knowledge of the properties of arguments, which is still an important component of GEK.

Additionally, different frequency variations in the training data could influence TLMs performance. Since the models' knowledge of the world is mediated by language, it is likely that an argument filler may or may not be predicted depending on the frequency of the word chosen to refer to it. We investigated this issue by testing the models on another diagnostic dataset obtained by replacing typical fillers with low-frequency synonyms.

The last question we explored is whether TLMs can be influenced by the way statements of event typicality are syntactically expressed. So, we evaluated TLMs by feeding them with sentences encoding typical events with a transformed and more complex syntactic form than the one used in the DTFit experiments.

Tuple	Expected	Preferred
mason mix __	cement (H=6.65, M=-8.41)	soup (H=1.95, M=-5.54)
climber climb __	rock (H=6.8, M=-5.29)	staircase (H=5.6, M=-4.05)
blacksmith pour __	metal (H=6.5, M=-4.03)	wine (H=1.6, M=-1.6)
chemist pour __	compound (H=6.25, M=-8.4)	juice (H=2.75, M=-5.18)
cat drink __	milk (H=5.6, M=-2.89)	coffee (H=1.45, M=-3.65)

Table 4: Examples of errors (BERT-base, $\text{Patient}_{\text{DTFit}}$). H= Human score, M=Model's log probability.

I. TLMs seem to prefer frequent collocations, but only when they are plausible. Errors reported in Table 4 suggest the tendency of TLMS to predict frequent complements of the verbs, irrespective of whether they are coherent with the rest of the tuple. We questioned to what extent salient local word co-occurrences make the models "blind" to the rest of the context and thus compromise the plausibility of their predictions. To investigate this behavior, we generated a new diagnostic dataset. The dataset is a small (31 pairs) subset of $\textbf{Patient}_{\text{DTFit}}$, where the atypical filler in each pair was replaced with another noun that has a very strong association with the verb in the tuple. We computed the association between the verb and its direct objects using Local Mutual Information (LMI) (Evert, 2008). Since LMI is computed by multiplying the Pointwise Mutual Information and the frequency of the two words in a grammatical relation, it assigns higher values to combinations that are both common and informative. We chose the new atypical fillers among the words with the highest LMIs. We chose words that give rise to odd events when integrated with the rest of the context. To approximate the word distributions encountered in the training data, we extracted LMI values from a 2018 dump of English Wikipedia and we evaluated only the BERT model (base and large) on the new dataset, as Wikipedia is a considerable part of the training only for this model. Examples of the new test pairs are the following: *The terrorist released the **hostage/ album**, The truck hit the **car/ ball**, The soldier heard the **command/ case**.*

To evaluate BERT performance, we computed the accuracy scores on the diagnostics dataset in the same way as in the main experiment (binary classification task). Results show that the models generally assign low probabilities to atypical fillers. They choose the atypical event in some cases (9 in BERT-base, 6 in large), but mainly when the contrast between the atypical event and our expectations is less evident (*The smuggler sold the **property*** is preferred to **weapon**, *The soldier throw the **ball*** is preferred to **bomb**).

As already observed in the main experiment, BERT seems to be able to look beyond salient local associations and build representations of global events flexibly. However, this issue should be further explored for the other roles as well. For instance, given the sentence *The engineer completed the project in the __*, the models must consider more contextual elements to make the correct prediction.

On the other hand, even if SDM design aims at capturing this aspect of GEK, the manipulations we made in this dataset cause a drop in the model performance (14 pairs out of 31 are classified wrongly). This drop is probably due to aspects of the implementation such as data sparsity. Specifically, if there are no events in which the subject occurs with a direct object, the prototype of the patient is built only from the verb's most associated patients, disregarding the fact they are implausible given the whole context.

II. TLMs know more about what is typical than what is possible. The use of typicality datasets such as DTFit for the estimation of the models' GEK has some limitations. TLMS' ability to reproduce combinations encountered frequently during training could be the reason for high performances in the typicality task, since what is most typical often occurs most frequently. However, GEK is not just memory of exemplars, but it requires fine-grained knowledge of the properties of objects and it involves reasoning processes such as abstraction and comparison between objects and prototypical concepts.

To evaluate TLMS on a setting where frequency variations in the training corpus have a minor impact, we used the dataset realized by Wang et al. (2018) (henceforth, **Wang2018**). This dataset represents a benchmark for the task of semantic physical plausibility (Bagherinezhad et al., 2016), that is, distinguishing an atypical but physically plausible event such as *The student climbed the ship* from an atypical and physically implausible one such as *The student climbed the water*. The dataset contains agent-verb-patient (SVO) triples divided into plausible and implausible. From the original dataset, which contains 1,540 plausible and 1,540 implausible triples, we derived two subsets containing pairs of triples differing either for the agent or for the patient role filler (obtaining 222 and 394 pairs respectively).

Table 3 reports the resulting accuracy values. In general, the models' scores are lower than in the typicality task (min. 0.64, max. 0.77), and in some cases they are not much higher than random performance. Moreover, in many cases the models could be facilitated by the existence of an association between the plausible filler and the verb of the event, as in *The ant **built** the **wall*** and in *The chair **absorbed** the **water***. Nevertheless, the results demonstrate that the notion of plausibility is harder to model compared to typicality, and invite caution when making claims about TLMS world and event knowledge. In fact, the results suggest that even if it were true that TLMS develop some generalization skills from training, they still miss many predictions about possible events, which instead humans easily make on the basis of their commonsense knowledge.

This dataset is also difficult for SDM, which obtains scores lower than those of the TLMS (0.65 for Agent and 0.66 for Patient). Even if SDM should be better at reproducing generalization through the construction of prototypical fillers, the model's distributional representations seem to fail to capture the specific properties that are relevant for the dataset items, namely physical properties of objects (liquid-solid, large-small, etc.). The lack of such properties constitutes a limitation of distributional models of word meaning based on text data only, which is why, in previous studies, world knowledge was explicitly injected into the models for the physical plausibility task (Wang et al., 2018).

III. TLMS do not extend fit judgments to low frequency synonyms. To test whether TLMS consider an entity more or less likely to take part in an event depending on the word used to refer to that entity, we evaluated them on a new diagnostic dataset of 39 pairs, generated from a subset of **Patient**$_{\text{DTFit}}$. In this setting, the typical filler in each pair was replaced with a low-frequency word that is semantically related to the original one. To choose an appropriate substitute, we first extracted a set of synonyms according to two lexical resources (WordNet, Lexico.com). Then, we picked a word that 1) is less frequent than the original filler and 2) has a frequency lower than 300,000. For the same reasons described in the first additional experiment, we extracted statistics from a 2018 dump of English Wikipedia and evaluated only BERT on the new dataset. Examples of substitutions are the following: *The botanist examined the **plant** → **flora***, *The waiter cleared the **restaurant** → **tavern***, *The veterinarian examined the **dog** → **puppy***. It is interesting to observe that these variations pose serious difficulties to the models, as their accuracy on the diagnostics dataset is close or lower to the random level (BERT-base: 0.37, BERT-large: 0.53). For example, BERT considers *The terrorist released the **captive*** as less probable than *The terrorist released the **/book***, and the same occurs for *The mother prepared the **provisions/gun***, and *The carver built the **bust/house***.

These results cast doubts that current TLMS can constitute plausible models of event knowledge: they tend to reproduce the patterns that are frequently observed in the data, and their good performance is disrupted once these are replaced with semantically equivalent, but less frequent ones. This means that they lack the abstract semantic knowledge of human subjects, whose predictions are more flexible thanks to inference mechanisms such as generalization to concepts sharing semantic features. At least in principle, models aiming at building prototypes of ideal role fillers (such as the distributional models of thematic fit) are more cognitively realistic, since they are less dependent on specific words. However, they may still show sub-optimal performance in this diagnostic dataset as they are based on the quality of the distributional representations, which is lower for words that have low frequency in corpora. This is confirmed by the performance of SDM on the dataset (the accuracy is 0.51).

	transitive	cleft	wh-interrogative
Agent$_{\text{DTFit}}$	0.64	-0.13	0.62
Patient$_{\text{DTFit}}$	0.64	0.26	0.51
Instrument$_{\text{DTFit}}$	0.5	0.10	0.6
Time$_{\text{DTFit}}$	0.66	0.33	0.64
Location$_{\text{DTFit}}$	0.73	0.67	0.73

Table 5: Spearman Correlation for DTFit datasets using RoBERTa-large and input sentences with different word orders.

IV. TLMS can be influenced by the surface structure of sentences Finally, we analyzed to what extent TLMS' ability to predict the fit of a word in a given role arises from the observation of recurrent word order patterns during pre-training (e.g., the fact that an actor's award-winning event is canonically expressed with active sentences, in which *award* follows the words *actor* and *won*), rather than being based on a deep understanding of the semantic relations between the words.

To explore this issue, we modified DTFit tuples to create two different versions of the dataset, each with examples of a syntactic construction different from the English canonical word order. Specifically, we experimented with **cleft** (*It was the award that the actor won, It was on the ring that the boxer delivered the punch*) and **wh-interrogative** sentences (*Which award did the actor win?, On which ring did the boxer deliver the punch?*).

We evaluated this new set of sentences using RoBERTa-large (cf. Table 5). We observe that the model is not particularly affected by the interrogative structure. Conversely, the model suffers from the cleft construction for all semantic roles except for Location (ρ=0.67). If we ask the model to generate the most likely words to appear in that position, we observe that word predictions in the new construction are more general and less dependent on the GEK associated with the other words in the sentence, proving that TLMS are affected by the surface syntactic shape of the linguistic input, since the cleft construction is less frequent and presents a less canonical word order. For instance, given the sentence *It was with the [MASK] that the guard opened the door*, RoBERTa generates the following possible fillers: *gun* (P=0.044), *crowd* (P=0.020), *sword* (P=0.016), and then *key* (P=0.016), while in the active sentence *key* is correctly predicted as the most probable word (P=0.22). In this specific case, it seems that the model only looks at the word nearby (*guard*) to make a prediction, disregarding the entire context. Generally, the agent role shows the worst results, obtaining -0.13. Note that SDM is not affected by these variations by design, since its predictions are based on semantic roles derived from the syntactic analysis of the sentence, which is explicitly provided to the model.

6 Conclusions

In this paper, we tested Transformer-based Language Models on tasks related to Generalized Event Knowledge. In the main experiment, we evaluated their ability to model event typicality, that is, discern typical from atypical events, on a dataset designed for this task, DTFit. Results show that TLMS scores positively correlate with human judgments. However, they do not significantly outperform the distributional prototype-based model (SDM) that we selected for comparison. This confirms the ability of SDM to dynamically update the semantic representation of a sentence, which was recently shown for the challenging task of logical metonymy interpretation (Rambelli et al., 2020).

However, we decided to go beyond the simple evaluation against human judgments. We carried out several additional small-scale experiments with the specific aim to understand which factors could affect the predictions of TLMS. The results suggest that models are often too dependent on what they observe during training and lack some key aspects of human event knowledge. In particular, we observed that, in some cases, they are unable to compose all elements of the input to make predictions, and they tend to rely more on salient local associations between words. However, further analysis is needed. Secondly, their performance drop on the physical plausibility task, which requires the ability to infer physical properties necessary for an object to participate in a given event. Lastly, their probabilities are dependent on the specific words that have to be predicted rather than on their meaning, and on the canonical word order in which these words tend to occur. Noticeably, even a distributional model of event knowledge (SDM) showed similar limitations, generally likely to be due to data sparsity and inherent limitations of distributional representations obtained from text data.

To conclude, we believe that the experiments we reported are the first step towards a deep investigation of "how general" is the Generalized Event Knowledge in computational models. Future work might include the creation of a larger version of our diagnostic datasets, in order to make available to NLP researchers a more robust benchmark for tasks related to Generalized Event Knowledge.

Acknowledgements

This work, carried out within the Institut Convergence ILCB (ANR-16-CONV-0002), has benefited from support from the French government, managed by the French National Agency for Research (ANR) and the Excellence Initiative of Aix-Marseille University (A*MIDEX). We thank the anonymous reviewers for their insightful feedback.

References

Hessam Bagherinezhad, Hannaneh Hajishirzi, Yejin Choi, and Ali Farhadi. 2016. Are Elephants Bigger than Butterflies? Reasoning about Sizes of Objects. In *Proceedings of AAAI*.

Marco Baroni, Silvia Bernardini, Adriano Ferraresi, and Eros Zanchetta. 2009. The WaCky Wide Web: A Collection of Very Large Linguistically Processed Web-Crawled Corpora. *Language Resources and Evaluation*, 43(3):209–226.

Marco Baroni and Alessandro Lenci. 2010. Distributional Memory: A General Framework for Corpus-Based Semantics. *Computational Linguistics*, 36(4):673–721.

Klinton Bicknell, Jeffrey L Elman, Mary Hare, Ken McRae, and Marta Kutas. 2010. Effects of Event Knowledge in Processing Verbal Arguments. *Journal of Memory and Language*, 63(4):489–505.

Emmanuele Chersoni, Philippe Blache, and Alessandro Lenci. 2016. Towards a Distributional Model of Semantic Complexity. In *Proceedings of the COLING Workshop on Computational Linguistics for Linguistic Complexity*.

Emmanuele Chersoni, Alessandro Lenci, and Philippe Blache. 2017. Logical Metonymy in a Distributional Model of Sentence Comprehension. In *Proceedings of *SEM*.

Emmanuele Chersoni, Ludovica Pannitto, Enrico Santus, Alessandro Lenci, and Chu-Ren Huang. 2020. Are Word Embeddings Really a Bad Fit for the Estimation of Thematic Fit? In *Proceedings of LREC*.

Emmanuele Chersoni, Enrico Santus, Alessandro Lenci, Philippe Blache, and Chu-Ren Huang. 2021. Not All Arguments Are Processed Equally: A Distributional Model of Argument Complexity. *Language Resources and Evaluation*, pages 1–28.

Emmanuele Chersoni, Enrico Santus, Ludovica Pannitto, Alessandro Lenci, Philippe Blache, and C-R Huang. 2019. A Structured Distributional Model of Sentence Meaning and Processing. *Natural Language Engineering*, 25(4):483–502.

Andy Clark. 2013. Whatever Next? Predictive Brains, Situated Agents, and the Future of Cognitive Science. *Behavioral and Brain Sciences*, 36(3):181–204.

Jacob Devlin, Ming-Wei Chang, Kenton Lee, and Kristina Toutanova. 2019. BERT: Pre-training of Deep Bidirectional Transformers for Language Understanding. In *Proceedings of NAACL*.

Katrin Erk. 2007. A Simple, Similarity-Based Model for Selectional Preferences. In *Proceedings of ACL*.

Katrin Erk, Sebastian Padó, and Ulrike Padó. 2010. A Flexible, Corpus-Driven Model of Regular and Inverse Selectional Preferences. *Computational Linguistics*, 36(4):723–763.

Stefan Evert. 2008. Corpora and Collocations. *Corpus Linguistics. An International Handbook*, 2:1212–1248.

Todd R Ferretti, Ken McRae, and Andrea Hatherell. 2001. Integrating Verbs, Situation Schemas, and Thematic Role Concepts. *Journal of Memory and Language*, 44(4):516–547.

Yoav Goldberg. 2019. Assessing BERT's Syntactic Abilities. *arXiv preprint arXiv:1901.05287*.

Clayton Greenberg, Vera Demberg, and Asad Sayeed. 2015a. Verb Polysemy and Frequency Effects in Thematic Fit Modeling. In *Proceedings of the NAACL Workshop on Cognitive Modeling and Computational Linguistics*.

Clayton Greenberg, Asad B Sayeed, and Vera Demberg. 2015b. Improving Unsupervised Vector-Space Thematic Fit Evaluation via Role-Filler Prototype Clustering. In *Proceedings of HLT-NAACL*.

Xudong Hong, Asad Sayeed, and Vera Demberg. 2018. Learning Distributed Event Representations with a Multi-task Approach. In *Proceedings of *SEM*.

Ganesh Jawahar, Benoît Sagot, and Djamé Seddah. 2019. What Does BERT Learn About the Structure of Language? In *Proceedings of ACL*.

Wei-Jen Ko, Greg Durrett, and Junyi Jessy Li. 2019. Linguistically-informed Specificity and Semantic Plausibility for Dialogue Generation. In *Proceedings of NAACL*.

Geoffrey Neil Leech. 1992. 100 Million Words of English: The British National Corpus (BNC). *Language Research*, 28.

Alessandro Lenci. 2011. Composing and Updating Verb Argument Expectations: A Distributional Semantic Model. In *Proceedings of the ACL Workshop on Cognitive Modeling and Computational Linguistics*.

Yinhan Liu, Myle Ott, Naman Goyal, Jingfei Du, Mandar Joshi, Danqi Chen, Omer Levy, Mike Lewis, Luke Zettlemoyer, and Veselin Stoyanov. 2019. Roberta: A Robustly Optimized BERT Pretraining Approach. *arXiv preprint arXiv:1907.11692*.

Yuval Marton and Asad Sayeed. 2021. Thematic Fit Bits: Annotation Quality and Quantity for Event Participant Representation. *arXiv preprint arXiv:2105.06097*.

Kazunaga Matsuki, Tracy Chow, Mary Hare, Jeffrey L Elman, Christoph Scheepers, and Ken McRae. 2011. Event-Based Plausibility Immediately Influences On-Line Language Comprehension. *Journal of Experimental Psychology: Learning, Memory, and Cognition*, 37(4):913.

Ken McRae and Kazunaga Matsuki. 2009. People Use their Knowledge of Common Events to Understand Language, and Do So as Quickly as Possible. *Language and Linguistics Compass*, 3(6):1417–1429.

Ken McRae, Michael Spivey-Knowlton, and Michael Tanenhaus. 1998. Modeling the Influence of Thematic Fit (and other Constraints) in On-Line Sentence Comprehension. *Journal of Memory and Language*, 38(3):283–312.

Eleni Metheniti, Tim Van de Cruys, and Nabil Hathout. 2020. How Relevant Are Selectional Preferences for Transformer-based Language Models? In *Proceedings of COLING*.

Ulrike Padó. 2007. *The Integration of Syntax and Semantic Plausibility in a Wide-Coverage Model of Human Sentence Processing*. Ph.D. thesis.

Ian Porada, Kaheer Suleman, and Jackie Chi Kit Cheung. 2019. Can a Gorilla Ride a Camel? Learning Semantic Plausibility from Text. In *Proceedings of the EMNLP Workshop on Commonsense Inference in Natural Language Processing*.

Alec Radford, Jeffrey Wu, Rewon Child, David Luan, Dario Amodei, and Ilya Sutskever. 2019. Language Models Are Unsupervised Multitask Learners. *OpenAI Blog*, 1(8):9.

Giulia Rambelli, Emmanuele Chersoni, Alessandro Lenci, Philippe Blache, and Chu-Ren Huang. 2020. Comparing Probabilistic, Distributional and Transformer-Based Models on Logical Metonymy Interpretation. In *Proceedings of AACL-IJCNLP*.

Enrico Santus, Emmanuele Chersoni, Alessandro Lenci, and Philippe Blache. 2017. Measuring Thematic Fit with Distributional Feature Overlap. In *Proceedings of EMNLP*.

Asad Sayeed and Vera Demberg. 2014. Combining Unsupervised Syntactic and Semantic Models of Thematic Fit. In *Proceedings of CLIC.it*.

Asad Sayeed, Vera Demberg, and Pavel Shkadzko. 2015. An Exploration of Semantic Features in an Unsupervised Thematic Fit Evaluation Framework. *Italian Journal of Computational Linguistics*, 1(1).

Asad Sayeed, Clayton Greenberg, and Vera Demberg. 2016. Thematic Fit Evaluation: An Aspect of Selectional Preferences. In *Proceedings of the ACL Workshop on Evaluating Vector Space Representations for NLP*.

Ottokar Tilk, Vera Demberg, Asad Sayeed, Dietrich Klakow, and Stefan Thater. 2016. Event Participant Modelling with Neural Networks. In *Proceedings of EMNLP*.

Bram Vandekerckhove, Dominiek Sandra, and Walter Daelemans. 2009. A Robust and Extensible Exemplar-based Model of Thematic Fit. In *Proceedings of EACL*.

Paolo Vassallo, Emmanuele Chersoni, Enrico Santus, Alessandro Lenci, and Philippe Blache. 2018. Event Knowledge in Sentence Processing: A New Dataset for the Evaluation of Argument Typicality. In *Proceedings of the LREC Workshop on Linguistic and Neuro-Cognitive Resources*.

Su Wang, Greg Durrett, and Katrin Erk. 2018. Modeling Semantic Plausibility by Injecting World Knowledge. In *Proceedings of NAACL*.

Thomas Wolf, Lysandre Debut, Victor Sanh, Julien Chaumond, Clement Delangue, Anthony Moi, Pierric Cistac, Tim Rault, Rémi Louf, Morgan Funtowicz, et al. 2019. HuggingFace's Transformers: State-of-the-art Natural Language Processing. *arXiv preprint arXiv:1910.03771*.

Hongming Zhang, Hantian Ding, and Yangqiu Song. 2019. SP-10K: A Large-scale Evaluation Set for Selectional Preference Acquisition. In *Proceedings of ACL*.

Can Transformer Language Models Predict Psychometric Properties?

Antonio Laverghetta Jr., Animesh Nighojkar, Jamshidbek Mirzakhalov, and **John Licato**
Advancing Machine and Human Reasoning (AMHR) Lab
Department of Computer Science and Engineering
University of South Florida
Tampa, FL, USA
{alaverghett,anighojkar,mirzakhalov,licato}@usf.edu

Abstract

Transformer-based language models (LMs) continue to advance state-of-the-art performance on NLP benchmark tasks, including tasks designed to mimic human-inspired "commonsense" competencies. To better understand the degree to which LMs can be said to have certain linguistic reasoning skills, researchers are beginning to adapt the tools and concepts of the field of *psychometrics*. But to what extent can the benefits flow in the other direction? I.e., can LMs be of use in predicting what the psychometric properties of test items will be when those items are given to human participants? We gather responses from numerous human participants and LMs (transformer- and non-transformer-based) on a broad diagnostic test of linguistic competencies. We then use the responses to calculate standard psychometric properties of the items in the diagnostic test, using the human responses and the LM responses separately. We then determine how well these two sets of predictions match. We find cases in which transformer-based LMs predict psychometric properties consistently well in certain categories but consistently poorly in others, thus providing new insights into fundamental similarities and differences between human and LM reasoning.[1]

1 Introduction

The current generation of transformer-based language models (TLMs) (Vaswani et al., 2017) continues to surpass expectations, consistently achieving state-of-the-art results on many natural language processing (NLP) benchmark tasks. Especially surprising is their remarkable performance on benchmark tasks designed to assess "commonsense" reasoning (e.g., Wang et al., 2018, 2019), possibly owing to their ability to encode and retrieve a surprising amount of structural knowledge (Goldberg, 2019; Hu et al., 2020; Cui et al., 2020; Petroni et al., 2019; Davison et al., 2019), despite initial worries that all connectionist language models in general would suffer the same limitations as previous generations (Sun, 1992, 1995; McClelland, 1995; Klahr, 1999; McLaughlin, 2009).

Understanding how TLMs reason is a complex task made more difficult by the fact that the sizes of contemporary TLMs are so large as to effectively render them black boxes. As such, researchers are continually searching for new methods to understand the strengths and limitations of TLMs. One promising approach is to draw from *psychometrics*, a sub-field of psychology particularly suited to dealing with perhaps the most mysterious black box of them all: the human mind. Psychometrics is concerned with psychological measurement—i.e., how to measure latent attributes like reasoning skills, attitudes, and personality traits. Psychometricians have developed tools to measure such properties even when the mechanisms that give rise to them are not fully understood, thus suggesting a possible fruitful application of those tools to complex artificial black boxes like TLMs. Although some have called for bridging the gap between psychometrics and AI (Bringsjord and Schimanski, 2003; Bringsjord, 2011; Bringsjord and Licato, 2012; Dowe and Hernández-Orallo, 2012; Hernández-Orallo et al., 2016; Wilcox et al., 2020), the amount of work attempting to do so is limited: although some existing work attempts to use advances in psychometrics to benefit the study of TLMs, none to our knowledge have used SOTA TLMs (or even LMs in general) to benefit psychometrics.

To illustrate, assume that someone wishes to design a test to assess the degree to which a person possesses mastery of some cognitive skill $\mathcal{S}$. A good place to start is for a panel of experts to de-

[1] Code and data to reproduce our experiments can be found on Github: https://github.com/Advancing-Machine-Human-Reasoning-Lab/transformer-psychometrics

Proceedings of the 10th Conference on Lexical and Computational Semantics, pages 12–25
August 5–6, 2021, Bangkok, Thailand (online) ©2021 Association for Computational Linguistics

sign a set of test items (questions) $\mathcal{I}$, such that they believe solving $\mathcal{I}$ requires $\mathcal{S}$. However, although many NLP benchmarks tend to consider this sufficient, the items in $\mathcal{I}$ only have *face validity*, in that they only have been demonstrated to superficially test for $\mathcal{S}$. To go beyond face validity, one must assess $\mathcal{I}$'s psychometric properties by establishing their *validity* (how well the items actually measure the phenomenon $\mathcal{S}$ they purport to measure), *reliability* (how stable the items are as measurements), and *fairness* (how well the items are free from biases against certain sub-populations of subjects).[2] But establishing these psychometric properties can be prohibitively costly, requiring large numbers of human participants to answer the items in $\mathcal{I}$ and iteratively refine them. This drawback motivates the central research question of our paper: **Can TLMs be used to predict psychometric properties of test items?** If so, the benefit for psychometric practitioners[3] is enormous, as it can reduce the need for multiple rounds of costly empirical testing. But the benefits for NLP are significant as well: knowing how the psychometric properties of items differ when applied to artificial versus human populations will give us unique insight into how they solve such problems, and how they can be improved.

Main Contributions of this Paper: We present the first exploration into how well TLMs can be used to predict certain psychometric properties of linguistic test items. To do this, we identified a subset of items from the GLUE broad coverage diagnostic (Wang et al., 2018), and collected human responses on these items in order to assess simple psychometric properties, designing a novel user validation procedure to do so. We then assess the performance of 240 LMs on these diagnostic items. Our resulting analysis clearly shows that TLMs excel in modeling psychometric properties in certain sub-categories of linguistic skills, thus providing fruitful directions for future work.

2 Related Work

What reason do we have to suspect that TLMs can predict the psychometric properties of test items? Although TLMs were not primarily designed to compute in a human-like way, there are some reasons to suspect that they may have the ability to effectively model at least some aspects of human linguistic reasoning: They consistently demonstrate superior performance (at least compared to other LMs) on human-inspired linguistic benchmarks (Wang et al., 2018, 2019), and they are typically pre-trained using a lengthy process designed to embed deep semantic knowledge, resulting in efficient encoding of semantic relationships (Zhou et al., 2020; Petroni et al., 2019; Davison et al., 2019; Cui et al., 2020). Common optimization tasks for pre-training transformers, such as the masked LM task (Devlin et al., 2018) are quite similar to the word prediction tasks that are known to predict children's performance on other linguistic skills (Borovsky et al., 2012; Neuman et al., 2011; Gambi et al., 2020). Finally, TLMs tend to outperform other LMs in recent work modeling human reading times, eye-tracking data, and other psychological and psycholinguistic phenomena (Merkx and Frank, 2021; Schrimpf et al., 2020b,a; Hao et al., 2020; Bhatia and Richie, 2020; Laverghetta Jr. and Licato, 2021; Laverghetta Jr. et al., 2021).

There are many studies probing TLMs in various ways, a body of work sometimes called "BERTology" (Rogers et al., 2021; Belinkov and Glass, 2019). However, work explicitly bridging psychometrics with AI is less common. Xue (2019) augmented the DINA (De La Torre, 2009) and DINO (Templin and Henson, 2006) cognitive diagnostic models (Sessoms and Henson, 2018) with a feed-forward neural network that used a semi-supervised learning objective. The architecture achieved superior results to multiple baselines. Ahmad et al. (2020) created a deep learning architecture for extracting psychometric dimensions related to health-care, specifically numeracy, literacy, trust, anxiety, and drug experiences. Their architecture did not use transformers, and relied instead on a sophisticated combination of convolutional and recurrent layers in order to extract representations of emotions, demographics, and syntactic patterns, among others. Eisape et al. (2020) examined the correlation between human and LM next-word predictions and proposed a procedure for achieving more human-like cloze probabilities. In NLP, methods from item response theory (IRT) (Reckase, 2009) have been particularly popular. Lalor et al. (2018) used IRT models to study the impact of question difficulty on the performance of deep models on several NLP tasks. In a follow-up study, Lalor and

[2]Note however that we focus only on validity and reliability in this work.

[3]In other words, professionals responsible for designing standardized tests or other evaluations meant to assess latent attributes of individuals.

Yu (2020) used IRT models to estimate the competence of LSTM (Hochreiter and Schmidhuber, 1997) and BERT models during training. This allowed them to create a dynamic curriculum learning (Bengio et al., 2009) algorithm, which achieved superior performance to the same models trained using a static scheduler for several tasks. Sedoc and Ungar (2020) used IRT to efficiently assess chat-bots. Martínez-Plumed et al. (2019) used IRT to analyze the performance of machine learning classifiers in a supervised learning task. IRT has also been used to evaluate machine translation systems (Otani et al., 2016) and speech synthesizers (Oliveira et al., 2020), and also in computer vision (RichardWebster et al., 2018).

This literature clearly indicates that there has been a lot of interest in applying psychometrics to AI. So far, most of this effort has focused on specific use cases, and has not attempted to broadly assess commonalities between machine and human reasoning. Most similar to our current work is Lalor et al. (2019), who showed that deep models could achieve a strong correlation with IRT parameters fitted using human data on several NLP datasets. However, they compared the human responses to LSTMs and neural semantic encoders (Munkhdalai and Yu, 2017), and did not consider TLMs. Furthermore, they focused on the SNLI dataset, which is less challenging than the GLUE diagnostic and does not group questions based on fine-grained linguistic competencies.

Besides the GLUE diagnostic, other taxonomies have been proposed, such as TaxiNLI (Joshi et al., 2020b). Although TaxiNLI includes some types of reasoning which have no clear analogue in GLUE, many of their categories are quite similar.[4] Since the TaxiNLI questions were also taken from the MNLI dataset, we were concerned they would be too easy for some of the larger TLMs we planned to evaluate. We, therefore, chose to focus specifically on the challenging GLUE diagnostic set and leave TaxiNLI for future work.

3 Gathering Language Model Data

The GLUE and SuperGLUE benchmarks (Wang et al., 2018, 2019) are suites of NLP tasks designed to test the general linguistic capabilities of LMs. Included as part of the GLUE benchmark is a set of diagnostic questions, called the broad coverage diagnostic, which are all formatted as natural language inference (NLI) problems. NLI problems consist of two sentences: a premise (p) and hypothesis (h), and solving such a problem involves assessing whether p textually entails h. There are typically three choices: either p does textually entail h (entailment), p entails that h is impossible (contradiction), or h's truth can not be determined from p alone (neutral). The NLI task is therefore quite general and can encompass a wide variety of other "commonsense" reasoning tasks. The broad coverage diagnostic was manually curated by linguistics and NLP experts and is meant to assess broad psycholinguistic competencies of LMs across multiple categories. For instance, the *propositional structure* category contains questions that exploit propositional logic operators; e.g., p = "The cat sat on the mat." and h = "The cat did not sit on the mat." The diagnostic covers four main categories of linguistic competencies: *lexical semantics*, *predicate-argument structure*, *logic*, and *knowledge and common sense*. These categories are further divided into multiple sub-categories, each of which covers a specific and interesting phenomenon in language. The GLUE diagnostic thus aims to be a comprehensive test of linguistic reasoning skills, making it suitable for our present study.

To evaluate our models, we selected a subset of the GLUE diagnostic questions that were a member of only one sub-category, to better isolate factors. In most cases, there were enough questions in a single sub-category that we could just drop all questions that belonged to multiple sub-categories, further details on this preprocessing can be found in Appendix A. After performing preprocessing, we had 811 remaining diagnostic questions encompassing 20 sub-categories. Each sub-category had at least 15 questions, and we selected 7 of the sub-categories to use in our experiments:

1. *morphological negation* (MN)
2. *prepositional phrases* (PP)
3. *lexical entailment* (LE)
4. *quantifiers* (Q)
5. *propositional structure* (PS)
6. *richer logical structure* (RLS)
7. *world knowledge* (WK)

[4] Both GLUE and TanxiNLI test for temporal reasoning, but place them at different levels in the taxonomy.

We selected these 7 sub-categories based on how much the average performance of the LMs improved after pre-training and finetuning. A substantial performance improvement indicated the category was solvable by the models, and would therefore provide a meaningful comparsion to the human data. We gathered responses to the diagnostic from a wide array of TLMs, including BERT (Devlin et al., 2018), RoBERTa (Liu et al., 2019), T5 (Raffel et al., 2020), ALBERT (Lan et al., 2020), XLNet (Yang et al., 2019), ELECTRA (Clark et al., 2020), Longformer (Beltagy et al., 2020), SpanBERT (Joshi et al., 2020a), DeBERTa (He et al., 2020), and ConvBERT (Jiang et al., 2020). Each of these models differs from the others along one or more factors, including underlying architecture, pre-training objective and data, or the general category the model belongs to (autoregressive, autoencoding, or sequence-to-sequence). For most of these models we used the Transformers (Wolf et al., 2020) implementation, the exception being T5, which was implemented in PyTorch Lightning (Falcon and .al, 2019). We use LSTM-based LMs (Hochreiter and Schmidhuber, 1997) as a baseline, further details on the LMs can be found in Appendix A.

We used the SNLI (Bowman et al., 2015), MNLI (Williams et al., 2018), and ANLI (Nie et al., 2020) training and dev sets to finetune our models. We found that the amount of finetuning data had a significant impact on final diagnostic performance. Therefore, to increase the variance in our results as much as possible we used the following training set partitions for all model configurations:

- SNLI alone
- MNLI alone
- SNLI + MNLI
- SNLI + MNLI + ANLI

Both the train and dev sets were shuffled before every trial. We finetuned our models for between 5 to 10 epochs. We used the reported Matthews correlation (Matthews, 1975) on the dev set during training to determine when the performance had saturated; when this correlation stopped consistently increasing for at least a few dev set evaluations we stopped training. We evaluated on the dev set every 15,000 steps. All the transformer's key hyperparameters were selected in a similar way to the study by Lalor et al. (2019). For all models, we used a learning rate of $1 * 10^{-5}$ and a max sequence length of 175. Since running even a small grid search to optimize the hyperparameters of each model would have dramatically increased the number of trials, we instead chose to fix these hyperparameters to be similar to what was used in prior work (e.g. Devlin et al., 2018). We also found that nearly all models consistently achieved a Matthews correlation of about 0.5 or higher on the dev set, and thus concluded that our hyperparameters were suitable. It is important to note that our goal in finetuning was not to completely optimize the model's performance on these NLI datasets. Rather, since the diagnostic is formatted as an NLI task, we hoped that finetuning would help the models to learn what the output labels should be.[5] To evaluate these models, we experimented with four different training regimes:

- **Zero shot:** The model is initialized with random weights in the hidden layers and is evaluated on the diagnostic without any training. This is meant to test whether there is any property of the architecture itself which is useful for solving the diagnostic.
- **Pre-train, no finetune:** The model is pre-trained but not finetuned.
- **No pre-train, finetune:** The model weights are initialized randomly, but we finetune the model before evaluating it.
- **Pre-train and finetune:** The model is pre-trained and finetuned.

For BERT, we experimented with both Devlin et al.'s pre-trained models, and a BERT model we trained from scratch. Our BERT model had an identical architecture to *bert-base* and was pre-trained on Google's One Billion Words corpus (Chelba et al., 2014). We used the same hyperparameters from the BERT paper (Devlin et al., 2018), using a learning rate of $4 * 10^{-5}$, a max sequence length of 128, a warmup ratio of 0.01, and a weight decay of 0.01. We used the Transformers library to pre-train this model, and saved every end-of-epoch checkpoint. We pre-trained for 52 epochs and used every 10th checkpoint to gather diagnostic data separately. This allowed us to study the effect pre-training had on diagnostic performance.

[5]Finetuning T5 is necessary to avoid random output.

In summary, this process allowed us to vary the underlying architecture, the number of trainable parameters, and the amount of finetuning data used in each trial. This allowed us to treat each trained model as effectively being a different "individual" (and we will refer to them as such), which might have a radically different cognitive profile from its counterparts. For example, a *roberta-base* model that was pre-trained and finetuned on all 3 NLI datasets might produce very different response patterns than a *roberta-large* model evaluated zero-shot. We used three Tesla V100 GPUs with 32GB of video memory each, as well as preemptable GPUs on Google Colab,[6] to train all models. Wherever possible, we used Apex[7] to speed up training.

4 Human Studies

As our purpose in gathering this LM data was to evaluate it against human performance, we additionally ran a human study. To do this, we recruited workers on Amazon Mechanical Turk (mTurk[8]) to complete our subset of GLUE diagnostic questions. While mTurk makes conducting large-scale human studies convenient, there are also well-documented problems with participants not completing tasks in good faith (Berinsky et al., 2014, 2016; Keith et al., 2017). There are multiple techniques for filtering out bad-faith participants, such as the use of "attention check" questions, sometimes called "instructional manipulation checks" (Hauser and Schwarz, 2015), which are designed so that a good-faith participant would be unlikely to get them incorrect. But this alone would not suffice for our purposes here, as we want a certain amount of low-scoring participants on some sub-categories, so that the population variances on sub-category items would better reflect their actual variances.[9] Therefore, we designed a procedure for distinguishing bad-faith from low-performing participants.

We first obtained attention checks from the ChaosNLI dataset (Nie et al., 2020), which gathered over 450,000 human annotations on questions from SNLI and MNLI. Since each question in ChaosNLI was annotated by 100 different workers, if inter-annotator agreement for a given question is high, we conclude that question is likely extremely easy to solve. These questions were also in the same format as the diagnostic questions, which made it less likely that workers would realize they were being given an attention check. We gathered 36 questions from ChaosNLI where the agreement for the correct label was at least 90%. The labels for this subset were perfectly balanced. These were enough questions to ensure that each phase of our trials used a unique set of attention check questions.

The human studies were split up into 5 phases, and workers who did sufficiently well in a given phase were given a qualification to continue to the next phase:

1. **On-boarding:** A qualifying HIT (human intelligence task) open to any worker located in the United States, who had completed at least 50 HITs with an approval rating of at least 90%. The HIT consisted of 5 attention check questions, given to each worker in the same order. We gathered responses from up to 200 workers.

2. **Phase 1:** Included questions from *morphological negation*, and 3 attention checks. We gathered up to 45 responses.

3. **Phase 2:** Included questions from *lexical entailment* and *prepositional phrases*, as well as 6 attention checks. We gathered up to 36 responses.

4. **Phase 3:** Included questions from *quantifiers* and *propositional structure*, as well as 6 attention checks. We gathered up to 27 responses.

5. **Phase 4:** Included questions from *richer logical structure* and *world knowledge*, as well as 6 attention checks. We gathered responses from all accepted workers from Phase 3.

In each phase, questions were randomly ordered, except for attention checks which were spread evenly throughout the survey. We used Qualtrics[10] to create the surveys for each HIT and collect the responses. Participants were first presented with

[6]https://colab.research.google.com

[7]https://github.com/NVIDIA/apex

[8]https://www.mturk.com

[9]If we only kept high-performing participants, the item variances would be skewed to be low and roughly the same, which would not reflect the true variances we would expect to see from a large population of good-faith participants.

[10]https://www.qualtrics.com

instructions for the task and some examples, which were based on the instructions originally given to annotators for the MNLI dataset.[11] The questions from each category were a randomly chosen subset of 15 questions tested on the LMs for that category, balanced for each label. For each question, workers also had to provide a short justification statement on why they believed their answer was correct, which was used to help filter out bad faith participants. To validate the responses to our surveys, we developed the following authentication procedure:

Stage 1: Look for duplicate IPs or worker IDs, indicating that the worker took the HIT more than once. If there are any, reject the second and future HITs, but keep the first submission.
Stage 2: If the worker's overall score was less than 40%, reject the HIT. If their overall score was greater than 60%, accept the HIT. For workers who scored between 40% and 60%, we still rejected the HIT if they got less than 75% of the attention checks correct.
Stage 3: Finally, examine the justifications of all workers not previously rejected. Here we were looking for simple, but clear, reasons for why workers chose their answer. We included this step because we found in a pilot study that workers sometimes provided nonsensical justifications for their answers even when they did well on the survey, making it unclear whether they were truly paying attention. We checked that the justifications appeared relevant to the question (some workers seemed to paste random text from other websites into the justification), that they did not paste part of the question for their justification, that they did not use the same justification for every question, and that they did not use short nonsensical phrases for their justification (some workers simply wrote "good" or "nice" as their justification). This allowed us to keep some low-scoring participants who had put genuine effort into the task.

Manual inspection of the resulting responses suggested that workers who passed stage 3 consistently gave higher quality responses than those who did not. These workers gave more detailed justifications that clearly articulated their thought process, often citing specific details from the question. On the other hand, workers who failed to give good justifications also tended to perform quite poorly, generally scoring at or below random chance, which further indicated that they were not actually paying attention. We, therefore, believe the use of justifications helped us gather higher-quality responses. Further details on the human study can be found in Appendix B.

[11] https://nyu-mll.github.io/GLUE-human-performance/mnli.html

5 Experimental Results

Using the procedures described in §3 and §4, we gathered results from 27 human participants and 240 neural LMs (183 transformer-based and 57 LSTM-based). In addition to the LSTMs, we also include a true random baseline which simply guesses randomly on every question. In the following experiments, we use the human performance on each category as the basis for analyzing the performance of the artificial populations, specifically in terms of how well each artificial population's responses correlate with the human data.

Category	D_T	D_L	D_R
MN	**-0.28, $<$0.5**	0.27, $>$0.5	-0.14, $>$0.5
PP	**0.86, $<$0.001**	0.47, $<$0.1	0.42, $<$0.5
LE	**0.62, $<$0.05**	0.17, $>$0.5	-0.22, $<$0.5
Q	**0.57, $<$0.05**	-0.22, $<$0.5	0.41, $<$0.5
PS	**0.93, $<$0.001**	0.27, $<$0.5	0.37, $<$0.5
RLS	0.28, $<$0.5	-0.03, $>$0.5	**-0.37, $<$0.5**
WK	**0.79, $<$0.001**	0.46, $<$0.1	-0.25, $<$0.5

Table 1: Given D_H, Spearman correlation and p-values were calculated with transformer-based (D_T), LSTM-based (D_L), and random (D_R) estimates of problem difficulty (percentage of the population that got the item correct). Note here we have bolded cells whose correlations (absolute values) were highest, but their p-values were not always significant.

5.1 Classical Test Theory

We began by examining how well TLMs could predict simple problem difficulty in the human data. This measure comes from classical test theory and is calculated simply as how many members of the population get a given item right. For each item i in a given sub-category in our subset of the GLUE diagnostic, we calculated the percentage of human participants who got that question correct (D^i_H), and then the corresponding percentage for the TLMs (D^i_T), LSTM-based LMs (D^i_L), and the random baseline (D^i_R). We then calculated the Spearman correlation (Spearman, 1961) between D^i_H and each of the other populations. Results are shown in Table 1. In almost all cases, TLMs achieve a much stronger correlation with the human data than either baseline, and most were statistically significant. The main exceptions are *morphological negation* (MN) and *richer logical structure* (RLS), both of which fail to produce strong correlations. As we will see, this pattern will repeat in other measurements as well.

IIC-based Clustering An important idea in psychometrics is that questions that rely on the same skills should have similar chances of being answered correctly by a given participant (Rust and Golombok, 2014). Whether questions rely on similar skills can be tested using the inter-item correlation (IIC) between two items, where high IIC suggests that the items rely on similar underlying reasoning skills. Thus, it can be assumed that if items cluster together when using IIC as a distance metric, they rely on similar underlying cognitive skills. To explore this, given a correlation measure c ranging from -1 to 1, we convert it into a distance metric by taking $1 - c$. We use this metric to apply k-medoids clustering to the diagnostic questions, using the silhouette method (Rousseeuw, 1987) to find the optimal number of clusters. For each subcategory, we perform clustering using human, transformer, LSTM, and random data separately (H, T, L, and R respectively). We use the k-medoids implementation from scikit-learn extra[12] and use scikit-learn (Pedregosa et al., 2011) to calculate the silhouette coefficient.

After clustering, for each pair of items (i, j) we define $C^D_{i,j}$ as 1 if i and j are in the same cluster as determined by dataset $D \in \{H, T, L, R\}$. Finally, to determine how well clusters from the LM responses match the human responses, we calculate Pearson correlation (Pearson, 1895) between C^H and each of C^T, C^L, and C^R. Results are shown in Table 2. Similar to Table 1, we see statistically significant correlations from TLMs in every subcategory, except for *morphological negation* (MN), where TLMs again achieve only weak correlation.

Per Model Analysis The previous results give us some insights into the performance of the entire TLM population. However, individual transformers might differ somewhat in the specific skills they are proficient in. To study this, we performed the same simple problem difficulty experiment, but this time only used the diagnostic results from a single transformer architecture (for instance just BERT). We did this for each architecture, and then

[12] https://github.com/scikit-learn-contrib/scikit-learn-extra

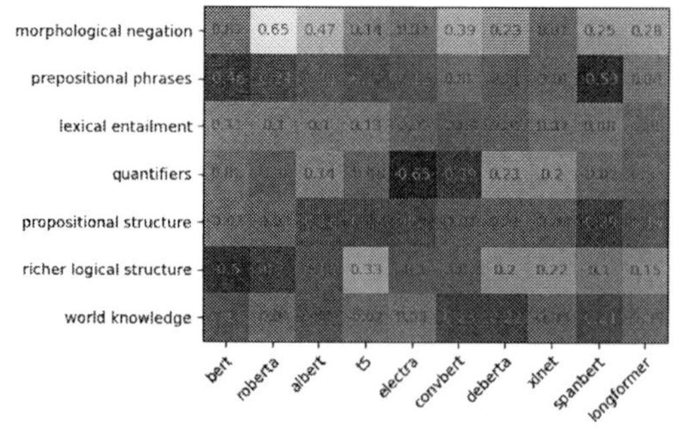

Figure 1: Change in correlation for each TLM architecture on each category, compared to the entire TLM population. Best viewed in color.

on each diagnostic sub-category, we computed the difference between the single architecture's correlation and the overall correlation from Table 1. The heatmap in Figure 1 shows the results, with cooler colors indicating a stronger decrease in correlation and warmer colors indicating a stronger increase. In many cases, the correlation is almost the same as the value reported in Table 1. However, in some cases the difference is striking. For example, RoBERTa gets a much stronger correlation on *morphological negation* than any other model. Overall, it appears that most models are achieving close to the mean correlation, but there are a few significant differences.

Category	C_T	C_L	C_R
MN	0.18, <0.1	**0.40, <0.001**	-0.14, <0.5
PP	**0.31, <0.01**	-0.15, <0.5	-0.01, >0.5
LE	**0.31, <0.01**	-0.03, >0.5	-0.16, <0.5
Q	**0.24, <0.05**	-0.01, >0.5	0.06, >0.5
PS	**0.51, <0.001**	0.03, >0.5	0.04, >0.5
RLS	**0.46, <0.001**	-0.07, <0.5	0.04, >0.5
WK	**0.28, <0.01**	0.00, >0.5	-0.09, <0.5

Table 2: Pearson correlation and p-values for how well items clustered using human responses match the clusters which used transformer-based (C_T), LSTM-based (C_L), and random (C_R) items.

5.2 Item Response Theory

Models from classical test theory have an important shortcoming: they provide no clear way to separate the characteristics of the test taker and the test items. In practice, the observed performance on a test is affected by both the test taker and the test itself. This intuition is formalized in a psychometrics approach known as item response theory (IRT), in which both item characteristics and individual ability are modeled and used to predict performance (Baker and Kim, 2004). IRT models are often regarded as more informative than classical models and have become standard tools when designing evaluation scales. Formally, let j be an individual taking a test, i be an item on that test, and θ_j be that individual's latent ability. Then the probability that j answers i correctly is defined as:

$$P(y_i = 1|\theta_j) = c_i + \frac{1 - c_i}{1 + e^{-a_i(\theta_j - b_i)}} \quad (1)$$

Where a_i, b_i, and c_i are *item parameters* and $y_i = 1$ indicates a correct answer. a_i is the discrimination parameter, which refers to how effective the item is for picking out high versus low ability test takers. b_i is the difficulty parameter, which models how easy or difficult the item is. Finally, c_i is the probability of guessing correctly. If both guessing and discrimination are held constant, we get the one-parameter or Rasch model (Rasch, 1993). Given a large number of human responses to a set of items, parameters for IRT models can be estimated using the marginal maximum likelihood method and expectation maximization (Bock and Aitkin, 1981).

Since TLMs correlated well with humans using the classical techniques we tested, we wished to examine whether this would still hold using IRT models. To do this, we used the diagnostic results from each population to fit Rasch models. We used the ltm R package to fit all models (Rizopoulos, 2006). This gave us separate difficulty parameter estimates b_i for each item i, for each population. To determine how well the difficulty parameters matched between populations, we calculated the Pearson correlation between the b_i using our human response data (H), and the b_i obtained using the other populations (T, L, R). Results are shown in Table 3. As before, TLMs consistently get a stronger correlation than either baseline on most sub-categories, except for *morphological negation* (MN) and *richer logical structure* (RLS). Interestingly, LSTM-based LMs achieved statistically significant and stronger correlations than TLMs on certain sub-categories: *world knowledge* (WK) and *prepositional phrases* (PP). The only other experiment where LSTM-based LMs achieved stronger correlation was reported in Table 2, where they achieved superior correlation to TLMs on *morphological negation* (MN).

Category	D_T	D_L	D_R
MN	0.08, >0.5	**0.29, <0.5**	0.19, >0.5
PP	0.48, <0.1	**0.69, <0.01**	-0.25, <0.5
LE	**0.88, <0.001**	-0.06, >0.5	0.14, >0.5
Q	**0.61, <0.05**	0.03, >0.5	0.12, >0.5
PS	**0.61, <0.05**	0.05, >0.5	-0.25, <0.5
RLS	0.16, >0.5	-0.05, >0.5	**-0.31, <0.5**
WK	0.52, <0.05	**0.59, <0.05**	-0.1, >0.5

Table 3: Pearson correlation and p-values for transformer-based (D_T), LSTM-based (D_L), and random (D_R) estimates of problem difficulty computed using Rasch models.

6 Discussion

Our analysis has revealed some interesting patterns that would have been difficult to discern using traditional evaluation metrics. Overall, TLMs perform consistently better than either of our baselines in modeling human psychometric properties. However, this improvement is also not uniform across all psycholinguistic categories. In fact, we have found some regularities in this regard. For instance, TLMs failed to achieve a strong correlation on *morphological negation* in all cases. This might be explained by two facts: there is little relative variance in the human responses in this sub-category, and the average accuracy of human participants was above 90%, as opposed to LM accuracy of 55%. This sub-category also tests for reasoning over negation, which prior studies found that transformers struggle with (Rogers et al., 2021). This ability to analyze the specific kinds of reasoning transformers have become proficient in is a clear advantage psychometrics have over typical NLP evaluations. The NLP community is becoming increasingly aware of the need to construct more fine-grained evaluation benchmarks (Wang et al., 2018; Joshi et al., 2020b), and we believe our work complements these efforts nicely.

Of course, this study also has limitations. The number of human participants in our study was somewhat small compared to typical psychometrics studies, which makes it difficult to draw stronger conclusions. One of the main criticisms IRT models draw is that they can require thousands of responses to get good estimates of the latent parameters (Min and Aryadoust, 2021). As stated earlier, practical limitations on population size is a common problem in psychometrics research, one which our present work hopes to alleviate somewhat. Future work will need to repeat our experiments with much larger population sizes, and also take measures to ensure sufficient diversity in the study population (e.g., age, income, education level, English fluency, etc.). Improvements in the computational efficiency of TLMs is likely also necessary for our approach to be practical, as it is unlikely most pyschometricians have access to extensive GPU resources. One possible solution would be to identify a subset of TLMs that preserves the psychometric properties of the entire population, which might allow us to achieve similar results with fewer models.

Furthermore, although we reported in detail on certain psychometrics measures where our method demonstrated promising results for TLMs, it is worth reporting that certain other measures we examined did not appear to align well. For example, item-total correlations using human data did not appear to correlate with any LM data better than with the random baseline. Likewise, our LMs failed to predict average inter-item correlations between either random subsets of items or our diagnostic sub-categories. More work is needed to better understand why.

Finally, while our experiments have given us some insights into the validity and reliability of the diagnostic items, it is unclear whether our approach can allow us to measure their fairness. Although it is an important property, fairness is somewhat more controversial than other psychometric properties, in part because there are multiple interpretations of what constitutes test bias (Warne et al., 2014). Being able to probe the fairness of items would have interesting downstream applications. For instance, it might indicate whether a diagnostic gives an unfair advantage to certain types of classifiers.

7 Conclusion

We believe our work offers a clear path forward for bridging psychometrics and AI. The use of psychometrics measures gives us a more nuanced understanding of the latent abilities of LMs than single-valued measures like accuracy or F_1 can provide. Furthermore, the increasingly powerful ability of TLMs to model human "commonsense" reasoning and knowledge suggests new ways to predict psychometrics properties of test items, reducing the need for costly human empirical data.

Acknowledgments

This material is based upon work supported by the Air Force Office of Scientific Research under award numbers FA9550-17-1-0191 and FA9550-18-1-0052. Any opinions, findings, and conclusions or recommendations expressed in this material are those of the authors and do not necessarily reflect the views of the United States Air Force.

References

Faizan Ahmad, Ahmed Abbasi, Jingjing Li, David G Dobolyi, Richard G Netemeyer, Gari D Clifford, and Hsinchun Chen. 2020. A deep learning architecture for psychometric natural language processing. *ACM Transactions on Information Systems (TOIS)*, 38(1):1–29.

Frank B Baker and Seock-Ho Kim. 2004. *Item response theory: Parameter estimation techniques*. CRC Press.

Yonatan Belinkov and James Glass. 2019. Analysis methods in neural language processing: A survey. *Transactions of the Association for Computational Linguistics*, 7:49–72.

Iz Beltagy, Matthew E. Peters, and Arman Cohan. 2020. Longformer: The long-document transformer. *arXiv preprint arXiv:2004.05150*.

Yoshua Bengio, Jérôme Louradour, Ronan Collobert, and Jason Weston. 2009. Curriculum learning. In *Proceedings of the 26th annual international conference on machine learning*, pages 41–48.

Adam J. Berinsky, Michele F. Margolis, and Michael W. Sances. 2014. Separating the shirkers from the workers? making sure respondents pay attention on self-administered surveys. *American Journal of Political Science*, 58(3):739–753.

Adam J. Berinsky, Michele F. Margolis, and Michael W. Sances. 2016. Can we turn shirkers into workers. *Journal of Experimental Social Psychology*, 66:20–28.

Sudeep Bhatia and Russell Richie. 2020. Transformer Networks of Human Concept Knowledge.

R Darrell Bock and Murray Aitkin. 1981. Marginal maximum likelihood estimation of item parameters: Application of an em algorithm. *Psychometrika*, 46(4):443–459.

Arielle Borovsky, Jeffrey L. Elman, and Anne Fernald. 2012. Knowing a lot for one's age: Vocabulary skill and not age is associated with anticipatory incremental sentence interpretation in children and adults. *Journal of Experimental Child Psychology*, 112(4):417–436.

Samuel R. Bowman, Gabor Angeli, Christopher Potts, and Christopher D. Manning. 2015. A large annotated corpus for learning natural language inference. In *Proceedings of the 2015 Conference on Empirical Methods in Natural Language Processing (EMNLP)*. Association for Computational Linguistics.

Selmer Bringsjord. 2011. Psychometric artificial intelligence. *Journal of Experimental & Theoretical Artificial Intelligence*, 23(3):271–277.

Selmer Bringsjord and John Licato. 2012. Psychometric artificial general intelligence: the piaget-macguyver room. In *Theoretical foundations of artificial general intelligence*, pages 25–48. Springer.

Selmer Bringsjord and Bettina Schimanski. 2003. What is artificial intelligence? psychometric ai as an answer. In *Proceedings of the 18th international joint conference on Artificial intelligence*, pages 887–893.

Ciprian Chelba, Tomas Mikolov, Mike Schuster, Qi Ge, Thorsten Brants, Phillipp Koehn, and Tony Robinson. 2014. One billion word benchmark for measuring progress in statistical language modeling. In *Fifteenth Annual Conference of the International Speech Communication Association*.

Kevin Clark, Minh-Thang Luong, Quoc V. Le, and Christopher D. Manning. 2020. Electra: Pre-training text encoders as discriminators rather than generators. In *ICLR 2020 : Eighth International Conference on Learning Representations*.

Leyang Cui, Sijie Cheng, Yu Wu, and Yue Zhang. 2020. Does bert solve commonsense task via commonsense knowledge? *arXiv preprint arXiv:2008.03945*.

Joe Davison, Joshua Feldman, and Alexander Rush. 2019. Commonsense knowledge mining from pre-trained models. In *Proceedings of the 2019 Conference on Empirical Methods in Natural Language Processing and the 9th International Joint Conference on Natural Language Processing (EMNLP-IJCNLP)*, pages 1173–1178, Hong Kong, China. Association for Computational Linguistics.

Jimmy De La Torre. 2009. Dina model and parameter estimation: A didactic. *Journal of educational and behavioral statistics*, 34(1):115–130.

Jacob Devlin, Ming-Wei Chang, Kenton Lee, and Kristina N. Toutanova. 2018. Bert: Pre-training of deep bidirectional transformers for language understanding. In *Proceedings of the 2019 Conference of the North American Chapter of the Association for Computational Linguistics: Human Language Technologies, Volume 1 (Long and Short Papers)*, pages 4171–4186.

David L. Dowe and José Hernández-Orallo. 2012. Iq tests are not for machines, yet. *Intelligence*, 40(2):77–81.

Tiwalayo Eisape, Noga Zaslavsky, and Roger Levy. 2020. Cloze Distillation Improves Psychometric Predictive Power. In *Proceedings of the 24th Conference on Computational Natural Language Learning*, pages 609–619.

WA Falcon and .al. 2019. Pytorch lightning. *GitHub. Note: https://github.com/PyTorchLightning/pytorch-lightning*, 3.

Chiara Gambi, Priya Jindal, Sophie Sharpe, Martin J. Pickering, and Hugh Rabagliati. 2020. The relation between preschoolers' vocabulary development and their ability to predict and recognize words. *Child Development*, n/a(n/a).

Yoav Goldberg. 2019. Assessing bert's syntactic abilities. *CoRR*, abs/1901.05287.

Yiding Hao, Simon Mendelsohn, Rachel Sterneck, Randi Martinez, and Robert Frank. 2020. Probabilistic predictions of people perusing: Evaluating metrics of language model performance for psycholinguistic modeling. In *Proceedings of the Workshop on Cognitive Modeling and Computational Linguistics*, pages 75–86.

David J. Hauser and Norbert Schwarz. 2015. It's a trap! instructional manipulation checks prompt systematic thinking on "tricky" tasks. *SAGE Open*, 5(2).

Pengcheng He, Xiaodong Liu, Jianfeng Gao, and Weizhu Chen. 2020. Deberta: Decoding-enhanced bert with disentangled attention.

José Hernández-Orallo, Fernando Martínez-Plumed, Ute Schmid, Michael Siebers, and David L. Dowe. 2016. Computer models solving intelligence test problems: Progress and implications. *Artificial Intelligence*, 230:74 – 107.

Sepp Hochreiter and Jürgen Schmidhuber. 1997. Long Short-Term Memory. *Neural Computation*, 9(8):1735–1780.

Jennifer Hu, Jon Gauthier, Peng Qian, Ethan Wilcox, and Roger Levy. 2020. A systematic assessment of syntactic generalization in neural language models. In *Proceedings of the 58th Annual Meeting of the Association for Computational Linguistics*, pages 1725–1744, Online. Association for Computational Linguistics.

Zi-Hang Jiang, Weihao Yu, Daquan Zhou, Yunpeng Chen, Jiashi Feng, and Shuicheng Yan. 2020. Convbert: Improving bert with span-based dynamic convolution. *Advances in Neural Information Processing Systems*, 33.

Mandar Joshi, Danqi Chen, Yinhan Liu, Daniel S Weld, Luke Zettlemoyer, and Omer Levy. 2020a. Spanbert: Improving pre-training by representing and predicting spans. *Transactions of the Association for Computational Linguistics*, 8:64–77.

Pratik Joshi, Somak Aditya, Aalok Sathe, and Monojit Choudhury. 2020b. Taxinli: Taking a ride up the nlu hill. In *Proceedings of the 24th Conference on Computational Natural Language Learning*, pages 41–55.

Melissa G. Keith, Louis Tay, and Peter D. Harms. 2017. Systems perspective of amazon mechanical turk for organizational research: Review and recommendations. *Frontiers in Psychology*, 8:1359.

David Klahr. 1999. The Conceptual Habitat: In What Kind of System Can Concepts Develop? In Ellin Kofsky, editor, *Conceptual Development : Piaget's Legacy*, chapter 6. Lawrence Erlbaum Associates.

John P Lalor, Hao Wu, Tsendsuren Munkhdalai, and Hong Yu. 2018. Understanding deep learning performance through an examination of test set difficulty: A psychometric case study. In *Proceedings of the Conference on Empirical Methods in Natural Language Processing. Conference on Empirical Methods in Natural Language Processing*, volume 2018, page 4711. NIH Public Access.

John P Lalor, Hao Wu, and Hong Yu. 2019. Learning latent parameters without human response patterns: Item response theory with artificial crowds. In *Proceedings of the Conference on Empirical Methods in Natural Language Processing. Conference on Empirical Methods in Natural Language Processing*, volume 2019, page 4240. NIH Public Access.

John P Lalor and Hong Yu. 2020. Dynamic data selection for curriculum learning via ability estimation. In *Proceedings of the Conference on Empirical Methods in Natural Language Processing. Conference on Empirical Methods in Natural Language Processing*, volume 2020, page 545. NIH Public Access.

Zhenzhong Lan, Mingda Chen, Sebastian Goodman, Kevin Gimpel, Piyush Sharma, and Radu Soricut. 2020. Albert: A lite bert for self-supervised learning of language representations. In *ICLR 2020 : Eighth International Conference on Learning Representations*.

Antonio Laverghetta Jr. and John Licato. 2021. Modeling age of acquisition norms using transformer networks. In *Proceedings of The 34th International Florida Artificial Intelligence Research Society Conference (FLAIRS-34)*. AAAI Press.

Antonio Laverghetta Jr., Animesh Nighojkar, Jamshidbek Mirzakhalov, and John Licato. 2021. Predicting Human Psychometric Properties Using Computational Language Models. In *Proceedings of the 86th Annual Meeting of the Psychometric Society*.

Yinhan Liu, Myle Ott, Naman Goyal, Jingfei Du, Mandar Joshi, Danqi Chen, Omer Levy, Mike Lewis, Luke Zettlemoyer, and Veselin Stoyanov. 2019. Roberta: A robustly optimized bert pretraining approach. *arXiv preprint arXiv:1907.11692*.

Fernando Martínez-Plumed, Ricardo BC Prudêncio, Adolfo Martínez-Usó, and José Hernández-Orallo. 2019. Item response theory in ai: Analysing machine learning classifiers at the instance level. *Artificial Intelligence*, 271:18–42.

Brian W Matthews. 1975. Comparison of the predicted and observed secondary structure of t4 phage lysozyme. *Biochimica et Biophysica Acta (BBA)-Protein Structure*, 405(2):442–451.

J.L. McClelland. 1995. A Connectionist Perspective on Knowledge and Development. In T.J. Simon and Graeme S Halford, editors, *Developing Cognitive Competence: New Approaches to Process Modeling*. Psychology Press.

Brian P McLaughlin. 2009. Systematicity Redux. *Synthese*, 170(2):251–274.

Danny Merkx and Stefan L. Frank. 2021. Human sentence processing: Recurrence or attention? In *Proceedings of the Workshop on Cognitive Modeling and Computational Linguistics*, pages 12–22, Online. Association for Computational Linguistics.

Shangchao Min and Vahid Aryadoust. 2021. A systematic review of item response theory in language assessment: Implications for the dimensionality of language ability. *Studies in Educational Evaluation*, 68:100963.

Tsendsuren Munkhdalai and Hong Yu. 2017. Neural semantic encoders. In *Proceedings of the 15th Conference of the European Chapter of the Association for Computational Linguistics: Volume 1, Long Papers*, pages 397–407, Valencia, Spain. Association for Computational Linguistics.

Susan B. Neuman, Ellen H. Newman, and Julie Dwyer. 2011. Educational effects of a vocabulary intervention on preschoolers' word knowledge and conceptual development: A cluster-randomized trial. *Reading Research Quarterly*, 46(3):249–272.

Yixin Nie, Adina Williams, Emily Dinan, Mohit Bansal, Jason Weston, and Douwe Kiela. 2020. Adversarial NLI: A new benchmark for natural language understanding. In *Proceedings of the 58th Annual Meeting of the Association for Computational Linguistics*. Association for Computational Linguistics.

Yixin Nie, Xiang Zhou, and Mohit Bansal. 2020. What can we learn from collective human opinions on natural language inference data. In *Proceedings of the 2020 Conference on Empirical Methods in Natural Language Processing (EMNLP)*, pages 9131–9143.

Chaina Santos Oliveira, C. C. Tenório, and R. Prudêncio. 2020. Item response theory to estimate the latent ability of speech synthesizers. In *ECAI*.

Naoki Otani, Toshiaki Nakazawa, Daisuke Kawahara, and Sadao Kurohashi. 2016. Irt-based aggregation model of crowdsourced pairwise comparison for evaluating machine translations. In *Proceedings of the 2016 Conference on Empirical Methods in Natural Language Processing*, pages 511–520.

K Pearson. 1895. Notes on regression and inheritance in the case of two parents proceedings of the royal society of london, 58, 240-242.

F. Pedregosa, G. Varoquaux, A. Gramfort, V. Michel, B. Thirion, O. Grisel, M. Blondel, P. Prettenhofer, R. Weiss, V. Dubourg, J. Vanderplas, A. Passos, D. Cournapeau, M. Brucher, M. Perrot, and E. Duchesnay. 2011. Scikit-learn: Machine learning in Python. *Journal of Machine Learning Research*, 12:2825–2830.

Jeffrey Pennington, Richard Socher, and Christopher Manning. 2014. Glove: Global vectors for word representation. In *Proceedings of the 2014 Conference on Empirical Methods in Natural Language Processing (EMNLP)*, pages 1532–1543.

Fabio Petroni, Tim Rocktäschel, Sebastian Riedel, Patrick Lewis, Anton Bakhtin, Yuxiang Wu, and Alexander Miller. 2019. Language models as knowledge bases? In *Proceedings of the 2019 Conference on Empirical Methods in Natural Language Processing and the 9th International Joint Conference on Natural Language Processing (EMNLP-IJCNLP)*, pages 2463–2473.

Colin Raffel, Noam Shazeer, Adam Roberts, Katherine Lee, Sharan Narang, Michael Matena, Yanqi Zhou, Wei Li, and Peter J. Liu. 2020. Exploring the limits of transfer learning with a unified text-to-text transformer. *Journal of Machine Learning Research*, 21(140):1–67.

Georg Rasch. 1993. *Probabilistic models for some intelligence and attainment tests.* ERIC.

Mark D Reckase. 2009. Multidimensional item response theory models. In *Multidimensional item response theory*, pages 79–112. Springer.

Brandon RichardWebster, So Yon Kwon, Christopher Clarizio, Samuel E Anthony, and Walter J Scheirer. 2018. Visual psychophysics for making face recognition algorithms more explainable. In *Proceedings of the European Conference on Computer Vision (ECCV)*, pages 252–270.

Dimitris Rizopoulos. 2006. ltm: An r package for latent variable modeling and item response theory analyses. *Journal of statistical software*, 17(5):1–25.

Anna Rogers, Olga Kovaleva, and Anna Rumshisky. 2021. A primer in bertology: What we know about how bert works. *Transactions of the Association for Computational Linguistics*, 8:842–866.

Peter J Rousseeuw. 1987. Silhouettes: a graphical aid to the interpretation and validation of cluster analysis. *Journal of computational and applied mathematics*, 20:53–65.

John Rust and Susan Golombok. 2014. *Modern psychometrics: The science of psychological assessment.* Routledge.

Martin Schrimpf, Idan Blank, Greta Tuckute, Carina Kauf, Eghbal A. Hosseini, Nancy Kanwisher, Joshua Tenenbaum, and Evelina Fedorenko. 2020a. Artificial neural networks accurately predict language processing in the brain. *bioRxiv*.

Martin Schrimpf, Idan Blank, Greta Tuckute, Carina Kauf, Eghbal A. Hosseini, Nancy Kanwisher, Joshua Tenenbaum, and Evelina Fedorenko. 2020b. The neural architecture of language: Integrative reverse-engineering converges on a model for predictive processing. *bioRxiv*.

João Sedoc and Lyle Ungar. 2020. Item response theory for efficient human evaluation of chatbots. In *Proceedings of the First Workshop on Evaluation and Comparison of NLP Systems*, pages 21–33.

John Sessoms and Robert A Henson. 2018. Applications of diagnostic classification models: A literature review and critical commentary. *Measurement: Interdisciplinary Research and Perspectives*, 16(1):1–17.

Charles Spearman. 1961. The proof and measurement of association between two things.

Nitish Srivastava, Geoffrey Hinton, Alex Krizhevsky, Ilya Sutskever, and Ruslan Salakhutdinov. 2014. Dropout: a simple way to prevent neural networks from overfitting. *The journal of machine learning research*, 15(1):1929–1958.

Ron Sun. 1992. On variable binding in connectionist networks. *ConnectionScience*, 4(2):93–124.

Ron Sun. 1995. Schemas, Logics, and Neural Assemblies. *Applied Intelligence*, 5.2:83–102.

Jonathan L Templin and Robert A Henson. 2006. Measurement of psychological disorders using cognitive diagnosis models. *Psychological methods*, 11(3):287.

Ashish Vaswani, Noam Shazeer, Niki Parmar, Jakob Uszkoreit, Llion Jones, Aidan N. Gomez, undefinedukasz Kaiser, and Illia Polosukhin. 2017. Attention is all you need. In *Proceedings of the 31st International Conference on Neural Information Processing Systems*, NIPS'17, page 6000–6010, Red Hook, NY, USA. Curran Associates Inc.

Alex Wang, Yada Pruksachatkun, Nikita Nangia, Amanpreet Singh, Julian Michael, Felix Hill, Omer Levy, and Samuel R. Bowman. 2019. Superglue: A stickier benchmark for general-purpose language understanding systems. In *Proceedings of NeurIPS*.

Alex Wang, Amanpreet Singh, Julian Michael, Felix Hill, Omer Levy, and Samuel Bowman. 2018. GLUE: A multi-task benchmark and analysis platform for natural language understanding. In *Proceedings of the 2018 EMNLP Workshop BlackboxNLP: Analyzing and Interpreting Neural Networks for NLP*, pages 353–355, Brussels, Belgium. Association for Computational Linguistics.

Russell T Warne, Myeongsun Yoon, and Chris J Price. 2014. Exploring the various interpretations of "test bias". *Cultural Diversity and Ethnic Minority Psychology*, 20(4):570.

Ethan Gotlieb Wilcox, Jon Gauthier, Jennifer Hu, Peng Qian, and Roger Levy. 2020. On the predictive power of neural language models for human real-time comprehension behavior.

Adina Williams, Nikita Nangia, and Samuel Bowman. 2018. A broad-coverage challenge corpus for sentence understanding through inference. In *Proceedings of the 2018 Conference of the North American Chapter of the Association for Computational Linguistics: Human Language Technologies, Volume 1 (Long Papers)*, pages 1112–1122. Association for Computational Linguistics.

Thomas Wolf, Lysandre Debut, Victor Sanh, Julien Chaumond, Clement Delangue, Anthony Moi, Pierric Cistac, Tim Rault, Rémi Louf, Morgan Funtowicz, Joe Davison, Sam Shleifer, Patrick von Platen, Clara Ma, Yacine Jernite, Julien Plu, Canwen Xu, Teven Le Scao, Sylvain Gugger, Mariama Drame, Quentin Lhoest, and Alexander M. Rush. 2020. Transformers: State-of-the-art natural language processing. In *Proceedings of the 2020 Conference on Empirical Methods in Natural Language Processing: System Demonstrations*, pages 38–45, Online. Association for Computational Linguistics.

Kang Xue. 2019. Computational diagnostic classification model using deep feedforward network based semi-supervised learning. In *25th ACM SIGKDD Conference on Knowledge Discovery and Data Mining (KDD) Workshop on Deep Learning for Education*.

Zhilin Yang, Zihang Dai, Yiming Yang, Jaime G. Carbonell, Ruslan Salakhutdinov, and Quoc V. Le. 2019. Xlnet: Generalized autoregressive pretraining for language understanding. In *Advances in Neural Information Processing Systems*, volume 32, pages 5753–5763.

Xuhui Zhou, Yue Zhang, Leyang Cui, and Dandan Huang. 2020. Evaluating commonsense in pre-trained language models. In *Proceedings of the AAAI Conference on Artificial Intelligence*, volume 34, pages 9733–9740.

A Additional Details on Language Model Experiments

To create the subset of the GLUE diagnostic, there were three cases where we needed to merge members of one sub-category into another to prevent overlap:

1. *negation* and *double negation* questions were merged into *morphological negation*.
2. *symmetry/collectivity* was merged into *core arguments*.
3. Questions in both *world knowledge* and *named entities* were merged into *named entities*.

Each of these was cases where the sub-categories overlapped highly. For a full listing of the sub-categories and their descriptions, see (Wang et al., 2018). We experimented with multiple different snapshots of each TLM, which differed in the number of trainable parameters. We obtained these snapshots from HuggingFace.[13] For each model we used a smaller version, designated with the *small* or *base* suffix, and a larger version, designated with the *base* or *large* suffix. For example, for BERT we experimented with both *bert-base* and *bert-large*, where *bert-large* had more trainable parameters. For ALBERT, we used the *base* and *xxlarge* versions.

For the LSTMs, we used a PyTorch implementation designed specifically for NLI.[14] We initialized the LSTM-based LMs with GloVe word embeddings (Pennington et al., 2014). We ran a non-exhaustive grid search to generate a population of LSTMs, changing the number of recurrent layers, size of the hidden layers, learning rate, and dropout (Srivastava et al., 2014) probability.

B Human Study Details

We paid workers the following amount for each phase:

- **On-boarding:** $0.50
- **Phase 1:** $3.60
- **Phase 2:** $7.20
- **Phase 3:** $7.20
- **Phase 4:** $7.20

Our payment structure was designed to incentivize workers to put forth their best effort when completing the task. Workers were informed that successfully completing each task would award them the opportunity to earn additional payment on each subsequent phase. However, if on a given phase a worker failed our authentication protocol

[13] https://huggingface.co/models

[14] https://github.com/pytorch/examples/tree/master/snli

we rejected their work and did not pay them. Workers were informed before starting every study that we would evaluate the quality of their work, and that it might be rejected if we found evidence that they did not put forth an honest effort.

Semantic shift in social networks

Bill Noble*, **Asad Sayeed***, **Raquel Fernández**†, **Staffan Larsson***

*Dept. of Philosophy, Linguistics and Theory of Science, University of Gothenburg
{bill.noble,asad.sayeed,staffan.larsson}@gu.se

†University of Amsterdam
raquel.fernandez@uva.nl

Abstract

Just as the meaning of words is tied to the communities in which they are used, so too is semantic change. But how does lexical semantic change manifest differently across different communities? In this work, we investigate the relationship between community structure and semantic change in 45 communities from the social media website Reddit. We use distributional methods to quantify lexical semantic change and induce a social network on communities, based on interactions between members. We explore the relationship between semantic change and the *clustering coefficient* of a community's social network graph, as well as community *size* and *stability*. While none of these factors are found to be significant on their own, we report a significant effect of their three-way interaction. We also report on significant word-level effects of frequency and change in frequency, which replicate previous findings.

1 Introduction

The mechanisms and patterns of semantic change have a long history of study in linguistics (e.g., Paul, 1886; Bloomfield, 1933; Blank, 1999). However, historical accounts of semantic change typically consider meaning at the language level and, as Clark (1996) points out, referring to Lewis's (1969) account of convention, the meaning of a word "does not hold for a word *simpliciter*, but for a word *in a particular community*". This gives rise questions of how semantic change manifests differently in different communities. In this work, we explore relationship between semantic change and several community characteristics, including social network structure.

Social network analysis has long been a tool of sociolinguists studying variation and change (e.g., Bloomfield, 1933; Milroy and Milroy, 1985; Eckert, 1988), but our work differs somewhat from that tradition in both methodology and focus. Sociolinguists typically work with the social networks *of individuals*—their *ego networks*—how many people each speaker is connected to, what kind of relationships they have and, sometimes, how people in their immediate network are connected to each other. The ego network is convenient for sociolinguists using ethnographic methods; it is usually infeasible to recreate the entire social network of a large community (Sharma and Dodsworth, 2020). By studying online communities, we are able to define and compute several community-level structural characteristics including *size*, *stability*, and *social network clustering* (Section 5).

Another way that our work differs from the variationist approach is that we consider change on the level of *meaning*. With a few exceptions (e.g., Hasan, 2009), sociolinguistic research studies variation in linguistic *form* (phonology, morphology and syntax). Indeed, mainstream sociolinguists have expressed skepticism that semantics can be a proper subject of variational analysis at all (Lavandera, 1978; Weiner and Labov, 1983), since the received definition of linguistic variation concerns multiple forms expressing the same content—i.e., *different ways of saying the same thing*. With semantics at the top of the traditional linguistic hierarchy, there is no higher-order constant to which two *meanings* can refer. In this work, we instead consider *semantic shift*, which refers to changes in the meaning of a given lexical form (Newman, 2015).

For more traditional sociolinguistic variables, *social indexicality*—the association of a variant with social identities and ideology—is the main factor that mediates diffusion (Eckert, 2019). Since semantic variation can itself carry social and idealogical meaning (Hasan, 2009), there is good reason to think that it may be sensitive to some of the same aspects of community structure.

The focus on semantic shift is also made possible

Proceedings of the 10th Conference on Lexical and Computational Semantics, pages 26–37
August 5–6, 2021, Bangkok, Thailand (online)

by computational methodology—we model word meaning with distributional semantics (Section 4), which allows us to quantify short-term lexical semantic shifts at the community level.

In this study, we model the social networks of 45 English-language communities from the social media website Reddit,[1] and use diachronic word vectors to measure semantic change between two time periods one year apart. Then, we use a multi-stage linear mixed effects statistical model to test the effect of various community features on word-level semantic change.

2 Related work

In this section, we review work that uses computational methods to study linguistic variation and change in social context.

Distributional semantics Distributional methods, which model the meaning of a word with the contexts in which it appears, are a popular way to detect and quantify semantic change.[2] Several recent studies use distributional semantics to examine short-term semantic shift at the community level. Azarbonyad et al. (2017) use diachronic word vectors to study semantic change in political and media discourse, including in UK parliamentary debates, finding that word meaning changes differently depending on the political viewpoint of the speaker. Stewart et al. (2017) use diachronic word vectors to measure semantic change in the VKontakte social network during the Russia-Ukriaine crisis and find that changes in word frequency are predictive of semantic shift. Del Tredici et al. (2019) studied short-term semantic shift in the /r/LiverpoolFC community on Reddit, empirically validating the diachronic word vector model proposed by Kim et al. (2014) by correlating cosine distance between vectors from two different time periods with semantic change judgments collected from members of the community. In another study Del Tredici and Fernández (2017) find variations in word meaning across different Reddit communities, including communities organized around the same topic.

Social network analysis In an early example of using social network analysis to study the language online communities, Paolillo (1999) categorizes the relationships of users of an IRC channel as strong or weak ties, based on interaction frequency. They find that tie strength predicts the use of some online and community-specific forms but not others and conjecture that this difference is related the social meaning of those forms. Kooti et al. (2012) examined early Twitter conventions for attributing the source tweet to someone else (i.e., indicating that it is a *retweet*). They examined social network features, such as the size of a user's ego network, but did not find such features to be very predictive of convention adoption compared to global trends.

Communication games in a laboratory setting have also been used to examine the effect of social network structure on linguistic change. Raviv et al. (2019) quantified the communicative success, systematicity and stability of languages developed by "communities" of participants, but did not find a significant effect across the three different network structures that were tested. Lev-Ari (2018) found that individuals with larger real-world ego networks had less malleable semantic representations in the lab, and use computer simulations to argue that individuals with smaller ego networks therefore play an important role in the community-level propagation of linguistic change.

3 Data

To investigate semantic change in different communities, we use comments collected from the social media website Reddit.[3] On Reddit, users create *posts*, which consist of a link, image, or user-generated text, along with a *comment* section. Comments are threaded: users can comment on the post or reply to another user's comment.

Reddit is divided into forums called *subreddits*, which are typically organized around a topic of interest. While some forums—especially those organized around relatively niche topics—have a small tightly-knit community of users, others have a much looser community structure, with any given user posting and commenting infrequently.

Our dataset consists of comments from 45 randomly selected subreddits that were active in the years 2015–2017. In addition to the subreddit corpora, we created a generic Reddit corpus, consisting of comments sampled from every subreddit, including communities not in our sample. For both the generic corpus and the community-specific corpora, we constructed separate datasets for 2015 and 2017, leaving a one-year gap between them.

[1] https://www.reddit.com

[2] See Tahmasebi et al. (2018), Tang (2018), and Kutuzov et al. (2018) for recent surveys.

[3] Obtained from pushshift.io (Baumgartner et al., 2020).

The generic corpus consists of 55M comments for 2015 and 54M for 2017. For each of the selected subreddits, we sampled comments from 2015 and 2017 to construct two datasets of 5.4M tokens each (averaging 158K comments).[4]

4 Semantic change model

In this section, we describe how we quantify semantic change. We adopt a modeling procedure similar to that of Del Tredici et al. (2019), which is adapted from Kim et al. (2014)'s diachronic skip-gram with negative sampling (SGNS) model (Section 4.1). We define *naïve cosine change* for the community-specific and "generic" lexicons (Section 4.2). In Section 4.3, we use a control procedure adapted from Dubossarsky and Weinshall (2017) to account for noise in the naïve metric.

4.1 Diachronic SGNS

The strategy laid out by Kim et al. (2014) is to train a standard skip-gram language model on a corpus from some time period t_0, and then for each subsequent time period t_{n+1}, initialize a model with the same architecture with word vectors from time period t_n.[5] Del Tredici et al. (2019) adapts this procedure for a low-data setting by first training a *base* model on some large corpus, and initializing the t_0 model with vectors from that model. We follow the same framework. We train a base model, $M_{G,2015}$, on the generic 2015 corpus. Then, for each community, c, $M_{c,2015}$ is initialized with word vectors from $M_{G,2015}$ and trained on the community-specific 2015 corpus. Then, $M_{c,2017}$ is initialized from $M_{c,2015}$ and trained on the community-specific 2017 corpus. Additionally, we train a generic 2017 model, $M_{G,2017}$, which is initialized from $M_{G,2015}$ and trained on the generic 2017 corpus. See the supplementary materials for details on vocabulary and skip-gram model hyperparameters.

In the following, will write $\vec{w}_{c,t}$ for the word vector from $M_{c,t}$, corresponding word w.

[4]See Appendix A and B for details on community selection and data preprocessing. Code for downloading the data and the running experiments can be found at `https://github.com/GU-CLASP/semantic-shift-in-social-networks`.

[5]It is not clear in the original paper if the t_{n+1} model is initialized with only the word vectors from the previous time period, or if internal weights and context vectors are included as well. It seems that most subsequent implementations only carry over the word vector weights, though, which allows for more flexibility with the vocabulary. We follow this approach.

4.2 Naïve cosine change

We define *naïve cosine change* as the angular distance between corresponding word vectors from the two different time periods.[6]

For a community c, naïve cosine change is defined for all words in the vocabulary as follows:

$$\Delta_c^{\cos}(w) = \frac{\cos^{-1}(\cos\operatorname{sim}(\vec{w}_{c,2015}, \vec{w}_{c,2017}))}{\pi} \tag{1}$$

where

$$\cos\operatorname{sim}(v_1, v_2) = \frac{v_1 \cdot v_2}{\|v_1\|\|v_2\|} \tag{2}$$

Generic naïve cosine change, $\Delta_G^{\cos}$, is defined analogously.

Generally speaking, naïve cosine change has a strong track record as a semantic change metric, performing well in both human-annotated and synthetic evaluations (Hamilton et al., 2016b; Shoemark et al., 2019; Schlechtweg et al., 2020). Especially relevant to this work, Del Tredici et al. (2019) found cosine change to correlate with aggregated semantic change judgments collected from members of the /r/LiverpoolFC community on Reddit.

Model drift can distort cosine change, although this is mainly a problem with many serially-trained time periods (Shoemark et al., 2019). In a pilot study, we experimented with post-hoc aligned vector spaces and a neighborhood-based change metric (Hamilton et al., 2016a), but found minimal differences from the naïve metric.

A more serious concern for our purposes is the fact that naïve cosine change is inherently biased towards words that appear in more variable contexts. In the following section, we examine this issue more closely and define a *rectified change* metric that controls for noise. We discuss other limitations of the model in the final discussion section.

4.3 Rectified change score

Consider Figure 1 (left). Although naïve cosine change ranges *a priori* from 0 to 1, very few words score below 0.1. Even some of the most common function words have naïve cosine change above 0.2. Dubossarsky and Weinshall (2017) demonstrate that this bias is due to differences in the variance of different words' context distributions—if

[6]Some authors use $1 - \cos\operatorname{sim}$ as the cosine change metric, but angular distance is easier to interpret since it is a distance metric and ranges from 0 to 1.

a word appears in highly variable contexts, the SGNS model is more likely to pick up on differences between time periods, even if those differences are mere happenstance and not reflective of actual change. This is especially a problem in our case where the amount of data is relatively small.

We adapt the *shuffle control condition* described by Dubossarsky and Weinshall (2017) to address this problem. For each subreddit, we shuffle the 2015 and 2017 corpora together and split them randomly to create *pseudo-diachronic* corpora with two "time periods". Then, we train diachronic SGNS models just as before, including initializing the "first" model with word vectors from $M_{G,2015}$. We do this $n = 10$ times for each community, giving us, for each sample i, and each vocabulary item w, a *pseudo*-naïve cosine change, $\Delta^{\cos}_{c,i}(w)$. Since no *genuine* change can possibly have taken place between the shuffled corpora, $\Delta^{\cos}_{c,i}(w)$ is a sample from the noise distribution that contributes to w's naïve cosine change, based purely on the nosiness of its context distribution in c.

Next, we take the mean, $\bar{x}_{c,w}$ and sample standard deviation (using Bessel's correction of $n-1$ degrees of freedom), $s_{c,w}$, of the samples and compute *rectified change*, which we define as the t-statistic of the genuine naïve cosine change, given the estimated noise distribution:The resulting metric, although it is still more variable for less frequent words, is unbiased by the variance of the underlying context distribution (Figure 1, right).

$$\Delta^*_c(w) = \frac{\Delta^{\cos}_c(w) - \bar{x}_{c,w}}{s_{c,w}\sqrt{1+1/n}} \tag{3}$$

We perform this same procedure with the generic change models (shuffling together the generic 2015 and 2017 corpora) and define *generic rectified change*, Δ^*_G, analogously.

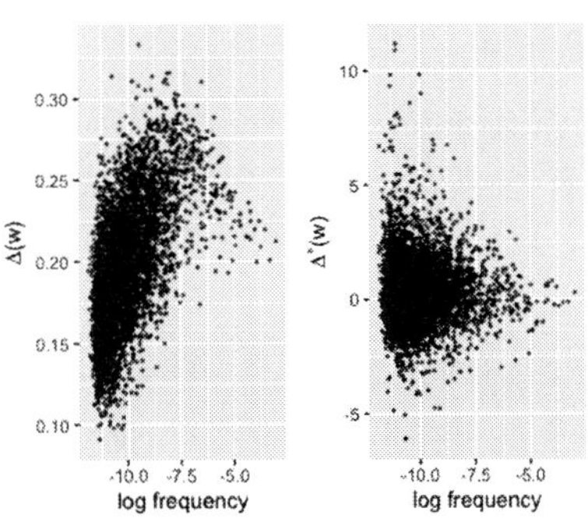

Figure 1: Naïve cosine change versus rectified change for words in the /r/toronto subreddit.

	$\Delta^{\cos}$	rank	Δ^*	rank	freq.
possibly	0.333	1	4.19	81	7.78
;	0.316	2	0.30	2519	33.89
definitely	0.316	3	2.23	450	29.68
heck	0.314	4	2.58	311	2.19
except	0.314	5	1.60	860	14.78
2016	0.260	303	11.19	1	1.54
rentals	0.245	576	10.91	2	1.53
foreign	0.218	1414	9.84	3	4.60
admission	0.221	1330	9.83	4	1.23
screening	0.245	582	9.34	5	1.21

Table 1: Top five tokens from /r/toronto, according to naïve cosine change and rectified change. Frequency is per 100k tokens.

Rectified change is a measure of how much higher (or lower) the measured naïve cosine change is than would be expected if the word's underlying context distribution hadn't changed at all. In other words, it quantifies the strength of the evidence that the word has changed. In our setup with 10 samples from the noise distribution, rectified change scores above 4.781 correspond to a 99.95% confidence that the change detected by the diachronic SGNS model was genuine. In addition to the analytical reasons for preferring rectified change and previous empirical work on historical change, we note that the highest scoring words for each community in our data are intuitively more varied and community-specific for rectified change. The naïve cosine change frequently ranks words with some kind of rhetorical or discourse connective function as the having changed the most (see Table 1 for examples).

5 Community features

In this section we characterize the structural features of the online communities in our dataset. Many of the features we define use the notion of *active members*. For a community c and time period t, the active members, $U_{c,t}$, is the set of members who made at least 10 posts in that period.

Size The size of a community may have an effect on semantic change. In communication game experiments, Raviv et al. (2019) found that larger communities of participants developed linguistic structure faster and more consistently than when they were grouped in smaller communities.

We define community size, $S_{2015} = |U_{c,2015}|$, as the number of active members in 2015.

Stability Community stability may also have an effect on semantic change. For example, communi-

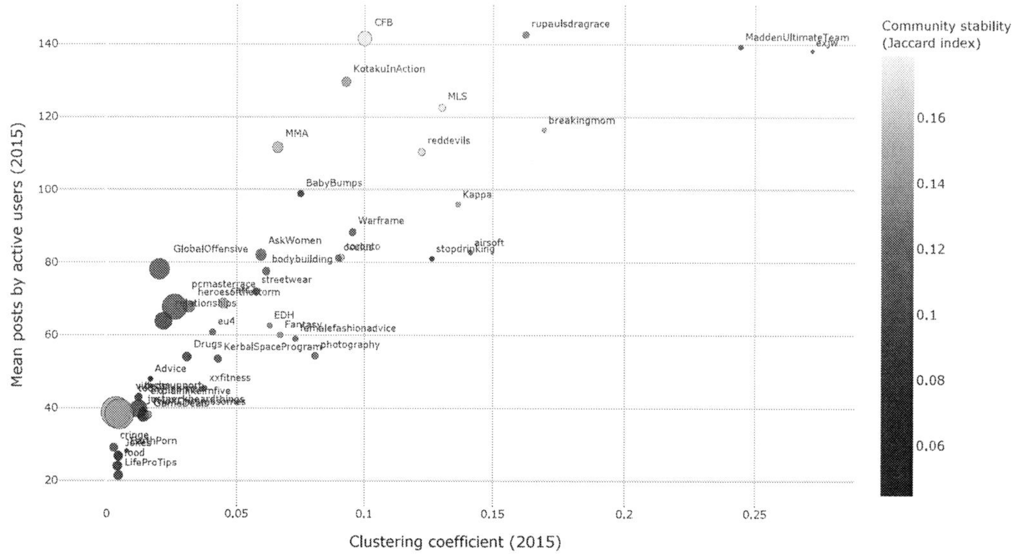

Figure 2: Community-level features for each of the 45 subreddits in our experiments. Dot size represents the community's active membership in 2015 (smallest = 1 679; largest = 118 625).

ties with stable membership have a better chance of building up community-specific common ground. On the other hand, stable communities may experience less change if such change tends to come from new community members, as some studies have suggested (Danescu-Niculescu-Mizil et al., 2013).

We define community stability as the Jaccard index between the sets of active members in 2015 and 2017. This metric, ranging from 0 to 1, captures how similar the community membership is between the two time periods.

$$T = \frac{|U_{c,t_0} \cap U_{c,t_1}|}{|U_{c,t_0} \cup U_{c,t_1}|} \quad (4)$$

Mean posts P_{2015} is the average number of posts per active members over the course of 2015.

5.1 Social network model

In this section, we define our model of social network structure and a measure of network connectivity, which we consider along with the other community features. First, we give some background and motivation for including this feature.

Social network connectivity can have seemingly-contradictory influences on linguistic change. Bloomfield (1933) observed that densely connected networks and strong social ties have a conservative influence on an individual's speech.

It is not clear whether this pattern will hold for semantic change since, as discussed by Sharma and Dodsworth (2020), different variables respond differently to different social network structures. We must also consider the evidence that an encounter with a novel or subtly unfamiliar word usage gives a speaker about the community's lexical *common ground* (Stalnaker, 2002; Clark, 1996). In more densely connected communities, such an exposure is better evidence that other speakers have been exposed to similar uses of the same word, either by the same speaker or, especially in the case of communities on social media, to the very same occurrence. For this reason, it could be that semantic change occurs faster in communities with dense clusters of strong social ties.

Clustering coefficient For each community, we define a graph model of its social network. For $a, b \in U_{c,2015}$, let $I(a, b)$ be the number of interactions between a and b in that community in 2015. Interactions are considered undirected (regardless of who is replying to whom) and we don't consider self-replies, meaning that $I(a, b) = I(b, a)$ and $I(a, a) = 0$. The two networks are thus defined:

$$G = \{\{a, b\} \mid I(a, b) > 1\} \quad (5)$$

Note that we do not consider a top-level comment to be an interaction between the commenter and the creator of the post for two reasons: First, posts frequently do not contain any text written by the author—they are often just a link or photo. Second, the author of the post is not always the addressee of top-level comments, whereas in replies to comments, the author of the parent comment is always salient (though replies may of course be made with a wider audience in mind).

The *clustering coefficient* (Watts and Strogatz, 1998), measures the graph's tendency to form dense, interconnected clusters of nodes. For an individual, i, the clustering coefficient C^i is defined as the proportion of possible connections that exist between individuals connected to i in G:

$$C^i = \frac{|\{\{j,k\} \in G \mid j,k \in N(i)\}|}{|N(i)|(|N(i)|-1)} \quad (6)$$

where $N(i) = \{j \in U \mid \{i,j\} \in G\}$ is the *neighborhood* of i. The clustering coefficient for the community as a whole is the mean clustering coefficient of its members:

$$C_G = \frac{\sum_{i \in U} C_G^i}{|U|} \quad (7)$$

Note that C^i is precisely the measure of ego network density used in many sociolinguistic studies (Milroy, 1987), meaning that we would expect communities with higher clustering coefficients to exhibit less sociolinguistic change. We don't know whether the same effect holds for semantic change.

6 Predictive model

We perform an exploratory analysis of the data using multi-stage regressions and model selection by backwards elimination with semantic change, as measured by Δ^*, as the dependent variable.[7]

Since we fit the mixed effects model at the word level, in addition to the community-level independent variables described in Section 5, we consider two word-level features as fixed effects. See Table 2 for the full list of fixed effects.

Word frequency Since word frequency known to interact with semantic change (Hamilton et al., 2016b). we include the frequency of the token in the 2015 community corpus (f_{2015}) as a feature.

Change in frequency Additionally, we include the change in frequency between 2015 and 2017 ($f_\Delta = f_{2017} - f_{2015}$) as a feature since previous work suggests that increases in the frequency of a word often accompany semantic change (Wijaya and Yeniterzi, 2011; Kulkarni et al., 2015; Del Tredici et al., 2019).

Effect		Varies by
Mean posts (2015)	P_{2015}	community
Size (2015)	S_{2015}	community
Stability	T	community
Clustering	C	community
Frequency (2015)	f_{2015}	token, community
Change in Frequency	f_Δ	token, community
Generic rectified change	Δ_G^*	token
Rectified change	Δ^*	token, community

Table 2: Fixed effect inputs to the statistical model. **Rectified change** is the dependent variable.

Community intercepts In addition to fixed effects, we use community-level random intercepts under the hypothesis that community topics have idiosyncratic reasons or lexical reasons for differences in semantic change rates to do with the community topics themselves, which we do not model.

6.1 Detecting multicollinearity

Before fitting the full model with interactions, we checked for multicollinearity via linear regressions with the standard `lm` function in R as well as the variance inflation factor (VIF) calculation provided by the `car` package in R. All the predictors were scaled and centered (n = 201 240 word-community combinations). We found that the distribution of Δ^* is fat-tailed (it is likely t-distributed). Nevertheless, it is bell-shaped and large enough that this should not be a problem. We ran a regression under the hypothesis $\Delta^* \sim S_{2015} + T + C + P_{2015} + \Delta_G^* + f_{2015} + f_\Delta$ (see Table 2) and calculated the VIF on this model. We found that P_{2015} had VIF higher than 2, the cutoff from Zuur et al. (2010). Removing it produced VIFs below the cutoff for the other predictors.[8]

We fit a linear mixed effects model (using the `lmer` command from the `lme4` package in R; Bates et al., 2015) with the remaining predictors

[7] The use of stepwise regression has been criticized for being a fallacious method for one-shot hypothesis testing but is a legitimate way to investigate the explanatory capacity of predictors. See `https://dynamicecology.wordpress.com/2013/10/16/in-praise-of-exploratory-statistics/` for a discussion of the issue.

[8] Initially we defined a separate clustering metric C_{weak} for the *weak ties* network, analogous to the network defined in Section 5.1 but with edges between community members with exactly one interaction. However, this features was highly colinear with C and had a very high VIF when we tested it at this stage, so it was also excluded from further analysis.

in order to take into account the individual semantic change characteristics of community and word. (Model code and output will be placed on the web upon publication.)

We performed a regression on the model equation $\Delta_c^* \sim (1|\text{community}) + S_{2015} * T * C + \Delta_G^* * f_{2015} * \Delta_f$; that is, we included interactions among the community-level and word-level predictors.

6.2 Results

For the regression results (table 3), we do not report statistical significance directly from `lmer`. Instead, using R's `anova` function, we performed backwards elimination model selection (by stepwise removal of interactions and factors), and we report statistical significance based on p-values derived from the χ^2 log-likelihood ratio between models.

We found that all word-level fixed effects and their three-way interaction were significant at $p < 0.05$ in the model in terms of a χ^2 likelihood ratio test. The three-way word-level interaction $\Delta_G^* \cdot f_{2015} \cdot f_\Delta$ had a p-value too small to represent ($\chi^2(4) = 6380.751$) relative to a model with all predictors without the interaction (so terms $\Delta_G^* + f_{2015} + f_\Delta$) along with all the other predictors and interactions. Relative to the model without the three-way word level interaction, removing each word-level predictor individually yielded $p_{\Delta_G^*} = 7.059 \times 10^{-81}$ ($\chi^2(1) = 362.759$), $p_{f_{2015}} = 1.605 \times 10^{-26}$ ($\chi^2(1) = 113.587$), and p_{f_Δ} was too small to measure ($\chi^2(2) = 2070.095$).

The three-way interaction for the community-level features was significant at $p = 0.014$ ($\chi^2(4) = 12.530$), but none of the two-way interactions or the individual predictors were significant.[9]

We plotted the three-way interaction in Figure 3. Clustering coefficient and size are held at the mean and plus or minus one standard deviation from the mean. At low levels of clustering, all levels of size have a positive linear relationship on rectified change with respect to increasing stability.

At mean levels of clustering, the lower and mean levels of size retain the positive relationship but flatten out, and the high size level becomes negative. At one standard deviation above the mean for clustering, only the lowest size level remains positively sloped relative to stability. Confidence intervals increase dramatically as clustering increases (as there are fewer examples with higher coefficients).

[9]This means that all the individual predictors and two-way interactions must be part of the model, but their significant effect is conditioned on one another.

Predictor	Coefficient	SE
(intercept)	0.250	0.069
S_{2015}	-0.076	0.146
T	0.041	0.046
C	-0.022	0.107
$S_{2015} \cdot T$	-0.088	0.076
$S_{2015} \cdot C$	-0.017	0.192
$T \cdot C$	-0.132	0.056
$S_{2015} \cdot T \cdot C$	-0.056	0.112
f_{2015}	-0.014	0.007
f_Δ	0.462	0.005
Δ_G^*	0.055	0.003
$f_{2015} \cdot f_\Delta$	-0.026	0.001
$f_{2015} \cdot \Delta_G^*$	-0.012	0.006
$f_\Delta \cdot \Delta_G^*$	0.251	0.004
$f_{2015} \cdot f_\Delta \cdot \Delta_G^*$	-0.014	0.000

Table 3: Fixed effect coefficients of the mixed effects model with standard errors. p-values for some predictors are reported in the text.

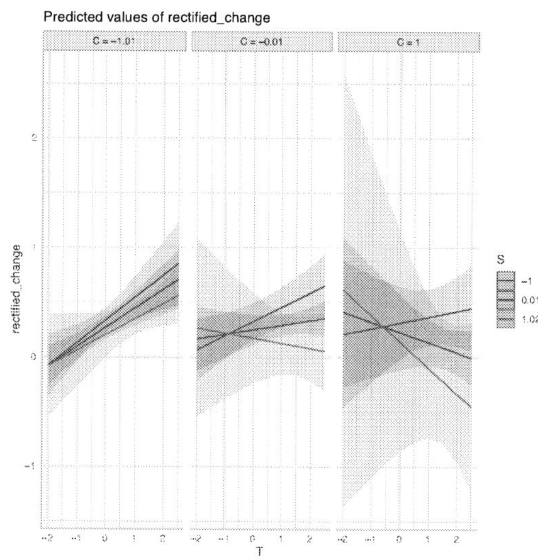

Figure 3: Plot of three-way interaction between community-level predictors vs. the rectified change using the `ggeffects` package. Each panel represents a fixed value for the clustering coefficient, specifically -1 st.dev. from the mean, the mean, and 1 st.dev from the mean. Similarly, each line represents the same three values for the size. The x-axis in each panel represents the group stability.

The effect of the random intercept is small (σ^2 = 0.019, SD = 0.138). This is the extent to which the type of community causes the intercept of rectified change to vary.

7 Discussion and conclusions

We conducted an exploratory statistical analysis of the relationship between semantic change and several word- and community-level predictive features. Rectified semantic change, our independent variable, protects the results from certain systematic biases inherent in the traditional cosine change metric. By looking at online communities, we were able to compute a clustering coefficient on the social network graph of each community, as well as several other community-level structural features.

Community features and semantic change We found all three word-level features to be significant. Together with the intercept, f_{Δ} dominates the mixed-effects model, with greater changes in frequency associated with higher semantic change. This is in line with previous findings (Wijaya and Yeniterzi, 2011; Kulkarni et al., 2015; Del Tredici et al., 2019), but our study is the first to demonstrate this effect while controlling for noise effects.

Although the effect is much smaller, there is a negative relationship between semantic change and baseline frequency, f. This agrees with previous results about historical change (Hamilton et al., 2016a; Dubossarsky and Weinshall, 2017), but we note that, while we cannot compare the regression coefficients directly, it appears that frequency may have a much smaller effect on semantic change in the short-term setting; however, testing this hypothesis would require further research.

Semantic change in the generic lexicon also predicts community-level change, though it has a smaller effect than f_{Δ}. The interaction between f_{Δ} and Δ_G suggests that changes in frequency can predict whether generic lexicon changes in meaning will be picked up by a particular community.

We found that the three-way interaction between size, stability, and clustering, was significant: For communities with low clustering, there is a positive linear relationship between stability and semantic change (regardless of community size). For communities with average or high clustering, however, the positive relationship between stability and change only appears to hold for smaller communities. Note, however that the confidence intervals increase dramatically as clustering increases, since our sample of communities found fewer examples with high clustering.

We did not find significant correlations for any of the community-level features on their own. It is possible that a larger study with more communities or a more diverse set of communities would reveal some more universal effect, but we cannot make any conclusions from these results. The fact that the three-way interaction has a significant effect while none of the individual features did on their own demonstrates the complexity of relationship between structural community characteristics and semantic change.

Assumptions and limitations of the semantic change model In spite of our efforts to control for biases of cosine change, there are still some caveats when interpreting the results.

Like most distributional models of semantics, the diachronic SGNS model associates each word form with a single vector, meaning it is not sensitive to polysemy or homonymy. If a word with multiple senses undergoes changes in the relative frequency with which those senses are used, this would be reflected in the vector representation of the token that both senses are associated with, even if the meaning of either sense hasn't changed on its own.[10] However, many theories of semantic change emphasize the role of changing sense distributions as a mechanism for lexical semantic change, so it is not necessarily contrary to our aims of quantifying semantic change over the lexicon.

A related weakness of distributional semantics has to do with the distinction between meaning-in-use and lexical meaning. Even if we assume that distributional context is a faithful (if noisy) representation of the situated meaning of a word (cf. Lücking et al., 2019; Bisk et al., 2020; Bender and Koller, 2020), it might not capture the word's full *meaning potential* (Norén and Linell, 2007)—in the extreme, a word may have common ground semantic content that *could* be activated, but that happens not to appear in the corpus.

Moreover, changes in the topics discussed by the community may cause changes in the context distribution of words that don't reflect actual change in meaning. Consider the words at the top of the list for /r/toronto (Table 1). It's possible that some of those words appear due to changes in the sociopolitical topics people were discussing on the forum between 2015 and 2017. Similarly, the top word, 2016, presumably still refers to the same year, though the year itself went from being in the future to being in the past. Whether or not such a change counts as a *change in meaning* is naturally beyond the scope of this paper.

[10]Contextualized word representations (Peters et al., 2018; Devlin et al., 2019) don't have this shortcoming and have recently been used to investigate semantic change (Giulianelli et al., 2020; Vani et al., 2020), but extracting one vector per occurrence is computationally expensive and has therefore only been applied to small sets of target words.

Future work This work offers some insight into how semantic change and community structure interact, but there are still many open questions, including how these results generalize to communities in different communicative settings and over different time frames. Future work should take a closer look at the *kinds* of change (e.g., Blank, 1999) taking place. For example, are the meanings of words broadening or narrowing? How are existing community-level communicative resources used to create new word uses? Given that we can identify statistically significant changes in meaning over a relatively short period of time, it would also be interesting to investigate the circumstances of individual changes. For example, do community members with more central social network position tend to innovate more? How are early innovative uses received by the community? Is there a correlation between semantic change in a given time period and the frequency of explicit *word meaning negotiation* (Myrendal, 2019) in the same period?

Acknowledgements

This work was supported by grant 2014-39 from the Swedish Research Council (VR) for the establishment of the Centre for Linguistic Theory and Studies in Probability (CLASP) at the University of Gothenburg. This work was also supported by the Marianne and Marcus Wallenberg Foundation grant 2019.0214 for the Gothenburg Research Initiative for Politically Emergent Systems (GRIPES). This project has received funding from the European Research Council (ERC) under the European Union's Horizon 2020 research and innovation programme (grant agreement No. 819455 Awarded to RF).

References

Hosein Azarbonyad, Mostafa Dehghani, Kaspar Beelen, Alexandra Arkut, Maarten Marx, and Jaap Kamps. 2017. Words are Malleable: Computing Semantic Shifts in Political and Media Discourse. In *Proceedings of the 2017 ACM on Conference on Information and Knowledge Management*, CIKM '17, pages 1509–1518, New York, NY, USA. Association for Computing Machinery.

Douglas Bates, Martin Mächler, Ben Bolker, and Steve Walker. 2015. Fitting Linear Mixed-Effects Models Using lme4. *Journal of Statistical Software*, 67(1):1–48.

Jason Baumgartner, Savvas Zannettou, Brian Keegan, Megan Squire, and Jeremy Blackburn. 2020. The Pushshift Reddit Dataset. *arXiv:2001.08435 [cs]*.

Emily M. Bender and Alexander Koller. 2020. Climbing towards NLU: On Meaning, Form, and Understanding in the Age of Data. In *ACL 2020*.

Yonatan Bisk, Ari Holtzman, Jesse Thomason, Jacob Andreas, Yoshua Bengio, Joyce Chai, Mirella Lapata, Angeliki Lazaridou, Jonathan May, Aleksandr Nisnevich, Nicolas Pinto, and Joseph Turian. 2020. Experience Grounds Language. In *Proceedings of the 2020 Conference on Empirical Methods in Natural Language Processing (EMNLP)*, pages 8718–8735, Online.

A. Christian Blank. 1999. Why do new meanings occur? A cognitive typology of the motivations for lexical semantic change. In Andreas Blank and Peter Koch, editors, *Historical Semantics and Cognition*. De Gruyter Mouton.

Leonard Bloomfield. 1933. *Language*, 14. impr edition. Allen & Unwin, London.

Herbert H. Clark. 1996. *Using Language*. Cambridge University Press.

Cristian Danescu-Niculescu-Mizil, Robert West, Dan Jurafsky, Jure Leskovec, and Christopher Potts. 2013. No country for old members: User lifecycle and linguistic change in online communities. In *Proceedings of the 22nd International Conference on World Wide Web*, WWW '13, pages 307–318, Rio de Janeiro, Brazil. Association for Computing Machinery.

Marco Del Tredici and Raquel Fernández. 2017. Semantic Variation in Online Communities of Practice. In *IWCS 2017 - 12th International Conference on Computational Semantics - Long Papers*.

Marco Del Tredici, Raquel Fernández, and Gemma Boleda. 2019. Short-Term Meaning Shift: A Distributional Exploration. In *Proceedings of the 2019 Conference of the North American Chapter of the Association for Computational Linguistics*, volume 1 (Long and Short Papers), pages 2069–2075, Minneapolis, Minnesota. Association for Computational Linguistics.

Jacob Devlin, Ming-Wei Chang, Kenton Lee, and Kristina Toutanova. 2019. BERT: Pre-training of Deep Bidirectional Transformers for Language Understanding. In *Proceedings of the 2019 Conference of the North American Chapter of the Association for Computational Linguistics: Human Language Technologies, Volume 1 (Long and Short Papers)*, pages 4171–4186, Minneapolis, Minnesota. Association for Computational Linguistics.

Haim Dubossarsky and Daphna Weinshall. 2017. Outta Control: Laws of Semantic Change and Inherent Biases in Word Representation Models. In *Proceedings of the 2017 Conference on Empirical Methods in Natural Language Processing*, pages 1136–

1145, Copenhagen, Denmark. Association for Computational Linguistics.

Penelope Eckert. 1988. Adolescent social structure and the spread of linguistic change. *Language in Society*, 17(2):183–207.

Penelope Eckert. 2019. The limits of meaning: Social indexicality, variation, and the cline of interiority. *Language*, 95(4):751–776.

Mario Giulianelli, Marco Del Tredici, and Raquel Fernández. 2020. Analysing Lexical Semantic Change with Contextualised Word Representations. In *Proceedings of the 58th Annual Meeting of the Association for Computational Linguistics*, pages 3960–3973, Online. Association for Computational Linguistics.

William L. Hamilton, Jure Leskovec, and Dan Jurafsky. 2016a. Cultural Shift or Linguistic Drift? Comparing Two Computational Measures of Semantic Change. In *Proceedings of the 2016 Conference on Empirical Methods in Natural Language Processing*, Austin, Texas. Association for Computational Linguistics.

William L. Hamilton, Jure Leskovec, and Dan Jurafsky. 2016b. Diachronic Word Embeddings Reveal Statistical Laws of Semantic Change. In *Proceedings of the 54th Annual Meeting of the Association for Computational Linguistics (Volume 1: Long Papers)*, pages 1489–1501, Berlin, Germany. Association for Computational Linguistics.

Ruqaiya Hasan. 2009. *Collected Works of Ruqaiya Hasan. Vol. 2, Semantic Variation: Meaning in Society and in Sociolinguistics*. Equinox, London ; Oakville.

Yoon Kim, Yi-I Chiu, Kentaro Hanaki, Darshan Hegde, and Slav Petrov. 2014. Temporal Analysis of Language through Neural Language Models. In *Proceedings of the ACL 2014 Workshop on Language Technologies and Computational Social Science*, pages 61–65, Baltimore, MD, USA. Association for Computational Linguistics.

Farshad Kooti, Winter A. Mason, Krishna P. Gummadi, and Meeyoung Cha. 2012. Predicting emerging social conventions in online social networks. In *Proceedings of the 21st ACM International Conference on Information and Knowledge Management - CIKM '12*, page 445, Maui, Hawaii, USA. ACM Press.

Vivek Kulkarni, Rami Al-Rfou, Bryan Perozzi, and Steven Skiena. 2015. Statistically Significant Detection of Linguistic Change. In *Proceedings of the 24th International Conference on World Wide Web - WWW '15*, pages 625–635, Florence, Italy. ACM Press.

Andrey Kutuzov, Lilja Øvrelid, Terrence Szymanski, and Erik Velldal. 2018. Diachronic word embeddings and semantic shifts: A survey. In *Proceedings of the 27th International Conference on Computational Linguistics*, pages 1384–1397, Santa Fe, New Mexico, USA. Association for Computational Linguistics.

Beatriz R. Lavandera. 1978. Where Does the Sociolinguistic Variable Stop? *Language in Society*, 7(2):171–182.

Shiri Lev-Ari. 2018. Social network size can influence linguistic malleability and the propagation of linguistic change. *Cognition*, 176:31–39.

David K. Lewis. 1969. *Convention: A Philosophical Study*. Wiley-Blackwell.

Andy Lücking, Robin Cooper, Staffan Larsson, and Jonathan Ginzburg. 2019. Distribution is not enough: Going Firther. In *Proceedings of the Sixth Workshop on Natural Language and Computer Science*, pages 1–10, Gothenburg, Sweden. Association for Computational Linguistics.

James Milroy and Lesley Milroy. 1985. Linguistic change, social network and speaker innovation. *Journal of Linguistics*, 21(02):339.

Lesley Milroy. 1987. *Language and Social Networks*. Wiley.

Jenny Myrendal. 2019. Negotiating meanings online: Disagreements about word meaning in discussion forum communication - Jenny Myrendal, 2019. *Discourse Studies*, 21(3):317–339.

John Newman. 2015. Semantic shift. In Nick Riemer, editor, *The Routledge Handbook of Semantics*. Routledge, London.

Kerstin Norén and Per Linell. 2007. Meaning potentials and the interaction between lexis and contexts: An empirical substantiation. *Pragmatics*, 17(3):387–416.

J.C. Paolillo. 1999. The virtual speech community: Social network and language variation on IRC. In *Proceedings of the 32nd Annual Hawaii International Conference on Systems Sciences. 1999. HICSS-32. Abstracts and CD-ROM of Full Papers*, volume Track2, pages 10 pp.–, Torun, Italy.

Hermann Paul. 1886. *Prinzipien der Sprachgeschichte*. Max Niemeyer.

Matthew Peters, Mark Neumann, Mohit Iyyer, Matt Gardner, Christopher Clark, Kenton Lee, and Luke Zettlemoyer. 2018. Deep Contextualized Word Representations. In *Proceedings of the 2018 Conference of the North American Chapter of the Association for Computational Linguistics: Human Language Technologies, Volume 1 (Long Papers)*, pages 2227–2237, New Orleans, Louisiana. Association for Computational Linguistics.

Limor Raviv, Antje Meyer, and Shiri Lev-Ari. 2019. Larger communities create more systematic languages. *Proceedings of the Royal Society B: Biological Sciences*, 286(1907):20191262.

Dominik Schlechtweg, Barbara McGillivray, Simon Hengchen, Haim Dubossarsky, and Nina Tahmasebi. 2020. SemEval-2020 Task 1: Unsupervised Lexical Semantic Change Detection. In *Proceedings of the Fourteenth Workshop on Semantic Evaluation*, pages 1–23, Barcelona (online). International Committee for Computational Linguistics.

Devyani Sharma and Robin Dodsworth. 2020. Language Variation and Social Networks. *Annual Review of Linguistics*, 6(1):341–361.

Philippa Shoemark, Farhana Ferdousi Liza, Dong Nguyen, Scott Hale, and Barbara McGillivray. 2019. Room to Glo: A Systematic Comparison of Semantic Change Detection Approaches with Word Embeddings. In *Proceedings of the 2019 Conference on Empirical Methods in Natural Language Processing and the 9th International Joint Conference on Natural Language Processing (EMNLP-IJCNLP)*, pages 66–76, Hong Kong, China. Association for Computational Linguistics.

Robert Stalnaker. 2002. Common Ground. *Linguistics and Philosophy*, 25(5-6):701–721.

Ian Stewart, Dustin Arendt, Eric Bell, and Svitlana Volkova. 2017. Measuring, Predicting and Visualizing Short-Term Change in Word Representation and Usage in VKontakte Social Network. In *Proceedings of the Eleventh International AAAI Conference on Web and Social Media (ICWSM 2017)*, page 4, Montréal, Québec, Canada.

Nina Tahmasebi, Lars Borin, and Adam Jatowt. 2018. Survey of Computational Approaches to Diachronic Conceptual Change. *arXiv:1811.06278 [cs]*, 1(1).

Xuri Tang. 2018. A state-of-the-art of semantic change computation. *Natural Language Engineering*, 24(5):649–676.

K. Vani, Sandra Mitrovic, Alessandro Antonucci, and Fabio Rinaldi. 2020. SST-BERT at SemEval-2020 Task 1: Semantic Shift Tracing by Clustering in BERT-based Embedding Spaces. *arXiv:2010.00857 [cs]*.

Duncan J. Watts and Steven H. Strogatz. 1998. Collective dynamics of 'small-world' networks. *Nature*, 393(6684):440–442.

E. Judith Weiner and William Labov. 1983. Constraints on the agentless passive. *Journal of Linguistics*, 19(1):29–58.

Derry Tanti Wijaya and Reyyan Yeniterzi. 2011. Understanding semantic change of words over centuries. In *Proceedings of the 2011 International Workshop on DETecting and Exploiting Cultural diversiTy on the Social Web - DETECT '11*, page 35, Glasgow, Scotland, UK. ACM Press.

Alain F. Zuur, Elena N. Ieno, and Chris S. Elphick. 2010. A protocol for data exploration to avoid common statistical problems. *Methods in Ecology and Evolution*, 1(1):3–14.

A Subreddit selection

We randomly selected 50 subreddits from the set of all forums with at least 15,000 comments per month for each of the 36 months in the 2015–2017 period. We initially selected 50 subreddits but excluded five from further analysis: two which were primarily non-English, two with particularly short average comment lengths, and one where our procedure for identifying template-generated posts failed (see Section B for details).

B Data preprocessing

Below we describe the preprocessing procedure we used to prepare training data for our diachronic SGNS models.

Duplicate comments Before any text normalization steps (described below), we sought to remove duplicate template-generated posts by bots and moderating tools. Since this automated content frequently appears in only one of the two time periods, it can have an outsized effect on the cosine change score of words included in the template.

We identified these posts by comparing the tail (after the first 50 characters) any two posts of more than 50 characters in length. Posts marked as duplicate under this criteria were discarded (keeping one such post in each category). This preserves "natural" human-written duplicates, which tend to be short, while catching most template-generated content, where form-filled deviations tend to be relegated to the beginning of the post. Unfortunately, this criteria missed posts by a bot in the /r/jailbreak subreddit, resulting rectified semantic change score outliers for certain words in the bot's template. As a result, we excluded this community from analysis in the mixed-effects model.

Normalization and tokenization The text of comments was normalized as follows. We removed markdown formatting, extracting only rendered text. We exclude the content of block quotes, code blocks, and tables. We tokenized comments using the SpaCy tokenizer with the default English model (version 2.2.3). We lower-cased all tokens and removed whitespace, including linebreaks. Additionally, we removed tokens containing certain characters present in the 2015 data but absent in 2017, apparently due to text encoding changes made by Reddit. The removed characters were mostly emojis and certain Hangul graphemes and none were particularly common in our data (see [link] for a list of excluded characters).

C Vocabulary and SGNS training proceedure

For each community c we maintain a separate vocabulary, V_c. Words with at least 50 occurances in *both* the 2015 and 2017 time periods are included in the vocabulary. Likewise, the generic Reddit models have vocabulary V_G, which includes words with at least 500 occurances in both time periods.

All models were trained with the Gensim (v. 3.8.1) SGNS implementation, with 200 dimensional vectors for 50 epochs (for both the generic and community-spcefic models). For all other hyperparameters, we maintain the default hyperparameters (length 5 context window, 5 negative samples per word, inital learning rate of 0.025, subsampling threshold of 1×10^{-5}, and negative sampling distribution exponent of 0.75).

For $M_{c,2015}$, we randomly initialize vectors for words in $V_c \setminus V_G$. Words in $V_G \setminus V_c$ have no vector representation in $M_{c,2015}$ or $M_{c,2017}$.

A Study on Using Semantic Word Associations to Predict the Success of a Novel

Syeda Jannatus Saba*[1], Biddut Sarker Bijoy*[1], Henry Gorelick[2], Sabir Ismail[3], Md Saiful Islam[1], Mohammad Ruhul Amin[2]

[1]Department of Computer Science & Engineering, Shahjalal University of Science & Tech.
[2]Department of Computer & Information Science, Fordham University
[3]Google LLC
`{syeda06,biddut12}@student.sust.edu,`
`hgorelick@fordham.edu, sabir.ismail01@gmail.com,`
`saiful-cse@sust.edu,mamin17@fordham.edu`

Abstract

Many new books get published every year, and only a fraction of them become popular among the readers. So the prediction of a book success can be a very useful parameter for publishers to make a reliable decision. This article presents the study of semantic word associations using the word embedding of book content for a set of Roget's thesaurus concepts for book success prediction. In this work, we discuss the method to represent a book as a spectrum of concepts based on the association score between its content embedding and a global embedding (i.e. fastText) for a set of semantically linked word clusters. We show that the semantic word associations outperform the previous methods for book success prediction. In addition, we present that semantic word associations also provide better results than using features like the frequency of word groups in Roget's thesaurus, LIWC (a popular tool for linguistic inquiry and word count), NRC (word association emotion lexicon), and part of speech (PoS). Our study reports that concept associations based on Roget's Thesaurus using word embedding of individual novel resulted in the state-of-the-art performance of 0.89 average weighted F1-score for book success prediction. Finally, we present a set of dominant themes that contribute towards the popularity of a book for a specific genre.

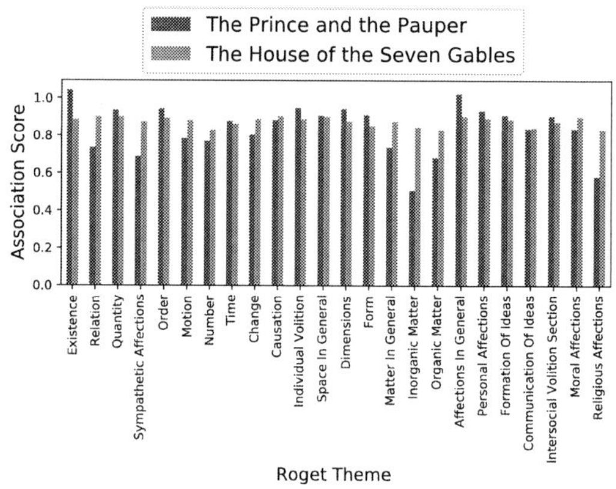

Figure 1: This figure represents average word embedding association scores for 24 themes as defined in the Roget's thesaurus. We observe that corresponding association scores for historical fiction books, such as the successful book *The Prince and the Pauper*, and the unsuccessful book *The House of the Seven Gables* are very different. The success of those books were defined using their corresponding *Goodreads-rating*.

1 Introduction

Every year a lot of literary fictions get published and only a few of them achieve the popularity. So it is very important to be able to predict the success of a book before the publisher commits a significant effort and resources for it. Many factors contribute to the success of a book. The story, plot, and character development, all have specific role in the popularity of a book. There are some other factors like the time when the book has been published, the author's reputation, the marketing strategy, etc that may also influence a book's popularity. In this paper, we only focus on understanding a set of concepts' associations extracted from the content of the book to predict its success.

According to the theory of word embedding, the vector representation of a word in the embedding space captures its semantic relationship with other words based on co-occurrence in the corpus. Kulkarni et al. (2015), and Hamilton et al. (2016a) developed methods for detecting the statistically significant linguistic change using word embedding. In the meantime, Caliskan et al. (2017) developed the concepts of word embedding association test (WEAT) to uncover the gender bias and ethnicity bias. Following these studies, Garg et al. (2018),

*Both authors contributed equally to this research.

Proceedings of the 10th Conference on Lexical and Computational Semantics, pages 38–51
August 5–6, 2021, Bangkok, Thailand (online) ©2021 Association for Computational Linguistics

and Jones et al. (2020) used 100 years of text data and demonstrated that word embedding can be used as a powerful tool to quantify historical trends and social change. For every time period, they warp the vector spaces into one unified coordinate system and construct a distance-based distributional time series for each word to track its linguistic displacement over time. Our idea is to use the associations of different semantically linked word groups or concepts in a book and investigate how its impact on book success prediction.

In this article, we study the efficacy of word associations to represent literature as a spectrum of individually organized concepts as a set of connoted words in the popular Roget's Thesaurus (Roget and Roget, 1886). We represent word association as the Euclidean distance between two words in the embedding space. To find the association of book content to a set of concepts, we compute the average Euclidean distance for each set of semantically linked word vectors of a book's normalized embedding space to the respective word representation in the global embedding space. The concept of word embedding normalization and the word association score has been used successfully in many recent research works for computing the gender associations (Jones et al., 2020).

In Figure 1, we show word associations of prominent themes for a successful book *The Prince and the Pauper* having *Goodreads-rating* > 3.5, and an unsuccessful book *The House of the Seven Gables* with a *Goodreads-rating* < 3.5. We observe that the average association score of each theme vary between these two books. We analyze the impact of these associations score for the success of each book, and obtain a set of dominant concepts that play an important role for a book success. In this paper, we include following research contributions:

- We developed necessary methods to represent a book as the spectrum of word associations for a set of semantically linked words.
- We present genre-wise book success prediction model using semantic word associations as features, and show that the model can achieve the best average weighted F1-score of 0.89.
- We derived a set of dominant features for each genre showing the impact of those features for interpreting the prediction of book success.

2 Related Work

In the earlier work, Ashok et al. (2013) used stylistic approaches, such as unigram, bigram, distribution of the part-of-speech, grammatical rules, constituents, sentiment, and connotation as features and used Liblinear SVM (Fan et al., 2008) for the classification task. They used books from total 8 genres, and they were able to achieve an average accuracy of 73.50% for all the genres.

van Cranenburgh and Koolen (2015) distinguished highly literary works from less literary works using textual features e.g. bigram. Vonnegut (1981); Reagan et al. (2016) worked on emotion along with the book for success prediction.

Maharjan et al. (2017) used a set of hand-crafted features in combination with recurrent neural network and generated feature representation to predict the success, and obtained an average accuracy of 73.50% for the 8 genres. They also performed several experiments, including using all the features from Ashok et al. (2013), sentiment concept (Cambria et al., 2018), different readability metrics, Doc2Vec (Le and Mikolov, 2014) representation of a book, and unaligned Word2Vec (Mikolov et al., 2015) model of the book.

In a more recent work by Maharjan et al. (2018a), they used the flow of the emotions across the book for success prediction and obtained an F1-score of 69%. They divided the book into some chunks, counted the frequency of emotional associations for each word using the NRC emotion lexicon (Mohammad and Turney, 2013), and used a recurrent neural network with an attention mechanism to predict both the genre and the success.

Jarmasz and Szpakowicz (2004); Jarmasz (2012) showed that Roget's has turned out to be an excellent resource for measuring semantic similarity and the words in Roget's word clusters have higher correlation than many other prominent word groups e.g., Wordnet Miller (1998). Guyon et al. (2002) used SVM weights for assigning ranks in the feature selection process. They verified that the top-ranked genes found by SVM have biological relevance to cancer and the SVM classifier with SVM selected features worked better than other classifiers in determining the relevant features along with the classification task.

3 Dataset

In this study, we use the dataset introduced by Maharjan et al. (2017), a publicly available dataset

Genre	Unsuccessful	Successful	Total
Detective Mystery	60	46	106
Drama	29	70	99
Fiction	30	81	111
Historical Fiction	16	65	81
Love Stories	20	60	80
Poetry	23	158	181
Science Fiction	48	39	87
Short Stories	123	135	258
Total	349	654	1,003

Table 1: The book dataset originally introduced by Maharjan et al. (2017) is used in this research work for success prediction. Each book in this dataset belongs to one of the eight genres. Here we have the most number of books from the Short Stories genre(258) and the least number of books from the Love Stories genre(80).

comprising of total 1,003 books. All of these books are downloaded from the Project Gutenberg[1]. Details of the dataset are given in Table 1. Each of these books are labeled as either successful (1) or unsuccessful (0). The definition of the success of a book is based on Goodreads[2] ratings. A book is considered successful if it had been rated by at least 10 Goodreads users and has a Goodreads rating $\geq$ 3.5 out of 5. In this corpus, there are 349 unsuccessful books and 654 successful books. After downloading the books we used the NLTK API for data processing (Bird et al., 2009). For each book, we extracted the part-of-speech (PoS) tag frequencies using the Stanford CoreNLPParser, the Roget's Thesaurus category frequencies (Roget and Roget, 1886; Manning et al., 2014).

Linguistic Models

We utilized four linguistic models for our quantitative analysis. Two of the models - PoS and NRC are our own implementation of models used in Ashok et al. (2013) and Maharjan et al. (2018a). Our two additional models have not been used to make these types of qualitative conclusions until now. The linguistic models used in our frequency and association analysis are described below.

PoS: Part of Speech or PoS is a category to which a word is assigned in accordance with its syntactic functions. PoS provides context and classification to words that helps with better understanding of the purpose of word choice. We used NLTK PoS tagger to label our tokens.

LIWC: Linguistic Inquiry and Word Count (Pennebaker et al., 2015) is a text analysis program that counts words in psychologically meaningful categories. We used 72 LIWC categories for our experiments.

NRC: The distribution of sentiments is one way of looking at books. We used ten categories from NRC (trust, fear, negative, sadness, anger, surprise, positive, disgust, joy, anticipation) to quantify shifts in sentiment across the book.

Roget's Thesaurus: It is composed of 6 primary classes and each class is composed of multiple themes. There are total 24 themes that are further divided into multiple concepts. We used 1,019 word categories from the Roget's Thesaurus for the book success prediction.

4 Methodology

In order to predict the success of a book, one of our major research questions was how we can represent a book properly. We explored a wide range of feature sets and performed multiple experiments in order to find the most suitable feature set that can represent the concept, emotion and writing style of a book. In this section, we discuss the relevant methods that we used for the study of book success prediction.

4.1 Frequency Distribution

We explore 4 different word frequency distributions, such as (1) Roget's Thesaurus, (2) LIWC, (3) NRC and (4) PoS as the feature sets for the book success prediction. We first experimented with frequency distribution of Roget word categories to predict the success of a book. To perform this task, we compute the unit normalized word frequency distribution for each book. Here, frequency is computed for word groups rather than individual words. If a word falls under multiple word group its frequency contributes to all of them. The frequency count of a word group is the summation of frequencies of all the underlying words in that group. And finally, we apply the classifier as discussed in the subsection 4.4 for the book success prediction using Roget's word group frequency distributions as a feature of individual book. We repeat the above steps for creating three other feature sets based on the word frequency distributions of LIWC, NRC, and PoS for each book.

4.2 Association Score

To represent a book as a vector of concept association score, we first create the word embedding vectors from the respective book's content. We

[1]https://www.gutenberg.org/

[2]https://www.goodreads.com

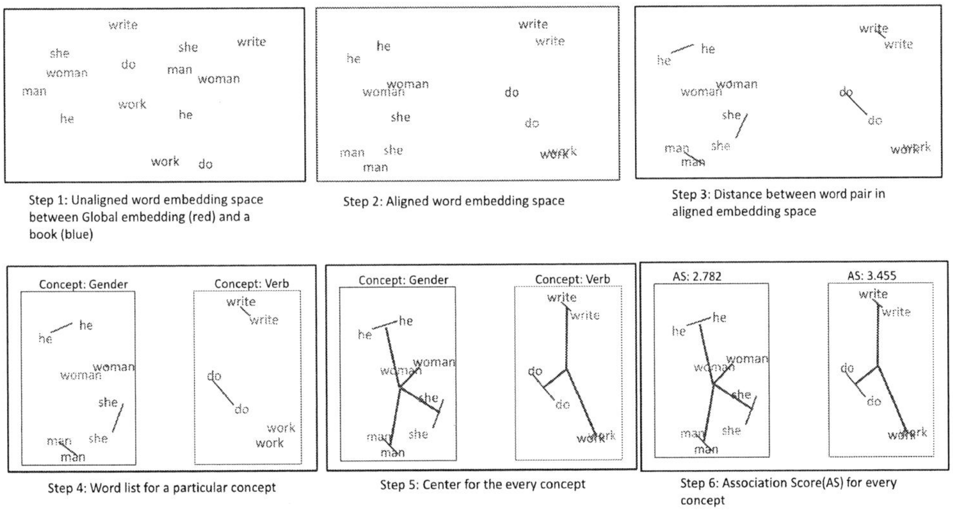

Figure 2: Steps in computing the concept association. At first, word vectors for the global embedding (fastText) and local embedding (individual book embedding) are aligned to a unified space (Steps 1 - 3). Then, for each word, we compute the Euclidean distance of its representative vector from the global and aligned local embedding. The Euclidean distance of all words of each concept are then averaged to calculate the association score (Steps 4 - 6).

then align each book embedding to a global embedding space so that each book can be analyzed with respect to a reference embedding space (Mikolov et al., 2018). To generate the word embedding of each book, we considered the fastText embedding generation methods (Bojanowski et al., 2017). On the contrary to Word2Vec and Glove, fastText treats each word in corpus like an atomic entity and generate a vector for each word. In fastText embedding, the vector representation for a word is created depending on its constituent character n-grams. This method generates better word embedding for rare words and out of vocabulary words.

To do the embedding space alignment, we use the methods described in the paper (Artetxe et al., 2018) including 4 other methods described in (Hamilton et al., 2016b; Kendall, 1989). Intuitively, we have two embedding space for each book, one is the original or local embedding of the book and the other is global fastText embedding. For every

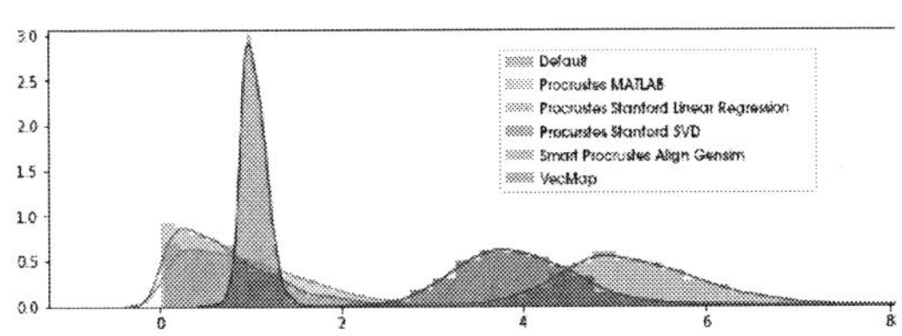

Figure 3: Distribution of the word association for Roget concept words using different alignments methods

word present in a book embedding, we calculate the Euclidean distance. The distribution of the distance using different alignment methods is shown in Figure 3 for the word embedding of 10 books. Ultimately, we use the method named VecMap (Artetxe et al., 2018) as it results in minimum distance after vector alignment.

To represent a book as a vector of concept association score, we first create the fastText word embedding vectors from the respective book's content. As a result, we obtain two individual embedding spaces, one for book and another for the global embedding space. We align the book embedding space to the global embedding space so that each book can be analyzed with respect to a reference embedding space (Refer to Figure 2: Steps 1 - 3). To find the concept association score, we compute the average Euclidean distance from the book's aligned embedding vectors to the global embedding vectors for each semantically linked word cluster. We depict the process in Figure 2 (Steps 4 - 6).

We use the wiki word embedding model (Bojanowski et al., 2017) as our global embedding space. It is trained on Wikipedia using fastText. For the compatibility of book embedding and global embedding, we use fastText to produce word embedding for each book individually. Each generated word vector is 300 dimensional. We use skip-gram as a training algorithm. We then tune the number of iterations over the book content (epochs) by

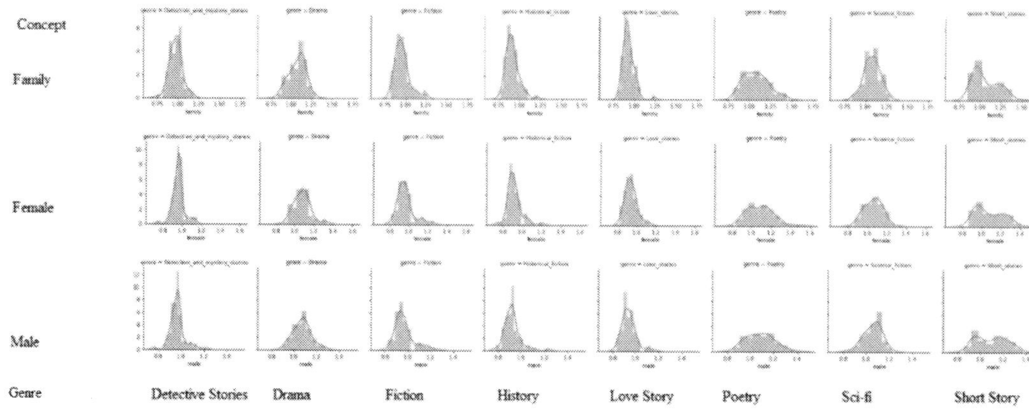

Figure 4: Association of different concepts with 8 genres. The x-axis is the mean association score of the words in a Roget concept, and the y-axis is the frequency observed for each book.

running 20 different experiments with a random selection of diverse values of epochs, and then select 50 as the epoch. To generate word embedding vectors for each book, we only consider those words that have a minimum word count 2.

Therefore, each book of the dataset is represented using a feature vector of length 1,019 following the word category definition in Roget's Thesaurus. Figure 4 shows the distribution of different Roget concept associations for 8 different genres. From these distributions, it is clear that different concepts have different impact on each genre. We also perform the *Kolmogorov-Smirnov Test* (kol, 2008) to check whether these distributions are different or not. In most of the cases, we find that a pair of the the distributions are significantly different from each other as per the statistical test. Finally, we apply the classifier described in subsection 4.4 on the set of association scores of each book for book success prediction task.

4.3 Feature Selection

The feature selection process selects a subset of features that can efficiently describe the input samples. As a result, this step eliminates the interdependent and irrelevant variables, reduce effects from noise, and finally improve classification performance. Among various feature selection methods, we use the filter method (John et al., 1994) to identify relevant features. In this method, all the features are ranked based on a score or weight that is used to denote the feature relevance. This list of features is optimized or shortened depending on a defined threshold to improve the model prediction. We set the limit of shortened and selected feature length as 50 to prevent the loss of important information about a book.

In our experiments, we use the weighted linear SVM as a classifier. To predict the class of any testing sample x, the decision function for this classifier is given below.

$$f(x) = sgn(w^T \phi(x) + b) \quad (1)$$

If $f(x) < 0$, the book is predicted as unsuccessful and if $f(x) > 0$ the book is predicted as successful. Here, feature weight vector w in Equation 1 is determined by training the linear SVM classifier. This weight vector w can be used to find out the relevance of each feature (Guyon et al., 2002) . The feature values $\phi(x)$ in Equation 1 can only be positive for the book success prediction using both frequency and association analysis as feature. So the larger the value $|w_i|$ is, the more it contributes for deciding the sign of the decision function. It is worth mentioning that linear SVM classifier with optimized feature set is intuitively an efficient process as both the tasks use the same decision model. Thus selection of decision boundary for SVM and selection of relevant features are tightly connected (Bron et al., 2015).

4.4 Model Evaluation

For our prediction task, we used weighted linear SVM (Fan et al., 2008) as a classifier with L2 regularization over training data. We used grid-search in order to tune regularization hyperparameter C for weighted linear SVM. To tune the weighted linear SVM parameter C, we used the tool gridsearchCV (Pedregosa et al., 2011) and performed a search over the values ranging $1e(-4to3)$. Then the best value of C was used as a regularization parameter for the weighted linear SVM. To mitigate the overfitting problem, we used 5-fold cross-validation to measure our performance. Thus, our dataset was randomly split into 5 equal segments, and results were averaged over 5 trials. In each trial, the model was trained on 4 segments and tested on the last segment.

We present the algorithms for *Association Score Calculation*, *Feature Ranking Based on Linear SVM Weights*, and *Training and Prediction* in the *Appendix Algorithms 1-3*.

5 Results

5.1 Baseline Model

Prior works have been done on book success prediction using the dataset introduced in Maharjan et al. (2017). Among them, some of the best weighted F1-scores for the book success prediction tasks are 0.69 for Book2Vec (DBoW+DMM) (Maharjan et al., 2017), 0.67 for the Emotion Flow (Maharjan et al., 2018a), 0.71 for Annotated char-3gram(AC3) (Maharjan et al., 2019), and 0.75 for the genre attention with RNN method (Maharjan et al., 2018b) which achieved the state-of-the-art performance. We set the weighted F1 score of 0.75 as our baseline result and proceed to our experiments.

5.2 Book Success Using Word Group Frequency

Our first set of experiments were devised using PoS, NRC and LIWC feature sets having 10, 44, 72 features respectively. As we decided 50 as the lowest number of selected features in subsection 4.3, we did not apply the feature selection method for PoS and NRC categories. Table 2 shows that feature set using PoS and NRC word frequencies could obtain average weighted F1 scores of 0.65 and 0.67 respectively. After employing the feature selection method for LIWC, we obtained an average weighted F1 score of 0.69 which is a slight improvement over the previous two methods but it still fails to outperform the baseline result.

5.3 Book Success Using Roget's Word Group Frequency

For this modeling task, we started with the semantic word association scores of 1,019 Roget's thesaurus concepts as features. As discussed in the methodology section, we performed feature selection for optimized model performance. As a result, this method yielded a performance gain of 0.88 average weighted F1 score beating the baseline results by a large margin (Table 2). In order to investigate the interpretability of the results we obtained from Roget frequency, we dived deeper into the analysis and explored the discriminative features for classifying successful and unsuccessful books for different genres. The visualization we produced for "Detective and Mystery Stories" is placed in the *Appendix Figure 9*. Although we obtained a result that outperformed the state-of-the-art performance using this analysis, it fails to discover more meaningful insights than association analysis that we discussed in the following subsections 5.4 and 5.5.

5.4 Book Success Using Word Association

As all our previous experiments are based on frequency distribution of lexical features, they failed to capture the essential semantic features that have an enormous impact on book success. To deal with this problem, we performed an association analysis using Roget's word groups that were cataloged based on semantic meaning as discussed in subsection 4.2. The feature selection result for each genre are presented in the Figure 5. It can be observed that as we keep filtering out irrelevant features, the performance for book success prediction for each genre increased. But after reaching a certain level, further feature reduction caused a monotonous decline in performance as it discarded important features. The best result obtained using Roget Association is an average weighted F1 score of 0.89 which outperforms not only the baseline results but also the state-of-art result we obtained using Roget's word group frequency (Table 2).

As mentioned earlier, our modeling experiments were performed using the genre-wise 5-fold cross validation. To further identify any overfitting characteristics in the modeling we computed the area under precision-recall curve (AUC of PR-curve). As our dataset is not balanced, we used PR-curve to validate or interpret our result. In the *Appendix Figure 1*, we show genre-wise precision-recall plots, where we draw a combined precision-recall curve of 5-fold cross-validation. Most of the combined results are above an AUC of 0.90 except Detective and Short Stories having that slightly less than 0.90 AUC. This proves that our model performed very well in this imbalanced dataset.

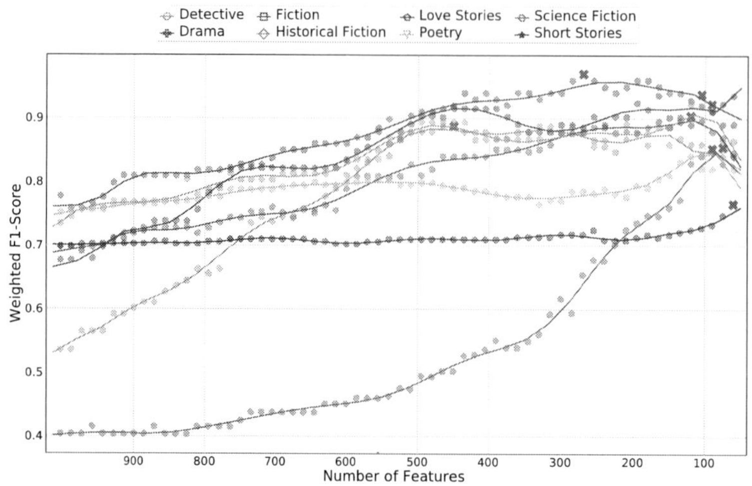

Figure 5: We performed feature selection process for each of the 8 genres. This figure represents the weighted F1-score achieved for different feature sets. Here the max length of the feature set is 1,019. Thus, at each iteration a single feature was filtered based on its weight. For each genre, we select the set of features that obtain the highest F1-score. The best performance for each genre for a particular feature set is marked with *X*. This plot shows an interesting insight that it is not necessary to use more than 500 concepts/features to represent a book.

Method	Genre (Weighted F1)								Average			
	Detect	Drama	Fiction	Hist	Love	Poet	Scien	Short	Acc.	W. F1	Pre	Rec
Roget Association	0.90	0.97	0.90	0.92	0.95	0.86	0.86	0.77	**0.89**	0.89	0.86	0.87
Roget Frequency	0.92	0.90	0.86	0.93	0.87	0.83	0.89	0.83	0.88	0.88	0.85	0.86
LIWC Frequency	0.68	0.68	0.69	0.74	0.74	0.82	0.49	0.70	0.69	0.69	0.63	0.64
PoS Frequency	0.70	0.68	0.66	0.65	0.61	0.77	0.47	0.68	0.64	0.65	0.6	0.61
NRC Frequency	0.58	0.69	0.62	0.72	0.65	0.75	0.59	0.72	0.66	0.67	0.62	0.62

Table 2: Genre-wise classification results

5.5 Result Interpretation

To explore the importance of semantic word associations in book success prediction, we present sunburst plot of reduced feature set. In figure 6, we observe that “Detective and Mystery” is the most interesting since it goes against expectations in a way that makes sense. Specifically, we would probably expect the *Intellectual Faculties*, *Related To Matter*, and *Abstract Relation* categories to be positively associated with stories about solving a crime/mystery using intellect, evidence, and abstract relationships. However, it appears that the most popular stories of this genre actually favor things that have less to do with evidence and more to do with characters and their choices/feelings. This is illustrated by the positive associations of *Voluntary Powers*, *Related To Space*, and *Sentiment and Moral Powers*. In other words, it seems readers like it best when a detective solves a mystery because he/she is "the good guy" who makes the right choices, rather than through real detective work.

Among all the 24 themes, *Intellectual Faculties* shows some interesting insights about the success prediction of a book. So we’ll discuss about the impact of this theme in classifying books across different genres. The top features that the weighted linear SVM classifier determined for successful poetry books are *Analogy*, *Obscurity*, *Overestimation*, etc. This sheds light on the writing style of many of the greatest poems where the poets show a connection between materialistic and abstract entities while keeping some room for the readers to perceive the same poem with their own different flavor of apprehension. This finding is further validated by the presence of *Perspicuity* as one of the top features for unsuccessful poetry books. For example, take the following poem -

O my Luve is like a red, red rose
That’s newly sprung in June;
O my Luve is like the melody
That’s sweetly played in tune.

— Robert Burns

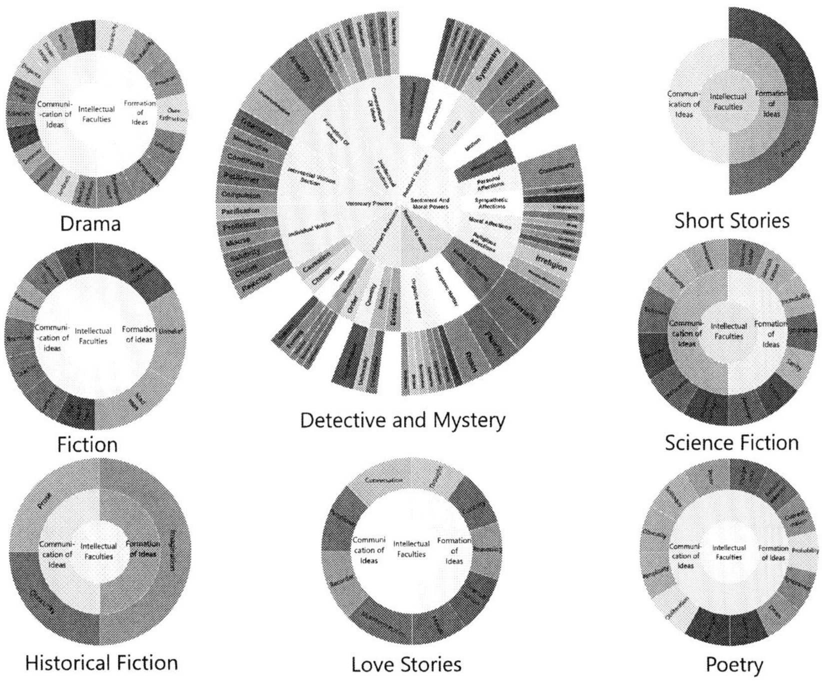

Figure 6: The large sunburst presents a comprehensive review of the most discriminative Roget classes, themes and concepts for a single genre, "Detective Mystery". While the small circles represent the disriminative feature distribution across multiple genres for a common Roget class, "Intellectual Faculties". We consider the top 30 discriminative features for both successful and unsuccessful books. Discriminative features for successful and unsuccessful books are colored with green and red respectively.

Here, the analogy between love and rose may arise a debate between the readers where one side will find the poem expressing that love is beautiful like a rose while the opposition might say this poem is indicating the delicacy and fragility of love. For the Love Stories genre, concepts like *Thought*, *Reasoning*, *Conversation*, *Perspicuity* work as important features for a successful book prediction. This goes against the normal way of thinking that a good love story book should only contain overflowing emotions, gestures that abandon earthly reasonings for the triumph of romance, etc. But it seems like the readers tend to prefer romantic books where lovers also consider their logical reasoning, worldly obligations while trying to win over their love. The 'Intellectual Faculties' section has an overall positive impact on detecting successful books of the Science Fiction genre. It is expected, as the main focus of successful science fiction books is towards many scientific revolutions or the main timeline of the story is set on futuristic utopian or dystopian civilization where new technology is introduced. We present the sunburst plot for all genres in the *Appendix Figures 2-8*.

6 Conclusion and Future Work

We present a novel study of word association of book content to predict the success of book and show that semantic word association features can be new vertical of the classification based task. Our empirical results demonstrate that word association and different types of concepts can be very useful to capture the book's literary content and can predict the book success with better accuracy. Rather than individual word frequency, the set of words with similar concepts has been proved to be more effective. We will continue our research work in this area and we intend to perform the experiments on a bigger data set in the future. We hypothesize that instead of preparing word embedding for individual book, we can retrain the global embedding using genre-wise data. This genre specialized embedding can help us to obtain a much better result for two reasons - as each embedding will be retrained on individual genre, the quality of generated embedding is expected to be better and it will represent the genre specific context for each word more explicitly.

References

2008. *Kolmogorov–Smirnov Test*. Springer New York, New York, NY.

Mikel Artetxe, Gorka Labaka, and Eneko Agirre. 2018. Generalizing and improving bilingual word embedding mappings with a multi-step framework of linear transformations. In *Proceedings of the Thirty-Second AAAI Conference on Artificial Intelligence*, pages 5012–5019.

Vikas Ganjigunte Ashok, Song Feng, and Yejin Choi. 2013. Success with style: Using writing style to predict the success of novels. In *Proceedings of the 2013 conference on empirical methods in natural language processing*, pages 1753–1764.

Steven Bird, Ewan Klein, and Edward Loper. 2009. *Natural language processing with Python: analyzing text with the natural language toolkit*. " O'Reilly Media, Inc.".

Piotr Bojanowski, Edouard Grave, Armand Joulin, and Tomas Mikolov. 2017. Enriching word vectors with subword information. *Transactions of the Association for Computational Linguistics*, 5:135–146.

Esther E Bron, Marion Smits, Wiro J Niessen, and Stefan Klein. 2015. Feature selection based on the svm weight vector for classification of dementia. *IEEE journal of biomedical and health informatics*, 19(5):1617–1626.

Aylin Caliskan, Joanna J Bryson, and Arvind Narayanan. 2017. Semantics derived automatically from language corpora contain human-like biases. *Science*, 356(6334):183–186.

Erik Cambria, Soujanya Poria, Devamanyu Hazarika, and Kenneth Kwok. 2018. Senticnet 5: Discovering conceptual primitives for sentiment analysis by means of context embeddings. In *Thirty-Second AAAI Conference on Artificial Intelligence*.

Andreas van Cranenburgh and Corina Koolen. 2015. Identifying literary texts with bigrams. In *Proceedings of the Fourth Workshop on Computational Linguistics for Literature*, pages 58–67, Denver, Colorado, USA. Association for Computational Linguistics.

Rong-En Fan, Kai-Wei Chang, Cho-Jui Hsieh, Xiang-Rui Wang, and Chih-Jen Lin. 2008. Liblinear: A library for large linear classification. *Journal of machine learning research*, 9(Aug):1871–1874.

Nikhil Garg, Londa Schiebinger, Dan Jurafsky, and James Zou. 2018. Word embeddings quantify 100 years of gender and ethnic stereotypes. *Proceedings of the National Academy of Sciences*, 115(16):E3635–E3644.

Isabelle Guyon, Jason Weston, Stephen Barnhill, and Vladimir Vapnik. 2002. Gene selection for cancer classification using support vector machines. *Machine learning*, 46(1):389–422.

William L Hamilton, Jure Leskovec, and Dan Jurafsky. 2016a. Diachronic word embeddings reveal statistical laws of semantic change. *arXiv preprint arXiv:1605.09096*.

William L Hamilton, Jure Leskovec, and Dan Jurafsky. 2016b. Diachronic word embeddings reveal statistical laws of semantic change. *arXiv preprint arXiv:1605.09096*.

Mario Jarmasz. 2012. Roget's thesaurus as a lexical resource for natural language processing. *arXiv preprint arXiv:1204.0140*.

Mario Jarmasz and Stan Szpakowicz. 2004. Roget's thesaurus and semantic similarity. *Recent Advances in Natural Language Processing III: Selected Papers from RANLP*, 2003:111.

George H John, Ron Kohavi, and Karl Pfleger. 1994. Irrelevant features and the subset selection problem. In *Machine Learning Proceedings 1994*, pages 121–129. Elsevier.

Jason J Jones, Mohammad Ruhul Amin, Jessica Kim, and Steven Skiena. 2020. Stereotypical gender associations in language have decreased over time. *Sociological Science*, 7:1–35.

David G Kendall. 1989. A survey of the statistical theory of shape. *Statistical Science*, pages 87–99.

Vivek Kulkarni, Rami Al-Rfou, Bryan Perozzi, and Steven Skiena. 2015. Statistically significant detection of linguistic change. In *Proceedings of the 24th International Conference on World Wide Web*, pages 625–635.

Quoc Le and Tomas Mikolov. 2014. Distributed representations of sentences and documents. In *International conference on machine learning*, pages 1188–1196.

Suraj Maharjan, John Arevalo, Manuel Montes, Fabio A González, and Thamar Solorio. 2017. A multi-task approach to predict likability of books. In *Proceedings of the 15th Conference of the European Chapter of the Association for Computational Linguistics: Volume 1, Long Papers*, pages 1217–1227.

Suraj Maharjan, Sudipta Kar, Manuel Montes-y Gómez, Fabio A Gonzalez, and Thamar Solorio. 2018a. Letting emotions flow: Success prediction by modeling the flow of emotions in books. *arXiv preprint arXiv:1805.09746*.

Suraj Maharjan, Deepthi Mave, Prasha Shrestha, Manuel Montes, Fabio A. González, and Thamar Solorio. 2019. Jointly learning author and annotated character n-gram embeddings: A case study in literary text. In *Proceedings of the International Conference on Recent Advances in Natural Language Processing (RANLP 2019)*, pages 684–692, Varna, Bulgaria. INCOMA Ltd.

Suraj Maharjan, Manuel Montes, Fabio A. González, and Thamar Solorio. 2018b. A genre-aware attention model to improve the likability prediction of books. In *Proceedings of the 2018 Conference on Empirical Methods in Natural Language Processing*, pages 3381–3391, Brussels, Belgium. Association for Computational Linguistics.

Christopher D. Manning, Mihai Surdeanu, John Bauer, Jenny Finkel, Steven J. Bethard, and David McClosky. 2014. The Stanford CoreNLP natural language processing toolkit. In *Association for Computational Linguistics (ACL) System Demonstrations*, pages 55–60.

Tomas Mikolov, Kai Chen, Gregory S Corrado, and Jeffrey A Dean. 2015. Computing numeric representations of words in a high-dimensional space. US Patent 9,037,464.

Tomas Mikolov, Edouard Grave, Piotr Bojanowski, Christian Puhrsch, and Armand Joulin. 2018. Advances in pre-training distributed word representations. In *Proceedings of the International Conference on Language Resources and Evaluation (LREC 2018)*.

George A Miller. 1998. *WordNet: An electronic lexical database*. MIT press.

Saif M. Mohammad and Peter D. Turney. 2013. Crowdsourcing a word-emotion association lexicon. 29(3):436–465.

F. Pedregosa, G. Varoquaux, A. Gramfort, V. Michel, B. Thirion, O. Grisel, M. Blondel, P. Prettenhofer, R. Weiss, V. Dubourg, J. Vanderplas, A. Passos, D. Cournapeau, M. Brucher, M. Perrot, and E. Duchesnay. 2011. Scikit-learn: Machine learning in Python. *Journal of Machine Learning Research*, 12:2825–2830.

James Pennebaker, Roger Booth, Ryan Boyd, and Martha Francis. 2015. Linguistic inquiry and word count: Liwc2015.

Andrew J Reagan, Lewis Mitchell, Dilan Kiley, Christopher M Danforth, and Peter Sheridan Dodds. 2016. The emotional arcs of stories are dominated by six basic shapes. *EPJ Data Science*, 5(1).

P.M. Roget and J.L. Roget. 1886. *Thesaurus of English Words and Phrases: Classified and Arranged So as to Facilitate the Expression of Ideas and Assist in Literary Composition*. T. Y. Crowell.

K. Vonnegut. 1981. *Palm Sunday: An autobiographical collage*. New York: Delacorte Press.

Appendix

Algorithm 1: Association Score Calculate

Input: Books $b_i, i = 1, ..., n.$
Roget Concepts $r_i, i = 1, ..., c$
Global Word Embedding E_G
Output: The association vector $a_i, i = 1, ..., n$

for $i \leftarrow 1$ **to** n **do**
    $P_{b_i} = Embedding(b_i)$
    $E_{b_i} = Align(P_{b_i}, E_G)$
    for $j \leftarrow 1$ **to** c **do**
        $W_G = Words(E_G)$
        $W_{b_i} = Words(E_{b_i})$
        $W_{r_j} = Words(r_j)$
        $W = W_G \cap W_{b_i} \cap W_{r_j}$
        for $k \leftarrow 1$ **to** $len(W)$ **do**
            $VG_{W_k} = E_G[W_k]$
            $VL_{W_k} = E_{b_i}[W_k]$
            $D_k = \sqrt{\sum_{l=1}^{L} (VG_{W_k,l} - VL_{W_k,l})^2}$
        end
        $a_{i,j} = AVG(D)$
    end
end

Algorithm 2: Feature Ranking Based on Linear SVM Weights

Input: Training sets, $(x_i, y_i), i = 1, ..., l.$
Output: Sorted feature ranking list.

1. Use grid search to find the best parameter *C*.
2. Train a L2-loss linear SVM model using the best *C*.
3. Sort the features according to the absolute values of weights in the model.

Algorithm 3: Training and Prediction

Input: Training sets, testing sets.
Output: Predictions on nested subsets.

1. Use a feature ranking algorithm to compute the sorted feature list $f_j, j = 1, ..., n.$
2. For each feature size $m \in \{50, 51, ..., n\}$.
   (a) Generate the new training set that has only the first m features in the sorted feature list, $f_j, j = 1, ..., m.$
   (b) Use grid search to find the best parameter C.
   (c) Train the L2-loss linearSVM model on the new training set.
   (d) Predict the testing set using the model.

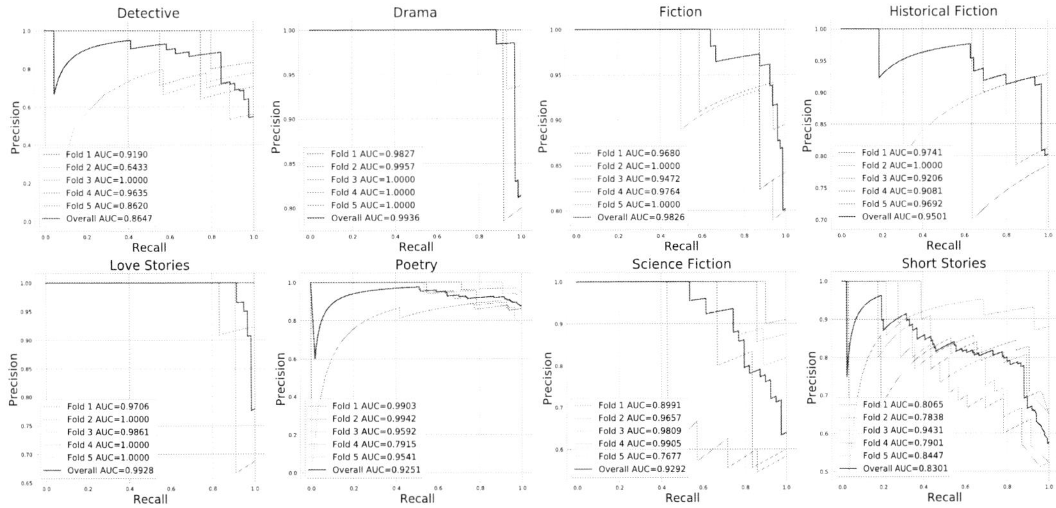

Figure 1: The precision-recall (PRC) plot shows precision values for corresponding sensitivity (recall) values for the association analysis. This PRC plot provides a model-wide evaluation.

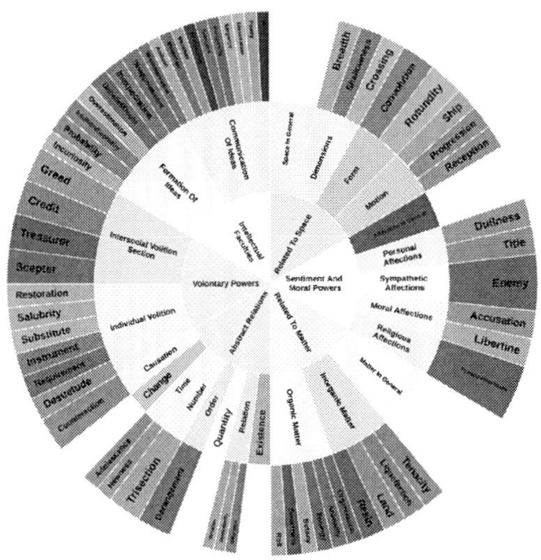

Figure 2: This figure presents a comprehensive review of the most discriminative Roget classes, themes and concepts for Roget Association Analysis of Drama genre. We consider the top 30 discriminative features for both successful and unsuccessful books. Discriminative features for successful and unsuccessful books are colored with green and red respectively.

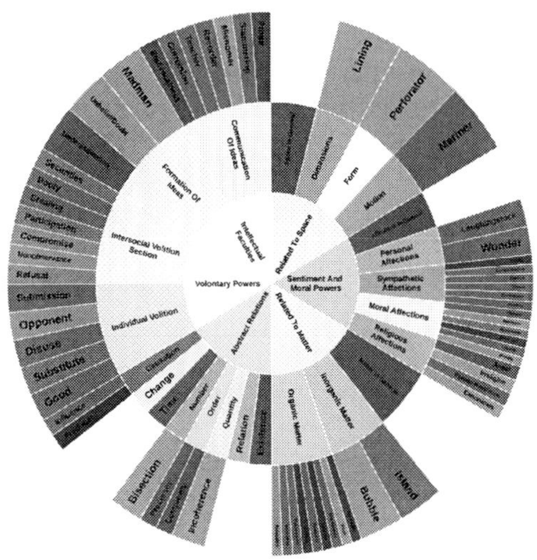

Figure 3: This figure presents a comprehensive review of the most discriminative Roget classes, themes and concepts for Roget Association Analysis of Fiction genre. We consider the top 30 discriminative features for both successful and unsuccessful books. Discriminative features for successful and unsuccessful books are colored with green and red respectively.

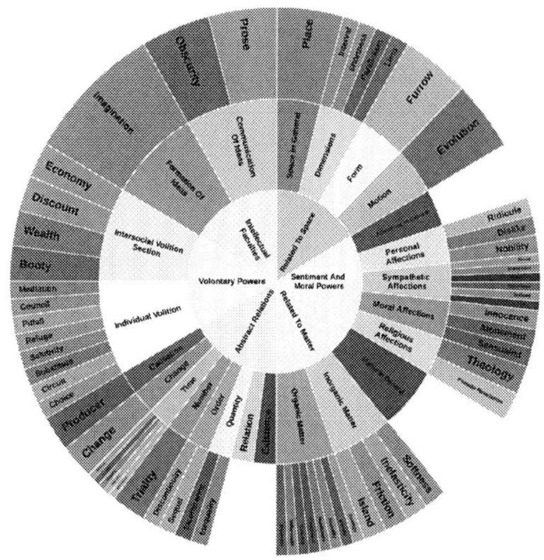

Figure 4: This figure presents a comprehensive review of the most discriminative Roget classes, themes and concepts for Roget Association Analysis of Historical Fiction genre. We consider the top 30 discriminative features for both successful and unsuccessful books. Discriminative features for successful and unsuccessful books are colored with green and red respectively.

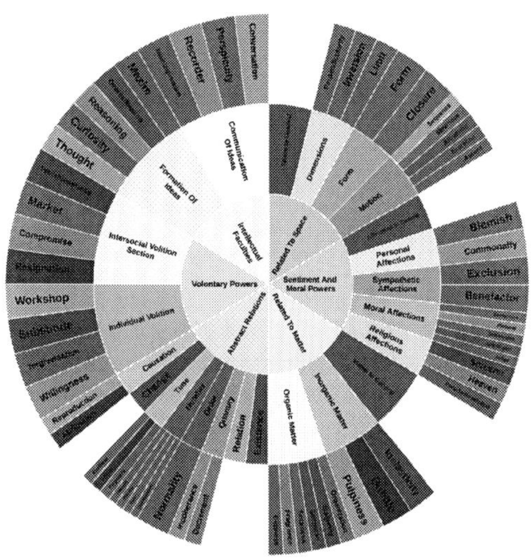

Figure 5: This figure presents a comprehensive review of the most discriminative Roget classes, themes and concepts for Roget Association Analysis of Love Stories genre. We consider the top 30 discriminative features for both successful and unsuccessful books. Discriminative features for successful and unsuccessful books are colored with green and red respectively.

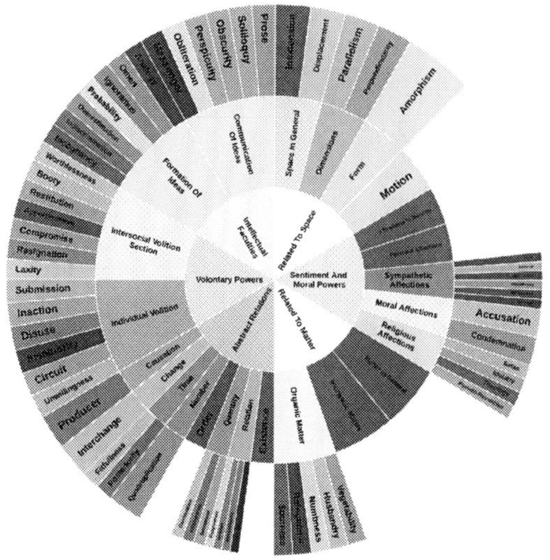

Figure 6: This figure presents a comprehensive review of the most discriminative Roget classes, themes and concepts for Roget Association Analysis of Poetry genre. We consider the top 30 discriminative features for both successful and unsuccessful books. Discriminative features for successful and unsuccessful books are colored with green and red respectively.

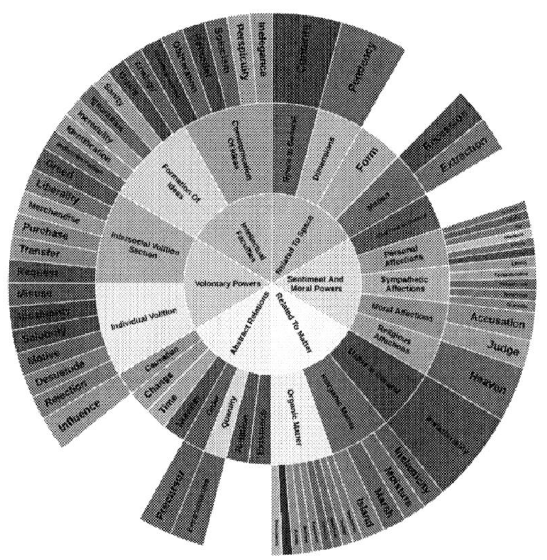

Figure 7: This figure presents a comprehensive review of the most discriminative Roget classes, themes and concepts for Roget Association Analysis of Science Fiction genre. We consider the top 34 and 26 discriminative features for successful and unsuccessful books respectively. Discriminative features for successful and unsuccessful books are colored with green and red respectively.

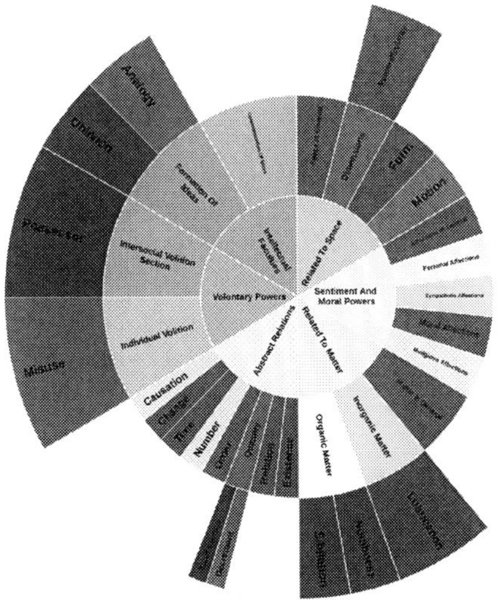

Figure 8: This figure presents a comprehensive review of the most discriminative Roget classes, themes and concepts for Roget Association Analysis of Short Stories genre. We consider the top 36 and 24 discriminative features for successful and unsuccessful books respectively. Discriminative features for successful and unsuccessful books are colored with green and red respectively.

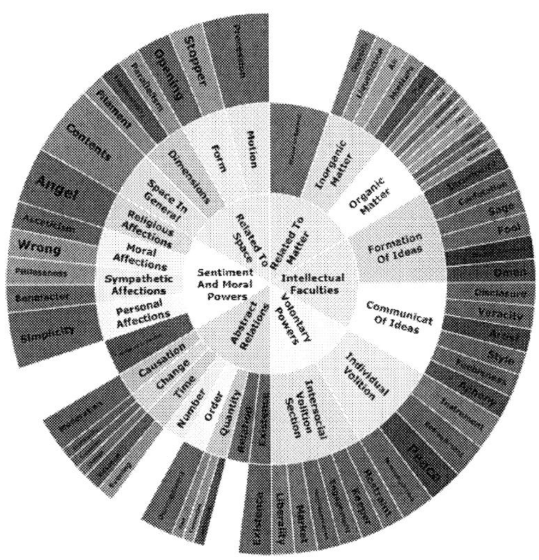

Figure 9: This figure presents a comprehensive review of the most discriminative Roget classes, themes and concepts for Roget Frequency Analysis of Detective and Mystery genre. We consider the top 30 discriminative features for both successful and unsuccessful books. Discriminative features for successful and unsuccessful books are colored with green and red respectively.

Recovering Lexically and Semantically Reused Texts

Ansel MacLaughlin*, **Shaobin Xu***, **David A. Smith**
Khoury College of Computer Science
Northeastern University
{ansel, shaobinx, dasmith}@ccs.neu.edu

Abstract

Writers often repurpose material from existing texts when composing new documents. Because most documents have more than one source, we cannot trace these connections using only models of document-level similarity. Instead, this paper considers methods for local text reuse detection (LTRD), detecting *localized* regions of lexically or semantically similar text embedded in otherwise unrelated material. In extensive experiments, we study the relative performance of four classes of neural and bag-of-words models on three LTRD tasks – detecting plagiarism, modeling journalists' use of press releases, and identifying scientists' citation of earlier papers. We conduct evaluations on three existing datasets and a new, publicly-available citation localization dataset. Our findings shed light on a number of previously-unexplored questions in the study of LTRD, including the importance of incorporating document-level context for predictions, the applicability of of-the-shelf neural models pretrained on "general" semantic textual similarity tasks such as paraphrase detection, and the trade-offs between more efficient bag-of-words and feature-based neural models and slower pairwise neural models.

1 Introduction

When composing documents in many genres—from news reports, to scientific papers, to political speeches—authors obtain ideas and inspiration from source documents and present them in the form of direct copies, quotations, summaries, or paraphrases. In the simplest case, e.g. in congressional bills, writers include text from earlier versions of the same document along with new material (Wilkerson et al., 2015). In news media, journalists often paraphrase or quote speeches, press releases, and interviews (Niculae et al., 2015; Tan et al., 2016). In academia, citations of papers usually appear along with summaries of their contributions (Qazvinian and Radev, 2010). These are instances of lexical and semantic **local text reuse**, where both source and target documents contain lexically or semantically similar passages, surrounded by text that is unrelated or dissimilar. Often, reused text is presented without explicit links or citations, making it hard to track information flow.

While many state-of-the-art (SoTA) NLP architectures have been trained on the closely-related tasks of document- and sentence-pair similarity detection (Reimers and Gurevych, 2019) and ad-hoc retrieval (Dai and Callan, 2019), prior methods for local text-reuse detection (LTRD) are mostly limited to lexical matching (Lee, 2007; Clough et al., 2002; Leskovec et al., 2009; Wilkerson et al., 2015; Smith et al., 2014) with some dictionary expansion (Moritz et al., 2016). To our knowledge, only Zhou et al. (2020) has applied neural models to this problem, proposing hierarchical neural models that use a cross-document attention mechanism to model local similarities between two candidate documents.

In this paper, we conduct a large-scale evaluation of several lexical overlap and SoTA neural models for LTRD. Among the neural models, we benchmark not only the hierarchical neural models proposed by Zhou et al. (2020), but also study the effectiveness of three classes of models not yet applied to LTRD: **1)** BERT-based (Devlin et al., 2019) passage encoders trained on generic paraphrase, semantic textual similarity, and IR data (Reimers and Gurevych, 2019); **2)** feature-based BERT models with direct sentence-level supervision; and **3)** fine-tuned BERT-based models for sequence-pair tasks.

We conduct evaluations on four datasets, including **1)** PAN and S2ORC (Zhou et al., 2020), benchmark LTRD datasets for plagiarism detection and

*Equal contribution.

Proceedings of the 10th Conference on Lexical and Computational Semantics, pages 52–66
August 5–6, 2021, Bangkok, Thailand (online) ©2021 Association for Computational Linguistics

citation localization; **2)** Pr2News (MacLaughlin et al., 2020), a dataset of text reuse in news articles labeled with a mix of expert, non-expert, and heuristic annotation; **3)** ARC-Sim, a new, publicly available[1] citation localization dataset created using citation links in the ACL ARC (Bird et al., 2008).

Our experiments address a number of previously-unexplored questions in the study of LTRD, including **1)** the impact of training on weakly-supervised data on model accuracy; **2)** the effectiveness of SoTA neural models trained on "general" semantic similarity data for LTRD tasks; **3)** the importance of incorporating document-level context; **4)** the effects of domain-adaptive pretraining (Gururangan et al., 2020) on the accuracy of fine-tuned BERT models; and **5)** the trade-offs between more efficient lexical overlap and feature-based neural models and slower pairwise neural models.

2 Related Work

LTRD methods have been applied in many domains, including tracking short "memes" in news and social media (Leskovec et al., 2009), tracing specific policy language embedded in proposed legislation (Wilkerson et al., 2015; Funk and Mullen, 2018), studying reuse of scripture in historical and theological writings (Lee, 2007; Moritz et al., 2016), tracing information propagation in news and social media (Tan et al., 2016; Clough et al., 2002; MacLaughlin et al., 2020), and detecting plagiarism on the web (Potthast et al., 2013; Sánchez-Pérez et al., 2014; Vani and Gupta, 2017). Most applications, however, use only *lexical* overlap and alignment methods to detect reuse, sometimes with lemmatization and dictionary curation.

Our work builds on the recent efforts of Zhou et al. (2020), who demonstrate the efficacy of hierarchical neural models in detecting instances of non-literal reuse where authors paraphrase, summarize, and heavily edit source content. However, as discussed in §1, we conduct a much larger set of experiments beyond those of Zhou et al. (2020). In addition to the hierarchical neural models with document-level supervision proposed by Zhou et al. (2020), we evaluate four sets of models: lexical overlap models, SoTA neural models trained for general paraphrase detection, hierarchical neural models with sentence-level supervision, and fine-tuned sequence-pair BERT models. Further, in addition to evaluating models on the benchmark LTRD datasets introduced by Zhou et al. (2020), we conduct experiments on two more challenging datasets: ARC-Sim, a new citation localization dataset with hard negative examples, and Pr2News (MacLaughlin et al., 2020), a dataset of text reuse in science news articles with heuristically-labeled training data.

Also related to our work is research studying sentence-pair problems, e.g. paraphrase detection (PD) (Dolan and Brockett, 2005), semantic textual similarity (STS) (Cer et al., 2017) and textual entailment, (Bowman et al., 2015), and document-ranking problems, e.g. ad-hoc retrieval (Croft et al., 2009). In fact, it is trivial to adapt existing approaches to sentence-pair and document ranking problems to LTRD. As discussed in §3, we cast LTRD as sentence classification and ranking, identifying which sentences in a target text are lexically or semantically reused from some portion of the source. Thus, in order to adapt sentence-pair models to this task, we simply compute scores for all pairs of (source sentence, target sentence), and use some function (e.g. *max*) to aggregate the scores for each target sentence. Similarly, one can adapt existing ad-hoc retrieval approaches by treating each target sentence as a query and computing a score with the corresponding source. These approaches, however, may suffer from a lack of contextualization and/or efficiency issues. Sentence-pair models that encode each source and target sentence separately, while efficient, might miss important contextualizing information in surrounding sentences. Similarly, neural IR models that process each target sentence as a separate query do not contextualize target sentences and also require a computationally-expensive forward pass for each query. We study the importance and impact of these limitations in our work, testing the effectiveness of multiple SoTA BERT-based architectures for sequence-pair similarity and ranking.

3 Problem Definition

Following Zhou et al. (2020), we define LTRD as two tasks: **document-to-document (D2D) alignment** and **sentence-to-document (S2D) alignment**. In D2D, for a given pair of documents (source document $\mathbf{S}$, target document $\mathbf{T}$), we aim to predict whether $\mathbf{T}$ reuses content from $\mathbf{S}$. Thus, each pair has a corresponding binary label of 1 if $\mathbf{T}$ reuses content, else 0. Note, this is different than

[1] https://github.com/maclaughlin/ARC-Sim

evaluating the similarity of the two documents as a whole, since, in this setting, only a small portion of $\mathbf{T}$ is adapted from $\mathbf{S}$, and most of it is possibly unrelated. In S2D, given an ($\mathbf{S}$, $\mathbf{T}$) pair, we aim to predict *which* specific sentences $\mathbf{t_i} \in \mathbf{T}$ contain reused S content. Thus, each pair has n corresponding labels, one label for each sentence $\mathbf{t_i} \in \mathbf{T}$.[2]

4 Models

We benchmark four classes of models on this task:

4.1 Lexical Overlap Models

We evaluate two unsupervised metrics:

- **TF-IDF Cosine Similarity**: Simple word overlap metrics are commonly-used baselines to measure the similarity between two passages for PD (Dolan and Brockett, 2005), STS (Reimers and Gurevych, 2019), document retrieval (Croft et al., 2009), and LTRD (Tan et al., 2016; Lee, 2007; Clough et al., 2002).
- **Rouge** (Lin, 2004): Since authors of derived documents often paraphrase and summarize source content, we evaluate Rouge, a popular summarization evaluation metric. We evaluate Rouge-{1, 2, L}, selecting the best configuration for each dataset using validation data.

We compute two versions of each metric: single-pair (sp) and all-pairs (ap). In sp, for a given document pair ($\mathbf{S}$, $\mathbf{T}$), we compute a score for each sentence $\mathbf{t_i} \in \mathbf{T}$ by computing its similarity to the *entire* $\mathbf{S}$. In ap, we compute a score for each sentence $\mathbf{t_i} \in \mathbf{T}$ by computing its similarity to *each sentence* $\mathbf{s_i} \in \mathbf{S}$, then selecting the maximum score over all $\mathbf{s_i}$. These scores are then thresholded to make binary predictions. For the D2D task, we predict $\mathbf{T}$ as positive if it contains at least one positively predicted sentence. For the S2D task, we evaluate the predicted score for each $\mathbf{t_i} \in \mathbf{T}$.

4.2 Pretrained Sentence-BERT Encoders

We evaluate Sentence-BERT (SBERT) (Reimers and Gurevych, 2019), a SoTA pretrained passage encoder for semantic-relatedness tasks. SBERT models are trained by 1) adding pooling (e.g. mean pooling) to the output of BERT; 2) training on pairs or triplets of passages to learn semantically meaningful passage representations; 3) at test time, computing the similarity between two passages as the cosine similarity between their pooled representations. We evaluate three SBERTs trained for different tasks:

- **Semantic Textual Similarity (STS)**: Roberta$_{LARGE}$ (Liu et al., 2019) trained on SNLI (Bowman et al., 2015) and MultiNLI (Williams et al., 2018) then fine-tuned on the STS-B (Cer et al., 2017) train set.
- **Paraphrase Detection (PD)**: distilled Roberta$_{BASE}$ (Sanh et al., 2019) fine-tuned on a large-scale paraphrase detection corpus.
- **Information Retrieval (IR)**: distilled Roberta$_{BASE}$ (Sanh et al., 2019) fine-tuned on MS MARCO (Campos et al., 2016).

Note, these pretrained SBERT models are *not* trained for LTRD. Instead, they are trained on large-scale datasets for other related tasks (PD, STS, IR). These experiments thus evaluate how well off-the-shelf tools generalize to a new task and domain.

Just as the lexical models, we evaluate in sp and ap settings. Following Reimers and Gurevych (2019), we embed each source document, source sentence, and target sentence separately, then compute cosine similarity for each pair.

4.3 Hierarchical Neural Models (HNM)

We also benchmark three HNM. Similar to SBERT (§4.2), HNM operate on frozen embeddings (Peters et al., 2019) which are computationally efficient since they only need to be calculated once (i.e. only one BERT forward pass for each source or target sentence). Unlike SBERT, however, HNM also have task-specific model architectures that learn to contextualize and align sentences.

BERT-HAN (shallow) (Zhou et al., 2020): this model mean pools frozen BERT embeddings to generate sentence representations, then uses a hierarchical attention network (HAN) (Yang et al., 2016) to add document-level context and a cross-document attention (CDA) mechanism to align passages across documents. See Zhou et al. (2020).

At training time, BERT-HAN only calculates loss at the document-pair level, i.e. D2D classification. There is no sentence-level supervision (S2D). At inference, two sets of predictions are output: 1) the D2D prediction, as during training; 2) the intermediate hidden representations of the sentences

[2] We could also study the sentence-to-sentence problem, learning to identify which source sentence(s) contain the content reused in a given target sentence, if any. However, as noted by Zhou et al. (2020), no datasets exist yet which contain such fine-grained annotation.

$\mathbf{t_i} \in \mathbf{T}$ are extracted, then ranked by their similarity to the final hidden representation of the entire source document $\mathbf{S}$.

GRU-HAN (deep) (Zhou et al., 2020): this model mirrors BERT-HAN, except with GloVe (Pennington et al., 2014) embeddings and a HAN with CDA at both the word and sentence level. It follows the same training and testing regime.

BCL-CDA: We adapt the BCL model from MacLaughlin et al. (2020) (originally designed for the task of intrinsic source attribution on Pr2News) for LTRD by adding a final CDA layer (Zhou et al., 2020). After generating contextualized representations of each source and target sentence with BCL, a CDA layer computes an attention-weighted representation of each target sentence, weighted by its similarity to the source sentences. The CDA-weighted and original target sentence representations are then concatenated and fed into a final layer for prediction.

At training time, BCL-CDA is supervised with target sentence labels. At testing time, it makes target sentence-level predictions (S2D) just as in training. We make a D2D prediction for each (S, T) pair by taking the max over its sentence-level predictions. See Appendix C for full model details.

4.4 Fine-tuned BERT-based Models

Finally, we evaluate fine-tuned BERT-based models for sequence pair classification. Unlike the other three classes of models described above, features for these fine-tuned models cannot be precomputed. Instead, at test time, a separate forward pass is required for each ($\mathbf{S}$, $\mathbf{T}$) or ($\mathbf{S}$, $\mathbf{t_i}$) pair. Thus, though these models might achieve better performance than feature-based alternatives (Peters et al., 2019), it may be unfeasible to test them on large collections where many pairwise computations would be required.

Sequence Pair Models: We fine-tune Roberta$_{Base}$ (Liu et al., 2019) using the standard setup for sequence-pair tasks such as PD, STS, and IR (Devlin et al., 2019; Akkalyoncu Yilmaz et al., 2019). We create an input example for each (source document $\mathbf{S}$, target sentence $\mathbf{t_i}$) pair:

$$[\texttt{CLS}] < \texttt{s}_1, ..., \texttt{s}_\texttt{n} > [\texttt{SEP}]\ \texttt{t}_\texttt{i}\ [\texttt{SEP}]$$

where $< \texttt{s}_1, ..., \texttt{s}_\texttt{n} >$ contains the source document, split into sentences, with each sentence separated by a special [SSS] token ("source sentence start") and $\texttt{t}_\texttt{i}$ is a single target sentence. We feed the [CLS] representation into a final layer to make a prediction for $\texttt{t}_\texttt{i}$. Thus, making a prediction for an entire ($\mathbf{S}$, $\mathbf{T}$) document pair requires n forward passes, one for each $\mathbf{t_i} \in \mathbf{T}$.

Table 1: Dataset statistics: the total number of (source $\mathbf{S}$, target $\mathbf{T}$) example pairs, the average # of sentences and words in each $\mathbf{S}$ and $\mathbf{T}$, and the average # of positively labeled $\mathbf{T}$ sentences in each *positive* ($\mathbf{S}$, $\mathbf{T}$) pair. For Pr2News, we report the average # of $\mathbf{T}$ sentences with label > 0 in the human-labeled val and test sets.

		Avg. Source		Avg. Target		
Dataset	# Examples	# Sents	# Words	# Sents	# Words	# Positive
PAN	18,903	23.7	527.6	22.4	538.5	14.0
S2ORC	188,311	7.2	190.7	11.5	335.8	1.2
Pr2News	64,779	35.3	934.7	30.1	761.3	8.7
ARC-Sim	105,381	5.0	126.6	16.7	400.8	1.2

Domain-adapted Sequence Pair Models: As shown by Gururangan et al. (2020), further pretraining BERT-based models on in-domain text improves performance on a variety of tasks. We explore the effects of DAPT for LTRD, testing Roberta models domain-adapted on either biomedical publications, computer science publications or news data. We fine-tune these models as above.

Sequential Sequence Pair Models: Since the fine-tuned models discussed above operate on a single $\mathbf{t_i}$ at a time, they cannot leverage information from the surrounding target context. Following the success of BERT-based models for sequential sentence classification (Cohan et al., 2019), we construct new input examples containing the full source and target documents, split into sentences:

$$[\texttt{CLS}]< \texttt{s}_1, ..., \texttt{s}_\texttt{n} >[\texttt{SEP}]< \texttt{t}_1, ..., \texttt{t}_\texttt{n} >[\texttt{SEP}]$$

Again, $< \texttt{s}_1, ..., \texttt{s}_\texttt{n} >$ contains the source sentences. Similarly, $< \texttt{t}_1, ..., \texttt{t}_\texttt{n} >$ contains the target sentences, with each separated by a special [TSS] token ("target sentence start"). We feed the final [TSS] representations into a multi-layer feed-forward network to make a prediction for each target sentence.

Each pair is labeled with all corresponding target sentence labels. Since many pairs exceed Roberta's 512 Wordpiece length limit, we use Longformer$_{Base}$ (Beltagy et al., 2020), a Roberta-based model with an adapted attention pattern to handle up to 4,096 tokens. We put global attention on the [SSS] and [TSS] tokens to allow the model to capture cross-document sentence similarity.

5 Datasets

We benchmark the proposed models on four different datasets (Table 1). See Appendix A for further dataset stastics and preprocessing details.

5.1 PAN (Zhou et al., 2020)

PAN contains pairs of (**S**, **T**) web documents where **T** has potentially plagiarized **S**. Positive pairs contain synthetic plagiarism, generated by methods such as back-translation (Potthast et al., 2013). Negative examples are created by replacing **S** with another, unplagiarized source text, $\tilde{\mathbf{S}}$, sampled from the corpus. D2D labels are binary: plagiarized or not. The S2D labels for $\mathbf{t_i} \in \mathbf{T}$ are 1 if $\mathbf{t_i}$ plagiarizes **S**, else 0 (labels in negative pairs are 0).

5.2 Pr2News (MacLaughlin et al., 2020)

Pr2News contains pairs of (press release **S**, science news article **T**), where each **T** has reused content from **S**. There are three aspects of this dataset which are unlike the others we study: **1)** All (**S**, **T**) pairs are positive and contain reuse. Thus, we only evaluate the S2D task. **2)** While the val and test sets are human-annotated, the (**S**, **T**) pairs in the training set are labeled using a heuristic (TF-IDF cosine similarity). Though there has been some success training neural models on scores generated by word-overlap heuristics for the problems of document retrieval (Dehghani et al., 2017) and source attribution (MacLaughlin et al., 2020), applications of weakly-supervised models have not yet been studied on human-labeled LTRD test sets. **3)** Target sentences, $\mathbf{t_i} \in \mathbf{T}$, in the val and test sets are labeled on a 0-3 ordinal scale, ranging from no reuse (0) to near or exact duplication (3).

5.3 S2ORC (Zhou et al., 2020)

S2ORC is a citation localization dataset, containing (abstract **S**, paper section **T**) pairs. Citation localization consists of identifying which $\mathbf{t_i} \in \mathbf{T}$, if any, cite the source. All citation marks are removed from the texts, so models can only make predictions by comparing the language of **S** and **T**, not just simply identify citation marks. Positive examples are created by sampling scientific papers from the broader S2ORC corpus (Lo et al., 2020), finding sections in those papers that contain citation(s) to another paper in the corpus, and pairing together the (cited source abstract **S**, citing section **T**). Negative pairs are created by pairing **T** with $\tilde{\mathbf{S}}$, the abstract of a paper it does *not* cite. The D2D labels are 0 for negative pairs, 1 for positive. The S2D labels for $\mathbf{t_i} \in \mathbf{T}$ are 1 if $\mathbf{t_i}$ contains a citation of **S**, else 0. S2D labels for negative pairs are all 0.

The design of this dataset follows the assumption that the citing sentence(s) in **T** often paraphrase or summarize some portion of the cited paper, which is, in turn, summarized by its abstract **S**. This assumption, however, may be incorrect if the citing sentence is a poor summary of the cited paper (Abu-Jbara and Radev, 2012) or it refers to content in the cited paper which is not included in the abstract. Nevertheless, this assumption allows for easy creation of large-scale, real-world LTRD datasets. This is in contrast to Pr2News, which is substantially smaller due its reliance on human-annotated val and test labels, and PAN, which uses automatic methods to generate synthetic examples. We discuss the trade-offs of using citation marks to generate LTRD datasets in §5.4.

5.4 ARC-Sim

Motivated by the design of S2ORC, we propose a new citation localization dataset[3] built on the ACL Anthology Conference Corpus (ARC) (Bird et al., 2008). Just as S2ORC, we construct our dataset using citations links between papers. Thus, we first break up each ARC paper by section, then use ParsCit (Councill et al., 2008) to find all sections that cite another paper in ARC. Positive examples are pairs (abstract **S**, paper section **T**) where **S** is cited by at least one $\mathbf{t_i} \in \mathbf{T}$. Using this method we generate 61,131 positive (**S**, **T**) pairs. Most (88%) **T** contain only one positive sentence.

To create negative examples, we pair each **S** from the positive samples with a new section, $\tilde{\mathbf{T}}$, that does not cite it. Importantly, $\tilde{\mathbf{T}}$ is sampled from the *same* target paper as the original **T**. This generates 44,250 negative pairs.[4] We argue that these negative samples method will be both more *difficult* and *realistic* than those in S2ORC. In S2ORC, negatives are generated by sampling a new source $\tilde{\mathbf{S}}$ to pair with **T**. However, due to the large scale of the corpus, $\tilde{\mathbf{S}}$ and **T** are often completely unrelated (e.g. Bio vs. CS). These examples, therefore, are trivial and can be easily classified using simple lexical overlap. In ARC-Sim, however, negatives are generated by sampling a new section $\tilde{\mathbf{T}}$ from the *same* paper as **T**. We hypothesize that differentiating between these positive and negative examples will **1)** be more difficult since $\tilde{\mathbf{T}}$ is likely still topically related to **S** and may contain some spurious lexical or semantic overlap; **2)** be more indicative of real-world performance, since real users may

[3] Available for download here.

[4] We sample 1 negative pair per (source abstract, target paper), so target papers that cite the source in more than 1 section will have more positive examples than negative.

need to identify which specific sections in a full target paper reuse content from the source. Further preprocessing and dataset split information is detailed in Appendix A. We use the same labeling scheme as S2ORC.

With dataset creation complete, we sample a set of 50 positive pairs from the val set to analyze in depth. Three expert annotators (authors of this paper) perform the LTRD task, predicting which $\mathbf{t_i} \in \mathbf{T}$ reuse content from $\mathbf{S}$. Five pairs are marked by all annotators (Fleiss' Kappa: 0.83). The remaining 45 are split into 15 per annotator. Overall, we find that annotators mark more sentences as reused (avg. 1.6 sents / target) than the true citation labels (1.3 / target). This is reasonable since $\mathbf{T}$ often only cites $\mathbf{S}$ once, even if it discusses $\mathbf{S}$ in multiple sentences (Qazvinian and Radev, 2010). These false negatives are one disadvantage of using citation marks as supervision. Further, we find that annotators and ground truth often, but not always, agree – annotators identify at least one true citing sentence in 72% of pairs. This difference is mostly due to **1)** citing sentences that discuss source content not described in the source abstract; **2)** OCR errors that can make text hard to read. On the whole, we find that ACL-Sim is a useful LTRD dataset, but there are clear avenues for improvement, such as manually annotating reused sentences without citation marks and improving OCR.

6 Evaluation Settings & Metrics

D2D Metrics: We evaluate the D2D task as $(\mathbf{S}, \mathbf{T})$ pair classification using F1 score. A positive label indicates that $\mathbf{T}$ reuses content from $\mathbf{S}$. A negative label indicates no text reuse. There is no D2D task for Pr2News since all examples are positive.

S2D Metrics: We evaluate S2D in two settings: *corpus level* (i.e. evaluating *all* target sentences from all pairs at once), and *document level* (i.e. evaluating the sentences in each target document w.r.t each other, then averaging scores across documents). The metrics for each setting depend on the dataset. At the corpus level, we evaluate binary-label datasets (PAN, S2ORC, ARC-Sim) with sentence-level F1 and ordinal-label datasets (Pr2News: 0-3 scale), with spearman's correlation (ρ) and NDCG@N (where N is the number of target sentences in the test set). At the document level, we evaluate binary-label datasets with mean average precision (MAP) and top-k accuracy (Acc@k), defined as the proportion of test examples where a positively-labeled sentence in $\mathbf{T}$ is ranked in the top k by the model. We evaluate ordinal-label datasets with NDCG@$\{1,3,5\}$. Note, in order for these document-level metrics to be meaningful, $\mathbf{T}$ must contain at least one positive sentence. Thus, our document-level evaluations are *only* calculated on the positive $(\mathbf{S}, \mathbf{T})$ pairs in each dataset.[5] Since Pr2News only contains positive examples, we use the full test set for all evaluations.

BERT-HAN & GRU-HAN: Since both HAN models are trained on document-level, not sentence-level, labels, we cannot train them on Pr2News, where all document-level labels are positive. Thus, we skip evaluating the HAN models on this dataset.

Domain-adapted RoBERTa Models: We evaluate three DAPT models: 1) Biomed-DAPT for S2ORC and Pr2News since they contain biomedical texts, 2) News-DAPT for Pr2News since the target documents are news articles, 3) CS-DAPT model for S2ORC and ARC-Sim since they contain CS papers.[6] We do not apply DAPT to PAN since no models are adapted to a similar domain.

7 Results & Discussion

As seen in Tables 2 & 3, BERT-based models finetuned on LTRD data perform the best in general, outperforming lexical overlap, SBERT, and HNM. Overall, models achieve their best performances on PAN. We suspect that this is because many positive $(\mathbf{S}, \mathbf{T})$ pairs are easy, containing many plagiarized passages with high lexical overlap, and since many negative $(\tilde{\mathbf{S}}, \mathbf{T})$ pairs are topically unrelated and share little lexical or semantic overlap. On the other end of the spectrum is ARC-Sim, where models score relatively poorly. We hypothesize that this is because most $\mathbf{T}$ only contain one citing sentence and since, as discussed in §5.4, we focus on selecting hard negative target texts, $\tilde{\mathbf{T}}$, sampled from the same document as the original $\mathbf{T}$.

[5]We confirmed that Zhou et al. (2020) calculate their document-level metrics, MRR, P@5 and P@10, across *all* $(\mathbf{S}, \mathbf{T})$ pairs. For the negative pairs, they give models full credit on the S2D task if their corresponding D2D prediction is correct. We argue that this is not indicative of model performance, and thus conduct our document-level evaluations on *only positive* pairs.

[6]CS- and Biomed-DAPT models are adapted on an internal version of the S2ORC corpus (Lo et al., 2020). Since the S2ORC LTRD dataset is randomly sampled from that same corpus, it is possible that the DAPT models are pretrained on some portion of the S2ORC LTRD test set. We do not believe this overlap exists for any other (DAPT, LTRD dataset) pairs.

Table 2: D2D and S2D results on PAN and S2ORC.

Setting	Model	PAN						S2ORC					
		D2D-F1	S2D-F1	MAP	Acc@1	Acc@3	Acc@5	D2D-F1	S2D-F1	MAP	Acc@1	Acc@3	Acc@5
Single-pair baselines	TF-IDF	84.5	69.6	92.4	97.3	99.8	99.8	90.4	27.1	52.9	36.0	65.9	79.6
	Rouge	82.8	59.5	92.2	98.1	99.7	99.9	71.3	21.3	47.1	30.2	58.0	73.0
	SBERT-STS	78.8	32.8	76.6	91.7	99.0	**100.0**	83.3	23.6	48.0	30.4	59.6	75.4
	SBERT-PD	80.8	36.8	80.8	95.1	99.2	99.8	87.6	22.2	44.4	26.7	54.5	71.2
	SBERT-IR	76.0	41.6	77.5	89.5	98.3	99.5	89.9	25.4	50.6	33.5	62.5	77.6
All-pairs baselines	TF-IDF	86.7	79.4	94.5	97.7	99.7	**100.0**	91.1	26.5	51.1	33.6	63.7	78.8
	Rouge	91.8	80.8	94.9	98.2	99.7	99.8	74.9	21.3	45.4	27.4	56.6	73.8
	SBERT-STS	89.3	74.4	93.1	98.2	99.8	99.9	85.9	24.6	48.3	30.5	60.3	76.3
	SBERT-PD	90.8	76.1	94.4	98.5	99.8	99.9	88.6	21.7	42.9	24.8	53.2	70.3
	SBERT-IR	87.3	71.8	91.8	97.9	99.4	99.8	90.8	25.5	50.4	32.8	62.7	78.0
Hierarchical Neural Models	Bert-Han (Shallow)	74.6	44.3	54.6	46.2	74.5	86.4	90.8	10.0	37.7	19.4	46.2	63.1
	Gru-Han (Deep)	77.2	44.3	54.0	42.8	76.0	89.4	91.8	10.2	40.4	21.5	50.0	68.1
	BCL-CDA	74.1	68.8	81.1	78.1	90.5	94.6	88.6	37.2	58.9	42.5	72.3	84.9
Fine-tuned BERT	Roberta	**95.0**	**82.2**	**96.8**	**99.2**	**99.9**	**100.0**	88.8	54.2	76.7	65.7	88.3	94.4
	Biomed-Roberta	–	–	–	–	–	–	90.3	54.0	77.6	66.8	89.2	94.7
	CS-Roberta	–	–	–	–	–	–	89.9	54.1	**77.7**	**67.2**	**89.3**	**94.9**
	$\text{Longformer}_{sequential}$	76.6	68.3	89.6	90.7	96.3	98.5	**96.6**	**58.5**	75.5	63.6	88.0	94.4

7.1 Impact of Weak Supervision

In general, the supervised BERT-based models outperform the unsupervised lexical overlap baselines. The exception to this finding is Pr2News, where the lexical overlap baselines Rouge_{ap} and Rouge_{sp} have the best corpus-level and document-level S2D scores, respectively. This result is perhaps not unexpected, since, unlike other datasets, the labeling methods of Pr2News differ substantially between training (heuristic generated by TFIDF_{ap} scores), validation (non-expert-labeled) and test (expert-labeled). However, our results still contrast Dehghani et al. (2017), who, working on a document ranking task, find that weakly-supervised neural models consistently outperform the unsupervised methods used to label their training data. We hypothesize that our negative finding might be due, in part, to the small scale of Pr2News and our reliance on only a single heuristic as the supervision signal source. To address this, future work could explore applications on larger weakly-supervised LTRD datasets, e.g. closer in scale to the 50M document collection of Dehghani et al. (2017), and improving the weak-supervision signal to better reflect human judgements, e.g. through combination of multiple heuristics (Boecking et al., 2021).

7.2 Effectiveness of Off-the-shelf Tools

Next, we take a closer look at the performances of SBERT (Reimers and Gurevych, 2019). Note, these off-the-shelf models are trained on the related tasks of either PD, STS, or IR, *not* on our LTRD datasets. Though PD, STS, and IR receive substantially more attention in the NLP and IR literature, prior research has not yet explored the generalizability of models trained on these tasks to LTRD. We focus in particular on SBERT-PD, since Reimers and Gurevych (2019) recommend it for various applications and claim that it achieves strong results on various similarity and retrieval tasks. Examining our results, however, we find the opposite – SBERT performs worse in general than the lexical overlap baselines, and SBERT-PD performs no better than SBERT-IR (though both better than SBERT-STS). We suspect that the SBERT models would perform better if they were fine-tuned on in-domain LTRD data. However, since we aimed to evaluate the effectiveness of an off-the-shelf tool, we did not test this hypothesis.

7.3 Importance of Document-level Context

To examine the importance of incorporating document-level context for LTRD, we compare the results of Roberta and Longformer.[7] As noted in §4, input to both models follows the standard BERT sequence-pair setup (Devlin et al., 2019). However, Roberta operates on pairs of source documents and single target sentences $(\mathbf{S}, \mathbf{t_i})$, while Longformer operates on full document pairs $(\mathbf{S}, \mathbf{T})$, making predictions for all target sentences simultaneously.

From Tables 2 & 3, we see that modeling target document context does not consistently improve performance. While Longformer outperforms Roberta on the D2D and corpus-level S2D tasks on most datasets, Roberta consistently scores higher on document-level S2D. To investigate the discrepancy between Longformer's strong corpus-level S2D performance and its relatively weaker document-level S2D scores, we examine S2ORC

[7]Longformer is initialized from Roberta_{Base}, but has additional parameters and is further pretrained on a long-document corpus. Thus, though we cannot disentangle these effects from the benefits of incorporating document-level context, we believe our experiments provide a relatively fair comparison between two SoTA models for short vs. long input sequences.

Table 3: D2D and S2D results on ARC-Sim and S2D results on Pr2News.

Setting	Model	ARC-Sim						Pr2News				
		D2D-F1	S2D-F1	MAP	Acc@1	Acc@3	Acc@5	ρ	NDCG@N	NDCG@1	NDCG@3	NDCG@5
Single-pair baselines	TF-IDF	77.4	18.4	44.8	30.1	52.5	65.5	60.0	90.8	76.0	70.0	71.0
	Rouge	75.3	14.6	36.6	21.8	42.4	55.5	64.5	94.2	**77.3**	**77.0**	**77.7**
	SBERT-STS	76.3	15.0	39.6	23.6	47.0	61.4	35.5	81.6	40.3	42.8	49.2
	SBERT-PD	77.2	16.6	41.4	25.8	48.1	62.5	36.4	82.6	48.7	51.2	55.4
	SBERT-IR	76.9	16.9	41.3	25.7	49.2	62.8	35.3	79.7	54.0	54.7	54.5
All-pairs baselines	TF-IDF	77.3	18.3	43.1	27.6	51.4	64.3	66.7	97.1	66.7	69.8	72.8
	Rouge	75.1	12.9	35.9	20.2	42.0	56.4	**67.2**	**97.3**	69.7	74.6	77.4
	SBERT-STS	76.7	15.8	39.2	23.1	46.7	60.8	58.0	94.8	59.2	61.1	64.4
	SBERT-PD	77.2	16.6	40.4	24.4	47.8	61.3	63.0	96.4	70.3	70.8	71.4
	SBERT-IR	77.4	16.9	40.2	24.3	47.9	62.5	56.1	94.2	56.3	62.4	63.3
Hierarchical Neural Models	Bert-Han (Shallow)	78.7	7.5	35.5	19.8	41.1	56.5	–	–	–	–	–
	Gru-Han (Deep)	79.7	22.1	43.5	27.2	53.2	67.3	–	–	–	–	–
	BCL-CDA	79.9	30.8	55.3	38.5	67.7	80.4	26.3	80.2	24.3	32.5	37.1
Fine-tuned BERT	Roberta	82.0	41.6	**69.7**	**57.0**	**81.8**	**90.4**	60.5	93.7	71.3	68.6	71.4
	Biomed-Roberta	–	–	–	–	–	–	60.1	93.3	68.6	66.2	69.9
	News-Roberta	–	–	–	–	–	–	60.6	93.4	68.3	67.8	70.6
	CS-Roberta	81.6	44.0	69.5	56.7	81.7	89.8	–	–	–	–	–
	Longformer$_{sequential}$	**84.5**	**46.5**	68.3	55.0	80.9	88.8	62.7	95.9	69.5	70.4	70.8

and ARC-Sim. At the corpus-level, Roberta mostly makes false positives (FP) errors, while Longformer makes roughly equal FP and FN errors (and fewer errors overall). For both models, most of these FPs occur in positive (**S**, **T**) pairs, i.e. pairs where at least one $\mathbf{t_i}$ cites **S**. As discussed in §5, these errors are reasonable, since **T** often only cites **S** once, even if it discusses **S** in multiple sentences (Qazvinian and Radev, 2010). Roberta's more-frequent FP errors, however, do not affect its document-level scores as much. Since, at the document-level, we evaluate how well models *rank* the $\mathbf{t_i}$ in each **T** w.r.t each other, models perform well if they score positive sentences higher than negatives (no reuse). Indeed, though Roberta predicts high scores for many negatives, it does better than Longformer at scoring positives higher, leading to better ranking performance.

Next, we first perform error analysis on PAN, the only dataset where Roberta outperforms Longformer across all metrics. We find that Roberta makes few D2D errors, of which most (80%) are FPs. Longformer, on the other hand, not only makes substantially more errors overall, but splits them roughly equally between FPs and FNs. These FNs are especially surprising since many positive examples in PAN have high lexical overlap. On the other hand, for the corpus-level S2D task, we find that both models have similar numbers of TPs and FNs, but that Longformer generates an order of magnitude more FPs, i.e. predicting that negative target sentences contain reuse.

7.4 Effects of Domain-adaptive Pretraining

We next examine the benefits of DAPT. Gururangan et al. (2020) find that further pretraining Roberta on text from a new domain improves downstream performance, provided that this new domain is similar to the downstream task. To examine whether this finding holds for LTRD, we conduct DAPT evaluations on three datasets – S2ORC, ARC-Sim and Pr2News. Unlike Gururangan et al. (2020), however, we find mixed results. On ARC-Sim and Pr2News, standard Roberta models outperform the corresponding DAPT models on most metrics. The ARC-Sim findings are especially surprising, since its domain (NLP papers) is substantially different from Roberta's standard pretraining data (books, news, web documents) and since Gururangan et al. (2020) show strong performance gains from DAPT on a classification dataset also based on ACL-ARC. Moving on to S2ORC, our findings are reversed, with both DAPT models outperforming Roberta. However, as noted in §6, since the extra pretraining data for these DAPT models is sampled from the same corpus as S2ORC, we cannot be sure how much of this boost is due to DAPT models pretraining on S2ORC's test data.

7.5 Trade-offs between Models

Finally, we discuss the trade-offs between models, focusing on differences in performance and relative computational efficiency. On one end of the efficiency spectrum are the lexical overlap metrics (TFIDF, Rouge-{1,2}) which are easily scaled to large document collections by simply keeping track of the ngrams in each source or target passage, then computing word-overlap scores for each (**S**, **T**) pair.[8] As discussed in §4, we evaluate these metrics in two settings, *sp* and *ap*, depending on whether we compute similarity scores between target sen-

[8] Rouge-L cannot be scaled as easily as the other lexical overlap baselines. However, it performs worse than Rouge-1 and -2 on all validation sets and is not applied to any test data.

tences and entire source documents or with each source sentence separately (then compute an aggregate score). Though no single metric or evaluation setting consistently achieves the best performance, these models provides a very strong baseline, especially on the D2D task.

In the middle of the efficiency spectrum are SBERT and HNM. Though these models require an expensive forward pass to generate an embedding for each source or target passage, these embeddings can then be saved and reused. Scores for each (**S**, **T**) pair can be computed relatively quickly by either computing cosine similarity scores (SBERT) or running the pair through a lighter-weight task-specific architecture (HNM). However, we find mixed and negative results regarding their effectiveness. Specifically, as discussed in §7.2, off-the-shelf SBERT models generally lag behind the computationally-cheaper lexical overlap baselines. Results are slightly more positive, though, for the HNMs. BCL-CDA, the best HNM, achieves the second best performance on two datasets (S2ORC, ARC-Sim). However, it still lags behind the best model, fine-tuned BERT, by a significant margin. Further, it performs worse than lexical overlap baselines on the other datasets, PAN and Pr2News. Turning next to the HAN models, we find that though they achieve competitive D2D performance on two of the three datasets, they have very weak S2D scores. We suspect that this is because they are only trained on the D2D task – at test time, they make sentence-level predictions by computing similarity scores between hidden source and target representations extracted from a pretrained D2D model. Due to this training formulation, the HAN models fail to learn sentence-level representations that are useful for prediction. See Appendix B for a discussion of our efforts to replicate the results from the HAN models on our datasets.

Lastly, the least efficient models are fine-tuned BERTs, which require a separate forward pass to compute a score for each (**S**, **T**) or (**S**, $\mathbf{t_i}$) pair. As is the trend with other NLP tasks, though, these computationally-intense and parameter-rich models achieve the best average performance. This finding is clearest on S2ORC and ARC-Sim, where few $\mathbf{t_i}$ contain reuse and that reuse is non-literal (e.g. paraphrase). On these datasets, the best fine-tuned BERT outperforms the next-best model (BCL-CDA) by an average of 6.3% (D2D) and 15.5% (S2D). However, on datasets where target documents directly copy large spans of source content with minimal changes (PAN) or where large-scale supervised training data is unavailable (Pr2News), fine-tuned BERT provides much less or no improvement over the lexical overlap metrics.

8 Conclusion

We study methods for local text reuse detection, identifying passages in a target document that lexically or semantically reuse content from a source. Through evaluations on four datasets, including a new citation localization dataset, we confirm the strong performance of BERT models fine-tuned on our task. However, we also find that lexical-overlap methods, e.g. TFIDF, provide strong baselines, frequently outperforming off-the-shelf neural passage encoders and hierarchical neural models.

Based on these findings, we suggest practitioners take one of two approaches: **1)** in instances with little labeled training data or where most reuse is exact (i.e. copying), use traditional lexical overlap models; **2)** in instances with large-scale labeled training data and where much of the reuse is non-literal (e.g. summarization, paraphrasing), use a lexical overlap method to filter possible (**S**, **T**) pairs, then run a more expensive fine-tuned BERT on that subset. We suggest users opt for fine-tuned BERT models over pretrained passage encoders (SBERT) or HNMs for this second step since they achieve substantially higher performance. Suggestion #2 follows current approaches to neural IR, where neural models only rerank smaller lists of documents retrieved by a cheaper lexical overlap method, e.g. TF-IDF. Performance *may* be further boosted by fine-tuning BERT-based models that incorporate document-level context (i.e. Longformer) or ones that are adapted to the target domain of interest (i.e. DAPT), but often the standard Roberta$_{Base}$ achieves highly competitive results.

Acknowledgements

Ansel MacLaughlin was supported by a National Endowment for the Humanities Digital Humanities Advancement Grant (HAA-263837-19) and a Northeastern University Dissertation Completion Fellowship.

References

Martín Abadi, Ashish Agarwal, Paul Barham, Eugene Brevdo, Zhifeng Chen, Craig Citro, Greg S. Corrado,

Andy Davis, Jeffrey Dean, Matthieu Devin, Sanjay Ghemawat, Ian Goodfellow, Andrew Harp, Geoffrey Irving, Michael Isard, Yangqing Jia, Rafal Jozefowicz, Lukasz Kaiser, Manjunath Kudlur, Josh Levenberg, Dandelion Mané, Rajat Monga, Sherry Moore, Derek Murray, Chris Olah, Mike Schuster, Jonathon Shlens, Benoit Steiner, Ilya Sutskever, Kunal Talwar, Paul Tucker, Vincent Vanhoucke, Vijay Vasudevan, Fernanda Viégas, Oriol Vinyals, Pete Warden, Martin Wattenberg, Martin Wicke, Yuan Yu, and Xiaoqiang Zheng. 2015. TensorFlow: Large-scale machine learning on heterogeneous systems. Software available from tensorflow.org.

Amjad Abu-Jbara and Dragomir Radev. 2012. Reference scope identification in citing sentences. In *Proceedings of the 2012 Conference of the North American Chapter of the Association for Computational Linguistics: Human Language Technologies*, pages 80–90, Montréal, Canada. Association for Computational Linguistics.

Zeynep Akkalyoncu Yilmaz, Shengjin Wang, Wei Yang, Haotian Zhang, and Jimmy Lin. 2019. Applying BERT to document retrieval with birch. In *Proceedings of the 2019 Conference on Empirical Methods in Natural Language Processing and the 9th International Joint Conference on Natural Language Processing (EMNLP-IJCNLP): System Demonstrations*, pages 19–24, Hong Kong, China. Association for Computational Linguistics.

Iz Beltagy, Matthew E. Peters, and Arman Cohan. 2020. Longformer: The long-document transformer. *ArXiv*, abs/2004.05150.

Steven Bird, Robert Dale, Bonnie Dorr, Bryan Gibson, Mark Joseph, Min-Yen Kan, Dongwon Lee, Brett Powley, Dragomir Radev, and Yee Fan Tan. 2008. The ACL Anthology reference corpus: A reference dataset for bibliographic research in computational linguistics. In *Proceedings of the Sixth International Conference on Language Resources and Evaluation (LREC'08)*, Marrakech, Morocco. European Language Resources Association (ELRA).

Steven Bird and Edward Loper. 2004. NLTK: The natural language toolkit. In *Proceedings of the ACL Interactive Poster and Demonstration Sessions*, pages 214–217, Barcelona, Spain. Association for Computational Linguistics.

Benedikt Boecking, W. Neiswanger, E. Xing, and A. Dubrawski. 2021. Interactive weak supervision: Learning useful heuristics for data labeling. In *ICLR*.

Samuel R. Bowman, Gabor Angeli, Christopher Potts, and Christopher D. Manning. 2015. A large annotated corpus for learning natural language inference. In *Proceedings of the 2015 Conference on Empirical Methods in Natural Language Processing*, pages 632–642, Lisbon, Portugal. Association for Computational Linguistics.

Daniel Fernando Campos, T. Nguyen, M. Rosenberg, Xia Song, Jianfeng Gao, Saurabh Tiwary, Rangan Majumder, L. Deng, and Bhaskar Mitra. 2016. Ms marco: A human generated machine reading comprehension dataset. *ArXiv*, abs/1611.09268.

Daniel Cer, Mona Diab, Eneko Agirre, Iñigo Lopez-Gazpio, and Lucia Specia. 2017. SemEval-2017 task 1: Semantic textual similarity multilingual and crosslingual focused evaluation. In *Proceedings of the 11th International Workshop on Semantic Evaluation (SemEval-2017)*, pages 1–14, Vancouver, Canada. Association for Computational Linguistics.

Paul Clough, Robert Gaizauskas, Scott S.L. Piao, and Yorick Wilks. 2002. Measuring text reuse. In *Proceedings of the 40th Annual Meeting of the Association for Computational Linguistics*, pages 152–159, Philadelphia, Pennsylvania, USA. Association for Computational Linguistics.

Arman Cohan, Iz Beltagy, Daniel King, Bhavana Dalvi, and Dan Weld. 2019. Pretrained language models for sequential sentence classification. In *Proceedings of the 2019 Conference on Empirical Methods in Natural Language Processing and the 9th International Joint Conference on Natural Language Processing (EMNLP-IJCNLP)*, pages 3693–3699, Hong Kong, China. Association for Computational Linguistics.

Isaac Councill, C. Lee Giles, and Min-Yen Kan. 2008. ParsCit: an open-source CRF reference string parsing package. In *Proceedings of the Sixth International Conference on Language Resources and Evaluation (LREC'08)*, Marrakech, Morocco. European Language Resources Association (ELRA).

W. Croft, Donald Metzler, and Trevor Strohman. 2009. *Search Engines - Information Retrieval in Practice*. Pearson.

Zhuyun Dai and J. Callan. 2019. Deeper text understanding for ir with contextual neural language modeling. *Proceedings of the 42nd International ACM SIGIR Conference on Research and Development in Information Retrieval*.

M. Dehghani, Hamed Zamani, A. Severyn, J. Kamps, and W. Croft. 2017. Neural ranking models with weak supervision. *Proceedings of the 40th International ACM SIGIR Conference on Research and Development in Information Retrieval*.

Jacob Devlin, Ming-Wei Chang, Kenton Lee, and Kristina Toutanova. 2019. BERT: Pre-training of deep bidirectional transformers for language understanding. In *Proceedings of the 2019 Conference of the North American Chapter of the Association for Computational Linguistics: Human Language Technologies, Volume 1 (Long and Short Papers)*, pages 4171–4186, Minneapolis, Minnesota. Association for Computational Linguistics.

William B. Dolan and Chris Brockett. 2005. Automatically constructing a corpus of sentential paraphrases. In *Proceedings of the Third International Workshop on Paraphrasing (IWP2005)*.

Kellen Funk and Lincoln Mullen. 2018. The spine of American law: Digital text analysis and U.S. legal practice. *The American Historical Review*, 123(1):1–39.

Suchin Gururangan, Ana Marasović, Swabha Swayamdipta, Kyle Lo, Iz Beltagy, Doug Downey, and Noah A. Smith. 2020. Don't stop pretraining: Adapt language models to domains and tasks. In *Proceedings of the 58th Annual Meeting of the Association for Computational Linguistics*, pages 8342–8360, Online. Association for Computational Linguistics.

Diederik P. Kingma and Jimmy Ba. 2015. Adam: A method for stochastic optimization. In *3rd International Conference on Learning Representations, ICLR 2015, San Diego, CA, USA, May 7-9, 2015, Conference Track Proceedings*.

John Lee. 2007. A computational model of text reuse in ancient literary texts. In *Proceedings of the 45th Annual Meeting of the Association of Computational Linguistics*, pages 472–479, Prague, Czech Republic. Association for Computational Linguistics.

Jure Leskovec, Lars Backstrom, and Jon Kleinberg. 2009. Meme-tracking and the dynamics of the news cycle. In *KDD*, pages 497–506.

Chin-Yew Lin. 2004. ROUGE: A package for automatic evaluation of summaries. In *Text Summarization Branches Out*, pages 74–81, Barcelona, Spain. Association for Computational Linguistics.

Y. Liu, Myle Ott, Naman Goyal, Jingfei Du, Mandar Joshi, Danqi Chen, Omer Levy, M. Lewis, Luke Zettlemoyer, and Veselin Stoyanov. 2019. Roberta: A robustly optimized bert pretraining approach. *ArXiv*, abs/1907.11692.

Kyle Lo, Lucy Lu Wang, Mark Neumann, Rodney Kinney, and Daniel Weld. 2020. S2ORC: The semantic scholar open research corpus. In *Proceedings of the 58th Annual Meeting of the Association for Computational Linguistics*, pages 4969–4983, Online. Association for Computational Linguistics.

Thang Luong, Hieu Pham, and Christopher D. Manning. 2015. Effective approaches to attention-based neural machine translation. In *Proceedings of the 2015 Conference on Empirical Methods in Natural Language Processing*, pages 1412–1421, Lisbon, Portugal. Association for Computational Linguistics.

Ansel MacLaughlin, J. Wihbey, Aleszu Bajak, and D. A. Smith. 2020. Source attribution: Recovering the press releases behind health science news. In *ICWSM*.

Christopher D. Manning, Mihai Surdeanu, John Bauer, Jenny Finkel, Steven J. Bethard, and David McClosky. 2014. The Stanford CoreNLP natural language processing toolkit. In *ACL*, pages 55–60.

Maria Moritz, Andreas Wiederhold, Barbara Pavlek, Yuri Bizzoni, and Marco Büchler. 2016. Non-literal text reuse in historical texts: An approach to identify reuse transformations and its application to Bible reuse. In *Proceedings of the 2016 Conference on Empirical Methods in Natural Language Processing*, pages 1849–1859, Austin, Texas. Association for Computational Linguistics.

Vlad Niculae, Caroline Suen, Justine Zhang, Cristian Danescu-Niculescu-Mizil, and J. Leskovec. 2015. Quotus: The structure of political media coverage as revealed by quoting patterns. *Proceedings of the 24th International Conference on World Wide Web*.

Adam Paszke, Sam Gross, Francisco Massa, Adam Lerer, James Bradbury, Gregory Chanan, Trevor Killeen, Zeming Lin, Natalia Gimelshein, Luca Antiga, Alban Desmaison, Andreas Kopf, Edward Yang, Zachary DeVito, Martin Raison, Alykhan Tejani, Sasank Chilamkurthy, Benoit Steiner, Lu Fang, Junjie Bai, and Soumith Chintala. 2019. Pytorch: An imperative style, high-performance deep learning library. In H. Wallach, H. Larochelle, A. Beygelzimer, F. d'Alché-Buc, E. Fox, and R. Garnett, editors, *Advances in Neural Information Processing Systems 32*, pages 8024–8035. Curran Associates, Inc.

Jeffrey Pennington, Richard Socher, and Christopher Manning. 2014. GloVe: Global vectors for word representation. In *Proceedings of the 2014 Conference on Empirical Methods in Natural Language Processing (EMNLP)*, pages 1532–1543, Doha, Qatar. Association for Computational Linguistics.

Matthew E. Peters, Sebastian Ruder, and Noah A. Smith. 2019. To tune or not to tune? adapting pretrained representations to diverse tasks. In *Proceedings of the 4th Workshop on Representation Learning for NLP (RepL4NLP-2019)*, pages 7–14, Florence, Italy. Association for Computational Linguistics.

Martin Potthast, Tim Gollub, Matthias Hagen, Martin Tippmann, Johannes Kiesel, Paolo Rosso, Efstathios Stamatatos, and Benno Stein. 2013. Overview of the 5th international competition on plagiarism detection. In *Working Notes Papers of the CLEF 2013 Evaluation Labs*.

Vahed Qazvinian and Dragomir R. Radev. 2010. Identifying non-explicit citing sentences for citation-based summarization. In *Proceedings of the 48th Annual Meeting of the Association for Computational Linguistics*, pages 555–564, Uppsala, Sweden. Association for Computational Linguistics.

Nils Reimers and Iryna Gurevych. 2017. Reporting score distributions makes a difference: Performance study of LSTM-networks for sequence tagging. In *Proceedings of the 2017 Conference on Empirical Methods in Natural Language Processing*, pages 338–348, Copenhagen, Denmark. Association for Computational Linguistics.

Nils Reimers and Iryna Gurevych. 2019. Sentence-BERT: Sentence embeddings using Siamese BERT-networks. In *Proceedings of the 2019 Conference on Empirical Methods in Natural Language Processing and the 9th International Joint Conference on Natural Language Processing (EMNLP-IJCNLP)*, pages 3982–3992, Hong Kong, China. Association for Computational Linguistics.

M. Sánchez-Pérez, G. Sidorov, and Alexander Gelbukh. 2014. A winning approach to text alignment for text reuse detection at pan 2014. In *CLEF*.

Victor Sanh, Lysandre Debut, Julien Chaumond, and Thomas Wolf. 2019. Distilbert, a distilled version of bert: smaller, faster, cheaper and lighter. *ArXiv*, abs/1910.01108.

David A. Smith, Ryan Cordell, Elizabeth Maddock Dillon, Nick Stramp, and John Wilkerson. 2014. Detecting and modeling local text reuse. In *JCDL*.

Chenhao Tan, Adrien Friggeri, and Lada A. Adamic. 2016. Lost in propagation? unfolding news cycles from the source. In *ICWSM*.

K. Vani and D. Gupta. 2017. Detection of idea plagiarism using syntax-semantic concept extractions with genetic algorithm. *Expert Syst. Appl.*, 73:11–26.

John Wilkerson, David A. Smith, and Nick Stramp. 2015. Tracing the flow of policy ideas on legislatures: A text reuse approach. *American Journal of Political Science*, 59(4):943–956.

Adina Williams, Nikita Nangia, and Samuel Bowman. 2018. A broad-coverage challenge corpus for sentence understanding through inference. In *Proceedings of the 2018 Conference of the North American Chapter of the Association for Computational Linguistics: Human Language Technologies, Volume 1 (Long Papers)*, pages 1112–1122, New Orleans, Louisiana. Association for Computational Linguistics.

Zichao Yang, Diyi Yang, Chris Dyer, Xiaodong He, Alex Smola, and Eduard Hovy. 2016. Hierarchical attention networks for document classification. In *Proceedings of the 2016 Conference of the North American Chapter of the Association for Computational Linguistics: Human Language Technologies*, pages 1480–1489, San Diego, California. Association for Computational Linguistics.

Xuhui Zhou, Nikolaos Pappas, and Noah A. Smith. 2020. Multilevel text alignment with cross-document attention. In *Proceedings of the 2020 Conference on Empirical Methods in Natural Language Processing (EMNLP)*, pages 5012–5025, Online. Association for Computational Linguistics.

A Data Preprocessing

Table 4 lists the training, validation and test set sizes for each dataset. Each split is separated into the number of positive examples that contain reuse and the number of negative examples that do not. Below we discuss the data preprocessing steps we follow for each dataset:

ARC-Sim We create this dataset using papers from the ACL Anthology Conference Corpus (Bird et al., 2008). Since we use citation marks to identify instances of text reuse, we use ParsCit (Councill et al., 2008) to first identify all in-line citation marks. We then create examples by matching together a section in a paper that contains a citation with the abstract of the cited paper (assuming the cited paper is also in the ACL ARC). Since citation marks have a distinctive lexical pattern, we remove them all after matching the pairs. We then split sections and abstracts into sentences using Stanford CoreNLP (Manning et al., 2014), keeping track of where the original citation was in order to generate S2D labels. We create negative examples by matching a cited abstract together with another section from the same paper as the original citing section (the new section is selected so that it does not cite the paper). Finally, for computational feasibility, we limit source documents to 20 sentences and target sections to 50, the 90th percentiles in the data. We remove pairs where the citation occurs after the 50th sentence in the target section. We split the dataset into train/val/test by cited abstract S, yielding the splits detailed in Table 4.

PAN: We download the public dataset. We filter out 1) malformed positive pairs that do not contain any positively-labeled sentences or contain positively-labeled sentences with no words; 2) extremely long pairs which cause GPU memory issues for our models, removing (source, target) pairs that contain more than 4,000 tokens total (80th percentile). Following Zhou et al. (2020), we split documents into sentences and tokenize them using NLTK (Bird and Loper, 2004).

For the hierarchical neural models (BERT-HAN, GRU-HAN, BCL-CDA), we follow Zhou et al. (2020) and cap documents at a predefined number of sentences so that the models fit in GPU memory. We cap source documents at 50 sentences (90th percentile). We split examples with target documents containing more than 45 sentences (90th percentile) into multiple examples, i.e. (source document, first 45 sentences of target document), (source docu-

Table 4: Number of examples in the training, validation and test sets of each dataset, split into numbers of positive and negative examples. Pr2News contains no negative examples.

	Train		Val		Test	
Dataset	# Pos	# Neg	# Pos	# Neg	# Pos	# Neg
PAN	6,152	7,567	1,243	1,336	1,253	1,352
S2ORC	74,807	75,861	9,262	9,562	9,258	9,561
Pr2News	64,684	–	45	–	50	–
ARC-Sim	50,197	36,227	5,269	3,852	5,665	4,171

ment, next 45 sentences of target document), and so on. Predictions for split examples are merged back together at test time.

S2ORC: We download the public dataset. As for PAN, we filter out malformed positive pairs that do not contain any positively-labeled sentences or contain positively-labeled sentences with no words. S2ORC examples, are, in general, short and do not require length-based filtering. Following Zhou et al. (2020), we split documents into sentences and tokenize them using NLTK (Bird and Loper, 2004).

For the hierarchical neural models (BERT-HAN, GRU-HAN, BCL-CDA), we cap source documents at 20 sentences (99th percentile). We split examples with target documents containing more than 29 sentences (99th percentile) into multiple examples and merge back predictions at test time.

Pr2News: We obtain the preprocessed and filtered Pr2News dataset from MacLaughlin et al. (2020, §4-5), who created it with data from Altmetric. We evaluate models on the provided test set of 50 expert-labeled (press release, news article) pairs. We use the set of 45 non-expert-labeled (press release, news article) pairs as our validation set (we filter out the 5 spurious validation set pairs noted by MacLaughlin et al. (2020)). Finally, we use the remaining 64,684 pairs labeled with their TF-IDF cosine similarity heuristic as training data. For pairs with more than one matched press release, we select the press release with the highest TFIDF cosine similarity to the news article.

For the hierarchical neural models (BERT-HAN, GRU-HAN, BCL-CDA), we cap source documents at 54 sentences (90th percentile). We split examples with target documents containing more than 57 sentences (90th percentile) into multiple examples and merge back predictions at test time.

B Implementation of BERT-HAN and GRU-HAN

Although we use the official source code from Zhou et al. (2020) to run the HAN models, our results differ on PAN and S2ORC from their originally reported results (mostly slightly, but, in one instance, substantially). With the exception of using BERT_{BASE} as the passage encoder for BERT-HAN instead of BERT_{LARGE}, we follow their recommended hyperparameters. But, as compared with the results from Zhou et al. (2020), on the D2D task (measured by F1), BERT-HAN's scores are substantially lower on PAN and slightly lower on S2ORC. GRU-HAN's scores, on the other hand, are very slightly higher on both PAN and S2ORC. We hypothesize that the minor differences in performance are due to **1)** differences in model random initialization (Reimers and Gurevych, 2017); **2)** differences in the datasets – as noted in Appendix A, we filtered out some examples from PAN and S2ORC since they contained some malformed positive examples with either no positively-labeled sentences or positively-labeled sentences that were empty strings; **3)** for BERT-HAN, we use BERT_{BASE} as the encoder rather than BERT_{LARGE}. Despite these factors, BERT-HAN's large performance drop on PAN is still surprising. However, we emphasize that even when using Zhou et al. (2020)'s original numbers, BERT-HAN still lags behind both our lexical overlap baselines and fine-tuned BERT models, so our overall takeaways from §7 still stand.

For the S2D task, our results are not directly comparable to the original numbers of Zhou et al. (2020) for two reasons:

1. We use different metrics – we use MAP and Acc@k, while they use MRR and P@k. MAP is more appropriate than MRR since there are often multiple positively-labeled target sentences. Acc@k is more appropriate than P@k when k is greater than the number of

positively-labeled target sentences. When there are fewer than k positively-labeled target sentences in an example, a perfect system will still have a P@k < 1. Systems receive a perfect Acc@k score, on the other hand, if at least one positively-labeled target sentence appears anywhere in the top k.

2. We evaluate on different sets of the data – as noted in §6 , Zhou et al. (2020) calculate their S2D ranking metrics (MRR, P@k) on all test examples, both positive and negative. However, these metrics cannot be computed on negative examples where no target sentences contain reuse. We confirmed with Zhou et al. (2020) that, in these instances, they give their models full credit if the corresponding D2D prediction is correct, i.e. the model predicts that the target document contains no reuse. Since many negative examples in PAN and S2ORC are easy to classify, this manner of calculation substantially inflates the results. To address this, we calculate our S2D ranking metrics (MAP, Acc@k) on only the subset of positive examples. Calculating in this way shows substantially decreased S2D performance for the HAN models.

C Model Hyperparameters & Best Configurations

Below, we discuss all searched hyperparameters (HP) for each model. For all models, we search for a threshold, $t \in [0, 1]$, to differentiate between positive and negative sentence and document predictions (not used for the Pr2News dataset). Table 5 lists the optimal HP values for each dataset (as selected by average performance on the val set).

All neural models, with the exception of BCL-CDA (Tensorflow: Abadi et al. (2015)) were implemented in Pytorch (Paszke et al., 2019) and run on 16GB or 32GB Nvdia P100s or V100s.

TF-IDF: We search over n-gram size (unigrams or unigrams & bigrams).

Rouge: We search over three different Rouge measures, Rouge-{1, 2, L}.

Sentence-BERT: None except threshold. We test the following pretrained Sentence-BERT models: Semantic Textual Similarity: stsb-roberta-large, Paraphrase Detection: paraphrase-distilroberta-base-v1, Information Retrieval: msmarco-distilroberta-base-v2.

BERT-HAN (shallow): We use the suggested batch size (256), HAN hidden dimension size (50), and early stopping criterion (no improvement on val set for 5 epochs). We perform a search over Adam (Kingma and Ba, 2015) learning rates $\in$ {1e-5, 2e-5, 5e-5, 1e-4}. We use BERT$_{BASE}$ as the sentence encoder instead of BERT$_{LARGE}$ for efficiency reasons. For the S2ORC and ARC-Sim datasets, we find that BERT-HAN's S2D performance is substantially higher when we rank sentences by the complement of their scores, i.e. $score_{new} = 1 - score_{old}$. This, in effect, inverts the predicted target sentence ranking for each document (we select this transformation based on val set results). We are only able to achieve results roughly on par with those reported in Zhou et al. (2020) using this trick. This trick is not necessary for the PAN dataset nor for the GRU-HAN model.

GRU-HAN (deep): We use batch size 128 and 50 dimensional GloVe embeddings. Otherwise, the HPs are the same as for BERT-HAN.

BCL-CDA: We adapt the BCL model from MacLaughlin et al. (2020) for LTRD as follows (see MacLaughlin et al. (2020) for details of the BCL model): Each source and target sentence is fed into frozen BERT$_{BASE}$ separately. We then use a CNN with 1-max pooling over time to aggregate the token representations from BERT's second to last layer into a single representation for each sentence. We search over CNN filter size $\in \{3,5,7\}$ and number of filters $\in$ {50, 100, 200}. The sentence representations in each source or target document are then contextualized with document-level BiLSTMs (two separate BiLSTMs for source or target documents). We search over hidden dimension size $\in \{64, 128\}$ (same dimensionality for both BiLSTMs). After the BiLSTM layer, we are left with $s_i \in \mathbf{S}$ and $t_i \in \mathbf{T}$, contextualized sentence representations for the sentences in the source and target documents. Next, we use a sentence-level CDA layer to compute $\tilde{t}_i$, an attention-weighted (Luong et al., 2015, §3.1: general attention) representation of t_i, weighted by its similarity to the sentences $s_i \in \mathbf{S}$. Finally, we concatenate $[\tilde{t}_i;t_i]$ and feed this to a final layer to make a prediction for each target sentence.

We set dropout at 0.2, batch size at 32, and search over the max number of epochs (10, with early stopping). We optimize with Adam with learning rate $\in$ {1e-4, 5e-4}. For the PAN, S2ORC and ARC-Sim datasets, we use weighted cross-

Table 5: Best HP configurations for all models across all datasets. t is the classification threshold (only for PAN, S2ORC and ARC-Sim). BERT-HAN and GRU-HAN have two thresholds, one for document classification, the other for sentence classification. All other models have a single, sentence-level threshold. n-gram is the n-gram range for TF-IDF (unigrams or unigrams and bigrams). For the neural models: e is epochs, lr is learning rate, and w is the weight placed on positive examples in weighted cross-entropy loss (weight on negative examples is 1). For BCL-CDA, fs is the CNN filter size, nf is number of CNN filters, and lhd is the BiLSTM hidden dimension. '–' indicates that there are no HPs to be optimized. '×' indicates that the model is not trained on that dataset.

		PAN	S2ORC	ARC-Sim	Pr2News
Single-pair baselines	TF-IDF	$t = 0.10$, n-gram = 1 & 2	$t = 0.04$, n-gram = 1 & 2	$t = 0.04$, n-gram = 1 & 2	n-gram = n-gram = 1 & 2
	Rouge	$t = 0.03$, rouge = R-2	$t = 0.02$, rouge = R-2	$t = 0.02$, rouge = R-2	rouge = R-2
	Roberta$_{mean}$ (STS)	$t = 0.46$	$t = 0.48$	$t = 0.48$	–
	DistilRoberta$_{mean}$ (PD)	$t = 0.41$	$t = 0.39$	$t = 0.42$	–
	DistilRoberta$_{mean}$ (IR)	$t = 0.38$	$t = 0.38$	$t = 0.44$	–
All-pairs baselines	TF-IDF	$t = 0.17$, n-gram = 1 & 2	$t = 0.14$, n-gram = 1	$t = 0.14$, n-gram = 1	n-gram = 1 & 2
	Rouge	$t = 0.40$, rouge = R-1	$t = 0.27$, rouge = R-1	$t = 0.24$, rouge = R-1	rouge = R-2
	Roberta$_{mean}$ (STS)	$t = 0.63$	$t = 0.53$	$t = 0.52$	–
	DistilRoberta$_{mean}$ (PD)	$t = 0.58$	$t = 0.42$	$t = 0.45$	–
	DistilRoberta$_{mean}$ (IR)	$t = 0.61$	$t = 0.43$	$t = 0.48$	–
Frozen BERT	Bert-Han (Shallow)	doc $t = 0.41$, sent $t = 0$, lr =5e-5	doc $t = 0.34$, sent $t = 0.0$, lr =2e-5	doc $t = 0.33$, sent $t = 0.08$, lr = 1e-4	×
	Gru-Han (Deep)	doc $t = 0.34$, sent $t = 0$, lr = 1e-5	doc $t = 0.33$, sent $t = 0.01$, lr = 5e-5	doc $t = 0.42$, sent $t = 0.11$, lr = 1e-4	×
	BCL-CDA	$t = 0.57$, lr =5e-4, $e = 7$, $w = 5$, $fs = 5$, $nf = 50$, $lhd = 128$	$t = 0.44$, lr =5e-4, $e = 5$, $w = 5$, $fs = 3$, $nf = 50$, $lhd = 128$	$t = 0.74$, lr =1e-4, $e = 3$, $w = 15$, $fs = 5$, $nf = 200$, $lhd = 64$	lr =5e-4, e =7, $fs = 7$, $nf = 200$, $lhd = 128$
Fine-tuned BERT	Biomed-Roberta$_{single}$	×	$t = 0.34$, lr = 2e-5, $e = 2$, $w = 3$	×	lr = 3e-5, $e = 1$
	CS-Roberta$_{single}$	×	$t = 0.47$, lr = 2e-5, $e = 3$, $w = 3$	$t = 0.51$, lr = 2e-5, $e = 5$, $w = 10$	×
	News-Roberta$_{single}$	×	×	×	lr = 3e-5, $e = 1$
	Roberta$_{single}$	$t = 0.91$, lr =3e-5, $e = 4$, $w = 1$	$t = 0.4$, lr = 2e-5, $e = 4$, $w = 3$	$t = 0.39$, lr = 2e-5, $e = 3$, $w = 5$	lr = 2e-5, $e = 2$
	Longformer$_{seq}$	$t = 0.52$, $lr = 5e-5$, $e = 9$, $w = 5$	$t = 0.41$, lr =3e-5, e =19, w =5	$t = 0.53$, lr =3e-5, e =12, $w = 5$	$lr = 5e-5$, $e = 7$

entropy loss since the datasets are unbalanced (many more negative sentences than positive). We search over the weight w to put on examples from the positive class. Weights vary by dataset since datasets are not equally imbalanced: PAN $\in \{1, 3, 5\}$, S2ORC $\in \{3, 5, 10\}$, ARC-Sim $\in \{10, 15, 20\}$. Following MacLaughlin et al. (2020), we use MAE loss for Pr2News.

Fine-tuned RoBERTa$_{BASE}$, DAPT, and Longformer: We search over Adam learning rate $\in \{$2e-5, 3e-5, 5e-5$\}$. We use batch size 32 (with gradient accumulation to ensure that batches fit in GPU memory) and train models for 10 epochs at most (20 for Longformer), with early stopping. For PAN, S2ORC and ARC-Sim, following BCL-CDA, we search over weight w for weighted cross-entropy loss. We search over the same w ranges for each dataset as for BCL-CDA, except for ARC-Sim, where we search over $w \in \{5, 10, 20\}$. We use MAE loss for Pr2News.

Generating Hypothetical Events for Abductive Inference

Debjit Paul
Research Training Group AIPHES
Institute for Computational Linguistics
Heidelberg University
paul@cl.uni-heidelberg.de

Anette Frank
Research Training Group AIPHES
Institute for Computational Linguistics
Heidelberg University
frank@cl.uni-heidelberg.de

Abstract

Abductive reasoning starts from some observations and aims at finding the most plausible explanation for these observations. To perform abduction, humans often make use of temporal and causal inferences, and knowledge about how some hypothetical situation can result in different outcomes. This work offers the first study of how such knowledge impacts the *Abductive α**NLI*** task – which consists in choosing the more likely explanation for given observations. We train a specialized language model $LM_{\mathcal{I}}$ that is tasked to generate *what could happen next* from a hypothetical scenario that evolves from a given event. We then propose a multi-task model $\mathcal{MTL}$ to solve the α**NLI task**, which predicts a plausible explanation by a) considering different *possible events* emerging from candidate hypotheses – events generated by $LM_{\mathcal{I}}$ – and b) selecting the one that is most *similar* to the observed outcome. We show that our $\mathcal{MTL}$ model improves over prior vanilla pre-trained LMs fine-tuned on αNLI. Our manual evaluation and analysis suggest that learning about possible next events from different hypothetical scenarios supports abductive inference.

1 Introduction

Abductive reasoning (AR) is inference to the best explanation. It typically starts from an incomplete set of observations about everyday situations and comes up with what can be considered the most likely possible explanation given these observations (Pople, 1973; Douven, 2017). One of the key characteristics that make abductive reasoning more challenging and distinct from other types of reasoning is its non-monotonic character (Strasser and Antonelli, 2019) i.e., even the most likely explanations are not necessarily correct. For example, in Figure 1, the most likely explanation for *Observation 1: "wet grass outside my house"* is that *"it has been raining"*. However, when a new piece of information (observation or evidence) becomes available, the explanation must possibly be retracted, *showing the defeasible character of abduction.* With the new observation (*"the sprinkler was switched on"*) the most plausible explanation changes to *"Sprinkler caused the grass to be wet"*. Humans, in such situations, could induce or validate such abductive inferences by performing hypothetical reasoning (such as *"What would happen if the sprinkler was switched on?"*) to arrive at a plausible explanation for *"wet grass outside my house"*.

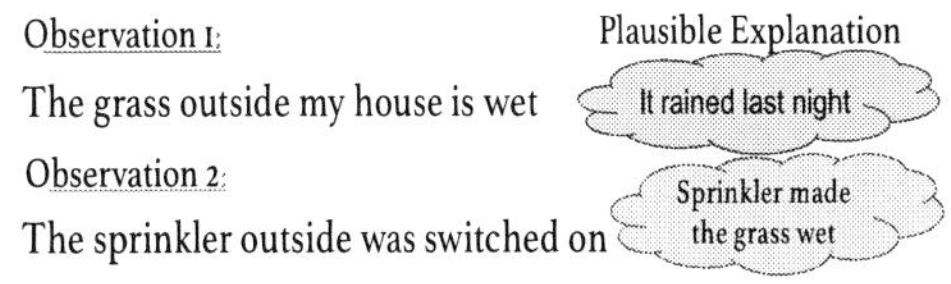

Figure 1: Motivational example illustrating Abductive Reasoning and its non-monotonic character.

In this work, we focus on the α**NLI task** (Bhagavatula et al., 2020), where given two observations (O_1 at time t_1, O_2 at time t_2, with $t_1 < t_2$) as an incomplete context, the task is to predict which of two given hypothesized events (H_1 or H_2) is more plausible to have happened between O_1 and O_2. Figure 2 illustrates this with an example: given observations O_1*: "Priya decided to try a new restaurant."* and O_2*: "Priya thought her food was delicious."*, the task is to predict whether H_1 or H_2 is the more plausible explanation given observations O_1 and O_2. Both H_1 and H_2 are different plausible hypothetical situations that can evolve from the same observation (premise) O_1.

In this paper, we hypothesize that learning how different hypothetical scenarios (H_1 and H_2) can result in different outcomes (e.g., $O_2^{H_j}$, Fig. 2) can help in performing abductive inference. In order to decide which H_i, is *more plausible* given observa-

Proceedings of the 10th Conference on Lexical and Computational Semantics, pages 67–77
August 5–6, 2021, Bangkok, Thailand (online) ©2021 Association for Computational Linguistics

Figure 2: Motivational example for αNLI : The top box (red) shows the observations and two callout clouds (green) contain the hypotheses. The implications ($O_i^{H_i}$) – generated by the LM conditioned on each hypothesis and the observations – are given in pink colored boxes.

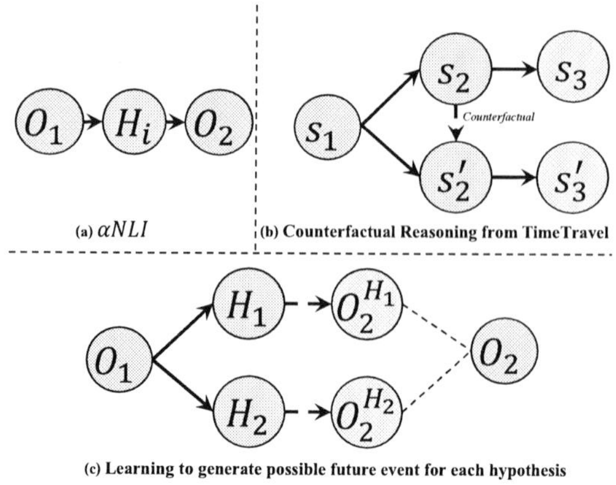

Figure 3: Different reasoning schemes and settings for our task and approach. The arrows denote the direction (temporal flow) of the reasoning chain. The dotted arrow in (b) denotes the derivation of a counterfactual situation s_2' from a factual s_2. In (c), the dotted arrows denote the learned inference; the dotted lines indicate the similarity between O_2 and $O_2^{H_i}$.

tions, we assume each H_i to be *true* and generate a *possible next event* $O_2^{H_i}$ for each of them independently (e.g.: *What will happen if Priya's ordered food was microwaved and precooked?*). We then compare the generated sentences ($O_2^{H_1}$, $O_2^{H_2}$ in Fig. 2) to what has been observed (O_2) and choose as most plausible hypothesis the one whose implication is closest to observation O_2.

We design a language model ($LM_{\mathcal{I}}$) which, given observations and a hypothesis, generates a possible event that could happen next, given one hypothesis. In order to train this language model, we use the TIMETRAVEL (TT) corpus (Qin et al., 2019) (a subpart of the *ROCStories* corpus[1]). We utilize the $LM_{\mathcal{I}}$ model to generate a possible next event for each hypothesis, given the observations. We then propose a multi-task learning model $\mathcal{MTL}$ that jointly chooses from the generated possible next events ($O_2^{H_1}$ or $O_2^{H_2}$) the one most similar to the observation O_2 and predicts the most plausible hypothesis (H_1 or H_2).

Our contributions are: i) To our best knowledge, we are the first to demonstrate that a model that learns to perform hypothetical reasoning can support and improve abductive tasks such as αNLI. We show that ii) for αNLI our multi-task model outperforms a strong BERT baseline (Bhagavatula et al., 2020).

Our code is made publicly available.[2]

2 Learning about Counterfactual Scenarios

The main idea is to learn to generate assumptions, in a given situation, about *"What could have happened (next) if we had done X?" or "What could happen (next) if we do X?"* (Bhatt and Flanagan, 2010). Figure 3(a) depicts the αNLI task framework. We hypothesize that getting to know *what will happen (next) if any of two hypotheses occurs*, will help us verifying which of them is more plausible (see Fig. 3(c)). Therefore, we encourage the model to learn how different hypothetical events (including counterfactual events) evolving from the same premise (s_1) can lead to different or similar outcomes (see Fig. 3(b)).

Accordingly, we teach a pre-trained GPT-2 (Radford et al., 2019) language model how to generate *a sequence of* possible subsequent events given different hypothetical situations in a narrative setting. Training such a model on narrative texts encourages it to learn causal and temporal relations between events. We train a conditional language model, $LM_{\mathcal{I}}$, which generates a possible event that could happen next, given some counterfactual scenarios for a given story.

We train this model on the TIMETRAVEL (TT) dataset (Qin et al., 2019), by fine-tuning GPT-2 to learn about possible next events emerging from a situation in a story, given some alternative, counterfactual event. The TT dataset consists of five-sentence instances S=(s_1,s_2,..,s_5)[3] from the ROCStories corpus[1] plus additional crowd-sourced sen-

[1]We ensure that αNLI testing instances are held out.

[2]`https://github.com/Heidelberg-NLP/HYPEVENTS`

[3]s_1 = *premise*, s_2 = *initial context*, $s_{3:5}$ = original ending

O_1: *Dotty was being very grumpy.*
O_2: *She felt much better afterwards.*
H_1: Dotty ate something bad.
H_2: **Dotty call some close friends to chat.**
$O_2^{H_1}$: *She started to feel sick.*
$O_2^{H_2}$: *They all tried to make her happy.*

Table 1: Example of generated possible next events $O_2^{H_j}$ using the $LM_{\mathcal{I}}$ model. **Bold** hypothesis (H_2) is more plausible.

tences $s'_{2:5}$, where s'_2 is counterfactual[4] to s_2 from the original story[5]. There are two reasons for using the TT dataset for our purposes: a) the domains on which GPT-2 was pretrained are broad[6] and different from the domain of ROCStories, b) the model can see how alternative situations can occur starting from the same premise s_1, resulting in similar or different outcomes. Note that, although intermediate situations may be counterfactual to each other, the future outcome can still be similar to the original ending due to *causal invariance* [7].

Concretely, the language model $LM_{\mathcal{I}}$ reads the premise (s_1) and the alternative event(s) (s_2 or s'_2), the masked token (serving as a placeholder for the missing possible next event(s) ($s_{3:i}$ or $s'_{3:i}$), then the rest of the story ($s_{i+1:5}$ or $s'_{i+1:5}$) and again the premise (s_1). We train the model to maximize the log-likelihood of the missing ground-truth sentence(s) ($s_{3:i}$).

$$\mathcal{L}^{LM_{\mathcal{I}}}(\beta) = log_{p_\beta}(s_{3:i}|[S]s_1, [M], s_{i+1:5}, [E], [S], s_1, s_2) \quad (1)$$
$$+log_{p_\beta}(s'_{3:i}|[S]s_1, [M], s'_{i+1:5}, [E], [S], s_1, s'_2)$$

where $i \in [3, 4]$, $s_i=\{w_1^{s_i}, .., w_n^{s_i}\}$ a sequence of tokens, $[S]$=start-of-sentence token, $[E]$=end-of-sentence token, $[M]$=mask token.

3 Generating Hypothetical Events to support the αNLI task

In this paper, we aim to investigate whether models perform better on the αNLI task when explicitly learning about events that could follow other events in a hypothetical scenario. We do so by introducing two methods $LM_{\mathcal{I}}$ + *BERTScore* and $LM_{\mathcal{I}}$ + $\mathcal{MTL}$ for unsupervised and supervised settings, respectively.

We first apply the trained model $LM_{\mathcal{I}}$ on the αNLI task, where the given observations O_1 and O_2, and alternative hypotheses H_j are fed as shown in (2) below.[8]

$$O_2^{H_j} = \beta([S], O_1, [M], O_2, [E], [S], O_1, H_j) \quad (2)$$

We generate a possible next event for each hypothetical event H_j, i.e., $O_2^{H_1}$ and $O_2^{H_2}$ (or: what will happen if some hypothesis H_j occurs given the observations), where $j \in [1, 2]$. Table 1 illustrates an example where different $O_2^{H_j}$ are generated using $LM_{\mathcal{I}}$. One of the challenges when generating subsequent events given a hypothetical situation is that there can be infinite numbers of possible next events. Therefore, to constrain this range, we chose to give future events (O_2) as input, such that the model can generate subsequent events in a constrained context.

3.1 Unsupervised Setting

In this setting, we do not train any supervised model to explicitly predict which hypothesis is more plausible given the observations. Instead, we apply the fine-tuned $LM_{\mathcal{I}}$ model to the αNLI data, generate possible next events $O_2^{H_j}$ given O_1 and H_j, as described above, and measure the similarity between such possible next events ($O_2^{H_j}$) and the observation (O_2) in an unsupervised way, using *BERTScore* (BS) (Zhang et al., 2020) [9]. We evaluate our hypothesis that the generated possible next event $O_2^{H_j}$ given the more plausible hypothesis H_j should be *more similar* to observation O_2. Table 1 illustrates an example where H_2 is the more plausible hypothesis. We impose the constraint that for a correctly predicted instance BS(${O_2}^{H^+}$, O_2) $>$ BS(${O_2}^{H^-}$, O_2) should hold, where H^+, H^- are the more plausible vs. implausible hypothesis, respectively.

3.2 Supervised Setting

In this setting, displayed in Figure 4, we explore the benefits of training a multi-task $\mathcal{MTL}$ model that predicts i) the most plausible hypothesis and ii) which possible next event ($O_2^{H_j}$) is more similar

[4]a counterfactual s' states something that is contrary to s

[5]During our experiments we treat them as two separate instances: S_1=($s_{1:5}$) and S_2 = (s_1,$s'_{2:5}$).

[6]GPT-2 was trained on the WebText Corpus.

[7]the future events that are invariant under the counterfactual conditions (Qin et al., 2019)

[8]For definition of placeholders see (1).

[9]BERTScore is an automatic evaluation metric for text generation that leverages the pre-trained contextual embeddings from BERT and matches words in candidate and reference sentences by cosine similarity.

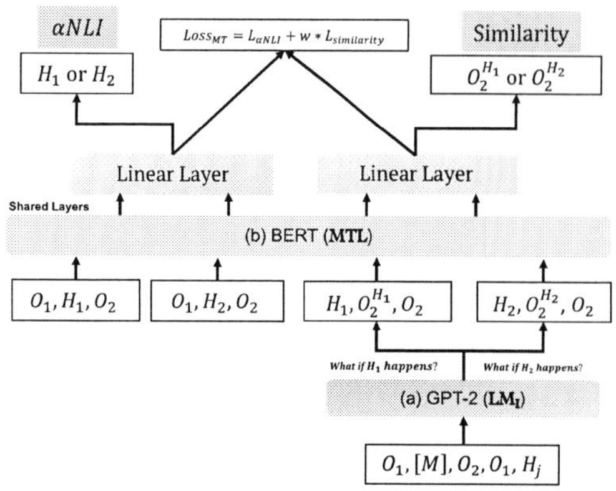

Figure 4: Overview of our $LM_{\mathcal{I}}$ + $\mathcal{MTL}$ model for αNLI: (a) language model $LM_{\mathcal{I}}$ takes the input in a particular format to generate different possible next events, (b) the $\mathcal{MTL}$ model learns to predict the best explanation (H_j) and possible next events ($O_2^{H_j}$) at the same time to perform the αNLI task.

to the observation (O_2). Multi-task learning aims to improve the performance of a model for a task by utilizing the knowledge acquired by learning related tasks (Ruder, 2019). We *hypothesize that* a) the possible next event $O_2^{H_j}$ of the more plausible hypothesis H_j should be most similar to observation O_2, and that b) learning which possible next event is more similar supports the model in the αNLI task (*inductive transfer*).

The architecture of $LM_{\mathcal{I}}$ + $\mathcal{MTL}$ model is shown in Figure 4. The model marked (a) in Figure 4 depicts the $LM_{\mathcal{I}}$ model as described in §3. The outputs of the $LM_{\mathcal{I}}$ model, which we get from Eq. (2) for both hypotheses are incorporated as an input to the $\mathcal{MTL}$ model. Concretely, we feed the $\mathcal{MTL}$ classifier a sequence of tokens as stated in part (b) of Figure 4, and aim to compute their contextualized representations using pre-trained BERT. The input format is described in Table 3. Similar to (Devlin et al., 2019), two additional tokens are added [CLS] at the start of each sequence input and [SEP] at the end of each sentence. In the shared layers (see Fig 4(b)), the model first transform the input sequence to a sequence of embedding vectors. Then it applies an attention mechanism that learns contextual relations between words (or sub-words) in the input sequence.

For each instance we get four [CLS] embeddings ($CLS_{H_j}, CLS_{O_2^{H_j}}$; $j \in [1, 2]$) which are then passed through two linear layers, one for the αNLI (main task) and another for predicting the similarity (auxiliary task) between $O_2^{H_j}$ and O_2. We compute the joint loss function $\mathcal{L} = \mathcal{L}_{\alpha NLI} + w * \mathcal{L}_{similarity}$; where w is a trainable parameter, $\mathcal{L}_{\alpha NLI}$ and $\mathcal{L}_{similarity}$ are the loss function for the αNLI task and auxiliary task, respectively.

Task	Train	Dev	Test
αNLI	169654	1532	3059
TimeTravel (NLG)	53806	2998	–

Table 2: Dataset Statistics: nb. of instances

Input Format	Output
[CLS] O_1 [SEP] H_i [SEP] O_2 [SEP]	H_1 or H_2
[CLS] H_i [SEP] $O_2^{H_i}$ [SEP] O_2[SEP]	$O_2^{H_1}$ or $O_2^{H_2}$

Table 3: Input and output format for the αNLI task: [CLS] is a special token used for classification, [SEP] a delimiter.

4 Experimental Setup

Data. We conduct experiments on the $\mathcal{ART}$ (Bhagavatula et al., 2020) dataset. Data statistics are given in Table 2. For evaluation, we measure accuracy for αNLI.

Hyperparameters. To train the $LM_{\mathcal{I}}$ model we use learning rate of $5e-05$. We decay the learning rate linearly until the end of training; batch size: 12. In the supervised setting for the α**NLI task**, we use the following set of hyperparameters for our $\mathcal{MTL}$ model with integrated $LM_{\mathcal{I}}$ model ($LM_{\mathcal{I}}$ + $\mathcal{MTL}$): batch size: $\{8, 16\}$; epochs: $\{3, 5\}$; learning rate: $\{2e\text{-}5, 5e\text{-}6\}$. For evaluation, we measure accuracy. We use Adam Optimizer, and dropout rate = 0.1. We experimented on GPU size of 11GB and 24GB. Training is performed using cross-entropy loss. The loss function is $\mathcal{L}_{\alpha NLI}$ + $w * \mathcal{L}_{similarity}$, where w is a trainable parameter. During our experiment we initialize $w = 1$. The input format is depicted in Table 3. We report performance by averaging results along with the variance obtained for 5 different seeds.

Baselines. We compare to the following baseline models that we apply to the αNLI task, training them on the training portion of the $\mathcal{ART}$ dataset (cf. Table 2).

- *ESIM + ELMo* is based on the ESIM model previously used for NLI (Chen et al., 2017). We use (a) ELMo to encode the observations and hypothesis, followed by (b) an attention

Model	Dev Acc.(%)	Test Acc.(%)
Majority *(from dev set)*◇	–	50.8
$LM_{\mathcal{I}}$ + BERTScore	62.27	**60.08**
Infersent ◇	50.9	50.8
ESIM + ELMo ◇	58.2	58.8
BERT_{Large} ◇	69.1	68.9±0.5
GPT-2 +$\mathcal{MTL}$	68.9±0.3	68.8±0.3
COMET +$\mathcal{MTL}$	69.4±0.4	69.1±0.5
$LM_{\mathcal{I}} + \mathcal{MTL}$	72.9±0.5	**72.2±0.6**
Human Performance	-	91.4

Table 4: Results on α**NLI task**, ◇ : as in Bhagavatula et al. (2020) (no unpublished leaderboard results). For each row, the best results are in bold, and performance of our models are in blue.

layer, (c) a local inference layer, and (d) another bi-directional LSTM inference composition layer, and (e) a pooling operation,

- *Infersent* (Conneau et al., 2017) uses sentence encoding based on a bi-directional LSTM architecture with max pooling.
- *BERT* (Devlin et al., 2019) is a LM trained with a masked-language modeling (MLM) and next sentence prediction objective.

As baselines for using the $\mathcal{MTL}$ model, we replace $LM_{\mathcal{I}}$ with alternative generative LMs:

- *GPT-2 + $\mathcal{MTL}$.* In this setup, we directly use the pretrained GPT-2 model and task it to generate a next sentence conditioned on each hypothesis ($O_2^{H_i}$) without finetuning it on the TIMETRAVEL data. We then use the supervised $\mathcal{MTL}$ model to predict the most plausible hypothesis and which of the generated observations is more similar to O_2.
- *COMET + $\mathcal{MTL}$.* In this setting, we make use of inferential *if-then* knowledge from ATOMIC (Sap et al., 2019a) as background knowledge. Specifically, we use COMET to generate objects with **Effect**[10] relations for each hypothesis as a textual phrase.

5 Results

In Table 4, we compare our models $LM_{\mathcal{I}}$ + BERTScore and $LM_{\mathcal{I}} + \mathcal{MTL}$ against the models proposed in Bhagavatula et al. (2020): a majority baseline, supervised models (*Infersent* and *ESIM+ELMo*), as well as $BERT_{Large}$. Bhagavatula et al. (2020) re-train the ESIM+ELMo and Infersent models on the $\mathcal{ART}$ dataset and fine-tuned the BERT model on the αNLI task and report the results.

We find that our **unsupervised** model with BERTScore ($LM_{\mathcal{I}}$ + BERTScore) outperforms (by +9.28 pp. and +1.28 pp.) strong ESIM+ELMo and Infersent baseline models. Table 5 shows some examples of our generation model $LM_{\mathcal{I}}$ along with the obtained BERTScores.

Unlike the unsupervised $LM_{\mathcal{I}}$ + BERTScore, our **supervised** $LM_{\mathcal{I}} + \mathcal{MTL}$ model also improves over the BERT_{Large} baseline, by +3.3 pp. We can attribute the improvement to the model having been jointly trained to assess the similarity and dissimilarity of possible next events $O_2^{H_j}$ and observations (O_2) along with the αNLI task. One of the advantages of training our proposed multi-task learning ($\mathcal{MTL}$) model, instead of directly feeding the possible next events $O_2^{H_j}$ as knowledge inputs is that it adds an explainable component to the model. One can view the generated next events $O_2^{H_j}$ as natural language rationales and our multi-task model explicitly chooses one of them. Hence, the multi-task framework makes the model more expressive. Finally, we compare, for the $\mathcal{MTL}$ model, our embedded generation model $LM_{\mathcal{I}}$ to pre-trained GPT-2 and COMET. Table 4 shows that $LM_{\mathcal{I}} + \mathcal{MTL}$ yields better performance compared to both *COMET* + $\mathcal{MTL}$ (+3.1 pp.) and *GPT-2* + $\mathcal{MTL}$ (+3.4 pp.) – the intuitive reason being that the next events generated by $LM_{\mathcal{I}}$ are more helpful than events generated using pretrained GPT-2 and objects generated by COMET.

Table 5 illustrates some examples where our $\mathcal{MTL}$ model not only chooses the correct hypothesis, but also a likely possible next event that is similar to the observation O_2. Interestingly, during training of $\mathcal{MTL}$ we initialize w = 1, and after training the model we found the w value had been adjusted to a range between 0.85 and 0.75, which intuitively shows both the effectiveness of our $LM_{\mathcal{I}}$ -generated possible next events, and their similarity to the given observations O_2.

5.1 Case Study

Table 5 displays possible next events, generated by our $LM_{\mathcal{I}}$ model – along with the BERTscore measured between the possible next events $O_2^{H_j}$ and observation O_2. We see two different scenarios:

[10] as a result PersonX feels; as a result PersonX wants; PersonX then

	Observation (O)	Given Hypotheses (H_j)	What *if* H_j happens? Generated possible next events $O_2^{H_j}$	MTL	Reasoning Type	BERT Score	Human Evaluation
a.	O_1: Jim got ready for his first date.	H_1: **Jim's date wasn't attracted to him.**	$O_1^{H_2}$: He tried to get her number. She never responded to him.	$H_1, O_2^{H_1}$	*Reaction*	**47.34**	Non-Contradiction
	O_2: Since then, she has ignored all of Jim's text messages.	H_2: Jim went on the date and said he didn't like the girl.	$O_2^{H_2}$: He told her that he didn't want to date her.			44.19	Contradiction
b.	O_1: Nate had the summer off before college.	H_1: **Nate spent the summer traveling and partying.**	$O_2^{H_1}$: Nate had a lot of fun.	$H_1, O_2^{H_1}$	*Motivation*	**49.02**	Non-Contradiction
	O_2: Nate's last summer before college was a total blast!	H_2:Nate decided to spend the entire summer working in the Mines.	$O_2^{H_2}$: Nate spent the summer working in the mines.			44.34	Redundancy
c.	O_1: Dotty was being very grumpy.	H_1: Dotty ate something bad.	$O_2^{H_1}$: She started to feel sick.	$H_2, O_2^{H_2}$	*Emotional Effect*	**0.604**	Contradiction
	O_2: She felt much better afterwards	H_2: **Dotty call some close friends to chat.**	$O_2^{H_2}$: They all tried to make her happy.			0.405	Non-Contradiction
d.	O_1: Cay had a crush on a boy in her class.	H_1: **Cay sent a love note to the boy.**	$O_2^{H_1}$: The boy responded and said he liked Cay.	$H_1, O_2^{H_1}$	*Emotional Effect*	**0.509**	Non-Contradiction
	O_2: He smiled at her after and said he liked her too!	H_2: She told him she did not like him.	$O_2^{H_2}$: The boy was very sad about it.			0.423	Contradiction

Table 5: Examples of generated possible next events for solving αNLI using our $LM_{\mathcal{I}}$ model. Column 3: Hypothesis and possible next events chosen by our $LM_{\mathcal{I}} + \mathcal{MTL}$ model; Column 4: Reasoning type between the hypothesis H_j and O_2; Column 5: BERTScore between the $O_2^{H_j}$ and O_2; Column5: Human evaluation of the possible next events with respect the observation O_2.

(i) examples (a), (b) and (d) depicting the scenario where possible next events and observation pairs *correctly* achieve higher BERTscores [11], (ii) example (c) depicting the scenario where an incorrect possible next event and observation pair achieves higher BERTscores than the correct one. Intuitive reasons for these scenarios are, for example, for (a): there is a higher word overlap and semantic similarity between a correct next event and observation O_2, for example (b): there is higher semantic similarity; whereas for example (c): although there is a higher semantic dissimilarity, the word overlap between the wrong possible next event (*"She started to feel sick."*) and the observation (*"She felt much better afterwards."*) is much higher.

6 Manual Evaluation

Since the automatic scores only account for word-level similarity between observations and generated possible next events, we conduct a manual evaluation study, to assess the quality of sentences generated by our $LM_{\mathcal{I}}$ model.

Annotation Study on $LM_{\mathcal{I}}$ generations. The annotation was performed by three annotators with computational linguistic background. We provide each of the three annotators with observations, hypotheses and sentences, as produced by our $LM_{\mathcal{I}}$ model, for 50 randomly chosen instances from the αNLI task. They obtain i) *generated sentences for a next possible event* for the *correct* and *incorrect hypothesis*, as well as ii) the *sentence stating observation* O_2.

We ask each annotator to rate the sentences according to four quality aspects as stated below.

Grammaticality: the sentence is i) grammatical, ii) not entirely grammatical but understandable, or iii) completely not understandable;

Redundancy: the sentence contains redundant or repeated information;

Contradiction: the sentence contains any pieces of information that are contradicting the given observation O_2 or not;

Relevance: the possible next event is i) relevant, ii) partially relevant, or iii) not relevant.

For each aspect, they are asked to judge the sentence generated for the correct hypothesis[12]. Only for **Contradiction**, they are asked to judge both sentences, for correct and the incorrect hypotheses.

Results and Discussion. Figures 5, 7, and 6 present the results of manual evaluations of the generation quality, according to the different criteria described above.

[11]BERTscore matches words in candidate and reference sentences by cosine similarity.

[12]The correct hypothesis was marked for the annotation.

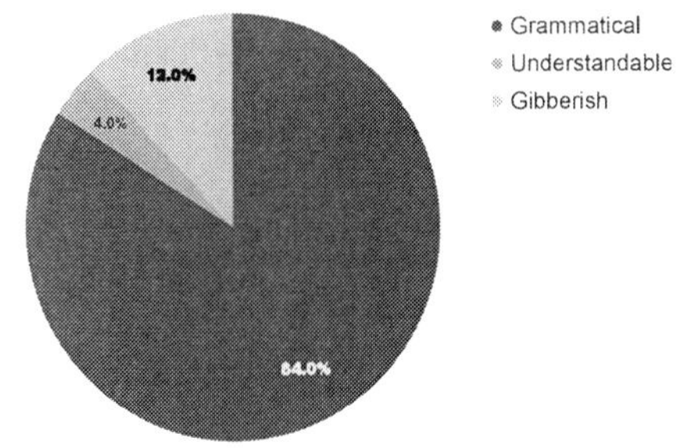

Figure 5: Human evaluation of the *grammaticality* of generated sentences: ratio of i) grammatical, ii) not entirely grammatical but understandable, iii) completely not understandable sentences.

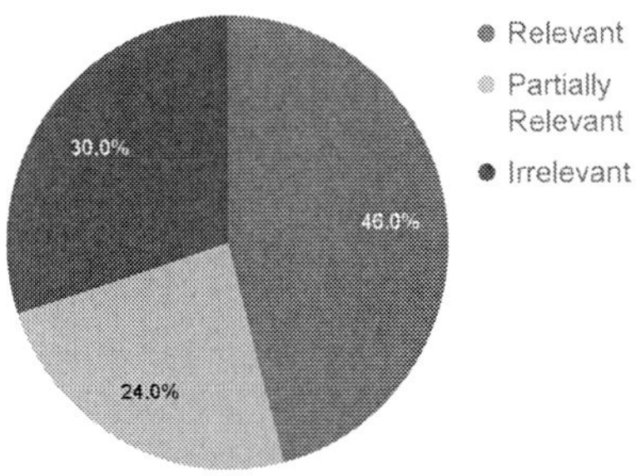

Figure 6: Human evaluation of the *Relevance* of generated sentences for possible next events.

For measuring inter-annotator agreement, we computed Krippendorff's α (Hayes and Krippendorff, 2007) for *Grammaticality* and *Relevance*, as it is suited for ordinal values, and Cohen's Kappa κ for *Redundancy* and *Contradiction*. We found α values are 0.587 and 0.462 for *Grammaticality* and *Relevance*, respectively (moderate agreement) and κ values 0.61 and 0.74 for *Redundancy* and *Contradiction* (substantial agreement). We aggregated the annotations from the three annotators using majority vote. Figure 5 shows that the majority of sentences (96%) are grammatical or understandable. Figure 7 shows that most sentences for correct labels are non-redundant (84%) and non-contradictory (88%), whereas for incorrect labels 39 instances are found to be contradictory with the observation O_2 (78%). The manual evaluation supports our hypothesis that the generated sentences for correct labels should be more similar (less contradictory) compared to the sentences generated for incorrect labels. Figure 6 shows the ratio of sentences considered by humans as relevant, partially relevant, and irrelevant. The results show that 46% of cases are relevant (based on majority agreement) and 24% of cases are partially relevant. This yields that the generated sentences are (partially) relevant

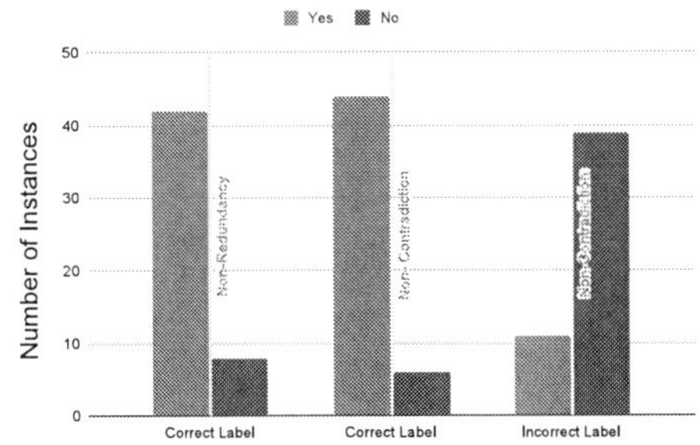

Figure 7: Human evaluation of *Redundancy* and *Contradiction* of generations for possible next events.

in most cases and thus should support abduction for both unsupervised ($LM_{\mathcal{I}}$ + BERTScore) and supervised ($LM_{\mathcal{I}}$ + $\mathcal{MTL}$) models.

Impact of Reasoning types. Finally, to better assess the performance of our model, we determine what *types of reasoning* underly the abductive reasoning tasks in our data, and examine to what extent our models capture or not these reasoning types. We consider again the 50 instances that were annotated by our previous annotators and manually classify them into different reasoning types. We broadly divided the data into 6 categories: (i) Motivation, (ii) Spatial-Temporal, (iii) Emotional, (iv) Negation, (v) Reaction, (vi) Situational fact. The most frequent type was Emotional (10), most infrequent was Spatial (7). We ask a new annotator to annotate the reasoning types for these 50 instances. Considering the relevance and contradiction categories from the previous annotations we determine that for Negation (8), Emotional (10), and Reaction (8) *all* generated events for *correct labels* are *partially or fully relevant and non-contradictory*. An intuitive reason can be that we train our $LM_{\mathcal{I}}$ model to learn how different counterfactual hypothetical events emerging from a single premise can lead to the same or different outcomes through a series of events. Some counterfactual events (s_2') are negations of the original event (s_2) in the TIMETRAVEL dataset. This may support the reasoning class Negation. For the other categories: Motivation, Spatial-temporal, and Situational fact, we detect errors regarding (missing) *Relevance* in 21%, 14% and 28% of cases, respectively. Table 6 illustrates an example from the class Situational Fact, where our generated next event is *irrelevant* and *redundant*.

O_1: *Jenna hit the weight hard in the gym.*
O_2: *She took a cold bath in order to alleviate her pain.*
H_1: Her neck pain stopped because of this.
H_2: **Jenna pulled a muscle lifting weights.**
$O_2^{H_1}$: *She decided to take a break .*
$O_2^{H_2}$: *Jenna lost weight in the gym.*

Table 6: Error Analysis: An example of generated possible next event $O_2^{H_j}$ from Situational Fact category.

7 Related Work

Commonsense Reasoning. There is growing interest in this research field, which led to the creation of several new resources on commonsense reasoning, in form of both *datasets*, such as SocialIQA (Sap et al., 2019b), CommonsenseQA (Talmor et al., 2019), CosmosQA (Huang et al., 2019) and *knowledge bases*, e.g. ConceptNet (Speer et al., 2017), ATOMIC (Sap et al., 2019a), or Event2Mind (Rashkin et al., 2018). Recently, many works proposed to utilize external *static* knowledge graphs (KGs) to address the bottleneck of obtaining relevant commonsense knowledge. Lin et al. (2019) proposed to utilize knowledge graph embeddings to rank and select relevant knowledge triples or paths. Paul and Frank (2019) proposed to extract subgraphs from KGs using graph-based ranking methods and further Paul et al. (2020) adopted the graph-based ranking method and proposed to *dynamically* extend the KG to combat sparsity. In concurrent work, Paul and Frank (2021) introduced a method to dynamically generate contextually relevant knowledge that guides a model while performing the narrative story completion task.

Both hypothetical reasoning and abductive reasoning are understudied problems in NLP. Recently, Tandon et al. (2019) proposed a first large-scale dataset of *"What if..."* questions over procedural text. They introduced the dataset to study the effect of perturbations in procedural text. Related to our work, Qin et al. (2019) investigated the capabilities of state-of-the-art LMs to rewrite stories with counterfactual reasoning. In our work we utilize this dataset to model how to generate possible next events emerging from different hypothetical and counterfactual events. Mostafazadeh et al. (2016) designed the narrative cloze task, a task to choose the correct ending of a story.[13] Conversely, Bhagavatula et al. (2020) proposed a task that requires reasoning about plausible explanations for narrative omissions. Our research touches on the issue of hypothetical reasoning about alternative situations. We found that making language models learn how different hypothetical events can evolve from a premise and result in similar or different future events forming from a premise and how these events can result in similar or different future events helps models to perform better in abduction.

Explainability. Despite the success of large pretrained language models, recent studies have raised some critical points such as: high accuracy scores do not necessarily reflect understanding (Min et al., 2019), large pretrained models may exploit superficial clues and annotation artifacts (Gururangan et al., 2018; Kavumba et al., 2019). Therefore, the ability of models to generate explanations has become desirable, as this enhances interpretability. Recently, there has been substantial effort to build datasets with natural language explanations (Camburu et al., 2018; Park et al., 2018; Thayaparan et al., 2020). There have also been numerous research works proposing models that are interpretable or explainable (Rajani et al., 2019; Atanasova et al., 2020; Latcinnik and Berant, 2020; Wiegreffe and Marasović, 2021). Our work sheds light in this direction, as our $\mathcal{MTL}$ model not only predicts the plausible hypothesis H_j but also generates possible next events $O_2^{H_j}$ and chooses the one that is closer to the given context, thereby making our model more expressive.

Abductive Reasoning. There has been longstanding work on theories of abductive reasoning (Peirce, 1903, 1965a,b; Kuipers, 1992, 2013). Researchers have applied various frameworks, some focused on pure logical frameworks (Pople, 1973; Kakas et al., 1992), some on probabilistic frameworks (Pearl, 1988), and others on Markov Logics (Singla and Mooney, 2011). Recently, moving away from logic-based abductive reasoning, Bhagavatula et al. (2020) proposed to study language-based abductive reasoning. They introduced two tasks: *Abductive Natural Language Inference (αNLI)* and *Generation (αNLG)*. They establish baseline performance based on state-of-the-art language models and make use of inferential structured knowledge from ATOMIC (Sap et al., 2019a) as background knowledge. Zhu et al. (2020) proposed to use a learning-to-rank framework to address the abductive reasoning task. Ji et al. (2020)

[13]Their dataset, ROCStories, was later extended in Qin et al. (2019) and Bhagavatula et al. (2020).

proposed a model GRF that enables pre-trained models (GPT-2) with dynamic multi-hop reasoning on multi-relational paths extracted from the external ConceptNet commonsense knowledge graph for the αNLG task. Paul and Frank (2020) have proposed a multi-head knowledge attention method to incorporate commonsense knowledge to tackle the αNLI task. Unlike our previous work in Paul and Frank (2020), which focused on leveraging structured knowledge, in this work, we focus on learning about what will happen next from different counterfactual situations in a story context through language model fine-tuning. Specifically, we study the impact of such forward inference on the αNLI task in a multi-task learning framework and show how it can improve performance over a strong BERT model.

8 Conclusion

We have introduced a novel method for addressing the abductive reasoning task by explicitly learning what events could follow other events in a hypothetical scenario, and learning to generate such events, conditioned on a premise or hypothesis. We show how a language model – fine-tuned for this capability on a suitable narrative dataset – can be leveraged to support abductive reasoning in the αNLI tasks, in two settings: an unsupervised setting in combination with *BertScore*, to select the proper hypothesis, and a supervised setting in a $\mathcal{MTL}$ setting.

The relatively strong performance of our proposed models demonstrates that learning to choose from generated hypothetical next events the one that is most similar to the observation, supports the prediction of the most plausible hypothesis. Our experiments show that our unsupervised $LM_{\mathcal{I}}$+*BERTScore* model outperforms some of the strong supervised baseline systems on αNLI. Our research thus offers new perspectives for training generative models in different ways for various complex reasoning tasks.

Acknowledgements

This work has been supported by the German Research Foundation as part of the Research Training Group "Adaptive Preparation of Information from Heterogeneous Sources" (AIPHES) under grant No. GRK 1994/1. We thank our annotators for their valuable annotations. We also thank NVIDIA Corporation for donating GPUs used in this research.

References

Pepa Atanasova, Jakob Grue Simonsen, Christina Lioma, and Isabelle Augenstein. 2020. Generating fact checking explanations. In *Proceedings of the 58th Annual Meeting of the Association for Computational Linguistics*, pages 7352–7364, Online. Association for Computational Linguistics.

Chandra Bhagavatula, Ronan Le Bras, Chaitanya Malaviya, Keisuke Sakaguchi, Ari Holtzman, Hannah Rashkin, Doug Downey, Wen tau Yih, and Yejin Choi. 2020. Abductive commonsense reasoning. In *International Conference on Learning Representations*.

M. Bhatt and G. Flanagan. 2010. Spatio-temporal abduction for scenario and narrative completion (a preliminary statement). In *ECAI*.

Oana-Maria Camburu, Tim Rocktäschel, Thomas Lukasiewicz, and Phil Blunsom. 2018. e-SNLI: Natural Language Inference with Natural Language Explanations. In S. Bengio, H. Wallach, H. Larochelle, K. Grauman, N. Cesa-Bianchi, and R. Garnett, editors, *Advances in Neural Information Processing Systems 31*, pages 9539–9549. Curran Associates, Inc.

Qian Chen, Xiaodan Zhu, Zhen-Hua Ling, Si Wei, Hui Jiang, and Diana Inkpen. 2017. Enhanced LSTM for natural language inference. In *Proceedings of the 55th Annual Meeting of the Association for Computational Linguistics (Volume 1: Long Papers)*, pages 1657–1668, Vancouver, Canada. Association for Computational Linguistics.

Alexis Conneau, Douwe Kiela, Holger Schwenk, Loïc Barrault, and Antoine Bordes. 2017. Supervised learning of universal sentence representations from natural language inference data. In *Proceedings of the 2017 Conference on Empirical Methods in Natural Language Processing*, pages 670–680, Copenhagen, Denmark. Association for Computational Linguistics.

Jacob Devlin, Ming-Wei Chang, Kenton Lee, and Kristina Toutanova. 2019. BERT: Pre-training of deep bidirectional transformers for language understanding. In *Proceedings of the 2019 Conference of the North American Chapter of the Association for Computational Linguistics: Human Language Technologies, Volume 1 (Long and Short Papers)*, pages 4171–4186, Minneapolis, Minnesota. Association for Computational Linguistics.

Igor Douven. 2017. Abduction. In Edward N. Zalta, editor, *The Stanford Encyclopedia of Philosophy*, summer 2017 edition. Metaphysics Research Lab, Stanford University.

Suchin Gururangan, Swabha Swayamdipta, Omer Levy, Roy Schwartz, Samuel Bowman, and Noah A Smith. 2018. Annotation artifacts in natural language inference data. In *Proceedings of the 2018 Conference of the North American Chapter of the*

Association for Computational Linguistics: Human Language Technologies, Volume 2 (Short Papers), pages 107–112.

A. Hayes and K. Krippendorff. 2007. Answering the call for a standard reliability measure for coding data. *Communication Methods and Measures*, 1:77 – 89.

Lifu Huang, Ronan Le Bras, Chandra Bhagavatula, and Yejin Choi. 2019. Cosmos QA: Machine reading comprehension with contextual commonsense reasoning. In *Proceedings of the 2019 Conference on Empirical Methods in Natural Language Processing and the 9th International Joint Conference on Natural Language Processing (EMNLP-IJCNLP)*, pages 2391–2401, Hong Kong, China. Association for Computational Linguistics.

Haozhe Ji, Pei Ke, Shaohan Huang, Furu Wei, Xiaoyan Zhu, and Minlie Huang. 2020. Language generation with multi-hop reasoning on commonsense knowledge graph. In *Proceedings of the 2020 Conference on Empirical Methods in Natural Language Processing (EMNLP)*, pages 725–736, Online. Association for Computational Linguistics.

Antonis C Kakas, Robert A. Kowalski, and Francesca Toni. 1992. Abductive logic programming. *Journal of logic and computation*, 2(6):719–770.

Pride Kavumba, Naoya Inoue, Benjamin Heinzerling, Keshav Singh, Paul Reisert, and Kentaro Inui. 2019. When Choosing Plausible Alternatives, Clever Hans can be Clever. In *Proceedings of the First Workshop on Commonsense Inference in Natural Language Processing*, pages 33–42, Hong Kong, China. Association for Computational Linguistics.

Theo AF Kuipers. 1992. Naive and refined truth approximation. *Synthese*, 93(3):299–341.

Theo AF Kuipers. 2013. *From instrumentalism to constructive realism: On some relations between confirmation, empirical progress, and truth approximation*, volume 287. Springer Science & Business Media.

Veronica Latcinnik and Jonathan Berant. 2020. Explaining question answering models through text generation. *arXiv preprint arXiv:2004.05569*.

Bill Yuchen Lin, Xinyue Chen, Jamin Chen, and Xiang Ren. 2019. Kagnet: Knowledge-aware graph networks for commonsense reasoning. In *Proceedings of the 2019 Conference on Empirical Methods in Natural Language Processing and the 9th International Joint Conference on Natural Language Processing (EMNLP-IJCNLP)*, pages 2822–2832.

Sewon Min, Eric Wallace, Sameer Singh, Matt Gardner, Hannaneh Hajishirzi, and Luke Zettlemoyer. 2019. Compositional questions do not necessitate multi-hop reasoning. In *Proceedings of the 57th Annual Meeting of the Association for Computational Linguistics*, pages 4249–4257, Florence, Italy. Association for Computational Linguistics.

Nasrin Mostafazadeh, Nathanael Chambers, Xiaodong He, Devi Parikh, Dhruv Batra, Lucy Vanderwende, Pushmeet Kohli, and James Allen. 2016. A corpus and cloze evaluation for deeper understanding of commonsense stories. In *Proceedings of the 2016 Conference of the North American Chapter of the Association for Computational Linguistics: Human Language Technologies*, pages 839–849, San Diego, California. Association for Computational Linguistics.

Dong Huk Park, L. Hendricks, Zeynep Akata, Anna Rohrbach, B. Schiele, T. Darrell, and M. Rohrbach. 2018. Multimodal explanations: Justifying decisions and pointing to the evidence. *2018 IEEE/CVF Conference on Computer Vision and Pattern Recognition*, pages 8779–8788.

Debjit Paul and Anette Frank. 2019. Ranking and selecting multi-hop knowledge paths to better predict human needs. In *Proceedings of the 2019 Conference of the North American Chapter of the Association for Computational Linguistics: Human Language Technologies, Volume 1 (Long and Short Papers)*, pages 3671–3681, Minneapolis, Minnesota. Association for Computational Linguistics.

Debjit Paul and Anette Frank. 2020. Social commonsense reasoning with multi-head knowledge attention. In *Findings of the Association for Computational Linguistics: EMNLP 2020*, pages 2969–2980, Online. Association for Computational Linguistics.

Debjit Paul and Anette Frank. 2021. COINS: Dynamically Generating COntextualized Inference Rules for Narrative Story Completion. In *Proceedings of the Joint Conference of the 59th Annual Meeting of the Association for Computational Linguistics and the 11th International Joint Conference on Natural Language Processing (ACL-IJCNLP 2021)*, Online. Association for Computational Linguistics. Long Paper.

Debjit Paul, Juri Opitz, Maria Becker, Jonathan Kobbe, Graeme Hirst, and Anette Frank. 2020. Argumentative Relation Classification with Background Knowledge. In *Proceedings of the 8th International Conference on Computational Models of Argument (COMMA 2020)*, volume 326 of *Frontiers in Artificial Intelligence and Applications*, pages 319–330. Computational Models of Argument.

Judea Pearl. 1988. *Probabilistic Reasoning in Intelligent Systems: Networks of Plausible Inference*. Morgan Kaufmann Publishers Inc., CA.

C. S. Peirce. 1903. *Pragmatism as the Logic of Abduction*. `https://www.textlog.de/7663.html`.

Charles Sanders Peirce. 1965a. *Collected papers of Charles Sanders Peirce*, volume 5. Harvard University Press. `http://www.hup.harvard.edu/catalog.php?isbn=9780674138001`.

Charles Sanders Peirce. 1965b. *Pragmatism and pragmaticism*, volume 5. Belknap Press of Harvard University Press. https://www.jstor.org/stable/224970.

Harry E Pople. 1973. On the mechanization of abductive logic. In *Proceedings of the 3rd international joint conference on Artificial intelligence*, pages 147–152.

Lianhui Qin, Antoine Bosselut, Ari Holtzman, Chandra Bhagavatula, Elizabeth Clark, and Yejin Choi. 2019. Counterfactual story reasoning and generation. In *2019 Conference on Empirical Methods in Natural Language Processing.*, Hongkong, China. Association for Computational Linguistics.

Alec Radford, Jeff Wu, Rewon Child, David Luan, Dario Amodei, and Ilya Sutskever. 2019. Language models are unsupervised multitask learners.

Nazneen Fatema Rajani, Bryan McCann, Caiming Xiong, and Richard Socher. 2019. Explain yourself! leveraging language models for commonsense reasoning. In *Proceedings of the 57th Annual Meeting of the Association for Computational Linguistics*, pages 4932–4942, Florence, Italy. Association for Computational Linguistics.

Hannah Rashkin, Maarten Sap, Emily Allaway, Noah A. Smith, and Yejin Choi. 2018. Event2Mind: Commonsense inference on events, intents, and reactions. In *Proceedings of the 56th Annual Meeting of the Association for Computational Linguistics (Volume 1: Long Papers)*, pages 463–473, Melbourne, Australia. Association for Computational Linguistics.

Sebastian Ruder. 2019. *Neural transfer learning for natural language processing*. Ph.D. thesis, NUI Galway.

Maarten Sap, Ronan Le Bras, Emily Allaway, Chandra Bhagavatula, Nicholas Lourie, Hannah Rashkin, Brendan Roof, Noah A. Smith, and Yejin Choi. 2019a. ATOMIC: an atlas of machine commonsense for if-then reasoning. In *The Thirty-Third AAAI Conference on Artificial Intelligence, AAAI 2019, The Thirty-First Innovative Applications of Artificial Intelligence Conference, IAAI 2019, The Ninth AAAI Symposium on Educational Advances in Artificial Intelligence, EAAI 2019, Honolulu, Hawaii, USA, January 27 - February 1, 2019.*, pages 3027–3035.

Maarten Sap, Hannah Rashkin, Derek Chen, Ronan Le Bras, and Yejin Choi. 2019b. Social IQa: Commonsense reasoning about social interactions. In *Proceedings of the 2019 Conference on Empirical Methods in Natural Language Processing and the 9th International Joint Conference on Natural Language Processing (EMNLP-IJCNLP)*, pages 4463–4473, Hong Kong, China. Association for Computational Linguistics.

Parag Singla and Raymond J Mooney. 2011. Abductive markov logic for plan recognition. In *Twenty-Fifth AAAI Conference on Artificial Intelligence*.

Robyn Speer, Joshua Chin, and Catherine Havasi. 2017. Conceptnet 5.5: An open multilingual graph of general knowledge. In *Thirty-First AAAI Conference on Artificial Intelligence*.

Christian Strasser and G. Aldo Antonelli. 2019. Nonmonotonic logic. In Edward N. Zalta, editor, *The Stanford Encyclopedia of Philosophy*, summer 2019 edition. Metaphysics Research Lab, Stanford University.

Alon Talmor, Jonathan Herzig, Nicholas Lourie, and Jonathan Berant. 2019. CommonsenseQA: A question answering challenge targeting commonsense knowledge. In *Proceedings of the 2019 Conference of the North American Chapter of the Association for Computational Linguistics: Human Language Technologies, Volume 1 (Long and Short Papers)*, pages 4149–4158, Minneapolis, Minnesota. Association for Computational Linguistics.

Niket Tandon, Bhavana Dalvi, Keisuke Sakaguchi, Peter Clark, and Antoine Bosselut. 2019. WIQA: A dataset for "what if..." reasoning over procedural text. In *Proceedings of the 2019 Conference on Empirical Methods in Natural Language Processing and the 9th International Joint Conference on Natural Language Processing (EMNLP-IJCNLP)*, pages 6076–6085, Hong Kong, China. Association for Computational Linguistics.

Mokanarangan Thayaparan, Marco Valentino, and André Freitas. 2020. A survey on explainability in machine reading comprehension. *arXiv preprint arXiv:2010.00389*.

Sarah Wiegreffe and Ana Marasović. 2021. Teach me to explain: A review of datasets for explainable nlp. ArXiv:2102.12060.

Tianyi Zhang, Varsha Kishore, Felix Wu, Kilian Q. Weinberger, and Yoav Artzi. 2020. BERTScore: Evaluating Text Generation with BERT. In *International Conference on Learning Representations*.

Yunchang Zhu, Liang Pang, Yanyan Lan, and Xueqi Cheng. 2020. $l2r^2$: Leveraging ranking for abductive reasoning. In *Proceedings of the 43rd International ACM SIGIR Conference on Research and Development in Information Retrieval*, SIGIR '20, page 1961–1964, New York, NY, USA. Association for Computing Machinery.

NeuralLog:
Natural Language Inference with Joint Neural and Logical Reasoning

Zeming Chen[†*] **Qiyue Gao**[†] **Lawrence S. Moss**[‡]
[†]Rose-Hulman Institute of Technology, Terre Haute, IN, USA
[‡]Indiana University, Bloomington, IN, USA
{chenz16,gaoq}@rose-hulman.edu
{lmoss}@indiana.edu

Abstract

Deep learning (DL) based language models achieve high performance on various benchmarks for Natural Language Inference (NLI). And at this time, symbolic approaches to NLI are receiving less attention. Both approaches (symbolic and DL) have their advantages and weaknesses. However, currently, no method combines them in a system to solve the task of NLI. To merge symbolic and deep learning methods, we propose an inference framework called NeuralLog, which utilizes both a monotonicity-based logical inference engine and a neural network language model for phrase alignment. Our framework models the NLI task as a classic search problem and uses the beam search algorithm to search for optimal inference paths. Experiments show that our joint logic and neural inference system improves accuracy on the NLI task and can achieve state-of-art accuracy on the SICK and MED datasets.

1 Introduction

Currently, many NLI benchmarks' state-of-the-art systems are exclusively deep learning (DL) based language models (Devlin et al., 2019; Lan et al., 2020; Liu et al., 2020; Yin and Schütze, 2017). These models often contain a large number of parameters, use high-quality pre-trained embeddings, and are trained on large-scale datasets, which enable them to handle diverse and large test data robustly. However, several experiments show that DL models lack generalization ability, adopt fallible syntactic heuristics, and show exploitation of annotation artifacts (Glockner et al., 2018; McCoy et al., 2019; Gururangan et al., 2018). On the other hand, there are logic-based systems that use symbolic reasoning and semantic formalism to solve NLI (Abzianidze, 2017; Martínez-Gómez et al., 2017; Yanaka et al., 2018; Hu et al., 2020). These systems show high precision on complex inferences involving difficult linguistic phenomena and present logical and explainable reasoning processes. However, these systems lack background knowledge and do not handle sentences with syntactic variations well, which makes them poor competitors with state-of-the-art DL models. Both DL and logic-based systems show a major issue with NLI models: they are too one-dimensional (either purely DL or purely logic), and no method has combined these two ap-

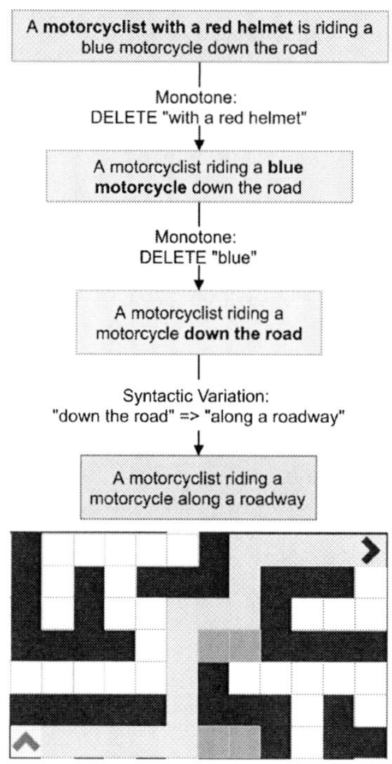

Figure 1: Analogy between path planning and an entailment inference path from the premise *A motorcyclist with a red helmet is riding a blue motorcycle down the road* to the hypothesis *A motorcyclist is riding a motorbike along a roadway*.

*The first two authors have equal contribution

Proceedings of the 10th Conference on Lexical and Computational Semantics, pages 78–88
August 5–6, 2021, Bangkok, Thailand (online) ©2021 Association for Computational Linguistics

proaches together for solving NLI.

This paper makes several contributions, as follows: first, we propose a new framework in section 3 for combining logic-based inference with deep-learning-based network inference for better performance on conducting natural language inference. We model an NLI task as a path-searching problem between the premises and the hypothesis. We use beam-search to find an optimal path that can transform a premise to a hypothesis through a series of inference steps. This way, different inference modules can be inserted into the system. For example, DL inference modules will handle inferences with diverse syntactic changes and logic inference modules will handle inferences that require complex reasoning. Second, we introduce a new method in section 4.3 to handle syntactic variations in natural language through sequence chunking and DL based paraphrase detection. We evaluate our system in section 6 by conducting experiments on the SICK and MED datasets. Experiments show that joint logical and neural reasoning show state-of-art accuracy and recall on these datasets.

2 Related Work

Perhaps the closest systems to NeuralLog are Yanaka et al. (2018), MonaLog (Hu et al., 2020), and Hy-NLI (Kalouli et al., 2020). Using Martínez-Gómez et al. (2016) to work with logic representations derived from CCG trees, Yanaka et al. (2018) proposed a framework that can detect phrase correspondences for a sentence pair, using natural deduction on semantic relations and can thus extract various paraphrases automatically. Their experiments show that assessing phrase correspondences helps improve NLI accuracy. Our system uses a similar methodology to solve syntactic variation inferences, where we determine if two phrases are paraphrases. Our method is rather different on this point, since we call on neural language models to detect paraphrases between two sentences. We feel that it would be interesting to compare the systems on a more theoretical level, but we have not done the comparison in this paper.

NeuralLog inherits the use of polarity marking found in MonaLog (Hu et al., 2020). (However, we use the dependency-based system of Chen and Gao (2021) instead of the CCG-based system of Hu and Moss (2018).) MonaLog did propose some integration with neural models, using BERT when logic failed to find entailment or contradiction. We are doing something very different, using neural models to detect paraphrases at several levels of "chunking". In addition, the exact algorithms found in Sections 3 and 4 are new here. In a sense, our work on alignment in NLI goes back to MacCartney and Manning (2009) where alignment was used to find a chain of edits that changes a premise to a hypothesis, but our work uses much that simply was not available in 2009.

Hy-NLI is a hybrid system that makes inferences using either symbolic or deep learning models based on how linguistically challenging a pair of sentences is. The principle Hy-NLI followed is that deep learning models are better at handling sentences that are linguistically less complex, and symbolic models are better for sentences containing hard linguistic phenomena. Although the system integrates both symbolic and neural methods, its decision process is still separate, in which the symbolic and deep learning sides make decisions without relying on the other side. Differently, our system incorporates logical inferences and neural inferences as part of the decision process, in which the two inference methods rely on each other to make a final decision.

3 Method

3.1 NLI As Path Planning

The key motivation behind our architecture and inference modules is that the Natural Language Inference task can be modeled as a path planning problem. Path planning is a task for finding an optimal path traveling from a start point to a goal containing a series of actions. To formulate NLI as path planning, we define the **premise** as the **start state** and the **hypothesis** as the **goal** that needs to be reached. The classical path planning strategy applies expansions from the start state through some search algorithms, such as depth-first-search or Dijkstra search, until an expansion meets the goal. In a grid map, two types of action produce an expansion. The vertical action moves up and down, and the horizontal action moves left and right. Similarly, language inference also contains these two actions. Monotonicity reasoning is a vertical action, where the monotone inference moves up and simplifies a sentence, and the antitone inference moves down and makes a sentence more specific. Syntactic variation and synonym replacement are horizontal actions. They change the form of a sentence while maintaining the original mean-

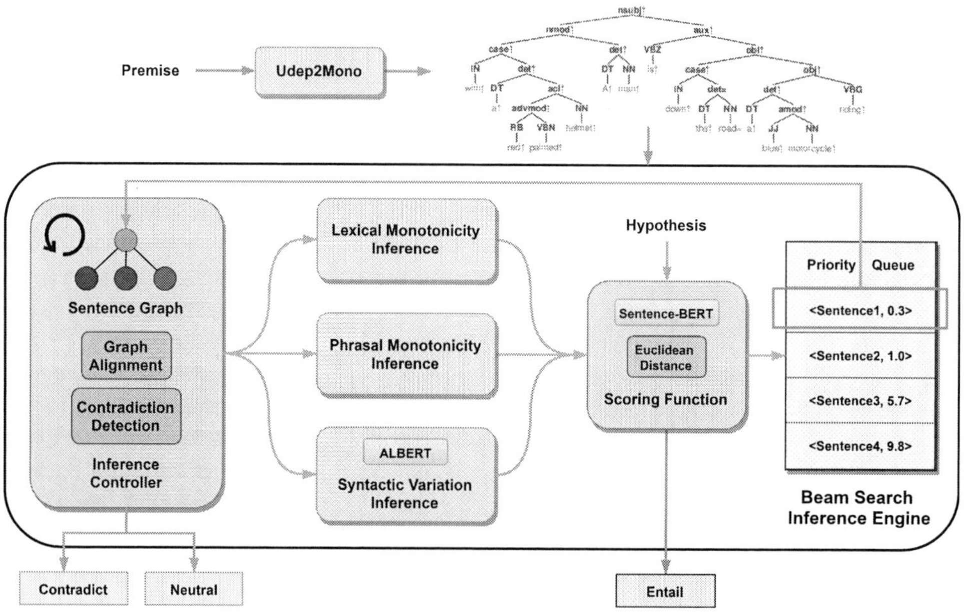

Figure 2: Overview system diagram of NeuralLog.

ing. Then, similar to path planning, we can continuously make inferences from the premise using a search algorithm to determine if the premise entails the hypothesis by observing whether one of the inferences can reach the hypothesis. If the hypothesis is reached, we can connect the list of inferences that transform a premise to a hypothesis to be the optimal path in NLI, a valid reasoning chain for entailment.

Figure 1 shows an analogy between an optimal path for the classical grid path planning problem and an example of an optimal inference path for NLI. On the top, we have a reasoning process for natural language inference. From the premise, we can first delete the modifier *with a red helmet*, then delete *blue* to get a simplified sentence. Finally, we can paraphrase *down the road* to *along a roadway* in the premise to reach the hypothesis and conclude the entailment relationship between these two sentences.

3.2 Overview

Our system contains four components: (1) a polarity annotator, (2) three sentence inference modules, (3) a search engine, and (4) a sentence inference controller. Figure 2 shows a diagram of the full system. The system first annotates a sentence with monotonicity information (polarity marks) using Udep2Mono (Chen and Gao, 2021). The polarity marks include monotone (↑), antitone (↓), and no monotonicity information (=) polarities. Next, the polarized parse tree is passed to the search engine. A beam search algorithm searches for the optimal inference path from a premise to a hypothesis. The search space is generated from three inference modules: lexical, phrasal, and syntactic variation. Through graph alignment, the sentence inference controller selects a inference module to apply to the premise and produce a set of new premises that potentially form entailment relations with the hypothesis. The system returns **Entail** if an inference path is found. Otherwise, the controller will determine if the premise and hypothesis form a contradiction by searching for counter example signatures and returns **Contradict** accordingly. If neither **Entail** nor **Contradict** is returned, the system returns **Neutral**.

3.3 Polarity Annotator

The system first annotates a given premise with monotonicity information using Udep2Mono, a polarity annotator that determines polarization of all constituents from universal dependency trees. The annotator first parses the premise into a binarized universal dependency tree and then conducts polarization by recursively marks polarity on each node . An example can be *Every*$^{\uparrow}$ *healthy*$^{\downarrow}$ *person*$^{\downarrow}$ *plays*$^{\uparrow}$ *sports*$^{\uparrow}$.

3.4 Search Engine

To efficiently search for the optimal inference path from a premise $\mathcal{P}$ to a hypothesis $\mathcal{H}$, we use a beam search algorithm which has the advantage of reducing search space by focusing on sentences with higher scores. To increase the search efficiency and accuracy, we add an inference controller that can guide the search direction.

Scoring In beam search, a priority queue $\mathcal{Q}$ maintains the set of generated sentences. A core operation is the determination of the highest-scoring generated sentence for a given input under a learned scoring model. In our case, the maximum score is equivalent to the minimum distance:

$$\mathbf{y}^{\star} = \arg\max_{\mathrm{s} \in \mathcal{S}} \mathrm{score}(\mathrm{s}, \mathcal{H})$$

$$\mathbf{y}^{\star} = \arg\min_{\mathrm{s} \in \mathcal{S}} \mathrm{dist}(\mathrm{s}, \mathcal{H})$$

where $\mathcal{H}$ is the hypothesis and $\mathcal{S}$ is a set of generated sentences produced by the three (lexical, phrasal, syntactic variation) inference modules. We will present more details about these inference modules in section 4. We formulate the distance function as the Euclidean distance between the sentence embeddings of the premise and hypothesis. To obtain semantically meaningful sentence embeddings efficiently, we use Reimers and Gurevych (2019)'s language model, Sentence-BERT (SBERT), a modification of the BERT model. It uses siamese and triplet neural network structures to derive sentence embeddings which can be easily compared using distance functions.

3.5 Sentence Inference Controller

In each iteration, the search algorithm expands the search space by generating a set of potential sentences using three inference modules: (1) lexical inference, (2) phrasal inference, and (3) syntactic variation inference. To guide the search engine to select the most applicable module, we designed a inference controller that can recommend which of the labels the overall algorithm should proceed with. For example, for a premise *All animals eat food* and a hypothesis *All dogs eat food*, only a lexical inference of *animals* to *dogs* would be needed. Then, the controller will apply the lexical inference to the premise, as we discuss below.

3.5.1 Sentence Representation Graph

The controller makes its decision based on graph-based representations for the premise and the hypothesis. We first build a sentence representation graph from parsed input using Universal Dependencies. Let $\mathcal{V} = \mathcal{V}_m \cup \mathcal{V}_c$ be the set of vertices of a sentence representation graph, where $\mathcal{V}_m$ represents the set of modifiers such as *tall* in Figure 5, and V_c represents the set of content words (words that are being modified) such as *man* in Figure 5. While content words in $\mathcal{V}_c$ could modify other content words, modifiers in $\mathcal{V}_m$ are not modified by other vertices. Let $\mathcal{E}$ be the set of directed edges in the form $\langle v_c, v_m \rangle$ such that $v_m \in \mathcal{V}_m$ and $v_c \in \mathcal{V}_c$. A sentence representation graph is then defined as a tuple $\mathrm{G} = \langle \mathcal{V}, \mathcal{E} \rangle$. Figure 3a shows an example graph.

3.5.2 Graph Alignment

To observe the differences between two sentences, we rely on graph alignment between two sentence representation graphs. We first align nodes from subjects, verbs and objects, which constitutes what we call a component level. Define G_p as the graph for a premise and G_h as the graph for a hypothesis. Then, $\mathcal{C}_p$ and $\mathcal{C}_h$ are component level nodes from the two graphs. We take the Cartesian product $\mathcal{C}_p \times \mathcal{C}_h = \{(\mathrm{c}_p, \mathrm{c}_h) : \mathrm{c}_p \in \mathcal{C}_p, \mathrm{c}_h \in \mathcal{C}_h\}$. In the first round, we recursively pair the child nodes of each c_p to child nodes of each c_h. We compute word similarity between two child nodes c_p^i and c_h^i and eliminate pairs with non-maximum similarity. We denote the new aligned pairs as a set $\mathcal{A}^*$. At the second round, we iterate through the aligned pairs in $\mathcal{A}^*$. If multiple child nodes from the first graph are paired to a child node in the second graph, we only keep the pair with maximum word similarity. In the final round, we perform the same check for each child node in the first graph to ensure that there are no multiple child nodes from the second graph paired to it. Figure 3b shows a brief visualization of the alignment process.

3.5.3 inference Module Recommendation

After aligning the premise graph $\mathcal{G}_p$ with hypothesis graph $\mathcal{G}_h$, the controller checks through each node in the two graphs. If a node does not get aligned, the controller considers to delete the node or insert it depending on which graph the node belongs to and recommends phrasal inference. If a node is different from its aligned node, the controller recommends lexical inference. If additional lexical or phrasal inferences are detected under this node, the controller decides that there is a more complex transition under this node and rec-

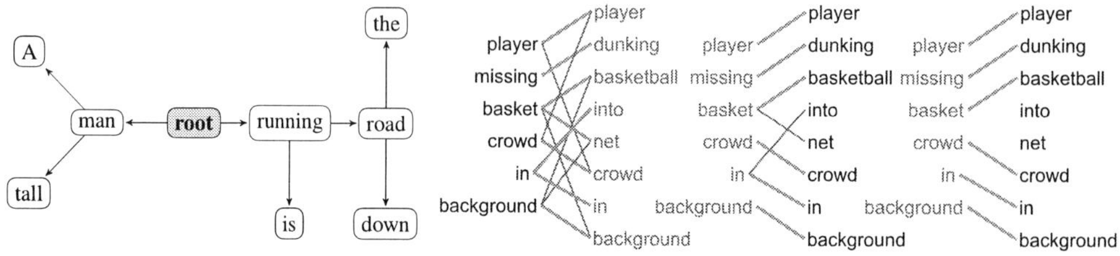

(a) Sentence representation graph

(b) Graph alignment visualization

Figure 3: (a) A sentence representation graph for *A tall man is running down the road.* (b) Visualization for the graph alignment. The lines between two words represent their similarity. The orange lines are the pairs with maximum similarities for a blue word. Through bi-directional alignment, we eliminate word pairs with non-maximum similarity and gets the final alignment pairs.

ommends a syntactic variation.

3.5.4 Contradiction Detection

We determine whether the premise and the hypothesis contradict each other inside the controller by searching for potential contradiction transitions from the premise to the hypothesis. For instance, a transition in the scope of the quantifier (*a* $\longrightarrow$ *no*) from the same subject could be what we call a contradiction signature (possible evidence for a contradiction). With all the signatures, the controller decides if they can form a contradiction as a whole. To avoid situations when multiple signatures together fail to form a complete contradiction, such as double negation, the controller checks through the contradiction signatures to ensure a contradiction. For instance, in the verb pair (*not remove*, *add*), the contradiction signature *not* would cancel the verb negation contradiction signature from *remove* to *add* so the pair as a whole would not be seen as a contradiction. Nevertheless, other changes from the premise to the hypothesis may change the meaning of the sentence. Hence, our controller would go through other transitions to make sure the meaning of the sentence does not change when the contradiction sign is valid. For example, in the neutral pair P: *A person is eating* and H: *No tall person is eating*, the addition of *tall* would be detected by our controller. But the aligned word of the component it is applied to, *person* in P, has been marked downward monotone. So this transition is invalid. This pair would then be classified as neutral.

For P2 and H2 in Figure 4, the controller notices the contradictory quantifier change around the subject *man*. The subject *man* in P2 is upward monotone so the deletion of *tall* is valid. Our controller also detects the meaning transition from *down the road* to *inside the building*, which affects the sentence's meaning and cancels the previous contradiction signature. The controller thus will not classify P2 and H2 as a pair of contradiction.

signature type	example
quantifier negation	**no** dogs $\Longrightarrow$ **some** dogs
verb negation	is **eating** $\Longrightarrow$ is **not eating**
noun negation	**some people** $\Longrightarrow$ **nobody**
action contradiction	is **sleeping** $\Longrightarrow$ is **running**
direction contradiction	The **turtle** is following the **fish** $\Longrightarrow$ The **fish** is following the **turtle**

Table 1: Examples of contradiction signatures.

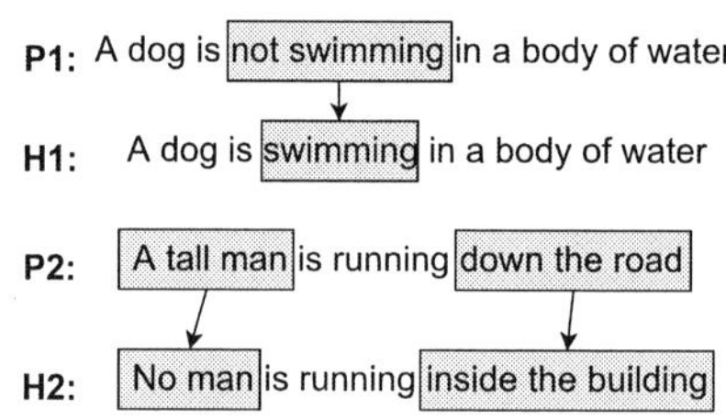

Figure 4: Example of contradiction signatures. P1 and H1 form a contradiction. P2 and H2 does not form a contradiction because the meaning after the verb *running* has changed.

4 Inference Generation

4.1 Lexical Monotonicity Inference

Lexical inference is word replacement based on monotonicity information for key-tokens including nouns, verbs, numbers, and quantifiers. The system uses lexical knowledge bases including WordNet (Miller, 1995) and ConceptNet (Liu and Singh, 2004). From the knowledge bases, we extract four word sets: hypernyms, hyponyms, synonyms, and antonyms. Logically, if a word has a monotone polarity ($\uparrow$), it can be replaced by its hypernyms. For example, *swim* $\leq$ *move*; then *swim* can be replaced with *move*. If a word has an antitone polarity ($\downarrow$), it can be replaced by its hyponyms. For example, *flower* $\geq$ *rose*. Then, *flower* can be replaced with *rose*. We filter out irrelevant words from the knowledge bases that do not appear in the hypothesis. Additionally, we handcraft knowledge relations for words like quantifiers and prepositions that do not have sufficient taxonomies from knowledge bases. Some handcrafted relations include: *all* = *every* = *each* $\leq$ *most* $\leq$ *many* $\leq$ *several* $\leq$ *some* = *a*, *up* $\perp$ *down*.

4.2 Phrasal Monotonicity Inference

Phrasal replacements are for phrase-level monotonicity inference. For example, with a polarized sentence *A* $^{\uparrow}$ *woman*$^{\uparrow}$ *who*$^{\uparrow}$ *is*$^{\uparrow}$ *beautiful*$^{\uparrow}$ *is*$^{\uparrow}$ *walking*$^{\uparrow}$ *in*$^{\uparrow}$ *the*$^{\uparrow}$ *rain*$^{=}$, the monotone mark $^{\uparrow}$ on *woman* allows an upward inference: *woman* $\sqsupseteq$ *woman who is beautiful*, in which the relative clause *who is beautiful* is deleted. The system follows a set of phrasal monotonicity inference rules. For upward monotonicity inference, modifiers of a word are deleted. For downward monotonicity inference, modifiers are inserted to a word. The algorithm traverses down a polarized UD parse tree, deletes the modifier sub-tree if a node is monotone ($\uparrow$), and inserts a new sub-tree if a node is antitone ($\downarrow$). To insert new modifiers, the algorithm extracts a list of potential modifiers associated to a node from a modifier dictionary. The modifier dictionary is derived from the hypothesis and contains word-modifier pairs for each dependency relation. Below is an example of a modifier dictionary from *There are no beautiful flowers that open at night*:

- **obl**: [head: *open*, mod: *at night*]
- **amod**: [head: *flowers*, mod: *beautiful*]
- **acl:relcl**: [head: *flowers*, mod: *that open at night*]

4.3 Syntactic Variation Inference

We categorize linguistic changes between a premise and a hypothesis that cannot be inferred from monotonicity information as *syntactic variations*. For example, a change from *red rose* to *a rose which is red* is a syntactic variation. Many logical systems rely on handcrafted rules and manual transformation to enable the system to use syntactic variations. However, without accurate alignments between the two sentences, these methods are not robust enough, and thus are difficult to scale up for wide-coverage input.

Recent development of pretrained transformer-based language models are showing state-of-art performance on multiple benchmarks for Natural Language Understanding (NLU) including the task for paraphrase detection (Devlin et al., 2019; Lan et al., 2020; Liu et al., 2020) exemplify phrasal knowledge of syntactic variation. We propose a method that incorporates transformer-based language models to robustly handle syntactic variations. Our method first uses a sentence chunker to decompose both the premise and the hypothesis into chunks of phrases and then forms a Cartesian product of chunk pairs. For each pair, we use a transformer model to calculate the likelihood of a pair of chunks being a pair of paraphrases.

4.3.1 Sequence Chunking

To obtain phrase-level chunks from a sentence, we build a sequence chunker to extract chunks from a sentence using its universal dependency information. Instead of splitting a sentence into chunks, our chunker composes word tokens recursively to form meaningful chunks. First, we construct a sentence representation graph of a premise from the controller. Recall that a sentence representation graph is defined as $G = \langle \mathcal{V}, \mathcal{E} \rangle$, where $\mathcal{V} = \mathcal{V}_m \cup \mathcal{V}_c$ is the set of modifiers ($\mathcal{V}_m$) and content words ($\mathcal{V}_c$), and $\mathcal{E}$ is the set of directed edges. To generate the chunk for a content word in $\mathcal{V}_c$, we arrange its modifiers, which are nodes it points to, together with the content word by their word orders in the original sentence to form a word chain. Modifiers that make the chain disconnected are discarded because they are not close enough to be part of the chunk. For instance, the chunk from the verb *eats* in the sentence *A person eats the food carefully* would not contain its modifier *carefully* because they are separated by the object *the food*. If the sentence is stated as *A person carefully eats the food*, *carefully* now is next to *eat* and it would be included in the chunk of the verb *eat*. To obtain chunks for a sentence, we iterate through each main component node, which is a node for subject, verb, or object, in the sentence's graph representation and construct verb phrases by combining verbs' chunks with their paired objects' chunks. There are cases when a word modifies other words and gets modified in the same time. They often occur when a chunk serves as a modifier. For example, in *The woman in a pink dress is dancing*, the phrase *in a pink dress* modifies *woman* whereas *dress* is modified by *in*, *a* and *pink*. Then edges from *dress* to *in*, *a*, *pink* with the edge from *woman* to *dress* can be drawn. Chunks *in a pink dress* and *the woman in a*

Type	Premise	Hypothesis
Verb Phrase Variation	Two men are standing near the water and are **holding fishing poles**	Two men are standing near the water and are **holding tools used for fishing**
Noun Phrase Variation	A man with climbing equipment is hanging from **rock which is vertical and white**	A man with equipment used for climbing is hanging from a **white, vertical rock**.

Table 2: Examples of phrasal alignments detected by the syntactic variation module

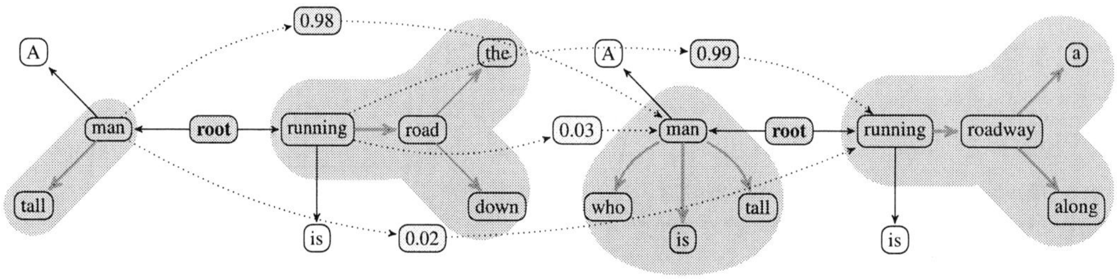

Figure 5: A graph representation of the monolingual phrase alignment process. Here the left graph represents the premise: *A tall man is running down the road.* The right graph represents the hypothesis *A man who is tall is running along a roadway.* The blue region represents phrase chunks extracted by the chunker from the graph. An alignment score is calculated for each pair of chunks. The pair ⟨ *tall man*, *man who is tall* ⟩ is a pair of paraphrases, and thus has a high alignment score (0.98). The pair ⟨ *tall man*, *running along a road way* ⟩ has two unrelated phrases, and thus has a low alignment score(0.03).

pink dress will be generated for *dress* and *woman* respectively.

4.3.2 Monolingual Phrase Alignment

After the chunker outputs a set of chunks from a generated sentence and from the hypothesis, the system selects chunk pairs that are aligned by computing an alignment score for each pair of chunks. Formally, we define $\mathcal{C}_s$ as the set of chunks from a generated sentence and $\mathcal{C}_h$ as the set of chunks from the hypothesis. We build the Cartesian product from $\mathcal{C}_s$ and $\mathcal{C}_h$, denoted $\mathcal{C}_s \times \mathcal{C}_h$. For each chunk pair $(c_{si}, c_{hj}) \in \mathcal{C}_s \times \mathcal{C}_h$, we compute an alignment score α:

$$\mathbf{y}_{\langle \mathbf{c_{si}}, \mathbf{c_{hi}} \rangle} = \text{ALBERT.forward}(\langle \mathbf{c_{si}}, \mathbf{c_{hi}} \rangle)$$

$$\alpha_{\langle \mathbf{c_{si}}, \mathbf{c_{hi}} \rangle} = \text{p}(\mathbf{c_{si}} \mid \mathbf{c_{hj}})$$

$$\alpha_{\langle \mathbf{c_{si}}, \mathbf{c_{hi}} \rangle} = \frac{\exp^{\mathbf{y}_{\langle \mathbf{c_{si}}, \mathbf{c_{hi}} \rangle 0}}}{\sum_{j=1}^{2} \exp^{\mathbf{y}_{\langle \mathbf{c_{si}}, \mathbf{c_{hi}} \rangle j}}}$$

If $\alpha > 0.85$, the system records this pair of phrases as a pair of syntactic variation. To calculate the alignment score, we use an ALBERT (Lan et al., 2020) model for the paraphrase detection task, fine tuned on the Microsoft Research Paraphrase Corpus (Dolan and Brockett, 2005). We first pass the chunk pair to ALBERT to obtain the logits. Then we apply a softmax function to the logits to get the final probability. A full demonstration of the alignment between chunks is shown in Figure 5.

5 Data

5.1 The SICK Dataset

The SICK (Marelli et al., 2014) dataset is an English benchmark that provides in-depth evaluation for compositional distribution models. There are 10,000 English sentence pairs exhibiting a variety of lexical, syntactic, and semantic phenomena. Each sentence pair is annotated as Entailment, Contradiction, or Neutral. we use the 4,927 test problems for evaluation.

5.2 The MED Dataset

The Monotonicity Entailment Dataset (MED), is a challenge dataset designed to examine a model's ability to conduct monotonicity inference (Yanaka et al., 2019a). There are 5382 sentence pairs in MED, where 1820 pairs are upward inference problems, 3270 pairs are downward inference problems, and 292 pairs are problems with no monotonicity information. MED's problems cover a variety of linguistic phenomena, such as lexical knowledge, reverse, conjunction and disjunction, conditional, and negative polarity items.

6 Evaluation

6.1 Experiment Setup

For Universal Dependency parsing, we follow Chen and Gao (2021)'s framework and use a parser

Model	P	R	acc.
ML/DL-based systems			
BERT (base, uncased)	86.8	85.4	86.7
Yin and Schütze (2017)	–	–	87.1
Beltagy et al. (2016)	–	–	85.1
Logic-based systems			
Abzianidze (2017)	98.0	58.1	81.4
Martínez-Gómez et al. (2017)	97.0	63.6	83.1
Yanaka et al. (2018)	84.2	77.3	84.3
Hu et al. (2020)	83.8	70.7	77.2
Abzianidze (2020)	94.3	67.9	84.4
Hybrid System			
Hu et al. (2020)+BERT	83.2	85.5	85.4
Kalouli et al. (2020)	–	–	86.5
Our System			
NeuralLog (full system)	88.0	**87.6**	**90.3**
– ALBERT-SV	68.9	79.3	71.4
– Monotonicity	74.5	75.1	74.7

Table 3: Performance on the SICK test set

from Stanford's natural language analysis package, Stanza (Qi et al., 2020). In the parser, we use a neural parsing model pretrained on the UD English GUM corpus (Zeldes, 2017) with 90.0 LAS (Zeman et al., 2018) evaluation score. For Sentence-BERT, we selected the BERT-large model pre-trained on STS-B (Cer et al., 2017). For ALBERT, we used textattack's ALBERT-base model pretrained on MRPC from transformers. For word alignment in the controller, we select Řehůřek and Sojka (2010)'s Gensim framework to calculate word similarity from pre-trained word embedding. We evaluated our model on the SICK and MED datasets using the standard NLI evaluation metrics of accuracy, precision, and recall. Additionally, we conducted two ablation tests focusing on analyzing the contributions of the monotonicity inference modules and the syntactic variation module.

6.2 Results

SICK Table 3 shows the experiment results tested on SICK. We compared our performance to several logic-based systems as well as two deep learning based models. As the evaluation results show, our model achieves the state-of-art performance on the SICK dataset. The best logic-based model is Abzianidze (2020) with 84.4 percent accuracy. The best DL-based model is Yin and Schütze (2017) with 87.1 percent accuracy. Our system outperforms both of them with 90.3 percent accuracy. Compare to Hu et al. (2020) + BERT, which also explores a way of combining logic-based methods and deep learning based methods, our system

Model	Up	Down	All
DeComp (Parikh et al., 2016)	71.1	45.2	51.4
ESIM (Chen et al., 2017)	66.1	42.1	53.8
BERT (Devlin et al., 2019)	82.7	22.8	44.7
BERT+ (Yanaka et al., 2019a)	76.0	70.3	71.6
NeuralLog (ours)	**91.4**	**93.9**	**93.4**

Table 4: Results comparing model compared to state-of-art NLI models evaluated on MED. **Up**, **Down**, and **All** stand for the accuracy on upward inference, downward inference, and the overall dataset.

shows higher accuracy with a 4.92 percentage point increase. In addition, our system's accuracy has a 3.8 percentage point increase than another hybrid system, Hy-NLI (Kalouli et al., 2020). The good performance proves that our framework for joint logic and neural reasoning can achieve state-of-art performance on inference and outperforms existing systems.

Ablation Test In addition to the standard evaluation on SICK, we conducted two ablation tests. The results are included in Table 3. First, we remove the syntactic variation module that uses neural network for alignment (−ALBERT-SV). As the table shows, the accuracy drops 18.9 percentage points. This large drop in accuracy indicates that the syntactic variation module plays a major part in our overall inference process. The result also proves our hypothesis that deep learning methods for inference can improve the performance of traditional logic-based systems significantly. Secondly, when we remove the monotonicity-based inference modules (−Monotonicity), the accuracy shows another large decrease in accuracy, with a 15.6 percentage point drop. This result demonstrates the important contribution of the logic-based inference modules toward the overall state-of-the-art performance. Compared to the previous ablation test which removes the neural network based syntactic variation module, the accuracy does not change much (only 3.3 differences). This similar performance indicates that neural network inference in our system alone cannot achieve state-of-art performance on the SICK dataset, and additional guidance and constrains from the logic-based methods are essential parts of our framework. Overall, we believe that the results reveal that both modules, logic and neural, contribute equally to the final performance and are both important parts that are unmovable.

MED Table 4 shows the experimental results tested on MED. We compared to multiple deep learning based baselines. Here, DeComp and ESIM are trained on SNLI and BERT is fine-tuned with MultiNLI. The BERT+ model is a BERT model fine-tuned on a combined training data with the HELP dataset, (Yanaka et al., 2019b), a set of augmentations for monotonicity reasoning, and the MultiNLI training set. Both models were tested in Yanaka et al. (2019a). Overall, our system (NeuralLog) outperforms all DL-based baselines in terms of accuracy, by a significant amount. Compared to BERT+, our system performs better both on upward (+15.4) and downward (+23.6) inference, and shows significant higher accuracy overall (+21.8). The good performance on MED validates our system's ability on accurate and robust monotonicity-based inference.

6.3 Error Analysis

For entailment, a large amount of inference errors are due to an incorrect dependency parse trees from the parser. For example, P: *A black, red, white and pink dress is being worn by a woman*, H: *A dress, which is black, red, white and pink is being worn by a woman*, has long conjunctions that cause the parser to produce two separate trees from the same sentence. Secondly, a lack of sufficient background knowledge causes the system to fail to make inferences which would be needed to obtain a correct label. For example, P: *One man is doing a bicycle trick in midair*, H: *The cyclist is performing a trick in the air* requires the system to know that *a man doing a bicycle trick* is a *cyclist*. This kind of knowledge can only be injected to the system either by handcrafting rules or by extracting it from the training data. For contradiction, our analysis reveals inconsistencies in the SICK dataset. We account for multiple sentence pairs that have the same syntactic and semantic structures, but are labeled differently. For example, P: *A man is folding a tortilla*, H: *A man is unfolding a tortilla* has gold-label **Neutral** while P: *A man is playing a guitar*, H: *A man is not playing a guitar* has gold-label **Contradiction**. These two pair of sentences clearly have similar structures but have inconsistent gold-labels. Both gold-labels would be reasonable depending on whether the two subjects refer to the same entity.

7 Conclusion and Future Work

In this paper, we presented a framework to combine logic-based inference with deep-learning based inference for improved Natural Language Inference performance. The main method is using a search engine and an alignment based controller to dispatch the two inference methods (logic and deep-learning) to their area of expertise. This way, logic-based modules can solve inference that requires logical rules and deep-learning based modules can solve inferences that contain syntactic variations which are easier for neural networks. Our system uses a beam search algorithm and three inference modules (lexical, phrasal, and syntactic variation) to find an optimal path that can transform a premise to a hypothesis. Our system handles syntactic variations in natural sentences using the neural network on phrase chunks, and our system determines contradictions by searching for contradiction signatures (evidence for contradiction). Evaluations on SICK and MED show that our proposed framework for joint logical and neural reasoning can achieve state-of-art accuracy on these datasets. Our experiments on ablation tests show that neither logic nor neural reasoning alone fully solve Natural Language Inference, but a joint operation between them can bring improved performance.

For future work, one plan is to extend our system with more logic inference methods such as those using dynamic semantics (Haruta et al., 2020) and more neural inference methods such as those for commonsense reasoning (Levine et al., 2020). We also plan to implement a learning method that allows the system to learn from mistakes on a training dataset and automatically expand or correct its rules and knowledge bases, which is similar to Abzianidze (2020)'s work.

Acknowledgements

We thank the anonymous reviewers for their insightful comments. We also thank Dr. Michael Wollowski from Rose-hulman Institute of Technology for his helpful feedback on this paper.

References

Lasha Abzianidze. 2017. LangPro: Natural language theorem prover. In *Proceedings of the 2017 Conference on Empirical Methods in Natural Language Processing: System Demonstrations*, pages 115–120, Copenhagen, Denmark. Association for Computational Linguistics.

Lasha Abzianidze. 2020. Learning as abduction: Trainable natural logic theorem prover for natural language inference. In *Proceedings of the Ninth Joint Conference on Lexical and Computational Seman-*

tics, pages 20–31, Barcelona, Spain (Online). Association for Computational Linguistics.

I. Beltagy, Stephen Roller, Pengxiang Cheng, Katrin Erk, and Raymond J. Mooney. 2016. Representing meaning with a combination of logical and distributional models. *Computational Linguistics*, 42(4):763–808.

Daniel Cer, Mona Diab, Eneko Agirre, Iñigo Lopez-Gazpio, and Lucia Specia. 2017. SemEval-2017 task 1: Semantic textual similarity multilingual and crosslingual focused evaluation. In *Proceedings of the 11th International Workshop on Semantic Evaluation (SemEval-2017)*, pages 1–14, Vancouver, Canada. Association for Computational Linguistics.

Qian Chen, Xiaodan Zhu, Zhen-Hua Ling, Si Wei, Hui Jiang, and Diana Inkpen. 2017. Enhanced LSTM for natural language inference. In *Proceedings of the 55th Annual Meeting of the Association for Computational Linguistics (Volume 1: Long Papers)*, pages 1657–1668, Vancouver, Canada. Association for Computational Linguistics.

Zeming Chen and Qiyue Gao. 2021. Monotonicity marking from universal dependency trees. *CoRR*, abs/2104.08659.

Jacob Devlin, Ming-Wei Chang, Kenton Lee, and Kristina Toutanova. 2019. BERT: Pre-training of deep bidirectional transformers for language understanding. In *Proceedings of the 2019 Conference of the North American Chapter of the Association for Computational Linguistics: Human Language Technologies, Volume 1 (Long and Short Papers)*, pages 4171–4186, Minneapolis, Minnesota. Association for Computational Linguistics.

William B. Dolan and Chris Brockett. 2005. Automatically constructing a corpus of sentential paraphrases. In *Proceedings of the Third International Workshop on Paraphrasing (IWP2005)*.

Max Glockner, Vered Shwartz, and Yoav Goldberg. 2018. Breaking NLI systems with sentences that require simple lexical inferences. In *Proceedings of the 56th Annual Meeting of the Association for Computational Linguistics (Volume 2: Short Papers)*, pages 650–655, Melbourne, Australia. Association for Computational Linguistics.

Suchin Gururangan, Swabha Swayamdipta, Omer Levy, Roy Schwartz, Samuel Bowman, and Noah A. Smith. 2018. Annotation artifacts in natural language inference data. In *Proceedings of the 2018 Conference of the North American Chapter of the Association for Computational Linguistics: Human Language Technologies, Volume 2 (Short Papers)*, pages 107–112, New Orleans, Louisiana. Association for Computational Linguistics.

Izumi Haruta, Koji Mineshima, and Daisuke Bekki. 2020. Combining event semantics and degree semantics for natural language inference. In *Proceedings of the 28th International Conference on Computational Linguistics*, pages 1758–1764, Barcelona, Spain (Online). International Committee on Computational Linguistics.

Hai Hu, Qi Chen, Kyle Richardson, Atreyee Mukherjee, Lawrence S. Moss, and Sandra Kuebler. 2020. MonaLog: a lightweight system for natural language inference based on monotonicity. In *Proceedings of the Society for Computation in Linguistics 2020*, pages 334–344, New York, New York. Association for Computational Linguistics.

Hai Hu and Larry Moss. 2018. Polarity computations in flexible categorial grammar. In *Proceedings of the Seventh Joint Conference on Lexical and Computational Semantics*, pages 124–129, New Orleans, Louisiana. Association for Computational Linguistics.

Aikaterini-Lida Kalouli, Richard Crouch, and Valeria de Paiva. 2020. Hy-NLI: a hybrid system for natural language inference. In *Proceedings of the 28th International Conference on Computational Linguistics*, pages 5235–5249, Barcelona, Spain (Online). International Committee on Computational Linguistics.

Zhenzhong Lan, Mingda Chen, Sebastian Goodman, Kevin Gimpel, Piyush Sharma, and Radu Soricut. 2020. Albert: A lite bert for self-supervised learning of language representations. In *International Conference on Learning Representations*.

Yoav Levine, Barak Lenz, Or Dagan, Ori Ram, Dan Padnos, Or Sharir, Shai Shalev-Shwartz, Amnon Shashua, and Yoav Shoham. 2020. SenseBERT: Driving some sense into BERT. In *Proceedings of the 58th Annual Meeting of the Association for Computational Linguistics*, pages 4656–4667, Online. Association for Computational Linguistics.

H. Liu and P. Singh. 2004. Conceptnet — a practical commonsense reasoning tool-kit. *BT Technology Journal*, 22(4):211–226.

Yinhan Liu, Myle Ott, Naman Goyal, Jingfei Du, Mandar Joshi, Danqi Chen, Omer Levy, Mike Lewis, Luke Zettlemoyer, and Veselin Stoyanov. 2020. Ro{bert}a: A robustly optimized {bert} pretraining approach.

Bill MacCartney and Christopher D. Manning. 2009. An extended model of natural logic. In *Proceedings of the Eighth International Conference on Computational Semantics (IWCS-8)*, Tilburg, Netherlands.

Marco Marelli, Stefano Menini, Marco Baroni, Luisa Bentivogli, Raffaella Bernardi, and Roberto Zamparelli. 2014. A SICK cure for the evaluation of compositional distributional semantic models. In *Proceedings of the Ninth International Conference on Language Resources and Evaluation (LREC'14)*, pages 216–223, Reykjavik, Iceland. European Language Resources Association (ELRA).

Pascual Martínez-Gómez, Koji Mineshima, Yusuke Miyao, and Daisuke Bekki. 2016. ccg2lambda: A compositional semantics system. In *Proceedings of ACL 2016 System Demonstrations*, pages 85–90, Berlin, Germany. Association for Computational Linguistics.

Pascual Martínez-Gómez, Koji Mineshima, Yusuke Miyao, and Daisuke Bekki. 2017. On-demand injection of lexical knowledge for recognising textual entailment. In *Proceedings of the 15th Conference of the European Chapter of the Association for Computational Linguistics: Volume 1, Long Papers*, pages 710–720, Valencia, Spain. Association for Computational Linguistics.

Tom McCoy, Ellie Pavlick, and Tal Linzen. 2019. Right for the wrong reasons: Diagnosing syntactic heuristics in natural language inference. In *Proceedings of the 57th Annual Meeting of the Association for Computational Linguistics*, pages 3428–3448, Florence, Italy. Association for Computational Linguistics.

George A. Miller. 1995. Wordnet: A lexical database for english. *Commun. ACM*, 38(11):39–41.

Ankur Parikh, Oscar Täckström, Dipanjan Das, and Jakob Uszkoreit. 2016. A decomposable attention model for natural language inference. In *Proceedings of the 2016 Conference on Empirical Methods in Natural Language Processing*, pages 2249–2255, Austin, Texas. Association for Computational Linguistics.

Peng Qi, Yuhao Zhang, Yuhui Zhang, Jason Bolton, and Christopher D. Manning. 2020. Stanza: A python natural language processing toolkit for many human languages. In *Proceedings of the 58th Annual Meeting of the Association for Computational Linguistics: System Demonstrations*, pages 101–108, Online. Association for Computational Linguistics.

Radim Řehůřek and Petr Sojka. 2010. Software Framework for Topic Modelling with Large Corpora. In *Proceedings of the LREC 2010 Workshop on New Challenges for NLP Frameworks*, pages 45–50, Valletta, Malta. ELRA. `http://is.muni.cz/publication/884893/en`.

Nils Reimers and Iryna Gurevych. 2019. Sentence-BERT: Sentence embeddings using Siamese BERT-networks. In *Proceedings of the 2019 Conference on Empirical Methods in Natural Language Processing and the 9th International Joint Conference on Natural Language Processing (EMNLP-IJCNLP)*, pages 3982–3992, Hong Kong, China. Association for Computational Linguistics.

Hitomi Yanaka, Koji Mineshima, Daisuke Bekki, Kentaro Inui, Satoshi Sekine, Lasha Abzianidze, and Johan Bos. 2019a. Can neural networks understand monotonicity reasoning? In *Proceedings of the 2019 ACL Workshop BlackboxNLP: Analyzing and Interpreting Neural Networks for NLP*, pages 31–40, Florence, Italy. Association for Computational Linguistics.

Hitomi Yanaka, Koji Mineshima, Daisuke Bekki, Kentaro Inui, Satoshi Sekine, Lasha Abzianidze, and Johan Bos. 2019b. HELP: A dataset for identifying shortcomings of neural models in monotonicity reasoning. In *Proceedings of the Eighth Joint Conference on Lexical and Computational Semantics (*SEM 2019)*, pages 250–255, Minneapolis, Minnesota. Association for Computational Linguistics.

Hitomi Yanaka, Koji Mineshima, Pascual Martínez-Gómez, and Daisuke Bekki. 2018. Acquisition of phrase correspondences using natural deduction proofs. In *Proceedings of the 2018 Conference of the North American Chapter of the Association for Computational Linguistics: Human Language Technologies, Volume 1 (Long Papers)*, pages 756–766, New Orleans, Louisiana. Association for Computational Linguistics.

Wenpeng Yin and Hinrich Schütze. 2017. Task-specific attentive pooling of phrase alignments contributes to sentence matching. In *Proceedings of the 15th Conference of the European Chapter of the Association for Computational Linguistics: Volume 1, Long Papers*, pages 699–709, Valencia, Spain. Association for Computational Linguistics.

Amir Zeldes. 2017. The GUM corpus: Creating multilayer resources in the classroom. *Language Resources and Evaluation*, 51(3):581–612.

Daniel Zeman, Jan Hajič, Martin Popel, Martin Potthast, Milan Straka, Filip Ginter, Joakim Nivre, and Slav Petrov. 2018. CoNLL 2018 shared task: Multilingual parsing from raw text to Universal Dependencies. In *Proceedings of the CoNLL 2018 Shared Task: Multilingual Parsing from Raw Text to Universal Dependencies*, pages 1–21, Brussels, Belgium. Association for Computational Linguistics.

Teach the Rules, Provide the Facts: Targeted Relational-knowledge Enhancement for Textual Inference

Ohad Rozen[1] **Shmuel Amar**[1] **Vered Shwartz**[2,3] **Ido Dagan**[1]
[1]Computer Science Department, Bar-Ilan University, Ramat-Gan, Israel
[2]Allen Institute for Artificial Intelligence
[3]Paul G. Allen School of Computer Science & Engineering, University of Washington
{ohadrozen,shmulikamar}@gmail.com, vereds@allenai.org, dagan@cs.biu.ac.il

Abstract

We present InferBert, a method to enhance transformer-based inference models with relevant relational knowledge. Our approach facilitates learning generic inference patterns requiring relational knowledge (e.g. inferences related to hypernymy) during training, while injecting on-demand the relevant relational facts (e.g. *pangolin* is an *animal*) at test time. We apply InferBERT to the NLI task over a diverse set of inference types (hypernymy, location, color, and country of origin), for which we collected challenge datasets. In this setting, InferBert succeeds to learn general inference patterns, from a relatively small number of training instances, while not hurting performance on the original NLI data and substantially outperforming prior knowledge enhancement models on the challenge data. It further applies its inferences successfully at test time to previously unobserved entities. InferBert is computationally more efficient than most prior methods, in terms of number of parameters, memory consumption and training time.

1 Introduction

Transformer-based pre-trained language models (LMs), such as BERT (Devlin et al., 2019) and GPT (Radford et al., 2018) have recently achieved human-level performance on standard natural language inference (NLI) benchmarks (Wang et al., 2019). However, the performance on this complex task is achieved in part thanks to large training sets that facilitate learning of dataset-specific biases and correlations, and thanks to the similar distributions between the training and test sets, that rewards such models (Poliak et al., 2018; Gururangan et al., 2018). This contrasts with humans, who can learn a generalized solution from fewer examples (Linzen, 2020). Indeed, NLI models often fail on examples involving various linguistic phenomena such as co-hyponymy (Glockner et al., 2018) and negation (Naik et al., 2018), which they are expected to acquire indirectly from the NLI training set.

Prior work proposed to provide ("inoculate") NLI models with a small number of phenomenon-specific training examples in order to teach the model to address them (Liu et al., 2019a). However, Rozen et al. (2019) showed that when the distributions of the training and test sets differ with respect to syntactic and lexical properties, the performance of such inoculated models drops, concluding that they do not learn a generalized notion of the phenomenon. In this paper we are motivated by the following question: *how can we facilitate learning of generalized inference patterns, with respect to a given linguistic phenomenon, from a relatively small number of examples?*

Ideally, we would like an NLI model to learn inference patterns detached from their original context, and to be able to apply them in new contexts involving different concrete facts. For example, an NLI model may learn that a word entails its hypernym in upward monotone sentences from training examples such as: *Alice ate a* *banana* → *Alice ate a* *fruit*. Then, to be able to apply this rule to a test instance with the premise *Bob saw a* *pangolin* and the hypothesis *Bob saw an* *animal*, it needs to know that *animal* is a hypernym of *pangolin*. Training a model on every possible hyponym-hypernym pair is incredibly inefficient and requires re-training a model whenever the vocabulary expands. Instead, we propose to *decouple the learning of generic inference patterns from that of the factual knowledge*.

To that end, we develop InferBert, a method to enhance language models with *relational* knowledge from a knowledge base (KB). In contrast to recent knowledge-enhancement approaches such as KnowBert (Peters et al., 2019) and Ernie (Zhang et al., 2019) that incorporate into LMs knowledge about individual entities (e.g. *pangolin*), we inform

Proceedings of the 10th Conference on Lexical and Computational Semantics, pages 89–98
August 5–6, 2021, Bangkok, Thailand (online)

the LM of the *relation* between a pair of entities that are involved in an inference instance, e.g. Hypernym(*pangolin*) = *animal*. This approach is agnostic to the identity of the specific entities, allowing models to learn inference patterns separately from the individual facts involved in particular instances.

To evaluate the ability of NLI models to learn inference patterns for specific linguistic phenomena, we follow the evaluation approach taken in previous work (Naik et al., 2018; Liu et al., 2019a; Richardson et al., 2020), which demonstrated the learning ability of models over a few chosen inference phenomena. We focus on 4 target semantic relations: hypernymy, location, country of origin, and color, for which we create challenge sets[1] (see Table 1 for examples). We construct the challenge sets such that there is no overlap between the training, validation, and test sets with respect to the target entities (e.g. *pangolin*), to allow testing whether the model had learned an inference phenomenon in a generic manner, rather than performing lexical memorization. The training sets are deliberately small (660-960 instances), aiming to challenge models with learning from a relatively small number of examples per semantic phenomenon.

Our results confirm that InferBert manages to generalize inference patterns to new facts, substantially improving performance on the challenge sets upon the knowledge-enhanced baselines (up to +17.5 points in accuracy from the next best model), all while maintaining the performance on the original MultiNLI test set (Williams et al., 2018).

Moreover, InferBert not only learns from a small number of training examples (which are insufficient for the baselines), it is also considerably more efficient than prior knowledge-enhanced LMs in terms of training time, resources, and memory. InferBert doesn't require LM pre-training, which is a computationally expensive process, and doesn't embed entities, only a small number of relations, substantially reducing the number of parameters with respect to some of the prior work (e.g. only 23% of KnowBert's parameters).

Finally, while InferBert is demonstrated on NLI, it is a general method and may benefit additional tasks such as question answering and co-reference resolution which may rely on relational knowledge between words in given instances.

[1]All datasets and resources are available at https://github.com/ohadrozen/inferbert.

Hypernymy	
P:	He killed another **jay** this season.
H:	He took life away from a **bird** this season.
Label:	Entailment
Relation:	Hypernym(jay)= bird
Location	
P:	It is not located in **Baytown**.
H:	It is located in all cities in **Texas** except for one.
Label:	Neutral
Relation:	LocationOf(Baytown)= Texas
Color	
P:	Tommy ordered tea and apricots.
H:	Tommy did not order any dark brown fruits.
Label:	Neutral
Relation:	none*
Country of Origin	
P:	**Viesgo** deal, from beginning to end, took less than five weeks.
H:	The minimum amount of time it has ever taken a **Spanish** company to close a deal is six weeks.
Label:	Contradiction
Relation:	CountryOfOrigin(Viesgo) = Spain

Table 1: An example from each phenomenon-specific challenge set. *By design, for half of the examples there is no corresponding relation (See Section 3.2).

2 Related Work

2.1 Probing NLI Models

In natural language inference (NLI; Bowman et al., 2015), originally referred as recognizing textual entailment (RTE; Dagan et al., 2013), the goal is to determine whether a first text unit (premise) entails, contradicts, or is neutral with respect to a second text (hypothesis). The decision involves various syntactic and semantic phenomena, including lexical and world knowledge, coreference resolution, geographical reasoning, etc. (Clark, 2018). While neural models have achieved human performance on the GLUE and SuperGLUE benchmarks (Wang et al., 2018, 2019), the success of such models is often due to learning non-generalizable dataset-specific patterns (Poliak et al., 2018; Gururangan et al., 2018; McCoy et al., 2019).

Various challenge sets were developed to test the capabilities of state-of-the-art NLI models in addressing specific semantic phenomena. For example, Glockner et al. (2018) showed that substituting a single term in the premise with a similar but mutually-exclusive term (e.g. *guitar* and *piano*) confused NLI models that predicted entailment. Naik et al. (2018) further showed that NLI models perform poorly on examples involving antonyms, numerical reasoning, and distractions such as high lexical overlap and spelling errors. NLI models also struggled with examples involving logic and monotonicity (Richardson et al., 2020; Yanaka et al., 2020; Geiger et al., 2020).[2] Finally, the GLUE benchmark dedicated a small set for diagnosing models' strengths and weaknesses on various phenomena (Wang et al., 2018).

Liu et al. (2019a) suggested that NLI models may perform poorly on specific phenomena they haven't observed enough during training, and proposed to "inoculate" LM-based models against challenge sets by fine-tuning them on a small number of phenomenon-specific training instances. Rozen et al. (2019) showed that the inoculation does not necessarily teach the model a generalized notion of the phenomenon of interest, and that when the challenge test set differs from the corresponding training sets in terms of, for example, syntactic complexity, the performance of the inoculated models drops. Richardson et al. (2020) highlighted the sensitivity of the inoculation training to hyper-parameters, that may result in "catastrophic forgetting", i.e. a substantial drop in performance on the original NLI task.

2.2 Knowledge-Enhanced Models

There is plenty of work on incorporating knowledge from KBs into neural models. Knowledge-based Inference Model (KIM; Chen et al., 2018) incorporated semantic relations from WordNet into an RNN-based NLI model, gaining a modest improvement on a challenge set. The incorporation at various components of the original NLI model is not straightforward to adapt to other models.

KnowBert (Peters et al., 2019) incorporated knowledge from Wikipedia and WordNet into a BERT model through entity embeddings, improving performance on relation extraction and entity typing. Ernie (Zhang et al., 2019) and K-Adapter (Wang et al., 2020a) both targeted similar downstream tasks. Ernie embeds entities and relations from a KB, and alters the BERT pre-training to predict entities in addition to words. K-Adapter does not re-train the LM weights, but takes a somewhat more efficient approach of training an additional neural component ("adapter") for each knowledge type as a plug-in for the LM. KEPLER (Wang et al., 2020b) learns entity embeddings from their textual descriptions. These entity-centric methods require *pre-training* the original LM or its plugins on the KB, while increasing training time and cost and storing the entity embeddings (increasing memory cost). In addition, by design, the knowledge can capture only entities seen during pre-training, thus requiring repeating the pre-training process each time the original input KB gets updated.

Finally, K-BERT (Liu et al., 2019b) is most similar to our model, incorporating knowledge regarding individual entities that occur in the input instance. Like our model, knowledge is augmented, per-instance, at inference time. Unlike our model, knowledge is augmented per entity, rather than per a relation between a pair of entities appearing in the inference instance. Further, K-BERT injects the KB knowledge in a textual form, which augments the input instance, while our model embeds directly structural knowledge. As we show in Section 6.1, this encoding is less effective than our structured incorporation method (Section 4.2), leading to weaker learning ability of different inference phenomena that require external knowledge.

3 Data

We focus on four types of semantic relations (Section 3.1), each corresponding to a set of *facts* in the form of semantic relation triplets. An NLI model may learn various *inference patterns* pertaining to the semantic relation type, such as "a word entails its hypernym in an upward monotone sentence".

To evaluate the models' ability to learn and apply these rules, we create an NLI challenge set for each semantic relation, that we derive from MultiNLI (Section 3.2). As usual, the goal is to determine the label of a premise-hypothesis pair (p, h) among entailment, neutral, and contradiction. For a given semantic relation, each instance in the corresponding challenge set requires applying an inference pattern associated with the semantic relation in order to determine the correct label (possibly along with other required inferences).

3.1 Semantic Relations

Hypernymy. An NLI system might learn that a term generally entails its generalization, for example "I ate an *apple*" entails "I ate a *fruit*".[3] The relevant facts for this semantic relation are pairs of (x, y) terms that appear in a direct or indirect

[2] The "Countries/Travel" genre in Richardson et al. (2020) is similar to our location phenomenon described in Section 3.1.

[3] The rule applies to upward monotone premises. Downward monotone premises (which typically include a negated predicate or certain quantifiers) reverse the inference direction.

KB entry: **Emporis** `CountryOfOrigin` (property): **Germany**
Extracted Premise: *These forms will be posted on **Apple** website.* Premise: *These forms will be posted on **Emporis** website.*
Manually created hypotheses: (1) *A company in **Germany** will make the forms available on its website.* (Entailment) (2) *The forms cannot be accessed from the website of any **German** company.* (Contradiction) (3) *Several **German** websites will feature the forms.* (Neutral)
Hypotheses with property replacement: (4) *A company in **France** will make the forms available on its website.* (Neutral) (5) *The forms cannot be accessed from the website of any **French** company.* (Neutral) (6) *Several **French** websites will feature the forms.* (Neutral)

Table 2: Example of premise and hypotheses generation from a MultiNLI premise. Hypotheses (1)-(3) were created by crowdworkers for the altered premise, based on the Wikidata fact that Emporis' country of origin is Germany. Hypotheses (4)-(6) were created by replacing *German* with another country of origin (*France*) and annotated for entailment.

Inference Type	Train	Dev	Test	All
Hypernymy	960	114	300	1374
Location	660	114	230	1004
Color	840	108	318	1266
Country of Origin	834	114	252	1200
Total	3294	450	1100	4844

Table 3: Statistics of our challenge set.

hypernymy relation in WordNet (Miller, 1995).[4]

Location. A model may learn that in some contexts, substituting a city name by the state in which it is located yields a factually correct generalization (e.g. "John visited *Chicago*" entails "John visited *Illinois*"). We retrieve entities from Wikidata (Vrandečić and Krötzsch, 2014), focusing on US locations using the `state` property.

Color. We retrieve entities from Wikidata and their `color` property. We substitute an entity (e.g. *banana*) for a generalization involving its color and hypernym (e.g. *yellow fruit*).

Country of Origin. We retrieve knowledge from Wikidata about companies and their country of origin, using the `country` property. We substitute an entity (e.g. *Apple*) for a generalization involving its country of origin (e.g. *American* organization).

3.2 Challenge Sets

Some of the semantic relations we focused on are very rare in the original MultiNLI dataset, e.g. by heuristically searching for instances that exhibit these phenomena we found that less than 0.05% of the data contained locations. We therefore create challenge sets focusing on each semantic relation. In order to create challenge examples in a similar style and domain, we base our examples on premises in MultiNLI.

For a given semantic relation r, we extract premises in the MultiNLI training set that contain an entity I_0^{tail} whose type corresponds to the relation argument. For example, for the *country of origin* semantic relation we extract premises containing company names (e.g. $I_0^{tail} = Apple$) in our data. For a given premise p, we modify it by replacing I_0^{tail} by a random entity I_1^{tail} of the same type in the KB (e.g. *Emporis*), and manually check that the sentence still makes sense. We specifically select replacement entities I_1^{tail} such that there exists a KB assertion $R(I_1^{tail}) = I_1^{head}$. For example, `CountryOfOrigin`(*Emporis*) = *Germany*.

From each premise p we created 6 hypotheses as follows (See Table 2). Similarly to Williams et al. (2018), we showed p to crowdsourcing workers and asked them to generate a hypothesis for each label (entailment, neutral and contradiction). Our instructions further specified that the hypothesis must include I_1^{head} (e.g. *Germany*) but not I_1^{tail} (e.g. *Emporis*). Examples (1)-(3) in Table 2 demonstrate the instances created at this step.

After creating 3 hypotheses, all of which include I_1^{head} by design, we replaced I_1^{head} with $\hat{I}_1^{head}$, where $\hat{I}_1^{head} \neq I_1^{head}$ is a random value of the

[4]Excluding instance hypernyms.

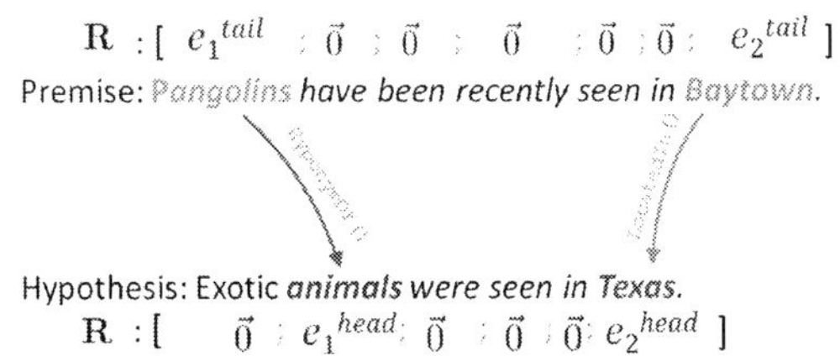

Embeddings	Relation	Side
e_1^{head}	Hypernymy	head (Hypernym)
e_1^{tail}	Hypernymy	tail (Hyponym)
e_2^{head}	Location	head (State)
e_2^{tail}	Location	tail (Location)
...		...

Figure 1: Relation embedding example. After extracting the related entity pairs for the relations r_1 =*hypernymy* and r_2 =*location*, we place the embedding vectors in $\mathbf{R}$ in the indices of the relevant tokens of the entities. For example, we place e_2^{head} in the index of *Texas* as this entity is the head in the relation *location*.

same property R (e.g. *France*). We then asked an annotator to label the new hypotheses with respect to p (Table 2, instances (4)-(6)).

The annotation task was performed using Amazon Mechanical Turk. To ensure the quality of the work, we required that workers had a minimum of 96% acceptance rate for prior HITs and pass a qualification test. We paid $1 for each premise. The test set was further validated by two trained annotators. The first annotator re-labeled an example, and, in case of disagreement with the original label (11.9% of the annotations), the second annotator also labeled the example, and the majority vote[5] was used.

Data Split. The statistics of the challenge sets are shown in Table 3. We split the datasets to 68%-9%-23% train, dev and test, respectively. The datasets are split lexically, i.e. such that head and tail entities in one set do not appear in the other sets. That way, a good performance on the test set indicates that the model learned a generalized notion of an inference rule rather than specific facts, and that it is capable of applying the rule when provided with the necessary yet not previously observed facts.

4 InferBert

We present InferBert, a BERT-based NLI model with a relational knowledge enhancement component. The key idea in InferBert is incorporating into the model relational knowledge (*facts*) from external knowledge resources regarding entities mentioned in the input instance. We adopt an inclusive definition of entity, which can refer either to a named entity (such as entries in Wikidata) or a common noun (such as WordNet lemmas).

As we discussed in Section 2.2, most prior work injects external knowledge into models through an entity's knowledge base embedding, which captures in a soft way its relationships with other KB entities. The limitation of such methods is the coupling of an inference pattern with the related factual knowledge. Suppose that a model observed during training that "*The boy ate an apple*" entails "*The boy ate a fruit*". The test example with the premise "*The woman has a dog*" and the hypothesis "*The woman has a pet*" is represented differently from the training example due to the distance between the entities (e.g. *apple* and *dog*) in the KB. Such a model is likely to fail on examples consisting of unseen entities.

We propose to decouple learning the *inference pattern* from the *facts* by directly embedding the semantic relations between entities in the text. In the above example, InferBert can access the KB during both the training and inference phases, and add an indicator that `fruit=Hypernym(apple)`. After observing enough training examples with the hypernym indicator, the model can learn a general rule like "a word entails its hypernym in certain common context". During inference, the model can apply this rule to unseen entities in the KB.

We first describe the KnowBert model (Peters et al., 2019, Section 4.1) which is the basis for InferBert. Next, we describe how we replace KnowBert's Knowledge Attention and Recontextualization component (KAR) by our Simplified KAR (S-KAR, Section 4.2).

4.1 KnowBert's KAR

KnowBert is a method to incorporate knowledge from KBs into transformer-based language models, which was specifically applied to BERTBASE. For a given input $X = (x_1, ..., x_N)$ of N word pieces, the BERT contextual embeddings are computed as $\mathbf{H_i} = \text{TransformerBlock}(\mathbf{H_{i-1}})$ where $\mathbf{H_i} \in \mathbb{R}^{N \times D}$ is the i-th hidden layer ($i \in \{1, ..., L\}$, and $L = 12$ layers) and D is BERT's embedding dimension. TransformerBlock operates over a query, key, and

[5]All three annotations were given an equal weight.

value, and is defined as $\text{TransformerBlock}(\mathbf{H_i}) = \text{MLP}(\text{MultiHeadAttn}(\mathbf{H_i}, \mathbf{H_i}, \mathbf{H_i}))$.

The Knowledge Attention and Recontextualization component (KAR) is added between BERT layers i and $i-1$, changing the embedding mechanism to: $\mathbf{H'_i} = \text{KAR}(\mathbf{H_i}, \mathcal{C})$, which is computed as follows:

Retrieval: The KB entity candidate selector provides a list of C potential entity links for X, along with their mention spans in X.

Disambiguation: Each mention span is represented by applying self-attention pooling over all word pieces in the span (after projection to the entity embedding dimension E), yielding $S \in \mathbb{R}^{C\times E}$. To select the relevant entities in the context, mention-span self-attention is applied to compute $S^e = \text{TransformerBlock}(S)$, followed by computing candidate entity scores ψ based on S^e.

Knowledge incorporation: The entity embeddings are averaged to $\tilde{e}$ based on their weight ψ, and are used to enhance the mention-span representations, yielding $S'^e = S^e + \tilde{e}$.

Recontextualization: The BERT word piece representations are recontextualized using a modified transformer layer in which S'^e is used as both the key and value for MultiHeadAttn. The resulting vectors $\mathbf{H'_i}$ are projected back into the BERT dimension D.

4.2 S-KAR

The main component of InferBert is the Simplified Knowledge Attention and Recontextualization component (S-KAR). Rather than enhancing BERT with KB entity embeddings, InferBert embeds the KB relations.

Similarly to KAR, S-KAR replaces BERT's embedding mechanism between two particular layers, computing: $\mathbf{H'_i} = \text{S-KAR}(\mathbf{H_i}, \mathcal{C})$, which is then used to compute the next layer: $\mathbf{H_{i+1}} = \text{TransformerBlock}(\mathbf{H'_i})$, and the remainder of BERT is run as usual. S-KAR operates as follows:

Retrieval: We follow KnowBert (Peters et al., 2019) and adopt a broad definition for a KB as a collection of (tail entity, relation, head entity) triplets, focusing on K relation types of interest: $\mathcal{R} = \{R_1, ..., R_K\}$. For each relation type R_k we learn two embedding vectors, e_k^{head} and e_k^{tail}, representing the head and the tail entity slots in this relation.[6]

We assume that for a given relation set $\mathcal{R}$, the KB is accompanied by a relation extractor, which takes a text X as input and returns a list of triplets:

$$\mathcal{C} = \{(\text{head}_m, \text{tail}_m, r_m) | m \in 1..|\mathcal{C}|, r_m \in \mathcal{R}\}$$

where head_m and tail_m are the indices of the first token of the head and tail entities in the text $(1, ..., N)$, and r_m is the relation, as illustrated in Figure 1.

Disambiguation: We focus on unambiguous entities, i.e. those with a single KB entry, with respect to relation type, and extract only entities of the relevant type.[7] For example, though *Pitcher* has multiple entries in Wikidata, only one of them is a location.

Knowledge incorporation: For a given list of triplets $\mathcal{C}$, S-KAR creates the relation embedding matrix $\mathbf{R} \in \mathbb{R}^{N\times E}$ such that the head embedding e_m^{head} is in index head_m, the related tail embedding vector e_m^{tail} is in index tail_m, and the remaining entries are set to $\vec{0}$. We incorporate this relation embeddings into the BERT vectors: $\mathbf{S'_i} = \mathbf{H_i^{proj}} + \mathbf{R}$, where $\mathbf{H_i^{proj}}$ is the projection of $\mathbf{H_i}$ into the relation embedding dimension $E = 768$.

Recontextualization: the recontextualization step is identical to KAR.

5 Experimental Setup

BERT model. Our model assumes access to a pre-trained BERT model with or without additional fine-tuning on the target downstream task. Specifically, we used the English uncased $\text{BERT}_{\text{BASE}}$ model (Devlin et al., 2019) fine-tuned on the MultiNLI dataset (Williams et al., 2018). Based on preliminary experiments, the S-KAR layer was inserted between the first and second layers of BERT.

Relational data. We retrieve relational data from WordNet and Wikidata (See Section 3.1). For a given premise p and hypothesis h we retrieve a relevant KB tuple list of triplets $\{(\text{head}_m, \text{tail}_m, r_m)\}$ (Section 4.2) when the head is in the premise, tail is

[6]We did not explore symmetric relations in this work, but they can be straightforwardly implemented by learning a single vector for both entity slots of the relation.

[7]We use spaCy NER (Honnibal and Montani, 2017) to extract the relevant entity types: LOC for locations, ORG for names of companies, and nouns for hyponyms and colors.

	Model	Entities	Hypernymy	Location	Color	Origin	MultiNLI*
LM-based Model	BERT	seen	64.7	77.6	62.2	70.6	-
		unseen	65.7	68.3	58.5	69.1	83.4
Knowledge-Enhanced Models	KnowBert	seen	74.0	83.5	67.2	78.2	-
		unseen	66.7	69.1	59.1	70.6	82.3
	K-BERT	seen	68.0	81.7	62.2	75.0	-
		unseen	68.3	67.6	56.6	71.4	83.2
	InferBert	seen	81.7	83.3	**77.2**	86.9	-
		unseen	**82.0**	**83.9**	72.0	**88.9**	82.3

Table 4: Performance on the challenge test sets and MultiNLI. Models were tested on either entities that appear in the training set (**seen**) or new entities (**unseen**). *Seen and unseen results are not relevant for MultiNLI.

in the hypothesis, and head $\neq$ tail. Since we focus on unambiguous entities (in the context of a given relation), we do not need to use an entity linker. We make sure that the target entities in the train, validation, and test sets are distinct, but that they all have entries in the relevant KB.

Training data. We train a single model on the combination of the challenge sets to learn phenomena related to all the semantic relations. To avoid "catastrophic forgetting", i.e. decrease in the performance on the original task (MultiNLI), we mix the challenge training set with a random sample of 10K MultiNLI training set instances and train on the mixed datasets. The training objective assigns more weight to the challenge examples: $\mathcal{L}'_{\text{BERT}} = \gamma \cdot \mathcal{L}_{\text{BERT}}$, where $\gamma > 1$ is a hyper-parameter fine-tuned on the validation set.

Training procedure. The model consists of a pre-trained BERT model and randomly initialized InferBert parameters (S-KAR weights and relation embeddings). To embed both sets of parameters in the same space, we follow KnowBert and train the model in two phases. In the first phase, we freeze the pre-trained BERT parameters and update only the S-KAR and the relation embeddings for 3 epochs. In the second phase we freeze the recently trained InferBert parameters and unfreeze the BERT parameters, training for another epoch.[8]

Baselines. We compare InferBert with two representative knowledge-informed models, KnowBert and K-BERT, as well as a $\text{BERT}_{\text{BASE}}$ NLI model. All the baselines are trained on MultiNLI and further fine-tuned on the the joint challenge set (mixed with a subset of MultiNLI).

For fair comparison, K-BERT used the same entity extraction mechanism, followed the same fine-tuning procedure, and was given access to the exact same data as InferBert. KnowBert, on the other hand, requires re-training a new model on new data. Because of its resource requirements, we used the available pre-trained KnowBert model. It is enhanced with knowledge about 470K entities from Wikipedia and all of WordNet, fully covering the knowledge in our hypernymy and location challenge sets, but only some of the entities in the color and country of origin sets[9]. Thus, the results for KnowBert on these two phenomena are not fully comparable to those of InferBert.

Hyper-parameters. Fine-tuning on MultiNLI followed the original hyper-parameters described in Devlin et al. (2019). When fine-tuning InferBert on the challenge sets, we selected the best hyper-parameter values based on the performance on the validation sets. The learning rate for S-KAR was chosen between 0.003-0.007 in steps of 0.001, and was set to 0.006. The rest of the parameters were trained with a learning rate of 9e-6 (selected between 3e-6 and 4e-5). We tested γ values among $\{2, 4, 6, 8, 10, 12\}$ and selected $\gamma = 4$. Fine-tuning was done on a single GeForce GTX 1080 GPU with batch size of 32. A single InferBert forward and backward pass took 0.35 seconds. K-BERT's best validation performance was achieved after 3 epochs with a learning rate of 3e-5 and KnowBert's after 4 epochs with a learning rate of 2e-5.

6 Experiments

We present the results of InferBert and the baselines on the various challenge sets (Section 6.1). We also test the ability of models to learn relational knowledge about entities seen during training (Section 6.2). Finally, we analyze InferBert's efficiency

[8]The first phase of KnowBert trains only the entity embeddings but not KAR, while we also include the S-KAR weights.

[9]All entities in our hypernymy challenge set are covered in WordNet, and all entities in our location set has corresponding entries in the Wikipedia subset used by KnowBert.

in terms of memory and runtime compared to the baselines (Section 6.3).

6.1 Performance on the Challenge Sets

Table 4 ("unseen" lines) shows the performance of InferBert and the baselines on the various challenge sets and on the MultiNLI[10] development set. The knowledge-enhanced baseline models slightly outperform BERT on all semantic relations. InferBert performs the best, with a large gap from the baselines (up to 20 points), demonstrating its ability to learn and generalize inference patterns and apply them to new relation instances, as well as to new entities.

K-BERT performs slightly better than KnowBert, yet worse than InferBert. We hypothesize that K-BERT and InferBert enjoy the advantage of having access to relational knowledge at inference time, which facilitates learning general inference patterns and applying them to new facts, on demand. With that said, the K-BERT method of incorporating relational knowledge as free text is less structured and likely leads to less efficient learning of inference patterns (with the limited amount of available training data).

InferBert retains a high performance on the MultiNLI matched development set, with 2.3% reduction from the original $\text{BERT}_{\text{BASE}}$ model (84.6%). KnowBert achieve similar performance, while K-BERT performs slightly better on it.

6.2 Seen vs. Unseen Entities

In contrast to our original test sets, in which the entities has not been seen during training, in this experiment we analyze how the models perform with entities that were all seen in the challenge training set. For that, we duplicated our test sets, while replacing test triplets (head, tail, relation) with others that are included in the training set. The rest of the words remained the same, and we made sure (manually) that the new test examples are analogously sensible and that their entailment labels have not changed. Results are shown in Table 4 in the *seen* rows. Evidently, InferBert shows impressive robustness when facing unseen entities, unlike other models that seem to depend significantly on seeing the test entities already in training time. In fact, when faced with new entities, the other models performance gets closer to that of original BERT (with no knowledge injected).

[10]We used MultiNLI dev-matched.

6.3 Efficiency Analysis

While large language models lead to performance boost on standard benchmarks, the NLP community had begun paying more attention to developing more resource-efficient NLP models (Moosavi et al., 2020). In the design of InferBert we took efficiency into consideration. First, InferBert is significantly less memory consuming than KnowBert, which stores up-front the embeddings for all entities in memory. KnowBert trained on Wikipedia and WordNet uses BERTBASE (110M parameters), to which it adds the KAR component (7.3M) and the embeddings of 471K entities (406M parameters), resulting in 523.3M parameters. Conversely, instead of entity embeddings, InferBert supports up to $K = 500$ relation types $\times$ 2 vectors (tail and head) $\times$ each with dimension $E = 768$, resulting in 768K parameters. The SKAR component takes up 8.3M parameters. Overall, InferBert has 119.1 parameters, only 23% of KnowBert's parameters. Second, as opposed to InferBert, KnowBert required a pre-training step in which the 471K instances (corresponding to KB entities) were processed.

InferBert achieved better performance than KnowBert on the challenge set with as little as 1,000 examples per relation (Table 4). We conjecture that the InferBert training is more data efficient as it is not required to learn about specific head or tail entities (e.g. *Emporis* and *Germany*) but about relationships, (e.g. `Hypernymy`) which occur more frequently in the training data.

Finally, we note that, similar to our model, K-BERT is also memory and parameter efficient since it does not store entity embeddings (as KnowBert does). Rather, it only involves fine-tuning the BERT parameters, thanks to representing the enhanced knowledge in textual form as part of the instance input. Our model does incorporate a modest number of additional parameters for structured relation embeddings, which, as shown in our experiment, leads to substantial performance gains over K-BERT's textual representations.

7 Conclusions

We presented InferBert, a generic and efficient method to incorporate relational knowledge into transformer-based inference models. Our approach targets specific inference phenomena that require external relational knowledge, allowing the model to learn generic inference patterns decoupled from the factual knowledge required for a particular instance, which is injected at inference time. Our experiments show that InferBert successfully applies the learned patterns to unseen facts, where other knowledge enhancement models fail. Unlike most prior work, InferBert does not require pre-training the LM on a KB, and consumes less memory.

Our work joins the effort of others to improve models by teaching them specific inference phenomena (Liu et al., 2019a; Richardson et al., 2020). A natural direction for future work would be to apply our methodology to a broader range of inference phenomena and adapt them for additional inference tasks.

Acknowledgments

The work described herein was supported in part by grants from Intel Labs, Facebook, the Israel Science Foundation grant 1951/17, the Israeli Ministry of Science and Technology and the German Research Foundation through the German-Israeli Project Cooperation (DIP, grant DA 1600/1-1).

References

Samuel R. Bowman, Gabor Angeli, Christopher Potts, and Christopher D. Manning. 2015. A large annotated corpus for learning natural language inference. In *Proceedings of the 2015 Conference on Empirical Methods in Natural Language Processing*, pages 632–642, Lisbon, Portugal. Association for Computational Linguistics.

Qian Chen, Xiaodan Zhu, Zhen-Hua Ling, Diana Inkpen, and Si Wei. 2018. Neural natural language inference models enhanced with external knowledge. In *Proceedings of the 56th Annual Meeting of the Association for Computational Linguistics (Volume 1: Long Papers)*, pages 2406–2417, Melbourne, Australia. Association for Computational Linguistics.

Peter Clark. 2018. What knowledge is needed to solve the rte5 textual entailment challenge? *arXiv preprint arXiv:1806.03561*.

Ido Dagan, Dan Roth, Mark Sammons, and Fabio Massimo Zanzotto. 2013. Recognizing textual entailment: Models and applications. *Synthesis Lectures on Human Language Technologies*, 6(4):1–220.

Jacob Devlin, Ming-Wei Chang, Kenton Lee, and Kristina Toutanova. 2019. BERT: Pre-training of deep bidirectional transformers for language understanding. In *Proceedings of the 2019 Conference of the North American Chapter of the Association for Computational Linguistics: Human Language Technologies, Volume 1 (Long and Short Papers)*, pages 4171–4186, Minneapolis, Minnesota. Association for Computational Linguistics.

Atticus Geiger, Kyle Richardson, and Christopher Potts. 2020. Neural natural language inference models partially embed theories of lexical entailment and negation. In *Proceedings of the Third BlackboxNLP Workshop on Analyzing and Interpreting Neural Networks for NLP*, pages 163–173, Online. Association for Computational Linguistics.

Max Glockner, Vered Shwartz, and Yoav Goldberg. 2018. Breaking NLI systems with sentences that require simple lexical inferences. In *Proceedings of the 56th Annual Meeting of the Association for Computational Linguistics (Volume 2: Short Papers)*, pages 650–655, Melbourne, Australia. Association for Computational Linguistics.

Suchin Gururangan, Swabha Swayamdipta, Omer Levy, Roy Schwartz, Samuel Bowman, and Noah A. Smith. 2018. Annotation artifacts in natural language inference data. In *Proceedings of the 2018 Conference of the North American Chapter of the Association for Computational Linguistics: Human Language Technologies, Volume 2 (Short Papers)*, pages 107–112, New Orleans, Louisiana. Association for Computational Linguistics.

Matthew Honnibal and Ines Montani. 2017. spacy 2: Natural language understanding with bloom embeddings, convolutional neural networks and incremental parsing. *To appear*, 7(1):411–420.

Tal Linzen. 2020. How can we accelerate progress towards human-like linguistic generalization? In *Proceedings of the 58th Annual Meeting of the Association for Computational Linguistics*, pages 5210–5217, Online. Association for Computational Linguistics.

Nelson F. Liu, Roy Schwartz, and Noah A. Smith. 2019a. Inoculation by fine-tuning: A method for analyzing challenge datasets. In *Proceedings of the 2019 Conference of the North American Chapter of the Association for Computational Linguistics: Human Language Technologies, Volume 1 (Long and Short Papers)*, pages 2171–2179, Minneapolis, Minnesota. Association for Computational Linguistics.

Weijie Liu, Peng Zhou, Zhe Zhao, Zhiruo Wang, Qi Ju, Haotang Deng, and Ping Wang. 2019b. K-BERT: enabling language representation with knowledge graph. *CoRR*, abs/1909.07606.

Tom McCoy, Ellie Pavlick, and Tal Linzen. 2019. Right for the wrong reasons: Diagnosing syntactic heuristics in natural language inference. In *Proceedings of the 57th Annual Meeting of the Association for Computational Linguistics*, pages 3428–3448, Florence, Italy. Association for Computational Linguistics.

George A. Miller. 1995. Wordnet: A lexical database for english. *COMMUNICATIONS OF THE ACM*, 38:39–41.

Nafise Sadat Moosavi, Angela Fan, Vered Shwartz, Goran Glavaš, Shafiq Joty, Alex Wang, and Thomas Wolf, editors. 2020. *Proceedings of SustaiNLP: Workshop on Simple and Efficient Natural Language Processing*. Association for Computational Linguistics, Online.

Aakanksha Naik, Abhilasha Ravichander, Norman Sadeh, Carolyn Rose, and Graham Neubig. 2018. Stress test evaluation for natural language inference. In *Proceedings of the 27th International Conference on Computational Linguistics*, pages 2340–2353, Santa Fe, New Mexico, USA. Association for Computational Linguistics.

Matthew E. Peters, Mark Neumann, Robert Logan, Roy Schwartz, Vidur Joshi, Sameer Singh, and Noah A. Smith. 2019. Knowledge enhanced contextual word representations. In *Proceedings of the 2019 Conference on Empirical Methods in Natural Language Processing and the 9th International Joint Conference on Natural Language Processing (EMNLP-IJCNLP)*, pages 43–54, Hong Kong, China. Association for Computational Linguistics.

Adam Poliak, Aparajita Haldar, Rachel Rudinger, J. Edward Hu, Ellie Pavlick, Aaron Steven White, and Benjamin Van Durme. 2018. Collecting diverse natural language inference problems for sentence representation evaluation. In *Proceedings of the 2018 Conference on Empirical Methods in Natural Language Processing*, pages 67–81, Brussels, Belgium. Association for Computational Linguistics.

Alec Radford, Karthik Narasimhan, Tim Salimans, and Ilya Sutskever. 2018. Improving language understanding by generative pre-training. *URL https://s3-us-west-2. amazonaws. com/openai-assets/research-covers/language-unsupervised/language_ understanding_paper. pdf*.

Kyle Richardson, Hai Hu, Lawrence S Moss, and Ashish Sabharwal. 2020. Probing natural language inference models through semantic fragments. In *AAAI*.

Ohad Rozen, Vered Shwartz, Roee Aharoni, and Ido Dagan. 2019. Diversify your datasets: Analyzing generalization via controlled variance in adversarial datasets. In *Proceedings of the 23rd Conference on Computational Natural Language Learning (CoNLL)*, pages 196–205, Hong Kong, China. Association for Computational Linguistics.

Denny Vrandečić and Markus Krötzsch. 2014. Wikidata: a free collaborative knowledgebase. *Communications of the ACM*, 57(10):78–85.

Alex Wang, Yada Pruksachatkun, Nikita Nangia, Amanpreet Singh, Julian Michael, Felix Hill, Omer Levy, and Samuel R Bowman. 2019. Superglue: A stickier benchmark for general-purpose language understanding systems. In *Neurips*.

Alex Wang, Amanpreet Singh, Julian Michael, Felix Hill, Omer Levy, and Samuel Bowman. 2018. GLUE: A multi-task benchmark and analysis platform for natural language understanding. In *Proceedings of the 2018 EMNLP Workshop BlackboxNLP: Analyzing and Interpreting Neural Networks for NLP*, pages 353–355, Brussels, Belgium. Association for Computational Linguistics.

Ruize Wang, Duyu Tang, Nan Duan, Zhongyu Wei, Xuanjing Huang, Jianshu ji, Guihong Cao, Daxin Jiang, and Ming Zhou. 2020a. K-adapter: Infusing knowledge into pre-trained models with adapters.

Xiaozhi Wang, Tianyu Gao, Zhaocheng Zhu, Zhiyuan Liu, Juanzi Li, and Jian Tang. 2020b. KEPLER: A unified model for knowledge embedding and pretrained language representation. *TACL*.

Adina Williams, Nikita Nangia, and Samuel Bowman. 2018. A broad-coverage challenge corpus for sentence understanding through inference. In *Proceedings of the 2018 Conference of the North American Chapter of the Association for Computational Linguistics: Human Language Technologies, Volume 1 (Long Papers)*, pages 1112–1122, New Orleans, Louisiana. Association for Computational Linguistics.

Hitomi Yanaka, Koji Mineshima, Daisuke Bekki, and Kentaro Inui. 2020. Do neural models learn systematicity of monotonicity inference in natural language? In *Proceedings of the 58th Annual Meeting of the Association for Computational Linguistics*, pages 6105–6117, Online. Association for Computational Linguistics.

Zhengyan Zhang, Xu Han, Zhiyuan Liu, Xin Jiang, Maosong Sun, and Qun Liu. 2019. ERNIE: Enhanced language representation with informative entities. In *Proceedings of the 57th Annual Meeting of the Association for Computational Linguistics*, pages 1441–1451, Florence, Italy. Association for Computational Linguistics.

ParsFEVER: a Dataset for Farsi Fact Extraction and Verification

Majid Zarharan[†], **Mahsa Ghaderan**[†], **Amin Pourdabiri**[†], **Zahra Sayedi**[†]
Behrouz Minaei-Bidgoli[†], **Sauleh Eetemadi**[†], and **Mohammad Taher Pilehvar**[‡]
[†]Iran University of Science and Technology, Tehran, Iran
[‡]Tehran Institute for Advanced Studies, Tehran, Iran
{majid_zarharan,m_ghaderan,amin_pourdabiri,s_sayedi}@comp.iust.ac.ir, {b_minaei,sauleh}@iust.ac.ir, mp792@cam.ac.uk

Abstract

Training and evaluation of automatic fact extraction and verification techniques require large amounts of annotated data which might not be available for low-resource languages. This paper presents ParsFEVER: the first publicly available Farsi dataset for fact extraction and verification. We adopt the construction procedure of the standard English dataset for the task, i.e., FEVER, and improve it for the case of low-resource languages. Specifically, claims are extracted from sentences that are carefully selected to be more informative. The dataset comprises nearly 23K manually-annotated claims. Over 65% of the claims in ParsFEVER are many-hop (require evidence from multiple sources), making the dataset a challenging benchmark (only 13% of the claims in FEVER are many-hop). Also, despite having a smaller training set (around one-ninth of that in Fever), a model trained on ParsFEVER attains similar downstream performance, indicating the quality of the dataset. We release the dataset and the annotation guidelines at https://github.com/Zarharan/ParsFEVER.

1 Introduction

The spread of false information can lead to severe social and political problems (Wang, 2017). It would be extremely difficult to detect and track false information manually, given that the abundance of available technology has made it possible for these to be produced at scale and disseminated rapidly. Therefore, there has been a lot of interest in developing natural language technologies for fact-checking (Thorne and Vlachos, 2018). Unfortunately, similarly to many other fields of NLP that rely on manually curated datasets, fact-checking has remained restricted to a few high-resource languages for which large-scale annotated datasets are available.

In this paper, we present ParsFEVER, the first Farsi fact extraction and verification dataset. The dataset opens room for research in fact-checking and verification on low-resourced languages. ParsFEVER is constructed based on FEVER (Thorne et al., 2018), the most widely used dataset for fact-checking and fake news detection in English. We collected 22,906 claims by altering sentences extracted from introductory sections of 358 popular articles from Farsi Wikipedia. Annotators manually classified these claims into SUPPORTED, REFUTED, or NOTENOUGHINFO based on the provided reference pages. In addition, the annotators tagged those sentences which they used as evidence for this classification. Therefore, the dataset can be used for both fact-checking (a 3-class classification task) and evidence retrieval (which is a necessary step for the classification).

The quality of the dataset was evaluated using three different validation checks: (1) 5-way inter-annotator agreement, (2) agreement against super-annotators[1], and (3) manual validation by the authors. We also report experimental results for when ParsFEVER was used as a benchmark for the fact-checking task. In this task, given an input claim the model is expected to support or refute it and provide the corresponding evidence for this decision. If no enough evidence is found, NOTENOUGHINFO is returned. We evaluated the baseline system provided for FEVER on our dataset. The results indicate the more challenging nature of ParsFEVER: 50.0% (vs. 52.1% in FEVER) accuracy on a held-out test set on claim classification, and 28.1% (vs. 32.6% in FEVER) for evidence retrieval. Finally, we release ParsFEVER and related tools to allow further research on low-resource fact-checking, particularly in Farsi.

[1]The annotators who were responsible for training and leading other annotators.

Proceedings of the 10th Conference on Lexical and Computational Semantics, pages 99–104
August 5–6, 2021, Bangkok, Thailand (online) ©2021 Association for Computational Linguistics

2 Related Work

The only related datasets in Farsi are those of Zarharan et al. (2019) and Zamani et al. (2017). The former is a dataset for Farsi stance detection containing hundreds of instances in the news domain. Unlike ParsFEVER, the dataset does not provide any evidence for the claims; hence, it can only be used for a constrained fact-checking evaluation setting where evidences are already extracted for verifying stance. Also, the dataset of Zamani et al. (2017) is targeted towards rumor detection in Farsi tweets, which mostly relies on Twitter-specific features such as user profile information and response/retweet structure. In contrast, our dataset mostly focuses on lexical features.

ParsFEVER is mainly based on FEVER, a dataset widely used for fact extraction and verification in English. The dataset consists of around 185K claims generated by modifying sentences extracted from Wikipedia. The claims are classified as SUPPORTED, REFUTED, and NOTENOGHINFO. Despite being based on FEVER, our dataset has some fundamental differences that aim at making a more challenging benchmark for low-resourced languages. In the following section, we elaborate on the construction procedure of our dataset and the differences it has to that used for FEVER.

Other related datasets include HOVER (Jiang et al., 2020) and LIAR (Wang, 2017). HOVER is a dataset for many-hop fact extraction and claim verification. Unlike our dataset, which consists of single sentence claims, HOVER includes claims from one sentence up to one paragraph. It consists of 26K claims with SUPPORTED or NOTSUPPORTED labels. LIAR was instead derived from the short statements extracted from POLITIFACT.COM for fake news detection. This dataset contains 12.8K human-labeled instances.

Other related datasets in the social media domain include PHEME (Zubiaga et al., 2016b) and RumourEval (Zubiaga et al., 2016a). PHEME consists of 5,802 comment threads collected from Twitter, with approximately 103K tweets. This dataset has 1,972 and 3,830 threads labeled as rumour and non-rumour, respectively, resulting in an imbalanced dataset. RumourEval was released as part of the SemEval-2017 Task 8 (Derczynski et al., 2017). The dataset contains 330 rumour threads (4,842 tweets) from Twitter, annotated for both stance and veracity.

3 Dataset

Performing accurate fact-checking at scale requires a high-quality dataset along with the necessary algorithms and models. While there is a significant volume of research on the algorithms and models, they are generally language-agnostic. However, the datasets must be developed for each language independently. In this work, while using FEVER as a baseline, we modify their approach to make it more suitable for low-resource languages like Farsi.

Thorne et al. (2018) processed the June 2017 Wikipedia dump with Stanford CoreNLP (Manning et al., 2014) to collect sentences from the introductory sections of approximately 5K popular pages. In addition to this set of *primary* pages, all the related (*secondary*) pages[2] are retrieved. Following this procedure, we manually selected a set of 358 articles from the most popular Farsi pages crawled from fa.wikipedia.org. While FEVER provides an annotation tool, it leverages proprietary services which are not publicly available. Hence we developed our own Wikipedia crawler and annotation tools, which we release along with our dataset and annotation guidelines.

Table 1 shows two samples from ParsFEVER. In what follows in this section, we describe our procedure for constructing and validating the dataset.

3.1 Construction

The construction procedure of ParsFEVER consists of two phases; claim generation and claim labeling.

3.1.1 Phase 1 - claim generation

The objective of this phase was to generate claims for the 358 retrieved popular Wikipedia pages. We followed the following two steps.

(1) Sentence selection: In the construction of FEVER, this step was carried out in a random manner, i.e., a sentence was randomly selected from the corresponding Wikipedia page to serve as claim. Instead, we opted for a manual sentence selection. Specifically, each annotator was asked to carefully select a sentence from the introductory section of the corresponding page (primary page) in a way that directly relates to the article while containing as many (hyper-)links as possible. The last criteria were to guarantee a high number of many-hop claims. Many-hop[3] claims are essentially more

[2] Referenced pages from the main page.

[3] The number of hops of a claim is the same as the number of necessary evidence documents for the claim.

Verdict	*(English)*	Farsi
supports	**Claim:** Maryam Mirzakhani obtained the full score of the World Mathematical Olympiad in 1995 as an official student at the pre-university level. **Evidence:** *[Maryam_Mirzakhani]* In her junior and senior years of high school (Tehran Farzanegan School), she won a gold medal at the International Mathematical Olympiad in 1994 (Hong Kong) and 1995 (Canada). The following year, in Toronto, she became the first Iranian student to achieve a perfect score. *[Student]* A student is primarily a person who is under learning with the goal of acquiring knowledge. The term "student" denotes those enrolled in secondary schools and higher.	**Claim:** مریم میرزاخانی نمره کامل المپیاد جهانی ریاضی را در سال ۱۹۹۵ به عنوان محصل رسمی در سطح تحصیلات پیش از دانشگاه به دست آورد. **Evidence:** [مریم_میرزاخانی] میرزاخانی در دوران تحصیل در دبیرستان فرزانگان تهران، برنده مدال طلای المپیاد جهانی ریاضی در سال‌های ۱۹۹۴ (هنگ‌کنگ) و ۱۹۹۵ (کانادا) شد و در این سال به‌عنوان نخستین دانش‌آموز ایرانی نمره کامل را به دست آورد. [دانش‌آموز] دانش‌آموز از لحاظ لغوی به معنی کسی است که دانش می‌آموزد و در اصطلاح، برای اطلاق به محصلان رسمی در سطح تحصیلات پیش از دانشگاه به کار می‌رود.
refutes	**Claim:** Typhoid is not contagious at all. **Evidence:** *[Typhoid_fever]* Typhoid fever, also known as typhoid, is a disease caused by Salmonella serotype Typhi bacteria. *[Infection]* An infectious disease, also known as a transmissible disease or communicable disease, is an illness resulting from an infection. Some signs of infection affect the whole body, generally.	**Claim:** حصبه به هیچ وجه مسری نمی‌باشد. **Evidence:** [حِصبه] حصبه، تیفوئید یا تب تیفوئید یک بیماری عفونی است که در اثر عفونت باکتری Salmonella enterica سویه تیفی ایجاد می‌شود. [بیماری_عفونی] بیماری عفونی یا بیماری واگیر یا بیماری مسری (به انگلیسی: Infectious diseases یا transmissible diseases یا communicable diseases) به بیماری گویند که توسط عفونت منتقل و علائم و نشانه‌های بیماری ظاهر شود.

Table 1: Sample instances from ParsFEVER (English translations are shown for reference). For each instance, we show the claim, the corresponding label (verdict), and the evidence (text spans from Wikipedia articles, with the page title in brackets) used for this decision.

challenging as they require evidence retrieved from multiple pages. Specifically, we asked the annotators to produce their claims in a way that at least half of them would require information from other neighbouring Wikipedia pages (secondary pages, i.e., those pages that are linked within the original claim) with the help of a custom dictionary.[4] Consequently, more than 87% of the claims in FEVER need information from only a single Wikipedia page (one hop) (Jiang et al., 2020). However, over 65% of the claims in ParsFEVER are many-hop. After selecting an appropriate sentence, at least two and at most five claims were generated, constituting our set of original claims.

(2) Claim mutation: Following Thorne et al. (2018), we asked the annotators to mutate the original claims. Six types of mutations were considered: paraphrasing, negation, substituting an entity/relation with a similar/dissimilar one, and making the claim more general/specific. At most, five mutated claims were generated for each mutation type.

In both steps in claim generation, the annotators were asked to construct claims that only target one specific fact. This was to avoid multiple-target claims, which can potentially have contradictions. In addition, the claims are required to be based on the entity of focus on the primary page.

3.1.2 Phase 2 - claim labeling

In this stage, each mutated claim is labeled with one of the SUPPORTED, REFUTED, or NOTENOUGHINFO tags. This requires the annotators to identify the appropriate evidence. The annotator specifies one of the SUPPORTED and REFUTED tags only when a strong evidence exists: SUPPORTED if the reason supports the claim, and REFUTED otherwise. If this decision needs additional knowledge (dic-

[4] The dictionary comprises the list of terms (hyper)linked in the original sentence and all the other sentences from the corresponding Wikipedia page.

tionary), the evidence has to be updated with the corresponding new extra entries. Finally, in case the information on Wikipedia pages is not enough to justify the verdict, the claim is labeled as NOTENOUGHINFO.

To simplify the annotation process, we provide all sentences from the introductory section of the primary and secondary pages. We let the annotators use any combination of these sentences as evidence. In contrast, Thorne et al. (2018) just provided the first sentence of each secondary page. Thorne et al. (2018) defined the dictionary using the title of secondary pages and their first sentence. It is worth mentioning that the first sentence might not necessarily offer any valuable extra information. The annotators could easily add an arbitrary Wikipedia page by providing its URL. As a result, the system automatically adds all sentences from the introductory section of the page and its dictionary. At last, by using all the provided sentences in the annotation interface, the annotators record the sentences necessary to justify their verdict.

3.2 Annotators

Our annotation team had 14 native Farsi speakers, all of whom were involved in phase 1 and phase 2. All the annotators were trained for the task prior to the annotation. There was no intervention during the annotation process, and annotators were paired randomly for various instances in phase 2.

3.3 Validation

During claim labeling (task 2), we carried out a verification step to filter out noisy claims. As a result, around 2% of all generated claims were skipped by annotators for not satisfying the required quality criteria. Approximately 1% contained typos, and about 5% were flagged as too ambiguous, all of which were excluded from our dataset.

We implemented three forms of data validation for claim labeling: 5-way inter-annotator agreement, an agreement against super-annotators, and manual validation by the authors. To this end, we selected 3% of claims to be annotated by five annotators and calculated a 5-way inter-annotator agreement. The Fleiss k score was computed as 0.599, which is lower than that reported for FEVER (0.684). This can be attributed to the fact that ParsFEVER comprises significantly more many-hop instances, making the annotation task more challenging. Also, Table 2 shows the results of agreement against super-annotators of ParsFEVER compared to FEVER: 12 of the 14 annotators had an agreement of 87% with the super-annotators (the other two had 81% and 79%).

	Precision	**Recall**	**F1**
FEVER	95.42	72.36	82.30
ParsFEVER	86.95	85.23	86.08

Table 2: Agreement against super-annotators of ParsFEVER compared to FEVER.

	FEVER	**ParsFEVER**
IAA	0.84	0.71
Human	0.75	0.63

Table 3: The agreement of 500 randomly selected claims from ParsFEVER compared to FEVER (in terms of accuracy). IAA and Human respectively stand for Inter-annotator agreement and annotators' agreement against gold labels.

We also randomly selected 500 claims from ParsFEVER and FEVER to make another comparison. We asked two annotators to label each claim of the selected set for FEVER and ParsFEVER. Table 3 shows evidence and label agreement. The agreement of ParsFEVER is lower than FEVER. This is because most ParsFEVER claims are many-hop, resulting in a more challenging dataset (Jiang et al., 2020). Finally, if we ignore the correct evidence for ParsFEVER, the inter-annotator agreement and annotators' agreement against the dataset are 0.92 and 0.87 based on accuracy, respectively.

3.4 Dataset Statistics

Table 4 lists the distribution of instances across the three classes in the training, development, and test sets. Unlike FEVER which only includes mutated claims, in ParsFEVER we consider both mutated and original claims to improve training.

4 Experiments

Following Thorne et al. (2018), we implemented a full pipeline system for fact verification and extraction with the following three modules:

1. A document retrieval component (Chen et al., 2017) to find the most relevant page to a specific claim.

2. A sentence retrieval module to extract the evidence sentence (DrQA-based sentence retrieval module).

Split	SUP	REF	NEI
Training	6,253	4,008	5,685
Dev	841	824	861
Test	853	833	863
Total	7,947	5,665	7,409

Table 4: Distribution of instances in ParsFEVER across the three classes: SUPPORTED (SUP), REFUTED (REF), and NOTENOUGHINFO (NEI). The statistics are for the pruned dataset, i.e., after omitting claims which are ambiguous or contain typo (around 1,885 samples). Both mutated and original claims are included in the dataset.

3. Two recognizing textual entailment (RTE) models are used to classify the claim based on collected evidences as SUPPORTED, REFUTED, or NOTENOUGHINFO.

These models are based on MLP (Riedel et al., 2017), with a single hidden layer that benefits term frequencies and TF-IDF cosine similarity between the claim and evidence, and Decomposable Attention (Parikh et al., 2016, DA). Given that NOTENOUGHINFO instances are not associated with any evidence, they cannot be used for training the RTE models. To address this issue, Thorne et al. (2018) proposed two alternatives solutions: sampling a sentence (as evidence) from the nearest page to the claim (NP) or using the document retrieval component to uniformly select a random sentence (as evidence) from Wikipedia (RS).

4.1 Results

We customized the system based on Farsi. Following Thorne et al. (2018), we set $k = 5$ (k nearest documents to the claim for document retrieval) and $l = 5$ (top l-most similar sentences from the k-most relevant documents). We also checked for other values of the two parameters. However, no improvements were observed on the development set of ParsFEVER.

Table 5 shows the accuracy of the system on ParsFEVER and FEVER. ScoreEv and NoScoreEv respectively stand for accuracy score with respect to correct evidence retrieval and without considering the evidence. The first row in the table belongs to the best result reported by Thorne et al. (2018) using a decomposable attention model (DA) trained on NP. We show results on ParsFEVER using the full pipeline system when either NP or RS methods are used to provide evidence for NOTENOUGHINFO instances. DA generally performs better than MLP, particularly when combined with the NP strategy for sampling sentences. In fact, the best accuracy was achieved by DA/NP, with (ScoreEv) and without (NoScoreEv) the requirement to provide correct evidence with 28.06% and 50.02%, respectively.

Model		Accuracy (%)	
		NoScoreEv	ScoreEv
FEVER	DA/NP	52.09	32.57
ParsFEVER	MLP/NP	41.03	17.46
	MLP/RS	43.76	14.62
	DA/NP	50.02	28.06
	DA/RS	48.08	19.06

Table 5: Accuracy performance of FEVER's full pipeline system on ParsFEVER (best results for FEVER are reported).

5 Conclusion

We presented ParsFEVER, a novel and publicly available dataset for Farsi fact extraction and verification. We elaborated the construction procedure for this dataset, which focuses on having a rich dataset suitable for low-resource languages. Although this work uses Wikipedia as its source, other textual structures and corpora can also be used for fact extraction in this framework.

We evaluated the baseline system proposed for FEVER on our dataset. However, there have been recent developments in the field of fact-checking with models such as QABriefs (Angel et al., 2020). An immediate future work would be to take ParsFEVER as a more challenging benchmark (than FEVER) with significant many-hop operations as a benchmark for evaluating and analyzing existing fact-checking models. This analysis can also shed light on the ability of these models to go beyond the English languages and in low-resource settings.

6 Acknowledgments

The authors would like to thank the annotation team (especially Sepideh Sedghi, Masoume Afshari, Fatemeh Abvali, Baran Barbarestani and Najmeh Keynezhad) for their significant contribution in generating and labeling the claims. In addition, we would like to thank Mohammad Javad Pirhadi, who developed the annotation tools.

References

Jason Angel, Segun Taofeek Aroyehun, Antonio Tamayo, and Alexander Gelbukh. 2020. NLP-CIC at SemEval-2020 task 9: Analysing sentiment in code-switching language using a simple deep-learning classifier. In *Proceedings of the Fourteenth Workshop on Semantic Evaluation*, pages 957–962, Barcelona (online). International Committee for Computational Linguistics.

Danqi Chen, Adam Fisch, Jason Weston, and Antoine Bordes. 2017. Reading Wikipedia to answer open-domain questions. In *Proceedings of the 55th Annual Meeting of the Association for Computational Linguistics (Volume 1: Long Papers)*, pages 1870–1879, Vancouver, Canada. Association for Computational Linguistics.

Leon Derczynski, Kalina Bontcheva, Maria Liakata, Rob Procter, Geraldine Wong Sak Hoi, and Arkaitz Zubiaga. 2017. SemEval-2017 task 8: RumourEval: Determining rumour veracity and support for rumours. In *Proceedings of the 11th International Workshop on Semantic Evaluation (SemEval-2017)*, pages 69–76, Vancouver, Canada. Association for Computational Linguistics.

Yichen Jiang, Shikha Bordia, Zheng Zhong, Charles Dognin, Maneesh Singh, and Mohit Bansal. 2020. HoVer: A dataset for many-hop fact extraction and claim verification. In *Findings of the Association for Computational Linguistics: EMNLP 2020*, pages 3441–3460, Online. Association for Computational Linguistics.

Christopher Manning, Mihai Surdeanu, John Bauer, Jenny Finkel, Steven Bethard, and David McClosky. 2014. The Stanford CoreNLP natural language processing toolkit. In *Proceedings of 52nd Annual Meeting of the Association for Computational Linguistics: System Demonstrations*, pages 55–60, Baltimore, Maryland. Association for Computational Linguistics.

Ankur Parikh, Oscar Täckström, Dipanjan Das, and Jakob Uszkoreit. 2016. A decomposable attention model for natural language inference. In *Proceedings of the 2016 Conference on Empirical Methods in Natural Language Processing*, pages 2249–2255, Austin, Texas. Association for Computational Linguistics.

Benjamin Riedel, Isabelle Augenstein, Georgios P. Spithourakis, and Sebastian Riedel. 2017. A simple but tough-to-beat baseline for the fake news challenge stance detection task. *CoRR*, abs/1707.03264.

James Thorne and Andreas Vlachos. 2018. Automated fact checking: Task formulations, methods and future directions. In *Proceedings of the 27th International Conference on Computational Linguistics*, pages 3346–3359, Santa Fe, New Mexico, USA. Association for Computational Linguistics.

James Thorne, Andreas Vlachos, Christos Christodoulopoulos, and Arpit Mittal. 2018. FEVER: a large-scale dataset for fact extraction and VERification. In *Proceedings of the 2018 Conference of the North American Chapter of the Association for Computational Linguistics: Human Language Technologies, Volume 1 (Long Papers)*, pages 809–819, New Orleans, Louisiana. Association for Computational Linguistics.

William Yang Wang. 2017. "liar, liar pants on fire": A new benchmark dataset for fake news detection. In *Proceedings of the 55th Annual Meeting of the Association for Computational Linguistics (Volume 2: Short Papers)*, pages 422–426, Vancouver, Canada. Association for Computational Linguistics.

Somayeh Zamani, Masoud Asadpour, and Dara Moazzami. 2017. Rumor detection for persian tweets. In *2017 Iranian Conference on Electrical Engineering (ICEE)*, pages 1532–1536.

Majid Zarharan, Samane Ahangar, Fatemeh Sadat Rezvaninejad, Mahdi Bidhendi, Mohammad Taher Pilehvar, Behrouz Minaei, and Sauleh Eetemadi. 2019. Persian stance classification data set. In *Proceedings of the conference for Truth and Trust Online*.

Arkaitz Zubiaga, Maria Liakata, Rob Procter, Geraldine Wong Sak Hoi, and Peter Tolmie. 2016a. Analysing how people orient to and spread rumours in social media by looking at conversational threads. *PLOS ONE*, 11(3):1–29.

Arkaitz Zubiaga, Geraldine Wong Sak Hoi, Maria Liakata, and Rob Procter. 2016b. PHEME dataset of rumours and non-rumours. *figshare, Jun*.

BiQuAD: Towards QA based on deeper text understanding

Frank Grimm **Philipp Cimiano**
CIT-EC, Universität Bielefeld
{fgrimm, cimiano}@cit-ec.uni-bielefeld.de

Abstract

Recent question answering and machine reading benchmarks frequently reduce the task to one of pinpointing spans within a certain text passage that answers the given question. Typically, these systems are not required to actually understand the text on a deeper level that allows for more complex reasoning on the information contained. We introduce a new dataset called *BiQuAD* that requires deeper comprehension in order to answer questions in both extractive and deductive fashion. The dataset consist of $4,190$ closed-domain texts and a total of $99,149$ question-answer pairs. The texts are synthetically generated soccer match reports that verbalize the main events of each match. All texts are accompanied by a structured Datalog program that represents a (logical) model of its information. We show that state-of-the-art QA models do not perform well on the challenging long form contexts and reasoning requirements posed by the dataset. In particular, transformer based state-of-the-art models achieve F_1-scores of only 39.0. We demonstrate how these synthetic datasets align structured knowledge with natural text and aid model introspection when approaching complex text understanding.

1 Introduction

Most of the recent question answering benchmarks require systems to pinpoint the span of the answer to the question in the given text. In the well-known SQuAD 2.0 dataset (Rajpurkar et al., 2018), systems are able to extract the correct answer span in the following paragraph as an answer to the question: "*What tactic did researchers employ to offset the former deficit of work surrounding the complexity of algorithmic problems?*":

"*Before the actual research explicitly devoted to the complexity of algorithmic problems started off,* ***numerous foundations were laid out by various researchers****. Most influential among these was the definition of Turing machines by Alan Turing in 1936, which turned out to be a very robust and flexible simplification of a computer.*" (sample from Rajpurkar et al. (2018))

Results of state-of-the-art (SOTA) systems on these datasets have reached Exact Match (EM) and F_1 performances of 90.9 and 93.2, respectively [1]. Some of these models even outperform the human baseline (which lies at $F_1 = 89.4$ for SQuAD 2.0).

It is unclear to which extent the existing benchmarks actually require systems to comprehend texts and to what extent these systems rely on surface cues signalling a match between question and answer span. Most state-of-the-art models rely on transformer models such as BERT and ALBERT (Lan et al., 2020) that are pre-trained on supplementary tasks using large amounts of textual data (Devlin et al., 2019) and employ extensive self-attention mechanisms that have been shown to learn many of the features of a classic natural language processing (NLP) pipeline (Tenney et al., 2019). It has been shown for a number of tasks that such models rely on surface cues and on artifacts of the datasets. A recent example is the Argument Reading and Comprehension (ARC) task (Habernal et al., 2018). A deeper analysis of the data and the performance of transformer models has shown that they exploit only surface cues and artefacts of the data, failing to perform beyond chance when systematic (adversarial) modifications are applied on the dataset (Niven and Kao, 2019).

Our motivation in this paper is to introduce a new question answering dataset that requires a deeper understanding of the text to answer questions beyond merely matching answer spans. In particular, in our dataset, the answers to questions can often

[1] Current performance of 'FPNet (ensemble)' at the time of writing according to the SQuAD 2.0 leaderboard https://rajpurkar.github.io/SQuAD-explorer/.

Proceedings of the 10th Conference on Lexical and Computational Semantics, pages 105–115
August 5–6, 2021, Bangkok, Thailand (online)

not be found in the original text, but can be inferred on the basis of a deeper, structural, understanding. Examples are aggregation questions such as "*'How many goals did Marco Reus score in the first half of the match?'*" but also questions such as "*'Who won the game?'*", requiring a system to understand that a balanced score leads to a tie, making the question unanswerable. Since most models cannot keep track of all the goals and intermediate scores for the whole game this provides a significant challenge. The dataset we present is called *BiQuAD* and comprises of 99,149 question answer pairs on 4,190 documents, averaging 23 questions per document. The texts describe soccer matches that have actually taken place. The texts have been generated automatically on the basis of handcrafted templates from structured reports of soccer games. A model of each game is available in the form of a Datalog program representing the meaning of the text in terms of a model consisting of predicates relevant to the description of a soccer game. The questions are paraphrases of queries that can be answered over the model of the game. Similar to extensions from SQuAD 1.0 to 2.0 (Rajpurkar et al., 2018), a percentage of the generated questions in the dataset are deemed as *unanswerable*.

In this paper we present the dataset in more detail and describe its creation (section 3). Further, we present the results of state-of-the-art QA systems on this task in section 4. We show the limits of current state-of-the-art QA in answering questions for which the answer is not in the text but requires deeper inference on the basis of the information given in the text. We show that, in spite of text being artificially generated using 335 relatively simple templates, thus being very regular, this task is not solvable by the current state-of-the-art in question answering. Arguably, the current state-of-the-art focuses on extractive QA and was not designed for deeper understanding. We posit that results on our dataset show that extractive models in particular overfit on surface cues that do not require deeper text understanding. In particular, we show that while the state-of-the-art on Squad 2.0 for example yield results of EM and F_1-scores of 90.7 and 93.0, results of these models for our task range between 38.8 and 39.0 respectively.

2 Related Work

Datasets on machine reading and question answering tasks can be characterized by broad categories: *a)* open vs. closed (specific) domain, and *b)* text-comprehension based (e.g. extractive or Cloze-style) vs. knowledge based QA. Table 1 categorizes prominent datasets along these lines and provides an overview over the number of questions/-documents, how each dataset was collected (e.g. crowdsourcing / artificially generated) as well as the current state-of-the-art (SOTA) results. This list is necessarily non-exhaustive and we only showcase datasets that are either prominent examples of the space or noteworthy because of their relation to the work presented here.

Prominent datasets focusing on open-ended extractive QA include SQuAD 1.0 (Rajpurkar et al., 2016) and 2.0 (Rajpurkar et al., 2018), which have enjoyed wide popularity in the research community. Together with NewsQA (Trischler et al., 2017), these datasets represent the largest, crowd-sourced, extractive QA datasets available. Questions here are answered by correctly identifying a span in a context paragraph, with version 2.0 introducing a subclass of unanswerable questions. More recently, SQuAD versions in languages other than English have been developed (Croce et al., 2018; Mozannar et al., 2019; d'Hoffschmidt et al., 2020; Carrino et al., 2020). The TriviaQA (Joshi et al., 2017) dataset integrates the notion of external evidence (Wikipedia articles) for trivia and open domain question answering and broadens the task to information retrieval (IR) settings.

The RACE dataset (Lai et al., 2017) relies on a multiple choice setting and leverages data used for the assessment of reading comprehension by humans. It features simple reasoning challenges such as deducing relative values from mentions of absolute ones. Similarly, the Open Book QA (Mihaylov et al., 2018) requires models to involve common sense knowledge to solve the task successfully.

There are different ways to frame the task of answering questions by machine reading, including sentence retrieval (Momtazi and Klakow, 2015), multi-hop reasoning (Khot et al., 2020), and reasoning about multiple paragraphs or documents at the same time (Dua et al., 2019; Cao et al., 2019). Recent work has considered the development of reasoning-based QA systems (Weber et al., 2019) as well as the integration of external (Banerjee and Baral, 2020) and commonsense knowledge (Clark et al., 2020) into the QA process.

Other machine reading based QA datasets focus on answering questions on the basis of struc-

Dataset	Domain	Task Type	Samples ~	Acquisition Method	SOTA	
SQuAD 1.0, 2.0	Open	Extractive QA	150,000	Crowdsourcing	EM 90.724	F_1 93.011
NewsQA	Open	Extractive QA	120,000	Crowdsourcing	F_1 73.6	
TriviaQA	Open	Extractive QA	95,000	Semi-Automatic	EM 90.38	F_1 92.96
RACE	Open	Multiple Choice	100,000	Domain Experts	Accuracy 90.9	
Open Book QA	Open	Multiple Choice	6,000	Crowdsourcing	Accuracy 87.20	
LC-QuAD 2.0	Open	Graph Retrieval	30,000	Semi-Automatic	*tbd.*	
WikiHop	Open	Extractive QA	50,000	Graph Traversal	Accuracy 81.9	
MedHop	Closed	Extractive QA	2,500	Graph Traversal	Accuracy 60.3	
QASC	Open	Multiple Choice	10,000	Crowdsourcing	Accuracy 90	
QALD-9	Open	Graph Retrieval	700 * 11	Manual Annotation	Macro F_1 QALD 5.0	
SciQA	Closed	Document Retrieval	10,000	Automated Extraction	MAP 24.36*	
DROP	Both	Extractive QA	97000	Crowdsourcing	EM 90.10	F_1 87.04

Table 1: Overview of related QA datasets. Exact match (EM), F_1, Accuracy, Mean Average Precision (MAP) scores according to their respective leaderboards at the time of writing. *Best result on BioASQ 6b test batch 3 (Nentidis et al., 2018).

tured knowledge graphs. A prominent example is the series of Question Answering over Linked Data (QALD) evaluation campaigns (Usbeck et al., 2018), now in its 9th edition and going back to 2011. Solving the QALD tasks requires mapping natural language questions in multiple languages into a corresponding SPARQL query (Cimiano et al., 2013). While QALD provided only hundreds of training samples, recent datasets such as LC-QuAD 2.0 (Trivedi et al., 2017; Dubey et al., 2019) rely on automatic generation and human post-processing to generate sufficient sample counts required for modern deep learning architectures. A similar approach is taken by QASC (Khot et al., 2020) or WikiHop and MedHop (Welbl et al., 2018) that are aimed at multi hop inference across multiple documents, finding answers directly from the KG without the need to generate a query.

Most closed domain datasets are smaller than their open domain counterparts since annotation usually requires experts that are inherently harder to source. Datasets such as the biomedical question answering corpus BiQA (Lamurias et al., 2020) make use of user generated content from other sources instead.

The recent DROP dataset (Dua et al., 2019) focuses on complex reasoning tasks in form of both, open and closed domain, questions. The task combines the challenge of extractive QA with testing a models ability to perform limited numerical reasoning, e.g. by having to calculate date differences. At the time of this writing, graph-based models presented in (Chen et al., 2020) rank at the top of the DROP leaderboard with F_1 of 90.1, and EM of 87.0.[2]

Similar to DROP, we aim to bridge gaps required for deeper text understanding while simultaneously providing sample annotations that allow for proper model introspection. The synthetic nature of generated texts in *BiQuAD* provides an extensible way to test model capabilities for reasoning about various sub-categories. We provide long form text passages alongside structured representations, in the form of Datalog rules, as a way to either explicitly combine structured and unstructured information or a further way for model introspection by aligning neural model representations with their graphical and discrete counterparts.

3 Methods

This section outlines the methodology used to generate the dataset and in what way the state-of-the-art transformer architectures can provide a first baseline for the *BiQuAD* dataset.

3.1 Dataset Generation

The *BiQuAD* dataset consists of two different views on each match: a *Datalog* program representing a model of each text in terms of the main events in the match, as well as an artificially generated *match report* in natural language. Each of these match reports is accompanied by a set of, on average, 23 question/answer pairs generated in a similar fashion.The dataset is made available as fixed 60-20-20 training/development/test splits.

The Datalog programs and natural language match reports are extracted and generated on the basis of structured match reports available as part of

[2]https://leaderboard.allenai.org/drop/submissions/public

the "European Soccer Database" (ESDB),[3] which aggregates real minute-by-minute data on 14,196 historic soccer matches between 2008 and 2016 from various sources. It is licensed under the permissive Open Database License (ODbL) v1.0. We extract data following a scheme of match objects and associated events from the database, an overview of which is available in Fig. 1.

The structure presents a complete model of the facts contained in the database and subsequently all texts generated using its information. It contains information about the following eight types of events for each match: `cross` (medium- / long-range pass), `foul`, `shot on target` (goal shot attempts), `shot off target` (shots not reaching the goal or hitting the frame), `card` (yellow or red), `goal`, `possession` (special event reporting the minutes each team is in ball possession). The available details for each event vary from sub-types, e.g. indicating the type of card, the reason on why it was given, to the individual players involved in a foul or cross pass. These details are used to create a natural sounding output sentence from each event. The Datalog programs capture all these events in addition to the final result via logical predicates and provide thus the basis for structured querying, supporting aggregation questions.

The transformation of the data to Datalog programs relies on a number of rules that extract data from the ESDB and transforms it into Datalog clauses. The full set of rules, as well as a comprehensive overview, is available for download alongside the QA dataset itself. Applied to a full object hierarchy of a match and all its events in the ESDB this generates a set of Datalog programs and documents of various sizes. While some matches only describe major events, like goals or cards, the majority averages more than one event per minute.

The following example represents information on the overall outcome of a certain match in both Datalog (shown here in a standard variant) and text:

[3] `https://www.kaggle.com/hugomathien/soccer`

EXAMPLE 1.

```
match(M47).
match_league(M47, "Bundesliga").
match_hometeam(M47,"Borussia Dortmund").
match_awayteam(M47, "Bayern München").
match_score(M47, "2:1").
match_hometeam_goals(M47, "2").
match_awayteam_goals(M47, "1").
```

```
The Bundesliga match ended with the
home team Borussia Dortmund beating
Bayern München 2 to 1.
```

Text Generation: The natural language match report is generated via a set of templates defined for the different types of events. An additional set of templates describes the overall match in various degrees of detail. Similar to the above Datalog transformation, we represent transformations into text as natural language with dynamic placeholders:

EXAMPLE 2.

```
The {@data.league} game of
{@data.hometeam} versus {@data.awayteam}
ended {@data.score}.
```

For text generation we defined a total of 335 rules, with least 5 different rules for each relevant event, so that some language variation is introduced. Filter functions are used to postprocess the names of players by removing parts of the full name to check the ability of systems to detect and resolve co-references. Some rules also introduce explicit co-reference markers, allowing generated systems to replace a player's name that occurs in multiple subsequent events.

EXAMPLE 3.

```
The {@data.league} match ended with the
home team {@data.hometeam} beating
{@data.awayteam} {@data.home_goals}
to {@data.away_goals}.
```

Question Templates ($QT_{category}$) are used to generate (question, answer) pairs on the original Datalog program. They are used to construct a Datalog query that answers the question given structured knowledge, as well as their textual representation. The answer is then retrieved by executing the constructed query and, where possible, annotated in text form. The templates, outlined below, have each been designed to address a specific challenge for the QA task. Similar to how most SQuAD evaluations report performance on answerable and

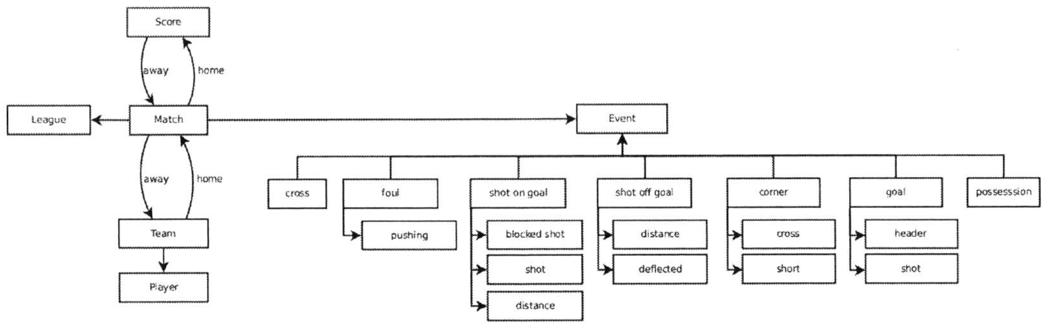

Figure 1: ESDB object model overview.

unanswerable questions separately, this allows researchers to evaluate their models along detailed axes and pinpoint potential for improvements. The dataset features the following nine types of questions:

- $QT_{Simple\ Facts}$ This template takes a fact from the Datalog program and randomly removes an entity, this generates cloze style questions answerable using a single sentence in the textual representation, e.g. "*Who won the game?*".
- $QT_{Multiple\ Facts}$ Questions that relate to multiple entities, akin to the extraction of relations with two arguments, such as "*Who did :event/player1 tackle?*".
- $QT_{Paraphrased\ Facts}$ This is an extension of $QT_{Simple\ Facts}$ that generates similar questions but is mapped to different text templates that change and omit entity labels (e.g. omitting the first name of a player or omitting a subsequent use of team names). These templates require models to learn inexact matching of labels to entities in the underlying knowledge base and introduce simple patterns of co-reference resolution.
- $QT_{Aggregation}$ (*min/max/count*): Events such as goals, cards, and fouls are discrete entries in the Datalog program. While some resulting questions might be available in text, e.g. "*How many goals did Team A score?*", some require further deduction via counting ("How many goals did Marco Reus score?"). This also includes comparisons between multiple entities, e.g. "Did :player1 score more goals than :player2?".
- $QT_{Unanswerable}$ Aligned with Rajpurkar et al. (2018), this template introduces an adversarial element to the dataset by generating questions that look valid but are in fact not answerable by the data. These questions are generated by randomly sampling another document and ensuring the resulting Datalog query does not yield a result for the current match. This leads to realistic questions that might even overlap in entities (e.g. player names) but make no sense in the context of the current document.
- $QT_{Temporal}$ This template generates questions relating to the temporal order of match events; it generates questions such as "*Who scored the first goal of the match?*" or "*Who scored the last goal in the first half of the match?*".
- $QT_{Aggregation\ Temporal}$ This template combines $QT_{Multiple\ Facts}$ and $QT_{Temporal}$ by asking questions such as "How many goals did Team A score in the second half of the match?" or "Did Team A score more goals in the first half of the match?" (comparison).

All templates contain placeholders such as `:event/player1` that are dynamically resolved via the knowledge in the Datalog program for each match and can refer to individual properties or entity names. Question templates may provide preconditions or constraints that have to be true in order for the question to be generated on any given match. This ensures that questions are answerable and compatible with the given match data.

A question about one player tackling another for example would generate the following Datalog query and text:

```
EXAMPLE 4.

Q(m, p1) :- event_match(e, m),
   event_player1(e, p1),
   event_player2(e, p2),
   event_type(e, "foulcommit"),
   event_subtype(e, "pull").
-------------------------------------
Who pulled {@data.player2|namefilter}?
```

The templates in category $QT_{Unanswerable}$ are generated in a second pass over the dataset, for each four answerable questions an unanswerable one is sampled randomly from another document in the corpus. The answer for the sampled question is dropped and the accompanying datalog query is used to validate that no answer exists for the question w.r.t. the current document. This reliably transforms templates that generate sensible and answerable questions into unanswerable ones.

Template annotations include a number of answer types (e.g. *text* or *numeric*) that are used to annotate the location of the answer within the context document. The datalog query of the question is automatically rewritten to obtain a sensible location within the text to annotate an answer. In the case of textual answers, the closest matches are annotated since the exact location might not contain the answer itself due to co-reference. For numerical answers we employ two strategies: *a)* temporal questions looking for the minute a particular event occurred are annotated at the appropriate marker and *b)* generic numeric answers are generated at the end of the document (ensuring that at least five multiple choices are presented, padded with random numbers if necessary).

All questions consist of four elements:

- Question in natural language.
- Datalog query corresponding to the question.
- Answer retrieved from the knowledge base.
- Metadata, such as the answer type (text, numeric) and question template category.

In Figure 2 we give an example excerpt from an automatically generated report for a single match. One of the questions w.r.t. this match in the dataset is the following:

- NL Question: How many goals did Fulham score in the first halftime?
- Datalog Query (excerpt):

```
Q(m, team) :- event_match(e, m),
    event_type(e, "goal"),
    event_team(e, team),
    event_minute(e) <= 45.
A :- sum(Q(m, "home")).
```

- Answer: *3 (three)*

The England Premier League match between Fulham and Norwich City ended 5:0.

2: Foul in minute 2: Handball by Johnson.
4: Anthony Pilkington takes the ball.
5: Sascha Riether pulls against Pilkingtons shirt.
6: Snodgrass takes the ball.
[...]
25: Dangerous play foul by Grant Holt on Mahamadou Diarra in minute 25.
26: Goal by Duff for Fulham.
29: Tierney shoots off.
30: In minute 30 John Arne Riise attempts a cross.
30: Incident between Fulham player Hangeland and Grant Holt results in penalty.
32: Dembele fouls Holt in minute 32 by obstructing.
[...]
87: Steve Sidwell scores for Fulham.
89: Opponent player is tackled from behind by Mahamadou Diarra.
92: Penalty against Brede Hangeland in minute 92 after incident with Morison.

Figure 2: Example match report excerpt between Fulham and Norwich City in 2012.

After generation, we generate fixed splits by shuffling all match report documents and dividing them into sets of train (60%), development (20%), and test (20%). The dataset, as well as an evaluation script and resources for generating it, are made available online. In order to provide a comparable baseline to existing state-of-the-art models the subset of QA pairs suitable for extractive QA is exported into a SQuAD-compatible data format.

3.2 Model

In order to provide first reference results for the *BiQuAD* dataset, we evaluate state-of-the-art vanilla transformer architectures on the task, in particular ALBERT (Lan et al., 2020). Based on hardware constraints and hyperparameter optimization using fine-tuned *base* models, all trainings ran for two epochs, with a learning rate of 3e−5 and a batch size of 8. The model itself uses a standard ALBERT architecture for question answering tasks following (Lan et al., 2020; Rajpurkar et al., 2018). The tasks were executed in a Linux cluster environment on GTX1080 Ti GPUs (CUDA10). A single additional hidden layer stores answer span logits (start and end of a span) and treats the first token (`[CLS]`) as an indicator for unanswerable questions. Optimization is performed through Adam (with $epsilon = 1\text{e}{-8}$).

Input Sequences in both models are constrained by the maximum sequence length they can process. Similar to the size of the parameter space, the specific maximum values (512 tokens for both models used here) depends on the maximum sequence length used during pre-training. We leverage the ability of the HuggingFace implementation (Wolf et al., 2019) to specify a *document stride*. This effectively extracts features in a sliding window approach over the full document and determines the answer by observing the maximal logit over all windows.

3.3 Evaluation

The evaluation of each model is performed in two major settings: *a)* single question-answering and *b)* document level question-answering. While the former aims to maintain compatibility with SQuAD-like datasets and optimizes on the overall ability of a model to extract individual answers from the textual description of a soccer match, the latter is designed to assess the overall ability of the model to cover lots of different questions on a particular complex text document.

Single Question Answering pairs are evaluated in accordance with the SQuAD paradigm of exact matches (EM) and F_1 scores (Rajpurkar et al., 2018):

- Exact Match (EM): Percentage of predictions completely matching the ground truth answer.

- F_1: Macro-averaged F_1 score. Here each answer and ground truth pair is treated as a bag-of-words to determine an inexact overlap and evaluate in a less strict manner. The calculation of individual F_1 scores follows the classical definition of $F_1 = 2\frac{Precision*Recall}{Precision+Recall}$ (van Rijsbergen, 1979). Unlike SQuAD our datasets only present a singular ground truth per question so it is unnecessary to search for a maximal F_1 score here.

For the purpose of error analysis, in this article we report these results on a per-category level, as well as distinguished by answerable and unanswerable questions. This not only showcases where a particular model might have problems with the dataset it is trained on, it also is of immense help when debugging errors and guiding decisions of where a model might require more training data.

Transfer Learning from open domain question answering datasets such as SQuAD 2.0 is used to assess how well the language structure itself can be used for extractive QA in the unseen data of our dataset. For this we evaluate the aforementioned experimental setup after training on the SQuAD 2.0 training split and evaluating on the test split of *BiQuAD* .

All results are reported on the development split, the test split is withheld from public release for use in an evaluation webservice. In the open source release of the *BiQuAD* dataset, evaluation scripts are provided in order to keep these evaluations consistent.[4] To aid in reproducibility, the MIT-licensed open source release also contains the scripts required to generate samples.

4 Results

This section provides an overview of the dataset and provides first results on the dataset by providing baselines relying on state-of-the-art transformer models.

4.1 Dataset

The dataset comprises 4,190 documents with play by play soccer matches and 99,149 questions ($\sim$ 23 per document) and is thus of similar size as comparable datasets. Each textual representation of a match contains an average of 82 sentences (759 words). The template based text generation yielded long form documents of rather factual and sober match descriptions. While syntactic and vocabulary variability is clearly limited due to this rule-based approach, co-reference and detailed event descriptions make texts non-trivial to reason about.

Albeit not being leveraged in the baseline models presented herein, the parallel construction of textual and structured descriptions enables the adoption of *BiQuAD* for use in further downstream tasks, such as relation extraction or knowledge base completion.

The dataset splits follow a 60-20-20 scheme, it contains a *training* split with 2,514 documents (58,807 QA pairs) and *Development and Test* splits with 838 documents (19,870 QA pairs) each.

4.2 Model Results

The following results outline the performance of SOTA models, as described in section 3, for question answering on the *BiQuAD* dataset.

Single Question Answering is evaluated on individual question answer pairs in the development dataset, table 2 shows the overall results. Individual question templates, and subsets such as answerable

[4] `https://github.com/ag-sc/BiQuAD`

$QT_{Answerable}$ and unanswerable $QT_{Unanswerable}$ questions. The latter distinction is important because both models regarded in this study explicitly model if a question is answerable in their architecture and are thus typically well equipped to make this decision.

Question Templates	EM	F_1
All	38.8	39.0
Answerable	25.4	25.8
Unanswerable	86.6	86.6
Simple Facts	25.0	21.6
Multiple Facts	29.7	30.1
Temporal	16.4	16.4
Aggregation	33.8	64.1
Aggregation Temporal	0.0	66.3

Table 2: Results for single QA setting, reported results on the public development split.

On the question of answerability, the models perform reasonably well. The fact that it does not achieve perfect scores here indicates that they are not able to exploit simple surface queues to make this decision and validates the approach to generate these samples as described in section 3. Other template categories indicate that the model cannot yet cope with more involved categories, such as the temporal reasoning category.

Transfer Learning results, presented in table 3, evaluate the QA pairs in the development set of *BiQuAD* on a model trained with the training data from SQuAD 2.0. The results show a strong ability to determine the answerability of questions but break down in other categories. This capability indicates that questions generated as unanswerable might often contain easily spotted and exploited surface clues, such as player names, that do not occur in the document in question.

The results presented here show that modern deep learning models such as ALBERT perform similarly well on the proposed dataset. While SQuAD-like datasets are commonly limited to the evaluation of subsets such as $QT_{Answerable}$ and $QT_{Unanswerable}$, the template based nature of *BiQuAD* allows for even further inspection.

5 Conclusion

We have introduced a challenging new QA dataset that emphasizes document-level text understanding. While most of the existing benchmark datasets require systems to extract answer spans from text or to select an answer given multiple choices, we have attempted to provide a dataset that requires answering questions beyond the content explicitly mentioned in the text, requiring inference and aggregation on top of the information given in the text. Our methodology builds on a structured database of soccer matches. From this database, it generates natural language reports of games relying on a set of handcrafted templates in addition to a Datalog logical representation of a text. For each document, 23 Datalog queries are generated and transformed into NL relying on a further set of handcrafted templates. The artificial nature of the dataset allows for clear cut error analysis and can guide the implementation of, especially closed domain, QA systems. Downsides introduced by synthetic generation include an unnaturally factual text style and the fact that relatively simple heuristics might be able to generate the correct answer for some of the question templates. These heuristics could potentially even target the soccer domain itself, as is common with many subtasks in closed domain corpora. We aim to alleviate these concerns in future work by extending *a)* the tooling around model introspection and *b)* coverage of further domains. These steps should further improve the way reasoning tasks are reflected in the dataset and establish *BiQuAD* , or the approach of synthetic corpora, as a modeling tool to be used alongside other corpora of natural texts in comparable or open domain settings.

Question Templates	EM	F_1
All	24.4	25.9
Answerable	3.7	5.7
Unanswerable	99.0	99.0
Simple Facts	6.5	6.8
Multiple Facts	16.9	24.1
Temporal	0.0	0.0
Aggregation	0.0	2.5
Aggregation Temporal	0.0	0.9

Table 3: Results for the transfer learning QA setting, reported results on the public development split.

We have provided baseline systems and show that existing state-of-the-art systems yield very low results on the dataset, with exact match and F_1-scores of 38.8 and 39.0, respectively. Results of $EM = 24.4, F_1 = 25.9$ in a transfer learning setup further strengthen the assumption that these models cannot sufficiently answer the type of reasoning tasks imposed by the dataset. While state-of-the-art systems perform well on standard extractive questions ($QT_{Multiple\ Facts,Aggregation}$), we show that on questions requiring inference and temporal reasoning, the baseline systems perform at F_1 below 20 even when encoding answers in a way compatible with extractive systems.

On the basis of these results and experience with other datasets, we can see that explicit modelling is required for various complex reasoning tasks. Many recent state-of-the-art models on QA achieve this complexity only in limited scopes, such as pure numeric reasoning, not deeper general text understanding. The parallel construction of structured Datalog knowledge about a closed world model may be used to *a)* develop models that combine textual information with external semantic knowledge or *b)* decode how a model performs reasoning tasks by linking text and structural knowledge when inspecting individual components such as attention layers. *BiQuAD* allows to model and inspect reasoning on specific categories without necessarily overfitting on any particular subtask. Our dataset is freely available and, in combination with other datasets of non-synthetic nature, will hopefully contribute to push the state of the art in machine reading further.

Acknowledgments We would like to thank the anonymous reviewers for their valuable feedback.

References

Pratyay Banerjee and Chitta Baral. 2020. Self-supervised knowledge triplet learning for zero-shot question answering. In *Proceedings of the 2020 Conference on Empirical Methods in Natural Language Processing (EMNLP)*, pages 151–162, Online. Association for Computational Linguistics.

Nicola De Cao, Wilker Aziz, and Ivan Titov. 2019. Question answering by reasoning across documents with graph convolutional networks. In *Proceedings of the 2019 Conference of the North American Chapter of the Association for Computational Linguistics: Human Language Technologies, NAACL-HLT 2019, Minneapolis, MN, USA, June 2-7, 2019, Volume 1 (Long and Short Papers)*, pages 2306–2317. Association for Computational Linguistics.

Casimiro Pio Carrino, Marta R. Costa-jussà, and José A. R. Fonollosa. 2020. Automatic spanish translation of squad dataset for multi-lingual question answering. In *Proceedings of The 12th Language Resources and Evaluation Conference, LREC 2020, Marseille, France, May 11-16, 2020*, pages 5515–5523. European Language Resources Association.

Kunlong Chen, Weidi Xu, Xingyi Cheng, Zou Xiaochuan, Yuyu Zhang, Le Song, Taifeng Wang, Yuan Qi, and Wei Chu. 2020. Question directed graph attention network for numerical reasoning over text. In *Proceedings of the 2020 Conference on Empirical Methods in Natural Language Processing (EMNLP)*, pages 6759–6768, Online. Association for Computational Linguistics.

Philipp Cimiano, Vanessa López, Christina Unger, Elena Cabrio, Axel-Cyrille Ngonga Ngomo, and Sebastian Walter. 2013. Multilingual question answering over linked data (QALD-3): lab overview. In *Information Access Evaluation. Multilinguality, Multimodality, and Visualization - 4th International Conference of the CLEF Initiative, CLEF 2013, Valencia, Spain, September 23-26, 2013. Proceedings*, pages 321–332.

Peter Clark, Oyvind Tafjord, and Kyle Richardson. 2020. Transformers as soft reasoners over language. In *Proceedings of the Twenty-Ninth International Joint Conference on Artificial Intelligence, IJCAI 2020*, pages 3882–3890. ijcai.org.

Danilo Croce, Alexandra Zelenanska, and Roberto Basili. 2018. Neural learning for question answering in italian. In *AI*IA 2018 – Advances in Artificial Intelligence*, pages 389–402, Cham. Springer International Publishing.

Jacob Devlin, Ming-Wei Chang, Kenton Lee, and Kristina Toutanova. 2019. BERT: pre-training of deep bidirectional transformers for language understanding. In *Proceedings of the 2019 Conference of the North American Chapter of the Association for Computational Linguistics: Human Language Technologies, NAACL-HLT 2019, Minneapolis, MN, USA, June 2-7, 2019, Volume 1 (Long and Short Papers)*, pages 4171–4186. Association for Computational Linguistics.

Martin d'Hoffschmidt, Wacim Belblidia, Quentin Heinrich, Tom Brendlé, and Maxime Vidal. 2020. Fquad: French question answering dataset. In *Proceedings of the 2020 Conference on Empirical Methods in Natural Language Processing: Findings, EMNLP 2020, Online Event, 16-20 November 2020*, pages 1193–1208. Association for Computational Linguistics.

Dheeru Dua, Yizhong Wang, Pradeep Dasigi, Gabriel Stanovsky, Sameer Singh, and Matt Gardner. 2019. DROP: A reading comprehension benchmark requiring discrete reasoning over paragraphs. In *Proceedings of the 2019 Conference of the North American Chapter of the Association for Computational Linguistics: Human Language Technologies, NAACL-HLT 2019, Minneapolis, MN, USA, June 2-7, 2019, Volume 1 (Long and Short Papers)*, pages 2368–2378. Association for Computational Linguistics.

Mohnish Dubey, Debayan Banerjee, Abdelrahman Abdelkawi, and Jens Lehmann. 2019. Lc-quad 2.0: A large dataset for complex question answering over wikidata and dbpedia. In *The Semantic Web - ISWC 2019 - 18th International Semantic Web Conference, Auckland, New Zealand, October 26-30, 2019, Proceedings, Part II*, volume 11779 of *Lecture Notes in Computer Science*, pages 69–78. Springer.

Ivan Habernal, Henning Wachsmuth, Iryna Gurevych, and Benno Stein. 2018. SemEval-2018 task 12: The argument reasoning comprehension task. In *Proceedings of The 12th International Workshop on Semantic Evaluation*, pages 763–772, New Orleans, Louisiana. Association for Computational Linguistics.

Mandar Joshi, Eunsol Choi, Daniel S. Weld, and Luke Zettlemoyer. 2017. Triviaqa: A large scale distantly supervised challenge dataset for reading comprehension. In *Proceedings of the 55th Annual Meeting of the Association for Computational Linguistics, ACL 2017, Vancouver, Canada, July 30 - August 4, Volume 1: Long Papers*, pages 1601–1611. Association for Computational Linguistics.

Tushar Khot, Peter Clark, Michal Guerquin, Peter Jansen, and Ashish Sabharwal. 2020. QASC: A dataset for question answering via sentence composition. In *The Thirty-Fourth AAAI Conference on Artificial Intelligence, AAAI 2020, The Thirty-Second Innovative Applications of Artificial Intelligence Conference, IAAI 2020, The Tenth AAAI Symposium on Educational Advances in Artificial Intelligence, EAAI 2020, New York, NY, USA, February 7-12, 2020*, pages 8082–8090. AAAI Press.

Guokun Lai, Qizhe Xie, Hanxiao Liu, Yiming Yang, and Eduard H. Hovy. 2017. RACE: large-scale reading comprehension dataset from examinations. In *Proceedings of the 2017 Conference on Empirical Methods in Natural Language Processing, EMNLP 2017, Copenhagen, Denmark, September 9-11, 2017*, pages 785–794. Association for Computational Linguistics.

Andre Lamurias, Diana Sousa, and Francisco M. Couto. 2020. Generating biomedical question answering corpora from q&a forums. *IEEE Access*, 8:161042–161051.

Zhenzhong Lan, Mingda Chen, Sebastian Goodman, Kevin Gimpel, Piyush Sharma, and Radu Soricut. 2020. ALBERT: A lite BERT for self-supervised learning of language representations. In *8th International Conference on Learning Representations, ICLR 2020, Addis Ababa, Ethiopia, April 26-30, 2020*. OpenReview.net.

Todor Mihaylov, Peter Clark, Tushar Khot, and Ashish Sabharwal. 2018. Can a suit of armor conduct electricity? A new dataset for open book question answering. In *Proceedings of the 2018 Conference on Empirical Methods in Natural Language Processing, Brussels, Belgium, October 31 - November 4, 2018*, pages 2381–2391. Association for Computational Linguistics.

Saeedeh Momtazi and Dietrich Klakow. 2015. Bridging the vocabulary gap between questions and answer sentences. *Inf. Process. Manage.*, 51(5):595–615.

Hussein Mozannar, Elie Maamary, Karl El Hajal, and Hazem M. Hajj. 2019. Neural arabic question answering. In *Proceedings of the Fourth Arabic Natural Language Processing Workshop, WANLP@ACL 2019, Florence, Italy, August 1, 2019*, pages 108–118. Association for Computational Linguistics.

Anastasios Nentidis, Anastasia Krithara, Konstantinos Bougiatiotis, Georgios Paliouras, and Ioannis Kakadiaris. 2018. Results of the sixth edition of the BioASQ challenge. In *Proceedings of the 6th BioASQ Workshop A challenge on large-scale biomedical semantic indexing and question answering*, pages 1–10, Brussels, Belgium. Association for Computational Linguistics.

Timothy Niven and Hung-Yu Kao. 2019. Probing neural network comprehension of natural language arguments. In *Proceedings of the 57th Annual Meeting of the Association for Computational Linguistics*, pages 4658–4664, Florence, Italy. Association for Computational Linguistics.

Pranav Rajpurkar, Robin Jia, and Percy Liang. 2018. Know what you don't know: Unanswerable questions for squad. In *Proceedings of the 56th Annual Meeting of the Association for Computational Linguistics, ACL 2018, Melbourne, Australia, July 15-20, 2018, Volume 2: Short Papers*, pages 784–789. Association for Computational Linguistics.

Pranav Rajpurkar, Jian Zhang, Konstantin Lopyrev, and Percy Liang. 2016. Squad: 100, 000+ questions for machine comprehension of text. In *Proceedings of the 2016 Conference on Empirical Methods in Natural Language Processing, EMNLP 2016, Austin, Texas, USA, November 1-4, 2016*, pages 2383–2392. The Association for Computational Linguistics.

C. J. van Rijsbergen. 1979. *Information Retrieval*. Butterworth.

Ian Tenney, Dipanjan Das, and Ellie Pavlick. 2019. BERT rediscovers the classical NLP pipeline. In *Proceedings of the 57th Conference of the Association for Computational Linguistics, ACL 2019, Florence, Italy, July 28- August 2, 2019, Volume 1: Long Papers*, pages 4593–4601. Association for Computational Linguistics.

Adam Trischler, Tong Wang, Xingdi Yuan, Justin Harris, Alessandro Sordoni, Philip Bachman, and Kaheer Suleman. 2017. Newsqa: A machine comprehension dataset. In *Proceedings of the 2nd Workshop on Representation Learning for NLP, Rep4NLP@ACL 2017, Vancouver, Canada, August 3, 2017*, pages 191–200. Association for Computational Linguistics.

Priyansh Trivedi, Gaurav Maheshwari, Mohnish Dubey, and Jens Lehmann. 2017. Lc-quad: A corpus for complex question answering over knowledge graphs. In *International Semantic Web Conference*, pages 210–218. Springer.

Ricardo Usbeck, Ria Hari Gusmita, Axel-Cyrille Ngonga Ngomo, and Muhammad Saleem. 2018. 9th challenge on question answering over linked data (QALD-9) (invited paper). In *Joint proceedings of the 4th Workshop on Semantic Deep Learning (SemDeep-4) and NLIWoD4: Natural Language Interfaces for the Web of Data (NLIWOD-4) and 9th Question Answering over Linked Data challenge (QALD-9) co-located with 17th International Semantic Web Conference (ISWC 2018), Monterey, California, United States of America, October 8th - 9th, 2018*, volume 2241 of *CEUR Workshop Proceedings*, pages 58–64. CEUR-WS.org.

Leon Weber, Pasquale Minervini, Jannes Münchmeyer, Ulf Leser, and Tim Rocktäschel. 2019. Nlprolog: Reasoning with weak unification for question answering in natural language. In *Proceedings of the 57th Conference of the Association for Computational Linguistics, ACL 2019, Florence, Italy, July 28- August 2, 2019, Volume 1: Long Papers*, pages 6151–6161. Association for Computational Linguistics.

Johannes Welbl, Pontus Stenetorp, and Sebastian Riedel. 2018. Constructing datasets for multi-hop reading comprehension across documents. *Transactions of the Association for Computational Linguistics*, 6:287–302.

Thomas Wolf, Lysandre Debut, Victor Sanh, Julien Chaumond, Clement Delangue, Anthony Moi, Pierric Cistac, Tim Rault, Rémi Louf, Morgan Funtowicz, and Jamie Brew. 2019. Huggingface's transformers: State-of-the-art natural language processing. *CoRR*, abs/1910.03771.

Evaluating Universal Dependency Parser Recovery of Predicate Argument Structure via CompChain Analysis

Sagar Indurkhya
LIDS/IDSS, Dept. of EECS
MIT
32 Vassar St.
Cambridge, MA 02139
indurks@mit.edu

Beracah Yankama
LIDS/IDSS, Dept. of EECS
MIT
32 Vassar St.
Cambridge, MA 02139
beracah@mit.edu

Robert C. Berwick
LIDS/IDSS, Dept. of EECS
MIT
Room 32D-728
32 Vassar St.
Cambridge, MA 02139
berwick@csail.mit.edu

Abstract

Accurate recovery of predicate-argument structure from a Universal Dependency (UD) parse is central to downstream tasks such as extraction of semantic roles or event representations. This study introduces *compchains*, a categorization of the hierarchy of predicate dependency relations present within a UD parse. Accuracy of compchain classification serves as a proxy for measuring accurate recovery of predicate-argument structure from sentences with embedding. We analyzed the distribution of compchains in three UD English treebanks, EWT, GUM and LinES, revealing that these treebanks are sparse with respect to sentences with predicate-argument structure that includes predicate-argument embedding. We evaluated the *CoNLL 2018 Shared Task* UDPipe (v1.2) baseline (dependency parsing) models as compchain classifiers for the EWT, GUMS and LinES UD treebanks. Our results indicate that these three baseline models exhibit poorer performance on sentences with predicate-argument structure with more than one level of embedding; we used compchains to characterize the errors made by these parsers and present examples of erroneous parses produced by the parser that were identified using compchains. We also analyzed the distribution of compchains in 58 non-English UD treebanks and then used compchains to evaluate the *CoNLL'18 Shared Task* baseline model for each of these treebanks. Our analysis shows that performance with respect to compchain classification is only weakly correlated with the official evaluation metrics (LAS, MLAS and BLEX). We identify gaps in the distribution of compchains in several of the UD treebanks, thus providing a roadmap for how these treebanks may be supplemented. We conclude by discussing how compchains provide a new perspective on the sparsity of training data for UD parsers, as well as the accuracy of the resulting UD parses.

1 Introduction

The Universal Dependencies (UD) project (De Marneffe et al., 2014; Nivre et al., 2016) is a multilingual annotation scheme for dependency grammars that has gained wide usage (Zeman et al., 2017; Kong et al., 2017; Qi et al., 2020). To this extent, automatically identifying whether a dependency parse[1] is correct or incorrect, as well as the potential source of such errors, becomes an important part of NLP pipelines. For example, such identification can prevent errors from propagating to downstream applications such as the identification of predicate-argument structure, involved in *semantic role labeling* and *sentiment analysis*.[2] Furthermore, embedding of sentences within sentences, and in particular embedding of predicate-argument structures within one another, is one of the ways in which humans have the capability to generate an infinity of different <sentences, meaning> pairings, and so it is important to evaluate whether a UD parser can accurately recover the predicate-argument structure of sentences with embedding. Thus, characterizing the limits of how accurately and consistently UD parsers assign predicate-argument structure in the context of correct UD annotation also becomes important (Nivre and Fang, 2017; Oepen et al., 2017; Fares et al., 2018; White et al., 2016; Reddy et al., 2017; Mille et al., 2018). That is the goal of this study.

In this study we introduce *compchains*, a categorization of the hierarchy of predicate dependency relations present within a Universal Dependency (UD) parse; this categorization serves as a proxy for

[1] This study only considers dependency parse trees annotated with UD. We refer to such a parse tree as a UD parse tree.

[2] Furthermore, (Surdeanu et al., 2003) has demonstrated that correct annotation of predicate-argument structure can improve the performance of information extraction systems.

Proceedings of the 10th Conference on Lexical and Computational Semantics, pages 116–128
August 5–6, 2021, Bangkok, Thailand (online) ©2021 Association for Computational Linguistics

predicate-argument structure. We use compchains to evaluate the accuracy of three (English) *CoNLL 2018 Shared Task* baseline models for the UDPipe dependency parser (Zeman et al., 2018). We found that the baseline model for the EWT UD treebank was more accurate than the baseline models for the LinES and GUM UD treebanks. We then use compchains to characterize the errors (relevant to predicate-argument structure) made by these models. We found that the accuracy of all three models dropped significantly when restricting the test set to samples with predicate-argument structure with embedding. Finally, we extended the analysis above to languages other than English, computing the distribution of compchains in 58 UD treebanks and evaluating the performance of the corresponding *CoNLL 2018 Shared Task* baseline models (for the UDPipe parser) as compchain classifiers. We conclude by discussing deficiencies in the distribution of predicate-argument structure with embedding present in the UD treebanks, as identified by our analysis.

2 Related Work

This section reviews prior work on the evaluation of (Universal) dependency parsers and the characterization of the errors these parsers make. The *CoNLL Shared Task* is a well established benchmark for evaluating the performance of multilingual (Universal) dependency parsers (Buchholz and Marsi, 2006; Nivre et al., 2007; Zeman et al., 2017, 2018). The task uses a number of metrics to evaluate the accuracy of the parser including: UAS (unlabeled attached score), LAS (labeled attachment score), CLAS (Content-word LAS) (Nivre and Fang, 2017), MLAS (Morphologically-aware LAS) and BLEX (BiLEXical Dependency Score). However, these metrics rely on the attachment accuracy (of dependency relations)[3] and do not take into account that errors cascade – i.e. if the parser incorrectly attaches a dependency relation, it may then be forced to make yet another incorrect attachment (Ng and Curran, 2015), thus making it difficult to identify the provenance of the error.

In light of this, efforts to further characterize the errors have proceeded in several directions. One direction involves studying whether and how the parsing errors are a result of the design of the dependency parser: (McDonald and Nivre, 2007) characterizes and compares the errors produced by graph-based dependency parsers (e.g. the MST-Parser by (McDonald and Pereira, 2006); see also (Kiperwasser and Goldberg, 2016; Cheng et al., 2016; Zhang et al., 2016)) and transition-based dependency parsers (e.g. the MaltParser by (Nivre et al., 2006)); (Zhang and Clark, 2008) shows how the two approaches to dependency parsing may be combined and documents the resulting improvement in performance.

An alternative direction involves characterizing the errors in the context of linguistic theory – e.g. (Kummerfeld et al., 2012) has introduced a method for classifying erroneous parse trees by repairing the tree with a series of tree-transformations, with each tree-transformation having a linguistic interpretation; (Mahler et al., 2017) has shown that it is possible to systematically break NLP systems for sentiment analysis by editing sentences with linguistically interpretable transformations. *In this study we pursue this latter direction, opting to characterize erroneous parse trees by classifying their predicate-argument structure using compchains.*

3 Compchains

Within a UD parse tree, predicate-argument structure[4] is encoded by *core argument* dependency relations, along with the special dependency relation *root*.[5] The *core-argument* dependency relations fall into two classes: *predicate* relations and *nominal* relations. In this study, we limit our attention to the two *predicate* dependency relations that encode embedding of clausal complements: (i) *ccomp* – a dependent, clausal complement, and (ii) *xcomp* – a clausal complement lacking a subject; the subject is determined by an argument that is external to the *xcomp*, usually the object (or otherwise subject) of the next higher clause.[6] We will focus on categorizing sequences of these two dependency relations (with POS marked as *Verb*) that originate from the root of a dependency tree (intuitively, the spine of the predicate-argument structure). This notion is formalized as follows:

Definition. A **compchain** is a finite sequence of dependency relations that traces a path starting at

[3]E.g. UAS (unlabeled attachment score) and LAS (labeled attachment score).

[4]See (Hale, 1993; Hale and Keyser, 2002) for further reference on predicate-argument structure.

[5]See `universaldependencies.org/u/dep/` for more details.

[6]*xcomp* is often used to model control/raising constructions in which an argument in the embedded clause establishes a syntactic relation with the predicate in the matrix clause.

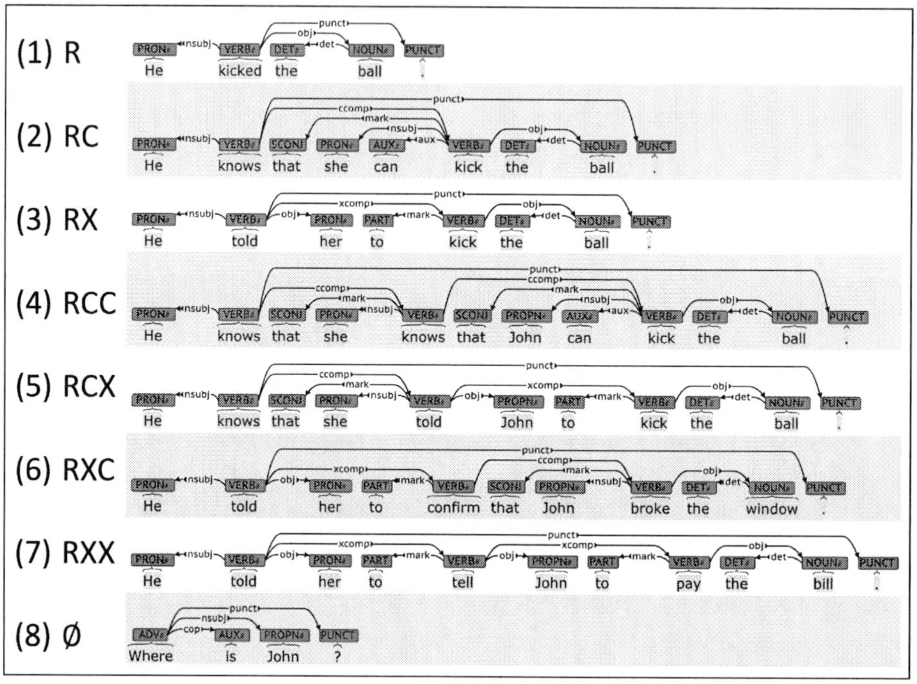

Figure 1: Examples of compchain classifications (left) for eight UD parses (right) produced by the UDv2.2 EWT baseline model using UDPipe 1.2. In each parse, the node with no incoming dependency relations is the *root*. Sentence 8 is classified as the ∅ compchain because the root is not marked as *VERB*.

the root node of a dependency parse tree and passing through only *xcomp* and *ccomp* dependency relations, subject to the constraints that: (i) every node in a compchain must have the POS tag of *Verb*; (ii) no node in a compchain should have a child dependency relation with POS *Verb* that is either an *xcomp* or *ccomp* and is not in the compchain as well.[7] We denote a compchain by listing the sequence of dependency relations, starting from the root of the tree, using the notation: R = *root*; X = *xcomp*; C = *ccomp*. E.g. we would denote the compchain $[root \rightarrow xcomp \rightarrow ccomp]$ as *RXC*. See Figure-1 for examples of UD parses and their compchain classifications.

One way to evaluate (indirectly) how well a UD parser can identify predicate-argument structure for sentences in a UD treebank is to evaluate whether the UD parse assigned by the parser to a sentence in the treebank has the same compchain as the compchain associated with the gold UD parse listed for that sentence (in the treebank); we refer to this task as **compchain classification**. *Performance on the compchain classification task is a proxy for performance on the task of classifying predicate-argument structure that includes predicate-argument embedding. If a UD parser performs poorly on the compchain classification task, predicate-argument structure cannot be reliably recovered from an (output) UD parse tree via top-down traversal of the sequence of dependency relations that forms the associated compchain.* See Figure-2 for examples of incorrect compchain classifications that reflect the parser recovering incorrect predicate-argument structure.

4 Experiments

4.1 Evaluation of English UD Treebanks

We evaluated the performance of the CoNLL'18 shared task baseline (parsing) models for English as *compchain classifiers* using three UD (v2.2) English treebanks: the English Web Treebank (EWT), with a total of 16,622 sentences (Silveira et al., 2014; Schuster and Manning, 2016); the English side of the English-Swedish Parallel Treebank (LinES), with a total of 4,564 sentences (Ahren-

[7]This constraint serves to ensure that if a UD parse tree has a compchain, it is unique and may be derived deterministically. This constraint also implies that some valid UD parse trees do not have a compchain – e.g. a parse in which there are two *xcomp* dependency relations that are both children of the same node. We use the symbol ∅ to denote that a UD parse tree has no compchain.

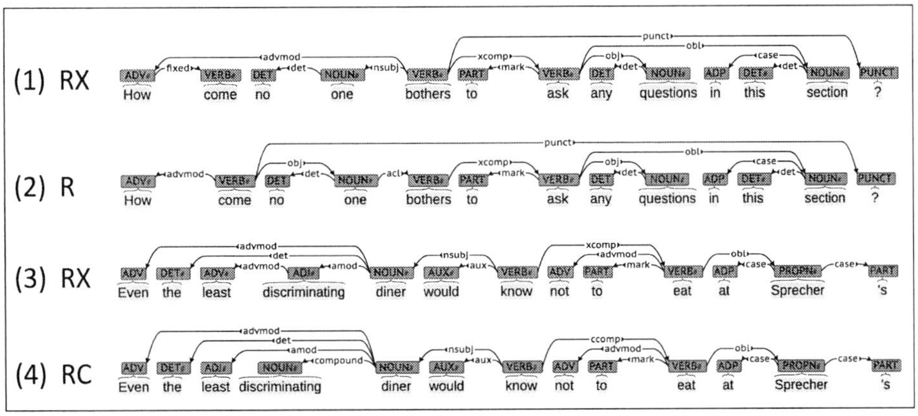

Figure 2: Examples of compchain classifications (left) for four UD parses (right). The parses in (1) and (2) are for the sentence *"How come no one bothers to ask any questions in this section?"* The parses in (3) and (4) are for the sentence *"Even the least discriminating diner would know not to eat at Sprecher's."* Both sentences were taken from the UDv2.2 English Web Treebank. (1) and (3) are gold parse from the treebank whereas (2) and (4) are produced by UDPipe using the CoNLL'18 baseline language model for UDv2.2 EWT. Both (2) and (4) are incorrectly classified, reflecting that these two parses encode misinterpretations (compared to the interpretations in their respective gold parses – i.e. (1) and (3)).

berg, 2007); and the GUM treebank, with a total of 4,390 sentences (Zeldes, 2017).[8]

We began by computing the distribution of compchains in each of the sections (train, dev, test) for each of the treebanks (see Table-1). We observed that although the training section of the EWT (UD) treebank includes a non-negligible number of UD parse trees that are classified (according to their corresponding Gold UD parse) as compchains with three or more dependency relations, the test section of the EWT (UD) treebank does not. This suggests that performing well on the task of parsing the test section of the EWT (UD) treebank need not indicate competency in parsing sentences with predicate-argument embedding of degree two or more. We also observed that the LinES and GUM treebanks have a negligible number of parse trees (across all sections) that are classified as compchains with three or more dependency relations – i.e. *RCC*, *RCX*, *RXC* and *RXX*.

Next, we evaluated the CoNLL'18 shared task baseline (parsing) models[9] for the three treebanks as compchain classifiers. We used UDPipe (v1.2), a transition-based non-projective dependency parser, to parse the test section of each of the three treebanks using the corresponding baseline model (Straka and Straková, 2017). We then classified the compchain of each UD parse and compared it to the compchain associated with the corresponding gold parse. We report the F-measures for this classification task in Table 2. We observed that the baseline model for EWT had the best performance as a compchain classifier. We also computed the per-compchain F-measures and observed that for all three baseline models, their per-compchain F1-score for *RX* was notably better than for *RC*. Here we observed a steep falloff in per-compchain F1-score as the number of dependency relations in a compchain increases. This suggests that either the parsers were not trained on enough examples of sentences with predicate-argument embedding, or that they did not adequately generalize from the limited number of examples that they were trained on.

Finally, we computed and analyzed the confusion matrix (i.e. error matrix) for each of the three baseline models, evaluating each model on the test section of its associated treebank. (see Figure 3) In each confusion matrix, off-diagonal entries count instances of parses with erroneous predicate-argument structure as indicated by the predicted compchain differing from the actual compchain (if two parse trees have different compchains, then their predicate-argument structure must differ as well). On-diagonal entries count instances of parses with correctly classified com-

[8] We used the pretrained word embeddings supplied with the CoNLL Shared Task for each of the three treebanks; these embeddings were produced with *word2vec* (Mikolov et al., 2013b,a).

[9] These UDPipe models were trained on the training section of the UDv2.2 EWT/LinES/GUM respectively. We also used the tagging and tokenization pipeline provided by UDPipe.

Compchain	EWT			LinES			GUM		
	Train	Dev	Test	Train	Dev	Test	Train	Dev	Test
∅	5230	985	1065	591	191	224	879	201	268
R	5500	815	806	1767	608	580	1661	413	419
RC	758	79	79	135	43	43	171	43	33
RX	808	100	104	202	65	50	158	43	41
RCC	47	4	6	1	0	2	8	1	2
RCX	94	7	9	17	1	6	10	2	1
RXC	48	6	3	10	2	6	6	0	2
RXX	39	2	2	12	2	3	13	3	3
Total	12543	2002	2077	2738	912	914	2914	707	769

Table 1: Distributions of compchains across the three treebanks. Counts for compchains with four or more dependency relations are not listed here because their presence in the three treebanks was negligible, although they are included in the "Total" count. Although there are very few compchains with three or more dependency relations (e.g. RCC) in the test sections of the treebanks, there are a non-negligible number of them in the training sections.

Compchain	EWT				LinES				GUM			
	F1	Prec.	Rec.	Support	F1	Prec.	Rec.	Support	F1	Prec.	Rec.	Support
∅	0.94	0.95	0.94	1065	0.74	0.72	0.75	224	0.85	0.81	0.9	268
R	0.89	0.89	0.9	806	0.85	0.87	0.83	580	0.85	0.89	0.81	419
RC	0.73	0.72	0.73	79	0.43	0.44	0.42	43	0.54	0.53	0.55	33
RX	0.79	0.8	0.79	104	0.53	0.44	0.66	50	0.64	0.57	0.73	41
RCC	0.67	0.67	0.67	6	0	0	0	2	0.4	0.33	0.5	2
RCX	0.4	0.5	0.33	9	0.25	0.5	0.17	6	0.5	0.33	1	1
RXC	0.33	0.33	0.33	3	0.55	0.6	0.5	6	0	0	0	2
RXX	1	1	1	2	0.44	0.33	0.67	3	0.4	0.5	0.33	3
W. Avg.	0.9	0.9	0.9	2077	0.78	0.78	0.77	914	0.82	0.83	0.82	769

Table 2: F-measures for the compchain classification of the parse trees in the EWT, LinES and GUM (UD) treebanks. The left most column refers to the *true* compchain from the appropriate UD treebank. Each row has the F1-score for the evaluation of the parser (as a compchain classifier) on sentences in the treebank that had the listed compchain, except for the bottom most row, which is the total (weighted) F1-score over all compchains – i.e. performance as a multi-way classifier.

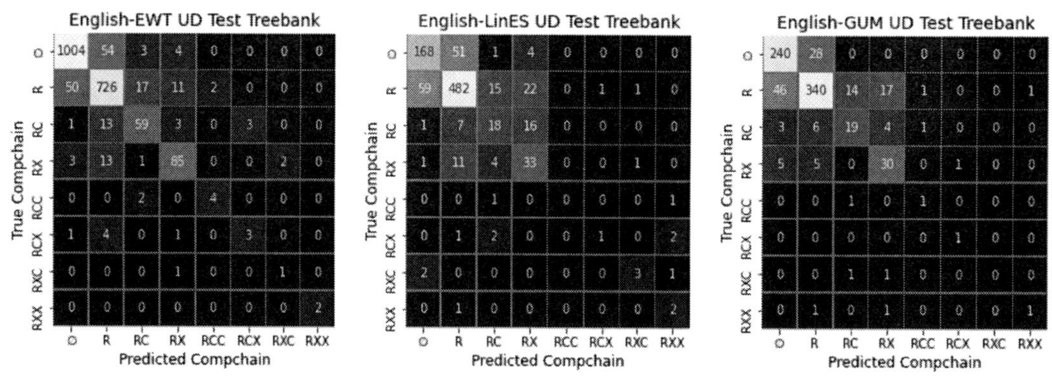

Figure 3: Confusion Matrices for Compchain Classification of the EWT, GUM and LinES UD (English) treebanks using their respective CoNLL'18 UDPipe Baseline Models.

pchains, which indicates that the parse may be correct (though it may well have errors not related to predicate-argument structure). We observed, for all three models, that compchains of length two or less were very rarely misclassified as compchains of length three or more, and that compchains of length two were often misclassified as the *R* compchain (see Figure-2 for an example of such a misclassification). We also observed that in the case of the baseline model for LinES, the compchain for *RC* is frequently misclassified as *RX*, but the compchain *RX* is rarely misclassified as *RC*; this asymmetry may reflect the difference in number of training examples in the LinES treebank – 135 in the case of *RC* and 202 in the case of *RX* (see Table-1).

4.2 Multilingual Evaluation of UD Treebanks

We also used the compchain classification task to evaluate the *CoNLL'18 shared task* baseline models (and the respective UD treebanks they were trained on) for languages other than English; this was motivated by the observation that since the UD treebanks are derived from a variety of textual sources, and thus have varying compchain distributions, we can use them collectively to evaluate and characterize the performance of the UDPipe dependency parser under various training conditions.

Figure 4 presents the distribution of compchains across 61 UD treebanks (including the three English treebanks analyzed earlier in this study).[10] Our analysis reveals that: (i) the UD treebanks for Hindi and Urdu have no instances of the compchain *RC* in either the training or test sections; (ii) the UD treebanks for Japanese, Korean, Turkish and Uyghur have no instances of the compchain *RC* in either the training or test sections; (iii) the UD treebanks for Hindi, Japanese, Turkish and Uyghur do not include *any* instances of compchains of length three or more (i.e. *RXX*, *RCC*, *RXC*, or *RCX*) in either the training or test sections.

We computed the F1-scores for the performance of each baseline model on the compchain classification task.[11] The F1-score for length-1 compchains is very weakly correlated with the F1-score for length-2 compchains, with $R^2 = 0.265$ (see Figure 5), and F1-scores for the two length-2 compchains (*RC* and *RX*) are also very weakly correlated, with $R^2 = 0.177$ (see Figure 6). This suggests that performance in recovering predicate-argument structures with differing embedding structures is largely unrelated and should be measured explicitly, just as the compchain classification task does. Additionally, we observe (as we did with the models trained on English treebanks) a rapid decline in the per-class F1-score as the length of the compchain increases, in particular for compchains of length two or more. (See Figure 7) This is revealing because, although the lack of compchains of length two or more in the UD treebanks suggests that we should not necessarily expect a dependency parser trained on the treebank to generalize out of the training domain, there is empirical evidence that humans *do* have the capacity to acquire a grammar from sentences with at most degree-1 embedding (corresponding to compchains of length 2) and then later correctly parse sentences with a degree of embedding of two or more (Wexler and Culicover, 1980; Morgan, 1986; Lightfoot, 1989); thus, the poor performance on compchains of length three or more suggests that the *CoNLL 2018 Shared Task* baseline models are not able to generalize beyond the distribution of syntactic structures they were trained upon, in contrast to human learners.

4.2.1 Impact of Word Ordering

Word ordering data (i.e. head-directionality) for each of the 61 languages in the UD treebanks was obtained from the WALS Online database (Dryer, 2013); we retrieved this information because the word ordering dictates whether a predicate precedes or succeeds its complement with respect to the linear ordering of the words in a sentence, and we wanted to understand whether this had an impact on the parser's performance on the compchain classification task. (See Table-5 in the appendix for the word-order of each language) The 47 languages with *verb-object* (VO) ordering had a median and mean weighted average F1-score of 0.85 and 0.88 respectively; the 18 languages with *object-verb* (OV) ordering had a median and mean weighted average F1-score of 0.86 and 0.85 respectively. It thus appears that the word-ordering does not appear to impact the weighted average F1-score. The F1-scores associated with compchains of length 2 (i.e. *RX* and *RC*) tell a different story: in the case of the *RC* compchain, the median F1-scores for *verb-object* and *object-verb* were 0.68 and 0.55 respectively, and in the case of the *RX* compchain, the median F1-scores for *verb-object* and *object-verb* were 0.72 and 0.42 respectively; thus for both compchains of length 2, models trained on *verb-object* ordered languages performed significantly better than models trained on *object-verb* ordered languages.[12] Given that the orderings of *verb-object* (i.e. head-initial) and *object-verb* (i.e. head-final) control whether a language will be associated with right-branching or left-branching structures respectively, our results suggest that the UDPipe

[10] See Table 4 in the appendix for a complete listing of the distribution of compchains in the Test and Training treebank for each of the 61 languages.

[11] See Table-5 for a complete listing of performance on the *compchain classification* task for each UD treebank using the associated baseline model, including a breakdown of performance per-compchain.

[12] These results also hold when comparing the mean F1-scores for compchains of length 1.

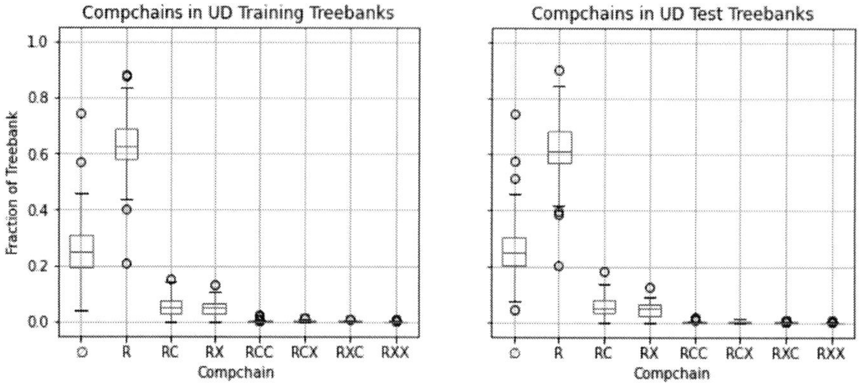

Figure 4: Distribution of Compchains in UD Training and Test Treebanks. 59 of the 61 languages had degree-2 compchains present in the test treebank; the languages with no degree-2 compchains in the test treebank were *turkish-imst* and *urdu-udtb*.

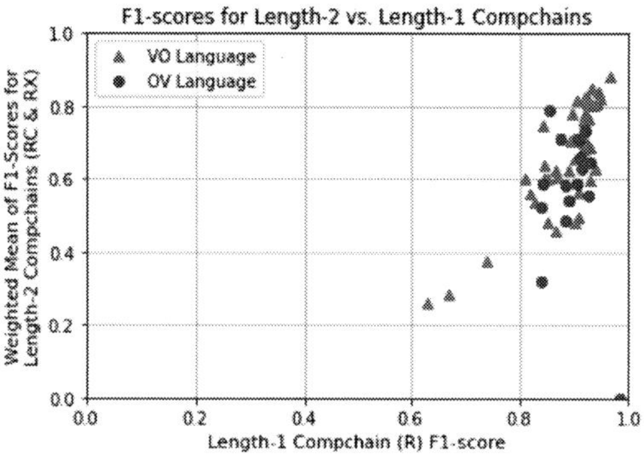

Figure 5: F1-scores for Length 2 vs. Length 1 compchains for each language in the UD treebank.

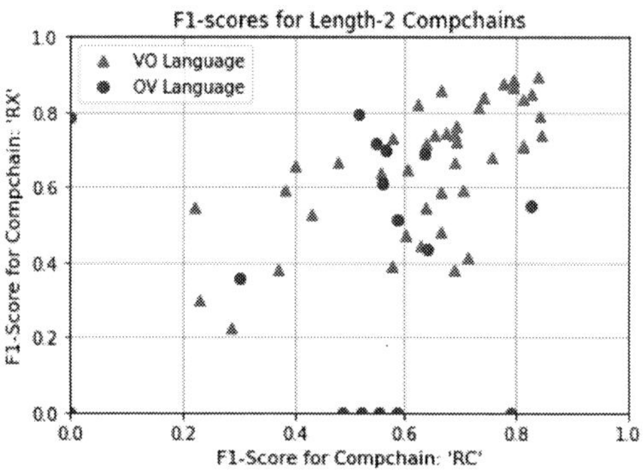

Figure 6: F1-scores for Length 2 compchains (i.e. *RC* and *RX*) for each language in the UD treebanks.

parser has difficulty dealing with left-branching structures.

4.2.2 Impact of Sentence Length

We carried out a regression analysis to investigate the relationship between the correctness of compchain classification and sentence length; this was

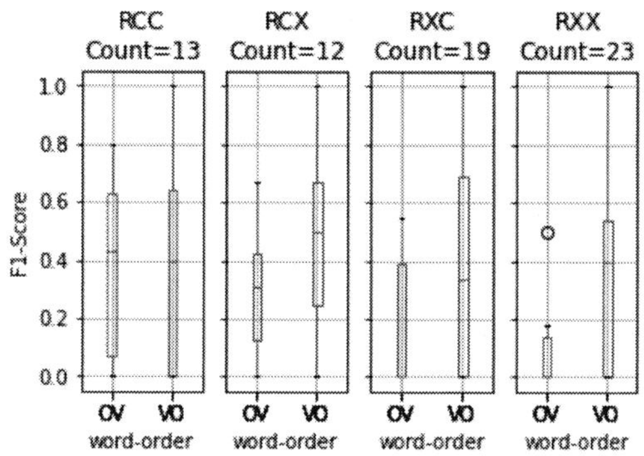

Figure 7: Distributions of F1-scores for length-3 compchains over all UD languages. For each length-3 compchain, F1-scores were reported for languages that had that compchain present in the test-treebank.

motivated by the observation that sentences with higher degrees of embedding, and thus longer compchains, tend to be longer sentences. We fitted a logistic function for each sentence in the test treebank, with the log of the sentence length (i.e. the number of tokens including punctuation) serving as the independent variable, and the (binary) dependent variable being whether the compchain associated with that sentence was correctly classified. We interpreted a good-fitting logistic function to indicate that compchain accuracy is dependent on sentence length. To evaluate the fit of the logistic function, we computed the Area Under Curve (AUC) measure of the Receiver Operator Characteristic (ROC) curve for the fitted logistic function. Figure 8 presents the distribution of AUCs for the test corpus of each of: (a) the 43 UD treebanks for languages with *verb-object* (VO) word-ordering, and (b) the 18 UD treebanks for langauges with

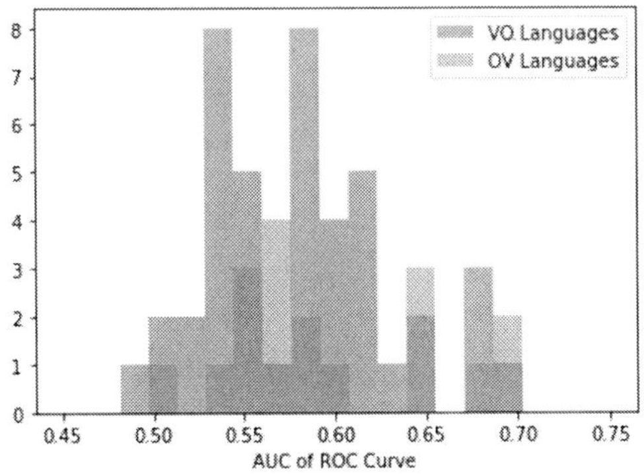

Figure 8: Histogram of Area-under-Curve (AUC) of Receiver Operator Characteristic (ROC) curve for Logistic Regression model of per-Sentence Compchain Classification Accuracy vs. log(Sentence Length). The AUC of ROC curve was computed for each UD test treebank.

object-verb (OV) word-ordering. We observe that the AUC for the majority of the treebanks falls between 0.55 and 0.65, and virtually none of the AUCs surpass 0.7, which is generally considered a minimum threshold for a binary-classifier to be considered accurate. Additionally, we observe that the OV languages tend to have a slightly higher AUC than the VO languages. We conclude that accuracy of compchain classification is weakly correlated with the log of the length of the sentence, and that this correlation is slightly higher for OV languages than for the VO languages. (Similar results were obtained when the analysis was carried out directly on the length of the sentence.)

4.2.3 Comparison with Other Eval. Metrics

In order to understand whether the compchain metric is simply a proxy for one of the three official evaluation metrics (LAS, BLEX and MLAS), we computed the pairwise linear correlation between each of the metrics for each of the 61 UD treebanks.[13] Table 3 presents the coefficient of determination for each pairing of the metrics. We observe that although LAS, MLAS and BLEX are all highly correlated with one another, they are weakly correlated with the compchain-metrics (i.e. weighted avg. of F1-score over all compchains and per-compchain F1-scores); notably, performance on compchain classification for *RX* is very weakly correlated with LAS, MLAS and BLEX ($R^2 < 0.1$).

[13]LAS, MLAS and BLEX scores for CoNLL Shared Task baseline models were obtained from `https://universaldependencies.org/conll18/baseline.html#baseline-results`.

	LAS	MLAS	BLEX
Compchain:W. Avg.	0.402	0.267	0.359
Compchain:R	0.329	0.180	0.277
Compchain:RC	0.399	0.305	0.388
Compchain:RX	0.074	0.089	0.096
LAS	1.000	0.780	0.918
MLAS	0.780	1.000	0.822
BLEX	0.918	0.822	1.000

Table 3: Coefficient of determination (R^2) for pairwise (linear) correlations of metric-scores over all CoNLL'18 Shared Task baseline models.

This suggests that the compchain metric is measuring an aspect of the parser's performance that is not brought to the fore by any of the three official evaluation metrics, and that *a baseline model having a good LAS, MLAS or BLEX score does not necessarily indicate that the model will correctly predict the embedding structure of a sentence with even a single level of embedding.*

5 Conclusion

In this study, we defined *compchains* and used them to evaluate how accurately a UD parser can parse sentences with predicate-argument structure that contains embedded clauses. We also used compchains to classify the errors, relevant to predicate-argument structure with embedding, made by a UD parser. Overall model performance on the compchain classification task (as measured by weighted F-measure) was found to be dominated by parse trees in the training set with no embedding (compchain *R*); closer inspection of per-compchain performance revealed that parser accuracy dropped precipitously as the degree of embedding in the predicate argument structure (i.e. length of compchain) increased. Finally, our results indicate that UD treebanks have very few parse trees with degree of embedding (i.e. length of compchain) greater than two. This presents an opportunity: if the test sets of the UD treebanks were augmented with parses with predicate-argument structure with degree of embeddings greater than two, then UD parsers can be evaluated in terms of their capacity to generalize from constructions (in the training set) with (mostly) low degree of embedding, just as a child must in some models of first language acquisition (Wexler and Culicover, 1980; Berwick, 1985; Lightfoot, 1989).

Acknowledgments

We would like to thank three anonymous reviewers for their valuable feedback and suggestions.

References

Lars Ahrenberg. 2007. Lines: An english-swedish parallel treebank. In *Proceedings of the 16th Nordic Conference of Computational Linguistics (NODALIDA 2007)*, pages 270–273.

Robert C. Berwick. 1985. *The acquisition of syntactic knowledge*. MIT press.

Sabine Buchholz and Erwin Marsi. 2006. Conll-x shared task on multilingual dependency parsing. In *Proceedings of the tenth conference on computational natural language learning*, pages 149–164. Association for Computational Linguistics.

Hao Cheng, Hao Fang, Xiaodong He, Jianfeng Gao, and Li Deng. 2016. Bi-directional attention with agreement for dependency parsing. *arXiv preprint arXiv:1608.02076*.

Marie-Catherine De Marneffe, Timothy Dozat, Natalia Silveira, Katri Haverinen, Filip Ginter, Joakim Nivre, and Christopher D Manning. 2014. Universal stanford dependencies: A cross-linguistic typology. In *LREC*, volume 14, pages 4585–4592.

Matthew S. Dryer. 2013. Order of subject, object and verb. In Matthew S. Dryer and Martin Haspelmath, editors, *The World Atlas of Language Structures Online*. Max Planck Institute for Evolutionary Anthropology, Leipzig.

Murhaf Fares, Stephan Oepen, Lilja Ovrelid, Jari Bjorne, and Richard Johansson. 2018. The 2018 shared task on extrinsic parser evaluation: on the downstream utility of english universal dependency parsers. In *Proceedings of the CoNLL 2018 Shared Task: Multilingual Parsing from Raw Text to Universal Dependencies*, pages 22–33.

Kenneth Hale. 1993. On argument structure and the lexical expression of syntactic relations. In Ken Hale and Samuel J. Keyser, editors, *The view from Building 20: Essays in linguistics in honor of Sylvain Bromberger*. MIT Press.

Kenneth Locke Hale and Samuel Jay Keyser. 2002. *Prolegomenon to a theory of argument structure*, volume 39. MIT press.

Eliyahu Kiperwasser and Yoav Goldberg. 2016. Simple and accurate dependency parsing using bidirectional lstm feature representations. *Transactions of the Association for Computational Linguistics*, 4:313–327.

Lingpeng Kong, Chris Alberti, Daniel Andor, Ivan Bogatyy, and David Weiss. 2017. Dragnn: A transition-based framework for dynamically connected neural networks. *arXiv preprint arXiv:1703.04474*.

Jonathan K Kummerfeld, David Hall, James R Curran, and Dan Klein. 2012. Parser showdown at the wall street corral: An empirical investigation of error types in parser output. In *Proceedings of the 2012 Joint Conference on Empirical Methods in Natural Language Processing and Computational Natural Language Learning*, pages 1048–1059. Association for Computational Linguistics.

David Lightfoot. 1989. The child's trigger experience: Degree-0 learnability. *Behavioral and Brain Sciences*, 12(2):321–334.

Taylor Mahler, Willy Cheung, Micha Elsner, David King, Marie-Catherine de Marneffe, Cory Shain, Symon Stevens-Guille, and Michael White. 2017. Breaking NLP: Using morphosyntax, semantics, pragmatics and world knowledge to fool sentiment analysis systems. In *Proceedings of the First Workshop on Building Linguistically Generalizable NLP Systems*, pages 33–39, Copenhagen, Denmark. Association for Computational Linguistics.

Ryan McDonald and Joakim Nivre. 2007. Characterizing the errors of data-driven dependency parsing models. In *Proceedings of the 2007 Joint Conference on Empirical Methods in Natural Language Processing and Computational Natural Language Learning (EMNLP-CoNLL)*.

Ryan McDonald and Fernando Pereira. 2006. Online learning of approximate dependency parsing algorithms. In *11th Conference of the European Chapter of the Association for Computational Linguistics*.

Tomas Mikolov, Kai Chen, Greg Corrado, and Jeffrey Dean. 2013a. Efficient estimation of word representations in vector space. *arXiv preprint arXiv:1301.3781*.

Tomas Mikolov, Ilya Sutskever, Kai Chen, Greg S Corrado, and Jeff Dean. 2013b. Distributed representations of words and phrases and their compositionality. In *Advances in neural information processing systems*, pages 3111–3119.

Simon Mille, Anja Belz, Bernd Bohnet, and Leo Wanner. 2018. Underspecified universal dependency structures as inputs for multilingual surface realisation. In *Proceedings of the 11th International Conference on Natural Language Generation*, pages 199–209.

James L Morgan. 1986. *From simple input to complex grammar.* The MIT Press.

Dominick Ng and James R Curran. 2015. Identifying cascading errors using constraints in dependency parsing. In *Proceedings of the 53rd Annual Meeting of the Association for Computational Linguistics and the 7th International Joint Conference on Natural Language Processing (Volume 1: Long Papers)*, volume 1, pages 1148–1158.

Joakim Nivre, Marie-Catherine De Marneffe, Filip Ginter, Yoav Goldberg, Jan Hajic, Christopher D Manning, Ryan T McDonald, Slav Petrov, Sampo Pyysalo, Natalia Silveira, et al. 2016. Universal dependencies v1: A multilingual treebank collection. In *LREC*.

Joakim Nivre and Chiao-Ting Fang. 2017. Universal dependency evaluation. In *Proceedings of the NoDaLiDa 2017 Workshop on Universal Dependencies, 22 May, Gothenburg Sweden*, 135, pages 86–95. Linköping University Electronic Press.

Joakim Nivre, Johan Hall, Sandra Kübler, Ryan McDonald, Jens Nilsson, Sebastian Riedel, and Deniz Yuret. 2007. The conll 2007 shared task on dependency parsing. In *Proceedings of the 2007 Joint Conference on Empirical Methods in Natural Language Processing and Computational Natural Language Learning (EMNLP-CoNLL)*.

Joakim Nivre, Johan Hall, Jens Nilsson, Svetoslav Marinov, et al. 2006. Labeled pseudo-projective dependency parsing with support vector machines. In *Proceedings of the Tenth Conference on Computational Natural Language Learning (CoNLL-X)*, pages 221–225.

Stephan Oepen, L Ovrelid, Jari Bjorne, Richard Johansson, Emanuele Lapponi, Filip Ginter, and Erik Velldal. 2017. The 2017 shared task on extrinsic parser evaluation towards a reusable community infrastructure. *Proceedings of the 2017 Shared Task on Extrinsic Parser Evaluation*, pages 1–16.

Peng Qi, Yuhao Zhang, Yuhui Zhang, Jason Bolton, and Christopher D. Manning. 2020. Stanza: A Python natural language processing toolkit for many human languages. In *Proceedings of the 58th Annual Meeting of the Association for Computational Linguistics: System Demonstrations*.

Siva Reddy, Oscar Tackstrom, Slav Petrov, Mark Steedman, and Mirella Lapata. 2017. Universal semantic parsing. *arXiv preprint arXiv:1702.03196*.

Sebastian Schuster and Christopher D Manning. 2016. Enhanced english universal dependencies: An improved representation for natural language understanding tasks. In *LREC*, pages 23–28. Portorož, Slovenia.

Natalia Silveira, Timothy Dozat, Marie-Catherine De Marneffe, Samuel R Bowman, Miriam Connor, John Bauer, and Christopher D Manning. 2014. A gold standard dependency corpus for english. In *LREC*, pages 2897–2904.

Milan Straka and Jana Straková. 2017. Tokenizing, pos tagging, lemmatizing and parsing ud 2.0 with udpipe. *Proceedings of the CoNLL 2017 Shared Task: Multilingual Parsing from Raw Text to Universal Dependencies*, pages 88–99.

Mihai Surdeanu, Sanda Harabagiu, John Williams, and Paul Aarseth. 2003. Using predicate-argument structures for information extraction. In *Proceedings of the 41st Annual Meeting of the Association for Computational Linguistics*.

Kenneth. Wexler and Peter W. Culicover. 1980. *Formal principles of language acquisition*. MIT Press.

Aaron Steven White, Drew Reisinger, Keisuke Sakaguchi, Tim Vieira, Sheng Zhang, Rachel Rudinger, Kyle Rawlins, and Benjamin Van Durme. 2016. Universal decompositional semantics on universal dependencies. In *Proceedings of the 2016 Conference on Empirical Methods in Natural Language Processing*, pages 1713–1723.

Amir Zeldes. 2017. The gum corpus: Creating multilayer resources in the classroom. *Lang. Resour. Eval.*, 51(3):581–612.

Daniel Zeman, Jan Hajič, Martin Popel, Martin Potthast, Milan Straka, Filip Ginter, Joakim Nivre, and Slav Petrov. 2018. CoNLL 2018 shared task: Multilingual parsing from raw text to universal dependencies. In *Proceedings of the CoNLL 2018 Shared Task: Multilingual Parsing from Raw Text to Universal Dependencies*, pages 1–21, Brussels, Belgium. Association for Computational Linguistics.

Daniel Zeman, Martin Popel, Milan Straka, Jan Hajic, Joakim Nivre, Filip Ginter, Juhani Luotolahti, Sampo Pyysalo, Slav Petrov, Martin Potthast, Francis Tyers, Elena Badmaeva, Memduh Gokirmak, Anna Nedoluzhko, Silvie Cinkova, Jan Hajic jr., Jaroslava Hlavacova, Václava Kettnerová, Zdenka Uresova, Jenna Kanerva, Stina Ojala, Anna Missilä, Christopher D. Manning, Sebastian Schuster, Siva Reddy, Dima Taji, Nizar Habash, Herman Leung, Marie-Catherine de Marneffe, Manuela Sanguinetti, Maria Simi, Hiroshi Kanayama, Valeria dePaiva, Kira Droganova, Héctor Martínez Alonso, Çağrı Çöltekin, Umut Sulubacak, Hans Uszkoreit, Vivien Macketanz, Aljoscha Burchardt, Kim Harris, Katrin Marheinecke, Georg Rehm, Tolga Kayadelen, Mohammed Attia, Ali Elkahky, Zhuoran Yu, Emily Pitler, Saran Lertpradit, Michael Mandl, Jesse Kirchner, Hector Fernandez Alcalde, Jana Strnadová, Esha Banerjee, Ruli Manurung, Antonio Stella, Atsuko Shimada, Sookyoung Kwak, Gustavo Mendonca, Tatiana Lando, Rattima Nitisaroj, and Josie Li. 2017. Conll 2017 shared task: Multilingual parsing from raw text to universal dependencies. In *Proceedings of the CoNLL 2017 Shared Task: Multilingual Parsing from Raw Text to Universal Dependencies*, pages 1–19. Association for Computational Linguistics.

Xingxing Zhang, Jianpeng Cheng, and Mirella Lapata. 2016. Dependency parsing as head selection. *arXiv preprint arXiv:1606.01280*.

Yue Zhang and Stephen Clark. 2008. A tale of two parsers: investigating and combining graph-based and transition-based dependency parsing using beam-search. In *Proceedings of the Conference on Empirical Methods in Natural Language Processing*, pages 562–571. Association for Computational Linguistics.

A Appendix

Table-4 presents the distribution of compchains across 61 UD treebanks (including the three English treebanks analyzed earlier in this study). Table-5 presents the F1-scores for the performance of each baseline models on the compchain classification task. The rows of Table 4 and Table 5 were seriated using the *Google OR-Tools library* so that rows with similar values appear close together: Table 4 is seriated so that languages with similar compchain distributions are clustered together; Table 5 is seriated so that languages with similar F1-scores are clustered together.

Computing Infrastructure: All experiments reported in this study were performed on a MacBook Pro (Retina, 15-inch, Late 2013) with a 2.3 GHz Intel Core i7 processor, and 16 GB of 1600 MHz DDR3 RAM. We used Python v3.7.9, Pandas v1.2.1 and Matplotlib v3.2.1.

(The remainder of this page intentionally blank. Please see the next page.)

Treebank	Total	R	RC	RX	RCC	RCX	RXC	RXX
vietnamese-vtb	1400/800	48.1/48.9	11.4/10.8	10.9/8.2	1.1/1.5	1.6/1.4	0.6/1.0	0.9/0.2
chinese-gsd	3997/500	52.6/53.4	11.1/11.4	10.0/8.6	1.2/0.6	1.5/1.0	1.1/0.8	0.9/0.4
catalan-ancora	13123/1846	65.0/66.5	10.1/7.9	5.8/6.1	0.6/0.2	0.6/0.5	0.2/0.1	0.2/0.2
serbian-set	2935/491	53.2/58.0	10.4/10.0	4.9/5.5	0.7/0.4	1.7/0.8	0.3/-	-/-
spanish-ancora	14305/1721	59.5/58.8	12.2/13.5	5.3/5.5	0.8/0.5	0.9/0.8	0.1/-	0.1/0.2
greek-gdt	1662/456	62.1/59.9	13.0/9.9	5.6/5.0	1.0/0.4	1.1/0.7	0.4/0.7	-/-
galician-ctg	2272/861	58.5/57.6	14.0/13.6	1.8/1.3	2.2/1.4	0.2/0.6	0.1/-	-/0.1
persian-seraji	4798/600	46.5/46.5	15.1/18.2	0.1/-	2.4/2.2	-/-	-/-	-/-
romanian-rrt	8043/729	72.4/71.9	10.1/12.1	1.5/2.3	0.7/1.2	0.1/-	0.0/-	-/-
korean-kaist	23010/2287	61.3/61.1	8.3/6.8	0.1/-	0.3/0.2	-/-	-/-	-/-
bulgarian-btb	8907/1116	66.1/64.7	9.5/14.0	3.5/1.3	0.7/0.6	0.3/0.1	0.3/-	0.1/-
slovak-snk	8483/1061	66.1/59.8	8.2/2.1	4.6/3.3	0.3/-	1.0/0.5	0.4/0.1	0.0/-
portuguese-bosque	8329/477	58.1/59.3	7.6/8.4	4.5/2.5	0.5/0.2	0.6/0.4	0.3/-	0.3/-
latin-proiel	15906/1260	67.9/64.6	7.6/6.7	5.3/6.0	0.4/0.6	0.3/0.6	0.2/0.1	0.1/0.1
latvian-lvtb	5424/1228	62.3/60.7	7.7/7.2	6.2/4.8	0.4/0.2	0.7/0.9	0.5/0.7	0.1/-
czech-fictree	10160/1291	63.7/59.5	7.7/8.1	6.3/8.1	0.3/0.4	1.0/1.0	0.5/0.7	0.0/-
hebrew-htb	5241/491	62.5/61.7	6.5/3.7	6.8/6.1	0.2/-	0.7/1.0	0.1/-	-/-
english-ewt	12543/2077	43.8/38.8	6.0/3.8	6.4/5.0	0.4/0.3	0.7/0.4	0.4/0.1	0.3/0.1
basque-bdt	5396/1799	72.5/74.1	5.8/5.3	5.9/5.3	0.1/0.1	0.7/0.8	0.3/0.4	0.1/-
swedish-lines	2738/914	63.3/65.4	6.5/6.0	5.7/6.2	0.2/0.1	0.6/0.4	0.3/0.4	0.2/0.3
english-gum	2914/769	57.0/54.5	5.9/4.3	5.4/5.3	0.3/0.3	0.3/0.1	0.2/0.3	0.4/0.4
ancient_greek-proiel	15015/1047	72.9/72.5	5.6/4.9	5.2/6.7	0.2/0.3	0.2/0.6	0.1/0.1	0.1/0.1
slovenian-ssj	6478/788	65.5/62.2	6.0/7.4	4.8/5.7	0.2/0.4	0.6/0.8	0.4/0.6	0.0/0.1
danish-ddt	4383/565	59.5/57.0	6.6/9.9	3.7/4.1	0.2/0.4	0.3/0.5	0.0/0.2	0.0/-
finnish-ftb	14981/1867	65.0/64.9	5.4/6.4	4.1/4.0	0.1/0.4	0.3/0.4	0.2/0.1	0.0/-
norwegian-bokmaal	15696/1939	59.8/63.2	5.0/6.0	3.0/3.2	0.1/0.1	0.2/0.4	0.1/0.1	0.0/0.1
norwegian-nynorsk	14174/1511	53.4/54.5	4.7/4.0	3.0/2.9	0.2/0.1	0.2/0.1	0.1/-	0.1/-
italian-postwita	5368/674	46.0/47.2	4.3/4.0	3.3/2.4	0.1/0.1	0.2/-	0.2/0.3	0.1/0.1
swedish-talbanken	4303/1219	66.7/66.0	3.7/5.0	2.3/2.5	0.1/0.1	0.1/-	0.1/0.2	0.0/-
arabic-padt	6075/680	20.8/20.3	4.0/4.4	0.6/0.7	0.1/-	0.1/0.1	0.1/-	-/-
korean-gsd	4400/989	69.9/70.7	4.8/5.6	-/-	0.2/0.3	-/-	-/-	-/-
afrikaans-afribooms	1315/425	71.1/73.2	3.8/3.3	0.3/0.2	0.2/-	-/-	-/-	-/-
uyghur-udt	1656/900	81.0/79.6	3.1/3.7	-/-	-/-	-/-	-/-	-/-
japanese-gsd	7164/557	65.9/62.5	2.0/2.0	-/-	-/-	-/-	-/-	-/-
turkish-imst	3685/975	63.3/61.1	0.1/-	-/-	-/-	-/-	-/-	-/-
urdu-udtb	4043/535	87.9/90.3	-/-	0.0/-	-/-	-/-	-/-	-/-
hindi-hdtb	13304/1684	87.5/84.7	-/-	0.0/0.1	-/-	-/-	-/-	-/-
dutch-lassysmall	5789/876	40.1/39.8	1.1/0.8	1.8/1.5	0.0/-	0.1/-	-/-	0.0/0.1
german-gsd	13814/977	69.0/59.5	2.0/9.6	2.1/3.3	0.0/0.3	0.1/0.1	0.1/0.1	0.1/-
hungarian-szeged	910/449	75.6/75.7	0.7/0.7	4.2/6.2	-/-	0.1/-	-/-	-/-
italian-isdt	13121/482	61.0/69.9	3.5/1.9	3.9/3.1	0.2/0.6	0.2/0.2	0.1/-	0.1/-
dutch-alpino	12269/596	63.2/63.9	4.6/5.5	4.8/4.4	0.3/0.3	0.3/0.7	0.2/1.0	0.2/-
estonian-edt	20827/2737	60.4/59.8	3.4/4.2	5.1/4.6	0.1/0.1	0.4/0.4	0.2/0.1	0.1/0.1
finnish-tdt	12217/1555	60.1/58.7	3.0/4.1	5.1/5.8	0.0/0.1	0.3/0.3	0.2/0.3	0.1/0.1
ukrainian-iu	4513/783	62.6/65.1	3.1/4.1	5.9/5.1	0.0/-	0.3/0.5	0.2/-	0.1/-
russian-syntagrus	48814/6491	60.6/60.9	3.4/2.8	6.6/6.5	0.0/0.0	0.4/0.3	0.2/0.2	0.1/0.1
ancient_greek-perseus	11476/1306	83.7/68.3	4.1/12.6	7.0/7.6	0.2/0.5	0.4/1.1	0.1/0.2	0.2/0.4
latin-ittb	15808/750	52.0/51.5	5.0/4.0	6.8/9.2	0.2/-	0.2/0.3	0.4/-	0.1/-
czech-pdt	68495/10148	53.8/54.6	4.9/4.6	6.9/6.6	0.2/0.2	0.9/0.9	0.3/0.3	0.1/0.1
croatian-set	6983/1057	53.8/55.2	5.8/8.6	7.4/6.5	0.2/0.1	1.1/1.1	0.3/0.8	0.0/0.1
gothic-proiel	3387/1029	75.4/77.5	6.7/6.3	8.6/7.7	0.2/0.3	0.5/0.5	0.1/-	0.1/0.2
old_church_slavonic-proiel	4123/1141	80.4/82.6	6.0/5.2	8.3/7.2	0.1/0.1	0.8/0.4	-/0.1	0.3/0.1
english-lines	2738/914	64.5/63.5	4.9/4.7	7.4/5.5	0.0/0.2	0.6/0.7	0.4/0.7	0.4/0.3
polish-sz	6100/1100	72.5/72.9	5.0/5.3	7.6/7.2	0.0/0.2	0.6/0.6	0.4/0.4	0.1/-
old_french-srcmf	13909/1927	79.2/78.6	4.8/4.0	7.7/8.2	0.1/0.1	0.4/0.4	0.2/0.2	0.2/0.1
french-gsd	14554/416	61.0/54.6	3.1/3.8	8.2/8.7	0.2/0.7	0.5/1.0	0.2/-	0.3/0.5
polish-lfg	13774/1727	80.9/79.7	2.8/2.7	8.4/8.9	0.0/0.1	0.3/0.6	0.2/0.2	0.1/0.1
czech-cac	23478/628	59.2/61.3	2.2/2.4	6.8/6.7	0.1/-	0.4/0.3	0.3/0.2	0.1/0.2
french-spoken	1153/726	49.6/52.6	1.6/4.8	7.7/4.5	0.1/0.1	0.2/0.8	0.2/-	0.1/0.1
indonesian-gsd	4477/557	62.0/63.9	2.2/2.9	9.0/7.7	0.1/0.2	0.3/0.2	0.1/-	0.7/0.9
french-sequoia	2231/456	44.1/41.9	3.0/3.5	13.2/12.9	-/-	1.0/1.1	1.0/0.7	0.6/0.4

Table 4: Distribution of Compchains in UD 2.2 Gold Treebanks. The column *Total* presents the number of trees in the training and test sections of each treebank, and is formatted as $Count_{Training}/Count_{Test}$; the columns for each compchain present the percent of trees with that compchain in the training and test sections of the treebank respectively – e.g. with respect to the English-EWT treebank, 6% of the 12543 trees in the training section have the compchain *RC* whereas only 3.8% of the 2077 trees in the test section have the compchain *RC*. A dash ("-") indicates an absence of trees with that compchain (i.e. 0%).

Treebank	Word Order	W. Avg	R	RC	RX	RCC	RCX	RXC	RXX
polish-lfg	verb-object	0.94	0.97	0.84	0.89	1.00	0.87	0.29	1.00
french-gsd	verb-object	0.89	0.92	0.62	0.81	0.80	0.75	-	1.00
spanish-ancora	verb-object	0.89	0.92	0.81	0.78	0.55	0.60	-	0.67
english-ewt	verb-object	0.90	0.89	0.73	0.79	0.67	0.40	0.33	1.00
croatian-set	verb-object	0.90	0.92	0.79	0.87	0.67	0.75	0.71	1.00
czech-pdt	verb-object	0.92	0.93	0.79	0.89	0.72	0.80	0.64	0.67
finnish-tdt	verb-object	0.89	0.92	0.74	0.68	0.50	0.75	0.67	0.40
slovenian-ssj	verb-object	0.88	0.91	0.84	0.79	0.50	0.67	0.80	0.40
russian-syntagrus	verb-object	0.93	0.95	0.83	0.85	0.50	0.59	0.74	0.44
catalan-ancora	verb-object	0.91	0.94	0.81	0.83	0.25	0.53	1.00	0.67
czech-cac	verb-object	0.92	0.94	0.67	0.86	-	1.00	1.00	1.00
norwegian-bokmaal	verb-object	0.90	0.92	0.84	0.74	0.00	0.83	0.80	0.67
french-sequoia	verb-object	0.86	0.86	0.71	0.78	0.00	0.80	0.50	0.80
english-lines	verb-object	0.78	0.85	0.43	0.53	0.00	0.25	0.55	0.44
latin-proiel	object-verb	0.86	0.92	0.57	0.70	0.36	0.40	0.33	0.50
english-gum	verb-object	0.82	0.85	0.54	0.64	0.40	0.50	0.00	0.40
bulgarian-btb	verb-object	0.85	0.91	0.58	0.39	0.55	0.67	0.00	-
portuguese-bosque	verb-object	0.85	0.89	0.72	0.50	0.50	1.00	-	-
italian-isdt	verb-object	0.91	0.94	0.60	0.72	0.40	1.00	0.00	-
serbian-set	verb-object	0.92	0.95	0.81	0.84	0.29	0.67	0.00	-
ukrainian-iu	verb-object	0.89	0.92	0.69	0.72	-	0.60	0.00	-
old_church_slavonic-proiel	verb-object	0.89	0.94	0.61	0.65	0.00	0.67	0.00	0.00
ancient_greek-proiel	object-verb	0.87	0.93	0.55	0.72	0.00	0.50	0.00	0.00
hebrew-htb	verb-object	0.77	0.83	0.63	0.78	-	0.25	-	-
latin-ittb	object-verb	0.85	0.87	0.52	0.79	-	0.00	-	-
dutch-lassysmall	object-verb	0.91	0.89	0.59	0.52	-	-	-	0.00
arabic-padt	verb-object	0.88	0.76	0.61	0.36	-	0.00	-	-
japanese-gsd	object-verb	0.94	0.95	0.76	-	-	-	-	-
uyghur-udt	object-verb	0.87	0.93	0.56	-	-	-	-	-
afrikaans-afribooms	verb-object	0.86	0.90	0.52	0.00	-	-	-	-
korean-kaist	object-verb	0.79	0.84	0.52	-	0.29	-	-	-
korean-gsd	object-verb	0.83	0.88	0.49	-	0.50	-	-	-
persian-seraji	object-verb	0.85	0.86	0.80	-	0.72	-	-	-
romanian-rrt	verb-object	0.85	0.92	0.71	0.41	0.57	-	-	-
german-gsd	object-verb	0.80	0.85	0.68	0.49	0.50	0.00	0.00	-
swedish-talbanken	verb-object	0.88	0.92	0.69	0.67	1.00	0.00	0.00	-
greek-gdt	object-verb	0.87	0.92	0.82	0.52	0.80	0.33	0.00	0.00
danish-ddt	verb-object	0.80	0.85	0.68	0.37	0.80	0.33	0.00	-
norwegian-nynorsk	verb-object	0.88	0.90	0.70	0.59	1.00	0.50	-	0.00
finnish-ftb	verb-object	0.85	0.89	0.69	0.74	0.67	0.43	0.33	0.00
basque-bdt	object-verb	0.85	0.91	0.64	0.69	0.67	0.29	0.44	0.00
old_french-srcmf	verb-object	0.88	0.93	0.64	0.72	0.67	0.35	0.50	0.40
swedish-lines	verb-object	0.84	0.89	0.67	0.59	0.50	0.50	0.75	0.00
czech-fictree	verb-object	0.89	0.92	0.78	0.88	0.25	0.69	0.78	-
polish-sz	verb-object	0.90	0.94	0.76	0.87	0.00	0.67	0.89	-
slovak-snk	verb-object	0.92	0.93	0.74	0.84	-	0.73	0.67	0.00
dutch-alpino	object-verb	0.83	0.89	0.56	0.61	0.00	0.67	0.55	-
latvian-lvtb	verb-object	0.80	0.86	0.57	0.74	0.00	0.58	0.55	-
estonian-edt	verb-object	0.87	0.90	0.68	0.74	0.00	0.53	0.33	0.22
french-spoken	verb-object	0.80	0.83	0.60	0.47	0.00	0.50	0.00	0.40
gothic-proiel	verb-object	0.82	0.91	0.38	0.59	0.00	0.33	-	0.67
italian-postwita	verb-object	0.85	0.87	0.63	0.60	0.00	0.00	0.00	1.00
indonesian-gsd	verb-object	0.81	0.87	0.22	0.55	0.00	0.00	0.00	0.50
ancient_greek-perseus	object-verb	0.70	0.84	0.30	0.36	0.00	0.17	0.00	0.18
hindi-hdtb	object-verb	0.97	0.98	-	0.00	-	-	-	-
urdu-udtb	object-verb	0.94	0.97	-	-	-	-	-	-
turkish-imst	object-verb	0.81	0.86	-	-	-	-	-	-
vietnamese-vtb	verb-object	0.51	0.63	0.21	0.29	0.20	0.08	0.00	0.00
chinese-gsd	verb-object	0.61	0.72	0.35	0.34	0.22	0.00	0.33	0.00
galician-ctg	verb-object	0.63	0.70	0.31	0.47	0.12	0.00	0.00	0.00
hungarian-szeged	object-verb	0.85	0.91	0.00	0.79	-	-	-	-

Table 5: F1-Scores for Compchains Classifications for each UD 2.2 Gold Treebanks. The test section of each gold treebank was parsed using the corresponding pre-trained UDPipe language model; the compchain classification was computed for each pair of gold and parsed treebanks, and we report: (i) the weighted average F1-score (over all compchains); (ii) the (per-class) F1-score for each compchain. Entries for which the F1-score could not be computed due to a lack of support are marked with a dash ("-").

InFillmore: Frame-Guided Language Generation with Bidirectional Context

Jiefu Ou[†‡] **Nathaniel Weir**[†] **Anton Belyy**[†] **Felix Yu** **Benjamin Van Durme**
Johns Hopkins University
jouaa@connect.ust.hk
{nweir,abel,fyu17,vandurme}@jhu.edu

Abstract

We propose a structured extension to bidirectional-context conditional language generation, or "infilling," inspired by Frame Semantic theory (Fillmore, 1976). Guidance is provided through two approaches: (1) model fine-tuning, conditioning directly on observed symbolic frames, and (2) a novel extension to disjunctive lexically constrained decoding that leverages frame semantic lexical units. Automatic and human evaluations confirm that frame-guided generation allows for explicit manipulation of intended infill semantics, with minimal loss in distinguishability from human-generated text. Our methods flexibly apply to a variety of use scenarios, and we provide an interactive web demo.[1]

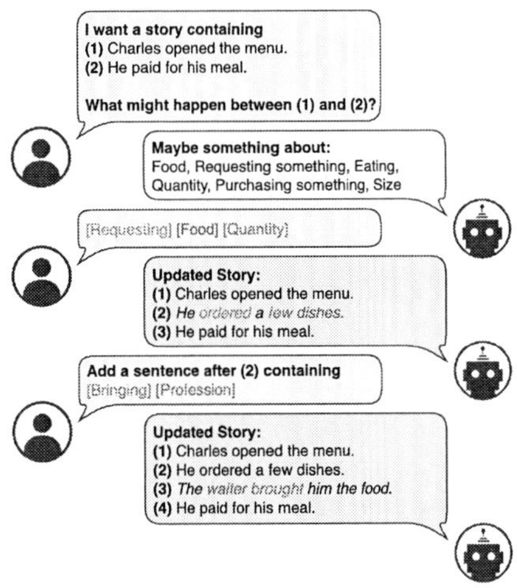

Figure 1: The proposed generation model, applied to the interactive story generation task. Similar to the existing infilling models, a user can insert or rewrite text spans at any position in a story. With the proposed extension, generation can be guided via explicit frame semantic constraints, either provided manually or suggested by the model based on surrounding context.

1 Introduction

A popular strategy for automatic story generation is to proceed in a coarse-to-fine manner: first by proposing a *story plan*, and then realizing it into natural language form using large pretrained neural language models (Fan et al., 2018; Goldfarb-Tarrant et al., 2019). In this work, we study the use of FrameNet frames (Baker et al., 1998) as representational units for such plan guidance.

In Frame Semantics (Fillmore, 1976; Fillmore and Baker, 2010), words evoke structural situation types (frames) that describe the common schematic relationships between lexical items. We hypothesize that these structured types can be used to effectively induce the semantic content of text generated by increasingly powerful pretrained language models, yielding a flexible, controllable and domain-general model for surface realization of story plans with a variety of dimensions for user guidance.

Based on this supposition, we fine-tune a recent infilling model (Donahue et al., 2020) with a frame-guided denoising objective. We contrast this approach with a novel method for frame-guided generation that modifies only the decoding step of a standard language model through lexical manipulation. The idea originates from the annotation scheme of FrameNet, where each semantic frame is annotated with a set of evocative lexical units (LUs). We posit that it is possible to guide the model's generation with frames *without* modifying its training procedure by instead lexically constraining its generation output to contain frame-associated LUs. Therefore, we develop an extension to lexically-constrained decoding that leverages LUs as ordered disjunctive constraint sets. Given a possibly multi-frame sequence and a generative model, our method en-

[†] Corresponding authors.
[‡] Work done during an internship at the Center for Language and Speech Processing, JHU.
[1] Codebase and demo available from https://nlp.jhu.edu/demos/infillmore.

Proceedings of the 10th Conference on Lexical and Computational Semantics, pages 129–142
August 5–6, 2021, Bangkok, Thailand (online) ©2021 Association for Computational Linguistics

forces the generation of one of the associated LUs for each frame in the sequence. This decoding method is implemented as a plug-and-play module that can be imposed on top of any standard generative language model.[2]

We evaluate through a sentence-infilling task based on ROCStories (Mostafazadeh et al., 2016), assessing performance on two dimensions: 1) the *quality* of generation, as measured through perplexity and human evaluation; and 2) the *fidelity*, which scores whether generated text evokes the frames used as guidance. We demonstrate that our methods utilize guidance to generate frame-evoking surface realizations without meaningfully detracting from the contextual narrative coherence. We also demonstrate the practical applicability of frame-guided generation in a variety of example use cases.

2 Related work

Controlled Generation Existing work employs a variety of pretraining strategies to guide and/or diversify text generation. Keskar et al. (2019) train large-scale language models on text prepended with *control codes*, allowing for guided content and style. PPLM (Dathathri et al., 2020) makes use of lightweight *attribute classifiers* that guide generation without requiring language model retraining. For diverse generation of sentences in a more general scenario, Weir et al. (2020) train models to condition on *semantic bit codes* obtained from hashing sentence embeddings.

Constrained Generation Separate lines of work employ *lexical constraints* to achieve the same goal of guided and diverse generation. As such, lexically constrained beam search methods such as Grid Beam Search (Hokamp and Liu, 2017) and Dynamic Beam Allocation (Post and Vilar, 2018; Hu et al., 2019a) were proposed as the decoding methods for causal generation with disjunctive positive constraints (Li et al., 2020b), paraphrasing (Hu et al., 2019b; Culkin et al., 2020), machine translation (Zhang et al., 2021), and abstractive summarization (Mao et al., 2020). Lu et al. (2020) generalize beam-search based methods with an algorithm that supports lexical constraints in the conjunctive normal form.

Parallel are the approaches that handle lexical constraints in an editing manner: starting with a sequence of keyword constraints and fleshing out a sentence via editing operations such as insertion or deletion (Miao et al., 2019; Liu et al., 2019; Sha, 2020; Susanto et al., 2020; **?**; Zhang et al., 2020). Finally, it is possible to satisfy lexical constraints in a soft manner as external memories (Li et al., 2020a, 2019) or constructing constraint-aware training data (Chen et al., 2020).

Story Generation Inspired by the traditional pipeline of Reiter and Dale (2000), recent work tackles generation of stories in a coarse-to-fine manner (Fan et al., 2018): based on a premise, a structured *outline* is generated first, and then an outline-condition model generates the full story. To represent the story outline, existing approaches typically either model it as a latent variable, or use symbolic representations such as key phrases (Xu et al., 2018; Yao et al., 2019; Goldfarb-Tarrant et al., 2019; Gupta et al., 2019; Rashkin et al., 2020), short summaries (Jain et al., 2017; Chen et al., 2019), verb-argument tuples (Martin et al., 2018), or PropBank predicates and arguments (Fan et al., 2019; Goldfarb-Tarrant et al., 2020). Our work can be viewed as an extension of this direction, where a *Content Planner* model generates an outline as a sequence of FrameNet frames, and our methods generate a surface form story.

3 Data

FrameNet FrameNet is a lexical database of English based on Fillmore's theory of Frame Semantics. It defines more than 1200 frames spanning various semantic domains, where each frame schematically describes a type of event, relation, or entity. A frame is defined with a set of corresponding *Frame Elements* (FEs): the participants in the frame with relational roles, and a set of *Lexical Units* (LUs): words that evoke the frame in text.

For example, the **Apply_heat** frame that describes the concept of cooking consists of core FEs *Food*, *Cook*, *Container*, *Heating_instrument*, and *Temperature_setting*, and has evocative LUs that include *fry, bake, boil,* and *broil*. Frame annotations provide a partial (albeit rich) picture of sentence meaning, i.e. information not governed by the syntax/semantics interface. We find that they serve as an effective, theory-grounded formalism for discrete semantic guidance of generation.

Conceptually, our choice to use FrameNet as guiding semantics builds upon trends in generative modeling of discourse (Ferraro and Van Durme, 2016) that treat text documents as mixtures of hi-

[2]Fairseq-based implementation and data to be released.

Story	Charles went shopping. He bought fruit. Then he left.
ILM	Charles went shopping. [blank] Then he left. *[sep] He bought fruit.*
S-FFL	[sep] [Food] He bought fruit.
A-FFL	[sep] [Commerce_buy] [Food] He bought fruit.

Figure 2: Training examples for frame-guided ILM models. Examples are fed from left to right, with the *italicized* portion of the ILM example replaced by the frame-injected sequences for FFL examples.

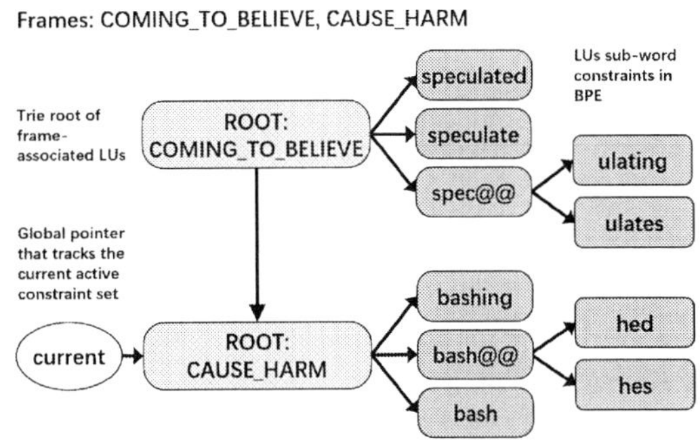

Figure 3: Example of LCD constraint representation in a list of 2 tries, corresponding to the given frames **Coming_to_believe** and **Cause_harm** (red). Other LUs are omitted for simplicity.

erarchical latent variables in accordance with classical theories of frame semantics (e.g. Minsky (1974); Fillmore (1976)). As described by Ferraro and Van Durme (2016), FrameNet frame information can be used to learn a hierarchical latent representation of sentence-level semantics that produces discourse models that better fit to natural text data. Our work then asks whether this information can be used to harness the increasingly powerful ability of recent neural language models for the purposes of controlled story generation.

ROCStories Mostafazadeh et al. (2016) introduce the ROCStories corpus, which comprises over 98K 5-sentence simple stories that can serve as a resource for commonsense narrative schema learning and story generation (Ippolito et al., 2020). We use this dataset to evaluate the performance of our methods (described in section 5).

4 Approach

4.1 Model Architecture

The Infilling by Language Modelling (ILM, Donahue et al., 2020) framework fine-tunes pretrained unidirectional language model such as GPT-2 (Radford et al., 2019) to generate target infill spans with bidirectional contexts. This allows the ILM model to flexibly generate text at any position in a document, as shown in Figure 1. In this work, we introduce FrameNet frame guidance into the ILM pipeline. We propose and compare methods based on 1) fine-tuning on frame-annotated data (4.2), and 2) imposing lexically-constrained beam search during decoding (4.3) with the original ILM.

4.2 Fine-Tuned "Framefilling" (FFL)

The ILM task definition comprises a context passage x containing **[blank]** tokens at points where the new spans must be generated.[3] The passage x is concatenated with a **[sep]** token and golden span infills (each separated by another **[sep]**) to form a fine-tuning instance for an off-the-shelf unidirectional language model such as GPT-2. We build on this setup by adding one or more frame ID tokens $F_1, F_2, \ldots$ (e.g. **[Food]**) as prefixes of each golden infill span, as shown in Figure 2. A model fine-tuned on this modified formulation, which we call a "framefilling" model (FFL for short), therefore conditions each infill on the bidirectional context as well as one or more control codes that guide the infill's semantic content. If an example contains multiple infills, subsequent infills are conditioned on the frames and text of previous infills.

We experiment with multiple variants of the FFL model, varying primarily in the level of frame guidance. We train a variant on infilling examples that contain a single frame ID (S-FFL), another on examples with a set of one or multiple frames (M-FFL; number of frames sampled from a geometric distribution with $p = .4$), and a final variant conditioned on all frames (covered by FrameNet v1.7) triggered by the infill (A-FFL). In all cases, the frame ID tokens are predicted by a state-of-the-art neural FrameNet parser (Xia et al., 2021).[4]

4.3 Lexically Constrained Decoding (LCD)

Given a sequence of frame ID tokens $F_1, F_2, ..., F_n$, we build a corresponding sequence of disjunctive lexical constraint sets $C_1, C_2, ..., C_n$, where C_i consists of all LUs of F_i with their morphologi-

[3]Our work focuses primarily on infilling single sentence spans, leaving arbitrary length spans, e.g. n-grams or full paragraphs, to the future work.

[4]We choose to evaluate these three variants in order to compare the coherence of a model trained with only low frame guidance (S-FFL), a model trained with only high (A-FFL), and a model (M-FFL) trained on a distribution of examples that comprises a superset of the first two.

cal variants. During decoding, our method forces the output to contain $c_1, c_2, ...c_n$, where $c_i \in C_i$.

Decoding with Ordered/Unordered Disjunctive Constraint Sets We develop a disjunctive lexically constrained decoding method (**LCD**) that extends implementations in Post and Vilar (2018); Hu et al. (2019a) and Li et al. (2020b). We also use Dynamic Beam Allocation (DBA) (Post and Vilar, 2018; Hu et al., 2019a) for beam assignment and next token selection, but we track our constraints differently. As shown in Figure 3, LCD represents a sequence of disjunctive constraint sets as a list of tries, one per frame, each covering a set of disjunctive lexical units (with morphological variants) based on the Byte Pair Encoding (BPE, Sennrich et al., 2016) adopted by GPT-2.

Based on this representation, we develop two versions of LCD: LCD-ordered and -unordered, the former of which requires that the constraint sets be completed in the order that the corresponding frame ID tokens are specified. By providing these two versions, we offer the user the flexibility to either enforce the frame-evoking narration being triggered in their desire order, or leave it to be determined by the generative model and decoder.

To track the generation progress through constraint sets, we use a global pointer to the currently active disjunctive set. Whenever the active set C_i is completed, the pointer is set to null. If unsatisfied sets remain, the next possible set(s) to be completed is C_{i+1} for LCD-ordered and $\{C_j : j \neq i \in \{1, 2, ..., n\} \mid C_j \text{ is not completed}\}$ for LCD-unordered. At the beginning of generation when no set is active, the next possible set(s) is C_0 for LCD-ordered and all sets for LCD-unordered. During the generation, when the pointer is null and a constraint token that starts any of the next possible set(s) is picked by DBA, the global pointer is set to the corresponding disjunctive set. Apart from the global pointer, the bookkeeping and unwinding mechanism within each trie is similar to the implementations in (Hu et al., 2019a) and (Li et al., 2020b), except that a trie is marked as finished and the global pointer is updated once any path in the trie is completed.

We implement LCD as an extension of the token generation constraint implementation in the `fairseq` library. Our LCD works very similarly to the disjunctive positive constraints decoding in (Li et al., 2020b), where the disjunctive sets are maintained in a single trie rather than our "list of tries" approach. However, we support explicit ordering of constraint sets, and we don't prune a sub-trie when the corresponding constraint set is finished.

5 Experiments

We test the effectiveness of our models on a frame-guided sentence infilling task derived from ROCStories. We use a state-of-the-art neural FrameNet parser (Xia et al., 2021) to obtain the set of frames evoked by each sentence in the dataset. We then present models with a five-sentence ROC story with one masked out. The model must infill the missing sentence given one or many frame ID tokens parsed from the masked-out sentence. For evaluations requiring generated outputs (all but perplexity), we use beam search with beam size 20. We find that beam search achieves higher frame fidelity and coherence than the random sampling approach used by Donahue et al. (2020).

We train our models (all GPT-2 'base') using the provided train split of ROCStories. For S/M/A-FFL, each example contains one/multiple/all frame ID tokens sampled randomly from the parser output. To test LCD, we re-train the original ILM using the identical ROCStories training data to our FFL models but without frame tokens (training details described in A.2). Unlike Donahue et al. (2020), we do not include story titles. We also use this ILM as a baseline with no guidance.

To investigate whether enforcing generated frame order impacts model performance, we evaluate both LCD-ordered and -unordered; we also evaluate FFL-ordered models fine-tuned to generate frames in the order in which they are provided.

5.1 Automatic Evaluation

We evaluate our frame-guided generation methods by measuring the rate at which they produce sentences that trigger the desired frame(s) and by measuring the perplexity score of the framefilling-trained language model on test examples.

Frame Fidelity We automatically evaluate whether a produced sequence triggers a given set of frames by running it through the same neural frame parser used to determine the desired frame from a gold human-generated sentence. Table 1 shows the rates at which methods correctly produce sentences that contain every specified frame.[5] For each

[5]Methods that condition on fewer frame IDs are evaluated using subsets of those for multi-frame models; e.g. if the

Fidelity ↑	Recall			Perfect Recall	
# Frames	Single	Multi	All	Multi	All
ILM (no guidance)	.169	.166	.165	.091	.026
ILM + LCD	**.584**	.595	.610	.418	.232
ILM + LCD-ord	–	**.598**	.626	**.427**	.255
FFL	.518	.559	.640	.381	.259
FFL (rand sample)	.461	.511	.601	.338	.224
FFL-ord	–	.585	**.669**	.415	**.298**

Table 1: Frame fidelity, computed as frame recall according to the neural frame parser (left). The per-example rate at which models perfectly predict frame sets is also given (right). Higher is better.

model, we evaluate the top-1 decoded sequence.

Perplexity The typical automatic evaluation metric for a language model is test data perplexity (PPL). Since LCD requires no training modification to the ILM model, we only compute the PPL for S/M/A-FFL and ILM on a test set of stories in which one of five sentences has been masked out.[6] Following Donahue et al. (2020), we evaluate models' PPL specifically on infill tokens and also compute PPL including the surrounding special tokens (separators and frame IDs). Because sequences for FFL models include one or more frame ID tokens, the token length for a given story example is different for ILM and each FFL variant; PPL therefore cannot be directly compared. To construct a scenario in which the ILM and FFL model perplexities *are* directly comparable, we train variants of both models for which every infill sequence is prepended with 5 special tokens, thus regularizing token length for every evaluated model.

5.2 Human Evaluation

In addition to automatic evaluation, we collect human judgements to assess models' ability to maintain coherent and plausible generation. We conduct two human evaluations that ask annotators to tell apart model- and human-generated sentences (Indistinguishability task) and rank model-generated sentences relative to one another (Relative Plausibility task). Details of our collection protocols and example interfaces are provided in Appendix D.

Indistinguishability Following Donahue et al., we present annotators with 5-sentence stories in which one sentence has been replaced by the output of an infilling model. Annotators must identify which sentence is model-generated.

For each model, we calculate the confusion rate $r = \frac{N_{confused}}{N_{all}}$, where $N_{confused}$ is the number of stories for which a human annotator fails to identify the machine-generated content, and N_{all} is the total number of stories. Results are shown in Table 3. Higher confusion rate is posited to mean more natural text infilling. Optimal performance is 80%, meaning the annotator is performing at chance.

Relative Plausibility We present human annotators with a 5-sentence story where one sentence is missing, and 10 candidate replacement sentences (the gold plus the infills of 9 different models). Annotators are tasked with ranking the candidate sentences (via drag-and-drop) based on how plausible they are relative to each other. Upon aggregating judgements, each model's score is calculated as the average relative rank of its output sentences that are assigned by annotators, as shown in Table 4.

M-FFL model must generate a set {**[Food] [Size]**}, the S-FFL must predict one of **[Food]** or **[Size]**.

[6] See Appendix C for model perplexity trained and evaluated with all five sentences having been masked.

Perplexity ↓	ILM	S-FFL	M-FFL	A-FFL	A-FFL (ord)
Infill Text	12.85	11.7	9.84	6.19	**5.05**
+ Sp Toks	7.24	8.32	9.5	8.95	**7.04**
w/ 5 Fr Slots	**4.06**	5.12	6.34	7.32	6.03

Table 2: Model perplexity over infill text tokens and infill text tokens + special tokens (<start to infill>, <end of infill>, <infill mask>). Lower is better.

6 Analysis

Fidelity From the results in Table 1, we find that ILM+LCD, FFL and FFL-ordered all perform similarly while substantially outperforming the baseline unguided ILM. This shows that our methods effectively produce text evoking the desired frame semantic content. Both methods benefit from the inclusion of gold frame order, more so for FFL.

There is a considerable gap between the performance of our models and perfect performance (1.0). This is because FFL operates only with soft "control code" constraints, and although LCD is strictly required to generate trigger LUs for every frame, it does not produce sentences that always successfully evoke the frame. While some of this gap might be the result of imperfections of the parser, we find word sense ambiguity to be a contributing problem. Many LUs, such as *work.v*, *see.v*, or *call.v* have multiple senses each associated with a different frame. Since neither LCD nor FFL imposes hard constraints on word sense, it is entirely

Confusion rate (%) ↑	# Frames		
	Single	Multi	All
ILM (no guidance)	**41**	**41**	**41**
ILM+LCD	35	31*	20*
FFL	33*	39	38
FFL-ordered	33*	38	37

Table 3: Confusion rate computed as the percentage of stories for which the annotator picks a wrong sentence as machine-generated. Higher is better. * denotes significant difference from the baseline (ILM) result, according to the two-sided McNemar test with $p < 0.05$.

Story
··· I danced terribly and broke a friend's toe. [blank]
Frame: [Request]

Gold [Request]
The next weekend, I was **asked** to please stay home.

ILM+LCD [Contacting]
I went home to **call** my friend and tell her I broke her toe.

Figure 4: From the lexical constraints on the LUs of the frame **Request** (as *asked.v* in the gold infill), the decoder selects *call.v*, but in the generated context *call* becomes a surfaces realization of frame **Contacting**.

possible for an unintended sense to be generated.

As illustrated in Figure 4, LCD forces picking the LU *call.v* for the target frame **Request**, but given the subsequent output *call my friend to tell her I was hurt*, the *call.v* unit takes on a sense that triggers the incorrect frame **Contacting**.

Perplexity Table 2 shows that the perplexity over purely the infill tokens is inversely proportional to the amount of frame guidance provided to the language model. However, we find that under the directly comparable 5 slot scenario, PPL computed over the infill tokens plus all surrounding special/frame tokens is *worse* for models with more frame tokens. As this work is predominantly concerned with the quality of generation given gold frame IDs, this is less of a concern; that the perplexity of infill tokens decreases considerably with the introduction of frame guidance shows that neural language models can be explicitly guided towards specific semantic spaces in accordance with the conceptual semantic structures underpinning human understanding of language.

Generation Quality Table 4 shows that in terms of human-judged relative plausibility, FFL outperforms all other models (including the unconstrained ILM) when conditioning on all frames, and underperforms ILM with only a small margin with multi-frame guidance. Table 3 shows that ILM outperforms FFL models and LCD on the Indistinguishability task in all cases, but with only a small margin in multi/all-frame cases comparing with FFLs. This is unsurprising, as ILM is optimized to replicate human-produced text under no constraints via semantic guidance. We observe as in the fidelity evaluation that LCD slightly outperforms FFL under single frame constraints in both human evaluations. From these results we can conclude that in the process of achieving effective controlled frame-guided language generation, the fine-tuned FFL model achieves competitive performance to its unconstrained ILM counterpart, especially in the presence of increased guiding information. Moreover, the compromise in quality for the LCD method is minimal particularly for single frame guidance.

Average rank (1..10) ↓	# Frames		
	Single	Multi	All
ILM (no guidance)	**5.48**	**5.48**	5.48
ILM+LCD	5.85*	6.38*	7.50*
FFL	5.88*	5.57	5.11
FFL-ordered	5.88*	5.53	**5.02***

Table 4: Average relative plausibility rank by human annotators. Lower is better. * denotes significant difference from the baseline (ILM) result, according to the two-sided Wilcoxon signed-rank test with $p < 0.05$.

Effect of Different Levels of Guidance Table 3 and Table 4 show that as the level of guidance (number of frames provided) increases, FFL and LCD models show opposite trends in quality: the former improves whereas the latter gets worse. We illustrate this effect in Figure 5.

For FFL, this indicates that generative capabilities would improve if the model were trained with more information about semantic content. This is a somewhat counterintuitive finding, given the effectiveness of the ILM model trained with no semantic information whatsoever beyond surface-level lexical information (words in the context).

For LCD, we posit that the increase in the size of lexical unit constraint sets amplifies the negative effects of the lexical units' word sense ambiguity, resulting in the downward trend. With more guiding frames, LCD has to search through a larger space of possible LU combinations and is therefore more prone to the misuse of LU (sense). More-

Story	
Ari spends $20 a day on pickles. He decides to make his own to save money. He puts the pickles in brine. [blank] Ari opens the jar to find perfect pickles.	
Gold	
Ari waits 2 weeks for his pickles to get sour.	
ILM Baseline	
He puts the pickles in a jar.	

	FFL	ILM+LCD
Single Frame: [Transition_to_State]	He ends up with a jar full of pickles.	He gets the pickles and puts them in jars.
Multiple Frames: [Cardinal_Numbers] [Transition_to_State]	He ends up with 5 jars of pickles.	He puts one in the jar and opens it to get a drink.
All Frames: [Cardinal_Numbers] [Measure_duration] [Transition_to_State][Chemical-sense_description]	He waits for a week for the pickles to get sour.	He waits for the pickles to thaw out of the jar to thaw one day he gets the pickles and eats them delicious.

Figure 5: Example infills by FFL, LCD and ILM baseline under single, multiple, and all frame guidance. Under single frame guidance, all decoding methods perform interchangeably. As the number of frames increases, FFL approaches a surface realization of frame-specified semantic content that resembles that of the gold infill. The unguided baseline ILM generates something relatively incoherent. Under "all frame" guidance, LCD fails to satisfy all constraints in one sentence and generates an additional sentence that corrupts quality.

over, we observe that in some cases with many (e.g. $\geq$ 5) frames, LCD cannot satisfy all constraints within one sentence and will start new sentences to complete unmet constraints. This is likely a contributing factor to LCD's lower scores under human evaluations.

7 Case Study: Interactive Generation

To demonstrate the practical applicability of our frame-guided infilling methods, we qualitatively explore them in a variety of human-in-the-loop use cases based on recent work in text generation. In the following cases, we use models for both frame ID inference and text infilling conditioned on surrounding context. For frame inference, we use the forward frame token probability of an unordered-frame M-FFL model trained as in Section 3, with the modification that training examples have between 0 and 4 surrounding sentences as context. This allows for more flexibilty than a model trained only on complete 5-sentence stories. We modify the training data by taking a random contiguous slice of each 5-sentence example. Figure 6 shows examples of each scenario. For infilling, we use FFL for **A**, **B** and **D** and LCD for **C**.

A. Iterative Story Refinement For a maximally free-form and extensible use case, we devise a scenario in the spirit of Goldfarb-Tarrant et al. (2019) in which a user interfaces with a model to collaboratively construct an open-domain story given any combination of text and/or frames. Over the course of a human-system dialog, the user can iteratively either choose for the model to predict new frames at specified locations in the context or select from candidate infills conditioned on selected frames. As discussed in Goldfarb-Tarrant et al. (2019), this type of process allows for a symbiotic relationship in which the user can correct, suggest or revise content generated by the machine and vice versa. Injecting frame guidance into this scenario enables for an extra degree of interactive flexibility in both suggestion and specification.

B. Generation from Story Skeleton Recent work (Fan et al., 2018; Goldfarb-Tarrant et al., 2019) has used pretrained neural language models for surface realization of structured story content. We approximate this task by having a model accept a seed sentence (i.e. a prompt) plus an ordered sequence of sets of frames specifying the content to appear in a story. We then use the frame-guided conditional generation to complete the text. Without the ability to handle explicit frame semantic guidance, this task would be incredibly difficult for a neural generation model.

C. Diverse Candidate Generation Weir et al. (2020) explore the task of diverse causal generation, in which a model must propose a set of semantically distinct causes or effects of an input sentence. Following their two-step approach, we devise a frame semantic model that 1) predicts the distinct frames that are likely to appear at a specified index before (for causes) or after (effects) the input sentence, then 2) run a separate beam search conditioned on each top-k predicted

A. Iterative Refinement

User: (I) Alice went to the grocery store. (II) [Commerce_buy]
System: (IIA) She bought all the ingredients for a cake. (IIB) She bought a new pair of shoes. (IIC) She bought a lot of fruits and veggies.
U: Choose (IIA) as (II) and infer content after (II)
S: [Food], [Cooking], [Ingredients], [Desirability], [Time_Collocation]
U: Choose [Desirability] [Cooking]
S: (I) Alice went to the grocery store. (II) She bought all the ingredients for a cake. *(III) She made the best cake she ever had.*
U: Infer content to replace (I)
S: [Food], [Deciding], [Social_Event], [Building], [Quantity]
U: choose [Social_Event]
S: *(I) Mary wanted to make a cake for her birthday.* (II) She bought all the ingredients for a cake. (III) She made the best cake she ever had.
U: Insert sentence about [Motion] at (II) and sentence about [Temporal_Collocation] at (IV)
S: (I) Mary wanted to make a cake for her birthday. *(II) She went to the store.* (III) She bought all the ingredients for a cake. *(IV) That afternoon, she baked the cake in the oven.* (V) She made the best cake she ever had.

B. Generation from Skeleton

User: (I) Bob went to Paris. (II) [Buildings] (III) [Experience] (IV) [Motion] 5 [Calendric_Unit]
System: (I) Bob went to Paris. *(II) He went to see the Louvre museum. (III) He saw lots of paintings and sculptures. (IV) He went to see the Eiffel Tower. (V) It was the best day of Bob's life.*

U: (I) Emma loved writing and wanted to be a writer. (II) [Deciding] (III) [Practice] (IV) [Publishing][Text] (V) [Fame]
S: (I) Emma loved writing and wanted to be a writer. *(II) She decided to enter a writing contest. (III) Emma's practice paid off and she won first prize. (IV) Emma was so proud of herself that she published a book. (V) Now Emma is a famous author.*

C. Diverse Candidate Generation

User: Infer candidates after (I) Charles slipped on a banana peel.
System: (IIA [Body_Parts]) He skinned his knee badly. (IIB [Motion_Directional]) He fell down on the ground. (IIC [Spatial_Contact]) He landed on his arm and broke it. (IID [Kinship]) His mother brought him to the emergency room. (IIE [Causation]) It caused him to fall down the stairs.

U: Infer candidates before (II) She hired a lawyer.
S: (IA [Submitting_Documents]) She filed a civil lawsuit. (IB [Trial]) She sued for breach of contract. (IC [Personal_Relationship]) She filed for divorce. (ID [Awareness]) She didn't know how to defend herself. (IE [Desiring]) she did not want to go to jail.

D. Counterfactual Story Rewriting

User: (I) Alec's daughter wanted more blocks to play with. (II) Alec figured that blocks would develop her scientific mind. (III) Alec bought blocks with letters on them. (IV) Alec's daughter made words with them rather than structures. (V) Alec was happy to see her developing her verbal ability. Replace (II) with "Alec could not afford to buy new blocks for his daughter" and rewrite the last three sentences.
Parser: (III) [Containers] (IV) [Text_Creation] (V) [Emotion_directed]
System: (I) Alec's daughter wanted more blocks to play with. (II) Alec could not afford to buy new blocks for his daughter. *(III) Alec's daughter begged him to buy her blocks. (IV) Alec wrote a letter to Santa Claus himself. (V) She was very happy when he wrote back.*

Figure 6: Example use cases of frame-guided infilling. **A.** depicts *human-in-the-loop iterative story refinement*, in which a user provides an initial context and/or intended frame semantic content and interacts with the model to predict and user-select new frame content and surface-realized context. **B.** depicts surface realization from a *frame semantic story skeleton*, i.e. a seed sentence and a sequence of frame sets to appear in the specified order. **C.** depicts *semantically diverse candidate generation* using model frame inference to identify distinct semantic content then using conditional generation to realize each candidate. **D.** depicts *counterfactual story revision*, in which one sentence (II) is replaced and subsequent sentences are rewritten using frames parsed from the originals.

frame. Using a frame-infused generation model for this purpose leverages the hierarchical semantic delineations contained within FrameNet, selecting human-interpretable semantic spaces from which to generate content. This is compared to other methods for diverse sampling, such as random and nucleus sampling (Holtzman et al., 2020), in which there is no notion of higher level semantic reasoning and a tendency to hallucinate content, or COD3S (Weir et al., 2020), which enables only moderate interpretability not based–as FrameNet is–in cognitive theories of semantic organization.

D. Counterfactual Story Revision Qin et al. (2019) introduce the task of generative counterfactual reasoning in narratives. Given an original story and a counterfactual event (i.e. the replacement of one original sentence), the task is to minimally revise the rest of the story according to the counterfactual replacement. We devise a frame semantic model for this task that 1) parses the frames of sentences following the replacement and 2) conditions the generation model on the replacement text and a sampled sequence of the parsed frames so as to produce a revised story whose frame semantics are similar to the original's. While previous approaches to this generation task condition only on surrounding context, our frame-injected model allows for explicit retention of semantic spaces.

8 Conclusion

We propose the application of frame semantics in the context of controlled text generation. We introduce two extensions of neural text generation that leverage FrameNet frames as guiding signals: 1) model fine-tuning with a frame-guided infilling objective; and 2) disjunctive lexically constrained decoding with frame-associated lexical units. Experimental results on a sentence infilling task and the case study involving an interactive story generation setup show that both of our methods can properly leverage the frame information to trigger surface realization of frame semantic content. Our results show that our methods enable explicit manipulation of semantics at the frame level with competitive generation quality, and we exhibit a variety of use cases that enable new dimensions of user guidance on generation.

Acknowledgments

This work was supported by DARPA KAIROS and NSF grant no. BCS-2020969. The U.S. Government is authorized to reproduce and distribute reprints for governmental purposes. The views and conclusions contained in this publication are those of the authors and should not be interpreted as representing official policies or endorsement.

References

Collin F. Baker, Charles J. Fillmore, and John B. Lowe. 1998. The Berkeley FrameNet project. In *COLING 1998 Volume 1: The 17th International Conference on Computational Linguistics*.

Gang Chen, Yang Liu, Huanbo Luan, Meng Zhang, Qun Liu, and Maosong Sun. 2019. Learning to predict explainable plots for neural story generation. *arXiv preprint arXiv:1912.02395*.

Guanhua Chen, Yun Chen, Yong Wang, and Victor O. K. Li. 2020. Lexical-constraint-aware neural machine translation via data augmentation. In *Proceedings of the Twenty-Ninth International Joint Conference on Artificial Intelligence, IJCAI 2020*, pages 3587–3593. ijcai.org.

Ryan Culkin, J. Hu, Elias Stengel-Eskin, Guanghui Qin, and Benjamin Van Durme. 2020. Iterative paraphrastic augmentation with discriminative span alignment. *arXiv preprint arXiv:2007.00320*.

Sumanth Dathathri, Andrea Madotto, Janice Lan, Jane Hung, Eric Frank, Piero Molino, Jason Yosinski, and Rosanne Liu. 2020. Plug and play language models: A simple approach to controlled text generation. In *8th International Conference on Learning Representations, ICLR 2020, Addis Ababa, Ethiopia, April 26-30, 2020*. OpenReview.net.

Chris Donahue, Mina Lee, and Percy Liang. 2020. Enabling language models to fill in the blanks. In *Proceedings of the 58th Annual Meeting of the Association for Computational Linguistics*, pages 2492–2501, Online. Association for Computational Linguistics.

Angela Fan, Mike Lewis, and Yann Dauphin. 2018. Hierarchical neural story generation. In *Proceedings of the 56th Annual Meeting of the Association for Computational Linguistics (Volume 1: Long Papers)*, pages 889–898, Melbourne, Australia. Association for Computational Linguistics.

Angela Fan, Mike Lewis, and Yann Dauphin. 2019. Strategies for structuring story generation. In *Proceedings of the 57th Annual Meeting of the Association for Computational Linguistics*, pages 2650–2660, Florence, Italy. Association for Computational Linguistics.

Francis Ferraro and Benjamin Van Durme. 2016. A unified bayesian model of scripts, frames and language. In *Proceedings of the Thirtieth AAAI Conference on Artificial Intelligence, February 12-17, 2016, Phoenix, Arizona, USA*, pages 2601–2607. AAAI Press.

Charles J Fillmore. 1976. Frame semantics and the nature of language. In *Annals of the New York Academy of Sciences: Conference on the origin and development of language and speech*, volume 280, pages 20–32. New York.

Charles J Fillmore and Collin Baker. 2010. A frames approach to semantic analysis. In *The Oxford handbook of linguistic analysis*.

Seraphina Goldfarb-Tarrant, Tuhin Chakrabarty, Ralph Weischedel, and Nanyun Peng. 2020. Content planning for neural story generation with aristotelian rescoring. In *Proceedings of the 2020 Conference on Empirical Methods in Natural Language Processing (EMNLP)*, pages 4319–4338, Online. Association for Computational Linguistics.

Seraphina Goldfarb-Tarrant, Haining Feng, and Nanyun Peng. 2019. Plan, write, and revise: an interactive system for open-domain story generation. In *Proceedings of the 2019 Conference of the North American Chapter of the Association for Computational Linguistics (Demonstrations)*, pages 89–97, Minneapolis, Minnesota. Association for Computational Linguistics.

Prakhar Gupta, Vinayshekhar Bannihatti Kumar, Mukul Bhutani, and Alan W Black. 2019. Writer-Forcing: Generating more interesting story endings. In *Proceedings of the Second Workshop on Storytelling*, pages 117–126, Florence, Italy. Association for Computational Linguistics.

Chris Hokamp and Qun Liu. 2017. Lexically constrained decoding for sequence generation using grid beam search. In *Proceedings of the 55th Annual*

Meeting of the Association for Computational Linguistics (Volume 1: Long Papers), pages 1535–1546, Vancouver, Canada. Association for Computational Linguistics.

Ari Holtzman, Jan Buys, Maxwell Forbes, and Yejin Choi. 2020. The curious case of neural text degeneration. *International Conference on Learning Representations*.

J. Edward Hu, Huda Khayrallah, Ryan Culkin, Patrick Xia, Tongfei Chen, Matt Post, and Benjamin Van Durme. 2019a. Improved lexically constrained decoding for translation and monolingual rewriting. In *Proceedings of the 2019 Conference of the North American Chapter of the Association for Computational Linguistics: Human Language Technologies, Volume 1 (Long and Short Papers)*, pages 839–850, Minneapolis, Minnesota. Association for Computational Linguistics.

J. Edward Hu, Rachel Rudinger, Matt Post, and Benjamin Van Durme. 2019b. PARABANK: monolingual bitext generation and sentential paraphrasing via lexically-constrained neural machine translation. In *The Thirty-Third AAAI Conference on Artificial Intelligence, AAAI 2019, The Thirty-First Innovative Applications of Artificial Intelligence Conference, IAAI 2019, The Ninth AAAI Symposium on Educational Advances in Artificial Intelligence, EAAI 2019, Honolulu, Hawaii, USA, January 27 - February 1, 2019*, pages 6521–6528. AAAI Press.

Daphne Ippolito, David Grangier, Douglas Eck, and Chris Callison-Burch. 2020. Toward better storylines with sentence-level language models. In *Proceedings of the 58th Annual Meeting of the Association for Computational Linguistics*, pages 7472–7478, Online. Association for Computational Linguistics.

Parag Jain, Priyanka Agrawal, Abhijit Mishra, Mohak Sukhwani, Anirban Laha, and Karthik Sankaranarayanan. 2017. Story generation from sequence of independent short descriptions. *arXiv preprint arXiv:1707.05501*.

Nitish Shirish Keskar, Bryan McCann, Lav R Varshney, Caiming Xiong, and Richard Socher. 2019. Ctrl: A conditional transformer language model for controllable generation. *arXiv preprint arXiv:1909.05858*.

Huayang Li, Guoping Huang, and L. Liu. 2020a. Neural machine translation with noisy lexical constraints. *IEEE/ACM Transactions on Audio, Speech, and Language Processing*, 28:1864–1874.

Ya Li, Xinyu Liu, Dan Liu, Xueqiang Zhang, and J. Liu. 2019. Learning efficient lexically-constrained neural machine translation with external memory. *arXiv preprint arXiv:1901.11344*.

Zhongyang Li, Xiao Ding, Ting Liu, J. Edward Hu, and Benjamin Van Durme. 2020b. Guided generation of cause and effect. In *Proceedings of the Twenty-Ninth International Joint Conference on Artificial Intelligence, IJCAI 2020*, pages 3629–3636. ijcai.org.

Dayiheng Liu, Jie Fu, Q. Qu, and J. Lv. 2019. Bfgan: Backward and forward generative adversarial networks for lexically constrained sentence generation. *IEEE/ACM Transactions on Audio, Speech, and Language Processing*.

Ximing Lu, Peter West, Rowan Zellers, Ronan Le Bras, Chandra Bhagavatula, and Yejin Choi. 2020. Neurologic decoding: (un)supervised neural text generation with predicate logic constraints. *arXiv preprint arXiv:2010.12884*.

Yuning Mao, X. Ren, Huai zhong Ji, and Jiawei Han. 2020. Constrained abstractive summarization: Preserving factual consistency with constrained generation. *arXiv preprint arXiv:2010.12723*.

Lara J. Martin, Prithviraj Ammanabrolu, Xinyu Wang, William Hancock, Shruti Singh, Brent Harrison, and Mark O. Riedl. 2018. Event representations for automated story generation with deep neural nets. In *Proceedings of the Thirty-Second AAAI Conference on Artificial Intelligence, (AAAI-18), the 30th innovative Applications of Artificial Intelligence (IAAI-18), and the 8th AAAI Symposium on Educational Advances in Artificial Intelligence (EAAI-18), New Orleans, Louisiana, USA, February 2-7, 2018*, pages 868–875. AAAI Press.

Ning Miao, Hao Zhou, Lili Mou, Rui Yan, and Lei Li. 2019. CGMH: constrained sentence generation by metropolis-hastings sampling. In *The Thirty-Third AAAI Conference on Artificial Intelligence, AAAI 2019, The Thirty-First Innovative Applications of Artificial Intelligence Conference, IAAI 2019, The Ninth AAAI Symposium on Educational Advances in Artificial Intelligence, EAAI 2019, Honolulu, Hawaii, USA, January 27 - February 1, 2019*, pages 6834–6842. AAAI Press.

Marvin Minsky. 1974. A framework for representing knowledge.

Nasrin Mostafazadeh, Nathanael Chambers, Xiaodong He, Devi Parikh, Dhruv Batra, Lucy Vanderwende, Pushmeet Kohli, and James Allen. 2016. A corpus and evaluation framework for deeper understanding of commonsense stories. *arXiv preprint arXiv:1604.01696*.

Jeffrey Pennington, Richard Socher, and Christopher Manning. 2014. GloVe: Global vectors for word representation. In *Proceedings of the 2014 Conference on Empirical Methods in Natural Language Processing (EMNLP)*, pages 1532–1543, Doha, Qatar. Association for Computational Linguistics.

Matt Post and David Vilar. 2018. Fast lexically constrained decoding with dynamic beam allocation for neural machine translation. In *Proceedings of the 2018 Conference of the North American Chapter of the Association for Computational Linguistics: Human Language Technologies, Volume 1 (Long Papers)*, pages 1314–1324, New Orleans, Louisiana. Association for Computational Linguistics.

Lianhui Qin, Antoine Bosselut, Ari Holtzman, Chandra Bhagavatula, Elizabeth Clark, and Yejin Choi. 2019. Counterfactual story reasoning and generation. In *Proceedings of the 2019 Conference on Empirical Methods in Natural Language Processing and the 9th International Joint Conference on Natural Language Processing (EMNLP-IJCNLP)*, pages 5043–5053, Hong Kong, China. Association for Computational Linguistics.

Alec Radford, Jeffrey Wu, Rewon Child, David Luan, Dario Amodei, and Ilya Sutskever. 2019. Language models are unsupervised multitask learners. *OpenAI blog*, 1(8):9.

Hannah Rashkin, Asli Celikyilmaz, Yejin Choi, and Jianfeng Gao. 2020. PlotMachines: Outline-conditioned generation with dynamic plot state tracking. In *Proceedings of the 2020 Conference on Empirical Methods in Natural Language Processing (EMNLP)*, pages 4274–4295, Online. Association for Computational Linguistics.

Ehud Reiter and Robert Dale. 2000. *Building natural language generation systems*. Cambridge university press.

Rico Sennrich, Barry Haddow, and Alexandra Birch. 2016. Neural machine translation of rare words with subword units. In *Proceedings of the 54th Annual Meeting of the Association for Computational Linguistics (Volume 1: Long Papers)*, pages 1715–1725, Berlin, Germany. Association for Computational Linguistics.

Lei Sha. 2020. Gradient-guided unsupervised lexically constrained text generation. In *Proceedings of the 2020 Conference on Empirical Methods in Natural Language Processing (EMNLP)*, pages 8692–8703, Online. Association for Computational Linguistics.

Raymond Hendy Susanto, Shamil Chollampatt, and Liling Tan. 2020. Lexically constrained neural machine translation with Levenshtein transformer. In *Proceedings of the 58th Annual Meeting of the Association for Computational Linguistics*, pages 3536–3543, Online. Association for Computational Linguistics.

Nathaniel Weir, João Sedoc, and Benjamin Van Durme. 2020. COD3S: Diverse generation with discrete semantic signatures. In *Proceedings of the 2020 Conference on Empirical Methods in Natural Language Processing (EMNLP)*, pages 5199–5211, Online. Association for Computational Linguistics.

Patrick Xia, Guanghui Qin, Siddharth Vashishtha, Yunmo Chen, Tongfei Chen, Chandler May, Craig Harman, Kyle Rawlins, Aaron Steven White, and Benjamin Van Durme. 2021. LOME: Large ontology multilingual extraction. In *Proceedings of the 16th Conference of the European Chapter of the Association for Computational Linguistics: System Demonstrations*, pages 149–159, Online. Association for Computational Linguistics.

Jingjing Xu, Xuancheng Ren, Yi Zhang, Qi Zeng, Xiaoyan Cai, and Xu Sun. 2018. A skeleton-based model for promoting coherence among sentences in narrative story generation. In *Proceedings of the 2018 Conference on Empirical Methods in Natural Language Processing*, pages 4306–4315, Brussels, Belgium. Association for Computational Linguistics.

Lili Yao, Nanyun Peng, Ralph Weischedel, Kevin Knight, Dongyan Zhao, and Rui Yan. 2019. Plan-and-write: Towards better automatic storytelling. In *AAAI*.

Jiacheng Zhang, Huanbo Luan, Maosong Sun, Feifei Zhai, Jingfang Xu, and Yang Liu. 2021. Neural machine translation with explicit phrase alignment. *IEEE/ACM Transactions on Audio, Speech, and Language Processing*, 29:1001–1010.

Yizhe Zhang, Guoyin Wang, Chunyuan Li, Zhe Gan, Chris Brockett, and Bill Dolan. 2020. POINTER: Constrained progressive text generation via insertion-based generative pre-training. In *Proceedings of the 2020 Conference on Empirical Methods in Natural Language Processing (EMNLP)*, pages 8649–8670, Online. Association for Computational Linguistics.

A Training Details

A.1 FFL

We finetune GPT-2 on examples of frame-guided infilling using the same training parameters (to the extend possible) as Donahue et al. (2020). We use the `fairseq` library to perform training and inference using the pretrained GPT-2 parameters provided by HuggingFace[7]. Training takes 1.5 hours using 8 Quadro RTX 6000 GPUs.

```
fairseq-train
--task framefilling
--sample-break-mode eos
--arch ilm_gpt2
--dropout 0.1
--attention-dropout 0.1
--clip-norm 1
-optimizer adam --adam-eps 1e-08
--lr 5e-5
--weight-decay 0.0
--max-epoch 100
--patience 3
```

A.2 ILM

To compare ILM with FFL on a uniform basis, we retrain ILM on sentence level infilling using the code provided by Donahue et al. (2020),[8] with same parameters and stopping criterion.

It is worth noticing that the original ILM is trained on stories from the ROCStories dataset with titles provided. However, the test set portion of ROCStories on which we formulate the frame-guided sentence infilling task are provided without title. We observe that the original ILM trained with title is problematic in infilling the first sentence of a story without title (Sometimes it outputs full stop only, or generate a new title in addition to the sentence). Therefore, we delete all titles in the training data when retraining ILM.

B LCD Diversification

Although the LCD algorithm will explore the prefix of each of the dozens of constraints typically associated with a frame, a few LUs will tend to dominate the final candidates throughout beam search — this is also observed in Li et al. (2020b). This problem is exacerbated by the rather broad definitions of some frames that cover both general, common LUs, and more specific LUs, whose likelihood will be dwarfed during decoding by the former. For example, the **Collaboration** frame contains LUs that depict the concept of collaboration from various perspectives: the act of collaborating (e.g. *collaborate.v*, *team up.v*), the participants in the collaboration (e.g. *collaborator.n*, *partner.n*), and the state of being in collaboration (e.g. *in cahoots.a*, *together.adv*), etc. However, in practice the general unit *together.adv* is more often selected by beam search to satisfy the constraint because of its generally higher likelihood. This dominant LU prevents other potentially diverse surface realizations of the frame triggered by other LUs.

To improve the lexical and semantic diversity in triggering frames, we construct disjunctive sets on a more fine-grained semantic level. We divide each set of LUs into k subsets using hierarchical clustering over the GloVe embeddings of LUs (Pennington et al., 2014). In particular, we use the `AgglomerativeClustering` class of **scikit-learn** [9] to perform hierarchical clustering over the GloVe embedding of LUs to divide each set of frame-associate LUs into subsets. In the experiments, we set number of clusters to 8. For multi-frame constraints, we set number of clusters to 4 for the frame with the most number of LUs and 2 for the frame with the second most of, we do not divide any LU sets for remaining frames (if any), this could ensure the total combination of multi-frame LU subsets equals 8. Figure 7 shows the clustering results of three frames: **Collaboration**, **Ingestion** and **Departing**, with number of clusters set to 4.

To ensure that the decoder will be able to explore all possible combinations of LUs, we build lists of tries for every combination of LU subsets. The constrained beam search is then run separately on each of them. To ensure that candidates from each LU subset are considered, final candidates are selected in a round-robin manner: the top-1 scored hypothesis is picked for each subset, followed by the top-2, and so on.

C Perplexity

We repeat the perplexity experiment from subsection 5.1, but instead of masking one out of five of a story's sentences at a time, we mask all five. This

[7]https://github.com/pytorch/fairseq/blob/master/fairseq/models/huggingface/hf_gpt2.py

[8]https://github.com/chrisdonahue/ilm

[9]https://scikit-learn.org/stable/modules/generated/sklearn.cluster.AgglomerativeClustering.html

Frames	**LUs clusters**
Collaboration	**cluster 1**: conspire, conspiracy, collusion, collude **cluster 2**: together, in league, in cahoots, work together, team up **cluster 3**: confederate **cluster 4**: partner, jointly, cooperation, associate, affiliated, collaboration, collaborator, cooperate, collaborate
Ingestion	**cluster 1**: have, put away, lap, put back, down **cluster 2**: feed, lunch, breakfast, snack, eat, drink **cluster 3**: swig, ingestion, quaff, swill, guzzle, sup, nosh, gulp, devour, gobble, ingest, consume, dine, nibble, imbibe, slurp, sip **cluster 4**: tuck, munch, feast, nurse
Departing	**cluster 1**: departure, depart, exit, leave **cluster 2**: vamoose, decamp, skedaddle **cluster 3**: exodus, disappearance, escape **cluster 4**: disappear, vanish, emerge

Figure 7: clustering examples of frame **Collaboration**, **Ingestion**, and **Departing**, morphological variants are excluded for demonstration purpose.

scenario can be considered a fully generative model of text in which no context is provided except for frame IDs specifying general semantic content for each sentence. Table 5 shows the resulting model perplexities.

Perplexity	ILM	S-FFL	M-FFL	A-FFL	A-FFL (ord)
Infill Text	13.88	11.07	8.76	5.45	**4.69**
+ Sp Toks	8.87	9.16	10.05	9.3	**7.43**
+ 5 Fr Slots	**4.66**	5.51	6.71	7.64	6.23

Table 5: Model perplexity over infill text tokens and infill text tokens + special tokens with all 5 ROCStory sentences masked out.

D Human Evaluation Details

Akin to Donahue et al. (2020), we sampled 100 stories from the test set of the ROCStories dataset. Masking one sentence at a time in each 5-sentence story, we obtained 500 masked stories. Each model was then tasked to infill a missing sentence in a masked story. We compared 10 models in total: 8 proposed in this paper (S/M/A-FFL, M/A-FFL-ordered, and the ordered variant[10] of S/M/A ILM+LCD), as well as the gold human infill and the ILM model. Below we further specify the details of each of the human evaluation tasks.

D.1 Indistinguishability

To achieve high comparability with Donahue et al. (2020), we conducted this evaluation as a Human Intelligence Task (HIT) on Amazon Mechanical Turk. To filter out malicious workers, we used a control model which always generates "This sentence was generated by a machine." or a synonymous sentence. We also validated that the gold human infill achieves 80% confusion rate (which was attained precisely in our run), which corresponds to picking 1 sentence out of 5 at random. Overall, 12 workers participated in the HIT, of which one was filtered by the control model. The annotator's interface can be seen on Figure 8.

[10]Based on the Frame Fidelity and the pilot HIT results, we chose to only evaluate the ordered variant, as the unordered LCD performed very similarly in terms of those metrics.

D.2 Relative Plausbility

Due to a relatively high complexity of this task, compared to the Indistinguishability task, the evaluation was conducted with a team of skilled annotators, comprised of four undergraduate students who have previously participated in NLP/AI annotation projects. On average, ranking 10 models' outputs for one story took 3 minutes 19 seconds for each worker. The annotator's interface can be seen on Figure 9.

You will be presented with **six** short stories, each comprised of **five** sentences.

For each story, please select **one** sentence out of **five** which you think was **the most likely** generated by a machine.

Note that some stories will appear multiple times. When you see a story re-appear, please answer **the same way** as in the previous response.

I. Identify one of the five sentences generated by a machine:

1. ○ Jill had been having a problem with mice in her home.
2. ○ She went to the animal shelter and adopted a cat.
3. ○ The cat turned out to be timid.
4. ○ Jill no longer had a mouse problem.
5. ○ She loved having her cat around.

II. Identify one of the five sentences generated by a machine:

1. ○ Jill had been having a problem with mice in her home.
2. ○ She went to the animal shelter and adopted a cat.
3. ○ Jill's cat took care of the mice.
4. ○ Jill no longer had a mouse problem.
5. ○ She loved having her cat around.

III. Identify one of the five sentences generated by a machine:

1. ○ Jill had been having a problem with mice in her home.
2. ○ She went to the animal shelter and adopted a cat.
3. ○ The cat turned out to be a dog.
4. ○ Jill no longer had a mouse problem.
5. ○ She loved having her cat around.

Figure 8: Interface shown to the workers during collection of indistinguishability judgments.

Given the story, please estimate how plausible the candidate sentences are relative to one another.

- Sort the candidates by relative plausibilities, from **most plausible** to **least plausible**, by drag-and-dropping the candidates into their respective order.
- After sorting the candidates, indicate the **relative plausibilities** using the vertical bar.
- Set the bar pin's value relative to the fixed candidates at the top and bottom of the bar (i.e. the most and least plausible candidates, respectively).
  - To set the plausibility for a particular candidate, select that candidate before clicking the bar.
  - Note that the bar pin does not appear until you have selected the value for the candidate for the first time.
  - Note that the bar pin for a given candidate cannot be moved past the two adjacent candidates.
- To switch the ranking of the candidates after the vertical bar appears, continue using the drag-and-drop feature.

Please calibrate your score for a specific candidate with respect to the scores you've given for other candidates in the same HIT (i.e. not relative to 0% and 100%).

Story: Jill had been having a problem with mice in her home. She went to the animal shelter and adopted a cat. **<X>**. Jill no longer had a mouse problem. She loved having her cat around.

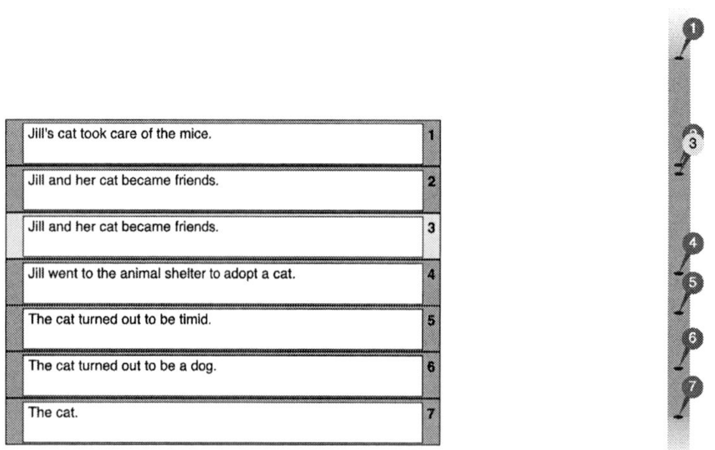

Figure 9: Interface shown to the workers during collection of relative plausibility judgments.

Realistic Evaluation Principles for Cross-document Coreference Resolution

Arie Cattan[1] **Alon Eirew**[1,2] **Gabriel Stanovsky**[3] **Mandar Joshi**[4] **Ido Dagan**[1]

[1]Computer Science Department, Bar Ilan University
[2]Intel Labs, Israel [3]The Hebrew University of Jerusalem
[4]Allen School of Computer Science & Engineering, University of Washington, Seattle, WA
arie.cattan@gmail.com alon.eirew@intel.com
gabis@cse.huji.ac.il mandar90@cs.washington.edu
dagan@cs.biu.ac.il

Abstract

We point out that common evaluation practices for cross-document coreference resolution have been unrealistically permissive in their assumed settings, yielding inflated results. We propose addressing this issue via two evaluation methodology principles. First, as in other tasks, models should be evaluated on predicted mentions rather than on gold mentions. Doing this raises a subtle issue regarding singleton coreference clusters, which we address by decoupling the evaluation of mention detection from that of coreference linking. Second, we argue that models should not exploit the synthetic topic structure of the standard ECB+ dataset, forcing models to confront the lexical ambiguity challenge, as intended by the dataset creators. We demonstrate empirically the drastic impact of our more realistic evaluation principles on a competitive model, yielding a score which is 33 F1 lower compared to evaluating by prior lenient practices.[1]

1 Introduction

Cross-document (CD) coreference resolution identifies and links textual mentions that refer to the same entity or event across multiple documents. For example, Table 1 depicts different news stories involving former U.S. president Barack Obama.

While subsuming the challenges of within-document (WD) coreference, CD coreference introduces additional unique challenges. Most notably, lexical similarity is often not a good indicator when identifying cross-document links, as documents are authored independently. As shown in Table 1, the same event can be referenced using different expressions ("nominated", "approached"), while two *different* events can be referenced using the same expression ("name"). Despite these challenges, reported state-of-the-art results on the popular CD coreference ECB+ benchmark (Cybulska and Vossen, 2014) are relatively high, reaching up to 80 F1 (Barhom et al., 2019; Meged et al., 2020).

Subtopic 1
Doc 1: *News that* ***Barack Obama*** *may name Dr. Sanjay Gupta of Emory University and CNN as* ***his*** *Surgeon...*
Doc 2: *CNN's management confirmed yesterday that Dr. Gupta had been approached by the Obama team.*
Subtopic 2
Doc 3: ***President Obama*** *will name Dr. Regina Benjamin as Surgeon General in a Rose Garden announcement...*
Doc 4: ***Obama*** *nominates new surgeon general: genius grant fellow Dr. Benjamin.* ***He*** *emphasizes* ***his*** *decision..*

Table 1: Example of sentences of from the ECB+. The underlined words represent events, same color represents a coreference cluster. Different documents describe the same event using different words (e.g name, approached), while the two predicates "name" in the two subtopics are *not* coreferring.

In this paper, we show that CD coreference models achieve these numbers using overly-permissive evaluation protocols, namely assuming gold entity and event mentions are given, rewarding singletons and bypassing the lexical ambiguity challenge. Accordingly, we present more realistic evaluation principles which better reflect model performance in real-world scenarios.

First, following well established standards in WD coreference resolution (Pradhan et al., 2012), we propose that CD coreference models should be also evaluated on predicted mentions. While recent models unrealistically assume that event mentions are given as part of the input, practical application on new texts and domains requires performing coreference on raw text, including automatic mention detection. Using predicted mentions raises a subtle point with regards to singletons (entities which are only referenced once). In particular, we

[1]https://github.com/ariecattan/coref

Proceedings of the 10th Conference on Lexical and Computational Semantics, pages 143–151
August 5–6, 2021, Bangkok, Thailand (online) ©2021 Association for Computational Linguistics

observe that ECB+'s inclusion of singletons inaccurately rewards models for predicting them, by conflating the evaluation of mention identification with that of coreference detection. To address this, we propose reporting of singleton identification performance in a separate metric, while reporting coreference results without singletons.

Second, we find that ECB+ does not accurately reflect real-world scenarios where prominent events can be referenced in documents spanning different subjects and domains. To facilitate its annotation, ECB+ mimics this phenomenon by artificially grouping documents dealing with the same event (e.g., the nomination of Sanjay Gupta in Table 1) into a *subtopic*, and further groups two similar subtopics into a larger *topic* document group (e.g., different nominations of government officials in Table 1). We observe that recent works exploit ECB+'s artificially simplistic structure by practically running the coreference model at the subtopic level, thus sidestepping a major lexical ambiguity challenge (e.g., mentions of "nomination" across subtopics do not co-refer). In contrast, in real-world scenarios such clustering is much harder to perform and is often not as easily delineated. For example, Barack Obama and events from his presidency can be referenced in news, literature, sport reports, and more. To address this, we propose that models report performance also at the topic level.

Finally, we show empirically that both of these evaluation practices artificially inflate results. An end-to end model that outperforms state-of-the-art results on previous evaluation settings drops by 33 F1 points when using our proposed evaluation scheme, pointing at weaknesses that future modelling work could explore.

2 Background

In this work, we will examine the evaluation of CD coreference on the popular ECB+ corpus (Cybulska and Vossen, 2014), constructed as an augmentation of the EECB and ECB datasets (Lee et al., 2012; Bejan and Harabagiu, 2010). As exemplified in Table 1, ECB+ groups its annotated documents into *subtopics*, consisting of different reports of the same real-world event (e.g., the nomination of Sanjay Gupta), and *topics*, which in turn consist of two lexically similar subtopics. Full ECB+ details are presented in Appendix A.

The ECB+ evaluation protocol largely follows that of CoNLL-2012, perhaps the most popular WD benchmark (Pradhan et al., 2012), with two major distinctions. First, barring a few notable exceptions (Yang et al., 2015; Choubey and Huang, 2017),[2] most recent CD models have unrealistically assumed that gold entity and event mentions are given as part of the input, reducing the task to finding coreference links between gold mentions (Bejan and Harabagiu, 2014; Cybulska and Vossen, 2015; Kenyon-Dean et al., 2018; Barhom et al., 2019; Meged et al., 2020). Second, while singletons are omitted on CoNLL-2012, they are exhaustively annotated in ECB+.

In the following section, we present a more realistic evaluation framework for CD coreference, taking into account the interacting distinctions of ECB+.

3 Realistic Evaluation Principles

In this paper, we suggest that CD coreference models should perform and be evaluated on predicted mentions. To achieve this, in Section 3.1, we will introduce the *singleton effect* on coreference evaluation and propose to decouple the evaluation of mention prediction from coreference resolution. In Section 3.2, we will establish guidelines allowing to better assess how models handle the ubiquitous lexical ambiguity challenge in real-world scenarios.

3.1 Decoupling Coreference Evaluation

Our goal is to propose a more reliable evaluation methodology of a coreference system over predicted mentions when singletons are included.

We use an example to show that evaluating singleton prediction with standard coreference metrics (B3, CEAF, LEA) could lead to counterproductive results which are hard to interpret (henceforth, we refer to this phenomenon as the *singleton effect*). Assume G denotes the gold clusters for Table 1 (for brevity, we omit some mentions), and $S1$ and $S2$ denote the output of two systems, which differ in their mention detection and coreference link performance:[3]

[2]However, as noted in (Barhom et al., 2019), they consider only the intersection between gold and predicted mentions, not penalizing models for false positive mention identification.

[3]This follows the natural distribution of singletons (about 50%), as illustrated in PreCo (Chen et al., 2018).

		MUC	B^3	CEAFe	LEA	CoNLL
CoNLL-2012	$S1$	75.0	53.1	44.4	42.1	57.5
	$S2$	**85.7**	**83.9**	**90.0**	**80.0**	**86.5**
With Singletons	$S1$	75.0	**77.6**	**77.8**	**69.0**	**76.8**
	$S2$	**85.7**	59.2	32.7	50.0	59.2

Table 2: Coreference results of $S1$ and $S2$ with (1) the standard CoNLL-2012 evaluation, where $S2$ does better and (2) when including singletons, where $S1$ does better. $S2$ predicts the coreference links better than $S1$ but $S1$ achieves higher results in (2) because $S1$ performs better the mention detection task.

G {News}, {Emory University}, {confirmed}, {yesterday}, {announcement}, {name, approached}, {names, nominates, decision}

$S1$ {News}, {Emory University}, {confirmed}, {yesterday}, {announcement, name, approached, names, nominates, decision}

$S2$ {News that}, {Emory}, {announcement, name, approached}, {names, nominates, decision}

$S1$ identified the mentions of the singleton clusters while $S2$ missed them and predicted incorrect span boundaries for the two first mentions ("News that" and "Emory"). Both $S1$ and $S2$ erroneously merged the singleton mention "announcement" with the cluster {name, approached}; however, $S1$ further included these mentions with the lexically-similar cluster {names, nominates, decision}, whereas $S2$ successfully separated them. In other words, $S1$ performs well on the mention detection task, but worse on the coreference linking, and $S2$ did the opposite.

Table 2 shows the results of $S1$ and $S2$ according to (1) the common CoNLL-2012 evaluation, where only non-singleton clusters are evaluated, and (2) using coreference metrics also on singleton prediction. With respect to (1), $S2$ achieves higher results according to all evaluation metrics. In (2), we see the opposite, the results of $S1$ are significantly higher than $S2$ w.r.t B^3 (+18.4), CEAF-e (+45.1), and LEA (+19), but not w.r.t MUC, a link-based metric. Indeed, these evaluation metrics reward $S1$ in both recall and precision for all predicted singletons, while penalizing $S2$ for the wrong and missing singleton spans. Since singletons are abundant in natural text, they contribute greatly to the overall score. However, as observed by Rahman and Ng (2009), a model's ability to identify that these singletons do not belong to any coreference cluster is already captured in the evaluation metrics, and additional penalty is not desired. In Appendix B, we introduce the aforementioned evaluation metrics for coreference resolution (MUC, B^3, CEAF and LEA) and explain how singletons affect them.

To address the *singleton effect*, we suggest decoupling the evaluation of the two coreference substasks, mention detection and coreference linking, allowing to better analyze coreference results and to compare systems more appropriately.[4]

Mention detection is typically a span detection task and should be evaluated using standard span metrics on all detected mentions, including singletons. In particular, we use the span F1 metric and consider a predicted mention as correct if it has an exact match with a gold mention, as common in named entity recognition (Tjong Kim Sang and De Meulder, 2003). Using such evaluation in our above example, $S1$ achieves 100 F1 and $S2$ achieves 66.7 F1 (recall: 60, precision: 75).

For the coreference evaluation, we propose to follow CoNLL-2012 and apply coreference metrics only on non-singleton (gold and predicted) clusters, as singletons are already evaluated under the mention detection evaluation. We note also that even when omitting singletons, coreference metrics still penalize models for making coreference errors involving singletons (as $S2$ is penalized for linking "announcement" to a cluster).

We further show empirically (§4.2) that when evaluating using gold mentions, the *singleton effect* is amplified and harms the validity of the current CD evaluation protocol. Evidently, a dummy baseline that predicts no coreference links and puts each input gold mention in a singleton cluster achieves non-negligible performance (Luo, 2005), while state-of-the-art results are artificially inflated.

3.2 Confronting Lexical Ambiguity

As mentioned previously, the same event can be described in documents from different topics, while documents in the same topic may describe *different* events (e.g. different nominations as surgeon general, as shown in Table 1). Such settings pose a lexical ambiguity problem, where models encounter identical or lexically-similar words that should be assigned to different coreference clusters. Accordingly, while topical document clustering is useful for CD coreference resolution in general, it does not solve the ambiguity problem and models still need to make subtle disambiguation distinctions (e.g nomination of Sanjay Gupta vs. nomination of Regina Benjamin). Aiming at simulating this chal-

[4]This also makes possible to compare coreference results across datasets that include/omit singletons, addressing an issue raised by Stoyanov et al. (2009).

		MUC			B^3			$CEAFe$			LEA			CoNLL
		R	P	F_1	R	P	F_1	R	P	F_1	R	P	F_1	F_1
Subtopic Clustering	Singleton baseline$^+$	0	0	0	45.2	100	62.3	86.7	39.2	54.0	35.0	35.0	35.0	38.8
	Singleton baseline$^-$	0	0	0	0	0	0	0	0	0	0	0	0	0
	Barhom et al. (2019)$^+$	78.1	84.0	80.9	76.8	86.1	81.2	79.6	73.3	76.3	64.6	72.3	68.3	79.5
	Barhom et al. (2019)$^-$	78.1	84.0	80.9	61.2	73.5	66.8	63.2	48.9	55.2	58.4	71.2	64.2	67.6
	Meged et al. (2020)$^+$	78.8	84.7	81.6	75.9	85.9	80.6	81.1	74.8	**77.8**	64.7	73.4	68.8	80.0
	Meged et al. (2020)$^-$	78.8	84.7	81.6	60.4	73.8	66.4	65.5	49.5	56.4	57.2	71.2	63.4	68.1
	Our model – Gold$^+$	85.1	81.9	**83.5**	82.1	82.7	**82.4**	75.2	78.9	77.0	68.8	72.0	**70.4**	**81.0**
	Our model – Gold$^-$	85.1	81.9	83.5	70.8	70.2	70.5	68.2	52.3	59.2	68.2	67.6	67.9	71.1
	Our model – Predicted$^+$	61.7	67.4	64.5	57.8	68.4	62.6	57.2	65.5	61.1	46.6	57.7	51.6	62.7
	Our model – Predicted$^-$	61.7	67.4	64.5	47.6	56.9	51.8	53.0	41.9	46.8	44.4	53.8	48.7	54.4
Topic Level	Our model – Gold$^+$	80.1	76.3	**78.1**	77.4	71.7	**74.5**	73.1	77.8	**75.4**	62.9	59.1	**61.0**	**76.0**
	Our model – Gold$^-$	80.1	76.3	78.1	63.4	54.1	58.4	56.3	44.2	49.5	59.7	49.6	54.2	62.0
	Our model – Predicted$^+$	61.5	62.5	62.0	55.6	56.1	55.8	52.8	66.7	59.0	43.4	46.2	44.8	58.9
	Our model – Predicted$^-$	61.5	62.5	62.0	44.7	41.4	43.0	43.9	37.9	40.7	40.9	37.4	39.1	48.6

Table 3: Event coreference on ECB+ test, while including($^+$)/excluding($^-$) singletons in the evaluation, showing that (1) including singletons in coreference metrics inflate performance in all models, (2) using predicted mentions (see rows marked "Predicted") over gold mentions harms performance, (3) topic level evaluation (bottom part) is markedly lower than subtopic performance, showing that models struggle with lexical ambiguity, and (4) our model outperforms previous models on most F1 scores (see numbers in bold).

lenge on a manageable annotation task, the ECB+ authors (Cybulska and Vossen, 2014) augmented each topic in the original ECB with an additional subtopic of the same event type, allowing to challenge models with lexical ambiguity (as mentioned in Section 2).

However, recent works (Barhom et al., 2019; Meged et al., 2020) predict coreference clusters separately on each subtopic, using a simple unsupervised document clustering during preprocessing. Such clustering performs near perfectly on ECB+ because of its synthetic structure, where each topic includes exactly two subtopics with only a few coreference links across different subtopics. Yet, document clustering is not expected to perform as well in realistic settings where coreferring events can spread multiple topics. More importantly, this bypasses intentions behind the inclusion of subtopics in the ECB+'s and avoids challenging the coreference models on lexical ambiguity. Indeed, the ECB+ authors, in a subsequent work, did not apply a topic clustering (Cybulska and Vossen, 2015).

We therefore recommend that models report results also at the *topic* level (when document clustering is not applied). This will conform to ECB+'s purpose and follows the original evaluation setup of the ECB+ corpus (Bejan and Harabagiu, 2014).

4 Experiments

We show empirically that each of the previous evaluation practices (using gold mentions, singleton inclusion, and subtopic clustering) artificially inflates the results (§4.2). As recent CD coreference models are designed to perform on gold mentions (§2), we cannot use them to set baseline results on predicted mentions. We therefore develop a simple and efficient end-to-end model for CD coreference resolution by combining the successful single document *e2e-coref* (Lee et al., 2017) with common CD modeling approaches.

4.1 Model

We briefly describe the general architecture of our model, further details are explained in (Cattan et al., 2021) and Appendix C. Given a set of documents, our model operates in four sequential steps: (1) following Lee et al. (2017), we encode all possible spans up to a length n with the concatenation of four vectors: the output representations of the span boundary (first and last) tokens, an attention-weighted sum of token representations in the span, and a feature vector denoting the span length (2) we train a mention detector on the ECB+ mentions, and keep further spans with a positive score,[5] (3) we generate positive and negative coreference pairs on the predicted mentions and train a pairwise scorer, and (4) apply an agglomerative clustering on the pairwise similarity scores to form the coreference clusters at inference.

[5]Here, we deviate from Cattan et al. (2021) who dynamically prune spans during training, because we need to predict singleton clusters.

4.2 Results

We first evaluate our model under the current evaluation setup (gold mentions, singletons, subtopic) and compare it with two recent neural state-of-the-art models (Barhom et al., 2019; Meged et al., 2020). In addition, we test a dummy *singleton* baseline which puts each gold mention in a singleton cluster and re-evaluate all baselines while omitting singletons. The results in Table 3 show that our model surpasses current state-of-the-art results in previous settings, supporting its relevance for setting baseline results over predicted mentions. The mention detection performance of our model is 80.1 F1 (Recall 76 and Precision 84.7).

The results corroborate the importance of our proposed evaluation enhancements. First, the performance drops dramatically when using predicted mentions (e.g. from 71.1 to 54.4 F1 at the subtopic level). Second, for all models, the results are significantly higher when including singletons in coreference metrics, because, as explained in Section 3.1, models are rewarded for singleton prediction. Indeed, the model performs better in mention detection than in coreference linking, confirming the importance of decoupling the evaluation of the two subtasks. Finally, performance is lower at the *topic* level than at the *subtopic* level (62.0 vs. 71.1 F1 using gold mentions and 48.6 vs. 54.4 F1 using predicted mentions), indicating that models struggle with lexical ambiguity (§3.2). Taken together, evaluating over raw text without singletons while not clustering into fine-grained subtopics, leads to a performance drop of 33 F1 points, indicating the vast room for improvement under realistic settings.

5 Conclusion

We established two realistic evaluation principles for CD coreference resolution: (1) predicting mentions and (2) facing the lexical ambiguity challenge. We also set baseline results for future work on our evaluation methodology using a SOTA model.

Acknowledgment

We thank Shany Barhom for fruitful discussion and sharing code, and Yehudit Meged for providing her coreference predictions. The work described herein was supported in part by grants from Intel Labs, Facebook, the Israel Science Foundation grant 1951/17, the Israeli Ministry of Science and Technology, the German Research Foundation through the German-Israeli Project Cooperation (DIP, grant DA 1600/1-1), and from the Allen Institute for AI.

Ethical Considerations

Model As described in the supplementary material (§C), our cross-document coreference model does not contain any intentional biasing or ethical issues, and our experiments were conducted on a single 12GB GPU, with relatively low compute time.

References

Amit Bagga and Breck Baldwin. 1998. Entity-based cross-document coreferencing using the vector space model. In *36th Annual Meeting of the Association for Computational Linguistics and 17th International Conference on Computational Linguistics, Volume 1*, pages 79–85, Montreal, Quebec, Canada. Association for Computational Linguistics.

Shany Barhom, Vered Shwartz, Alon Eirew, Michael Bugert, Nils Reimers, and Ido Dagan. 2019. Revisiting joint modeling of cross-document entity and event coreference resolution. In *Proceedings of the 57th Annual Meeting of the Association for Computational Linguistics*, pages 4179–4189, Florence, Italy. Association for Computational Linguistics.

C. Bejan and Sanda M. Harabagiu. 2014. Unsupervised event coreference resolution. *Computational Linguistics*, 40:311–347.

Cosmin Bejan and Sanda Harabagiu. 2010. Unsupervised event coreference resolution with rich linguistic features. In *Proceedings of the 48th Annual Meeting of the Association for Computational Linguistics*, pages 1412–1422, Uppsala, Sweden. Association for Computational Linguistics.

Arie Cattan, Alon Eirew, Gabriel Stanovsky, Mandar Joshi, and Ido Dagan. 2021. Cross-document coreference resolution over predicted mentions. In *Findings of the Association for Computational Linguistics: ACL 2021*, Online. Association for Computational Linguistics.

Hong Chen, Zhenhua Fan, Hao Lu, Alan Yuille, and Shu Rong. 2018. PreCo: A large-scale dataset in preschool vocabulary for coreference resolution. In *Proceedings of the 2018 Conference on Empirical Methods in Natural Language Processing*, pages 172–181, Brussels, Belgium. Association for Computational Linguistics.

Prafulla Kumar Choubey and Ruihong Huang. 2017. Event coreference resolution by iteratively unfolding inter-dependencies among events. In *Proceedings of the 2017 Conference on Empirical Methods in Natural Language Processing*, pages 2124–2133, Copenhagen, Denmark. Association for Computational Linguistics.

Agata Cybulska and Piek Vossen. 2014. Using a sledgehammer to crack a nut? lexical diversity and event coreference resolution. In *Proceedings of the Ninth International Conference on Language Resources and Evaluation (LREC'14)*, pages 4545–4552, Reykjavik, Iceland. European Language Resources Association (ELRA).

Agata Cybulska and Piek Vossen. 2015. Translating granularity of event slots into features for event coreference resolution. In *Proceedings of the The 3rd Workshop on EVENTS: Definition, Detection, Coreference, and Representation*, pages 1–10, Denver, Colorado. Association for Computational Linguistics.

Mandar Joshi, Omer Levy, Luke Zettlemoyer, and Daniel Weld. 2019. BERT for coreference resolution: Baselines and analysis. In *Proceedings of the 2019 Conference on Empirical Methods in Natural Language Processing and the 9th International Joint Conference on Natural Language Processing (EMNLP-IJCNLP)*, pages 5803–5808, Hong Kong, China. Association for Computational Linguistics.

Kian Kenyon-Dean, Jackie Chi Kit Cheung, and Doina Precup. 2018. Resolving event coreference with supervised representation learning and clustering-oriented regularization. In *Proceedings of the Seventh Joint Conference on Lexical and Computational Semantics*, pages 1–10, New Orleans, Louisiana. Association for Computational Linguistics.

Heeyoung Lee, Marta Recasens, Angel Chang, Mihai Surdeanu, and Dan Jurafsky. 2012. Joint entity and event coreference resolution across documents. In *Proceedings of the 2012 Joint Conference on Empirical Methods in Natural Language Processing and Computational Natural Language Learning*, pages 489–500, Jeju Island, Korea. Association for Computational Linguistics.

Kenton Lee, Luheng He, Mike Lewis, and Luke Zettlemoyer. 2017. End-to-end neural coreference resolution. In *Proceedings of the 2017 Conference on Empirical Methods in Natural Language Processing*, pages 188–197, Copenhagen, Denmark. Association for Computational Linguistics.

Yinhan Liu, Myle Ott, Naman Goyal, Jingfei Du, Mandar Joshi, Danqi Chen, Omer Levy, Mike Lewis, Luke Zettlemoyer, and Veselin Stoyanov. 2019. RoBERTa: A robustly optimized BERT pretraining approach. *arXiv preprint arXiv:1907.11692*.

Xiaoqiang Luo. 2005. On coreference resolution performance metrics. In *Proceedings of Human Language Technology Conference and Conference on Empirical Methods in Natural Language Processing*, pages 25–32, Vancouver, British Columbia, Canada. Association for Computational Linguistics.

Yehudit Meged, Avi Caciularu, Vered Shwartz, and Ido Dagan. 2020. Paraphrasing vs coreferring: Two sides of the same coin. In *Findings of the Association for Computational Linguistics: EMNLP 2020*, pages 4897–4907, Online. Association for Computational Linguistics.

Nafise Sadat Moosavi and Michael Strube. 2016. Which coreference evaluation metric do you trust? a proposal for a link-based entity aware metric. In *Proceedings of the 54th Annual Meeting of the Association for Computational Linguistics (Volume 1: Long Papers)*, pages 632–642, Berlin, Germany. Association for Computational Linguistics.

Sameer Pradhan, Alessandro Moschitti, Nianwen Xue, Olga Uryupina, and Yuchen Zhang. 2012. CoNLL-2012 shared task: Modeling multilingual unrestricted coreference in OntoNotes. In *Joint Conference on EMNLP and CoNLL - Shared Task*, pages 1–40, Jeju Island, Korea. Association for Computational Linguistics.

Altaf Rahman and Vincent Ng. 2009. Supervised models for coreference resolution. In *Proceedings of the 2009 Conference on Empirical Methods in Natural Language Processing*, pages 968–977, Singapore. Association for Computational Linguistics.

Veselin Stoyanov, Nathan Gilbert, Claire Cardie, and Ellen Riloff. 2009. Conundrums in noun phrase coreference resolution: Making sense of the state-of-the-art. In *Proceedings of the Joint Conference of the 47th Annual Meeting of the ACL and the 4th International Joint Conference on Natural Language Processing of the AFNLP*, pages 656–664, Suntec, Singapore. Association for Computational Linguistics.

Erik F. Tjong Kim Sang and Fien De Meulder. 2003. Introduction to the CoNLL-2003 shared task: Language-independent named entity recognition. In *Proceedings of the Seventh Conference on Natural Language Learning at HLT-NAACL 2003*, pages 142–147.

Marc Vilain, John Burger, John Aberdeen, Dennis Connolly, and Lynette Hirschman. 1995. A model-theoretic coreference scoring scheme. In *Sixth Message Understanding Conference (MUC-6): Proceedings of a Conference Held in Columbia, Maryland, November 6-8, 1995*.

Bishan Yang, Claire Cardie, and Peter Frazier. 2015. A hierarchical distance-dependent Bayesian model for event coreference resolution. *Transactions of the Association for Computational Linguistics*, 3:517–528.

A The ECB+ Dataset

Documents in ECB+ were selected from various topics in the Google News archive in English, while annotation was performed separately for each topic. ECB+ statistics are shown in Table 4. As opposed to Ontonotes, only a few sentences are exhaustively annotated in each document, and the annotations include singletons.

In addition, it is worth noting that the ECB+ authors kept the entities from EECB (Lee et al., 2012) only if they participate in events in the annotated sentences, while leaving all other entities. Accordingly, "Los Angeles" and "Los Angeles hospital" are marked as coreferent in the sentences *"Yesterday in **Los Angeles**, pin-up icon Bettie Page succumbed to complications..* and *"Pinup icon Bettie Page died Thursday evening at **a hospital in Los Angeles..**"* because they refer to the location of the same event. This differs from the standard entity coreference resolution since detecting those entities involves an additional challenge of extracting event participants, for example, using a Semantic Role Labeling system.

	Train	Validation	Test
# Topics	25	8	10
# Documents	594	196	206
# Sentences	1037	346	457
# Mentions	3808/4758	1245/1476	1780/2055
# Singletons	1116/814	280/205	632/412
# Clusters	411/472	129/125	182/196

Table 4: ECB+ statistics. # Clusters do not include singletons. The slash numbers for # Mentions, # Singletons, and # Clusters represent event/entity statistics. As recommended by the authors in the release note, we follow the split of Cybulska and Vossen (2015) that uses a curated subset of the dataset.

B Singleton Effect on Coreference Metrics

Here, we briefly introduce the different evaluation metrics for coreference resolution (MUC, B^3, CEAF and LEA) and explain how singletons affect them. As mentioned in the paper, all evaluation metrics penalize models for wrongly linking a singleton to a cluster or singletons together. However, B3, CEAF and LEA further reward models for predicting singleton clusters, as explained below.

MUC Introduced by (Vilain et al., 1995), MUC is an early link-based evaluation metric for coreference resolution. Recall and precision are measured based on the minimal number of coreference links needed to align gold and predicted clusters, as follows:

$$Recall = \frac{\sum_{k_i \in K}(|k_i| - |p(k_i)|)}{\sum_{k_j \in K}(|k_j| - 1)} \quad (1)$$

where $p(k_i)$ is the set of different predicted clusters that contain one or more mention of the gold cluster k_i. The precision is obtained by switching the role of the predicted and the gold clusters. Since MUC scores are calculated over the coreference links, singletons do not affect this metric, as observed in our illustrative example in the paper (Section 3.1).

B^3 B^3 (Bagga and Baldwin, 1998) is a mention-based evaluation metric, the recall and precision correspond to the average of individual mention scores. The recall is defined as the proportion of its true corefering mentions that the system links, over all the gold corefering mentions that are linked to it, as follows:

$$Recall(m_i) = \frac{|Rm_i \cap Km_i|}{|Km_i|} \quad (2)$$

where Rm_i and Km_i are respectively the system and the gold cluster containing the mention m_i. The precision is obtained by switching the role of the predicted and gold clusters.

Here, all mentions m_i (including singleton mentions) are scored in Eq. 2 and participate in the overall recall and precision score. Therefore, a singleton that was successfully predicted will be rewarded 100% in both precision and recall, missing singletons will affect the recall and extra-singletons will affect the precision.

CEAF Introduced by Luo (2005), CEAF assumes that each predicted cluster should be mapped to only one gold cluster and vice versa. Using the Kuhn-Munkres algorithm, CEAF first finds the best one-to-one mapping $g(*)$ of the predicted clusters to the gold clusters, according to a similarity function ϕ. Given this mapping, predicted clusters are compared to their corresponding gold clusters, as follows:

$$Recall = \frac{\sum_{r_i \in R} \phi(r_i, g^*(r_i))}{\sum_{k_i \in K} \phi(k_i, k_i)} \quad (3)$$

where R is the set of predicted clusters, K the set of gold clusters, $g^*(r_i)$ the gold cluster aligned to the predicted cluster r_i, and $\phi()$ the similarity function. The precision is obtained by switching the role of the predicted and gold clusters in the denominator. There are two variants of CEAF based on ϕ, (1) a mention-based CEAFm defined as the number of shared mentions between the two clusters $\phi(r_i, k_i) = |r_i \cap k_i|$ and (2) an entity-based metric CEAFe: $\phi(r_i, k_i) = 2\frac{|r_i \cap k_i|}{|r_i|+|k_i|}$. Here again, a predicted singleton cluster that appears also in the gold will be obviously mapped to it and will be rewarded 100% in both recall and precision.

LEA Recently proposed by Moosavi and Strube (2016), LEA is the most recent evaluation metric, designed to overcome shortcomings in previous evaluation metrics, notably the *mention identification effect* in B^3 and CEAF. LEA is a Link-Based Entity-Aware metric, which assigns a score to each coreference cluster, based on all coreference links $(n \times (n-1)/2)$ in the cluster, as follows:

$$Recall = \frac{\sum_{k_i \in K}(|k_i| \times \sum_{r_j \in R} \frac{link(k_i \cap r_j)}{link(k_i)})}{\sum_{k_z \in K} |k_z|} \quad (4)$$

where $link(k_i)$ is the total number of links in the gold cluster k_i, $link(k_i, r_j)$ is the total number of links in the predicted cluster r_j that appears in the gold cluster k_i, and $|k_i|$ is the number of mentions in the gold cluster k_i in order to give higher importance to large clusters. The precision is calculated by switching the role of the gold clusters K and the predicted clusters R. Singleton clusters are also rewarded because they have self-links (links to themselves). However, since each cluster score is weighted by the size of the cluster, the *singleton effect* is less important in LEA, as we can see in the paper (Table 3).

C Our Coreference Model

As mentioned in the paper (§4.1), our model is inspired by the single document coreference resolver *e2e-coref* (Lee et al., 2017). The *e2e-coref* model forms the coreference clusters by linking each mention to an antecedent span appearing before it in the text. However, in the CD setting, there is no linear ordering between the documents. We therefore implement a new model while modifying the clustering method and the optimization function of the original *e2e-coref* model, as elaborated below.[6]

[6]Please refer to Cattan et al. (2021) for more details, results and ablations of the model.

Span Representation Given a set of documents, the first step consists of encoding each document separately using RoBERTa$_{LARGE}$ (Liu et al., 2019). Long documents are split into non overlapping segments of up to 512 word-piece tokens and are encoded independently (Joshi et al., 2019). We then, following Lee et al. (2017), represent each possible span up to a length n with the concatenation of four vectors: the output representations of the span boundary (first and last) tokens, an attention-weighted sum of token representations in the span, and a feature vector denoting the span length. We use g_i to refer to the vector representation of the span i.

Mention Scorer We train a mention detector $s_m(i)$ using a simple MLP on top of these span representations, indicating whether i is a mention in ECB+. This is possible because singleton mentions are annotated in ECB+ (§A). Unlike the *e2e-coref*, we keep further only detected mentions in both training and inference. We also tried the joint approach but the performance drops by 0.4 CoNLL F1 and the run-time was longer.

Pairwise Scorer Given the predicted mentions, we first generate positive and negative training pairs as follows. The positive instances consist of all the pairs of mentions that belong to the same coreference cluster, while the negative examples are sampled (20x the number of positive pairs) from all other pairs. This sampling reduces the computation time, and limits the unbalanced negative ratio between training pairs. Then, for each pair of mentions i and j, we concatenate 3 vectors: g_i, g_j, and the element-wise multiplication $g_i \circ g_j$, and feed it to a simple MLP, which outputs a score $s(i, j)$ indicating the likelihood that mentions i and j belong to the same cluster, which we optimize using the binary cross-entropy loss on the pair label. Due to memory constraints, we freeze output representations from RoBERTa instead of fine-tuning all parameters.

Agglomerative Clustering As common in recent CD coreference models (Yang et al., 2015; Choubey and Huang, 2017; Kenyon-Dean et al., 2018; Barhom et al., 2019; Meged et al., 2020), we use an agglomerative clustering on the pairwise scores $s(i, j)$ to form the coreference clusters at inference time. The agglomerative clustering step merges the most similar cluster pairs until their pairwise similarity score falls below a tuned threshold

τ.

Technical Details We conduct our experience on a single GeForce GTX 1080 Ti 12GB GPU. Our model has 14M parameters. On average, the training takes 30 minutes and inference over all the test set takes 3 minutes.

Disentangling Online Chats with DAG-Structured LSTMs

Duccio Pappadopulo[*1], **Lisa Bauer**[*2], **Marco Farina**[1], **Ozan İrsoy**[1], **Mohit Bansal**[2]
[1]Bloomberg [2]UNC Chapel Hill
{dpappadopulo, mfarina19, oirsoy}@bloomberg.net
{lbauer6, mbansal}@cs.unc.edu

Abstract

Many modern messaging systems allow fast and synchronous textual communication among many users. The resulting sequence of messages hides a more complicated structure in which independent sub-conversations are interwoven with one another. This poses a challenge for any task aiming to understand the content of the chat logs or gather information from them. The ability to disentangle these conversations is then tantamount to the success of many downstream tasks such as summarization and question answering. Structured information accompanying the text such as user turn, user mentions, timestamps, is used as a cue by the participants themselves who need to follow the conversation and has been shown to be important for disentanglement. DAG-LSTMs, a generalization of Tree-LSTMs that can handle directed acyclic dependencies, are a natural way to incorporate such information and its non-sequential nature. In this paper, we apply DAG-LSTMs to the conversation disentanglement task. We perform our experiments on the Ubuntu IRC dataset. We show that the novel model we propose achieves state of the art status on the task of recovering *reply-to* relations and it is competitive on other disentanglement metrics.

1 Introduction

Online chat and text messaging systems like Facebook Messenger, Slack, WeChat, WhatsApp, are common tools used by people to communicate in groups and in real time. In these venues multiple independent conversations often occur simultaneously with their individual utterances interspersed.

It is reasonable to assume the existence of an underlying *thread* structure partitioning the full conversation into disjoint sets of utterances, which ideally represent independent sub-conversations.

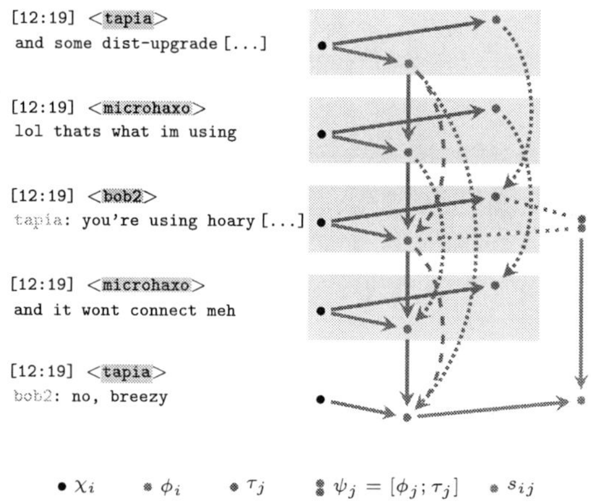

Figure 1: Excerpt from the IRC dataset (*left*) and our reply-to classifier architecture (*right*). Blue dots represent a unidirectional DAG-LSTM unit processing the states coming from the children of the current node. Red dots represent the GRU units performing thread encoding. At this point in time, we are computing the score (log-odds) of fifth utterance replying to the third.

The task of identifying these sub-units, *disentanglement*, is a prerequisite for further downstream tasks among which question answering, summarization, and topic modeling (Traum et al., 2004; Shen et al., 2006; Adams and Martell, 2008; Elsner and Charniak, 2010). Additional structure can generally be found in these logs, as a particular utterance could be a response or a continuation of a previous one. Such *reply-to* relationships implicitly define threads as the connected components of the resulting graph topology, and can then be used for disentanglement (Mehri and Carenini, 2017; Dulceanu, 2016; Wang et al., 2008; Gaoyang Guo et al., 2018).

Modeling work on conversation disentanglement spans more than a decade. Elsner and Charniak (2008, 2010) use feature based linear models to find

∗ Equal contribution

Proceedings of the 10th Conference on Lexical and Computational Semantics, pages 152–159
August 5–6, 2021, Bangkok, Thailand (online)

pairs of utterances belonging to the same thread and heuristic global algorithms to assign posts to threads. Mehri and Carenini (2017) and Jiang et al. (2018), while also adopting similar heuristics, use features extracted through neural models, LSTMSs (Hochreiter and Schmidhuber, 1997) and siamese CNNs (Bromley et al., 1993) respectively. Wang et al. (2011) follow a different approach by modeling the interactions between the predicted reply-to relations as a conditional random field.

One challenge in building automatic systems that perform disentanglement is the scarcity of large annotated datasets to be used to train expressive models. A remarkable effort in this direction is the work of Kummerfeld et al. (2019a) and the release of a dataset containing more that $77k$ utterances from the IRC `#Ubuntu` channel with annotated reply-to structure. In the same paper, it is shown how a set of simple handcrafted features, pooling of utterances GloVe embeddings (Pennington et al., 2014), and a feed-forward classifier can achieve good performances on the disentanglement task. Most of the follow-up work on the dataset relies on BERT (Devlin et al., 2019) embeddings to generate utterance representations (Zhu et al., 2020; Gu et al., 2020; Li et al., 2020). Zhu et al. (2020) use an additional transformer module to contextualize these representations, while Gu et al. (2020); Li et al. (2020) use an LSTM. Two exceptions are Liu et al. (2020), which models thread membership in an online fashion and discards reply-to relationships, and the recent Yu and Joty (2020a) which uses pointer networks (Vinyals et al., 2015).

In this short paper, we use DAG-structured LSTMs (İrsoy et al., 2019) to study disentanglement. As a generalization of Tree-LSTMs (Tai et al., 2015a), DAG-LSTMs allow to faithfully represent the structure of a conversation, which is more properly described as a directed acyclic graph (DAG) than a sequence. Furthermore, DAG-LSTMs allow for the systematic inclusion of structured information like user turn and mentions in the learned representation of the conversation context. We enrich the representation learned by the DAG-LSTM by concatenating to it a representation of the thread to which the utterance belongs. This *thread encoding* is obtained by means of a GRU unit (Cho et al., 2014) and captures thread specific features like style, topic, or persona. Finally we manually construct new features to improve username matching, which is crucial for detecting user mentions, one of the most important features for disentanglement.

Our results are summarized in Table 1. The DAG-LSTM significantly outperforms the BiLSTM baseline. Ablation studies show the importance of the new features we introduce. When augmented by thread encoding and a careful handling of posts predicted to be thread starters, the DAG-LSTM architecture achieves state of the art performances on *reply-to* relation extraction on the IRC Ubuntu dataset and it is competitive on the other metrics which are relevant to disentanglement.

2 Methodology

2.1 Problem Statement

A multi-party chat C is a sequence of posts $(c_i)_i$, $i = 1, \dots, |C|$. For each *query* post c_i we look for the set of *link* posts $\mathcal{R}(c_i)$ such that c_i replies to, or *links to*, c_j for $c_j \in \mathcal{R}(c_i)$. When a post c is a conversation starter we define, consistently with Kummerfeld et al. (2019a), $\mathcal{R}(c) = \{c\}$, that is c replies to itself, it is a *self-link*. This reply-to binary relation defines a DAG over C. By taking the union of the reply-to relation with its converse and by calculating its transitive closure, we obtain an equivalence relation on C whose equivalence classes are threads, thus solving the disentanglement problem.

We frame the problem as a sequence classification task. For each query post c_i we consider its L preceding posts $\mathcal{O}_{c_i} \equiv \{c_{i-L-1}, \dots, c_i\}$ and predict one of them as its link. In the IRC Ubuntu dataset, predicting a single link per query post is a good approximation, holding true for more than 95% of the annotated utterances. We use $L = 50$ in the following. As described in Sections 2.2 and 2.3, for each query utterance c_i, we construct a contextualized representation, $\phi_i \equiv \phi(c_i, C)$. We do the same for each of the links $c_j \in \mathcal{O}_{c_i}$, using a representation ψ that can in principle differ from ϕ. We then calculate $p(c_i \text{ replies-to } c_j) \equiv p(c_j|c_i)$ as

$$p(c_j|c_i) \equiv \frac{\exp(s_{ij})}{\sum_{c_k \in \mathcal{O}_{c_i}} \exp(s_{ik})}, \qquad (1)$$

where $s_{ij} \equiv s(\phi_i, \psi_j, f_{ij})$ is a real-valued scoring function described in Section 2.4 and f_{ij} are additional features. The parameters of the resulting model are learned by maximizing the likelihood associated to Eq. 1. At inference time we predict $\hat{j} = \text{argmax}_{c_j \in \mathcal{O}_{c_i}} p(c_j|c_i)$.

2.2 Contextual Post Representation

The construction of the ϕ and ψ representations closely follows İrsoy et al. (2019). Every post c_i is represented as a sequence of tokens $(t^i_n)_n$. An embedding layer maps the tokens to a sequence of d_I-dimensional real vectors $(\omega^i_n)_n$. We use the tokenizer and the word embeddings from Kummerfeld et al. (2019a), $d_I = 50$. We generate a representation χ_i of c_i by means of a single BiLSTM layer unrolled over the sequence of the token embeddings $(v^i_n)_n \equiv \text{BiLSTM}[(\omega^i_n)_n]$ followed by elementwise max-affine pooling $\chi_i = \max_n \text{Affine}[(v^i_n)_n]$.

To obtain the contextualized representations ϕ, we use a DAG-LSTM layer. This is an N-ary Tree-LSTM (Tai et al., 2015a) in which the sum over children in the recursive definition of the memory cell is replaced with an elementwise max operation (see Appendix). This allows the existence of multiple paths between two nodes (as it is the case if a node has multiple children) without the associated state explosion (İrsoy et al., 2019). This is crucial to handle long sequences, as in our case.

At each time step the DAG-LSTM unit receives the utterance representation χ_i of the current post c_i as the input and all the hidden and cell states coming from a labeled set of children, $\mathcal{C}(c_i)$, see Figure 1. In our case $\mathcal{C}(c_i)$ contains three elements: the previous post in the conversation (c_{i-1}), the previous post by the same user of c_i, the previous post by the user mentioned in c_i if any. More dependencies can be easily added making this architecture well suited to handle structured information. The DAG-LSTM is unrolled over the sequence $(\{\chi_i, \mathcal{C}(c_i)\})_i$, providing a sequence of contextualized post representations $(\phi_i)_i$. We also consider a bidirectional DAG-LSTM defined by a second unit processing the reversed sequence $\tilde{c}_i \equiv c_{|C|-i+1}$. Forward and backward DAG-LSTM representations are then concatenated to obtain ϕ.

2.3 Thread Encoding

The link post representation ψ can coincide with the query one, $\psi_j \equiv \phi_j$. One potential issue with this approach is that ψ does not depend on past thread assignments. Furthermore, thread-specific features such as topic and persona, cannot be easily captured by the hierarchical but sequential model described in the previous section. Thus we augment the link representations by means of *thread encoding* (Liu et al., 2020). Given a query, c_i, and a link c_j posts pair, we consider the thread $\mathcal{T}(c_j) = (c_{t_i})$, $t_i < t_{i+1}$, $t_{|\mathcal{T}(c_j)|} = j$, to which c_j has been assigned. We construct a representation τ_j of such thread by means of a GRU cell, $\tau_j = \text{GRU}[(\chi(c))_{c\in\mathcal{T}(c_j)}]$. ψ_j is then obtained by concatenating ϕ_j and τ_j. At training time we use the gold threads to generate the τ representations, while at evaluation time we use the predicted ones.

2.4 Scoring Function

Once query and link representations are constructed we use the scoring function in Eq. 1 to score each link against the query utterance, with s a three-layer feed-forward neural network. The input of the network is the concatenation $[\phi_i; \psi_j; f_{ij}]$, where f_{ij} are the 77 features introduced by Kummerfeld et al. (2019a). We augment them by 42 additional features based on Levenshtein distance and longest common prefix between query's username and words in the link utterance (and viceversa). These are introduced to improve mention detection by being more lenient on spelling mistakes (see 2.5 for precise definitions).

2.5 User Features

While IRC chats allow systematically tagging other participants (a single mention per post), users can address each other explicitly by typing usernames. This allows for abbreviations and typos to be introduced, which are not efficiently captured by the set of features used by Kummerfeld et al. (2019b). To ameliorate this problem we construct additional features. Given a pair of utterances c_1 and c_2 we define the following:

- Smallest Levenshtein distance (D_L) between $c_1(c_2)$'s username and each of the word in $c_2(c_1)$; 5 bins, $D_L = i$ for $i = 0, \ldots, 4$ or $D_L > 4$.

- Largest length of common prefix (ℓ) between $c_1(c_2)$'s username and each of the word in $c_2(c_1)$; 5 bins, $\ell = i$ for $i = 3, \ldots, 6$ or $\ell > 6$.

- Binary variable indicating whether $c_1(c_2)$'s username is a prefix of any of the words in $c_2(c_1)$.

These amount to a total of 42 additional features for each pair of posts.

Model	Graph			Cluster		
	P	R	F	P	R	F
Kummerfeld et al.	73.7	71.0	72.3	34.6	38.0	36.2
Zhu et al.*	73.2	69.2	70.6	35.8	32.7	34.2
Li et al.*				42.3	<u>46.2</u>	44.1
Yu and Joty	74.7	72.7	73.7	33.0	38.9	36.0
+ self.	<u>74.8</u>	<u>72.7</u>	<u>73.7</u>	42.2	40.9	41.5
+ joint train, self.	74.5	71.7	73.1	<u>44.9</u>	44.2	<u>44.5</u>
BiLSTM (↓)	73.9	71.2	72.5	31.3	37.5	34.1
DAG-LSTM	74.9	72.2	73.6	37.3	42.3	39.6
− user features (↓)	74.0	71.3	72.6	33.6	39.7	36.4
− mention link	74.5	71.8	73.1	33.5	38.3	35.7
+ self. (↑)	74.9	72.6	73.8	41.1	41.1	41.1
+ thread enc.	75.0	72.3	73.7	37.3	**42.5**	39.7
+ thread enc., self.	**75.2**	**72.7**	**73.9**	**42.4**	41.7	**42.0**

Table 1: Results of our experiments (*bottom*, best in bold) and literature (*top*, best underlined). The ↑(↓) sign indicates the model being significantly better (worse) ($p < 0.05$) than the DAG-LSTM entry based on a McNemar test (McNemar, 1947) conducted on the *test* set. User features and mention links are included in this baseline model, thread encoding and self-link threshold tuning are not. Starred entries use contextual embeddings.

3 Results

3.1 Evaluation

We conduct our experiments on the Ubuntu IRC dataset for disentanglement (Kummerfeld et al., 2019a; Kim et al., 2019). We focus on two evaluation metrics defined in Kummerfeld et al. (2019a): *graph* F_1, the F-score calculated using the number of correctly predicted reply-to pairs; *cluster* F_1, the F-score calculated using the number of matching threads of length greater than 1.

3.2 Experiments

As a baseline, we use a BiLSTM model in which $\phi_i (= \psi_i)$ is obtained as the hidden states of a bidirectional LSTM unrolled over the sequence $(\chi_i)_i$. The base DAG-LSTM model uses both username and mentions to define the children set $\mathcal{C}$ of an utterance. Bidirectionality is left as a hyperparameter. All our experiments use the same architecture from section 2 to construct the utterance representation χ. We train each model by minimizing the negative log-likelihood for Eq. 1 using Adam optimizer (Kingma and Ba, 2019). We tune the hyperparameters of each architecture through random search.[1] Table 1 shows the test set performances of the models which achieve the best graph F_1 score over the dev set. Optimizing graph over cluster score is motivated by an observation: dev set cluster F_1 score displays a much larger variance than graph F_1 score, which is roughly four-fold after subtracting the score rolling average. By picking the iteration with the best cluster F_1 score we would be more exposed to fluctuation and to worse generalization, which we observe.

[1] We refer to the Appendix for details.

Model	Self-links		
	P	R	F
BiLSTM	79.6	94.6	86.5
DAG-LSTM	82.8	93.8	88.0
+ self-links threshold	87.7	92.4	90.0
DAG-LSTM + thread enc.	81.4	93.8	87.2
+ self-links threshold	89.8	90.6	90.2

Table 2: Thread starters (*self-links*) performances for our models in Table 1, before and after thresholding.

3.3 Self-Links Threshold Tuning

As noted by Yu and Joty (2020b), the ability of the model to detect self-links is crucial for its final performances. In line with their findings, we also report that all our models are skewed towards high recall for self-link detection (Table 2).

To help with this, we introduce two thresholds θ and δ, which we compare with $\hat{p}$, the argmax probability Eq. 1, and Δp, the difference between the top-2 predicted probabilities. Whenever the argmax is a self-link: if $p < \theta$, we predict the next-to-argmax link, otherwise we predict both the top-2 links if also $\Delta\hat{p} < \delta$. On the dev set, we first fine-tune θ to maximize the self-link F_1 score and the fine-tune δ to maximize the cluster F_1 score.

3.4 Results Discussion

Table 1 shows our main results. Our DAG-LSTM model significantly outperforms the BiLSTM baseline. We perform ablation studies on our best DAG-LSTM model showing that while both user features and mention link provide a performance improvement for both cluster and graph score, only user features ablation results in a significant change. Self-links threshold tuning improves performances, particularly on cluster score for both models, highlighting the importance of correctly identifying thread starters.

The DAG-LSTM model with thread encoding achieves state of the art performances in predicting *reply-to* relations. This is particularly interesting especially when we compare with models employing contextual embeddings like Zhu et al. (2020). For the cluster scores, the best model is the pointer network model of Yu and Joty (2020a), which is anyway within less than 0.5% of the best contextual model, and within 2.5% of our model. The difference mainly arises from a difference in recall and corresponds to an absolute difference of less than 10 true positive clusters on the test set. Further comparisons with existing literature are limited by code not being available at the moment.

4 Conclusions

In this paper we apply, for the first time, DAG-LSTMs to the disentanglement task; they provide a flexible architecture that allows to incorporate into the learned neural representations the structured information which comes alongside multi-turn dialogue. We propose thread encoding and a new set of features to aid identification of user mentions.

There are possible directions left to explore. We modeled the reply-to relationships in a conversation by making an assumption of conditional independence of reply-to assignments. This is possibly a poor approximation and it would be interesting to lift it. A challenge with this approach is the computational complexity resulting from the large dimension of the output space of the reply-to classifier. We notice that thread encoding allows a non-greedy decoding strategy through beam search which would be interesting to further explore.

Acknowledgments

We thank the reviewers for their useful feedback. We thank Andy Liu, Camilo Ortiz, Huayan Zhong, Philipp Meerkamp, Rakesh Gosangi, Raymond (Haimin) Zhang for their initial collaboration. We thank Jonathan Kummerfeld for discussions. This work was performed while Lisa interned at Bloomberg, and was later supported by DARPA MCS Grant N66001-19-2-4031, NSF-CAREER Award 1846185, and a NSF PhD Fellowship. The views are those of the authors and not of the funding agencies.

References

P. H. Adams and C. H. Martell. 2008. Topic Detection and Extraction in Chat. In *2008 IEEE International Conference on Semantic Computing*, pages 581–588.

Jane Bromley, James W Bentz, Léon Bottou, Isabelle Guyon, Yann LeCun, Cliff Moore, Eduard Säckinger, and Roopak Shah. 1993. Signature Verification Using a "Siamese" Time Delay Neural Network. *International Journal of Pattern Recognition and Artificial Intelligence*, 7(04):669–688.

Kyunghyun Cho, Bart van Merriënboer, Dzmitry Bahdanau, and Yoshua Bengio. 2014. On the Properties of Neural Machine Translation: Encoder–Decoder Approaches. In *Proceedings of SSST-8, Eighth Workshop on Syntax, Semantics and Structure in Statistical Translation*, pages 103–111.

Jacob Devlin, Ming-Wei Chang, Kenton Lee, and Kristina Toutanova. 2019. BERT: Pre-training of deep bidirectional transformers for language understanding. In *Proceedings of the 2019 Conference of the North American Chapter of the Association for Computational Linguistics: Human Language Technologies, Volume 1 (Long and Short Papers)*, pages 4171–4186, Minneapolis, Minnesota. Association for Computational Linguistics.

Andrei Dulceanu. 2016. Recovering Implicit Thread Structure in Chat Conversations. *Romanian Journal of Human-Computer Interaction*, 9(3).

Micha Elsner and Eugene Charniak. 2008. You Talking to Me? a Corpus and Algorithm for Conversation Disentanglement. *ACL-08: HLT*, page 834.

Micha Elsner and Eugene Charniak. 2010. Disentangling Chat. *Computational Linguistics*, 36(3):389–409.

Gaoyang Guo, Chaokun Wang, Jun Chen, Pengcheng Ge, and Weijun Chen. 2018. Who is Answering Whom? finding "Reply-To" Relations in Group Chats with Deep Bidirectional LSTM Networks. *Cluster Computing*, pages 1–12.

Jia-Chen Gu, Tianda Li, Quan Liu, Xiaodan Zhu, Zhen-Hua Ling, and Yu-Ping Ruan. 2020. Pre-Trained and Attention-Based Neural Networks for Building Noetic Task-Oriented Dialogue Systems. In *AAAI 2020 Workshop on The Eighth Dialog System Technology Challenge*.

Sepp Hochreiter and Jürgen Schmidhuber. 1997. Long Short-Term Memory. *Neural computation*, 9(8):1735–1780.

Jyun-Yu Jiang, Francine Chen, Yan-Ying Chen, and Wei Wang. 2018. Learning to Disentangle Interleaved Conversational Threads with a Siamese Hierarchical Network and Similarity Ranking. In *Proceedings of the 2018 Conference of the North American Chapter of the Association for Computational Linguistics: Human Language Technologies, Volume 1 (Long Papers)*, pages 1812–1822.

Seokhwan Kim, Michel Galley, Chulaka Gunasekara, Sungjin Lee, Adam Atkinson, Baolin Peng, Hannes Schulz, Jianfeng Gao, Jinchao Li, Mahmoud Adada, et al. 2019. The Eighth Dialog System Technology Challenge. *arXiv preprint arXiv:1911.06394*.

Diederik P Kingma and J Adam Ba. 2019. A Method for Stochastic Optimization. arxiv 2014. *arXiv preprint arXiv:1412.6980*, 434.

Jonathan K Kummerfeld, Sai R Gouravajhala, Joseph J Peper, Vignesh Athreya, Chulaka Gunasekara, Jatin Ganhotra, Siva Sankalp Patel, Lazaros C Polymenakos, and Walter Lasecki. 2019a. A Large-Scale Corpus for Conversation Disentanglement. In *Proceedings of the 57th Annual Meeting of the Association for Computational Linguistics*, pages 3846–3856.

Jonathan K. Kummerfeld, Sai R. Gouravajhala, Joseph J. Peper, Vignesh Athreya, Chulaka Gunasekara, Jatin Ganhotra, Siva Sankalp Patel, Lazaros C Polymenakos, and Walter Lasecki. 2019b. A large-scale corpus for conversation disentanglement. In *Proceedings of the 57th Annual Meeting of the Association for Computational Linguistics*, pages 3846–3856, Florence, Italy. Association for Computational Linguistics.

Tianda Li, Jia-Chen Gu, Xiaodan Zhu, Quan Liu, Zhen-Hua Ling, Zhiming Su, and Si Wei. 2020. Dialbert: A Hierarchical Pre-Trained Model for Conversation Disentanglement. *CoRR*, abs/2004.03760.

Hui Liu, Zhan Shi, Jia-Chen Gu, Quan Liu, Si Wei, and Xiaodan Zhu. 2020. End-to-End Transition-Based Online Dialogue Disentanglement. In *Proceedings of the Twenty-Ninth International Joint Conference on Artificial Intelligence, IJCAI-20*, pages 3868–3874. International Joint Conferences on Artificial Intelligence Organization. Main track.

Quinn McNemar. 1947. Note on the Sampling Error of the Difference between Correlated Proportions or Percentages. *Psychometrika*, 12(2):153–157.

Shikib Mehri and Giuseppe Carenini. 2017. Chat Disentanglement: Identifying Semantic Reply Relationships with Random Forests and Recurrent Neural Networks. In *Proceedings of the Eighth International Joint Conference on Natural Language Processing (Volume 1: Long Papers)*, pages 615–623.

Jeffrey Pennington, Richard Socher, and Christopher D Manning. 2014. Glove: Global Vectors for Word Representation. In *Proceedings of the 2014 conference on empirical methods in natural language processing (EMNLP)*, pages 1532–1543.

Dou Shen, Qiang Yang, Jian-Tao Sun, and Zheng Chen. 2006. Thread Detection in Dynamic Text Message Streams. In *Proceedings of the 29th Annual International ACM SIGIR Conference on Research and Development in Information Retrieval*, SIGIR '06, page 35–42, New York, NY, USA. Association for Computing Machinery.

Kai Sheng Tai, Richard Socher, and Christopher D Manning. 2015a. Improved Semantic Representations from Tree-Structured Long Short-Term Memory Networks. In *Proceedings of the 53rd Annual Meeting of the Association for Computational Linguistics and the 7th International Joint Conference on Natural Language Processing (Volume 1: Long Papers)*, pages 1556–1566.

Kai Sheng Tai, Richard Socher, and Christopher D. Manning. 2015b. Improved semantic representations from tree-structured long short-term memory networks. In *Proceedings of the 53rd Annual Meeting of the Association for Computational Linguistics and the 7th International Joint Conference on Natural Language Processing (Volume 1: Long Papers)*, pages 1556–1566, Beijing, China. Association for Computational Linguistics.

David R. Traum, Susan Robinson, and Jens Stephan. 2004. Evaluation of multi-party virtual reality dialogue interaction. In *Proceedings of the Fourth International Conference on Language Resources and Evaluation (LREC'04)*, Lisbon, Portugal. European Language Resources Association (ELRA).

Oriol Vinyals, Meire Fortunato, and Navdeep Jaitly. 2015. Pointer Networks. In *Advances in Neural Information Processing Systems*, pages 2692–2700.

Hongning Wang, Chi Wang, ChengXiang Zhai, and Jiawei Han. 2011. Learning Online Discussion Structures by Conditional Random Fields. In *Proceedings of the 34th International ACM SIGIR Conference on Research and Development in Information Retrieval*, SIGIR '11, page 435–444, New York, NY, USA. Association for Computing Machinery.

Yi-Chia Wang, Mahesh Joshi, William Cohen, and Carolyn Rosé. 2008. Recovering Implicit Thread Structure in Newsgroup Style Conversations. In *AAAI*.

Tao Yu and Shafiq Joty. 2020a. Online Conversation Disentanglement with Pointer Networks. In *Proceedings of the 2020 Conference on Empirical Methods in Natural Language Processing (EMNLP)*, pages 6321–6330.

Tao Yu and Shafiq Joty. 2020b. Online conversation disentanglement with pointer networks. In *Proceedings of the 2020 Conference on Empirical Methods in Natural Language Processing (EMNLP)*, pages 6321–6330, Online. Association for Computational Linguistics.

Henghui Zhu, Feng Nan, Zhiguo Wang, Ramesh Nallapati, and Bing Xiang. 2020. Who Did They Respond To? Conversation Structure Modeling Using Masked Hierarchical Transformer. In *Proceedings of the AAAI Conference on Artificial Intelligence*.

Ozan İrsoy, Rakesh Gosangi, Haimin Zhang, Mu-Hsin Wei, Peter Lund, Duccio Pappadopulo, Brendan Fahy, Neophytos Neophytou, and Camilo Ortiz. 2019. Dialogue Act Classification in Group Chats with DAG-LSTMs. In *SIGIR 2019 Workshop on Conversational Interaction Systems*.

A Appendix

A.1 DAG-LSTM Equations

A DAG-LSTM is a variation on the Tree-LSTM (Tai et al., 2015b) architecture, that is defined over DAGs. Given a DAG, G, we assume that for every vertex v of G, the edges $e(v, v')$ connecting the children $v' \in \mathcal{C}(v)$ to v can be assigned a unique label $\ell_{v,v'}$ from a fixed set of labels.

A pair of states vectors (h_v, c_v) and an input x_v are associated to every vertex v. The DAG-LSTM equations define the states (h_v, c_v), as a function of the input x_v and the states of its children:

$$(h_v, c_v) = \text{DAG-LSTM}(x_v; \{(h_w, c_w) | w \in \mathcal{C}(v)\}). \quad (2)$$

The equations defining such functions are the following:

$$i_v = \sigma\Big(W_{ix}x_v + \sum_{v' \in \mathcal{C}(v)} W_{ih}^{\ell_{v,v'}} h_{v'}\Big) \quad (3)$$

$$f_{vv'} = \sigma\Big(W_{fx}x_v + \sum_{v'' \in \mathcal{C}(v)} W_{fh}^{\ell_{v,v'}\ell_{v,v''}} h_{v''}\Big) \quad (4)$$

$$c_v = i_v \odot u_v + \max_{v' \in \mathcal{C}(v)} f_{vv'} \odot c_{v'} \quad (5)$$

$$h_v = o_v \odot \tanh(c_v) \quad (6)$$

The equations for the o and u gates are the same as those for the i gate by replacing everywhere $i \to o, u$. Bias vectors are left implicit in the definition of i, f, o, and u. $\odot$ represents Hadamard product and max in Eq. 5 represent elementwise max operation.

A bidirectional DAG-LSTM, is just a pair of independent DAG-LSTM, one of which is unrolled over the time reversed sequence of utterances. The output of a bidirectional DAG-LSTM is the concatenation of the h states of the forward and backward unit for a given utterance.

A.2 Training and Hyperparameter Tuning

We use adjudicated training, development, and test sets from (Kummerfeld et al., 2019b). Each of these dataset is composed a set of conversation (153 in the training set and 10 in both development and test set) each representing a chunk of contiguous posts from the IRC `#Ubuntu` channel. Each of these conversation contains strictly more than 1000 posts (exactly 1250 and 1500 for dev and test set respectively). Annotations are available for all but the first 1000 posts in every conversation. We apply some preprocessing to these conversations. We chunk the annotated section of every training conversation in contiguous chunks of 50 posts each, starting from the first annotated post. [2] To each of these chunks we attach a past context of 100 posts and a future context of 50, resulting in 200 utterances long chunks. For each of these chunks we keep only those annotated links for which the response utterance lies in the central 50 posts. We do not chunk development and test set, but drop the first 900 post in every conversation.

The various architectures we consider share the same set of parameters to fine-tune. One parameter d_h controls the dimension of the hidden state of the LSTMs and one parameter d_{FF} controls the dimension of the hidden layers of the feed-forward scorer. We use word dropout, apply dropout after the max-affine layer, and apply dropout after activation at every layer of the feed-forward scorer. We clip all gradient entries at 5. We use a single layer of LSTMs and DAG-LSTMs to build the χ and ϕ, ψ representations and we do not dropout any of their units. Similarly we use a single layer GRU for the thread encoder. We list all the hyperparameters in Table 3 together with their range and distribution used for the random search.

Hyperparameter optimization is performed by running 100 training jobs for the base BiLSTM architecture, DAG-LSTM, and DAG-LSTM with thread encoding. Our published results are from the best among these runs. The best sets of parameters we find for each of these architectures are:

- BiLSTM: $d_h = 256$, $d_{FF} = 128$, no word and max-affine dropout, a feed forward-dropout equal to 0.3, and a learning rate of 2.4×10^{-4}.
- DAG-LSTM: $d_h = 64$, $d_{FF} = 256$, no word and max-affine dropout, a feed forward-dropout equal to 0.3, and a learning rate of 7.3×10^{-4}.
- DAG-LSTM with thread encoding: $d_h = d_{FF} = 256$, word and max-affine dropout equal to 0.3, a feed forward-dropout equal to 0.5, and a learning rate of 7.9×10^{-4}.

User feature and mention link ablations are obtained by fixing all parameters of the best DAG-LSTM run (removing the feature we are experimenting with) and running 10 jobs by only changing the random seed.

[2]This may result in the last chunk to have less than 50 posts. This happens for 45 conversations.

Parameter	Domain	Distribution
d_h	$\{64, 128, 256\}$	categorical
d_{FF}	$\{64, 128, 256\}$	categorical
word dropout	$\{0, 0.3, 0.5\}$	categorical
max-affine dropout	$\{0, 0.3, 0.5\}$	categorical
feed-forward dropout	$\{0, 0.3, 0.5\}$	categorical
learning rate	$[10^{-5}, 10^{-3}]$	log-uniform
BiDAG-LSTM	{true, false}	categorical

Table 3: Hyperparameters of the model architectures. During hyperparameter optimization, we perform a random search according to the distributions described above. Categorical distributions have uniform probability mass function.

Each training job is performed on a single GPU and, depending on the architectures, takes from 6 to 12 hours.

A.3 Significance Estimates

We use McNemar test (McNemar, 1947) to evaluate the significance of performance differences between model. Given two models M_A and M_B, we define $n_{A\overline{B}}$ as the number of links correctly predicted by A but not by B. Under the null hypothesis both $n_{A\overline{B}} \sim \text{Bin}(n_{A\overline{B}}, n, 1/2)$, where $n \equiv n_{A\overline{B}} + n_{B\overline{A}}$. We define a model A to be *significantly* better than a model B if the null hypothesis is excluded at 95% confidence level.

Toward Diverse Precondition Generation

Heeyoung Kwon[1], **Nathanael Chambers**[2], **and Niranjan Balasubramanian**[1]
[1]Stony Brook University, Stony Brook, New York
[2] US Naval Academy, Annapolis, MD
{heekwon, niranjan}@cs.stonybrook.edu
nchamber@usna.edu

Abstract

Language understanding must identify the logical connections between events in a discourse, but core events are often unstated due to their commonsense nature. This paper fills in these missing events by generating *precondition events*. Precondition generation can be framed as a sequence-to-sequence problem: given a target event, generate a possible precondition. However, in most real-world scenarios, an event can have *several* preconditions, requiring diverse generation – a challenge for standard seq2seq approaches. We propose DiP, a **Di**verse **P**recondition generation system that can generate unique and diverse preconditions. DiP uses a generative process with three components – an event sampler, a candidate generator, and a post-processor. The event sampler provides control codes (precondition triggers) which the candidate generator uses to focus its generation. Unlike other conditional generation systems, DiP automatically generates control codes without training on diverse examples. Analysis against baselines reveals that DiP improves the diversity of preconditions significantly while also generating more preconditions.

1 Introduction

Preconditions are an important part of language understanding with numerous applications, ranging from event understanding to story generation. They provide the semantic glue to understand (or generate) the chains of events common in narrative text. How can we build intelligent systems to fill in these chains, or to identify semantically related events in context? Kwon et al. (2020) took a first step by introducing a precondition generation task, where given a target event mention the goal is to generate text that describes a precondition for the target. They released the 'PeKo' dataset for training, and showed that a GPT-2 model can be fine-tuned on input/output sequence pairs.

TARGET: [BLANK] to **fill** Mr. Lavelle 's seat, for a term that expires on Dec. 31, 2008.
The Senate **voted** overwhelmingly on Thursday
The Senate **voted** on Wednesday
The Senate **voted** overwhelmingly on Wednesday
The Senate **voted** overwhelmingly on Tuesday
Mr. Lavelle was **appointed** by Gov. Eliot Spitzer

Table 1: Top 5 preconditions generated from GPT-2 with beam search decoding. Key problem: the top 4 preconditions are almost identical.

While PeKo is useful, it is constrained by annotating a single relation for each target event. This is contrast to the real-world where most events have many preconditions. For example, "*opening* a door" has several preconditions like *approaching* the door, *turning* a key in the door, and *pushing* the door. PeKo's annotation limits the ability of models to learn to generate multiple and *diverse* preconditions[1]. In this work, we address the challenge of generating more preconditions for each target event while still maintaining quality.

Generating non-repetitive diverse outputs is a challenge for any conditional language generation system. Our analysis of the GPT-2 based model shows that this is also the case for preconditions. Table 1 shows such top preconditions for an example event. Standard sampling techniques produce high-levels of lexical and semantic redundancy. In the absence of any explicit mechanisms to force diversity, the model just produces minor variations of the same event as preconditions. To obtain diverse candidate preconditions, we have to start looking lower in the model's ranked lists of probable preconditions, thereby sacrificing quality.

How can we induce a model to generate diverse outputs without losing quality? Context sensitivity might help with quality, but it also hinders diversity. To address this we introduce a three-stage

[1]In order to observe diverse preconditions for the same (or similar) target event we would need a much larger training set.

Proceedings of the 10th Conference on Lexical and Computational Semantics, pages 160–172
August 5–6, 2021, Bangkok, Thailand (online) ©2021 Association for Computational Linguistics

generative process, which we call DiP. In the first stage, DiP uses an event sampler whose only goal is to generate event trigger words as precondition candidates. In the second stage, DiP forces the generative model to use the candidate triggers from the first stage to produce the full description of the precondition event. In the third stage, DiP re-ranks and filters the generated descriptions using a precondition classifier (also trained from the same training data).[2] A brief example is shown here:

Target Event: I apologized for the debacle of the day before, and `[BLANK]` to **help** me make it right

Stage 1	**Stage 2**	**Stage 3**
trying	I am **trying** now	*delete*
use	I **use** my time	*delete*
used	I **used** my time	#2
asked	**asked** me	#3
hired	**hired** a new staff	#1

Experiments on the PeKo dataset show that DiP produces more diverse and better quality preconditions compared to standard beam decoding, as well as an iterative filtering extension that applies a standard repetition penalty in a sampling strategy. Analyses show that DiP is able to better balance the need for diversity against quality. While the iterative repetition penalty method generates lexically diverse outputs, it often introduces irrelevant information rather than producing distinct types of preconditions. Our human evaluation shows that DiP on the other hand is able to produce text that is more likely to be preconditions.

All code and data are available at `https://stonybrooknlp.github.io/DiP/`.

2 Related Work

Most work on logical preconditions has focused on identification/extraction from text. For example, Sil et al. (2010) identified preconditions using a SVM-based score function with hand-crafted PMI and WordNet based features. Branavan et al. (2012) extracted domain-specific precondition relations from instructions for the game of Minecraft. This paper is instead focused on generating novel preconditions. To the best of our knowledge, only the prior PeKo work (Kwon et al., 2020) has attempted this. We are building on those initial ideas.

There has been research for diverse generation using control codes or latent variables. Some works use explicit cues to control text generation. Huang et al. (2018) used emotion embeddings to generate dialogue responses in a specific mood. Keskar et al. (2019) trained a LM with human readable control codes, which describe domain, style, or topics. Then the model learns to generate text conditioned on a given code. The model requires manually predefined control codes and a corresponding training corpus for each code.

Other diverse generation works learn latent representations or codes from input text, and then generate text conditioned on those codes. Shu et al. (2019) applied a sentence embedding to generate syntactically diverse translations. They find that syntax-based encoding with TreeLSTM (Socher et al., 2011) yields better diversity than a contextual encoding using BERT (Devlin et al., 2019) or FastText (Bojanowski et al., 2017). Bao et al. (2020) used K categorical latent variables to control the generation context of dialogue responses and pick the highest probability response from the responses generated using the latent variables. COD3S (Weir et al., 2020) is designed to generate diverse causal relations. It uses locality-sensitive hashing (LSH) (Indyk and Motwani, 1998) on representations from Sentence-BERT (Reimers and Gurevych, 2019). Conditioning on these 16-bit LSH signatures, it generates cause/effect sentences using a Transformer architecture (Vaswani et al., 2017) but with a limited vocabulary size of 10K.

These previous approaches have some drawbacks – they either require explicit control codes and training examples, or they have low interpretability of their codes. Our approach addresses these two limitations: control codes are learned from non-diverse input text and the codes are human-readable events. And these approaches are not directly comparable to our method without proper modification, which would not be fair comparisons. Thus, we present our own baselines for evaluation, and these baselines serve as a proxy of ablation studies as well.

3 Diverse Precondition Generation

This section describes our diverse precondition generation task and our methodology for solving it. Our proposed approach does not require additional diverse training examples.

3.1 Generation Task

This paper follows the precondition definitions from Kwon et al. (2020):

Precondition Definition – "Given a target event mention t and a candidate event mention p, we

[2]We will release the source code upon acceptance.

assert p is *a precondition event for t* if p is necessary for t to happen i.e., t likely would not have occurred without p, in the current text context."
Precondition Generation – "Given a target event t, generate an event p that is a precondition for t."

The precondition generation task is defined over sentences that contain both a target and a precondition event. The precondition part is masked and a model is asked to reconstruct the sentence including its precondition. For masking, the syntactic subtree of a precondition is replaced with `[BLANK]`. In order to indicate the events of interest – target and precondition – we use special tokens <event> .. </event> and <pre> .. </pre>.

For our new task, instead of generating the entire sentence, we only generate a precondition clause that would fit into the input's `[BLANK]`. Since a precondition could be stated in either preceding or succeeding position of its target event, we modeled this as a text infilling task. This approach is inspired by Donahue et al. (2020) and this modification allows the model to focus solely on generating preconditions because the model doesn't need to copy over its input text. Thus, the model can learn faster and more efficiently.

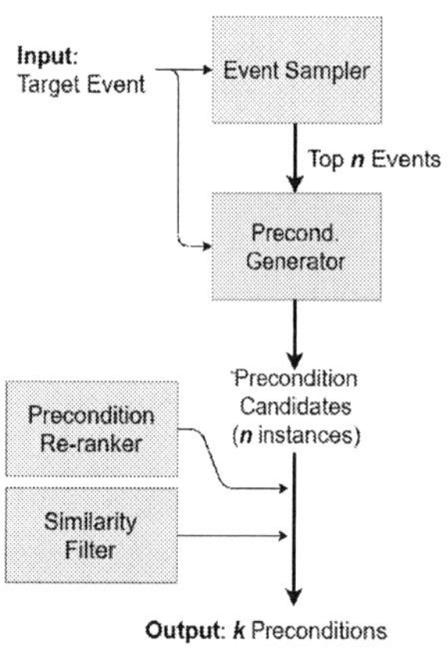

Figure 1: The DiP pipeline. Candidates are generated conditioned on the Event Sampler. The Re-ranker and Similarity Filter improve quality/diversity.

3.2 Diverse Precondition Generator

Generating preconditions is a difficult task even for a single output setting (Kwon et al., 2020). With the training data derived from existing news articles, generative models only get to see one possible precondition for each target event. Not surprisingly the top candidates in beam search tend to be focused towards a specific type of precondition event with minor variations. This suggests that we need to provide explicit guidance to the model to explore diverse candidates.

How can we get such diverse guidance? A main strength of large generative language models is that they learn to generate text that fits with the input context. If we can get the input context to be less specific then we can aim to get more general outputs. We can exploit this behavior by training a separate event sampler that is fed a reduced version of the target event description. For example, we can denote the target event by just the event trigger and its arguments. The event sampler learns to predict possible precondition event triggers based on this reduced context. This task forces the sampler to learn a more general mapping between target and precondition events that can produce a diverse set of starting points for generating the precondition events. We can then train another generative model to condition on the precondition trigger in addition to the input sentence. This gives us a model whose outputs we can control by providing different possible precondition triggers. Not all precondition triggers may yield high quality preconditions. To further assist the model, we also devise a precondition re-ranker.

Our overall system, shown in Figure 1, consists of three components – an event sampler, a candidate generator, and a post processor (Precondition re-ranker and Similarity filter). The first two stages are used for generation – they use two separate generation models, and the last is employed to improve the quality of generated preconditions. We refer to this system as DiP short for Diverse Preconditions.

3.2.1 Event Sampler

The event sampler provides possible precondition event triggers given a target event. This can be formulated as a sequence to sequence problem where the input sequence is a target event and the output sequence is a precondition event trigger. Since our goal here is to get diverse precondition events, we can experiment with input contexts of different levels of detail. To get more general precondition events, we use just the target event triggers as the input. To get more specific preconditions, we can use larger contexts surrounding the target event trigger as the input. During inference, we sample top n event triggers based on their probability.

Formally, let x' be a subset of the full description x of the target event. The sampler can be seen as a generative model that outputs event triggers e for the preconditions of the target event.

$$\hat{e} = \arg\max_{e} \log p(e|x')$$

The generative model is trained to maximize the probability for the correct precondition trigger e and during inference can be used to sample a candidate set of top n precondition event triggers.

3.2.2 Candidate Generator

The candidate generator, as the name suggests, is a language model that we fine-tune for generating precondition candidates. We want this model to generate preconditions corresponding to the triggers from the event sampler. To this end, in addition to the full target event description x, we also provide a precondition trigger marked by a special token – `<E> precondition_event` – at the end of the input. This can be seen as a form of a control code similar to those used in Keskar et al. (2019); Weir et al. (2020). The crucial difference, however, is that the codes in our case are dynamically generated conditioned on the input and not restricted to a predefined set.

Formally, the candidate generator is a language model that generates a description of the precondition event c_i conditioning on the full description of the target event x and a given precondition trigger e_i from the event sampler.

$$\hat{c_i} = \arg\max_{c_i} \log p(c_i|x, e_i)$$

The model is trained to maximize the probability of the observed precondition text for the target event when provided with the correct precondition trigger. Note that during training, the precondition trigger provided as input always appears in the correct precondition description output ($\hat{c_i}$). This encourages the model to learn to incorporate the trigger provided at the end of the input as part of its output. During inference, the model generates a set of preconditions one for each of the top n triggers obtained from the event sampler.

3.2.3 Post Processor

Precondition Re-ranker We use a precondition re-ranker to reorder the generated candidates based on how likely they are to be preconditions of the target event. Note that the generative model is implicitly trained for a similar objective. However, the model is also forced to include the input precondition trigger which could make it harder to focus on ensuring the result is indeed a precondition. Therefore, we introduce a separate precondition classifier that scores the generated candidates. Note that the original PeKo dataset is already setup for training such a classifier (Kwon et al., 2020). Each instance in this dataset consists of an input text that includes a pair of marked event triggers (target, candidate) and a label that indicates whether the candidate is a precondition of the event denoted by the target trigger. The output from the precondition generator is essentially equivalent to an instance from this dataset. We build a classifier that scores a pair of events in text, and we use this score as an indicator of the precondition quality of the generated candidates and re-rank them based on this score.

Iterative Redundancy Filtering The resulting candidates are a mix of candidate precondition events from different triggers. To further avoid redundancy we also include an explicit filtering step, where we post-process the generated text based on their pairwise similarity. Specifically, we start with the highest ranked instance in the output set, and iteratively walk down the ranked list and add instances to the output if the highest similarity score they have with any of the current output set is lower than a certain threshold.

4 Evaluation

Our goal is to investigate the impact of our DiP approach for generating diverse and high-quality preconditions. We closely follow Kwon et al. (2020) for the experimental setup and the GPT-2 based generation system for our evaluation.

4.1 Datasets

For the fine-tuning task, we use the precondition generation instances in the PeKo dataset. In addition, we also create a large additional pre-training dataset that includes temporal generation instances. With this additional dataset we can perform a form of domain adaptive pre-training (DAPT) introduced by Gururangan et al. (2020). The main idea here is to create generation instances where the model gets to see a target event but now is required to produce an event that temporally precedes the target event. Since preconditions are supposed to be temporally preceding this temporal generation task can be seen as a more permissive yet related generation task, which is then subsequently restricted to only preconditions in the fine-tuning stage. We use the CAEVO (Chambers et al., 2014) system

Target Event	The Metropolitan Transportation Authority recently ***canceled*** some large projects
Trigger Only	took, canceled, succeeded, began, scheduled, died, rejected, decision, filed, pushed
±3 tokens	planned, took, began, expected, needed, approved, designed, intended, completed, brought
±5 tokens	planned, intended, took, began, aimed, devised, completed, expected, designed, needed
Target Event	They tried to ***rebuild*** their shattered nation
Trigger Only	took, rebuilt, losing, sustained, lost, opened, came, bought, died, used
±3 tokens	took, lost, war, losing, reached, brought, moved, began, fled, came
±5 tokens	took, lost, war, collapsed, left, failed, abandoned, came, laid, began

Table 2: Top 10 generated event triggers from the event sampler. As more context is provided, the model generate more specific events related to the provided context.

Input Text	Generation Target
`[BLANK]` that donations be ***made*** to the Crohn's and Colitis Foundation or NYBOT Futures and Options for Kids in memory of Harry. `<E>` requests	In lieu of flowers, the family ***requests***
`[BLANK]` to ***start*** trading an important Nymex product, West Texas intermediate crude oil. `<E>` inspired	Nymex's foray also ***inspired*** ICE
Mr. Robbins played hard and fluidly, `[BLANK]` to ***give*** his solos funk and shape. `<E>` landing	***landing*** heavily on unexpected notes

Table 3: Examples of training instance pairs for the candidate generator. Unlike Kwon et al. (2020), we add the precondition event at the end of the input to help the model utilize the event trigger when generating a precondition.

to obtain temporally related event pairs from the NYT corpus (Sandhaus, 2008). This yields 1.1 million instances and each instance contains one temporal relation (BEFORE/AFTER). Note that all systems are trained using the same pre-training and fine-tuning strategy using both datasets.

4.2 Baselines

Beam Search As a baseline, we use text infilling GPT-2 system (inspired by (Donahue et al., 2020) with a standard beam search decoding strategy. This beam search decoder can provide multiple responses up to its beam size. We expect this simple baseline to contain high-levels of redundancy in its outputs.

Repetition Penalized Sampling (RPS) For a stronger baseline, we use a decoding strategy that can generate diverse preconditions by penalizing previously generated precondition event triggers. This is done by an iterative decoding process applied to the same GPT-2 generation model. Given a target event, the model generates k preconditions in an iterative manner. When the model generates a precondition trigger – after `<pre>` token – a repetition penalty is applied to deter the model from selecting previously generated precondition events. We adopt the penalized sampling from Keskar et al. (2019). Instead of using a list of all generated tokens, we use a list of precondition event triggers that are generated in the previous iterations. Given a list of generated precondition events t, the probability distribution p_i for the next trigger token x_i is defined as:

$$p_i = \frac{\exp\left(x_i/I(i \in t)\right)}{\sum_j \exp(x_j/I(j \in t))}$$
$$I(c) = \lambda \quad \text{if } c \text{ is true else } 1$$

We set $\lambda = 1.2$ as in Keskar et al. (2019). For decoding, we use Nucleus Sampling (Holtzman et al., 2020) which has been claimed to generate a higher quality of text. Finally, we test the RPS model with the post-processor from DiP, to confirm that the major gain of DiP is from the Event Sampler.

4.3 DiP Model

DiP has three modules – Event sampler, Candidate generator, and Precondition re-ranker. We train each module separately.

Event sampler We use the GPT-2 model for the event sampler. The model is trained on the same data instances described in Section 4.1, but instead of using the entire target-precondition pairs, we use target-precondition *event trigger* pairs. We train three event samplers with different levels of context – trigger only, 3 neighboring tokens, and 5 neighboring tokens – to understand how different context affect candidate precondition sampling. As Table 2 shows, adding more context help the model to generate more specific events related to describe situations while the model provides more general events if only a trigger is given.

Candidate generator The GPT-2 model is also used for the candidate generator. For training, as described in 3.2, we add `<E> precondition_event` at the end of input so

Model Diversity Evaluation

Model	Self-BLEU	Self-BLEURT
Beam Search	0.234	-0.450
RPS	0.016	-1.273
RPS+Post-proc.	0.013	-1.280
DiP	0.038	-1.111

Table 4: Diversity evaluation for different models. We evaluate top 10 preconditions for each model. RPS+Post-proc. produces the most diverse outputs followed by RPS and DiP with a small margin.

that the model can learn how to utilize the provided event trigger as a control code. Table 3 shows the training examples for the candidate generator.

Post-processor We train a precondition re-ranker using BERT (Devlin et al., 2019). The F1 score of the classifier is 71.91 with 64.65 of the precision. To remove possibly redundant preconditions using iterative redundancy filtering, we need to compute cosine similarity between the generated preconditions. We take the precondition classifier's [CLS] token representation as the embedding for preconditions. Since the similarity score distributions are different from instance to instance, instead of using a fixed value as the threshold, we set the threshold as $\mu + \sigma$ of each instance (the mean and the standard deviation of pairwise similarity scores). This filters out $\sim$16% of the most similar generated preconditions. For comparison with the baselines, we take top 10 preconditions from remaining outputs.

4.4 Automatic Evaluation Metrics

We use Self-BLEU (Zhu et al., 2018) and Self-BLEURT score to measure the diversity of generated preconditions. Self-BLEU measures how similar a set of sentences is to each other using BLEU score – the average of BLEU scores for the all pairs of sentences in the set. In addition to direct lexical overlap, we also measure semantic overlap using BLEURT (Sellam et al., 2020), which is a BERT-based learned evaluation metric that is trained on human ratings of sentence pairs. We refer to this metric as Self-BLEURT. For both metrics, a lower score implies more diverse preconditions.

4.5 Results

We compare the models on both diversity and quality. For diversity, we use an automatic evaluation, and for quality we used human annotators.

Automatic Diversity Evaluation:

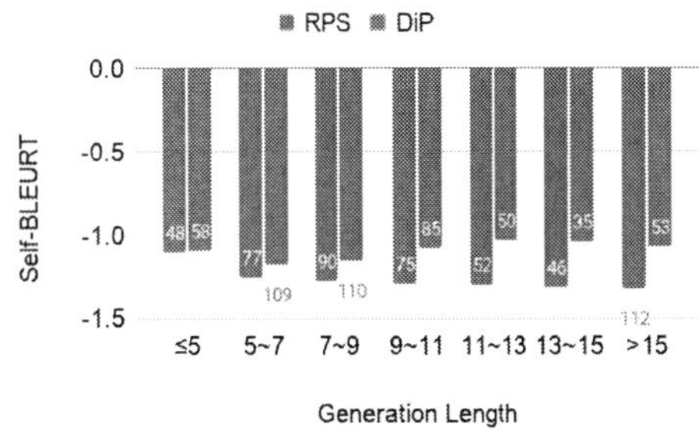

Figure 2: The Self-BLEURT scores across different lengths of generated text. The numbers indicate the number of instances in each bucket.

Quality of Preconditions

Model	Average Score	#Wins
RPS	0.954	30
DiP	**1.101**	**56**

Table 5: The Top 10 generated preconditions for each target event were scored on a 0-2 scale. A model "wins" a target if its average is highest. Using Bootstrapping with $n = 1000$ the 95% conf-interval for the RPS mean is (0.89, 1.01) and DiP is (1.05, 1.15).

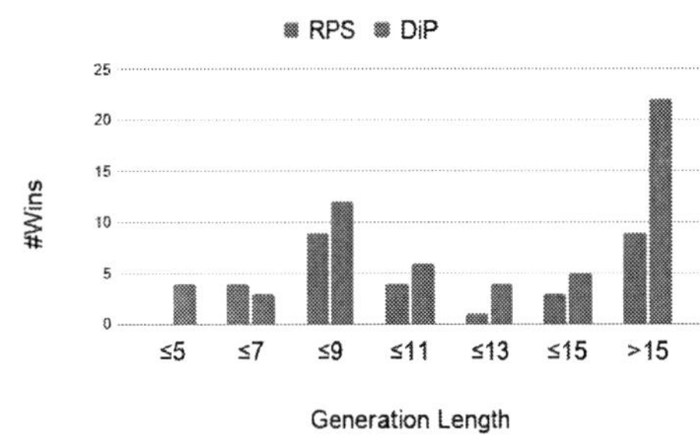

Figure 3: The number of wins across generation lengths. DiP wins more as the generations lengthen.

Table 4 shows the diversity metrics for all methods. We evaluated 5,000 preconditions generated for 500 target events. Comparing RPS+Post-proc to RPS, Post-proc shows little effect, we compare just RPS to DiP in the rest of the evaluations (See Appendix for more details between RPS and RPS+Post-proc).

In both metrics, DiP and RPS generate more diverse output than the beam search decoder. DiP is compatible to RPS in shorter preconditions, and RPS produces more diverse outputs when the generated text gets longer, as shown in Figure 2.

Manual Quality Evaluation:

The automatic evaluation only measures diversity. To see if the models generate legitimate preconditions, we conducted a manual evaluation for quality. We evaluated 960 generated outputs covering 96 distinct target events for both DiP and the RPS baseline. For each instance the annotators were presented with the top ten generated outputs from two systems. For each output the annotators provided a rating on a scale from 0 to 2, where 0 means not a precondition, 1 is a maybe, and 2 is definitely a precondition. We split the 96 instances across 8 different annotators[3].

Table 5 shows the results in terms of two metrics: one is the average score across all 96 instances, and another is the number of "Wins" where a model gets +1 point if the sum of its 10 precondition scores is higher than the other. In both metrics, DiP outperforms RPS. Moreover, as shown in Figure 3, DiP produces better preconditions across most output lengths and is best on longer outputs.

4.6 Analysis

Examples: Table 8 shows the top 5 generations from our main three systems. The beam search's failure on the diversity metric is easy to see with its repetitive output. Most verbs are the same. Both RPS and DiP are notably better in terms of diversity, but RPS introduces lots of irrelevant information that may have artificially increased its diversity score. Long irrelevant phrases are clear to see, and verb synonyms are common. In contrast, DiP generates more succinct and general preconditions, as well as fewer direct synonyms.

Context Specificity: Table 7 shows the diversity scores when different levels of context are provided to the event sampler. Diversity gets slightly worse with *more* context. This aligns with our observation from Table 2 that the event sampler with more context generates more context-specific precondition events, which now appear to be closer to each other semantically. This makes intuitive sense if you view context as closing a model's view of broader options.

Errors: We categorize 4 types of frequently observed errors from DiP. 1) **Rare target events**: some target event triggers are polysemious, and some meanings are rarely used in the newswire. Thus, the event sampler is biased toward generating precondition events based on more frequent usages of triggers. 2) **Conflict with sentence structure**: the candidate generator has no ability to modify the trigger for its syntactic context because it is trained only as copying over the event trigger. 3) **Re-ranking issue**: the re-ranker can induce errors due to its performance – 64.65 precision. 4) **Limited available context**: when the provided context of a target event is too limited, the model often fails to generate preconditions. Table 6 shows examples for each type of error.

[3]These were computer science graduate students

Rare target events	
`[BLANK]` my homework," and exercising like a demon at a nearby gym. She'd ***lost*** weight and viewed herself as training for a fight.	
Event	Generated Precondition
war	I ***war*** with the other women in my school, who had been working together on
died	She ***died*** of cancer in 1998, after her husband was killed by an electrician who had been working with him"
The word ***lost*** is usually used in the context of war, election, or obituary in the newswire. That may lead the event sampler to fail to generate proper precondition event triggers.	
Conflict with sentence structure	
The proposal from Mr. Levy that the Justice Department ***struck*** down, she added, would have violated nondiscrimination provisions of the consent decree and the Civil Rights Act of 1964 by `[BLANK]`.	
Event	Generated Precondition
created	***created*** a new state law requiring that a judge be present on the court
called	***called*** for a "state level ban on political activity" in New York City
The candidate generator is not able to modify the provided triggers according to the context.	
Re-ranking issue	
China's markets nearly ***disintegrated*** in 2005, and one 2003 poll found `[BLANK]`.	
Event	Generated Precondition
became (#4)	that the market ***became*** more popular than in 2000 (#2)
named (>#10)	that the country was ***named*** the world's largest economy (#4)
Generated sentences are not preconditions but ranked high after re-ranking (#4 → #2 and >#10 → #4).	
Limited available context	
`[BLANK]` to ***hit*** a short forehand and guided it wide.	
Event	Generated Precondition
batted	In the third round, he ***batted*** the ball with his left hand
pitched	In the first inning, the Mets ***pitched*** three consecutive hits
The target context is related to tennis, but preconditions are generated in the context of baseball because the provided context is too limited.	

Table 6: Examples from each type of errors. There are 4 types of frequently observed errors and the first 3 types are caused by each stage in DiP. The last one is due to data instances.

5 Conclusion

Real-world events often have multiple preconditions, but today's datasets do not, including the

Context	Self-BLEU	Self-BLEURT
Trigger only	0.038	-1.111
± 3 tokens	0.039	-1.103
± 5 tokens	0.040	-1.098

Table 7: Diversity evaluation for different samplers. Precondition candidates are generated from the event samplers given the input with a trigger only, a trigger with neighboring 3 tokens, or a trigger with 5 tokens.

latest PeKo, presenting a challenge for text-driven models. Vanilla generative models have high-levels of redundancy in their outputs and are thus not well suited for diverse generation. This work introduced an event sampler that overcomes the issue of target context specificity to provide diverse guidance to the generator. Coupled with a precondition ranker and similarity filter, this multi-stage generation setup yields more diverse and higher quality preconditions. Further, a new training corpus was not required. More generally, this approach can be seen as an instance of controllable diverse output generation for conditional language models.

Acknowledgements

This material is based on research that is supported in part by the Air Force Research Laboratory (AFRL), DARPA, for the KAIROS program under agreement number FA8750-19-2-1003 and in part by the National Science Foundation under the award IIS #2007290.

References

Siqi Bao, Huang He, Fan Wang, Hua Wu, and Haifeng Wang. 2020. PLATO: Pre-trained dialogue generation model with discrete latent variable. In *Proceedings of the 58th Annual Meeting of the Association for Computational Linguistics*, pages 85–96, Online. Association for Computational Linguistics.

Piotr Bojanowski, Edouard Grave, Armand Joulin, and Tomas Mikolov. 2017. Enriching word vectors with subword information. *Transactions of the Association for Computational Linguistics*, 5:135–146.

S.R.K. Branavan, Nate Kushman, Tao Lei, and Regina Barzilay. 2012. Learning high-level planning from text. In *Proceedings of the 50th Annual Meeting of the Association for Computational Linguistics (Volume 1: Long Papers)*, pages 126–135, Jeju Island, Korea. Association for Computational Linguistics.

Nathanael Chambers, Taylor Cassidy, Bill McDowell, and Steven Bethard. 2014. Dense event ordering with a multi-pass architecture. *Transactions of the Association for Computational Linguistics*, 2:273–284.

Jacob Devlin, Ming-Wei Chang, Kenton Lee, and Kristina Toutanova. 2019. BERT: Pre-training of deep bidirectional transformers for language understanding. In *Proceedings of the 2019 Conference of the North American Chapter of the Association for Computational Linguistics: Human Language Technologies, Volume 1 (Long and Short Papers)*, pages 4171–4186, Minneapolis, Minnesota. Association for Computational Linguistics.

Chris Donahue, Mina Lee, and Percy Liang. 2020. Enabling language models to fill in the blanks. In *Proceedings of the 58th Annual Meeting of the Association for Computational Linguistics*, pages 2492–2501, Online. Association for Computational Linguistics.

Suchin Gururangan, Ana Marasović, Swabha Swayamdipta, Kyle Lo, Iz Beltagy, Doug Downey, and Noah A. Smith. 2020. Don't stop pretraining: Adapt language models to domains and tasks. In *Proceedings of the 58th Annual Meeting of the Association for Computational Linguistics*, pages 8342–8360, Online. Association for Computational Linguistics.

Ari Holtzman, Jan Buys, Li Du, Maxwell Forbes, and Yejin Choi. 2020. The curious case of neural text degeneration. In *International Conference on Learning Representations*.

Chenyang Huang, Osmar Zaïane, Amine Trabelsi, and Nouha Dziri. 2018. Automatic dialogue generation with expressed emotions. In *Proceedings of the 2018 Conference of the North American Chapter of the Association for Computational Linguistics: Human Language Technologies, Volume 2 (Short Papers)*, pages 49–54, New Orleans, Louisiana. Association for Computational Linguistics.

Piotr Indyk and Rajeev Motwani. 1998. Approximate nearest neighbors: towards removing the curse of dimensionality. In *Proceedings of the thirtieth annual ACM symposium on Theory of computing*, pages 604–613.

Nitish Shirish Keskar, Bryan McCann, Lav R Varshney, Caiming Xiong, and Richard Socher. 2019. Ctrl: A conditional transformer language model for controllable generation. *arXiv preprint arXiv:1909.05858*.

Heeyoung Kwon, Mahnaz Koupaee, Pratyush Singh, Gargi Sawhney, Anmol Shukla, Keerthi Kumar Kallur, Nathanael Chambers, and Niranjan Balasubramanian. 2020. Modeling preconditions in text with a crowd-sourced dataset. In *Findings of the Association for Computational Linguistics: EMNLP 2020*, pages 3818–3828, Online. Association for Computational Linguistics.

Ilya Loshchilov and Frank Hutter. 2019. Decoupled weight decay regularization. In *International Conference on Learning Representations*.

Target Event: [BLANK] to ***maintain*** below-market rents.		
Beam Search	RPS	DiP
In the last few years, real estate prices have *risen* and real estate prices have dropped	Wilhelmina's stock *dropped* 8 percent in early 2005 after a lull, but more actively revived the strong dollar, lending to an expected influx of funds	The city has *reached* a deal with the tenants
In the last few years, real estate prices have *risen* and real estate investment trusts have grown	The City Council's 10-member City Planning Committee *voted* 11 to 6 yesterday	The city will *use* the money
In the last few years, real estate prices have *risen* and real estate prices have dropped, but rents have continued	property values are *rising*, rising as the vacancy rate is expected	In the 1980s, the city *moved* its building to a new site in the East River
In the last few years, real estate prices have *risen* and real estate investment trusts have grown in size	In less than a year, such improvements have *increased* through acquisitions and capitalization at New York City police stations, legal firms and cruise ships, suggesting that housing can be bought	The City Council *passed* a bill on Wednesday that would give the city the authority to build a new building at the site of the old Erez subway station, and
In the last few years, real estate prices have *risen* and real estate prices have dropped, and rents have risen in the last few years	Matthew Hallico, president of the General Electric Company in Manhattan, and Robert Chrisin, a sales vice partner at Ira G. Albrecht His comments about the incentive package *raised* many concerns about how it works, as well as what shareholders might do	In the 1980s, the city *began* a program
Target Event: By about 10 p.m., the proposals ***appeared*** dead for now [BLANK].		
Beam Search	RPS	DiP
Mr. Spitzer *took* office	after the judge, Col Richard Kultura of Thailand, *signaled* the end of his sentence	after the commission *filed* a proposal to provide $ 2 million in new money for the project
Mr. Spitzer *took* over	after city Hall *learned* it would begin public comment on ways it could add 27,000 new jobs to the island	after the Senate 's Democratic majority has *taken* over control of the House
the City Council *voted* on them	as they were *rejected* by legislative leaders	after the State Legislature *put* them on a vote
Mr. Spitzer *took* office in January	when Mayor Mark Meehan *heeded* all of his smaller complaints	when the State Legislature *used* the budget to cut a $ 2 billion tax break
the City Council *passed* them to the City Council	after the State Senate *voted* yes on key issues	after a suicide bomber *killed* a man in an Internet chat room
Target Event: [BLANK] to ***scout*** potential recruits.		
Beam Search	RPS	DiP
The N.F.L. and the N.B.A. have *taken* steps	The pending replacement of Carl Crawford has *enticed* some intelligence officials and top Qaeda leaders	The police *took* over the department 's operations , and they began
The N.F.L. and the N.F.L. have *taken* steps	Employees are *giving* them the opportunity	The department is *sending* a new system
The N.C.A.A. has *taken* steps	Most Somalis *want* a law that would enable them	The New York State Department of Education *began* a program last year
The N.F.L. and the N.B.A. have *taken* similar steps	Shortly after Katrina , Post servicemen were *chasing* selectors after the storm 's onset	The department has *sent* a handful of officers to the police
The N.F.L. and the N.F.L. have *taken* similar steps	Ever since college opened in 1983 , he *shopped* for school assignments	The N.C.A.A. *set* up a task force

Table 8: Top 5 generations from 3 systems. Red cells are invalid preconditions. Greyed out cells are repetitions from previous cells. DiP produces both valid *and* diverse preconditions.

Nils Reimers and Iryna Gurevych. 2019. Sentence-BERT: Sentence embeddings using Siamese BERT-networks. In *Proceedings of the 2019 Conference on Empirical Methods in Natural Language Processing and the 9th International Joint Conference on Natural Language Processing (EMNLP-IJCNLP)*, pages 3982–3992, Hong Kong, China. Association for Computational Linguistics.

Evan Sandhaus. 2008. The New York Times Annotated Corpus.

Thibault Sellam, Dipanjan Das, and Ankur Parikh. 2020. BLEURT: Learning robust metrics for text generation. In *Proceedings of the 58th Annual Meeting of the Association for Computational Linguistics*, pages 7881–7892, Online. Association for Computational Linguistics.

Raphael Shu, Hideki Nakayama, and Kyunghyun Cho. 2019. Generating diverse translations with sentence codes. In *Proceedings of the 57th Annual Meeting of the Association for Computational Linguistics*, pages 1823–1827, Florence, Italy. Association for Computational Linguistics.

Avirup Sil, Fei Huang, and Alexander Yates. 2010. Extracting action and event semantics from web text. In *2010 AAAI Fall Symposium Series*.

Richard Socher, Eric Huang, Jeffrey Pennin, Christopher D Manning, and Andrew Ng. 2011. Dynamic pooling and unfolding recursive autoencoders for paraphrase detection. *Advances in neural information processing systems*, 24:801–809.

Ashish Vaswani, Noam Shazeer, Niki Parmar, Jakob Uszkoreit, Llion Jones, Aidan N Gomez, Łukasz Kaiser, and Illia Polosukhin. 2017. Attention is all you need. In *Advances in neural information processing systems*, pages 5998–6008.

Nathaniel Weir, João Sedoc, and Benjamin Van Durme. 2020. COD3S: Diverse generation with discrete semantic signatures. In *Proceedings of the 2020 Conference on Empirical Methods in Natural Language Processing (EMNLP)*, pages 5199–5211, Online. Association for Computational Linguistics.

Thomas Wolf, Lysandre Debut, Victor Sanh, Julien Chaumond, Clement Delangue, Anthony Moi, Pierric Cistac, Tim Rault, Rémi Louf, Morgan Funtowicz, Joe Davison, Sam Shleifer, Patrick von Platen, Clara Ma, Yacine Jernite, Julien Plu, Canwen Xu, Teven Le Scao, Sylvain Gugger, Mariama Drame, Quentin Lhoest, and Alexander M. Rush. 2020. Transformers: State-of-the-art natural language processing. In *Proceedings of the 2020 Conference on Empirical Methods in Natural Language Processing: System Demonstrations*, pages 38–45, Online. Association for Computational Linguistics.

Yaoming Zhu, Sidi Lu, Lei Zheng, Jiaxian Guo, Weinan Zhang, Jun Wang, and Yong Yu. 2018. Texygen: A benchmarking platform for text generation models. In *The 41st International ACM SIGIR Conference on Research & Development in Information Retrieval*, pages 1097–1100.

A Appendix

A.1 Experimental Details

A.1.1 Data Split

For the dataset for pre-training, we split into train/dev/test with the ratio of 8:1:1. For PeKo dataset, we follow the setting from Kwon et al. (2020).

A.1.2 Infrastructure

All models are trained using NVIDIA Titan RTX (24GB of GDDR6 VRAM).

A.1.3 Parameters

We use Wolf et al. (2020) library for all transformer models. For the beam search baseline and RPS model we use the GPT-2 architecture, which has 124,445,184 trainable parameters. DiP model consists of two GPT-2 models for the event sampler and the candidate generator – 2 × 124,445,184 – and one BERT model for the re-ranker – 108,313,346 parameters. In total, DiP has 357,203,714 trainable parameters.

Optimizer: We use AdamW (Loshchilov and Hutter, 2019) for the optimizer across all models. For pre-trianing, we fix the learning rate as 1e-3. For fine-tuning, we experiment with [1e-4, 1e-5, 1e-6].

Event sampler: For pre-training, the epochs are set to 100 with the batch size of 128 for the trigger only, 64 for the ± 3 tokens, and 32 for the ± 5 tokens model. For fine-tuning, the epochs are set to 10 with the batch size of 32.

Candidate generator: For pre-training, the epochs are set to 100 with the batch size of 16. For fine-tuning, the epochs are set to 10 with the batch size of 16.

Precondition re-ranker: We use the classifier provided by the authors of Kwon et al. (2020) – `https://stonybrooknlp.github.io/PeKo/`.

All Models are picked based on the losses from the dev set.

A.2 Comparison between RPS and RPS+Post-processing

Table 9 shows the comparison between RPS and RPS+Post-processing. The effect of Post-processor on RPS system is considered neutral. There are some cases where the generation qualities are improved but also other cases where the qualities are compromised.

A.3 Manual Evaluation

Evaluation Instruction Figure 4 shows the evaluation instruction that we provided to annotators.

Evaluation rating distribution Table 10 shows the distribution of voted ratings by annotators. On average, DiP got higher ratings than RPS and RPS got highest votes in "Not a Precondition."

Target Event: [BLANK] to ***maintain*** below-market rents.	
RPS	RPS+Post-processor
Wilhelmina's stock *dropped* 8 percent in early 2005 after a lull, but more actively revived the strong dollar, lending to an expected influx of funds	Mr. Berg last year *signed* a two-year contract with the firm
The City Council's 10-member City Planning Committee *voted* 11 to 6 yesterday	Another landlord is *assembling* a plan
property values are *rising*, rising as the vacancy rate is expected	Ms. Cianci, 32, is *building* an intercom tower
In less than a year, such improvements have *increased* through acquisitions and capitalization at New York City police stations, legal firms and cruise ships, suggesting that housing can be bought	Her workers *hit* a brick floor a few years ago
Matthew Hallico, president of the General Electric Company in Manhattan, and Robert Chrisin, a sales vice partner at Ira G. Albrecht His comments about the incentive package *raised* many concerns about how it works, as well as what shareholders might do	Last week, Lloyd Pound, the influential Wall Street analyst, *gave* 75 percent shares of his money

Target Event: By about 10 p.m. , the proposals ***appeared*** dead for now [BLANK].	
RPS	RPS+Post-processor
after the judge, Col Richard Kultura of Thailand, *signaled* the end of his sentence	after negotiators from both parties *reconvened* in Davis Park to talk things out
after city Hall *learned* it would begin public comment on ways it could add 27,000 new jobs to the island	after the researchers *analyzed* DEMIC data on children and early adults whose ages began at 8 or 15
as they were *rejected* by legislative leaders	after Google *released* its pie-in-pie template during an extensive public presentation
when Mayor Mark Meehan *heeded* all of his smaller complaints	after the Council *passed* it on Monday
after the State Senate *voted* yes on key issues	after the developer, Trivata Films of New Orleans, *agreed* to pay up to $14 million over seven years

Target Event: [BLANK] to ***scout*** potential recruits.	
RPS	RPS+Post-processor
The pending replacement of Carl Crawford has *enticed* some intelligence officials and top Qaeda leaders	About the same time, Mr. Booker *elicited* state financing for another program that provided some of the funds through the Police Department's National Guard to help workers find mental illness or
Employees are *giving* them the opportunity	In 2005 , Mr. SCAD *sent* students from Iowa and Ohio to visit Johns Hopkins
Most Somalis *want* a law that would enable them	In championing the elite classes last week, public school teachers *mounted* an extensive publicity campaign to persuade parents
Shortly after Katrina , Post servicemen were *chasing* selectors after the storm 's onset	Joel Packer, a Detroit Pistons and assistant coach with Brigham *captured* a larger campus and invited the scouts
Ever since college opened in 1983 , he *shopped* for school assignments	As the trend forward moves into next season , larger colleges are *beginning* with faculty members from 75 sites on an extensive bioharker scholarship site

Table 9: Top 5 generation examples from RPS and RPS+Post-processor. Green colored events are considered legitimate preconditions and red colored ones are not. A red colored cell indicates invalid precondition text. As the examples show, the effect of Post-processor on RPS system is neutral – in some cases, the generation qualities are improved but compromised in other cases.

Evaluation rating distribution

Model	Not a Precond.	Maybe	Def. a Precond.
RPS	38.6%	27.3%	34.1%
DiP	29.8%	30.3%	39.9%

Table 10: Evaluation rating distribution. On average, DiP got higher ratings than RPS.

Evaluation for Diverse Precondition Generation

You will be asked to evaluate sets of generated sentences if they contain a precondition relation
Each set contains 20 generated preconditions given a target (seed) event.
-- 10 from our proposed model, other 10 from a baseline model

Please mark 0 ~ 2 if a {precond. event} is necessary for a [target event] to happen, where

0 -- Definitely No. A precondition relation doesn't hold between two marked events
1 -- Maybe. A precondition relation can hold in some senses
2 -- Definitely Yes. Two marked events are in a precondition relation

Things to keep in mind

1. Please ignore minor grammatical errors if you can understand the meaning of a sentence
2. Please evaluate based on the context.
   If a candidate precondition can cause (either directly or indirectly) the target event in the given context, you can consider it as a valid precondition
3. Instances from systems are randomly suffled, please don't be biased on columns
4. A precondition event must happen before its target event
5. Please mark your name on the right side, so that other people can know that which sheets are taken.

Example & Explanation

	Preconditio	Target	Score	Category	Explanation
I apologized for the debacle of the day before , and {hired} a new staff to [help] me make it right .	hired	help	2	Precondition	Hiring a new staff can help me make it right
I apologized for the debacle of the day before , and {used} my time to [help] me make it right .	used	help	2	Precondition / minor error	Some minor error is presented, but still understandable that using one's time to help
I apologized for the debacle of the day before , and I will {join} your friends as we try to change behavior and decide what tomorrow is to [help] me make it right .	join	help	0	Non-precondition / non-sensible	Phrase doesn't seem natural
I apologized for the debacle of the day before , and {told} the bloggers that I was going to [help] me make it right .	told	help	0	Non-precondition	"Told the bloggers" is not necessary to help
I apologized for the debacle of the day before , and I did n't {think} that I was going to [help] me make it right .	think	help	0	Non-precondition / negation	"didn't think" is not necessary to help
I apologized for the debacle of the day before , and {appeared} on my Web site to [help] me make it right .	appeared	help	1	Precondition	We can imagine "Appeared on my website" can indirectly help me in the context
I apologized for the debacle of the day before , and {put} in a few more hours to [help] me make it right .	put	help	2	Precondition	Spend time to help
I apologized for the debacle of the day before , and {signed} a letter to [help] me make it right .	signed	help	1	Precondition	Given the context, "signed a letter" might help me
I apologized for the debacle of the day before , and {assigned} the team to [help] me make it right .	assigned	help	2	Precondition	"assigned the team" to help me -- a direct way to help
I apologized for the debacle of the day before , and {paid} my way to a friend to [help] me make it right .	paid	help	2	Precondition	"pay a friend" to help me -- a direct way to help

Figure 4: Manual evaluation instruction

One Semantic Parser to Parse Them All: Sequence to Sequence Multi-Task Learning on Semantic Parsing Datasets

Marco Damonte **Emilio Monti**
Amazon Alexa AI
{dammarco,monti}@amazon.com

Abstract

Semantic parsers map natural language utterances to meaning representations. The lack of a single standard for meaning representations led to the creation of a plethora of semantic parsing datasets. To unify different datasets and train a single model for them, we investigate the use of Multi-Task Learning (MTL) architectures. We experiment with five datasets (GEOQUERY, NLMAPS, TOP, OVERNIGHT, AMR). We find that an MTL architecture that shares the entire network across datasets yields competitive or better parsing accuracies than the single-task baselines, while reducing the total number of parameters by 68%. We further provide evidence that MTL has also better compositional generalization than single-task models. We also present a comparison of task sampling methods and propose a competitive alternative to widespread proportional sampling strategies.

1 Introduction

Semantic parsing is the task of converting natural language into a meaning representation language (MRL). The commercial success of personal assistants, that are required to understand language, has contributed to a growing interest in semantic parsing. A typical use case for personal assistants is Question Answering (Q&A): the output of a semantic parser is a data structure that represents the underlying meaning of a given question. This data structure can be compiled into a query to retrieve the correct answer. The lack of a single standard for meaning representations resulted in the creation of a plethora of semantic parsing datasets, which differ in size, domain, style, complexity, and in the formalism used as an MRL. These datasets are expensive to create, as they normally require expert annotators. Consequently, the datasets are often limited in size.

Multi-task Learning (MTL; Caruana 1997) refers to jointly learning several tasks while sharing parameters between them. In this paper, we use MTL to demonstrate that it is possible to unify these smaller datasets together to train a single model that can be used to parse sentences in any of the MRLs that appear in the data. We experiment with several Q&A semantic parsing dataset for English: GEOQUERY (Zelle and Mooney, 1996), NLMAPS V2 (Lawrence and Riezler, 2018b), TOP (Gupta et al., 2018), and OVERNIGHT (Wang et al., 2015b). In order to investigate the impact of less related tasks, we also experiment on a non-Q&A semantic parsing dataset, targeting a broader coverage meaning representation: AMR (Banarescu et al., 2013), which contains sentences from sources such as broadcasts, newswire, and discussion forums.

Our baseline parsing architecture is a reimplementation of the sequence to sequence model by Rongali et al. (2020), which can be applied to any parsing task as long as the MRL can be expressed as a sequence. Inspired by Fan et al. (2017), we experimented with two MTL architectures: 1-TO-N, where we share the encoder but not the decoder, and 1-TO-1, where we share the entire network. Previous work (Ruder, 2017; Collobert and Weston, 2008; Hershcovich et al., 2018) has focussed on a lesser degree of sharing more closely resembling the 1-TO-N architecture, but we found 1-TO-1 to consistently work better in our experiments.

In this paper we demonstrate that the 1-TO-1 architecture can be used to achieve competitive parsing accuracies for our heterogeneous set of semantic parsing datasets, while reducing the total number of parameters by 68%, overfitting less, and improving on a compositional generalization benchmark (Keysers et al., 2019).

We further perform an extensive analysis of alternative strategies to sample tasks during training. A

Proceedings of the 10th Conference on Lexical and Computational Semantics, pages 173–184
August 5–6, 2021, Bangkok, Thailand (online) ©2021 Association for Computational Linguistics

number of methods to sample tasks proportionally to data sizes have been recently proposed (Wang et al., 2019b; Sanh et al., 2019; Wang et al., 2019a; Stickland and Murray, 2019), which are often used as de facto standards for sampling strategies. These methods rely on the hypothesis that sampling proportionally to the task sizes avoids overfitting the smaller tasks. We show that this hypothesis is not generally verified by comparing proportional methods with an inversely proportional sampling method, and a method based on the per-task loss during training. Our comparison shows that there is not a method that is consistently superior to the others across architectures and datasets. We argue that the sampling method should be chosen as another hyper-parameter of the model, specific to a problem and a training setup.

We finally run experiments on dataset pairs, resulting in 40 distinct settings, to investigate which datasets are most helpful to others. Surprisingly, we observe that AMR and GEOQUERY can work well as auxiliary tasks. AMR is the only graph-structured, non Q&A dataset, and was therefore not expected to help as much as more related Q&A datasets. GEOQUERY is the smallest dataset we tested, showing that low-resource datasets can help high-resource ones instead of, more intuitively, the other way around.

2 Sequence to Sequence Multi-Task Learning

MTL refers to machine learning models that sample training examples from multiple tasks and share parameters amongst them. During training, a batch is sampled from one of the tasks and the parameter update only impacts the part of the network relevant to that task.

The architecture for sequence to sequence semantic parsing that we use in this paper consists of an encoder, which converts the input sentence into a latent representation, and a decoder, which converts the latent representation into the output MRL (Jia and Liang, 2016; Konstas et al., 2017; Rongali et al., 2020). While the input to each task is always natural language utterances, each task is in general characterized by a different meaning representation formalism. It, therefore, follows that the input (natural language) varies considerably less than the output (the meaning representation). Parameter sharing can therefore more intuitively happen in the encoder, where we learn parameters that encode a representation of the natural language. Nevertheless, more sharing can also be allowed, by also sharing parts of the decoder (Fan et al., 2017). In this work, we experiment with two MTL architectures, as shown in Figure 1: 1-TO-N, where we share the encoder but not the decoder, and 1-TO-1, where we share the entire network. As different datasets normally use different MRLs, in the 1-TO-1 architecture we also need a mechanism to inform the network of which MRL to generate. We therefore augment the input with a special token that identifies the task, following Johnson et al. (2017).

3 Experimental Setup

In this section, we describe the datasets used, baseline architectures, and training details.

3.1 Data

While we focussed on Q&A semantic parsing datasets, we further consider the AMR dataset in order to investigate the impact of MTL between considerably different datasets. Table 1 shows a training example from each dataset. The sizes of all datasets are shown in Table 2.

Geoquery Questions and queries about US geography (Zelle and Mooney, 1996). The best results on this dataset are reported by Kwiatkowski et al. (2013) via Combinatory Categorial Grammar (Steedman, 1996, 2000) parsing.

NLMaps v2 Questions about geographical facts (Lawrence and Riezler, 2018b), retrieved from OpenStreetMap (Haklay and Weber, 2008). To our knowledge, we are the first to train a parser on the full dataset. Previous work trained a neural parser on a small subset of the dataset and used the rest to experiment with feedback data (Lawrence and Riezler, 2018a). We note that there exists a previous version of the dataset (Haas and Riezler, 2016), for which state-of-the-art results have been achieved with a sequence to sequence approach (Duong et al., 2017). We use the latest version of the dataset due to its larger size.

TOP Navigation and event queries generated by crowdsourced workers (Gupta et al., 2018). The queries are annotated to semantic frames comprising of intents and slots. The best results are achieved by a sequence to sequence model (Aghajanyan et al., 2020).

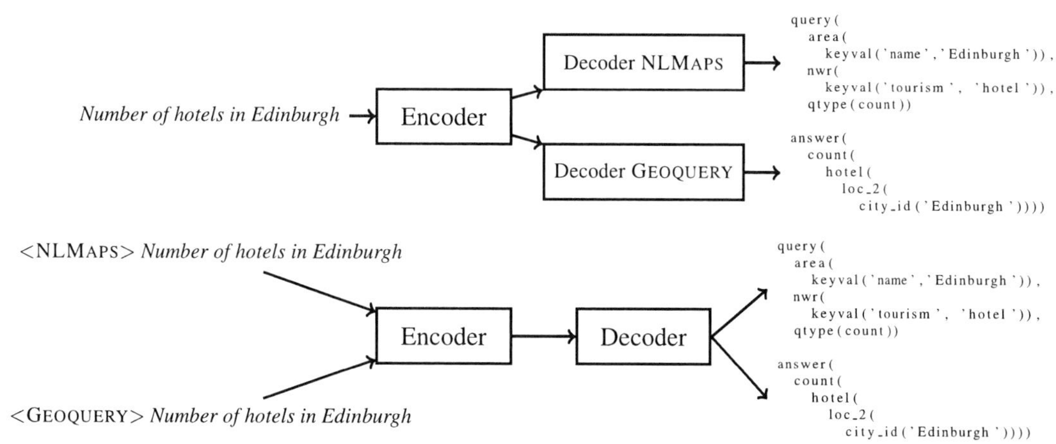

Figure 1: Two MTL architectures for two tasks (A and B): at the top 1-TO-N, where only the encoder is shared; at the bottom 1-TO-1, where we also share the decoder and we add a special token at the beginning of the input sentence.

Dataset	**Input**	**Output**

GEOQUERY	which is the shortest river	`answer(`
		`shortest(`
		`river(all)))`

NLMAPS	name Localities in Nantes	`query(`
		`area(keyval('name','Nantes')),`
		`nwr(keyval('place','locality')),`
		`qtype(findkey('name')))`

TOP	is traffic heavy downtown	`[IN:GET_INFO_TRAFFIC`
		`is traffic heavy in`
		`[SL:LOCATION`
		`downtown]]`

OVERNIGHT	show me all important meetings	`listValue(`
		`filter(`
		`filter(getProperty(`
		`singleton en.meeting)`
		`(string !type))`
		`(string is\_important)))`

AMR	this method will not pollute the environment	`(p / pollute-01 :polarity -`
		`:ARG0 (m / method`
		`:mod (t / this))`
		`:ARG1 (e / environment))`

Table 1: Training examples from each of the datasets used in our experiments. The output logical forms were simplified for the sake of readability.

Dataset	**Train**	**Dev**	**Test**	**Src Vocab**	**Tgt Vocab**
GEOQUERY	540	60	280	279	103
NLMAPS	16172	1843	10594	8628	1012
TOP	28414	4032	8241	11873	116
OVERNIGHT	18781	2093	5224	1921	311
AMR	36521	1368	1371	30169	28880

Table 2: Details of each dataset. "Train", "Dev", and "Test" are the number of examples (questions paired with MRLs) in the training, development, and test splits. "Src Vocab" is the vocabulary size for the input (natural language) and "Tgt Vocab" is the vocabulary size for the output (meaning representation).

Overnight This dataset (Wang et al., 2015b) contains Lambda DCS (Liang, 2013) annotations divided into eight domains: *calendar*, *blocks*, *housing*, *restaurants*, *publications*, *recipes*, *socialnetwork*, and *basketball*. Due to the small size of the domains, we merged them together. The current state-of-the-art results, on single domains, are reported by Su and Yan (2017), who frame the problem as a paraphrasing task. They use denotation (answer) accuracy as a metric, while we report parsing accuracies, a stricter metric.

AMR AMR (Banarescu et al., 2013) has been widely adopted in the semantic parsing community (Artzi et al., 2015; Flanigan et al., 2014; Wang et al., 2015a; Damonte et al., 2017; Titov and Henderson, 2007; Zhang et al., 2019). We used the latest version of the dataset (LDC2017T10), for which the best results were reported by Bevilacqua et al. (2021). The AMR dataset is different from the other datasets, not only in that it is not Q&A, but also in the formalism used to express the meaning representations. While for the other datasets the output logical forms can be represented as trees, in AMR each sentence is annotated as a rooted, directed graph, due to explicit representation of pronominal coreference, coordination, and control structures.

In order to use sequence to sequence architectures on AMR, a preprocessing step is required to remove variables in the annotations and linearize the graphs. In this work, we followed the linearization method by van Noord and Bos (2017).[1]

3.2 Baseline Parser

Our baseline parser is a reimplementation of Rongali et al. (2020): a single-task attentive sequence to sequence model (Bahdanau et al., 2015) with pointer network (Vinyals et al., 2015). The input utterance is embedded with a pretrained RoBERTa encoder (Liu et al., 2019), and subsequently fed into a Transformer (Vaswani et al., 2017) decoder. The encoder converts the input sequence of tokens $x_1, \ldots, x_n$ into a sequence of context-sensitive embeddings $e_1, \ldots, e_n$. At each time step t, the decoder generates an action a_t. There are two types of actions: output a symbol from the output vocabulary, or output a pointer to one of the input tokens x_i. The final softmax layer provides a probability distribution, for a_t, across all these possible actions. The probability with which we output a pointer to x_i is determined by the attention score on x_i. Finally, we use beam search to find the sequence of actions that maximize the overall output sequence probability.

3.3 Training

All models were trained with Adam (Kingma and Ba, 2014) on P3 AWS machines with one Tesla V100 GPU. To prevent overfitting, we used an early stopping policy to terminate training once the loss on the development set stops decreasing. To account for the effect of the random seed used for initialization, we train three instances of each model with different random seeds. We then report the average and standard deviation on the test set.

We evaluate all Q&A parsing models using the exact match metric, which is computed as the percentage of input sentences that are parsed without any mistake. AMR is instead evaluated using Smatch (Cai and Knight, 2013), which computes the F1 score of graphs' nodes and edges.[2]

We tuned hyper-parameters for each model based on exact match accuracies on their development sets. While AMR is typically evaluated on Smatch, to simplify the tuning of our models, we use exact match also for AMR and compute the Smatch score only for the final models. We performed manual searches (5 trials) for the following hyper-parameters: batch size (10 to 200), learning rate (0.04 to 0.08), number of layers (2 to 6) and units in the decoder (256 to 1024), number of attention heads (1 to 16), and dropout ratio (0.03 to 0.3). For the baseline, we selected the sets of hyper-parameters that maximize performance on the development set of each dataset. To tune the MTL model for each dataset would be costly: we instead selected the set of parameters that maximizes performance on the combination of all development sets. For analogous reasons, when presenting results on MTL between the 40 combinations of dataset pairs, we do not re-tune the models. Final hyper-parameters are shown in Appendix A.

4 Experiments

In Section 4.1, we compare several sampling methods for the 1-to-1 and 1-to-N architectures. In Section 4.2 we then compare the MTL models with the single-task baselines. We turn to the issue of

[1] https://github.com/RikVN/AMRwithdefaultsettings

[2] https://github.com/snowblink14/smatch

generalization in Section 4.3, where we use a recently introduced benchmark to evaluate the compositional generalization of our models. Finally, in Section 4.4 we report experiments between dataset pairs to find good auxiliary tasks.

4.1 Task Sampling

As discussed in Section 2, each training batch is sampled from one of the tasks. A simple sampling strategy is to pick the task uniformly, i.e., a training batch is extracted from task t with probability $p_t = 1/N$, where N is the number of tasks. Due to the considerable differences in the sizes of our datasets, we further investigate the impact of previously proposed sampling strategies that take dataset sizes into account:

- PROPORTIONAL (Wang et al., 2019b; Sanh et al., 2019), where p_t is proportional to the size of the training set of task t: D_t. That is: $p_t = D_t/(\sum_t D_t)$;
- LOGPROPORTIONAL (Wang et al., 2019a), where p_t is proportional to $log(D_t)$;
- SQUAREROOT (Stickland and Murray, 2019), where p_t is proportional to $\sqrt{D_t}$;
- POWER (Wang et al., 2019a), where p_t is proportional to $D_t^{0.75}$;
- ANNEALED (Stickland and Murray, 2019), where p_t is proportional to D_t^{α}, with α decreasing at each epoch. When using proportional sampling methods, smaller tasks can be forgotten or interfered with, especially in the final epochs and when the final layers are shared (Stickland and Murray, 2019). The method can therefore be particularly useful for the 1-TO-1 architecture, where the decoder is shared.

We further test two additional sampling strategies:

- INVERSE, where p_t is proportional to $1/D_t$. The idea behind proportional sampling methods is to avoid overfitting smaller tasks and underfitting larger tasks. However, to the best of our knowledge, this intuitive hypothesis has not been explicitly tested. We test the opposite strategy.
- LOSS, where p_t is proportional to $\mathcal{L}_t$, the loss on the development set for task t. This strategy therefore assigns higher sampling probabilities to harder tasks. This strategy is reminiscent of the active learning-inspired sampling method by Sharma et al. (2017).

The results are shown in Table 3 for 1-TO-N and in Table 4 for 1-TO-1. We note that the choice of a sampling method depends on the MTL architecture and the dataset we want to optimize. The choice appears to be more critical for 1-TO-N than for 1-TO-1: for instance, in the case of NLMAPS, the difference between the best sampling method and the worst is 4.3 for 1-TO-N and only 1.3 for 1-TO-1. This suggests that sampling methods are more relevant to train the dedicated layers. 1-TO-1 appears to work well also with PROPORTIONAL, which is expected to suffer for interference when sharing the final layers (Stickland and Murray, 2019). As expected, ANNEALED, which explicitly addresses interference, works particularly well for 1-TO-1.

We presented INVERSE as a way to test the intuition behind proportional strategies. Given the widespread use of proportional methods, we would expect PROPORTIONAL to largely outperform UNIFORM and INVERSE. We instead observe that in most cases it does not outperform INVERSE, and in some cases underperforms it. For 1-TO-1, it does not even match the results of UNIFORM. These results further suggest that there is not a generally superior sampling method, which should instead be picked as an additional hyper-parameter. They also highlight the need to further investigate sampling methods in MTL. The proposed LOSS method is faster and performs particularly well for 1-TO-N. Henceforth, we use LOSS for 1-TO-N and ANNEALED for 1-TO-1, which maximize the average accuracies across datasets.

4.2 One Semantic Parser to Parse Them All

Table 5 compares the MTL results for the chosen sampling methods with the single-task baselines. We also report state-of-the-art parsing accuracies of each dataset for reference. Note that 1-TO-1 has more parameters than 1-TO-N. This is due to the fact that the increased sharing of 1-TO-1 allowed us to train a larger model with 1024 hidden units instead of 512. In order to more directly compare the two MTL architectures, we also train a smaller 1-TO-1 model (1-TO-1-SMALL), which uses the same number of units as 1-TO-N. The re-

Sampling	Geoquery	NLMaps	TOP	Overnight	AMR	Time
UNIFORM	68.8 (±3.8)	81.4 (±2.6)	84.7 (±0.1)	67.0 (±0.8)	61.4 (±1.7)	22h (±2h)
PROP.	70.5 (±1.9)	82.0 (±0.5)	85.0 (±0.0)	68.1 (±0.4)	63.2 (±0.4)	20h (±2h)
LOGPROP.	70.7 (±1.6)	82.8 (±0.7)	85.2 (±0.1)	68.3 (±0.1)	62.9 (±0.5)	18h(±4h)
SQUAREROOT	71.1 (±2.5)	83.4 (±1.1)	84.7 (±0.0)	67.8 (±0.6)	63.6 (±1.0)	21h (±4h)
POWER	73.5 (±1.4)	84.2 (±0.5)	85.1 (±0.3)	68.3 (±0.4)	64.1 (±0.3)	23h (±7h)
ANNEALED	72.1 (±0.0)	82.1 (±0.2)	85.1 (±0.3)	67.8 (±0.2)	63.0 (±0.6)	19h (±2h)
INVERSE	69.9 (±2.4)	84.3 (±0.8)	84.9 (±0.2)	68.4 (±0.7)	64.2 (±0.7)	20h (±2h)
LOSS	73.3 (±1.9)	85.7 (±0.0)	85.2 (±0.1)	68.9 (±0.2)	64.2 (±0.4)	15h (±2h)

Table 3: Comparison of sampling strategies for the 1-TO-N architecture. We report the average over three runs with different random seeds. The standard deviation is in parentheses. All values reported are exact match, except for AMR, where SMATCH is reported. We also report training times (in hours).

Sampling	Geoquery	NLMaps	TOP	Overnight	AMR	Time
UNIFORM	78.5 (±1.4)	87.2 (±0.2)	86.8 (±0.2)	71.1 (±0.2)	66.7 (±0.5)	21h (±4h)
PROP.	77.7 (±1.0)	86.2 (±0.2)	86.5 (±0.2)	70.6 (±0.2)	65.7 (±0.6)	16h (±1h)
LOGPROP.	78.8 (±1.5)	87.2 (±0.1)	86.6 (±0.1)	71.0 (±0.3)	67.3 (±0.5)	23h (±3h)
SQUAREROOT	78.9 (±1.5)	86.8 (±0.1)	86.7 (±0.2)	70.9 (±0.0)	66.4 (±0.3)	17h (±0h)
POWER	78.9 (±0.6)	86.9 (±0.3)	86.6 (±0.1)	71.2 (±0.6)	67.2 (±0.5)	23h (±2h)
ANNEALED	79.8 (±0.7)	87.1 (±0.1)	86.4 (±0.2)	70.8 (±0.4)	67.7 (±0.3)	26h (±1h)
INVERSE	75.0 (±2.3)	87.3 (±0.4)	86.5 (±0.1)	71.2 (±0.5)	66.5 (±0.7)	20h (±3h)
LOSS	76.5 (±1.4)	87.5 (±0.2)	86.5 (±0.1)	71.1 (±0.1)	64.8 (±0.2)	11h (±3h)

Table 4: Comparison of sampling strategies for the 1-TO-1 architecture.

sults indicate that sharing also the decoder provides generally better results, even for the smaller model. Remarkably, compared to the single-task baseline, 1-TO-1 achieves a 68% reduction in the number of learnable parameters. Smaller models can have positive practical impacts as they decrease memory consumption hence reducing costs and carbon footprint (Schwartz et al., 2019). We accomplish this without sacrificing parsing accuracies, which are competitive and in some cases higher than the baselines. This result is particularly promising, as we purposedly included a heterogeneous set of tasks and we use the same set of hyper-parameters for all of them. We can therefore train a single model with accurate parsing for a wide range of datasets, with fewer parameters.

4.3 Generalization

Table 5 also shows that MTL models are slower to converge. This is due to the regularization effect of training multiple tasks (Ruder, 2017): as the loss on the development set keeps improving, the early stopping policy allows the MTL models to be trained for more epochs, resulting in longer training times. This regularization effect allows MTL to have better generalization (Caruana, 1997; Ruder, 2017). In Figure 2 we compare the single-task TOP baseline against the 1-TO-1 model trained on all datasets and evaluated on TOP. We show training and development accuracies as a function of the epochs. We observe that the baseline overfits earlier (early stopping is triggered earlier) and generalizes less (the gap between dev set and training set is larger) compared to the MTL model.

We further evaluate our models on the CFQ dataset (Keysers et al., 2019), designed to test compositional generalization. The idea behind datasets such as CFQ is to include test examples that contain unseen compositions of primitive elements (such as predicates, entities, and question types). To achieve this, a test set is sampled to maximize the compound divergence with the training set, hence containing unseen compositions (MCD). The dataset also contains a second test set, obtained with a random split. A parser that generalizes well is expected to achieve good results on both test sets. Table 6 shows the results of our MTL model when

Model	Geoquery	NLMaps	TOP	Overnight	AMR	Time	Pars
SOTA	89.0	64.4(±0.1)*	87.1	80.6*	84.5		
BASELINE	77.6(±2.2)	87.2(±0.7)	85.3(±0.4)	70.2(±0.9)	67.2(±0.3)	7h(±0h)	721M
1-TO-N	73.3(±1.9)	85.7(±0.0)	85.2(±0.1)	68.9(±0.2)	64.2(±0.4)	15h(±2h)	203M
1-TO-1	79.8(±0.7)	87.1(±0.1)	86.4(±0.2)	70.8(±0.4)	67.7(±0.3)	26h(±1h)	231M
1-TO-1-SMALL	76.7(±1.4)	85.0(±0.8)	85.9(±0.2)	69.7(±0.8)	64.9(±1.3)	20h(±5h)	169M

Table 5: Results of multitasking between all five datasets, compared to the baseline single-task parsers and state-of-the-art results (SOTA) on these datasets. PARS indicates the total number of parameters (in millions). Results marked with * are not directly comparable, as discussed in Section 3.1.

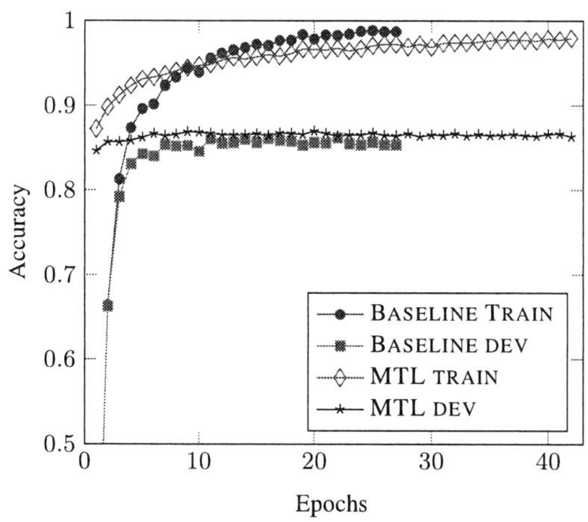

Figure 2: Accuracies on training and dev split at each epoch for the TOP baseline and 1-TO-1 MTL parser trained on all datasets and evaluated on TOP.

Model	MCD	Random
KEYSERS	17.9 (±0.9)	98.5 (±0.2)
BASELINE	14.9 (±1.5)	84.9 (±0.7)
1-TO-N	16.8 (±0.6)	95.9 (±0.0)
1-TO-1	18.9 (±0.8)	95.6 (±0.1)

Table 6: Results on the CFQ dataset. KEYSERS refers to the results reported by Keysers et al. (2019) for the TRANSFORMER model. MCD reports the average of the three released MCD test sets.

adding CFQ as the sixth task.[3] We consider the relative improvements for MCD and RANDOM, as the baseline values are considerably different. We note larger improvements on MCD (+27%) than on RANDOM (+13%) when MTL is used. The results provide initial evidence that the MTL models result in better compositional generalization than the single-task baselines.

4.4 Auxiliary Tasks

Finally, we trained MTL models on dataset pairs to find what datasets are good auxiliary tasks (i.e., tasks that are helpful to other tasks). Note that we do not tune the hyper-parameters of each pairwise model, as we would need to do a costly hyper-parameter search over 40 models. The results are shown in Table 7. The problem of choosing auxiliary tasks has been shown to be challenging (Alonso and Plank, 2016; Bingel and Søgaard, 2017; Hershcovich et al., 2018). Similar to task sampling methods, there is not an easy recipe to choose the auxiliary tasks. However, our results elicit the following surprising observations:

1. AMR is the only dataset to use graph-structured MRL, due to explicit representation of pronominal coreference, coordination, and control structures. It is also the only non-Q&A dataset. Nevertheless, we note that AMR is a competitive auxiliary task, possibly due to its large size and scope. It is also surprising that AMR is often more helpful in the 1-TO-1 setup, where the whole network is shared and more related tasks are expected to be preferred.

2. Transfer learning is often used to provide low-resource tasks with additional data from a higher-resource task. However, in our experiments, GEOQUERY, our smallest dataset, appears to be helpful for the larger TOP dataset.

5 Related Work

A number of alternative meaning representations and semantic parsing datasets have been developed in recent years, spanning from broad-range meaning representations such as Parallel Meaning Bank

[3]For comparison with Keysers et al. (2019), we report mean and 95%-confidence interval radius of 5 runs.

Model		Geoquery	NLMaps	TOP	Overnight	AMR
BASELINE		77.6(±2.2)	87.2(±0.7)	85.3(±0.4)	70.2(±0.9)	67.2(±0.3)
1-TO-N	+GEOQUERY	N/A	86.1 (±0.3)	85.8 (±0.0)	69.2 (±0.6)	63.3 (±2.1)
	+NLMAPS	77.6 (±0.9)	N/A	85.6 (±0.1)	68.2 (±0.5)	64.4 (±0.5)
	+TOP	79.4 (±0.3)	83.0 (±1.0)	N/A	61.9 (±1.9)	65.3 (±0.5)
	+OVERNIGHT	75.7 (±0.8)	85.5 (±0.2)	85.0 (±0.3)	N/A	64.1 (±0.7)
	+AMR	82.0 (±0.4)	85.9 (±0.5)	85.8 (±0.1)	69.0 (±0.4)	N/A
1-TO-1	+GEOQUERY	N/A	87.4 (±0.6)	86.5 (±0.1)	70.9 (±0.8)	66.3 (±0.3)
	+NLMAPS	80.0 (±1.8)	N/A	86.4 (±0.3)	69.7 (±1.6)	67.3 (±0.1)
	+TOP	80.5 (±1.5)	85.4 (±0.5)	N/A	65.8 (±1.2)	66.8 (±0.5)
	+OVERNIGHT	77.3 (±1.5)	87.0 (±0.3)	86.2 (±0.4)	N/A	67.0 (±0.3)
	+AMR	77.7 (±0.2)	86.9 (±0.3)	86.7 (±0.3)	70.9 (±0.1)	N/A

Table 7: Experiments on dataset pairs. The rows are the auxiliary tasks and the columns are the main tasks.

(Abzianidze et al., 2017) and UCCA (Abend and Rappoport, 2013), to domain-specific datasets such as LCQUAD (Dubey et al., 2019) and KQA Pro (Shi et al., 2020).

Following previous work on semantic parsing (Jia and Liang, 2016; Konstas et al., 2017; Fan et al., 2017; Hershcovich et al., 2018; Rongali et al., 2020), the baseline parser used in this work is based on the popular attentive sequence to sequence framework (Sutskever et al., 2014; Bahdanau et al., 2015). Pointer networks (Vinyals et al., 2015) have demonstrated the importance of decoupling the job of generating new output tokens from that of copying tokens from the input. To achieve this, our models use copy mechanisms, following previous work on semantic parsing (Rongali et al., 2020). We further rely on pre-trained embeddings (Liu et al., 2019).

Compositional generalization has recently attracted attention (Neyshabur et al., 2017; Lake and Baroni, 2018; Finegan-Dollak et al., 2018; Hupkes et al., 2018; Keysers et al., 2019). We used the CFQ dataset (Keysers et al., 2019), with the purpose of assessing their compositional generalization.

MTL (Caruana, 1997; Ruder, 2017) based on sequence to sequence models has been used to address several NLP problems such as syntactic parsing (Luong et al., 2016) and Machine Translation (Dong et al., 2015; Luong et al., 2016). For the task of semantic parsing, MTL has been employed as a way to transfer learning between domains (Damonte et al., 2019) and datasets (Fan et al., 2017; Lindemann et al., 2019; Hershcovich et al., 2018; Lindemann et al., 2019). A shared task on multi-framework semantic parsing with a particular focus on MTL has been recently introduced (Oepen et al., 2019). The 1-TO-N and 1-TO-1 models have been previously experimented with by Fan et al. (2017), with the latter being an MTL variant of the models used for multilingual parsing by Johnson et al. (2017). An alternative to MTL for transfer learning is based on pre-training on a task and fine-tuning on related tasks (Thrun, 1996). It has been investigated mostly for machine translation tasks (Zoph et al., 2016; Johnson et al., 2017; Bansal et al., 2019) but also for semantic parsing (Damonte et al., 2019).

6 Conclusions

We used MTL to train joint models for a wide range of semantic parsing datasets. We showed that MTL provides large parameter count reduction while maintaining competitive parsing accuracies, even for inherently different datasets. We further discussed how generalization is another advantage of MTL and we used the CFQ dataset to suggest that MTL achieves better compositional generalization. We leave it to future work to further investigate this type of generalization in the context of MTL. We compared several sampling methods, indicating that proportional sampling is not always optimal, showing room for improvements, and introducing a loss-based sampling method as a competitive and promising alternative. We were surprised to see the positive impact of low-resource (GEOQUERY) and less-related (AMR) datasets can have as auxiliary tasks. Challenges in finding optimal sampling strategies and auxiliary tasks suggest that they should be treated as hyper-parameters to be tuned.

Acknowledgments

The authors would like to thank the three anonymous reviewers for their comments and the Amazon Alexa AI team members for their feedback.

References

Omri Abend and Ari Rappoport. 2013. Universal conceptual cognitive annotation (ucca). In *Proceedings of the 51st Annual Meeting of the Association for Computational Linguistics (Volume 1: Long Papers)*, pages 228–238.

Lasha Abzianidze, Johannes Bjerva, Kilian Evang, Hessel Haagsma, Rik Van Noord, Pierre Ludmann, Duc-Duy Nguyen, and Johan Bos. 2017. The parallel meaning bank: Towards a multilingual corpus of translations annotated with compositional meaning representations. *arXiv preprint arXiv:1702.03964*.

Armen Aghajanyan, Jean Maillard, Akshat Shrivastava, Keith Diedrick, Mike Haeger, Haoran Li, Yashar Mehdad, Ves Stoyanov, Anuj Kumar, Mike Lewis, et al. 2020. Conversational semantic parsing. *arXiv preprint arXiv:2009.13655*.

Héctor Martínez Alonso and Barbara Plank. 2016. When is multitask learning effective? semantic sequence prediction under varying data conditions. *arXiv preprint arXiv:1612.02251*.

Yoav Artzi, Kenton Lee, and Luke Zettlemoyer. 2015. Broad-coverage CCG semantic parsing with AMR. *Proceedings of EMNLP*.

Dzmitry Bahdanau, Kyunghyun Cho, and Yoshua Bengio. 2015. Neural machine translation by jointly learning to align and translate. In *Proceedings of ICLR*.

Laura Banarescu, Claire Bonial, Shu Cai, Madalina Georgescu, Kira Griffitt, Ulf Hermjakob, Kevin Knight, Philipp Koehn, Martha Palmer, and Nathan Schneider. 2013. Abstract meaning representation for sembanking. *Linguistic Annotation Workshop*.

Sameer Bansal, Herman Kamper, Karen Livescu, Adam Lopez, and Sharon Goldwater. 2019. Pretraining on high-resource speech recognition improves low-resource speech-to-text translation. In *Proceedings of the 2019 Conference of the North American Chapter of the Association for Computational Linguistics: Human Language Technologies, Volume 1 (Long and Short Papers)*, pages 58–68.

Michele Bevilacqua, Rexhina Blloshmi, and Roberto Navigli. 2021. One spring to rule them both: Symmetric amr semantic parsing and generation without a complex pipeline. In *Proceedings of AAAI*.

Joachim Bingel and Anders Søgaard. 2017. Identifying beneficial task relations for multi-task learning in deep neural networks. In *Proceedings of EACL*.

Shu Cai and Kevin Knight. 2013. Smatch: an evaluation metric for semantic feature structures. *Proceedings of ACL*.

Rich Caruana. 1997. Multitask learning. *Machine learning*, 28(1):41–75.

Ronan Collobert and Jason Weston. 2008. A unified architecture for natural language processing: Deep neural networks with multitask learning. In *Proceedings of ICML*.

Marco Damonte, Shay B Cohen, and Giorgio Satta. 2017. An incremental parser for abstract meaning representation. In *Proceedings of EACL*.

Marco Damonte, Rahul Goel, and Tagyoung Chung. 2019. Practical semantic parsing for spoken language understanding. In *Proceedings of the 2019 Conference of the North American Chapter of the Association for Computational Linguistics: Human Language Technologies, Volume 2 (Industry Papers)*, pages 16–23.

Daxiang Dong, Hua Wu, Wei He, Dianhai Yu, and Haifeng Wang. 2015. Multi-task learning for multiple language translation. In *Proceedings of ACL*.

Mohnish Dubey, Debayan Banerjee, Abdelrahman Abdelkawi, and Jens Lehmann. 2019. Lc-quad 2.0: A large dataset for complex question answering over wikidata and dbpedia. In *International Semantic Web Conference*, pages 69–78. Springer.

Long Duong, Hadi Afshar, Dominique Estival, Glen Pink, Philip Cohen, and Mark Johnson. 2017. Multilingual semantic parsing and code-switching. In *Proceedings of CoNLL 2017*.

Xing Fan, Emilio Monti, Lambert Mathias, and Markus Dreyer. 2017. Transfer learning for neural semantic parsing. In *Proceedings of the 2nd Workshop on Representation Learning for NLP*.

Catherine Finegan-Dollak, Jonathan K Kummerfeld, Li Zhang, Karthik Ramanathan, Sesh Sadasivam, Rui Zhang, and Dragomir Radev. 2018. Improving text-to-sql evaluation methodology. In *Proceedings of the 56th Annual Meeting of the Association for Computational Linguistics (Volume 1: Long Papers)*, pages 351–360.

Jeffrey Flanigan, Sam Thomson, Jaime G Carbonell, Chris Dyer, and Noah A Smith. 2014. A discriminative graph-based parser for the abstract meaning representation. *Proceedings of ACL*.

Sonal Gupta, Rushin Shah, Mrinal Mohit, Anuj Kumar, and Mike Lewis. 2018. Semantic parsing for task oriented dialog using hierarchical representations. In *Proceedings of the 2018 Conference on Empirical Methods in Natural Language Processing*, pages 2787–2792.

Carolin Haas and Stefan Riezler. 2016. A corpus and semantic parser for multilingual natural language querying of openstreetmap. In *Proceedings of the 2016 Conference of the North American Chapter of the Association for Computational Linguistics: Human Language Technologies*, pages 740–750.

Mordechai Haklay and Patrick Weber. 2008. Openstreetmap: User-generated street maps. *Ieee Pervas Comput*, 7(4):12–18.

Daniel Hershcovich, Omri Abend, and Ari Rappoport. 2018. Multitask parsing across semantic representations. In *Proceedings of the 56th Annual Meeting of the Association for Computational Linguistics (Volume 1: Long Papers)*, pages 373–385.

Dieuwke Hupkes, Anand Singh, Kris Korrel, German Kruszewski, and Elia Bruni. 2018. Learning compositionally through attentive guidance. *arXiv preprint arXiv:1805.09657*.

Robin Jia and Percy Liang. 2016. Data recombination for neural semantic parsing. *arXiv preprint arXiv:1606.03622*.

Melvin Johnson, Mike Schuster, Quoc V Le, Maxim Krikun, Yonghui Wu, Zhifeng Chen, Nikhil Thorat, Fernanda Viégas, Martin Wattenberg, Greg Corrado, et al. 2017. Google's multilingual neural machine translation system: Enabling zero-shot translation. *Transactions of the Association for Computational Linguistics*, 5:339–351.

Daniel Keysers, Nathanael Schärli, Nathan Scales, Hylke Buisman, Daniel Furrer, Sergii Kashubin, Nikola Momchev, Danila Sinopalnikov, Lukasz Stafiniak, Tibor Tihon, et al. 2019. Measuring compositional generalization: A comprehensive method on realistic data. *arXiv preprint arXiv:1912.09713*.

Diederik P Kingma and Jimmy Ba. 2014. Adam: A method for stochastic optimization. *arXiv preprint arXiv:1412.6980*.

Ioannis Konstas, Srinivasan Iyer, Mark Yatskar, Yejin Choi, and Luke Zettlemoyer. 2017. Neural amr: Sequence-to-sequence models for parsing and generation. *Proceedings of ACL*.

Tom Kwiatkowski, Eunsol Choi, Yoav Artzi, and Luke Zettlemoyer. 2013. Scaling semantic parsers with on-the-fly ontology matching. In *Proceedings of the 2013 conference on empirical methods in natural language processing*, pages 1545–1556.

Brenden Lake and Marco Baroni. 2018. Generalization without systematicity: On the compositional skills of sequence-to-sequence recurrent networks. In *International Conference on Machine Learning*, pages 2873–2882.

Carolin Lawrence and Stefan Riezler. 2018a. Counterfactual learning from human proofreading feedback for semantic parsing. *arXiv preprint arXiv:1811.12239*.

Carolin Lawrence and Stefan Riezler. 2018b. Improving a neural semantic parser by counterfactual learning from human bandit feedback. *Institute for Computational Linguistics*.

Percy Liang. 2013. Lambda dependency-based compositional semantics. *arXiv preprint arXiv:1309.4408*.

Matthias Lindemann, Jonas Groschwitz, and Alexander Koller. 2019. Compositional semantic parsing across graphbanks. In *Proceedings of the 57th Annual Meeting of the Association for Computational Linguistics*, pages 4576–4585.

Yinhan Liu, Myle Ott, Naman Goyal, Jingfei Du, Mandar Joshi, Danqi Chen, Omer Levy, Mike Lewis, Luke Zettlemoyer, and Veselin Stoyanov. 2019. Roberta: A robustly optimized bert pretraining approach. *arXiv preprint arXiv:1907.11692*.

Thang Luong, Quoc V Le, Ilya Sutskever, Oriol Vinyals, and Lukasz Kaiser. 2016. Multi-task sequence to sequence learning.

Behnam Neyshabur, Srinadh Bhojanapalli, David McAllester, and Nati Srebro. 2017. Exploring generalization in deep learning. In *Proceedings of NIPS*.

Rik van Noord and Johan Bos. 2017. Dealing with coreference in neural semantic parsing. In *Proceedings of the 2nd Workshop on Semantic Deep Learning*.

Stephan Oepen, Omri Abend, Jan Hajic, Daniel Hershcovich, Marco Kuhlmann, Tim O'Gorman, Nianwen Xue, Jayeol Chun, Milan Straka, and Zdenka Urešová. 2019. Mrp 2019: Cross-framework meaning representation parsing. In *Proceedings of CoNLL*.

Subendhu Rongali, Luca Soldaini, Emilio Monti, and Wael Hamza. 2020. Don't parse, generate! a sequence to sequence architecture for task-oriented semantic parsing. *Proceedings of The Web Conference*.

Sebastian Ruder. 2017. An overview of multi-task learning in deep neural networks. *arXiv preprint arXiv:1706.05098*.

Victor Sanh, Thomas Wolf, and Sebastian Ruder. 2019. A hierarchical multi-task approach for learning embeddings from semantic tasks. In *Proceedings of the AAAI Conference on Artificial Intelligence*, volume 33, pages 6949–6956.

Roy Schwartz, Jesse Dodge, Noah A Smith, and Oren Etzioni. 2019. Green ai. *arXiv preprint arXiv:1907.10597*.

Sahil Sharma, Ashutosh Jha, Parikshit Hegde, and Balaraman Ravindran. 2017. Learning to multi-task by active sampling. *arXiv preprint arXiv:1702.06053*.

Jiaxin Shi, Shulin Cao, Liangming Pan, Yutong Xiang, Lei Hou, Juanzi Li, Hanwang Zhang, and Bin He. 2020. Kqa pro: A large diagnostic dataset for complex question answering over knowledge base. *arXiv preprint arXiv:2007.03875*.

Mark Steedman. 1996. Surface structure and interpretation. The MIT Press.

Mark Steedman. 2000. The syntactic process. The MIT Press.

Asa Cooper Stickland and Iain Murray. 2019. Bert and pals: Projected attention layers for efficient adaptation in multi-task learning. In *International Conference on Machine Learning*, pages 5986–5995.

Yu Su and Xifeng Yan. 2017. Cross-domain semantic parsing via paraphrasing. In *Proceedings of EMNLP*.

Ilya Sutskever, Oriol Vinyals, and Quoc V Le. 2014. Sequence to sequence learning with neural networks. In *Proceedings of NIPS*.

Sebastian Thrun. 1996. Is learning the n-th thing any easier than learning the first? In *Advances in neural information processing systems*, pages 640–646.

Ivan Titov and James Henderson. 2007. A latent variable model for generative dependency parsing. In *Proceedings of IWPT*.

Ashish Vaswani, Noam Shazeer, Niki Parmar, Jakob Uszkoreit, Llion Jones, Aidan N Gomez, Łukasz Kaiser, and Illia Polosukhin. 2017. Attention is all you need. In *Advances in neural information processing systems*, pages 5998–6008.

Oriol Vinyals, Meire Fortunato, and Navdeep Jaitly. 2015. Pointer networks. In *Proceedings of NIPS*.

Alex Wang, Jan Hula, Patrick Xia, Raghavendra Pappagari, R Thomas McCoy, Roma Patel, Najoung Kim, Ian Tenney, Yinghui Huang, Katherin Yu, et al. 2019a. Can you tell me how to get past sesame street? sentence-level pretraining beyond language modeling. In *Proceedings of the 57th Annual Meeting of the Association for Computational Linguistics*, pages 4465–4476.

Alex Wang, Amanpreet Singh, Julian Michael, Felix Hill, Omer Levy, and Samuel Bowman. 2019b. Glue: A multi-task benchmark and analysis platform for natural language understanding. In *7th International Conference on Learning Representations, ICLR 2019*.

Chuan Wang, Nianwen Xue, and Sameer Pradhan. 2015a. A transition-based algorithm for AMR parsing. *Proceedings of NAACL*.

Yushi Wang, Jonathan Berant, and Percy Liang. 2015b. Building a semantic parser overnight. In *Proceedings of ACL*.

John M Zelle and Raymond J Mooney. 1996. Learning to parse database queries using inductive logic programming. In *Proceedings of the national conference on artificial intelligence*.

Sheng Zhang, Xutai Ma, Kevin Duh, and Benjamin Van Durme. 2019. Broad-coverage semantic parsing as transduction. In *Proceedings of the 2019 Conference on Empirical Methods in Natural Language Processing and the 9th International Joint Conference on Natural Language Processing (EMNLP-IJCNLP)*, pages 3777–3789.

Barret Zoph, Deniz Yuret, Jonathan May, and Kevin Knight. 2016. Transfer learning for low-resource neural machine translation. In *Proceedings of the 2016 Conference on Empirical Methods in Natural Language Processing*, pages 1568–1575.

A Hyper-parameters

Table 8 reports the final hyper-parameters used for our experiments.

Model		Batch	lr	Layers	Units	Heads	Dropout
BASELINE	GEOQUERY	100	0.05	3	512	4	0.1
	NLMAPS	50	0.05	4	512	16	0.05
	TOP	200	0.05	3	512	4	0.04
	OVERNIGHT	10	0.05	3	700	4	0.03
	AMR	10	0.05	4	512	4	0.03
1-TO-N		10	0.05	3	512	4	0.1
1-TO-1		10	0.05	3	1024	4	0.1
1-TO-1-SMALL		10	0.05	3	512	4	0.1

Table 8: Hyper-parameter selected for baselines and MTL models. From left to right the hyper-parameters are: batch size, learning rate, number of layers and units in the decoder, number of attention heads, and dropout ratio.

Multilingual Neural Semantic Parsing for Low-Resourced Languages

Menglin Xia
Amazon Research Cambridge
ximengli@amazon.com

Emilio Monti
Amazon Research Cambridge
monti@amazon.com

Abstract

Multilingual semantic parsing is a cost-effective method that allows a single model to understand different languages. However, researchers face a great imbalance of availability of training data, with English being resource rich, and other languages having much less data. To tackle the data limitation problem, we propose using machine translation to bootstrap multilingual training data from the more abundant English data. To compensate for the data quality of machine translated training data, we utilize transfer learning from pretrained multilingual encoders to further improve the model. To evaluate our multilingual models on human-written sentences as opposed to machine translated ones, we introduce a new multilingual semantic parsing dataset in English, Italian and Japanese based on the Facebook Task Oriented Parsing (TOP) dataset. We show that joint multilingual training with pretrained encoders substantially outperforms our baselines on the TOP dataset and outperforms the state-of-the-art model on the public NLMaps dataset. We also establish a new baseline for zero-shot learning on the TOP dataset. We find that a semantic parser trained only on English data achieves a zero-shot performance of 44.9% exact-match accuracy on Italian sentences.

1 Introduction

Semantic parsing is defined as the task of parsing a natural language sentence into a logical form that represents its meaning. The logical form, or sometimes called the meaning representation language (MRL) expression, can be executed against a knowledge base to extract information; therefore, semantic parsing often finds its application in question answering, code generation, information retrieval, etc. Due to its wide range of applications, semantic parsing has drawn a lot of research interest. Among them, neural semantic parsing methods have gained popularity in recent years due to their good results (Dong and Lapata, 2018). Neural semantic parsing often formulates the task as a machine translation problem and uses neural networks to translate the sentences into MRL expressions.

Multilingual neural semantic parsing is a cost-effective method that allows a single model to understand different languages. However, similar to other machine-learning based approaches, neural semantic parsing requires large amounts of training data. To understand texts in different languages, semantic parsing models need training data for each target language. Unfortunately, researchers face a great imbalance of availability of training data for semantic parsing: while we have lots of data in English, the data in non-English languages is often scarce. Although there is a growing number of datasets published for semantic parsing in English, very few datasets are available in other languages. Moreover, manually annotating data for semantic parsing is difficult and time-consuming, as it requires a lot of training and effort for annotators to write MRLs.

Instead of manually annotating semantic parsing data in low-resourced languages, can we bootstrap training data for multilingual semantic parsing from the more abundant English data? In this paper, we aim to tackle the data limitation problem for multilingual semantic parsing with machine translation. We machine translate English sentences into target non-English languages and make use of the alignment information in the English MRL to create MRL annotations in other languages (see Section 3). We then describe our methods to build multilingual semantic parsing models on the machine translated training data (see Section 4). To train the multilingual semantic parser, we mix the training data from all languages together and train a model from scratch (see Section 4.1). We base our neural semantic parser on the sequence-to-sequence model with pointer mecha-

Proceedings of the 10th Conference on Lexical and Computational Semantics, pages 185–194
August 5–6, 2021, Bangkok, Thailand (online) ©2021 Association for Computational Linguistics

nism (Sutskever et al., 2014; Vinyals et al., 2015), where both the natural language question and the target MRL are treated as sequences of tokens and the parser learns from the training data a mapping to translate questions into MRLs.

The machine translation-based data generation method allows us to easily extend English data to other languages. However, the quality of the bootstrapped training data is constrained by the accuracy of the machine translation model and other components of the generation method, such as alignment. To mitigate the problem of data quality of the machine translated training data, we make use of transfer learning with pretrained multilingual encoders to further improve the multilingual semantic parsing model (see Section 4.2).

To evaluate the model performance on sentences written by human as opposed to machine translated ones, we introduce a new multilingual semantic parsing dataset based on the Facebook Task Oriented Parsing (TOP) dataset (Gupta et al., 2018). We compare our method against several baselines, including monolingual models and a popular technique in literature that relies on translating the utterances and using an English model to understand them (see Section 4.3). We report the experimental results and our analysis in Section 5. To show that our multilingual semantic parsing models also work with human-generated training data and to compare them against previous work, we report the performance of our models on the public multilingual NLMaps dataset in Section 5.3.

Apart from bootstrapping training data, zero-shot learning is also a technique that allows a multilingual model to generalize to low-resourced languages. We study how the multilingual semantic parsers with pretrained encoders can generalize to other languages in a zero-shot scenario (see Section 5.4).

Our main contributions are as follows:

1. We propose a method to automatically generate training data for multilingual semantic parsing from existing English data via machine translation and we use pretrained multilingual encoders to compensate for the data quality. We release a new multilingual semantic parsing dataset in English, Italian and Japanese based on the public TOP dataset, with ~30k machine-translated training and validation data and ~8k manually translated test data for each language. The dataset is available for download at: `https://github.com/awslabs/multilingual-top`.

2. We show that our multilingual semantic parsing model achieves state-of-the-art performance, outperforming several baselines on the TOP dataset and existing work on the public NLMaps dataset.

3. We establish a new baseline for zero-shot learning on the TOP dataset with semantic parsing model finetuned from pretrained multilingual encoders.

2 Background and Related Work

Semantic parsing has been studied for a few decades. Earlier methods on semantic parsing rely on defining semantic rules to parse the input sentence (Zelle and Mooney, 1996; Zettlemoyer and Collins, 2005). With recent advances in neural networks, there is a trend of formulating semantic parsing as a machine translation problem. In particular, the sequence-to-sequence model (Sutskever et al., 2014) is commonly used in recent works on semantic parsing (Dong and Lapata, 2018; Jia and Liang, 2016; Zhong et al., 2017). Typically, they use a neural network encoder to encode the utterance sentence into a latent vector representation and use a decoder conditioned on the latent representation to predict the MRL as a sequence of symbols.

Due to the research interest in semantic parsing, many public datasets have been made available for English semantic parsing, ranging from small datasets that contain only a few hundred or a few thousand examples, such as GeoQuery (Zelle and Mooney, 1996) and ATIS (Dahl et al., 1994), to larger datasets with tens of thousands of question-logical form pairs, such as WikiSQL (Zhong et al., 2017) and Overnight (Wang et al., 2015).

Multilingual semantic parsing, however, has only begun to draw research attention in more recent years. Therefore, very few datasets have been published for semantic parsing in non-English languages. So far, almost all of the multilingual semantic parsing datasets are manually translated from their English versions. Due to the cost of manual translation, they are limited to small datasets. For example, Jones et al. (2012) translated the GeoQuery dataset into German, Greek, and Thai. Susanto and Lu (2017) translated the ATIS dataset into Indonesian and Chinese. Haas and Riezler (2016) created the NLMaps dataset which contains around 2,400 queries to a geographic database in English. The authors translated the queries into German but kept the MRL annotation the same as that for English. Apart from the semantic parsing datasets for question answering, there are some multilingual datasets with other logical form representations, such as multilingual GraphQuestions with graphs as the meaning representation (Reddy et al., 2017), Parallel Meaning Bank with DRT (Discourse Representation Theory) representation (Abzianidze et al., 2017), and multilingual AMR test set with Abstract Meaning Representation (Damonte and Cohen, 2018). The logical form representation in these datasets are very different from the MRLs used for question answering and thus cannot be easily harnessed by many semantic parsers.

Among the limited literature on multilingual semantic parsing, several different methods have been proposed. The first attempts on multilingual semantic parsing (Haas and Riezler, 2016; Damonte and Cohen, 2018) use statistical/neural machine translation methods to translate non-English questions into English and rely on using an English semantic parser to parse all the utterances. Annotation projection is an alternative technique to deal with the lack of multilingual data. It maps the annotation from one language to another using word alignment. It has been applied to many NLP applications, including POS tagging (Yarowsky et al., 2001), role-labeling (Akbik et al., 2015), semantic CCG parsing (Evang and Bos, 2016), and AMR parsing (Damonte and Cohen, 2018). In addition, Susanto and Lu (2017) approached multilingual semantic parsing with a multi-task learning technique. They used separate encoders to encode sentences in different languages and used a shared decoder to predict the MRL. Duong et al. (2017) used cross-lingual word embeddings in a sequence-to-sequence model. They observed that using cross-lingual word embeddings improves the results on both English and German over their baseline models on the NLMaps dataset. They also compared training a model with a single encoder on multilingual data against training with separate encoders for each language and found that keeping separate encoders actually harms semantic parsing accuracy. Based on their observation, we will use a single encoder for multiple languages in our experiments.

Question:
```
Any festivals this weekend
```

Hierarchical intent-slot representation:
```
[IN:GET_EVENT Any
[SL:CATEGORY_EVENT festivals ]
[SL:DATE_TIME this weekend ] ]
```

Adapted MRL representation:
```
[IN:GET_EVENT
[SL:CATEGORY_EVENT festivals ]
[SL:DATE_TIME this weekend ] ]
```

Table 1: An example of the English TOP dataset

3 Multilingual Semantic Parsing Data

To tackle the data scarcity problem for multilingual semantic parsing, we aim to utilize machine translation to automatically generate training data from the more abundant English data for other languages. In this section, we introduce the English semantic parsing dataset we are using and describe our strategy to bootstrap training data for multilingual semantic parsing.

3.1 English Semantic Parsing Data

We use the Facebook Task Oriented Parsing (TOP) dataset (Gupta et al., 2018) as our source English semantic parsing data. The TOP dataset contains around 44k navigation and event questions created by crowd-sourced workers. The questions are annotated to semantic frames comprising of hierarchical intents and slots. We adapted the original intent-slot representation to a representation that is more similar to other question answering MRLs. More specifically, we dropped the text mentions in the intent label and kept only the entity text in the slot label. The resulting MRL is still a valid meaning representation because the text in the intent label does not affect the execution of the query on a knowledge base. Table 1 shows an example of the original TOP data and its corresponding MRL representation in the adapted task.

We also remove the utterances where the root intent is `IN:UNSUPPORTED`, as it is a noisy catch-all class for out-of-domain utterances. The final dataset contains 28,414 training, 4,032 validation, and 8,241 test data points.

3.2 Bootstrapping Multilingual Semantic Parsing Data

Creating multilingual semantic parsing data from the English data is not a trivial task, because the

Question (English):
`Any festivals|`x_0 `this|`x_1 `weekend|`x_1

MRL:
`[IN:GET_EVENT`
`[SL:CATEGORY_EVENT` x_0 `]`
`[SL:DATE_TIME` x_1 `] ]`

Table 2: Replacing text in the MRL with placeholder tokens and marking the positions of placeholder tokens in the question (on the same example as in Table 1).

MRL annotation is highly intertwined with the input question. Directly translating the text in the MRL into another language is likely to generate an incorrect MRL, as it may not match the translation of the input question. In order to obtain valid multilingual equivalents of both the natural language question and its meaning representation, rather than translating the MRL directly, we apply a similar method to annotation projection. We make use of the text alignment information between the question and the MRL to ensure that the translated MRL matches with the translated question. This is done in three steps:

Step 1: First, we reformat the question-MRL pair in English by replacing the text tokens in the MRL with placeholder tokens $x_0, x_1, ...$ that correspond to text tokens in the question. We also mark the positions of placeholder tokens in the question. Table 2 gives an example.

Step 2: We then use the Amazon Machine Translation Service[1] to translate the natural language question into the target language. Next, we use the fast align algorithm (Dyer et al., 2013) to align the text between the translation and the original English sentence so as to identify the positions of the placeholder tokens in the translation. Figure 1 illustrates the alignment of texts between the source English sentence and its Italian translation and the identified placeholder tokens in the translation.

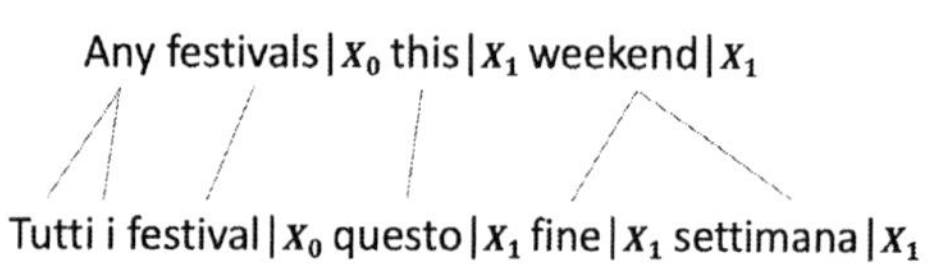

Figure 1: Using fast align algorithm to identify corresponding placeholder tokens in the translation.

Step 3: Finally, to obtain a valid MRL in the target language, we substitute the placeholder tokens in the MRL back with their corresponding text tokens in the translation. In this way, a valid pair of question and its MRL annotation in the target language is created (see Table 3).

Question (Italian):
`Tutti i festival questo fine settimana`

MRL:
`[IN:GET_EVENT`
`[SL:CATEGORY_EVENT festival ]`
`[SL:DATE_TIME questo fine settimana ] ]`

Table 3: English semantic parsing data translated into Italian

Following this method, we generate training data for Italian and Japanese semantic parsing from the English TOP dataset. We machine translated the training and validation splits of the TOP dataset into the two target languages.

In order to evaluate the performance of our multilingual models on human-written sentences rather than machine-translated ones, we hire professional translators to manually translate the test set into Italian and Japanese. Table 4 shows the data distribution of the multilingual TOP dataset. It should be noted that as the fast align algorithm may fail to align the tokens between the translation and the source text, especially when the source and target languages are dissimilar, we may lose some data points in the automatic multilingual data generation process. Overall, the vast majority of the training data can be bootstrapped successfully following our method (97.9% data for Italian and 89.9% for Japanese).

Language	Train	Dev	Test
English	28414	4032	8241
Italian	27830	3955	8241
Japanese	25544	3629	8241

Table 4: The distribution of the multilingual TOP dataset

4 Multilingual Semantic Parsing Models

4.1 Model Architecture

Following the work of the state-of-the-art semantic parsers in English (Dong and Lapata, 2018; Rongali et al., 2020), we base our multilingual semantic parsing model on the sequence-to-sequence

[1] `https://aws.amazon.com/translate/`

method. We train a model that is similar in architecture to the Transformer encoder-decoder model described in Vaswani et al. (Vaswani et al., 2017). More specifically, we use a multilayer bidirectional Transformer encoder to encode the input question and a Transformer decoder to predict the MRL as a sequence of tokens. An encoder-decoder attention layer in the decoder learns to attend to the input tokens. We also implement an attention-based pointer mechanism (Vinyals et al., 2015) to learn to copy text tokens from the input question. We concatenate the attention scores from the attention layer with the output vocabulary distribution from the final layer of the decoder. We then feed the concatenated vector to a Softmax layer to obtain a final probability distribution of possible actions. At each time step, the decoder either generates a symbol from the output vocabulary or outputs a pointer to one of the input tokens based on the scores from the final probability distribution. We use beam-search at inference time to select the prediction that maximizes the probability of the entire sequence. To train our baseline multilingual semantic parsing model, we mix the data from all languages together and train a single model from scratch to parse all questions. We apply Byte-Pair Encoding (BPE) tokenization (Sennrich et al., 2016) to preprocess the data. BPE tokenization learns to break rare words into subword units. It is frequently used in machine translation and has contributed to better translation quality in many shared tasks (Denkowski and Neubig, 2017). For multilingual tasks, we believe that subword representation helps to encode shared information between similar languages, and therefore facilitates multilingual semantic parsing.

4.2 Multilingual Semantic Parsing with Pretrained Encoders

Transfer learning is a technique that aims to transfer information from a model trained on a source task to improve performance of the model on a target task. For neural network models, transfer learning typically consists of two stages: a pretraining stage and a finetuning stage. In the pretraining stage, the model is trained on the source task. In the finetuning stage, the knowledge of the trained model is transferred to the target task and adapted on that task. Existing literature has shown that transferring knowledge from pretrained models can improve the downstream performance on many NLP tasks (Devlin et al., 2019).

As all our non-English semantic parsing training data are automatically generated from machine translation, it may not be as natural as real human-written sentences. We believe that transferring knowledge from a model that is pretrained on a huge amount of authentic multilingual text will allow our multilingual semantic parser to learn a better representation for the input utterance and to generalize better on real human-written sentences. To do that, we first initialize the encoder parameters with pretrained encoder parameters. We compare two state-of-the art multilingual encoders for initializing the multilingual semantic parser: the multilingual BERT (mBERT) model (Vaswani et al., 2017) and the XLM-R model (Conneau and Lample, 2019). Both models cover all the languages required in our semantic parsing tasks. The mBERT model is based on the multi-layer Transformer architecture. It is trained using the masked language objective and the next sentence prediction objective (Devlin et al., 2019) on Wikipedia texts for the top 100 languages with the largest Wikipedia dumps. In our experiment, we use the public multilingual cased BERT-Base model[2] (12-layer, 768-hidden, 12 heads) to initialize our semantic parsing encoder. The XLM-R model is a Transformer model trained using multilingual masked language model objectives (Conneau and Lample, 2019). It is trained for 100 languages on the CommonCrawl corpus, which is several orders of magnitude larger than the Wikipedia dump, especially for low-resourced languages. We use the public XLM-R Base model[3] (12-layer, 768-hidden, 12 heads) in our experiment.

After initializing the semantic parsing model with pretrained encoder parameters, we finetune the models on the mixed multilingual semantic parsing data. To effectively adapt the pretrained encoder to our data, we implement gradual unfreezing (Howard and Ruder, 2018) in the finetuning steps. Instead of tuning all encoder layers from the beginning, which may cause the model to forget what it learnt in pretraining, we slowly unfreeze the encoder layer weights to be tuned, from not changing the weights at all in the beginning until we finetune all the layers.

[2]https://github.com/google-research/bert/blob/master/multilingual.md

[3]https://github.com/pytorch/fairseq/tree/master/examples/xlmr

4.3 Baselines

We compare our multilingual semantic parsing models against two groups of baselines: monolingual models trained for each target language and a common method in previous research that also makes use of machine translation.

4.3.1 Monolingual Baselines

We investigate how our multilingual semantic parsing models compare to monolingual models trained on each language separately. In accordance with the multilingual models, we build two types of monolingual baselines: monolingual models without pretraining and monolingual models finetuned from pretrained encoders. We use the same model architecture as the multilingual models for the monolingual baselines. For the monolingual pretrained encoders, we use the public English RoBERTa (Liu et al., 2019) model to initialize the English model, because semantic parsers finetuned from the English RoBERTa model have achieved state-of-the-art result on the original TOP dataset (Rongali et al., 2020). As there is no public RoBERTa model available for Italian and Japanese, we use Italian and Japanese BERT models trained on Wikipedia data instead.

In addition to using monolingual pretrained encoders, we also investigate a baseline with multilingual pretrained encoders (mBERT and XLM-R) finetuned on monolingual data for each target language.

4.3.2 Multilingual Semantic Parsing through Machine Translation

An alternative to multilingual semantic parsing is to translate all non-English languages into English and use an English semantic parsing model to understand the translated utterances (Haas and Riezler, 2016). We compare our multilingual semantic parsing models against this method. We train an semantic parser on the English training data by finetuning from the RoBERTa model. We then use the Amazon Machine Translation Service to translate the Italian and Japanese sentences in the TOP test set into English. The translated texts are fed into the English semantic parser to get their MRL predictions. We use the MRL annotation of the English test set as the gold-standard for evaluation.

5 Experiments and Results

5.1 Experiment Setup

We measure the performance of the semantic parsing models by exact match accuracy. By its definition, an MRL prediction is considered accurate only if the entire predicted sequence is exactly the same as the gold-standard MRL. The models are trained on AWS P3 instances with Tesla V100 GPU. We use the Adam optimizer in training and introduce early stopping if the loss doesn't improve on the validation set. We tune the hyperparameters for each model by random search on the validation set and report the results on the test set.

5.2 Results and Analysis on the TOP Dataset

Table 5 shows the performance of the multilingual models on the TOP dataset and Table 6 shows the results of the baselines models. Comparing the multilingual models against the monolingual baselines, we find that training semantic parsing models on multilingual data jointly outperforms models trained on monolingual data only, even without using a pretrained encoder. The joint training is not only helpful for non-English languages, where the training data were machine translated, but it is also helpful for English, with or without a multilingual pretrained encoder.

In addition, we observe that transfer learning from pretrained encoders can improve the multilingual model performance further. Among the multilingual models, finetuning from pretrained XLM-R model achieves the best performance, which yields a parsing accuracy of 85.1% for English, 62.4% for Italian, and 36.3% for Japanese. It substantially outperforms the monolingual baselines as well as the method that relies on machine translating utterances into English and using the English semantic parser to understand the utterances. The results prove that bootstrapping training data from English using machine translation is an effective method for constructing training data for multilingual semantic parsing.

On the other hand, constrained by the method we created our training data, the semantic parsing accuracy is heavily dependent on the machine translation quality. The better the machine translation model is, the more similar the automatically generated multilingual training data can be to real data. We measured the BLEU scores of the machine translation models on a random sample of English-Italian and English-Japanese sentences and found

Languages	multilingual (no pretraining)	mBERT	XLM-R
English	79.1%	84.6%	**85.1%**
Italian	57.4%	61.4%	**62.4%**
Japanese	31.9%	34.2%	**36.3%**
Mixed	56.1%	60.1%	**61.2%**

Table 5: Results on the multilingual TOP dataset

Languages	monolingual baselines				machine translated
	no pretraining	monolingual BERTs	mBERT	XLM-R	to English
English	78.3%	85.3%	83.3%	83.8%	85.3% (English model)
Italian	55.9%	55.1%	59.8%	60.2%	35.3%
Japanese	28.0%	32.1%	33.0%	32.5%	15.1%

Table 6: Results from baseline models on the multilingual TOP dataset

that the BLEU scores are 57.5 for Italian and 27.2 for Japanese, which shows that the English-Italian machine translation model is substantially more accurate than the English-Japanese one. Therefore, we observe a big difference between the semantic parsing accuracy for Italian and for Japanese.

During error analysis, we find that a large group of errors in Italian semantic parsing is due to the inclusion or exclusion of articles copied in the MRL, which has minimal influence over the understanding. Table 7 gives an example. As a heuristic solution, we filter out articles from both the expectation and the prediction and the exact match accuracy rises from 62.4% to 75.4% by our best performing model. Similarly, a large group of errors in Japanese is due to the inclusion or omission of postpositions and grammatical particles in the MRL when they are copied from the input question. If we filter out the postpositions and grammatical particles from the gold-standard and the predicted MRLs, the exact match accuracy is raised from 36.3% to 52.3%.

Question (Italian):
`dove posso vedere i fuochi d'artificio questa sera`

Gold-standard MRL:
`[IN:GET_EVENT [SL:CATEGORY_EVENT i fuochi d'artificio ] [SL:DATE_TIME questa sera ]]`

Predicted MRL:
`[IN:GET_EVENT [SL:CATEGORY_EVENT fuochi artificio ] [SL:DATE_TIME questa sera ]]`

Table 7: An example of missing article "i" in Italian semantic parsing

5.3 Experiment on the NLMaps Dataset

Apart from experimenting on the machine translated training data, we also want to see how our multilingual models perform with training data created by human and how our models compare to existing work. Therefore, we report the results of our models on the multilingual NLMaps dataset. The multilingual NLMaps dataset (Haas and Riezler, 2016) is one of the largest multilingual semantic parsing dataset published in previous literature. It contains around 2,400 English utterances and their manual translation into German. The queries are paired with a MRL representation that can be executed on a geographic database. Because NLMaps doesn't have a validation set, we randomly split 10% of the training data as the validation set and trained our models on the remaining 90% of the data. The resulting dataset contains 1,350 training utterance-MRL pairs, 150 validation pairs and 880 test pairs for both English and German.

Table 8 shows the results. Our best performing model on the NLMaps dataset is the multilingual semantic parser finetuned from the mBERT model, which yields an accuracy of 79.7% for English and 79.5% for German. The best result reported on the multilingual NLMaps dataset in literature was by Duong et al. (2017). However, their model was trained on the full training dataset for 10k iterations without splitting a separate validation set. Therefore, we retrain our best performing model under the same condition and present the result in Table

Languages	monolingual baselines				multilingual (no pretraining)	mBERT	XLM-R
	no pretraining	monolingual BERTs	mBERT	XLM-R			
English	73.5%	74.1%	75.7%	63.3%	72.1%	**79.7%**	74.3%
German	68.0%	70.3%	71.6%	59.5%	66.9%	**79.5%**	73.9%
Mixed	-	-	-	-	69.5%	**79.6%**	74.1%

Table 8: Results on the multilingual NLMaps dataset

Languages	Our best (mBERT)	Duong et al. (2017)
English	**85.9%**	85.7%
German	**85.5%**	82.3%

Table 9: Comparing the mBERT-based model with SOTA model on the NLMaps dataset (trained on the full training data for 10k iterations)

9. The result shows that our multilingual model outperforms the state-of-the-art model in German by 3.2% while keeping the same level of accuracy in English (with a slight improvement of 0.2%).

On the NLMaps dataset, we find that training the model on mixed multilingual data does not outperform a monolingual model if the models are trained without using a pretrained encoder. However, joint multilingual training is still helpful when a pretrained encoder is used. For example, when we finetune the mBERT model on English and German data separately, the resulting models yield an accuracy of 75.7% for English and 71.6% for German, which are markedly lower than the results from the mBERT model finetuned on mixed multilingual data. In addition, we find that using pretrained multilingual mBERT model outperforms pretrained monolingual BERT models.

5.4 Experiment on Zero-shot Learning

Encoder weights unfreezing rate		Italian	Japanese
unfreeze all	mBERT	24.9%	4.6%
	XLM-R	36.1%	1.7%
unfreeze 10%	mBERT	28.6%	**7.3%**
	XLM-R	**44.9%**	4.9%
freeze all	mBERT	16.0%	2.5%
	XLM-R	15.6%	3.9%

Table 10: Zero-shot learning on the TOP dataset

Zero-shot learning is a problem setup in which a model is tested on tasks that are not observed at training time. It studies the model's ability to generalize to unseen tasks. For multilingual models, we are interested in the zero-shot performance of a model when it is trained on one language and

Question (Italian):
```
Concerti di Beyonce questo fine
settimana
```
Predicted MRL:
```
[IN:GET_EVENT [SL:CATEGORY_EVENT Concerti
] [SL:NAME_EVENT Beyonce ] [SL:DATE_TIME
questo fine settimana ] ]
```

Table 11: An example of correct zero-shot prediction

tested on other languages. To explore the zero-shot ability of our multilingual semantic parsers on the TOP dataset, we train a model with pretrained multilingual encoder on the English training data and apply the model to Italian and Japanese test data directly without further finetuning. We experiment with different ratios for unfreezing the pretrained encoder weights when tuning the models on the English data. Table 10 shows the results. We find that setting a small unfreezing rate to the pretrained encoder leads to a higher zero-shot accuracy.

Multilingual models trained only on English data can achieve 44.9% zero-shot accuracy when parsing Italian sentences, even though it has not seen any Italian semantic parsing data in training. Table 11 shows an example. However, their zero-shot performance on Japanese sentences is very poor. This is not surprising as English and Italian are more similar and they share a lot more BPE subword units than English and Japanese.

6 Conclusion

In this paper, we describe our method to build multilingual semantic parsing models when the multilingual data is limited. We introduce a new multilingual semantic parsing dataset in English, Italian and Japanese based on the public TOP dataset, with training and validation data automatically generated from English and 8k test data manually translated. The multilingual TOP test set is so far the largest dataset for multilingual semantic parsing, which will be useful for future research. By leveraging joint multilingual training and transfer learning from pretrained encoders, our semantic parsing models outperform several baselines on the TOP dataset and the state-of-the-art on the NLMaps dataset. We show that semantic parsing models with pretrained multilingual encoders can generalize from English to Italian with 44.9% zero-shot accuracy. However, we find that there is a gap between Italian and Japanese semantic parsing with our method. In future work, we plan to improve our models with both language-invariant and language-specific encodings and apply our method to more languages.

References

Lasha Abzianidze, Johannes Bjerva, Kilian Evang, Hessel Haagsma, Rik van Noord, Pierre Ludmann, Duc-Duy Nguyen, and Johan Bos. 2017. The parallel meaning bank: Towards a multilingual corpus of translations annotated with compositional meaning representations. In *Proceedings of the 15th Conference of the European Chapter of the Association for Computational Linguistics: Volume 2, Short Papers*, pages 242–247, Valencia, Spain. Association for Computational Linguistics.

Alan Akbik, Laura Chiticariu, Marina Danilevsky, Yunyao Li, Shivakumar Vaithyanathan, and Huaiyu Zhu. 2015. Generating high quality proposition Banks for multilingual semantic role labeling. In *Proceedings of the 53rd Annual Meeting of the Association for Computational Linguistics and the 7th International Joint Conference on Natural Language Processing (Volume 1: Long Papers)*, pages 397–407, Beijing, China. Association for Computational Linguistics.

Alexis Conneau and Guillaume Lample. 2019. Cross-lingual language model pretraining. In *Advances in Neural Information Processing Systems*, pages 7057–7067.

Deborah A. Dahl, Madeleine Bates, Michael Brown, William Fisher, Kate Hunicke-Smith, David Pallett, Christine Pao, Alexander Rudnicky, and Elizabeth Shriberg. 1994. Expanding the scope of the atis task: The atis-3 corpus. In *HUMAN LANGUAGE TECHNOLOGY: Proceedings of a Workshop held at Plainsboro, New Jersey, March 8-11, 1994.*

Marco Damonte and Shay B. Cohen. 2018. Cross-lingual abstract meaning representation parsing. In *Proceedings of the 2018 Conference of the North American Chapter of the Association for Computational Linguistics: Human Language Technologies, Volume 1 (Long Papers)*, pages 1146–1155, New Orleans, Louisiana. Association for Computational Linguistics.

Michael Denkowski and Graham Neubig. 2017. Stronger baselines for trustable results in neural machine translation. In *Proceedings of the First Workshop on Neural Machine Translation*, pages 18–27, Vancouver. Association for Computational Linguistics.

Jacob Devlin, Ming-Wei Chang, Kenton Lee, and Kristina Toutanova. 2019. BERT: Pre-training of deep bidirectional transformers for language understanding. In *Proceedings of the 2019 Conference of the North American Chapter of the Association for Computational Linguistics: Human Language Technologies, Volume 1 (Long and Short Papers)*, pages 4171–4186, Minneapolis, Minnesota. Association for Computational Linguistics.

Li Dong and Mirella Lapata. 2018. Coarse-to-fine decoding for neural semantic parsing. In *Proceedings of the 56th Annual Meeting of the Association for Computational Linguistics (Volume 1: Long Papers)*, pages 731–742, Melbourne, Australia. Association for Computational Linguistics.

Long Duong, Hadi Afshar, Dominique Estival, Glen Pink, Philip Cohen, and Mark Johnson. 2017. Multilingual semantic parsing and code-switching. In *Proceedings of the 21st Conference on Computational Natural Language Learning (CoNLL 2017)*, pages 379–389, Vancouver, Canada. Association for Computational Linguistics.

Chris Dyer, Victor Chahuneau, and Noah A. Smith. 2013. A simple, fast, and effective reparameterization of IBM model 2. In *Proceedings of the 2013 Conference of the North American Chapter of the Association for Computational Linguistics: Human Language Technologies*, pages 644–648, Atlanta, Georgia. Association for Computational Linguistics.

Kilian Evang and Johan Bos. 2016. Cross-lingual learning of an open-domain semantic parser. In *Proceedings of COLING 2016, the 26th International Conference on Computational Linguistics: Technical Papers*, pages 579–588, Osaka, Japan. The COLING 2016 Organizing Committee.

Sonal Gupta, Rushin Shah, Mrinal Mohit, Anuj Kumar, and Mike Lewis. 2018. Semantic parsing for task oriented dialog using hierarchical representations. *CoRR*.

Carolin Haas and Stefan Riezler. 2016. A corpus and semantic parser for multilingual natural language querying of OpenStreetMap. In *Proceedings of the 2016 Conference of the North American Chapter of the Association for Computational Linguistics: Human Language Technologies*, pages 740–750, San Diego, California. Association for Computational Linguistics.

Jeremy Howard and Sebastian Ruder. 2018. Universal language model fine-tuning for text classification. In *Proceedings of the 56th Annual Meeting of the Association for Computational Linguistics (Volume 1: Long Papers)*, pages 328–339, Melbourne, Australia. Association for Computational Linguistics.

Robin Jia and Percy Liang. 2016. Data recombination for neural semantic parsing. In *Proceedings of the 54th Annual Meeting of the Association for Computational Linguistics (Volume 1: Long Papers)*, pages 12–22, Berlin, Germany. Association for Computational Linguistics.

Bevan Jones, Mark Johnson, and Sharon Goldwater. 2012. Semantic parsing with Bayesian tree transducers. In *Proceedings of the 50th Annual Meeting of the Association for Computational Linguistics (Volume 1: Long Papers)*, pages 488–496, Jeju Island, Korea. Association for Computational Linguistics.

Yinhan Liu, Myle Ott, Naman Goyal, Jingfei Du, Mandar Joshi, Danqi Chen, Omer Levy, Mike Lewis, Luke Zettlemoyer, and Veselin Stoyanov. 2019. Roberta: A robustly optimized BERT pretraining approach. *CoRR*, abs/1907.11692.

Siva Reddy, Oscar Täckström, Slav Petrov, Mark Steedman, and Mirella Lapata. 2017. Universal semantic parsing. *CoRR*, abs/1702.03196.

Subendhu Rongali, Luca Soldaini, Emilio Monti, and Wael Hamza. 2020. Don't parse, generate! a sequence to sequence architecture for task-oriented semantic parsing. *arXiv preprint arXiv:2001.11458*.

Rico Sennrich, Barry Haddow, and Alexandra Birch. 2016. Neural machine translation of rare words with subword units. In *Proceedings of the 54th Annual Meeting of the Association for Computational Linguistics (Volume 1: Long Papers)*, pages 1715–1725, Berlin, Germany. Association for Computational Linguistics.

Raymond Hendy Susanto and Wei Lu. 2017. Neural architectures for multilingual semantic parsing. In *Proceedings of the 55th Annual Meeting of the Association for Computational Linguistics (Volume 2: Short Papers)*, pages 38–44, Vancouver, Canada. Association for Computational Linguistics.

Ilya Sutskever, Oriol Vinyals, and Quoc V Le. 2014. Sequence to sequence learning with neural networks. In *Advances in neural information processing systems*, pages 3104–3112.

Ashish Vaswani, Noam Shazeer, Niki Parmar, Jakob Uszkoreit, Llion Jones, Aidan N. Gomez, Lukasz Kaiser, and Illia Polosukhin. 2017. Attention is all you need. *CoRR*.

Oriol Vinyals, Meire Fortunato, and Navdeep Jaitly. 2015. Pointer networks. In C. Cortes, N. D. Lawrence, D. D. Lee, M. Sugiyama, and R. Garnett, editors, *Advances in Neural Information Processing Systems 28*, pages 2692–2700. Curran Associates, Inc.

Yushi Wang, Jonathan Berant, and Percy Liang. 2015. Building a semantic parser overnight. In *Proceedings of the 53rd Annual Meeting of the Association for Computational Linguistics and the 7th International Joint Conference on Natural Language Processing (Volume 1: Long Papers)*, pages 1332–1342, Beijing, China. Association for Computational Linguistics.

David Yarowsky, Grace Ngai, and Richard Wicentowski. 2001. Inducing multilingual text analysis tools via robust projection across aligned corpora. In *Proceedings of the First International Conference on Human Language Technology Research*.

John M. Zelle and Raymond J. Mooney. 1996. Learning to parse database queries using inductive logic programming. In *Proceedings of the Thirteenth National Conference on Artificial Intelligence - Volume 2*, AAAI'96, page 1050–1055. AAAI Press.

Luke S. Zettlemoyer and Michael Collins. 2005. Learning to map sentences to logical form: Structured classification with probabilistic categorial grammars. In *Proceedings of the Twenty-First Conference on Uncertainty in Artificial Intelligence*, UAI'05, page 658–666, Arlington, Virginia, USA. AUAI Press.

Victor Zhong, Caiming Xiong, and Richard Socher. 2017. Seq2sql: Generating structured queries from natural language using reinforcement learning. *CoRR*.

Script Parsing with Hierarchical Sequence Modelling

Fangzhou Zhai, Iza Škrjanec and **Alexander Koller**
Dept. of Language Science and Technology
Saarland Informatics Campus
Saarland University
{fzhai, skrjanec, koller}@coli.uni-saarland.de

Abstract

Scripts (Schank and Abelson, 1977) capture commonsense knowledge about everyday activities and their participants. Script knowledge has been shown to be useful in a number of NLP tasks, such as referent prediction, discourse classification, and story generation. A crucial step for the exploitation of script knowledge is ***script parsing***, the task of tagging a text with the events and participants from a certain activity. This task is challenging: it requires information both about the ways events and participants are usually realized in surface language as well as the order in which they occur in the world. We show how to do accurate script parsing with a hierarchical sequence model. Our model improves the state of the art of event parsing by over 16 points F-score and, for the first time, accurately tags script participants.

1 Introduction

Script knowledge is a category of common sense knowledge that describes how people conduct everyday activities sequentially (Schank and Abelson, 1977). Script knowledge of a specific **scenario**, e.g. GROCERY SHOPPING, includes the **events** that comprise the scenario, the **participants** involved, and the relations between them. Script knowledge is useful for various downstream NLP applications, such as referent prediction (Ahrendt and Demberg, 2016; Modi et al., 2017), discourse sense classification (Lee et al., 2020), story generation (Zhai et al., 2019, 2020).

Script parsing identifies pre-defined sets of script events and participants from surface text (see Figure 1). For a specific scenario, script parsing essentially boils down to determining what each verb and each NP (which we term **candidate**) refers to in the context of that scenario.

Script parsing is an under-investigated, complex task. It is highly contextualized and corresponds to each specific scenario. The task is challenging even for humans: the inter-annotator agreement is quite modest, at 0.64 and 0.77 Fleiss' κ for event and participant parsing, respectively (Modi et al., 2016). Various factors need to be taken into consideration for this task. (1) At the local level, the basic semantics of the candidates. (2) At the discourse level, the sequence of events and participants should sketch a reasonable agenda for the activity. For example, the events must occur in a feasible order; when an NP is a dependent of an adjacent verb, the predicted participant type must be one that participates in the predicted event. In Figure 1, the same verb *found* was assigned different event classes: ***found** bike pump* as *get tools* whereas ***found** a small glass shard* as *examine tire*. One would have to consider the arguments of the verb, and potentially where it appears in the story to make the decision: what happens after 'check' as *examine tire* is not likely to be *get tools*. Apart from the modelling difficulties, annotated corpora are quite limited in size, given the high cost. Many event / participant classes have less that 10 instances across these corpora, occasionally missing from a validation set generated by random split.

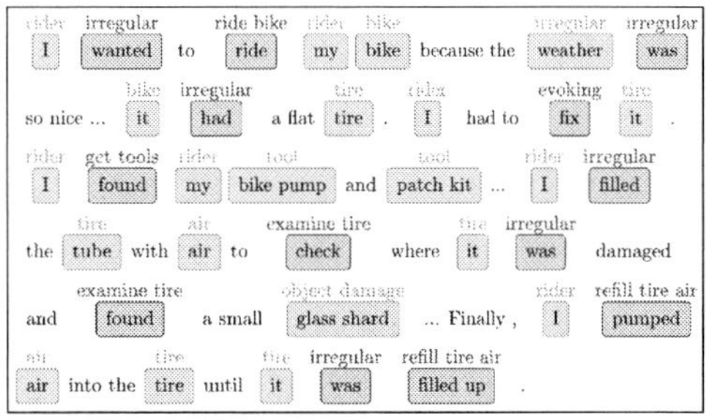

Figure 1: Descriptions of FIXING A FLAT TIRE from InScript. Script parsing identifies events and participants from surface text.

We contribute the following to the area of script

Proceedings of the 10th Conference on Lexical and Computational Semantics, pages 195–201
August 5–6, 2021, Bangkok, Thailand (online) ©2021 Association for Computational Linguistics

parsing: methodology-wise, **(1)** we propose a hierarchical sequence model, which learns patterns in different granularity levels with different sequence models. **(2)** We investigate data augmentation approaches to this task. In terms of results, **(3)** we achieve accurate participant parsing results for the first time and **(4)** improve the state of the art in event parsing by over 16 points F1-score.

2 Related Work

Theoretical considerations of scripts in AI (as described by Schank and Abelson, 1977; Barr and Feigenbaum, 1981) were analyzed in a wide coverage empirical study by Regneri et al. (2010), who crowdsourced event descriptions of several everyday activities (scenarios). They applied unsupervised methods to compute a graph representation of the script's temporal structure. As a direct extension, Modi et al. (2016) and Wanzare et al. (2016) collected the **InScript** and **DeScript** corpora of event descriptions and manually annotated the scenario-specific types of events and participants to accommodate aligning surface text with data-driven script knowledge. The goal is to identify spans of the text that refer to the events and participants that are typically involved in a script. For the case of the script about fixing a bike, the typical events include riding a bike, noticing a flat tire, getting tools, repairing the tire and testing it. These events and participants are pre-defined for each activity and the task is to label the tokens with these abstract classes, whereby the surface forms vary.

The model by Ostermann et al. (2017) is the state of the art for event parsing over InScript which was formulated as a sequence tagging task. The authors used a linear CRF to identify the script events. Its features include syntax, FrameNet (Ruppenhofer et al., 2006) features, pre-trained word embeddings and a number of script-related features encoding script-specific aspects like event order.

Our work shares many similarities with Berant et al. (2014). To do question answering in the biological domain, they first build a graph representation of events, participants and their relations given a text about a biological process. Token spans that denote an occurrence of an event are considered event triggers. However, unlike our approach, these events are not based on a pre-defined set. They separately train a model for identifying event triggers and a model for finding plausible argument candidates. The features used rely on syntax, semantic roles and some external domain resources. In contrast, we propose a model that jointly learns how to identify as well as label events and participants.

Much of the previous work on inferring script knowledge from text is focused around completing an event chain by predicting the missing event (Chambers and Jurafsky, 2008; Jans et al., 2012; Pichotta and Mooney, 2014; Rudinger et al., 2015), the missing text (Bisk et al., 2019) or both (Pichotta and Mooney, 2016). These approaches consider surface forms of event verbs and syntactic relation types of their arguments (*subj*, *obj*), while our task operates on abstract event and participant types.

3 Method

3.1 Data and Pre-processing

Our work is based on two English corpora, InScript and DeScript. InScript (Modi et al., 2016) includes around 100 stories about each of 10 daily activities (scenarios), e.g., GOING GROCERY SHOPPING, TAKING A BATH, and RIDING IN A PUBLIC BUS. The corpus annotates surface text with event and participant classes, and specifies the candidates according to their syntactic dependency (see Figure 1 for an excerpt from InScript). DeScript (Wanzare et al., 2016) includes, among others, 50 process descriptions for each of the 10 scenarios in InScript. These process descriptions are telegram-style short phrases, like '*Find hole in tire. Plug hole. Find tire pump. Insert tire pump into tire. Pump tire until full of air*'. The events in these texts are annotated with the same set of labels as InScript. DeScript has no participant annotations. We mainly perform experiments on InScript, whereas DeScript is used as auxiliary training data.

For each of the 10 scenarios in the InScript corpus, the authors (Modi et al., 2016) designed prototypical scenario-specific event and participant classes. For example, the story about FIXING A FLAT TIRE in Figure 1 shows that typically this activity includes a bike rider, a bike, tools and a tire. These participants are involved in the events of riding a bike, getting tools, fixing the tire, and checking it.

Following Ostermann et al. (2017), we distinguish between **regular events**, events corresponding to the crucial steps of the respective scenario, and **irregular events**, the ones that take place in the course of the story, but are not directly related to the scenario's core event chain. For example, in Figure 1, *the weather* ***was*** *nice* is considered an irregular event as it does not directly relate to the core steps of the scenario, fixing a flat tire. We collapse the classes UNREL, RELNSCR, OTHER and UNKNOWN into a single irregular event class for each scenario. 12,902 (33.5%) events in InScript are regular, whereas 4,185 (89.1%) events in DeScript are regular. We also distinguish **regular participants** from **irregular participants** in a similar manner. The identification of irregular candidates is a crucial component of a script parser, as naturally occurring text very often includes such content, making the text more interesting and personal.

The 10 scenarios vary in complexity (TAKING A BATH VS. FLYING IN AN AIRPLANE) and specificity (RIDING A PUBLIC BUS VS. REPAIRING A FLAT TIRE). This is reflected in the class sizes of regular events and regular participants. On average, each scenario has 19.2 regular event and 18.9 regular participant classes. TAKING A FLIGHT has the largest class sizes for events and participants (29 and 26, respectively), while PLANTING A TREE has the smallest (14 and 15, respectively).

3.2 Model

We train a scenario agnostic model that parses all InScript scenarios. Thus our model implicitly contains a *scenario detection* model, which determines the scenario that a piece of text is about. Our model consists of two sequence models: **(1)** a **word sequence model** that captures how each event and participant is usually realized in surface language, and **(2)** an **event sequence model** that operates on the event level, which models the sequence of events and participants to capture procedural script knowledge.

The Hierarchical Model. Figure 2 shows the model architecture. The model takes as input a story x from corpus d, an ordered set of indices I that specifies the positions of the candidates. It assigns an event / participant label to each of these candidates as output. These labels are pre-defined in InScript and specific to each scenario. The set of candidates consists of all NPs and verbs in the text. We use the InScript tokens as annotated in it; yet they could also be extracted with a syntactic parser.

The **word sequence model** encodes the entire story with pre-trained contextualized word embeddings into a list of vectors (we use *xlnet-base-cased*

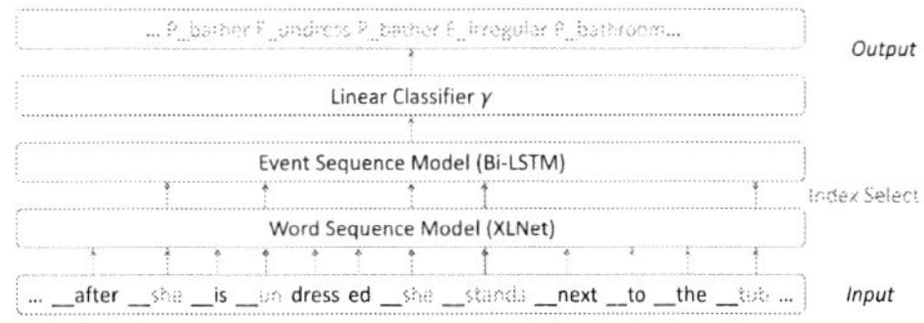

Figure 2: The model architecture. Note that index selection is performed before the Bi-LSTM layer.

(Yang et al., 2019)):

$$\tilde{x} = \text{XLNet}(x) \quad (1)$$

Next, to accommodate sequence modelling at the discourse level, we only keep the representations in $\tilde{x}$ that corresponds to the candidates, namely, the NP heads and the verbs. Their positions in $\tilde{x}$ are specified by the ordered set of indices I. We directly take the vector representation of these tokens and ignore the rest to form a sub-sequence of $\tilde{x}$. This operation is termed **index_select** in the Pytorch library:

$$c = \tilde{x}.index\_select(I) \quad (2)$$

Now, we apply the event sequence model ψ (a Bi-LSTM) on it, to yield the features $\tilde{c}$ for linear classifier γ, to generates a distribution over the labels for each token:

$$p(y|x, I; \theta_\psi, \theta_\gamma) = softmax(\gamma_{\theta_\gamma}(\psi_{\theta_\psi}(c))) \quad (3)$$

The model is trained by optimizing data likelihood:

$$\theta^* = \underset{\theta_\psi, \theta_\gamma}{\text{argmax}} \sum_{x,I} log(p(y|x, I; \theta_\psi, \theta_\gamma)) \quad (4)$$

3.3 Addressing Data Sparsity

The class distribution is skewed. Some classes are quite small: the largest regular event class has 397 instances (e.g., *get groceries* in GROCERY SHOPPING), whereas there are 26 classes with less than 10 instances (e.g., *get receipt* in GROCERY SHOPPING, *scalp massage* in TAKING A BATH), which means they are hard to learn reliably. Our efforts to address this are two-fold.

Domain Adaptation. Firstly, we use DeScript as additional training data. We experiment with two domain adaptation methods. Most straightforwardly, **(1)** *Data concatenates*, which concatenates DeScript with the original InScript train set. Having noticed InScript and DeScript varying greatly in

Index	Model	Train set	Events		Participants	
			Macro-F1	Micro-F1	Macro-F1	Micro-F1
1.	*Ostermann*	In	58.1	66.0	n/a	n/a
2.	*fine-tuned XLNet*	In	62.1^{1}	79.3^{1}	79.7^{345}	77.2
3.	*no_index_select*	In	63.3^{1}	78.3^{1}	74.3	87.1^{2}
4.	*hierarchical*	In	70.1^{123}	83.7^{123}	78.7^{3}	89.3^{23}
5.	*concatenate*	In, De	69.3^{123}	82.5^{123}	79.1^{3}	89.9^{23}
6.	*corpus_embedding*	In, De	74.9^{12345}	82.9^{123}	78.6^{3}	89.4^{23}
7.	*hierarchical*^{BT}	In, BT	**75.1**^{1234568}	**85.7**^{1234568}	80.3^{123456}	**90.3**^{1234568}
8.	*corpus_embedding*^{BT}	In, De, BT	74.3^{12345}	83.8^{123456}	**80.9**^{123456}	89.5^{12345}

$^{1-8}$: performance improvement over the respective model is significant at $\alpha = 0.05$ according to independent T-test.

Table 1: Results. The highest metrics in each column are displayed in boldface. Thanks to a larger training set, the optimization of **7.** and **8.** are quite stable, thus its performance difference compared to others can be significant despite small margins.

the style of their language, we also perform explicit domain modelling with **(2)** *Corpus embedding*. We follow Stymne et al. (2018) to train a vector representation (the **corpus embedding**) for each corpus to capture corpus-specific patterns. We concatenate the corpus representation with each candidate representation, to substitute the input term ($\psi_{\theta_\psi}(c)$) to the linear classifier γ with

$$\tilde{c} = \psi_{\theta_\psi}(c; \eta_{\theta_\eta}(d)) \quad (5)$$

Here $\eta(\cdot)$ denotes the corpus embeddings.

Data Augmentation. Secondly, we augment InScript via back-translation (Bojar and Tamchyna, 2011; Sennrich et al., 2016; Xie et al., 2020) to paraphrase the original data and help the model generalize better over the surface text. The stories are translated to French and back with Google Translate. The participant and event annotations are mapped to the paraphrases according to heuristics based on word-level semantics and string matching. The new data was concatenated with the original InScript and both were treated as a single domain. See the appendix for more implementation details[1]. In the example below, the event verb takes a different tense and surface form in the back-translation.

O : when I_{rider} was $riding_{ride}$ my_{rider} $bike_{bike}$ this past summer

Fr : l'été dernier, je montais mon vélo

BT : when I_{rider} $rode_{ride}$ my_{rider} $bike_{bike}$ this summer

[1]Our code, data and virtual environment are shared at `https://github.com/coli-saar/SSP_sem`.

4 Experiments

4.1 Ablations and Baselines

We randomly split (80/10/10) InScript by entire stories to create the train/val/test sets. We have two external baselines: (1) the SotA model from Ostermann et al. (2017); (2) a fine-tuned XLNet, for which we train a linear classifier, apart from tuning its pre-trained parameters. As for our models, *Hierarchical* is the hierarchical model described by formulas (1)-(4). For *no_index_select*, we ablate the index selection (thus $c = x$) to neutralize the event sequence model. Its event sequence model now takes every token of the story as input, and still operates on the token level. The variants *concatenate* and *corpus_embedding* exploit DeScript with respective domain adaptation methods.

4.2 Results

The results are shown in Table 1. A fine-tuned XLNet already outperforms *Ostermann*. Yet our model variants deliver further, substantial improvements. All our models outperform *Ostermann* by a considerable margin, on both event macro and micro F1. We also see that all micro-F1s are noticeably higher than the respective macro-F1s. This difference is due to the data including many small classes that are in general harder to learn.

hierarchical see substantial improvements over *no_index_select*, which fails to perform sequence modelling at the discourse level. We also note that *hierarchical* improved both micro-F1s. Analysis shows that the hierarchical models are generally better at addressing the most frequent yet problematic class, the irregular candidates. These candidates do not participate in the core event chain, a decision better made after taking the structure of the candidate sequences into consideration. That is exactly the job of our event sequence model.

Participant parsing yields much higher scores than event parsing. The reason is, a large proportion of errors come from the *irregular* candidates (see also Section 5). However, irregular participants (19.6%) are proportionally fewer than irregular events (66.5%). Moreover, a lot of participant candidates refer to the protagonist (31.0%), an easy class usually realized with first person pronouns, making participant parsing generally easier.

For the variants that performs domain adaptation, *corpus_embedding* is clearly a better way to exploit DeScript, due to the apparent difference between the language styles of both corpora. *hierarchical*^{BT} sees a larger improvement over *hierarchical* as it has paraphrased InScript as additional training data, which is larger and a more similar domain than DeScript to InScript. These improvements over *hierarchical* are more prominent in event macro-F1s, which means these models are generally better at tagging smaller event classes, achieving our original goal to alleviate the issues caused by the uneven class sizes. Further addition of DeScript on top of *hierarchical*^{BT} (model 8.) does not yield further significant improvement, but sees, overall, a modest performance drop: with the addition of back-translated data thus a larger, relatively homogeneous training set, the domain difference between DeScript and InScript is beginning to outweigh the benefit of having DeScript.

5 Error Analysis

We manually classified the validation set errors made by our best-performing model, *hierarchical*^{BT}, case by case. A breakdown is presented in Table 2.

Noisy Corpus Labels. The corpus annotations of these instances are possibly incorrect. This is quite common, given the complexity (thus the moderate inter-annotator agreement) of the task. For example, in a story about BORROWING A BOOK FROM A LIBRARY, ... *I had to* ***get*** *a library card* ... is a clear match for the event *obtain card*, as is predicted by our model; but in the corpus it was annotated as 'irregular', a mistake probably due to the light verb 'get' seemingly irrelevant to the scenario at first glance by the original annotator.

False Positives of *irregular*. A large proportion of errors feature a wrongly predicted *irregular*. We identified two main sources of such errors: (1) small class sizes; (2) instances that are particularly difficult because pragmatic inference is needed to make the right decision. As an example, ... ***get*** *materials for the assignment* ... corresponds to the event class *evoking_library*, i.e. it evokes the scenario of BORROWING A BOOK FROM A LIBRARY without explicitly referring to a scenario event. However, without taking the situational context of the scenario into consideration, it cannot be inferred that '***get*** *materials for the assignment*' actually means '*borrow a book from a library*'.

Wrong Category. A small number of events are tagged as participants and vice versa, e.g. some homonyms of verbs and nouns (*board* or *love*).

Type	Events	Participants
Noisy corpus label	23%	26%
False irregular predictions	49%	37%
Wrong category	2%	4%
Others	26%	33%

Table 2: A breakdown of the error types.

6 Conclusion

We present the first model that achieves high performance on both event and participant parsing. The model adopts a hierarchical design to model both the sequence of tokens and the sequence of script events and participants. Further exploitation of domain adaptation and data augmentation methods yields a substantial performance boost. This work has established methods to accurately parse both script events and participants, in a supervised learning framework. Our next step is approaching this complex task with less supervision, to lift the requirement on finely-annotated data, thus enabling wide-coverage script parsing.

Acknowledgments

We thank Simon Ostermann for providing the data from his experiments and his help all along the way of re-implementing his model. We thank Vera Demberg for the useful comments and suggestions. We also thank the anonymous reviewers for the valuable comments. This research was funded by the German Research Foundation (DFG) as part of SFB 1102 (Project-ID 232722074) "Information Density and Linguistic Encoding".

References

Simon Ahrendt and Vera Demberg. 2016. Improving event prediction by representing script participants. In *Proceedings of the 2016 Conference of the North American Chapter of the Association for Computational Linguistics: Human Language Technologies*, pages 546–551.

Avron Barr and Edward Feigenbaum. 1981. *The Handbook of Artificial Intelligence: Volume 2*. William Kaufman Inc, Los Altos, CA.

Jonathan Berant, Vivek Srikumar, Pei-Chun Chen, Abby Vander Linden, Brittany Harding, Brad Huang, Peter Clark, and Christopher D. Manning. 2014. Modeling biological processes for reading comprehension. In *Proceedings of the 2014 Conference on Empirical Methods in Natural Language Processing (EMNLP)*, pages 1499–1510, Doha, Qatar. Association for Computational Linguistics.

Yonatan Bisk, Jan Buys, Karl Pichotta, and Yejin Choi. 2019. Benchmarking hierarchical script knowledge. In *Proceedings of the 2019 Conference of the North American Chapter of the Association for Computational Linguistics: Human Language Technologies, Volume 1 (Long and Short Papers)*, pages 4077–4085.

Ondřej Bojar and Aleš Tamchyna. 2011. Improving translation model by monolingual data. In *Proceedings of the Sixth Workshop on Statistical Machine Translation*, pages 330–336, Edinburgh, Scotland. Association for Computational Linguistics.

Nathanael Chambers and Dan Jurafsky. 2008. Unsupervised learning of narrative event chains. *Proceedings of ACL-08: HLT*, pages 789–797.

Bram Jans, Steven Bethard, Ivan Vulić, and Marie Francine Moens. 2012. Skip n-grams and ranking functions for predicting script events. In *Proceedings of the 13th Conference of the European Chapter of the Association for Computational Linguistics*, pages 336–344, Avignon, France. Association for Computational Linguistics.

I-Ta Lee, Maria Leonor Pacheco, and Dan Goldwasser. 2020. Weakly-supervised modeling of contextualized event embedding for discourse relations. In *Findings of the Association for Computational Linguistics: EMNLP 2020*, pages 4962–4972, Online. Association for Computational Linguistics.

Ashutosh Modi, Tatjana Anikina, Simon Ostermann, and Manfred Pinkal. 2016. Inscript: Narrative texts annotated with script information. In *Proceedings of the Tenth International Conference on Language Resources and Evaluation (LREC'16)*, pages 3485–3493.

Ashutosh Modi, Ivan Titov, Vera Demberg, Asad Sayeed, and Manfred Pinkal. 2017. Modeling semantic expectation: Using script knowledge for referent prediction. *Transactions of the Association for Computational Linguistics*, 5:31–44.

Simon Ostermann, Michael Roth, Stefan Thater, and Manfred Pinkal. 2017. Aligning script events with narrative texts. In *Proceedings of the 6th Joint Conference on Lexical and Computational Semantics (* SEM 2017)*, pages 128–134.

Karl Pichotta and Raymond Mooney. 2014. Statistical script learning with multi-argument events. In *Proceedings of the 14th Conference of the European Chapter of the Association for Computational Linguistics*, pages 220–229, Gothenburg, Sweden. Association for Computational Linguistics.

Karl Pichotta and Raymond J. Mooney. 2016. Using sentence-level LSTM language models for script inference. In *Proceedings of the 54th Annual Meeting of the Association for Computational Linguistics (Volume 1: Long Papers)*, pages 279–289, Berlin, Germany. Association for Computational Linguistics.

Michaela Regneri, Alexander Koller, and Manfred Pinkal. 2010. Learning script knowledge with web experiments. In *Proceedings of the 48th Annual Meeting of the Association for Computational Linguistics*, pages 979–988.

Rachel Rudinger, Pushpendre Rastogi, Francis Ferraro, and Benjamin Van Durme. 2015. Script induction as language modeling. In *Proceedings of the 2015 Conference on Empirical Methods in Natural Language Processing*, pages 1681–1686, Lisbon, Portugal. Association for Computational Linguistics.

Josef Ruppenhofer, Michael Ellsworth, Myriam Schwarzer-Petruck, Christopher R Johnson, and Jan Scheffczyk. 2006. Framenet ii: Extended theory and practice.

Roger C Schank and Robert P Abelson. 1977. *Scripts, plans, goals, and understanding: An inquiry into human knowledge structures*. Psychology Press.

Rico Sennrich, Barry Haddow, and Alexandra Birch. 2016. Improving neural machine translation models with monolingual data. In *Proceedings of the 54th Annual Meeting of the Association for Computational Linguistics (Volume 1: Long Papers)*, pages 86–96, Berlin, Germany. Association for Computational Linguistics.

Sara Stymne, Miryam de Lhoneux, Aaron Smith, and Joakim Nivre. 2018. Parser training with heterogeneous treebanks. In *Proceedings of the 56th Annual Meeting of the Association for Computational Linguistics (Volume 2: Short Papers)*, pages 619–625, Melbourne, Australia. Association for Computational Linguistics.

Lilian DA Wanzare, Alessandra Zarcone, Stefan Thater, and Manfred Pinkal. 2016. Descript: A crowd-sourced database of event sequence descriptions for the acquisition of high-quality script knowledge. In *Proceedings of the Tenth International Conference on Language Resources and Evaluation (LREC'16)*, pages 3494–3501.

Qizhe Xie, Zihang Dai, Eduard Hovy, Thang Luong, and Quoc Le. 2020. Unsupervised data augmentation for consistency training. In *Advances in Neural Information Processing Systems*, volume 33, pages 6256–6268. Curran Associates, Inc.

Zhilin Yang, Zihang Dai, Yiming Yang, Jaime Carbonell, Russ R Salakhutdinov, and Quoc V Le. 2019. Xlnet: Generalized autoregressive pretraining for language understanding. In *Advances in neural information processing systems*, pages 5753–5763.

Fangzhou Zhai, Vera Demberg, and Alexander Koller. 2020. Story generation with rich details. In *Proceedings of the 28th International Conference on Computational Linguistics*, pages 2346–2351, Barcelona, Spain (Online). International Committee on Computational Linguistics.

Fangzhou Zhai, Vera Demberg, Pavel Shkadzko, Wei Shi, and Asad Sayeed. 2019. A hybrid model for globally coherent story generation. In *Proceedings of the Second Workshop on Storytelling*, pages 34–45, Florence, Italy. Association for Computational Linguistics.

Incorporating EDS Graph for AMR Parsing

Ziyi SHOU and **Fangzhen LIN**
Department of Computer Science
The Hong Kong University of Science and Technology
{zshou,flin}@cse.ust.hk

Abstract

AMR (Abstract Meaning Representation) and EDS (Elementary Dependency Structures) are two popular meaning representations in NLP/NLU. AMR is more abstract and conceptual, while EDS is more low level, closer to the lexical structures of the given sentences. It is thus not surprising that EDS parsing is easier than AMR parsing. In this work, we consider using information from EDS parsing to help improve the performance of AMR parsing. We adopt a transition-based parser and propose to add EDS graphs as additional semantic features using a graph encoder composed of LSTM layer and GCN layer. Our experimental results show that the additional information from EDS parsing indeed gives a boost to the performance of the base AMR parser used in our experiments.

1 Introduction

Semantic parsing has long been considered a difficult task and an important step to natural language understanding. A number of meaning representation formalisms have been proposed. Well-known ones include EDS (Elementary Dependency Structures; Oepen and Lønning, 2006), UCCA (Universal Conceptual Cognitive Annotation; Abend and Rappoport, 2013), and AMR (Abstract Meaning Representation; Banarescu et al., 2013). Among them, AMR is more abstract from surface tokens and tries to capture the meaning of a sentence using concepts that may not appear in the sentence. If one views an AMR encoding as a graph, the AMR graph is always composed of fewer nodes than other meaning representations and some nodes in the AMR graph cannot be anchored to tokens or strings of tokens in the sentence. But EDS tries to build a meaning representation using lexical terms that are presented in the sentence, and nodes in their parse trees are anchored. In comparison, AMR has a much more fine-grained classification for the named entities, total of 124 entity types (Lin and Xue, 2019). Thus not surprisingly, AMR parsers do not perform as well as the ones for EDS. Currently the parsing accuracies for AMR are in low 80s, while they can be high 90s for EDS. In this paper, we propose to use EDS improve the performance of the AMR parser.

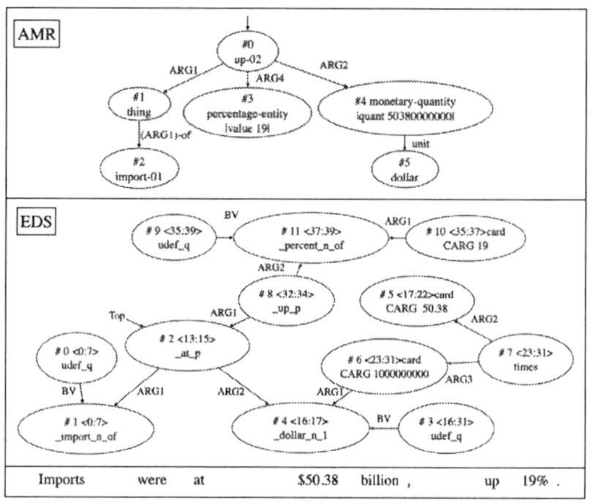

Figure 1: AMR and EDS graph for "Imports were at \$50.38 billion, up 19%.", #20011008 sentence from the WSJ Corpus, Penn Treebank (Marcus et al., 1993). Take node #3 in AMR as an example. "percentage-entity" is the node label, "value" is the property of this node, and "19" is the specific value. For node #10 in EDS, "<35:37>" indicates the span of the corresponding surface string; "card" is the node label, "CARG" which means "constant argument" is the property, and "19" is the value.

To see how information from EDS parsing can be of use to AMR, consider the following sentence "Imports were at \$50.38 billion, up 19%." from the Wall Street Journal Corpus, Penn Treebank (Marcus et al., 1993). Its graph encodings in AMR and EDS are shown in Figure 1. We mentioned that AMR is more abstract. This can be seen in the

Proceedings of the 10th Conference on Lexical and Computational Semantics, pages 202–211
August 5–6, 2021, Bangkok, Thailand (online) ©2021 Association for Computational Linguistics

example as the graph for AMR is a lot smaller, and the nodes are labeled with conceptual entities. Nevertheless, EDS and AMR edges are labeled using the same semantic roles (e.g., ARG1, ARG2), indicating the relationship between a predicate and its arguments (Lin and Xue, 2019). In this example, there are some correspondences between their nodes. For example, the AMR nodes *"percentage-entity"*, *"dollar"*, and *"import-01"* correspond to the EDS nodes *"_percent_n_of"*, *"_dollar_n_1"*, and *"_import_n_of"*, respectively. In our task, the most important feature of EDS is anchoring. From the EDS graph, each node has a corresponding span of text. Conversely, we can find all related EDS nodes for each token based on the indexes. This suggests that EDS parsing may serve as an intermediate to AMR parsing, which motivated this work.

To incorporate EDS parsing into an AMR parser, we propose an EDS encoder composed of LSTM networks that capture the contextual information and a Graph Convolutional Network (GCN, Kipf and Welling, 2017) that extracts the structure knowledge. We feed EDS into our proposed encoder and produce token-level features. These EDS token-level features are concatenated to word embedding of tokens and participate in the AMR parsing process. To demonstrate the effectiveness of our approach, we use the AMR dataset from MRP 2019 (Oepen et al., 2019) and take as our baseline model the HIT-SCIR (Che et al., 2019), which was the best overall system at MRP 2019 and the 2nd best for AMR. Our experimental results show that our EDS-enhanced parsers clearly outperform the baseline model. In fact, some of our new models beat the best score of the official submitted AMR parsers in this benchmark. We also observed that the biggest improvements happened to be on those test data that are least similar to the training data.

The rest of this paper is organized as follows: Second 2 gives a brief overview on AMR parsers; Section 3 is concerned with the baseline system we adopt and our EDS-enhanced model. We present experimental settings and experimental results in Section 4 and conclude in Section 5.

2 Related Work

We classify AMR parsing systems into grammar-based, graph-based, and transition-based ones. The grammar-based ones generate AMR graphs directly from grammar trees. Several early AMR parsing systems were of this type. For example, Artzi et al. (2015) used combinatory categorial grammar (CCG) parsing to construct AMR, while Peng et al. (2015) made use of synchronous Hyperedge Replacement Grammar (SHRG). Generally speaking, grammar-based ones suffer from information loss during the processes of both grammar tree generation and AMR conversion. They predated the current deep learning approaches.

Modern AMR parsers use deep learning methods. Depending on how the eventual AMR graphs are generated, we can divide them into graph-based and transition-based. Both approaches are popular and their performances are competitive. Briefly, a graph-based system splits AMR parsing into two tasks, concept identification and edge prediction, and then combines them to generate a final AMR graph. The idea seems to appear first in Flanigan et al. (2014), and is used in Lyu and Titov (2018); Zhang et al. (2019a); Cai and Lam (2020); Zhou et al. (2020). A transition-based system, however, uses a sequence of transition actions to construct the graph incrementally. We can include the systems in Wang et al. (2015); Ballesteros and Al-Onaizan (2017); Naseem et al. (2019); Che et al. (2019); Astudillo et al. (2020) in this category.

As we mentioned, our work is about incorporating EDS information into AMR parsing. We note that Brandt et al. (2016) considered adding preposition semantic role labeling to an AMR parser but found that the extra information did not seem to help. Hershcovich and Arviv (2019) used a multi-task learning model but found multi-task TUPA consistently falls behind the single-task one for AMR. Arviv et al. (2020) used multi-task learning on EDS and UCCA parsing, however, EDS didn't bring any benefits to UCCA parsing. Adding extra semantic information like EDS is not easy. It matters how EDS graphs are encoded and incorporated into AMR parsing. We conduct our work with the AMR dataset from MRP 2019, and pick one of the best performing systems there, HIT-SCIR (Che et al., 2019), as our baseline model. Our experimental results show that adding EDS information can indeed give a significant boost to the baseline model. We believe our method is general and can be applied to other AMR parsing systems.

3 Model

3.1 Baseline: A Transition-based Parser

Our baseline model is a transition-based system HIT-SCIR (Che et al., 2019). However, in our experiments, we use BERT-base instead of BERT-large for word embeddings (Devlin et al., 2019) due to our constraints on computing resources. Nevertheless, when the BERT-base baseline model is enhanced with EDS information, it still outperforms the best AMR parser at MRP 2019.

Task Formalization The main task of a transition-based model is to generate a sequence of actions to construct an AMR graph. The sequence of actions is predicted one at a time, and the graph is also constructed incrementally.

A state in HIT-SCIR is a tuple (S, L, B, E, V), where S is a stack holding processed words, L is a list holding tokens popped out of S that will be pushed back in the future, and B is a buffer holding tokens waiting to be processed. E is the sets of labeled dependency edges and V is a set of graph nodes include concept nodes and surface tokens. The initial state of AMR parser was $([0], [\ ], [w_1, \dots, w_n], [\ ], V)$, where V only contains surface tokens. During parsing, each token should be parsed individually, and AMR nodes and edges would be generated through the selection of actions. The final state should be $([0], [\ ], [\ ], E, V')$, where list L and buffer B is empty.

Oracle An action sequence bridges the input sentence and the AMR graph. So the basic requirement for the transition-based method is alignments. Given a gold AMR graph and alignments, one can convert the graph to an action sequence for model training. For each state s, HIT-SCIR decides one of the actions to apply and this is what we called *oracle* parser. To solve the problem of parsing concept nodes from surface strings, HIT-SCIR extends the basic oracle following previous work (Liu et al., 2018). The transition inventory is the following:

- MERGE is to connect the top two tokens in the buffer to a single token waiting for being converted to a concept node.

- CONFIRM$_X$ is for converting the top element of buffer to a concept node X.

- NEW$_X$ generates a new node X and pushing into the buffer.

- ENTITY$_X$ does the same thing as CONFIRM$_X$ but adding internal properties of entity X, such as *year* of a *date-entity*.

- LEFT-EDGE$_X$ and RIGHT-EDGE$_X$ add an edge with label X between w_j and w_i, where w_i is the top element of stack and w_j is the top element of buffer. But they can be performed only when the top of buffer is a concept node.

- SHIFT is performed when no dependency exists between w_j and any word in S other than w_i, which pushes all words in list and w_j into stack S. It is only allowed to perform when the top of buffer is a concept node.

- REDUCE is performed only when w_i has head and is not the head or child of any word in buffer, which pops w_i out of stack.

- PASS will be chosen when neither SHIFT or REDUCE can be performed, which moves w_i to the front of list.

- DROP pops the top of buffer when it is a token.

- FINISH pops the root node and marks the state as terminal.

Stack-LSTM HIT-SCIR follows Ballesteros and Al-Onaizan (2017) and uses Stack-LSTM to model AMR states. The output vector of this LSTM will consider the stack pointer instead of the rightmost position of the sequence.

The system models S, L, B and action history with multiple stack-LSTMs, which supports PUSH and POP operations. Parsing states from multiple stack LSTMs are fed into the action oracle classifier at once. The possibility of action under state s is calculated as

$$p(a|s) = \frac{\exp\{g_a \cdot \text{STACK LSTM}(s) + b_a\}}{\sum_{a' \in \mathcal{A}} \exp\{g_{a'} \cdot \text{STACK LSTM}(s) + b_{a'}\}}$$

where the set $\mathcal{A}$ represents the actions listed in the previous paragraph; STACK LSTM(s) encodes the state s into a vector, g_a is the embedding of action a and b_a is the bias vector for action.

In our model, items in S, L and B are the combined embedding of tokens that concatenate the original BERT word embeddings and EDS encoding for the tokens, introduced in the following section.

3.2 EDS Incorporation

In order to incorporate the EDS annotation information in the AMR parsing, we extend the EDS graph to include tokens. We feed the extended EDS graph to our proposed EDS encoder and obtain token-level EDS features. Afterward, we concatenate token-level EDS features with word embedding and input them into the transition-based model.

EDS Extension Each node in the EDS graph has an explicit many-to-many anchoring onto substrings of the input sentence. It means that corresponding related EDS nodes for each token can be found based on the nodes' span. Therefore, we add a bottom layer consisting of the input sentence tokens. In this way, the updated embedding of tokens in this layer can be extracted as EDS features for each token.

In the preprocessing, the edges labeled as *contain* are added between token nodes and original nodes if their spans of strings intersect. Figure 2 is the example of an updated EDS graph for the sentence "*Not this year.*", #20010002 from WSJ. We only care about EDS labels in our experiments. We show *contain* edges as dash lines and original edges as solid lines. In Figure 2, the bottom

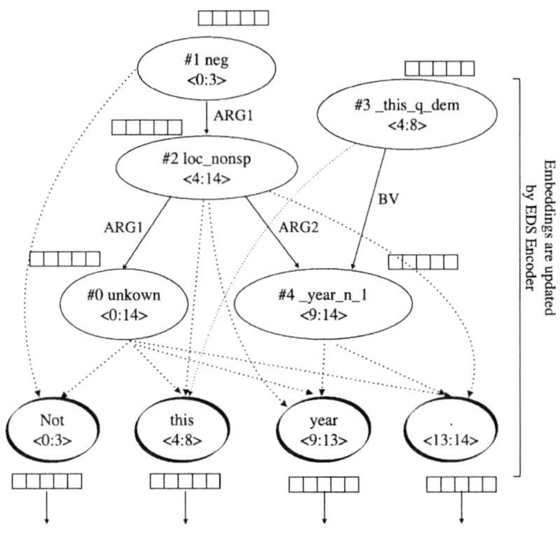

Figure 2: Example for adding *contain* edges in EDS graph. The bottom layer is the token nodes we add to the EDS graph. After EDS encoding, embeddings of token nodes are extracted and combined with original word embedding as extra semantic features.

four nodes are token nodes, whose embeddings are used as EDS features. For token node v_t, the hidden state at layer k is $h_{v_t}^k$. The calculation details can be found in the following paragraph. BERT splits each token into several pieces. The system extracts the first piece as its word embedding, denoted as BERT(t). Therefore, for each token t, we get embedding from two parts, BERT embedding BERT(t) and final hidden state h_{v_t} of corresponding new added node v_t. Then the concatenation of two vectors (BERT$(t)\|h_{v_t}$) would be pushed in the buffer, waiting for the next step of processing.

EDS Encoder The emergence of neural networks has had tremendous impacts on many fields, including graph data parsing systems. GCNs (Kipf and Welling, 2017; Marcheggiani and Titov, 2017) have emerged to be the neural networks of choice for encoding graphs. Our proposed EDS encoder consists of an LSTM layer to capture context information and GCN layers to encode structural knowledge.

EDS represents the meaning of a sentence in a directed graph where nodes represent logical predicates and edges to labeled arguments. The definition of EDS is $\mathcal{G} = \{\mathcal{V}, \mathcal{E}, L_{\mathcal{V}}, L_{\mathcal{E}}\}$ where $\mathcal{V}$ is a set of nodes (v, ℓ_v), $\mathcal{E}$ is a set of edges (v_i, v_j, ℓ_e) and $L_{\mathcal{V}}$, $L_{\mathcal{E}}$ are vocabularies for node labels and edge labels respectively.

To reinforce relations between nodes through layers, we add *self* edges (v_i, v_i) for every node in the graph and inverted edges (v_j, v_i) with label *inv_*ℓ_e for each directed edge (v_i, v_j) with label ℓ_e, including the new added *contain* edges. Therefore, $\mathcal{G}$ becomes $\{\mathcal{V}', \mathcal{E}', L_{\mathcal{V}'}, L_{\mathcal{E}'}\}$. $\mathcal{V}' = \mathcal{V} \cup \mathcal{T}$, where $\mathcal{T}$ is the set of token nodes. $\mathcal{E}' = \mathcal{E} \cup \{contain, self\} \cup \mathcal{I}$, where $\mathcal{I}$ is the set of inverted edges.

The goal of our EDS encoder is to update representation of each node considering the whole EDS graph. First, we adopt GCN to update word embedding based on their neighbors. Directed edges in the EDS graph represent the relationship of nodes, so we make the same assumption that the GCN parameters are label-specific as Marcheggiani and Titov (2017). Therefore, we calculate the hidden state of node v at k-th layer h_v^k as:

$$h_v^k = ReLU\left(\sum_{u \in \mathcal{N}(v)} W_{L(u,v)}^{(k-1)} h_u^{(k-1)} + b_{L(u,v)}^{(k-1)}\right)$$

where $\mathcal{N}(v)$ represents the neighbor nodes of v; ReLU is the rectifier linear unit activation function. However, to reduce the size of parameters and simplify the calculation, we classify edges into three kinds: *self* edge, edges in the original direction including *contain* and inverted edges. Therefore, instead of using $W_{L(u,v)}$, we define them as $W_{L(u,v)} = V_{dir(u,v)}$, where $dir(u, v)$ specifies the kind of edge.

EDS annotation in this experiment is automatically generated by EDS parser, so accepting all information from the EDS graph is risky. To solve this problem, we adopt gate schema. We calculate a scalar gate for each edge node pair in the form as:

$$g_{u,v}^{k} = \sigma\left(\hat{v}_{dir(u,v)}^{k} h_{u}^{k} + \hat{b}_{L(u,v)}^{k}\right)$$

where σ is the logistic sigmoid function; $\hat{v}_{dir(u,v)}^{k}$ and $\hat{b}_{L(u,v)}^{k}$ are weights and a bias for the gate. Therefore, the final formalism of the hidden state calculation is:

$$h_v^k = ReLU\Big(\sum_{u \in \mathcal{N}(v)} g_{u,v}^{(k-1)} (V_{dir(u,v)}^{(k-1)} h_u^{(k-1)} + b_{L(u,v)}^{(k-1)})\Big).$$

GCN introduced so far learns effective representation on the structure. Still, there is the limitation in that nodes can only be updated based on their immediate neighbors on each GCN layer. Nodes far away from each other with n-order in the graph are hard to encode on GCN models. Adding an LSTM layer can compensate for this limitation. The hidden states of LSTM instead of embedding of EDS nodes are fed into GCN layers, that is, $h_v^0 = \boldsymbol{s}_v$ where $\boldsymbol{s}_v$ is the final LSTM state of node v.

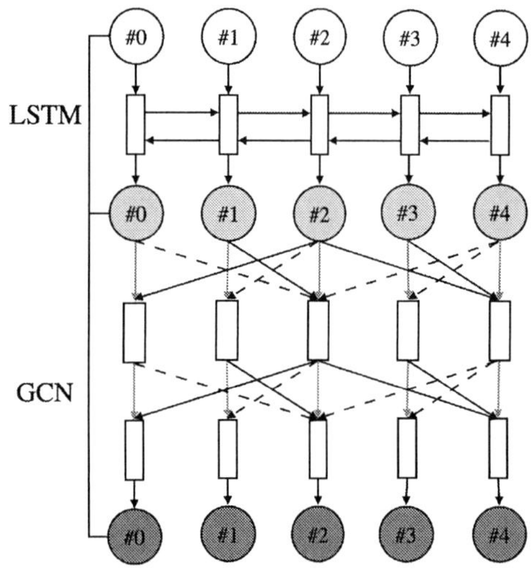

Figure 3: Example for EDS Encoder structure. Nodes embedding (circles) are sequentially fed into an LSTM layer and GCN layers. In GCN layers, solid lines are original edges in the EDS graph, dash lines represent the inverted edges and gray lines are *self* edges.

The structure of the EDS encoder is illustrated in Figure 3. The embeddings of EDS nodes (hollow circles) are first fed into an LSTM layer. After processing in the LSTM layer, contextual information is included in the light gray circles. After several GCN layers, dark gray circles that hold edges and neighbors information are the final hidden states of GCN layers.

4 Experiment

4.1 Experimental Setup

Our experiments were done using the toolkit AllenNLP (Gardner et al., 2018).

EDS Parser In this study, we adopted open-source distribution LOGON (Lønning and Oepen, 2006) to generate EDS annotations. LOGON [1] package contains ERG parsers and the ERG-to-EDS converter. Compared to the purely data-driven parsers, general-purpose grammatical knowledge encoded in the ERG aids EDS parsing (Oepen and Flickinger, 2019). We applied ERG release 1214 and use LOGON in one-best mode. However, LOGON failed to parse part of sentences due to limitation of search tree or other reasons (about 15% of data), so we used the EDS model of Che et al. (2019) to parse those sentences.

Baseline Model As we mentioned, we adopt HIT-SCIR as our baseline model. However, we use the smaller pre-trained model, BERT-base, for word embeddings due to GPU limitation. For alignments, the baseline model uses an enhanced rule-based aligner TAMR (Liu et al., 2018) to generate transition actions for AMR graph. More details on hyper-parameters can be found Table 3 in appendix. Our experiments were done using GeForce RTX 2080 Ti GPU. During model training, each epoch took about 4 hours on one GPU.

Dataset We use the dataset from MRP 2019 so that we can compare our models with the officially submitted models there. The shared task has constraints on which additional data or pretrained models can be used for reasons of comparability and fairness. Our models meet the requirements as both our baseline model (HIT-SCIR) and the EDS parser that we use to generate EDS graphs for use by the baseline model satisfy them.

There are 56,240 sentences in MRP 2019 AMR training set. The test set contains 1,998 sentences, and among them are 100 randomly selected sentences from the novel *The Little Prince*. MRP 2019 provided results for AMR parsing models on both

[1] `http://wiki.delph-in.net/LogonProcessing`

the entire test set (called All Data) and the subset of the setences from *The Little Prince* (called Lpps). The reason for the special interest on the latter was that the sentences from the novel are presumably least similar to the training data, which are mostly from the WSJ-corpus. Indeed, most models at MRP 2019 have lower scores on Lpps than on All Data. We will have more to say about this in the next section on our experimental results.

Metrics MRP 2019 used two metrics to evaluate the models: the standard SMATCH scorer (Cai and Knight, 2013) included in the open-source mtool software (the Swiss Army Knife of Meaning Representation) [2], and an MRP 2019 specific scorer that is similar to SMATCH but can compare two meaning representation graphs (the ground truth and the model output) according to certain fine-grained attributes such as edges, node labels and so on. We'll mainly use the SMATCH metric but also give MRP metric for the Lpps test set. We refer the reader to Oepen et al. (2019) for more details on MRP 2019 datasets and metrics.

4.2 Results

Results on Different Structures Our SMATCH experimental results are summarized in Table 1. To see the effects of different encodings of EDS graphs, we tried five EDS-enhanced systems. Among the five, three use only GCNs ([G1],[G2],[G3]), from single layer to three layers, and two with a single BiLSTM layer plus one or two GCN layers ([LG1],[LG2]). As can be seen from Table 1, LG1 achieves the highest F1 score, outperforming Amazon (Cao et al., 2019), the best overall AMR parser at MRP 2019.

We note that all our five EDS-enhanced systems perform better than HIT-SCIR, our reference baseline model. Interestingly, the number of GCN layers matters and it's not necessarily the more the better. The reason for GCN performance degradation in our work is possible to be over-smoothing, which was discussed in previous work (Li et al., 2018).

Among the three with GCN layers only ([G1],[G2],[G3]), the best is G2. When BiLSTM is added, one layer of GCN ([LG1]) is better than two ([LG2]). It's possible there is some theoretical explanation for this but we suspect it also has something to do with the dataset. For example, for All Data, the F1 score of BiLSTM plus one layer of GCN is the same as the one with two layers.

Results on Lpps Some interesting observations can be made on the Lpps test set. As we mentioned, this test set contains 100 random sentences from the book *The Little Prince*. These sentences seem to be quite different from those in the training set given at MRP 2019. So not surprisingly, most models have poorer performance on this test set except for Saarland (Donatelli et al., 2019) which somehow performs better in this test set than the All Data set. As for HIT-SCIR, its performance on Lpps is a lot worse than that on All Data. What is worthwhile noting is that our models, which are basically HIT-SCIR enhanced with EDS in various ways, boost its performance on Lpps significantly. Our best model is even better than Saarland on this test set. Compared to HIT-SCIT, it increases its F1 scores by 4.6% (from .680 to .726) on Lpps while only 1.1% on All Data (from .725 to .736). So the extra EDS information really pays off on this test set.

SMATCH is a general tool for computing the overall differences between two answers. To give a more fine-grained comparison between two meaning representations, MRP has its own scorer to compute what are called the Tops, Labels, Properties, Edges, and All scores, where the All scores are close to the SMATCH score. Table 2 gives MRP F1 scores for the Lpps test set for our baseline model HIT-SCIR and our EDS-enhanced models. Again we see that our models improve the performance of the baseline model significantly in all subtasks, especially in Labels and Properties. For F1 score on Tops, Labels, Properties, the model LG1 performs best, 5%, 6% and 9% improvement respectively. Whereas, G2 performs best in Edge F1 score, about 3% improvement.

Our model can handle these "out of domain" cases better because we have accurate EDS parsing for them. Consider the verb "look" in the sentence "I shall look as if I were suffering." In the baseline model, the predicted AMR node for it is "look-01", which is wrong. Our model with the extra information from EDS correctly labels it "look-02". The possible reason why the baseline model selects "look-01" is that "look-01" appears nearly twice as often as "look-02" in training data: the former 198 times and the latter 103. However, the EDS subgraph for the phrase "sb. look as if " is node(pron)-edge(arg1)-node(look-v)-

[2] https://github.com/cfmrp/mtool

System	Precision		Recall		F1	
	All Data	Lpps	All Data	Lpps	All Data	Lpps
Amazon (Cao et al., 2019)	.75	.70	.71	.71	.730	.704
Saarland (Donatelli et al., 2019)	.70	.73	.63	.71	.661	.722
SJTU-NICT (Li et al., 2019)	.75	.71	.68	.69	.714	.696
Suda-Alibaba (Zhang et al., 2019b)	.73	.66	.70	.69	.713	.674
HIT-SCIR (Che et al., 2019)	.77	.71	.69	.65	.725	.680
+EDS (GCNs, K=1)[G1]	.787	.738	.683	.671	.731	.703
+EDS (GCNs, K=2)[G2]	.780	.763	.691	.689	.733	.724
+EDS (GCNs, K=3)[G3]	.783	.752	.689	.674	.733	.711
+EDS (BiLSTM+GCNs, K=1)[LG1]	.785	.770	.692	.687	**.736**	**.726**
+EDS (BiLSTM+GCNs, K=2)[LG2]	.785	.774	.690	.678	.735	.723

Table 1: SMATCH scores on the evaluation data, "All Data" means results on all evaluation data and "Lpps" is results on 100 sentences of *The Little Prince*. In this table, the top part is the official results for four systems achieving competitive results in MRP 2019; the middle part is the results for our baseline model; the bottom part "+EDS" are our proposed EDS-enhanced models. For example, "GCNs, K=1" means EDS graph encoder consists of one GCN layer, denoted as [G1]; "BiLSTM+GCN, K=2" represents EDS graph encoder is composed of one BiLSTM layer and two GCN layers, denoted as [LG2].

System	Tops			Labels			Properties			Edges			All		
	P	R	F	P	R	F	P	R	F	P	R	F	P	R	F
HIT-SCIR	.81	.81	.81	.78	.74	.76	.51	.57	.54	.66	.56	.61	.722	.660	.689
+EDS [G1]	.84	.84	.84	.81	.77	.79	.77	.48	.59	.65	.57	.61	.746	.678	.710
+EDS [G2]	.82	.84	.83	.83	.78	.81	.76	.52	.62	.69	.59	**.64**	.771	.697	.732
+EDS [G3]	.83	.84	.83	.81	.77	.79	.73	.50	.59	.68	.58	.63	.761	.682	.720
+EDS [LG1]	.86	.86	**.86**	.85	.79	**.82**	.80	.52	**.63**	.68	.58	.62	.779	.695	**.734**
+EDS [LG2]	.83	.85	.84	.85	.78	.81	.84	.48	.61	.69	.58	.63	.783	.686	.732

Table 2: MRP scores of Lpps AMR sub tasks. In this table, HIT-SCIR is our baseline model (Che et al., 2019). "+EDS(G1)" to "+EDS(LG2)" correspond to the EDS-enhanced model "+EDS(GCNs, K=1)" to "+EDS(BiLSTM+GCNs, K=2)" in Table 1 according to the indexes.

edge(arg1)-node(as+if), which suggests "look-02". EDS graphs often encode multiple tokens as one node, and this helps predict edges more accurately. An example is "_blow_v_away" in "The wind blows them away." The baseline model predicts the edge label between "blow" and "away" as ":ARG2", whereas the gold answer is ":direction", which can be predicted by EDS-enhanced model. Here we believe the EDS subgraph "node(_blow_v_away)-edge(contain)-node(away)" affects the final result.

Results on gold EDS annotations Finally, we notice that MRP provided gold EDS annotation for Lpps test data. We tried our models using these gold EDS annotations on the Lpps test set, and observed that this actually resulted in a minor reduction in F1 scores, around 0.0001 worth than the model using silver EDS annotations. The reason the gold label actually performed a bit worse is because the model was trained using the actual EDS parsing results, so seems to "adapted" to the bias of the EDS parser used.

As a footnote, we remark here that we are aware of the new results on AMR parsers at MRP 2020 that were released in late November 2020. This work was done prior to MRP 2020. While MRP 2020 also used Lpps as a test set, the results there and our results here are not directly comparable as they were done using different training sets. Furthermore, the main purpose of this paper is about incorporating EDS graphs into AMR parsing, so the comparison with the baseline model is more meaningful.

5 Conclusions

In this study, we incorporate the EDS, a meaning representation that is more accessible than AMR, to improve the performance of AMR parsing. To encode EDS graphs for AMR parsing, we used both LSTM and GCN layers. As a case study, we enhanced a transition-based AMR parser with EDS graphs, and showed that on the AMR benchmarks that the baseline model already performs well, our EDS-enhanced parsers can further improve its performance. The improvements are especially noticeable on the Lpps (*The Little Prince*) test set where the baseline parser performs poorly and lags behind other AMR parsers at MRP 2019. In fact, on the Lpps test set, our EDS enhanced parsers outperform even the best one submitted there.

We can also see some other implications of this work. For us, the ultimate goal of semantic parsing is to use it in downstream tasks such as question answering, reasoning, and knowledge extraction from texts. Given that almost all meaning representations are graph-based, we believe our encoding of EDS graphs with LSTM and GCN layers can be applied in these downstream tasks. We are currently exploring this as a future work. Another insight from this work is about possible connections among different meaning representations. We have demonstrated the usefulness of EDS graphs for AMR parsing. It is likely they can also be useful for other frameworks, even vice versa. More generally, whether there is a universal semantic parser that can take advantages of information from each framework is an interesting question worth investigating.

References

Omri Abend and Ari Rappoport. 2013. UCCA: A semantics-based grammatical annotation scheme. In *Proceedings of the 10th International Conference on Computational Semantics (IWCS 2013) – Long Papers*, pages 1–12, Potsdam, Germany. Association for Computational Linguistics.

Yoav Artzi, Kenton Lee, and Luke Zettlemoyer. 2015. Broad-coverage ccg semantic parsing with amr. In *Proceedings of the 2015 Conference on Empirical Methods in Natural Language Processing*, pages 1699–1710.

Ofir Arviv, Ruixiang Cui, and Daniel Hershcovich. 2020. Huji-ku at mrp 2020: Two transition-based neural parsers. In *Proceedings of the CoNLL 2020 Shared Task: Cross-Framework Meaning Representation Parsing*, pages 73–82.

Ramón Fernandez Astudillo, Miguel Ballesteros, Tahira Naseem, Austin Blodgett, and Radu Florian. 2020. Transition-based parsing with stack-transformers. In *Proceedings of the 2020 Conference on Empirical Methods in Natural Language Processing: Findings*, pages 1001–1007.

Miguel Ballesteros and Yaser Al-Onaizan. 2017. Amr parsing using stack-lstms. In *Proceedings of the 2017 Conference on Empirical Methods in Natural Language Processing*, pages 1269–1275.

Laura Banarescu, Claire Bonial, Shu Cai, Madalina Georgescu, Kira Griffitt, Ulf Hermjakob, Kevin Knight, Philipp Koehn, Martha Palmer, and Nathan Schneider. 2013. Abstract meaning representation for sembanking. In *Proceedings of the 7th linguistic annotation workshop and interoperability with discourse*, pages 178–186.

Lauritz Brandt, David Grimm, Mengfei Zhou, and Yannick Versley. 2016. Icl-hd at semeval-2016 task 8: Meaning representation parsing-augmenting amr parsing with a preposition semantic role labeling neural network. In *Proceedings of the 10th international workshop on semantic evaluation (semeval-2016)*, pages 1160–1166.

Deng Cai and Wai Lam. 2020. AMR parsing via graph-sequence iterative inference. In *Proceedings of the 58th Annual Meeting of the Association for Computational Linguistics*, pages 1290–1301, Online. Association for Computational Linguistics.

Shu Cai and Kevin Knight. 2013. Smatch: an evaluation metric for semantic feature structures. In *Proceedings of the 51st Annual Meeting of the Association for Computational Linguistics (Volume 2: Short Papers)*, pages 748–752.

Jie Cao, Yi Zhang, Adel Youssef, and Vivek Srikumar. 2019. Amazon at mrp 2019: Parsing meaning representations with lexical and phrasal anchoring. In *Proceedings of the Shared Task on Cross-Framework Meaning Representation Parsing at the 2019 Conference on Natural Language Learning*, pages 138–148.

Wanxiang Che, Longxu Dou, Yang Xu, Yuxuan Wang, Yijia Liu, and Ting Liu. 2019. Hit-scir at mrp 2019: A unified pipeline for meaning representation parsing via efficient training and effective encoding. In *Proceedings of the Shared Task on Cross-Framework Meaning Representation Parsing at the 2019 Conference on Natural Language Learning*, pages 76–85.

Jacob Devlin, Ming-Wei Chang, Kenton Lee, and Kristina Toutanova. 2019. Bert: Pre-training of deep bidirectional transformers for language understanding. In *Proceedings of the 2019 Conference of the North American Chapter of the Association for Computational Linguistics: Human Language Technologies, Volume 1 (Long and Short Papers)*, pages 4171–4186.

Lucia Donatelli, Meaghan Fowlie, Jonas Groschwitz, Alexander Koller, Matthias Lindemann, Mario Mina, and Pia Weißenhorn. 2019. Saarland at mrp 2019: Compositional parsing across all graphbanks. In *Proceedings of the Shared Task on Cross-Framework Meaning Representation Parsing at the 2019 Conference on Natural Language Learning*, pages 66–75. Association for Computational Linguistics (ACL).

Jeffrey Flanigan, Sam Thomson, Jaime G Carbonell, Chris Dyer, and Noah A Smith. 2014. A discriminative graph-based parser for the abstract meaning representation. In *Proceedings of the 52nd Annual Meeting of the Association for Computational Linguistics (Volume 1: Long Papers)*, pages 1426–1436.

Matt Gardner, Joel Grus, Mark Neumann, Oyvind Tafjord, Pradeep Dasigi, Nelson F Liu, Matthew Peters, Michael Schmitz, and Luke Zettlemoyer. 2018. Allennlp: A deep semantic natural language processing platform. In *Proceedings of Workshop for NLP Open Source Software (NLP-OSS)*, pages 1–6.

Daniel Hershcovich and Ofir Arviv. 2019. Tupa at mrp 2019: A multi-task baseline system. In *Proceedings of the Shared Task on Cross-Framework Meaning Representation Parsing at the 2019 Conference on Natural Language Learning*, pages 28–39.

Thomas N. Kipf and Max Welling. 2017. Semi-supervised classification with graph convolutional networks. In *5th International Conference on Learning Representations, ICLR 2017, Toulon, France, April 24-26, 2017, Conference Track Proceedings*. OpenReview.net.

Qimai Li, Zhichao Han, and Xiao-Ming Wu. 2018. Deeper insights into graph convolutional networks for semi-supervised learning. In *Proceedings of the AAAI Conference on Artificial Intelligence*, volume 32.

Zuchao Li, Hai Zhao, Zhuosheng Zhang, Rui Wang, Masao Utiyama, and Eiichiro Sumita. 2019. Sjtu-nict at mrp 2019: Multi-task learning for end-to-end uniform semantic graph parsing. In *Proceedings of the Shared Task on Cross-Framework Meaning Representation Parsing at the 2019 Conference on Natural Language Learning*, pages 45–54.

Zi Lin and Nianwen Xue. 2019. Parsing meaning representations: is easier always better? In *Proceedings of the First International Workshop on Designing Meaning Representations*, pages 34–43.

Yijia Liu, Wanxiang Che, Bo Zheng, Bing Qin, and Ting Liu. 2018. An amr aligner tuned by transition-based parser. In *Proceedings of the 2018 Conference on Empirical Methods in Natural Language Processing*, pages 2422–2430.

Jan Tore Lønning and Stephan Oepen. 2006. Re-usable tools for precision machine translation. In *Proceedings of the COLING/ACL 2006 Interactive Presentation Sessions*, pages 53–56, Sydney, Australia. Association for Computational Linguistics.

Chunchuan Lyu and Ivan Titov. 2018. Amr parsing as graph prediction with latent alignment. In *Proceedings of the 56th Annual Meeting of the Association for Computational Linguistics (Volume 1: Long Papers)*, pages 397–407.

Diego Marcheggiani and Ivan Titov. 2017. Encoding sentences with graph convolutional networks for semantic role labeling. In *Proceedings of the 2017 Conference on Empirical Methods in Natural Language Processing*, pages 1506–1515.

Mitchell P. Marcus, Beatrice Santorini, and Mary Ann Marcinkiewicz. 1993. Building a large annotated corpus of English: The Penn Treebank. *Computational Linguistics*, 19(2):313–330.

Tahira Naseem, Abhishek Shah, Hui Wan, Radu Florian, Salim Roukos, and Miguel Ballesteros. 2019. Rewarding smatch: Transition-based amr parsing with reinforcement learning. In *Proceedings of the 57th Annual Meeting of the Association for Computational Linguistics*, pages 4586–4592.

Stephan Oepen, Omri Abend, Jan Hajic, Daniel Hershcovich, Marco Kuhlmann, Tim O'Gorman, Nianwen Xue, Jayeol Chun, Milan Straka, and Zdenka Uresova. 2019. MRP 2019: Cross-framework meaning representation parsing. In *CoNLL Shared Task*, pages 1–27.

Stephan Oepen and Dan Flickinger. 2019. The erg at mrp 2019: Radically compositional semantic dependencies. In *Proceedings of the Shared Task on Cross-Framework Meaning Representation Parsing at the 2019 Conference on Natural Language Learning*, pages 40–44.

Stephan Oepen and Jan Tore Lønning. 2006. Discriminant-based MRS banking. In *Proceedings of the Fifth International Conference on Language Resources and Evaluation (LREC'06)*, Genoa, Italy. European Language Resources Association (ELRA).

Xiaochang Peng, Linfeng Song, and Daniel Gildea. 2015. A synchronous hyperedge replacement grammar based approach for amr parsing. In *Proceedings of the Nineteenth Conference on Computational Natural Language Learning*, pages 32–41.

Chuan Wang, Nianwen Xue, and Sameer Pradhan. 2015. A transition-based algorithm for amr parsing. In *Proceedings of the 2015 Conference of the North American Chapter of the Association for Computational Linguistics: Human Language Technologies*, pages 366–375.

Sheng Zhang, Xutai Ma, Kevin Duh, and Benjamin Van Durme. 2019a. Amr parsing as sequence-to-graph transduction. In *Proceedings of the 57th Annual Meeting of the Association for Computational Linguistics*, pages 80–94.

Yue Zhang, Wei Jiang, Qingrong Xia, Junjie Cao, Rui Wang, Zhenghua Li, and Min Zhang. 2019b. Suda-alibaba at mrp 2019: Graph-based models with bert. In *Proceedings of the Shared Task on Cross-Framework Meaning Representation Parsing at the 2019 Conference on Natural Language Learning*, pages 149–157.

Qiji Zhou, Yue Zhang, Donghong Ji, and Hao Tang. 2020. AMR parsing with latent structural information. In *Proceedings of the 58th Annual Meeting of the Association for Computational Linguistics*, pages 4306–4319, Online. Association for Computational Linguistics.

Table 3 contains the values of hyper-parameters.

HYPER PARAMETER	VALUE
Word Embeddings	
source	BERT
dim	768
Model Parameters	
Action dim	128
Entity dim	64
Relation dim	64
Hidden dim	256
Dropout	0.2
Layer dropout	0.2
Recurrent dropout	0.2
EDS nodes embedding	64
EDS LSTM hidden dim	64
EDS GCN hidden dim	128
Trainer Parameters	
Learning rate scheduler	slanted triangular
Gradual unfreezing	True
Cut Frac	0.1
Ratio	32
Base learning rate	1×10^{-3}
BERT learning rate	5×10^{-5}
Batch size	6
Epoch	20
Gradient clipping	5
Gradient norm	5
Optimizer	Adam
β_1, β_2	0.9,0.999

Table 3: Hyper-parameters settings

Dependency Patterns of Complex Sentences and Semantic Disambiguation for Abstract Meaning Representation Parsing

Yuki Yamamoto* **Yuji Matsumoto**** **Taro Watanabe***

*Nara Institute of Science and Technology
{yamamoto.yuki.yt0, taro}@is.naist.jp
**RIKEN Center for Advanced Intelligence Project
{yuji.matsumoto}@riken.jp

Abstract

Abstract Meaning Representation (AMR) is a sentence-level meaning representation based on predicate argument structure. One of the challenges we find in AMR parsing is to capture the structure of complex sentences which expresses the relation between predicates. Knowing the core part of the sentence structure in advance may be beneficial in such a task. In this paper, we present a list of dependency patterns for English complex sentence constructions designed for AMR parsing. With a dedicated pattern matcher, all occurrences of complex sentence constructions are retrieved from an input sentence. While some of the subordinators have semantic ambiguities, we deal with this problem through training classification models on data derived from AMR and Wikipedia corpus, establishing a new baseline for future works. The developed complex sentence patterns and the corresponding AMR descriptions will be made public .

1 Introduction

Abstract Meaning Representation (AMR) is a sentence-level meaning representation based on predicate argument structure (Banarescu et al., 2013). AMR Parsing is the task of transforming a sentence into an AMR graph with nodes and edges, each representing a concept or relation. While early studies (Flanigan et al., 2014; Wang et al., 2015; Artzi et al., 2015; Pust et al., 2015) used dependency parsers to integrate syntactic features to their models, recent deep neural network-based approaches (Konstas et al., 2017; Peng et al., 2017; Zhang et al., 2019; Cai and Lam, 2020) tend to encode the input sentence as a sequence without considering its syntactic structure.

Generally speaking, syntactic and semantic structures share much in common. It is assumed

Code and resource are available at https://github.com/yama-yuki/skeletal-amr.

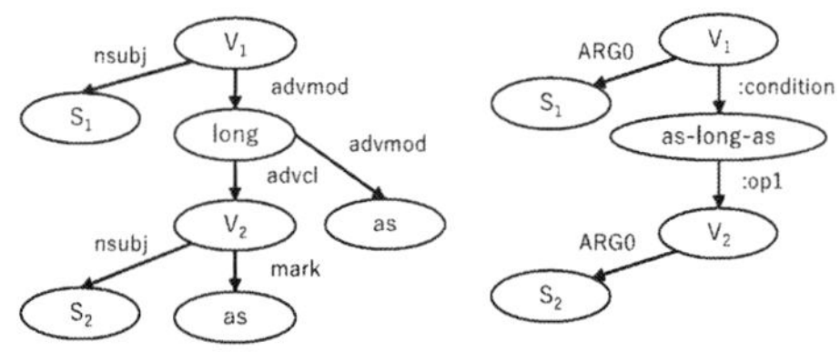

Figure 1: Representation of *as long as*-construction in dependency tree (left) and AMR graph (right).

that dependency trees and semantic role labeling structures have a strong correlation in that *nsubj* and *dobj* can be used interchangeably for ARG0 and ARG1 role (Xia et al., 2019). Since AMR is annotated based on PropBank frames (Palmer et al., 2005), the same could be said for AMR structures.

This holds to be true for a simple sentence, which is basically a matrix clause, comprised of a predicate and its arguments. However, it is not always the case with complex sentence constructions, each of which consists of a matrix clause and one or more subordinate clause(s). Consider Figure 1 which shows both dependency and AMR representation of a complex sentence with a subordinator *as long as*. While variables S's and V's are interchangeable between the representations, predicative relations and subordinator itself are expressed quite differently. Compared to uniform structures of simple sentences, various types of complex sentence are used in human language. This characteristics makes it challenging for existing AMR parsers to capture its structure correctly.

Among AMR parsers which are aware of syntactic structures, CAMR (Wang et al., 2015) directly transforms the result of dependency parsing into an AMR graph with transition-based algorithm. As Figure 2(a) shows an example parse with CAMR, existing parsers have trouble capturing the relation

Proceedings of the 10th Conference on Lexical and Computational Semantics, pages 212–221
August 5–6, 2021, Bangkok, Thailand (online) ©2021 Association for Computational Linguistics

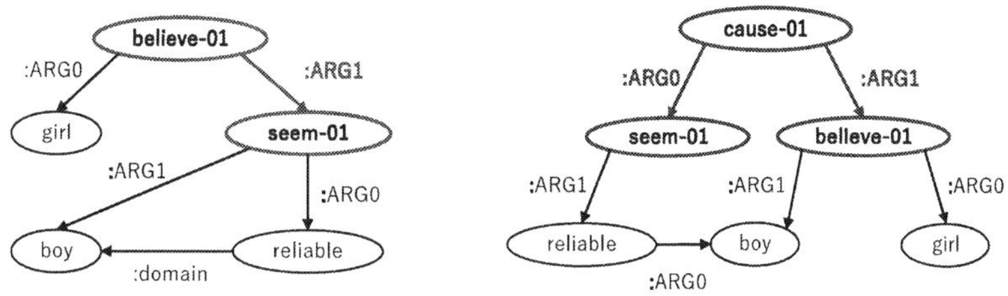

(a) Parser's Output AMR

(b) Correct AMR

Figure 2: Result of parsing "As the boy seemed reliable, the girl believed him." with CAMR.

between two clauses. In this case, CAMR predicts the relation between `believe-01` and `seem-01` as ARG1, though it should be represented as a causal relation with `cause-01` as shown in Figure 2(b). This is a crucial error as it incorrectly determines the very core structure of the output graph. We assume that the solution could be achieved either by retraining the parser on larger annotated data or providing the parser with the core structure of the input sentence in advance. The latter seems more reasonable in terms of the cost of annotation.

With the motivation to aid AMR parsing task, we present a method to retrieve all occurrences of complex sentence constructions from an input sentence using a dedicated pattern matcher. At the moment, there is no comprehensive resource that provides structural information about the relations between two clauses, particularly in AMR framework. Therefore, as our first step, we attempt to develop a pattern dictionary of English complex sentences together with the corresponding AMRs which represent the skeleton structure of the sentence (hereinafter referred to as "skeletal AMRs"). Then, we provide a pattern matcher which captures clausal relations between a superordinate and subordinate clauses in a complex sentence.

Our pattern matching approach faces the problem of syntactic and semantic ambiguities. When a complex sentence has more than one subordinate clause, we need to determine which pair of clauses are related. Consider the following example where two subordinate clauses appear in a single sentence.

(1) ... [<u>if</u> you wish to look at the comparative risks]$_{SUB1}$ [<u>if</u> we do not confront terrorist organizations in their staging areas]$_{SUB2}$, [how many people could die as a result of weapons of mass destruction at some point in the not too distant future]$_{MAT}$? (AMR: bolt-eng-DF-199-192783-6849434_0102.3)

While there has been studies regarding the syntactic scope of a subordinate clause such as Utsuro et al. (2000), this problem is beyond the scope of this paper. We rely on the output of the dependency parser, which we employ in our pattern matching system, to decide which pair of clauses are syntactically related.

Meanwhile, when a subordinator itself is ambiguous between several senses, we need to select the correct type of coherence relation between the clauses. Sentences in (2) show usages of a subordinator *since*, which is semantically ambiguous between causal and temporal senses.

(2) a. <u>Since</u> there is responsibility, we are not afraid. (AMR: bolt12_6455_6561.15)

b. Also <u>since</u> he turned 80, people had been paying more and more attention to Mao Zedong's birthday. (AMR: bolt12_10511_7302.5)

In order to resolve the semantic ambiguities of clause-level coherence relation, inspired by the work of Shi and Demberg (2019), we take finetuning-based approach with data augmentation method. With the support of weakly supervised data derived from Wikipedia, we achieve the scores of 75.65% and 83.94% on macro and micro F1 respectively, establishing a new baseline for coherence relation classification of complex sentence constructions in AMR framework.

To sum up, the contributions of this paper are the followings:

- We create a comprehensive resource of complex sentence constructions.
- We develop a pattern matching system which takes a sentence as an input and returns a corresponding skeletal AMR.

- We establish a new baseline for semantic disambiguation task of complex sentence constructions in AMR framework.

2 Related Works

While our focus is on clause-level relation of complex sentence constructions, not much study has been done specifically on this topic in AMR framework. Rather, the topic is dealt with in the field of discourse structures, where coherence relations between any text segments are the main focus.

In the studies of discourse parsing, various attempts have been made to capture coherence relations between pairs of sentences or clauses (Pitler et al., 2008; Rutherford et al., 2017; Qin et al., 2017; Bai and Zhao, 2018). These works basically rely on discourse frameworks such as Rhetorical Structure Theory (RST; Thompson and Mann 1987) or Penn Discourse Tree Bank (PDTB; Prasad et al. 2008).

Most recently, Shi and Demberg (2019) has presented a finetuning-based approach using the bidirectional encoder representation from transformers (BERT; Devlin et al. 2019). They designed their model to learn 11 classes to achieve the state-of-the-art performance on implicit discourse relation classification task in PDTB framework.

Their work was motivated by the method taken by Devlin et al. (2019) to pretrain BERT, which is called "next sentence prediction task" (NSP). In the process of pretraining using NSP, the model is presented with pairs of sentences. The model predicts whether the second sentence is the actual subsequent sentence. NSP enables BERT to represent a pair of sentences by packing them together as a single sequence.

Some studies have focused on discourse structure in AMR framework. Donatelli et al. (2018) enhances AMR by annontating tense and aspect phenomena at discourse-level. The work by O'Gorman et al. (2018) targets relations of sentences and provides annotation of coreference in multi-sentence AMR corpus. Yet, neither the structure of the complex sentence constructions nor the coherence relations between subordinate and matrix clauses have been much of a concern in this framework.

3 Pattern Matching System

In this section, we will give a description of our pattern matching system. The entire workflow is

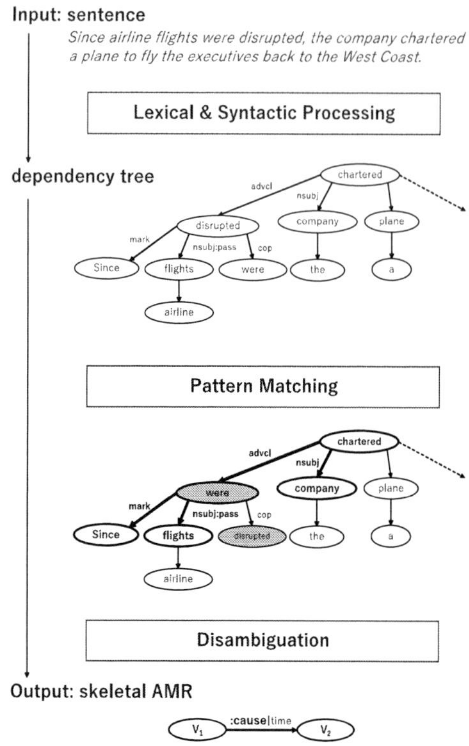

Figure 3: Pattern matching system workflow for a sentence "Since airline flights were disrupted, the company chartered a plane to fly the executives back to the West Coast.".

illustrated in Figure 3, where the system takes a sentence as an input and returns a skeletal AMR if it is a type of complex sentence construction. The disambiguation module will be described in the later section. We will use the sentence given as a running example throughout this paper.

3.1 Dictionary of Dependency Patterns

Complex sentence constructions in English grammar can be distinguished by their consisting subordinator. When creating a pattern dictionary, we refer to comprehensive studies on grammars (Quirk et al., 1985; Yamaguchi, 2013), which provide a typology of subordinators. To cover various types of constructions, we include simple (e.g. *if, because*), complex (e.g. *as if, so that*) and correlate (*e.g. no sooner ... than*) subordinators classified in Quirk et al. (1985). In addition to that, we also include the type of constructions involving degree and quantity which are introduced to AMR in Bonial et al. (2018).

Our pattern matching method depends not only

on lexical processing but also on syntactic processing. For syntactic framework, we follow the annotation of dependency structure in Universal Dependencies v2 format (UD; Nivre et al. 2020), which makes our patterns a form of dependency trees. The nodes in trees are represented either by a lemma form of a lexical entry or an abstract one defined by POS tags, where every edge has a dependency relation label. Regular expression is employed to place any form of a specific element. We provide these dependency patterns with a corresponding skeletal AMR that describes the core structure of an input sentence. Depending on the type of construction, a set of variables are used to take alignments between patterns and skeletons. At the moment, our dictionary includes 70 distinct patterns .

Figure 4 illustrates an example of a paired entry of a dependency pattern and skeletal AMR for *because*-construction:

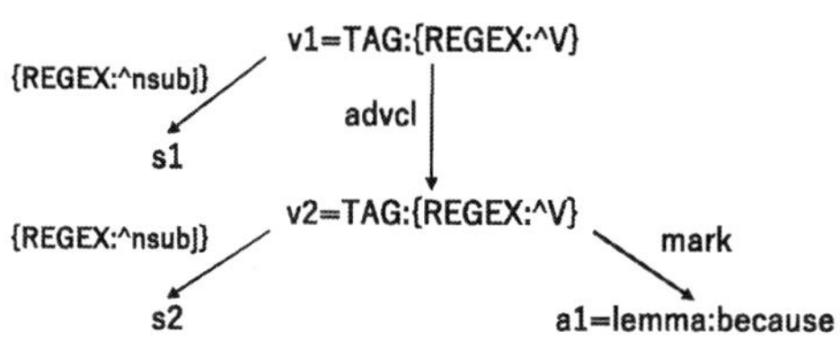

(a) Dependency Pattern

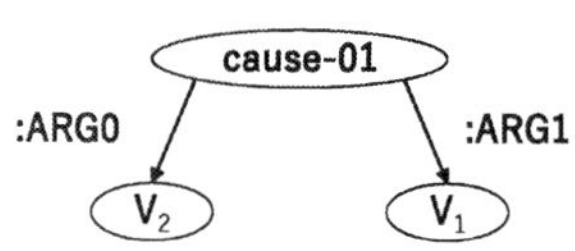

(b) Skeletal AMR

Figure 4: Pattern dictionary entry of complex sentence construction with simple subordinator *because*.

The dependency pattern in Figure 4(a) describes the simplest type of structure in our dictionary. The nodes that are represented as variables `s1` and `v1` capture a predicate and its argument in a matrix clause, whereas `s2` and `v2` capture a subordinate clause. Subordinators are basically described as a's, where their lemma forms are given as cues. **REGEX** operators are used on both nodes and edges to flexibly match possible elements. For example, the dependency relation of `{REGEX:^nsubj}` between `s`'s and `v`'s enables us to handle subjects of both the active (`nsubj`) and passive (`nsubj:pass`) voice. In the case of `TAG:{REGEX:^V}`, **REGEX** is used to represent any POS tag that starts from "V", meaning that it captures any form of a verb. Figure 4(b) shows the corresponding skeletal AMR, which represents a core relation between the two predicates. In all patterns in the dictionary, V_1 and V_2 act as slots for the predicates of the matrix and subordinate clauses.

Some subordinators could indicate more than one coherence relations. For example, Figure 5 shows the case of our running example with *since*, where the subordinator presents either (a) causal or (b) temporal relation:

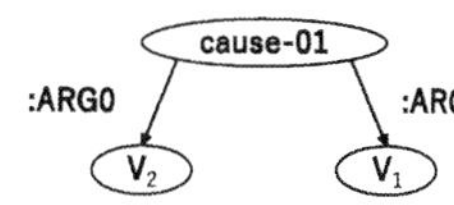

(a) Causal

(b) Temporal

Figure 5: Skeletal AMRs of ambiguous *since*.

In the pattern dictionary, rather than enumerating entries for every possible structure, we describe a primitive structure of skeletal AMR to dynamically generate the actual relation, which is in accordance with the Generative Lexicon approach (Pustejovsky, 1995). More specifically, we accomodate all possible relations separating them with a vertical bar on an edge of a skeletal AMR in the way described in Figure 6(b), which we call a "primitive skeleton":

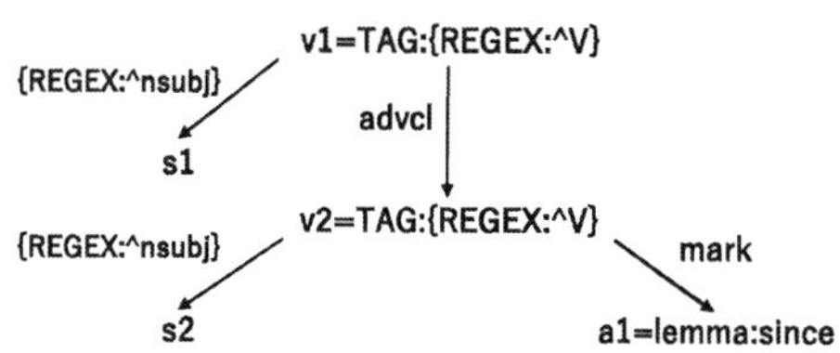

(a) Dependency Pattern

(b) Skeletal AMR

Figure 6: Pattern dictionary entry of complex sentence construction with simple subordinator *since*.

We make it available for users to add new patterns to the dictionary for further expansion.

The disambiguation step will follow after the pattern matcher returns the primitive skeleton. For simplicity and consistency, we use *shortcuts* to represent the relations if available, such as using a relational role `:cause` instead of a predicative frame `cause-01` that can be substitutionally used.

Aside the semantic ambiguity of relation mentioned above, structural ambiguity could be seen when several types of structure exists within the same relation. Compare Figure 5(b) and 7, where both skeletal AMRs represent temporal relation but show different structures:

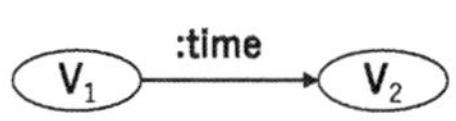

Figure 7: Skeletal AMR of *as*, *once*, etc. representing temporal relation.

Since the primitive skeleton only describes the simplest form, recovery step needs be taken to generate the final skeletal AMR for ambiguous subordinators. Therefore, we define a possible interpretation (such as Figure 5(b) and 7) for primitive skeleton of each ambiguous subordinator, which will be referred to after the skeletal AMR is disambiguated. This idea share similarity with the notion of *meaning postulates* (Carnap, 1952; Dowty, 1979). By following the definition, the structural ambiguity of skeletal AMRs will be resolved.

3.2 Pattern Matching Method

Our pattern matching method builds on the dependency matching module introduced by Honnibal et al. (2020) that matches subtrees within a dependency tree. The matcher works in naive manner, searching from the top to the bottom of the pattern dictionary. It is originally capable of handling recursive nature of clauses. Namely, even when an input sentence has more than two clauses, the matcher searches all possible patterns for all clause pairs in a single run.

Meanwhile, it suffers from the following situations: "overlap" where multiple patterns accidentally match with a pair of clauses and "copula" where the matcher fails to capture copular constructions due to the limitation of expressiveness of patterns. To account for these cases, we extend the matching method by incorporating additional functions.

Overlap Duplicated matching may occur within a single pair of clauses since some patterns share their forms.

(3) As if he were still in his old job, Mr.Wright enjoys a $120,000 annual office expense allowance.

When the target sentence is (3), the dependency matcher returns the following overlapping patterns:

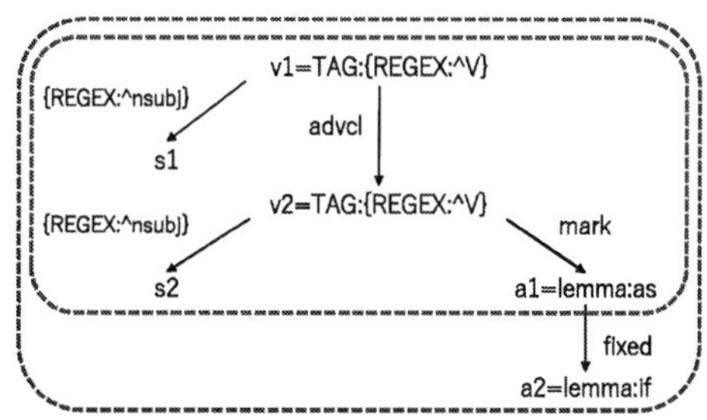

Figure 8: Overlap of patterns for *as* and *as if*.

This mostly occurs between simple and complex subordinators in Quirkian term (e.g. *as* and *as far as*, *if* and *even if*, etc.). To address this issue, we assign an ID for each entry in the pattern dictionary to refer to the type of subordinators. For example, *as* is assigned "#1.6.1", whereas *as if* is "#2.2.1". The first number in an ID represents the number of words consisting the subordinator. The second describes its sorted order while the third is organized by the structure of the pattern. When the matcher detects an overlap, it looks up the IDs to select the most desirable output. In the case of overlap between simple and complex subordinators, the matcher compares the first number in ID, selecting the pattern with more words. In this case, *as if* is regarded as the desirable pattern.

Copula Verbs that show a relationship between subjects and objects are referred to as copulas (e.g. "is" for "John is tall."). Since UD format refrains from using a copula as a head of its complement , the matcher cannot find a copular clause with complex sentence patterns alone. To avoid redundancy of creating additional patterns substituting `V`'s with copulas for each entry in dictionary, we make an extra pattern outside that describes a copula-complement structure:

For "John is tall.", UD treats "tall" as a head of "is".

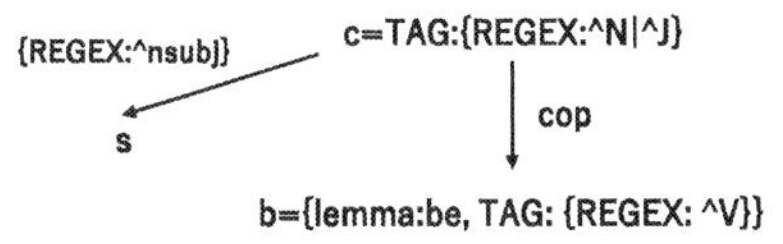

Figure 9: Dependency pattern of copular construction.

With the implementation of a converter, our system can detect copular clauses in complex sentences and convert it to a copular-headed structure when matched, in the way illustrated in the gray nodes in Figure 3.

4 Semantic Disambiguation Experiment

In this section, we describe details of our study on semantic disambiguation. We observe that the coherence relation between subordinate and superordinate clauses are commonly ambiguous among causal, conditional, concessional, and temporal senses. Considering that we are dealing with relations between clauses, which basically can be regarded as pairs of simple sentences, we can cast the problem of semantic ambiguity as a multi-class sentence-pair classification task. To be more specific, we assign the most typical class labels including CAUSE, COND, CONC, and TIME to make it a 4-class classification setting.

Throughout the experiment, we use the pretrained "bert-base-uncased" model for finetuning. BERT is pretrained under next sentence prediction as well as masked language modeling task. During pretraining, the model predicts the actual next sentence from a pair of candidate sentences. Thus, the model is expected to learn what the next sentence should look like. By finetuning BERT on a set of pairs of clauses, we can further expect the model to capture coherence relations between them.

Our input will be a separate pair of clauses with special tokens "[CLS]" and "[SEP]". While BERT takes the input in sequential manner, we would like the model to take advantage of dependency parsing, which we apply in the process of pattern matching. Therefore, we add artificial tags of " < " and " > " to indicate the head verb of each clause. The input format of our running example would look like: "[CLS] airlinc flights < wcrc > disruptcd [SEP] thc company < chartered > a plane to fly the executives back to the West Coast [SEP]".

4.1 Experimental Setup

For creating the dataset, we use the lateset release of AMR corpus (LDC2020T02), which provides 59.2k pairs of sentences and AMR graphs. To extract complex sentence constructions from the corpus, we use the STANZA pipeline (Qi et al., 2020) for lexical and syntactic processing of the sentences and employ our pattern matcher with all patterns in the dictionary. In order to check whether the corresponding AMR graph describes the relation we want for each class, we look for alignments between sentence tokens and AMR graphs . Finally, we split the sentence to obtain a pair of clauses and a subordinator.

While the data derived from AMR corpus can be regarded as "supervised", the amount is relatively small with the total of 1,933 pairs of subordinate and matrix clauses. As it consumes time and money to create more supervised data, we take weak supervision approach to augment training data. In other words, using specific subordinators that are known to be unambiguous in AMR corpus as linguistic cues, we seek to obtain complex sentences from larger corpus. We use raw data from Wikipedia for data augmentation to generate "weakly supervised" data. The list of subordinators used in this method is shown in Table 1. The distribution of each data, which we will refer to as AMR and WIKI data, is illustrated in Table 2. The data comprises *(subordinate clause, superordinate clause, subordinator, class label)* quadruplets.

Label	Subordinators
CAUSE	*because*
COND	*if, unless*
CONC	*although, though, even if*
TIME	*once, whenever*

Table 1: Subordinators used to create weakly supervised data (WIKI data).

Label	AMR	WIKI
CAUSE	442	27,264
COND	1,002	26,756
CONC	75	46,213
TIME	414	19,558
Total	1,933	119,791

Table 2: Distributions of labels in AMR and WIKI data.

We use the alignments provided in the corpus that are automatically generated.

We only target the simple structure such as the one presented in Figure 7, which we assume represent typical relation for each class.

Cosidering the size of AMR data, we make 5 splits of the data to perform 5-fold cross validation. When training on WIKI data, we average the scores of 5 runs with different random seeds to ensure stability. In addition, we perform grid search for hyperparameter tuning over the options in Table 3. All models will be evaluated using both Macro and micro F1 scores (F_M and F_m, respectively). Variances will be given in parentheses.

Hyperparameter	Values
batch size	16, 32, 64
learning rate	2e-05, 3e-05, 5e-05
epochs	3, 5, 10

Table 3: Hyperparameter options for grid search.

4.2 Baseline Model

As our baseline, we finetuned BERT solely on AMR data. To make best use of the data, we compared BERT→AMR with BERT→AMRs (with subordinators as a feature). One of BERT's "unused tags" is placed to specify the position of a subordinator in an input sequence: "[CLS] [unused_0] *subordinator* [unused_0] *subordinate clause* [SEP] *matrix clause* [SEP]". As presented in Table 4, it turned out that explicit information of subordinators was not effective in our experiment, as opposed to the general tendency in *explicit vs implicit* connective settings (Pitler et al., 2008). Therefore, we choose BERT→AMR as our baseline and seek for other ways to make use of subordinators.

Models	F_M	F_m
BERT→AMR	64.06(±.06)	74.29(±.03)
BERT→AMR*s*	22.43(±.02)	54.77(±.03)

Table 4: Performance of baseline models.

5 Use of Weakly Supervised Data

5.1 Approaches

In the experiments, we take several approaches to examine the effect of augmentated data on classification performance. For direct comparison of the training data, BERT→WIKI is solely finetuned on WIKI data to see whether the model would benefit from the larger weakly supervised data. BERT→MIX is finetuned on a combined set of data which consists of AMR data and certain amount of additional WIKI data. The amount of WIKI data used ranges from 2~20k, where we add 2k sentences at a time . We take this approach with an expectation that WIKI data would complement the inbalanced distribution of AMR data to perform better than the baseline or BERT→WIKI. Finally, we evaluate the model marked as BERT→WIKI→AMR which is first finetuned on WIKI data, then further finetuned on AMR data. This is conducted under our hypothesis that "prefinetuning" on WIKI data would make BERT model fit to our task than the original model, which is just pretrained on next sentence prediction task.

5.2 Results and Analyses

Models	F_M	F_m
BERT→AMR (baseline)	64.06(±.06)	74.29(±.03)
BERT→WIKI	47.67(±.00)	61.72(±.00)
BERT→MIX$_{8k}$	67.12(±.01)	77.50(±.00)
BERT→WIKI→AMR	**72.43(±.02)**	**81.22(±.00)**

Table 5: Performance of each approach. Only the best performing model is presented for BERT→MIX.

The scores of all approaches are presented together in Table 5. The results show that training on weakly supervised data by itself does not improve the baseline, with BERT→WIKI harming the performance by 16.39% points on F_M and 12.57% points on F_m. This may be attributed to the gap of construction types between WIKI and AMR data. Meanwhile, we see improvements of 3.06% and 3.21% when we add 8k amount of WIKI data to AMR data. The transition of scores by the amount of added data is presented in Figure 10. Both F_M and F_m show an increase as we combine AMR and WIKI data until they reach the peak at 8k. Further addition only lead to drop the model's performance. This suggests that too much amount of WIKI data dilutes the presence of supervised AMR data. We could predict that training on full addition of WIKI data would deteriorate its performance near to that of BERT→WIKI. Among all our approaches, BERT→WIKI→AMR achieved the best results with 8.37% and 6.93% increase as expected. This proves the effectiveness of prefinetuning on weakly supervised data when you have supervised data of a small size.

Additionally, we checked whether our preprocessing step of adding artificial tags ("<" and ">") in section 4 helped the model's performance. With

Train:Dev:Test=3:1:1 for each split.

Balanced data with 0.5k for each class label.

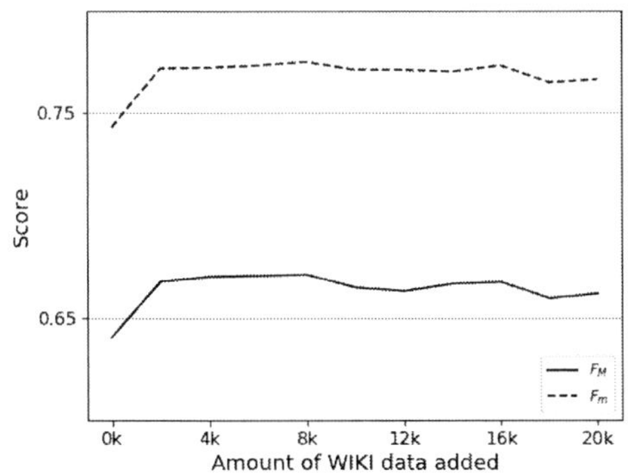

Figure 10: Score transitions of BERT→MIX by amount of WIKI data added. "k" stands for 1,000.

untagged version of BERT→WIKI→AMR scoring 71.21% for F_M and 80.47% for F_m, we see 1.22% and 0.75% increase for tagged version. We find that the improvements achieved are not as much as utilizing weakly supervised data, but still beneficial to some extent considering it is a by-product of dependency matching.

While it was not effective to use subordinators as features, it remains reasonable to take advantage of its information. Therefore, we make modifications to the trained models in Table 5. We first create a list of ambiguous subordinators and their possible labels (e.g. *since* is ambiguous between CAUSE and TIME). When we feed a complex sentence, its subordinator will be searched in the list to check whether it is potentially ambiguous. If it turns out to be true, a restriction will be applied to the softmax layer by lowering the probability of irrelevant class labels to 0. In other words, the models are modified to only look at possible labels defined in the list.

Models	F_M	F_m
BERT→AMR+*r*	67.11(±.05)	77.18(±.03)
BERT→MIX$_{8k}$+*r*	70.76(±.01)	80.52(±.00)
BERT→WIKI→AMR+*r*	**75.65(±.03)**	**83.94(±.01)**

Table 6: Performance with subordinator as restrictions on softmax layer.

The results after applying the restriction are shown in Table 6 with +*r* in model names. Compared to the performance in Table 5, we achieve overall improvements of 3.05∼3.64% on F_M and 2.72∼3.02% on F_m for all models. Table 7(a) and 7(b) present precision, recall, and F1 of BERT→AMR and BERT→AMR+*r* by labels.

The approach seems mostly effective except for CONC where the precision decreases by 5.75%. With further analysis on confusion matrices on the first split of data for cross validation in Table 8, we find the number of false positive errors of CONC increased. This is due to an error predicting sentences with *while*, which we regard ambiguous between CONC and TIME. When the correct label is TIME, the model first predicted CAUSE or COND. Even after the restriction was applied, the model predicted CONC. Overall, the restriction seems to help the models reduce false positive errors.

(a) BERT→AMR

Labels	*P*	*R*	*F*
CAUSE	60.51(±.07)	68.93(±.04)	64.34(±.04)
COND	84.00(±.02)	84.91(±.03)	84.43(±.02)
CONC	48.93(±.46)	43.16(±.19)	45.44(±.25)
TIME	72.96(±.21)	54.17(±.05)	62.01(±.08)

(b) BERT→AMR+*r*

Labels	*P*	*R*	*F*
CAUSE	63.71(±.07)	73.19(±.03)	68.00(±.03)
COND	89.17(±.02)	84.91(±.03)	86.97(±.02)
CONC	43.18(±.21)	43.16(±.19)	43.07(±.19)
TIME	73.25(±.18)	67.92(±.06)	70.40(±.10)

Table 7: Performance by labels.

(a) BERT→AMR

	Predicted Labels			
True Labels	CAUSE	COND	CONC	TIME
CAUSE	55	15	4	6
COND	10	179	1	6
CONC	4	5	12	1
TIME	10	12	0	26

(b) BERT→AMR+*r*

	Predicted Labels			
True Labels	CAUSE	COND	CONC	TIME
CAUSE	57	11	3	9
COND	10	179	1	6
CONC	4	5	12	1
TIME	7	3	5	33

Table 8: Confusion matrices of models trained on the first split of data for cross validation.

6 Conclusion

With the intention to capture the structure of complex sentence constructions in AMR framework, we proposed a pattern matching method using a list of dependency patterns and its corresponding skeletal AMRs. In the course of creating a comprehensive pattern dictionary, we observed semantically ambiguous entries. In order to resolve the semantic ambiguities, we framed the problem as a sentence-pair classification task and finetuned pretrained BERT models on data derived from AMR and Wikipedia corpus. Through the experiments, we found that the supplemental usage of weakly supervised data generated from Wikipedia effectively improves performance of the models compared to the one trained solely on small-sized supervised data. A natural next step will be to incorporate the presented method in AMR parsing task, which we leave for future work.

References

Yoav Artzi, Kenton Lee, and Luke Zettlemoyer. 2015. Broad-coverage CCG semantic parsing with AMR. In *Proceedings of the 2015 Conference on Empirical Methods in Natural Language Processing*, pages 1699–1710, Lisbon, Portugal. Association for Computational Linguistics.

Hongxiao Bai and Hai Zhao. 2018. Deep enhanced representation for implicit discourse relation recognition. In *Proceedings of the 27th International Conference on Computational Linguistics*, pages 571–583, Santa Fe, New Mexico, USA. Association for Computational Linguistics.

Laura Banarescu, Claire Bonial, Shu Cai, Madalina Georgescu, Kira Griffitt, Ulf Hermjakob, Kevin Knight, Philipp Koehn, Martha Palmer, and Nathan Schneider. 2013. Abstract meaning representation for sembanking. In *Proceedings of the 7th Linguistic Annotation Workshop and Interoperability with Discourse*, pages 178–186, Sofia, Bulgaria. Association for Computational Linguistics.

Claire Bonial, Bianca Badarau, Kira Griffitt, Ulf Hermjakob, Kevin Knight, Tim O ’ Gorman, Martha Palmer, and Nathan Schneider. 2018. Abstract meaning representation of constructions: The more we include, the better the representation. In *Proceedings of the Eleventh International Conference on Language Resources and Evaluation (LREC 2018)*.

Deng Cai and Wai Lam. 2020. AMR parsing via graph-sequence iterative inference. In *Proceedings of the 58th Annual Meeting of the Association for Computational Linguistics*, pages 1290–1301, Online. Association for Computational Linguistics.

Rudolf Carnap. 1952. Meaning postulates. *Philosophical Studies: An International Journal for Philosophy in the Analytic Tradition*, 3(5):65–73.

Jacob Devlin, Ming-Wei Chang, Kenton Lee, and Kristina Toutanova. 2019. BERT: Pre-training of deep bidirectional transformers for language understanding. In *Proceedings of the 2019 Conference of the North American Chapter of the Association for Computational Linguistics: Human Language Technologies, Volume 1 (Long and Short Papers)*, pages 4171–4186, Minneapolis, Minnesota. Association for Computational Linguistics.

Lucia Donatelli, Michael Regan, William Croft, and Nathan Schneider. 2018. Annotation of tense and aspect semantics for sentential AMR. In *Proceedings of the Joint Workshop on Linguistic Annotation, Multiword Expressions and Constructions (LAW-MWE-CxG-2018)*, pages 96–108, Santa Fe, New Mexico, USA. Association for Computational Linguistics.

David Dowty. 1979. *Word Meaning and Montague Grammar*. Reidel, Dordrecht.

Jeffrey Flanigan, Sam Thomson, Jaime G Carbonell, Chris Dyer, and Noah A Smith. 2014. A discriminative graph-based parser for the abstract meaning representation. In *Proceedings of the 52nd Annual Meeting of the Association for Computational Linguistics (Volume 1: Long Papers)*, pages 1426–1436.

Matthew Honnibal, Ines Montani, Sofie Van Landeghem, and Adriane Boyd. 2020. spaCy: Industrial-strength Natural Language Processing in Python. Zenodo.

Ioannis Konstas, Srinivasan Iyer, Mark Yatskar, Yejin Choi, and Luke Zettlemoyer. 2017. Neural amr: Sequence-to-sequence models for parsing and generation. *meeting of the association for computational linguistics*.

Joakim Nivre, Marie-Catherine de Marneffe, Filip Ginter, Jan Hajič, Christopher D Manning, Sampo Pyysalo, Sebastian Schuster, Francis Tyers, and Daniel Zeman. 2020. Universal dependencies v2: An evergrowing multilingual treebank collection. *arXiv preprint arXiv:2004.10643*.

Tim O'Gorman, Michael Regan, Kira Griffitt, Ulf Hermjakob, Kevin Knight, and Martha Palmer. 2018. AMR beyond the sentence: the multi-sentence AMR corpus. In *Proceedings of the 27th International Conference on Computational Linguistics*, pages 3693–3702, Santa Fe, New Mexico, USA. Association for Computational Linguistics.

Martha Palmer, Daniel Gildea, and Paul Kingsbury. 2005. The proposition bank: An annotated corpus of semantic roles. *Comput. Linguist.*, 31(1):71–106.

Xiaochang Peng, Chuan Wang, Daniel Gildea, and Nianwen Xue. 2017. Addressing the data sparsity issue in neural AMR parsing. In *Proceedings of the 15th Conference of the European Chapter of the Association for Computational Linguistics: Volume 1, Long Papers*, pages 366–375, Valencia, Spain. Association for Computational Linguistics.

Emily Pitler, Mridhula Raghupathy, Hena Mehta, Ani Nenkova, Alan Lee, and Aravind Joshi. 2008. Easily identifiable discourse relations. In *Coling 2008: Companion volume: Posters*, pages 87–90, Manchester, UK. Coling 2008 Organizing Committee.

Rashmi Prasad, Nikhil Dinesh, Alan Lee, Eleni Miltsakaki, Livio Robaldo, Aravind Joshi, and Bonnie Webber. 2008. The Penn Discourse TreeBank 2.0. In *Proceedings of the Sixth International Conference on Language Resources and Evaluation (LREC 2008)*, Marrakech, Morocco. European Language Resources Association (ELRA).

Michael Pust, Ulf Hermjakob, Kevin Knight, Daniel Marcu, and Jonathan May. 2015. Parsing English into Abstract Meaning Representation using syntax-based machine translation. In *Proceedings of the 2015 Conference on Empirical Methods in Natural Language Processing*, pages 1143–1154, Lisbon, Portugal. Association for Computational Linguistics.

James Pustejovsky. 1995. *The Generative Lexicon*. MIT Press, Cambridge, MA.

Peng Qi, Yuhao Zhang, Yuhui Zhang, Jason Bolton, and Christopher D. Manning. 2020. Stanza: A Python natural language processing toolkit for many human languages. In *Proceedings of the 58th Annual Meeting of the Association for Computational Linguistics: System Demonstrations*.

Lianhui Qin, Zhisong Zhang, Hai Zhao, Zhiting Hu, and Eric Xing. 2017. Adversarial connective-exploiting networks for implicit discourse relation classification. In *Proceedings of the 55th Annual Meeting of the Association for Computational Linguistics (Volume 1: Long Papers)*, pages 1006–1017, Vancouver, Canada. Association for Computational Linguistics.

Randolph Quirk, Sidney Greenbaum, Geoffrey Leech, and Jan Svartvik. 1985. *A Comprehensive Grammar of the English Language*. Longman, London.

Attapol Rutherford, Vera Demberg, and Nianwen Xue. 2017. A systematic study of neural discourse models for implicit discourse relation. In *Proceedings of the 15th Conference of the European Chapter of the Association for Computational Linguistics: Volume 1, Long Papers*, pages 281–291, Valencia, Spain. Association for Computational Linguistics.

Wei Shi and Vera Demberg. 2019. Next sentence prediction helps implicit discourse relation classification within and across domains. In *Proceedings of the 2019 Conference on Empirical Methods in Natural Language Processing and the 9th International Joint Conference on Natural Language Processing (EMNLP-IJCNLP)*, pages 5790–5796, Hong Kong, China. Association for Computational Linguistics.

S. A. Thompson and W. Mann. 1987. Rhetorical structure theory: A framework for the analysis of texts.

Takehito Utsuro, Shigeyuki Nishiokayama, Masakazu Fujio, and Yuji Matsumoto. 2000. Analyzing dependencies of Japanese subordinate clauses based on statistics of scope embedding preference. In *1st Meeting of the North American Chapter of the Association for Computational Linguistics*.

Chuan Wang, Nianwen Xue, and Sameer Pradhan. 2015. A transition-based algorithm for amr parsing. In *Proceedings of the 2015 Conference of the North American Chapter of the Association for Computational Linguistics: Human Language Technologies*, pages 366–375.

Qingrong Xia, Z. Li, Min Zhang, Meishan Zhang, G. Fu, Rui Wang, and Luo Si. 2019. Syntax-aware neural semantic role labeling. In *AAAI*.

Shunji Yamaguchi. 2013. *Eigo Koubun Zenkaisetsu* [The Perfect Study on English Sentence Structures]. Kenkyusha.

Sheng Zhang, Xutai Ma, Kevin Duh, and Benjamin Van Durme. 2019. Broad-coverage semantic parsing as transduction. In *Proceedings of the 2019 Conference on Empirical Methods in Natural Language Processing and the 9th International Joint Conference on Natural Language Processing (EMNLP-IJCNLP)*, pages 3786–3798, Hong Kong, China. Association for Computational Linguistics.

Neural Metaphor Detection with Visibility Embeddings

Gitit Kehat and **James Pustejovsky**
Department of Computer Science
Brandeis University
Waltham, MA 02453 USA
{gititkeh, jamesp}@brandeis.edu

Abstract

We present new results for the problem of sequence metaphor labeling, using the recently developed *Visibility Embeddings*. We show that concatenating such embeddings to the input of a BiLSTM obtains consistent and significant improvements at almost no cost, and we present further improved results when visibility embeddings are combined with BERT.

1 Introduction

When browsing through vision-language datasets, one can make the intuitive observation that their textual parts ("visual corpora") contain more physical language, mostly descriptive, which tends to be non-metaphorical by nature (See, for example, typical images from the Visual Genome dataset in Figure 1). Recently, this property was used to build visibility embeddings, which aim to provide a good estimation of a word's concreteness, a feature that has been long related to metaphoricity (Lakoff and Johnson, 1980; Turney et al., 2011).

Many metaphors indeed involve noticeable differences between the abstractness of words constructing them, like "clean conscience" (vs. "clean air"). Metaphors are not created in isolation, commonly do not stand alone as non-literal expressions, and are highly context-dependent in nature. Even the most concrete and physical text can be considered as metaphorical when mentioned in a different context than its original one, or in proximity to another text from the target domain. For example, a single use of a verb like "push" or "leak" can have both literal and metaphorical meanings, in relation to its context (see Figure 1).

Technically, the task of metaphor detection at the sentence level is commonly approached as one of the following two tasks:
(1) **Sequence Labeling**, in which each token in the sentence is classified as either "metaphorical" or "literal" (multiple outputs per sentence).
(2) **Classification** of a specific target word, usually the main verb (one output per sentence). This task is sometimes called "verb classification".

L: Water **leaking** on the road.
M: The news **leaked** out despite his secrecy.

L: A woman **pushing** a cart.
M: The liberal party **pushed** for reforms.

Figure 1: Images from the Visual Genome (Krishna et al., 2016) along with their literal ("L") description, and a metaphorical ("M") sentence with a similar verb from the MOH-X dataset (Mohammad et al., 2016) (concrete words in green and abstract words in red).

Recently, Kehat and Pustejovsky (2020) presented the simply constructed Visibility Embeddings (VE), which use references to visual/non-visual corpora to estimate word concreteness, and applied it to the task of verb-classification. In this paper we apply VE also to the sequence labeling task, and show how they consistently improve the result of a BiLSTM model with BERT. We also discuss possible problems when reporting results

Proceedings of the 10th Conference on Lexical and Computational Semantics, pages 222–228
August 5–6, 2021, Bangkok, Thailand (online) ©2021 Association for Computational Linguistics

on very small annotated datasets, and the effect on adding GloVe to the model input.

2 Background and Previous Work

2.1 Visibility Embeddings

Visibility embeddings (VE) were shown by (Kehat and Pustejovsky, 2020) to be useful for metaphor detection when concatenated to the input of BiLSTM models for the verb classification task. These simple and no-cost embeddings, are created by checking the occurrence of each word in a set of different visual and non-visual corpora, as a way to estimate its concreteness. They developed the *big visual corpus* (BVC), which contains the textual parts of multiple vision-language datasets, such as Visual Genome (Krishna et al., 2016), ImageNet (Deng et al., 2009), MSCOCO (Lin et al., 2014) and Flick r 30K (Young et al., 2014), as well as a "non-visual" corpus, $Brown - BVC$, which is the subtraction of the BVC from the Brown corpus (Francis and Kucera, 1964). These two corpora were previously shown (Kehat and Pustejovsky, 2017) to be highly concrete and highly abstract on average, respectively.

2.2 Metaphor Detection

The current state-of-the-art in metaphor detection is achieved by neural methods, enriched with contextual word embeddings (such as ELMo (Peters et al., 2018) and BERT (Devlin et al., 2019)), and commonly combined with varied linguistic features and metrics. Some notable results are the ones by Gao et al. (2018) who used ELMo and BiLSTM, Mao et al. (2019) who also experimented with BERT and features that rely on human metaphor processing, Dankers et al. (2019) who performed joint learning with emotion prediction, and Le et al. (2020) who used graph convolutional neural networks with dependency parse trees.

Impressive results[1] were presented in the 2018 Metaphor Detection Shared Task (Leong et al., 2018), with most of the groups using neural models with other linguistic elements like POS tags, WordNet features, concreteness scores and more (Wu et al., 2018; Swarnkar and Singh, 2018; Pramanick et al., 2018; Bizzoni and Ghanimifard, 2018), as well as in the more recent 2020 Shared Task (Leong et al., 2020), with the majority of groups using some variation of BERT in addition to the other features (Su et al., 2020; Gao and Zhang, 2002; Kuo and Carpuat, 2020; Torres Rivera et al., 2020; Kumar and Sharma, 2020; Hall Maudslay et al., 2020; Stemle and Onysko, 2020; Liu et al., 2020; Brooks and Youssef, 2020; Chen et al., 2020; Alnafesah et al., 2020; Li et al., 2020; Wan et al., 2020; Dankers et al., 2020).

Embedding-based approaches such as in Köper and Schulte im Walde (2017) and Rei et al. (2017) proved to work effectively on several annotated datasets. Different types of word embeddings were studied, including embeddings trained on corpora representing different levels of language mastery (Stemle and Onysko, 2018), and embeddings representing different dictionary categories in the form of binary vectors for each word (Mykowiecka et al., 2018). Previous work by Turney et al. (2011), Tsvetkov et al. (2014) and Köper and Schulte im Walde (2017) showed concreteness scores to be effective for Metaphor Detection, however, they all used fix concreteness score lists, such as the MRC (Coltheart, 1981) and the 40K list by Brysbaert et al. (2014), either as a reference or for training.

3 Model Details

As a base structure we use the simple BiLSTM architectures presented by Gao et al. (2018). The sequence labeling model (see Figure 2) consists of two layers, a BiLSTM and a feedforward layer, to get a label for each word in the sentence. We implemented the model in Python using the AllenNLP package (Gardner et al., 2017).

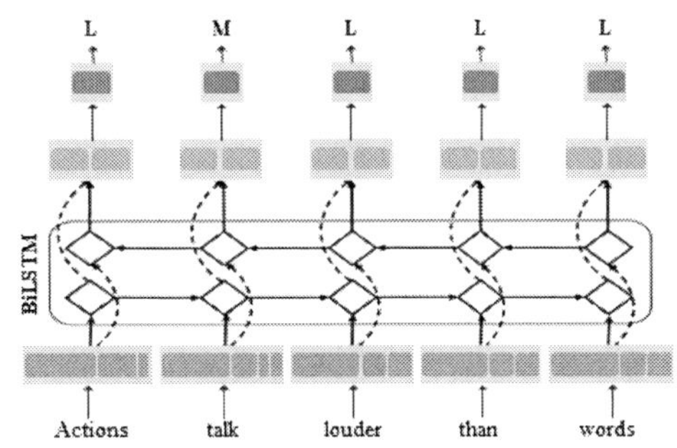

Figure 2: Simple sequence model with multiple outputs, one per word in the sentence.

We use a pretrained BERT model provided by the AllenNLP package, with 24 layers and 1024 hidden states, trained on cased English text. The

[1] yet not directly comparable to ours, since they used different train-test separations and evaluation, see Dankers et al. (2020)

input vector for the model consists of the concatenation of the 1024-dimensions BERT vector (using all the layers of the BERT model), the GloVe embeddings (Pennington et al., 2014) (not in all cases, see discussion in Section 4.3), and the VE of varied length (we experimented with vectors from length 50 and 300). Hyperparameters are fine-tuned on each dataset.

4 Experiment Setting and Results

We present results and comparison for two of the most common datasets for metaphor detection: **VUA** (Steen et al., 2010) and **MOH-X** (Mohammad et al., 2016). Annotated datasets for the validation and training of metaphor detection systems are not easily created, and require a level of expertise. The available datasets are therefore relatively small, hand crafted sets of several hundreds to a few thousands sentences, mostly only partially annotated for the metaphoricity of their main verb. As a result, the F1-scores vary highly, even with the slight change in parameters. In order to provide a consistent evidence to our algorithm's performance, we chose to compare not only the maximal F1-scores gained by each model, but also present a "parameterized" F1-score, over different learning rates. This would allow us to analyze the results while ignoring very highly-frequent fluctuations in the performance of the models.

4.1 VUA

We used the labels assigned to each token by the original VUA annotators. The verbs used for verb-testing are the ones used by Gao et al. (2018) (a large subset of all the verbs). Adding VE to the simple BiLSTM-BERT model achieves very high results (See Table 1). In order to provide more detailed comparison with previous models, results per POS are shown in Table 2.

Figure 3 demonstrates the consistent improvement gained by using VE by comparing four types of input vectors with different BERT - VE - GloVe combinations. Very similar learning rates (+-0.0001) can vary in up to +2 F1-Score, demonstrating the high variance those models have given the relatively small dataset. The random vector is of the same length and value range as the VE, with each value chosen randomly, to demonstrates that the length of the input vector has some effect on the results in terms of when the model reaches its maximum F1-score, as seen by the shifted gray line (BERT only). In this specific case, adding the GloVe vector improves the results (see discussion in Section 4.3).

	Model	P	R	F1
Verb Testing	Wu et al.*	60.0	76.3	67.2
	Gao et al.	68.2	71.3	69.7
	Mao et al.	69.3	72.3	70.8
	Su et al.*	78.9	81.9	80.4
	BERT+VE	72.2	75.0	73.6
All POS Testing	Wu et al.*	60.8	70.0	65.1
	Gao et al.	71.6	73.6	72.6
	Mao et al.	73.0	75.7	74.3
	Dankers et al.	—	—	76.8
	Su et al.*	75.6	78.3	76.9
	BERT+VE	77.1	77.8	**77.4**

Table 1: Sequence metaphor labeling on the VUA. Results denoted by * are not directly comparable.

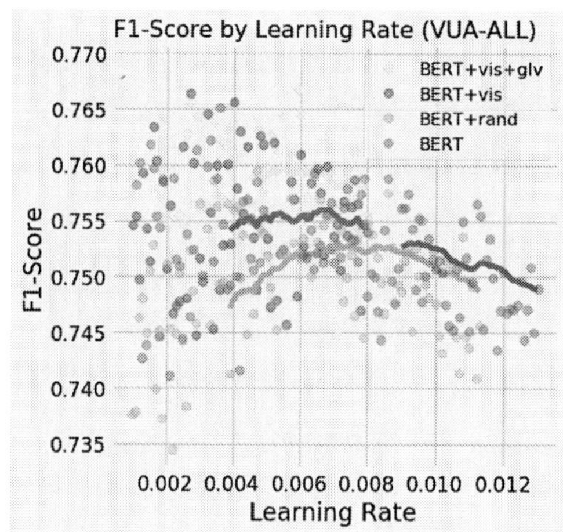

Figure 3: F1-scores as a function of the learning rate for VUA-ALL. The lines are moving averages of the corresponding points. **Yellow** - BERT + Visibility Embeddings + GloVe, **Red** - BERT + Visibility Embeddings, **Orange** - BERT + random vector, **Gray** - BERT only.

Figure 4 shows a similar comparison but in this case, the model is maximized on just the verbs of the classification task (as opposed to all words above). In all cases, adding visibility embeddings to the BERT embeddings achieves a no-cost improvement in the F1-score, both on average and as the maximal result gained for the model (over the given learning-rates gaps).

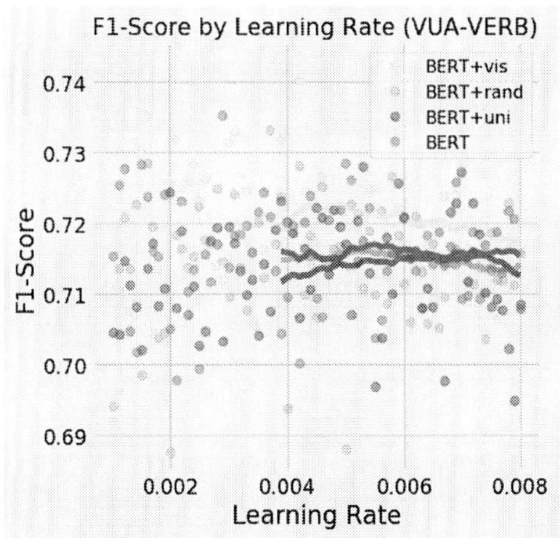

Figure 4: VUA target verbs testing. **Yellow** - BERT + Visibility Embeddings, **Orange** - BERT + random vector, **Red** - BERT with embeddings based on vocabulary (uniform positive value for all valid words), **Gray** - BERT only.

POS	P	R	F1
VERB	71.92	75.62	73.72
NOUN	71.33	67.85	69.55
ADP	89.36	91.55	90.44
ADJ	69.10	62.84	65.82

Table 2: Results by POS tags of the best model for VUA-All (BERT + GloVe + VE).

4.2 MOH-X

The MOH-X dataset (as a subset of the largest MOH dataset) was originally annotated for the main verbs only. It is small, and contains around 650 sentences. For the sequence labeling task, we use the default base case of assigning the rest of the tokens a "literal" label (as demonstrated in previous work). The results are presented in Table 3.

As a direct result from its size, testing on the MOH-X using ten-fold-CV with random splits yields fluctuating results. After conducting 50 random ten-fold-CVs (500 splits over all), we got an average F1-score of 82.3, with a maximum of 84.0 and a minimum of 81.0. Even though these two vary significantly, the minimum F1-score obtained is still higher in 1.0 F1-score point than the one recently reported by Mao et al. (2019) .

The above observation makes it hard to optimize and fine-tune the parameters of the model. We noticed that in general, higher F1-scores are gained for splits where the training set and evaluation set contain instances of the same verbs. Previously

Model	P	R	F1
Gao et al. (2018)	79.1	73.5	75.6
Le et al. (2020)	79.7	80.5	79.6
Mao et al. (2019)	77.5	83.1	80.0
BERT+VE	83.8	85.8	84.6
BERT+VE (rand-CV)	80.8	84.7	82.3

Table 3: Results on the MOH-X dataset using sequence labeling. Our model improves upon the previous state of the art by Mao et al. (2019).

reported results did not explicitly mention this issue. To maintain consistency with the results by Gao et al. (2018) and Le et al. (2020), we present our results both on their prechosen sets, as well as on randomly chosen splits (rand-CV).

4.3 Further Discussion

In some cases, adding the GloVe to the input vector does not help to improve the results, and even worsens them. This is true for both the sequence and classification tasks on the MOH-X dataset, and varies in the VUA (as can be seen in Figures 3, 4), though the differences are relatively small.

Concatenating GloVe to the input vector provides additional generalized non-domain-specific (the pre-trained GloVe was trained on Wikipedia) context for each word in a sentence. The MOH-X dataset contains shorter sentences, so on average, every word in the sentence has more weight when determining the metaphoricity of the target verb. In particular, when the verb is used metaphorically, the few other words in the sentence play a special role in giving us clues about it, say, when they belong to different domains. Adding the information from GloVe might smooth this effect.

When applied to the VUA, the Glove's effect is minimized, since it contains longer sentences and we have more words that are not directly related to the main metaphor presented by the target verb. In general, the VUA gets much lower results than the MOH-X on all performed tasks, since it was created from real sentences, while the MOH-X was handcrafted from WordNet sample sentences for the specific task of detecting non-direct language. in real world texts, we should expect similar lower performances.

5 Summary

We have presented new and improved results for sequence metaphor labeling for the VUA and MOH-X datasets using visibility embeddings and BERT as inputs for a simply constructed BiLSTM. We provided detailed comparison for the effect of adding VE to the model, and showed it to be a useful no-cost component to a metaphor detection system.

Acknowledgements

This work was supported by the US Defense Advanced Research Projects Agency (DARPA) and the Army Research Office (ARO) under contract #W911NF-15-C-0238 at Brandeis University. The points of view expressed herein are solely those of the authors and do not represent the views of the Department of Defense or the United States Government. Any errors or omissions are, of course, the responsibility of the authors.

References

Ghadi Alnafesah, Harish Tayyar Madabushi, and Mark Lee. 2020. Augmenting neural metaphor detection with concreteness. In *Proceedings of the Second Workshop on Figurative Language Processing*, pages 204–210, Online. Association for Computational Linguistics.

Yuri Bizzoni and Mehdi Ghanimifard. 2018. Bigrams and BiLSTMs two neural networks for sequential metaphor detection. In *Proceedings of the Workshop on Figurative Language Processing*, pages 91–101, New Orleans, Louisiana. Association for Computational Linguistics.

Jennifer Brooks and Abdou Youssef. 2020. Metaphor detection using ensembles of bidirectional recurrent neural networks. In *Proceedings of the Second Workshop on Figurative Language Processing*, pages 244–249, Online. Association for Computational Linguistics.

Marc Brysbaert, Amy Beth Warriner, and Victor Kuperman. 2014. Concreteness ratings for 40 thousand generally known english word lemmas. *Behavior research methods*, 46(3):904–911.

Xianyang Chen, Chee Wee (Ben) Leong, Michael Flor, and Beata Beigman Klebanov. 2020. Go figure! multi-task transformer-based architecture for metaphor detection using idioms: ETS team in 2020 metaphor shared task. In *Proceedings of the Second Workshop on Figurative Language Processing*, pages 235–243, Online. Association for Computational Linguistics.

Max Coltheart. 1981. The mrc psycholinguistic database. *The Quarterly Journal of Experimental Psychology Section A*, 33(4):497–505.

Verna Dankers, Karan Malhotra, Gaurav Kudva, Volodymyr Medentsiy, and Ekaterina Shutova. 2020. Being neighbourly: Neural metaphor identification in discourse. In *Proceedings of the Second Workshop on Figurative Language Processing*, pages 227–234, Online. Association for Computational Linguistics.

Verna Dankers, Marek Rei, Martha Lewis, and Ekaterina Shutova. 2019. Modelling the interplay of metaphor and emotion through multitask learning. In *Proceedings of the 2019 Conference on Empirical Methods in Natural Language Processing and the 9th International Joint Conference on Natural Language Processing (EMNLP-IJCNLP)*, pages 2218–2229, Hong Kong, China. Association for Computational Linguistics.

Jia Deng, Wei Dong, Richard Socher, Li-Jia Li, Kai Li, and Fei-Fei Li. 2009. Imagenet: A large-scale hierarchical image database. In *2009 IEEE Computer Society Conference on Computer Vision and Pattern Recognition (CVPR 2009), 20-25 June 2009, Miami, Florida, USA*, pages 248–255.

Jacob Devlin, Ming-Wei Chang, Kenton Lee, and Kristina Toutanova. 2019. BERT: Pre-training of deep bidirectional transformers for language understanding. In *Proceedings of the 2019 Conference of the North American Chapter of the Association for Computational Linguistics: Human Language Technologies, Volume 1 (Long and Short Papers)*, pages 4171–4186, Minneapolis, Minnesota. Association for Computational Linguistics.

W. Nelson Francis and Henry Kucera. 1964. Brown corpus. *Department of Linguistics, Brown University, Providence, Rhode Island*, 1.

Ge Gao, Eunsol Choi, Yejin Choi, and Luke Zettlemoyer. 2018. Neural metaphor detection in context. In *Proceedings of the 2018 Conference on Empirical Methods in Natural Language Processing*, pages 607–613, Brussels, Belgium. Association for Computational Linguistics.

Jianfeng Gao and Min Zhang. 2002. Improving language model size reduction using better pruning criteria. In *Proceedings of the 40th Annual Meeting of the Association for Computational Linguistics*, pages 176–182, Philadelphia, Pennsylvania, USA. Association for Computational Linguistics.

Matt Gardner, Joel Grus, Mark Neumann, Oyvind Tafjord, Pradeep Dasigi, Nelson F. Liu, Matthew Peters, Michael Schmitz, and Luke S. Zettlemoyer. 2017. Allennlp: A deep semantic natural language processing platform.

Rowan Hall Maudslay, Tiago Pimentel, Ryan Cotterell, and Simone Teufel. 2020. Metaphor detection using context and concreteness. In *Proceedings of the Second Workshop on Figurative Language Processing*, pages 221–226, Online. Association for Computational Linguistics.

Gitit Kehat and James Pustejovsky. 2017. Integrating vision and language datasets to measure word concreteness. In *Proceedings of the Eighth International Joint Conference on Natural Language Processing (Volume 2: Short Papers)*, pages 103–108, Taipei, Taiwan. Asian Federation of Natural Language Processing.

Gitit Kehat and James Pustejovsky. 2020. Improving neural metaphor detection with visual datasets. In *Proceedings of The 12th Language Resources and Evaluation Conference*, pages 5930–5935, Marseille, France. European Language Resources Association.

Maximilian Köper and Sabine Schulte im Walde. 2017. Improving verb metaphor detection by propagating abstractness to words, phrases and individual senses. In *Proceedings of the 1st Workshop on Sense, Concept and Entity Representations and their Applications*, pages 24–30, Valencia, Spain. Association for Computational Linguistics.

Ranjay Krishna, Yuke Zhu, Oliver Groth, Justin Johnson, Kenji Hata, Joshua Kravitz, Stephanie Chen, Yannis Kalantidis, Li-Jia Li, David A. Shamma, Michael S. Bernstein, and Fei-Fei Li. 2016. Visual genome: Connecting language and vision using crowdsourced dense image annotations. *CoRR*, abs/1602.07332.

Tarun Kumar and Yashvardhan Sharma. 2020. Character aware models with similarity learning for metaphor detection. In *Proceedings of the Second Workshop on Figurative Language Processing*, pages 116–125, Online. Association for Computational Linguistics.

Kevin Kuo and Marine Carpuat. 2020. Evaluating a Bi-LSTM model for metaphor detection in TOEFL essays. In *Proceedings of the Second Workshop on Figurative Language Processing*, pages 192–196, Online. Association for Computational Linguistics.

George Lakoff and Mark Johnson. 1980. *Metaphors we live by*. University of Chicago press.

Duong Le, My Thai, and Thien Nguyen. 2020. Multitask learning for metaphor detection with graph convolutional neural networks and word sense disambiguation. In *AAAI*, pages 8139–8146.

Chee Wee (Ben) Leong, Beata Beigman Klebanov, Chris Hamill, Egon Stemle, Rutuja Ubale, and Xianyang Chen. 2020. A report on the 2020 VUA and TOEFL metaphor detection shared task. In *Proceedings of the Second Workshop on Figurative Language Processing*, pages 18–29, Online. Association for Computational Linguistics.

Chee Wee (Ben) Leong, Beata Beigman Klebanov, and Ekaterina Shutova. 2018. A report on the 2018 VUA metaphor detection shared task. In *Proceedings of the Workshop on Figurative Language Processing*, pages 56–66, New Orleans, Louisiana. Association for Computational Linguistics.

Shuqun Li, Jingjie Zeng, Jinhui Zhang, Tao Peng, Liang Yang, and Hongfei Lin. 2020. ALBERT-BiLSTM for sequential metaphor detection. In *Proceedings of the Second Workshop on Figurative Language Processing*, pages 110–115, Online. Association for Computational Linguistics.

Tsung-Yi Lin, Michael Maire, Serge J. Belongie, James Hays, Pietro Perona, Deva Ramanan, Piotr Dollár, and C. Lawrence Zitnick. 2014. Microsoft COCO: common objects in context. In *Computer Vision - ECCV 2014 - 13th European Conference, Zurich, Switzerland, September 6-12, 2014, Proceedings, Part V*, pages 740–755.

Jerry Liu, Nathan O'Hara, Alexander Rubin, Rachel Draelos, and Cynthia Rudin. 2020. Metaphor detection using contextual word embeddings from transformers. In *Proceedings of the Second Workshop on Figurative Language Processing*, pages 250–255, Online. Association for Computational Linguistics.

Rui Mao, Chenghua Lin, and Frank Guerin. 2019. End-to-end sequential metaphor identification inspired by linguistic theories. In *Proceedings of the 57th Annual Meeting of the Association for Computational Linguistics*, pages 3888–3898, Florence, Italy. Association for Computational Linguistics.

Saif Mohammad, Ekaterina Shutova, and Peter Turney. 2016. Metaphor as a medium for emotion: An empirical study. In *Proceedings of the Fifth Joint Conference on Lexical and Computational Semantics*, pages 23–33, Berlin, Germany. Association for Computational Linguistics.

Agnieszka Mykowiecka, Aleksander Wawer, and Malgorzata Marciniak. 2018. Detecting figurative word occurrences using recurrent neural networks. In *Proceedings of the Workshop on Figurative Language Processing*, pages 124–127, New Orleans, Louisiana. Association for Computational Linguistics.

Jeffrey Pennington, Richard Socher, and Christopher D. Manning. 2014. Glove: Global vectors for word representation. In *Empirical Methods in Natural Language Processing (EMNLP)*, pages 1532–1543.

Matthew Peters, Mark Neumann, Mohit Iyyer, Matt Gardner, Christopher Clark, Kenton Lee, and Luke Zettlemoyer. 2018. Deep contextualized word representations. In *Proceedings of the 2018 Conference of the North American Chapter of the Association for Computational Linguistics: Human Language Technologies, Volume 1 (Long Papers)*, pages 2227–2237, New Orleans, Louisiana. Association for Computational Linguistics.

Malay Pramanick, Ashim Gupta, and Pabitra Mitra. 2018. An LSTM-CRF based approach to token-level metaphor detection. In *Proceedings of the Workshop on Figurative Language Processing*, pages 67–75, New Orleans, Louisiana. Association for Computational Linguistics.

Marek Rei, Luana Bulat, Douwe Kiela, and Ekaterina Shutova. 2017. Grasping the finer point: A supervised similarity network for metaphor detection. In *Proceedings of the 2017 Conference on Empirical Methods in Natural Language Processing*, pages 1537–1546, Copenhagen, Denmark. Association for Computational Linguistics.

Gerard J. Steen, Aletta G. Dorst, J. Berenike Herrmann, Anna A. Kaal, and Tina Krennmayr. 2010. Metaphor in usage. *Cognitive Linguistics*, 21(4):765–796.

Egon Stemle and Alexander Onysko. 2018. Using language learner data for metaphor detection. In *Proceedings of the Workshop on Figurative Language Processing*, pages 133–138, New Orleans, Louisiana. Association for Computational Linguistics.

Egon Stemle and Alexander Onysko. 2020. Testing the role of metadata in metaphor identification. In *Proceedings of the Second Workshop on Figurative Language Processing*, pages 256–263, Online. Association for Computational Linguistics.

Chuandong Su, Fumiyo Fukumoto, Xiaoxi Huang, Jiyi Li, Rongbo Wang, and Zhiqun Chen. 2020. DeepMet: A reading comprehension paradigm for token-level metaphor detection. In *Proceedings of the Second Workshop on Figurative Language Processing*, pages 30–39, Online. Association for Computational Linguistics.

Krishnkant Swarnkar and Anil Kumar Singh. 2018. Di-LSTM contrast : A deep neural network for metaphor detection. In *Proceedings of the Workshop on Figurative Language Processing*, pages 115–120, New Orleans, Louisiana. Association for Computational Linguistics.

Andrés Torres Rivera, Antoni Oliver, Salvador Climent, and Marta Coll-Florit. 2020. Neural metaphor detection with a residual biLSTM-CRF model. In *Proceedings of the Second Workshop on Figurative Language Processing*, pages 197–203, Online. Association for Computational Linguistics.

Yulia Tsvetkov, Leonid Boytsov, Anatole Gershman, Eric Nyberg, and Chris Dyer. 2014. Metaphor detection with cross-lingual model transfer. In *Proceedings of the 52nd Annual Meeting of the Association for Computational Linguistics, ACL 2014, June 22-27, 2014, Baltimore, MD, USA, Volume 1: Long Papers*, pages 248–258.

Peter D. Turney, Yair Neuman, Dan Assaf, and Yohai Cohen. 2011. Literal and metaphorical sense identification through concrete and abstract context. In *Proceedings of the 2011 Conference on Empirical Methods in Natural Language Processing, EMNLP 2011, 27-31 July 2011, John McIntyre Conference Centre, Edinburgh, UK, A meeting of SIGDAT, a Special Interest Group of the ACL*, pages 680–690.

Mingyu Wan, Kathleen Ahrens, Emmanuele Chersoni, Menghan Jiang, Qi Su, Rong Xiang, and Chu-Ren Huang. 2020. Using conceptual norms for metaphor detection. In *Proceedings of the Second Workshop on Figurative Language Processing*, pages 104–109, Online. Association for Computational Linguistics.

Chuhan Wu, Fangzhao Wu, Yubo Chen, Sixing Wu, Zhigang Yuan, and Yongfeng Huang. 2018. Neural metaphor detecting with CNN-LSTM model. In *Proceedings of the Workshop on Figurative Language Processing*, pages 110–114, New Orleans, Louisiana. Association for Computational Linguistics.

Peter Young, Alice Lai, Micah Hodosh, and Julia Hockenmaier. 2014. From image descriptions to visual denotations: New similarity metrics for semantic inference over event descriptions. *TACL*, 2:67–78.

Inducing Language-Agnostic Multilingual Representations

Wei Zhao[†] **Steffen Eger**[†] **Johannes Bjerva**[Ψ,Φ] **Isabelle Augenstein**[Φ]
[†]Technische Universität Darmstadt [Φ]University of Copenhagen [Ψ]Aalborg University
{zhao,eger}@aiphes.tu-darmstadt.de
jbjerva@cs.aau.dk
augenstein@di.ku.dk

Abstract

Cross-lingual representations have the potential to make NLP techniques available to the vast majority of languages in the world. However, they currently require large pretraining corpora or access to typologically similar languages. In this work, we address these obstacles by removing language identity signals from multilingual embeddings. We examine three approaches for this: (i) re-aligning the vector spaces of target languages (all together) to a pivot source language; (ii) removing language-specific means and variances, which yields better discriminativeness of embeddings as a by-product; and (iii) increasing input similarity across languages by removing morphological contractions and sentence reordering. We evaluate on XNLI and reference-free MT across 19 typologically diverse languages. Our findings expose the limitations of these approaches—unlike vector normalization, vector space re-alignment and text normalization do not achieve consistent gains across encoders and languages. Due to the approaches' additive effects, their combination decreases the cross-lingual transfer gap by 8.9 points (m-BERT) and 18.2 points (XLM-R) on average across all tasks and languages, however. Our code and models are publicly available.[1]

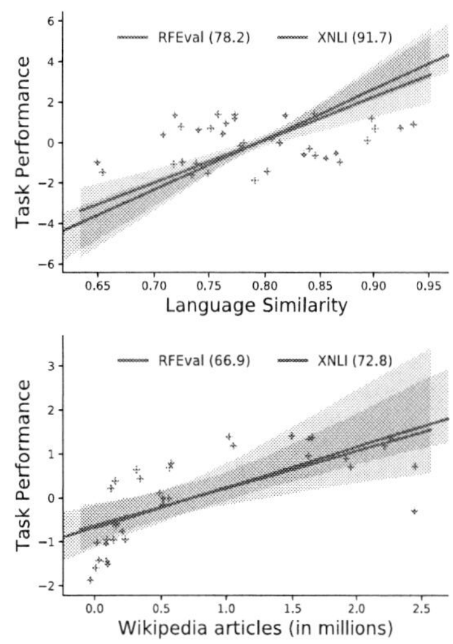

Figure 1: Zero-shot performance on XNLI and RFEval vs. language similarity to English (top), and data sizes in Wikipedia (bottom). Each point is a language; brackets give the Pearson correlation of points on the x- and y-axis. Zero-shot performance is based on the last layer of m-BERT and is standardized (zero mean, unit standard deviation) for better comparison.

1 Introduction

Cross-lingual text representations (Devlin et al., 2019; Conneau et al., 2019) ideally allow for transfer between *any* language pair, and thus hold the promise to alleviate the data sparsity problem for low-resource languages. However, until now, cross-lingual systems trained on English appear to transfer poorly to target languages dissimilar to English (Wu and Dredze, 2019; Pires et al., 2019) and for which only small monolingual corpora are available (Conneau et al., 2019; Hu et al., 2020; Lauscher et al., 2020), as illustrated in Fig. 1.[2]

As a remedy, recent work has suggested to train representations on larger multilingual corpora (Conneau et al., 2019) and, more importantly, to re-align them post-hoc so as to address the deficits of state-of-the-art contextualized encoders which have not seen any parallel data during training (Schuster et al., 2019; Wu and Dredze, 2019; Cao et al., 2020). However, re-mapping (i) can be costly, (ii) requires parallel data on word or sentence level, which may not be available abundantly in low-resource set-

[1]https://github.com/AIPHES/Language-Agnostic-Contextualized-Encoders

[2]We consider language similarity as the cosine similarity between the average representations of two languages over monolingual corpora from Wikipedia.

Proceedings of the 10th Conference on Lexical and Computational Semantics, pages 229–240
August 5–6, 2021, Bangkok, Thailand (online) ©2021 Association for Computational Linguistics

tings, and (iii) its positive effect has not yet been studied systematically.

Here, we explore *normalization* as an alternative to re-mapping. To decrease the distance between languages and thus allow for better cross-lingual transfer, we normalize (i) text inputs to encoders before vectorization to increase cross-lingual similarity, e.g., by reordering sentences according to typological features, and (ii) the representations themselves by removing their means and standard deviations, a common operation in machine and deep learning (LeCun et al., 1998; Rücklé et al., 2018). We evaluate vector normalization and post-hoc re-mapping across a typologically diverse set of 19 languages from five language families with varying sizes of monolingual corpora. However, input normalization is examined on a smaller sample of languages, as it is not feasible for languages whose linguistic features cannot be obtained automatically. We investigate two NLP tasks, and two state-of-the-art contextualized cross-lingual encoders—multilingual BERT (Devlin et al., 2019) and XLM-R (Conneau et al., 2019). Further, we provide a thorough analysis to investigate the effects of these techniques: (1) across layers; (2) to decrease the cross-lingual transfer gap, especially for low-resource and dissimilar languages; and (3) to eliminate language identity signals from multilingual representations and thus induce language-agnostic representations.

We evaluate on two cross-lingual tasks of varying difficulty: (1) zero-shot cross-lingual natural language inference (XNLI) measures the transfer ability of inference from source to target languages, where only the source language is annotated;and (2) reference-free machine translation evaluation (RFEval) measures the ability of multilingual embeddings to assign adequate cross-lingual semantic similarity scores to text from two languages, where one is frequently a corrupt automatic translation.

Our contributions: We show that: (i) input normalization leads to performance gains of up to 4.7 points on two challenging tasks; (ii) normalizing vector spaces is surprisingly effective, rivals much more resource-intensive methods such as re-mapping, and leads to more consistent gains; (iii) all three techniques—vector space normalization, re-mapping and input normalization—are orthogonal and their gains often stack. This is a very important finding as it allows for improvements on a much larger scale, especially for typologically dissimilar and low-resource languages.

2 Related Work

Cross-lingual Transfer Static cross-lingual representations have long been used for effective cross-lingual transfer and can even be induced without parallel data (Artetxe et al., 2017; Lample et al., 2018). In the monolingual case, static cross-lingual embeddings have recently been succeeded by contextualized ones, which yield considerably better results. The capabilities and limitations of the contextualized multilingual BERT (m-BERT) representations is a topic of vivid discourse. Pires et al. (2019) show surprisingly good transfer performance for m-BERT despite it being trained without parallel data, and that transfer is better for typologically similar languages. Wu et al. (2019) show that language representations are not correctly aligned in m-BERT, but can be linearly re-mapped. Extending this, Cao et al. (2020) find that jointly aligning language representations to be more useful than language-independent rotations. However, we show that the discriminativeness of the resulting embeddings is still poor, i.e., random word pairs are often assigned very high cosine similarity scores by the upper layers of original encoders, especially for XLM-R.

Libovický et al. (2019) further observe that m-BERT representations of related languages are seemingly close to one another in the cross-lingual embedding space. They show that removing language-specific means from m-BERT can eliminate language identity signals. In contrast, we remove both language-specific means and variances as well as morphological contractions, and reorder sentences to reduce linguistic gaps between languages. In addition, our analysis covers more languages from a typologically broader sample, and shows that vector space normalization is as effective as other recently proposed fixes for m-BERT's limitations (especially re-mapping), but is much cheaper and orthogonal to other solutions (e.g., input normalization) in that gains are almost additive.

Linguistic Typology in NLP. Structural properties of many of the world's languages can be queried via databases such as WALS (Dryer and Haspelmath, 2013). O'Horan et al. (2016); Ponti et al. (2019) suggest to inject typological information into models to bridge the performance gap between high- and low-resource languages. Bjerva and Augenstein (2018); de Lhoneux et al. (2018); Bjerva and Augenstein (2021) show that cross-

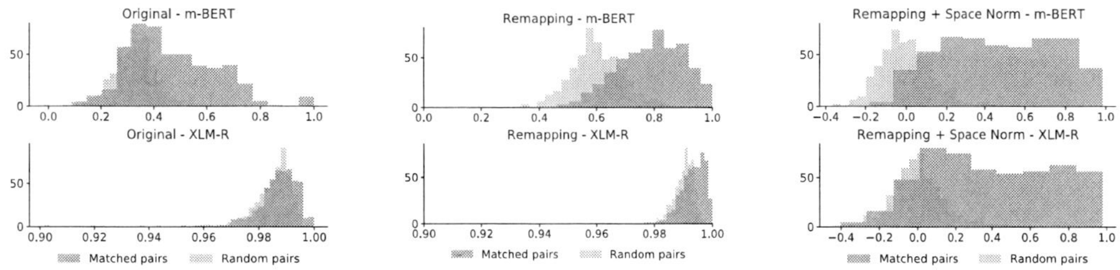

Figure 2: Histograms of cosine similarity scores of word pairs.

lingual transfer can be more successful between languages which share, e.g., morphological properties. We draw inspiration from Wang and Eisner (2016), who use dependency statistics to generate a large collection of synthetic languages to augment training data for low-resource languages. This intuition of modifying languages based on syntactic features can also be used in order to decrease syntactic and morphological differences between languages. We go further than using syntactic features, and remove word contractions and reorder sentences based on typological information from WALS.

3 Language-Agnostic Representations

Analyses by Ethayarajh (2019) indicate that random words are often assigned high cosine similarities in the upper layers of monolingual BERT. We examine this in a cross-lingual setting, by randomly selecting 500 German-English mutual word translations and random word pairs within parallel sentences from Europarl (Koehn, 2005). Fig. 2 (left) shows histograms based on the last layers of m-BERT (Devlin et al., 2019) and XLM-R (Conneau et al., 2019), respectively, which show that XLM-R wrongly assigns nearly perfect cosine similarity scores (+1) to both mutual word translations (matched word pairs) and random word pairs, whereas m-BERT sometimes assigns low scores to mutual translations. This reaffirms that both m-BERT and XLM-R have difficulty in distinguishing matched from random word pairs. Surprisingly, vector space re-mapping does not seem to help for XLM-R, but better separates random from matched pairs for m-BERT (Fig. 2 (middle)). In contrast, the joint effect of normalization and re-mapping leads to adequate separation of the two distributions for both m-BERT and XLM-R, increasing the discriminative ability of both encoders.

3.1 Vector space re-alignment

m-BERT and XLM-R induce cross-lingual vector spaces in an unsupervised way—no parallel data is involved at training time. To improve upon these representations, recent work has suggested to remap them, i.e., to use small amounts of parallel data to restructure the cross-lingual vector spaces. We follow the joint re-mapping approach of Cao et al. (2020), which has shown better results than rotation-based re-mapping.

Notation. Suppose we have k parallel corpora $C^1, \dots, C^k$, i.e., $C^\nu = \{(\mathbf{s}^1, \mathbf{t}^1), \dots, (\mathbf{s}^n, \mathbf{t}^n)\}$ is a set of corresponding sentence pairs from source and target languages, for $\nu = 1, \dots, k$. We denote the alignments of words in a sentence pair $(\mathbf{s}, \mathbf{t})$ as $a(\mathbf{s}, \mathbf{t}) = \{(i_1, j_1), \dots, (i_m, j_m)\}$, where (i, j) denotes that $\mathbf{s}_i$ and $\mathbf{s}_j$ are mutual translations. Let $f(i, \mathbf{u})$ be the contextual embedding for the i-th word in a sentence $\mathbf{u}$.

Joint Alignment via Fine-tuning. We align the monolingual sub-spaces of a source and target language by minimizing the distances of embeddings for matched word pairs in the corpus C^ν:

$$L(C^\nu, f_\Theta) = \sum_{(\mathbf{s},\mathbf{t}) \in C^\nu} \sum_{(i,j) \in a(\mathbf{s},\mathbf{t})} \|f_\Theta(i, \mathbf{s}) - f_\Theta(j, \mathbf{t}))\|_2^2 \tag{1}$$

where Θ are the parameters of the encoder f. As in Cao et al. (2020), we use a regularization term to avoid for the resulting (re-aligned) embeddings to drift too far away from the initial encoder state f_0:

$$R(C^\nu, f_\Theta) = \sum_{\mathbf{t} \in C^\nu} \sum_{i=1}^{\mathrm{len}(\mathbf{t})} \|f_\Theta(i, \mathbf{t}) - f_0(i, \mathbf{t})\|_2^2 \tag{2}$$

Like for the multilingual pre-training of m-BERT and XLM-R, we fine-tune the encoder f on the concatenation of k parallel corpora to handle resource-lean languages, which is in contrast to offline alignment with language-independent rotations (Aldarmaki and Diab, 2019; Schuster et al., 2019). Assume that English is a common pivot (source language) in all our k parallel corpora. Then the following objective function orients all non-English embeddings toward English:

$$\min_{\Theta} \sum_{\nu=1}^{k} L(C^{\nu}, f_{\Theta}) + R(C^{\nu}, f_{\Theta}) \quad (3)$$

In §5, we refer to the above described re-alignment step as JOINT-ALIGN.

3.2 Vector space normalization

We add a batch normalization layer that constrains all embeddings of different languages into a distribution with zero mean and unit variance:

$$\bar{f}(i, \mathbf{s}) = \frac{f(i, \mathbf{s}) - \mu_{\beta}}{\sqrt{\sigma_{\beta}^2 + \epsilon}} \quad (4)$$

where ϵ is a constant value for numerical stability, μ_{β} and σ_{β} are mean and variance, serving as per batch statistics for each time step in a sequence. In addition to a common effect during training, i.e., reducing covariate shift of input spaces, this additional layer in the cross-lingual setup may allow for 1) removing language identity signals, e.g. language-specific means and variances, from multilingual embeddings; and 2) increasing the discriminativeness of embeddings so that they can distinguish word pairs with different senses, as shown in Fig. 2 (right). We apply batch normalization to the last layer representations of m-BERT and XLM-R, and use a batch size of 8 across all setups. In §5, we refer to the above batch normalization step as NORM and contrast this with layer normalization. The latter yields batch-independent statistics, which are computed across all time steps for individual input sequences in a batch. This is predominantly used to stabilize the training process of RNN (Ba et al., 2016) and Transformer-based models (Vaswani et al., 2017).

3.3 Input normalization

In addition to joint alignment and vector space normalization, we investigate decreasing cross-linguistic differences between languages via the following surface form manipulation of input texts.

Removing Morphological Contractions. In many languages, e.g. Italian, prepositions and definite articles are often contracted. For instance, *de il* (*'of the'*) is usually contracted to *del*. This leads to a mismatch between, e.g., English and Italian in terms of token alignments, and increases the cross-lingual difference between the two. We segment an orthographic token (e.g. *del*) into several (syntactic) tokens (e.g. *de il*).[3] This yields a new sentence which no longer corresponds to typical standard Italian grammar, but which we hypothesise reduces the linguistic gap between Italian and English, thus increasing cross-lingual performance.

Sentence Reordering. Another typological feature which differs between languages, is the ordering of nouns and adjectives. For instance, WALS shows that Romance languages such as French and Italians often use noun-adjective ordering, e.g., *pomme rouge* in French, whereas the converse is used in English. Additionally, languages differ in their ordering of subjects, objects, and verbs. For instance, according to WALS, English firmly follows the subject-verb-object (SVO) structure, whereas there is no dominant order in German. We apply this reordering in order to decrease the linguistic gap between languages. For instance, when considering English and French, we reverse all noun-adjective pairings from French to match English. This alignment is done while considering a dependency tree. We re-align according to the typological features from WALS. Since such feature annotations are available for a large amount of languages, and can be obtained automatically with high accuracy (Bjerva et al., 2019a), we expect this method to scale to languages for which basic dependencies (such as noun-adjective attachment) can be obtained automatically. In §5, we refer to the above re-alignment step as TEXT.

4 Experiments

4.1 Transfer tasks

Cross-lingual embeddings are usually evaluated via zero-shot cross-lingual transfer for supervised text classification tasks, or via unsupervised cross-lingual textual similarity. For zero-shot transfer, fine-tuning of cross-lingual embeddings is done based on source language performance, and evaluation is performed on a held-out target language.

[3]We use UDPipe (Straka et al., 2016), which is a pipeline trained on UD treebank 2.5 (Nivre et al., 2020).

Language	Lang. family	Distance (EN-X)	Wiki-articles (in millions)	Sim level	Res level
Tagalog	α	29.3	0.08	low	low
Javanese	α	26.5	0.06	low	low
Bengali	γ	24.8	0.08	low	low
Marathi	γ	24.0	0.06	low	low
Estonian	η	23.8	0.20	low	middle
Hindi	γ	22.2	0.13	middle	low
Urdu	γ	21.7	0.15	middle	middle
Finnish	η	20.1	0.47	middle	middle
Hungarian	η	19.8	0.46	middle	middle
Afrikaans	β	19.6	0.09	middle	low
Malay	α	19.2	0.33	middle	middle
Spanish	δ	18.5	1.56	high	high
French	δ	18.2	2.16	high	high
Italian	δ	18.0	1.57	high	high
Indonesian	α	17.7	0.51	high	middle
Dutch	β	16.3	1.99	high	high
Portuguese	δ	16.2	1.02	high	high
German	β	15.6	2.37	high	high
English	β	0.0	5.98	high	high

Table 1: Languages used, with their language families: Austronesian (α), Germanic (β), Indo-Aryan (γ), Romance (δ), and Uralic (η). The cosine distances between target languages and English are measured using m-BERT.

This is, however, not likely to result in high quality target language embeddings and gives a false impression of cross-lingual abilities (Libovický et al., 2020). Zhao et al. (2020) use the more difficult task of reference-free machine translation evaluation (RFEval) to expose limitations of cross-lingual encoders, i.e., a failure to properly represent fine-grained language aspects, which may be exploited by natural adversarial inputs such as word-by-word translations.

XNLI. The goal of natural language inference (NLI) is to infer whether a premise sentence entails, contradicts, or is neutral towards a hypothesis sentence. Conneau et al. (2018) release a multilingual NLI corpus, where the English dev and test sets of the MultiNLI corpus (Williams et al., 2018) are translated to 15 languages by crowd-workers.

RFEval. This task evaluates the translation quality, i.e. similarity of a target language translation and a source language sentence. Following Zhao et al. (2020), we collect source language sentences with their system and reference translations, as well as human judgments from the WMT17 metrics shared task (Bojar et al., 2017), which contains predictions of 166 translation systems across 12 language pairs in WMT17. Each language pair has approximately 3k source sentences, each associated with one human reference translation and with the automatic translations of participating systems. As in Zhao et al. (2019, 2020), we use the Earth Mover Distance to compute the distances between source sentence and target language translations, based on the semantic similarities of their contextualized cross-lingual embeddings. We refer to this score as XMoverScore (Zhao et al., 2020) and report its Pearson correlation with human judgments in our experiments.

4.2 A Typologically Varied Language Sample

We evaluate multilingual representations on two sets of languages: (1) a default language set with 4 languages from the official XNLI test sets and 2 languages from the WMT17 test sets; (2) a diagnostic language set which contains 19 languages with different levels of data resources from a typologically diverse sample[4] covering five language families (each with at least three languages): Austronesian (α), Germanic (β), Indo-Aryan (γ), Romance (δ), and Uralic (η). For RFEval, we resort to pairs of translated source sentences and system translations. The former ones are translated from English human reference translations into 18 languages, obtained from Google Translate. For XNLI, we use translated test sets of all these languages from (Hu et al., 2020). Tab. 1 shows the overview of 19 languages which are labeled with 1) Similarity Level, i.e., the degree of similarity between target languages and English; and 2) Resource Level, i.e., the amount of data resources available in Wikipedia.

4.3 Cross-lingual Encoders

Our goal is to improve the cross-lingual abilities of established contextualized cross-lingual embeddings. These support around 100 languages and are pre-trained using monolingual language modeling.

m-BERT (Devlin et al., 2019) is pre-trained on 104 monolingual corpora from Wikipedia, with: 1) a vocabulary size of 110k; 2) language-specific tokenization tools for data pre-processing; and 3) two monolingual pre-training tasks: masked language modeling and next sentence prediction.

XLM-R (Conneau et al., 2019) is pre-trained on the CommonCrawl corpora of 100 languages, which contain more monolingual data than Wikipedia corpora, with 1) a vocabulary size of 250k; 2) a language-agnostic tokenization tool,

[4] This sample was chosen as it yields a large typological variety, with representatives from several language families across the world.

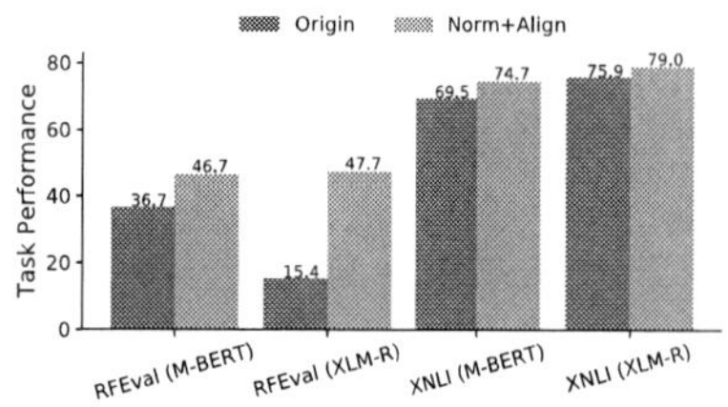

Figure 3: Results on RFEval are averaged over two language pairs (de-en and fi-en) from the WMT17 human translated test sets. Likewise, results on XNLI are averaged over four selected language pairs (en-fr, en-de, en-hi and en-es) from XNLI human translated test sets.

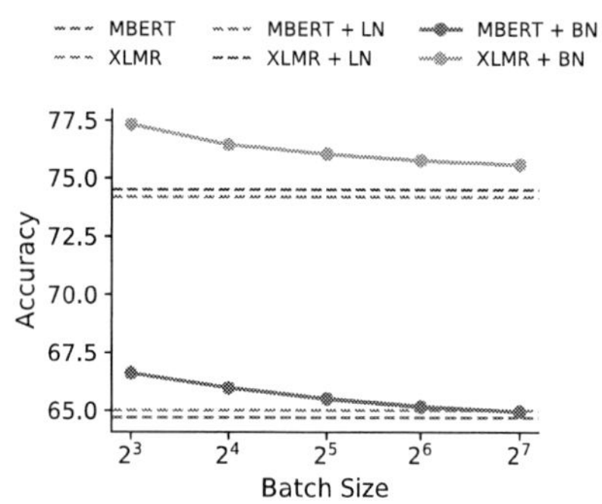

Figure 4: Results on XNLI on average across all language pairs. BN and LN denote batch and layer normalizations, respectively.

Sentence Piece (Kudo and Richardson, 2018) for data pre-processing; and 3) masked language modeling as the only monolingual pre-training task. We apply NORM, TEXT, JOINT-ALIGN and the combinations of these to the last layer of m-BERT and XLM-R, and report their performances on XNLI and RFEval in §5. To investigate the layer-wise effect of these modifications, we apply the modifications to individual layers and report the performances in §6. See the appendix for implementation details.

5 Results

Unlike re-mapping and vector space normalization, scaling input normalization to a large language sample is more difficult, as typological features differ across languages. Thus, we report the results of re-mapping and vector space normalization across 19 languages, while text normalization is evaluated on a smaller sample of languages.

Re-mapping and Vector Space Normalization. In Tab. 2, we show results on machine translated test sets. The m-BERT space modified by JOINT-ALIGN ⊕ NORM achieves consistent improvements on RFEval (+10.1 points) and XNLI (+7.6 points) on average. However, effects are different for XLM-R. The modified XLM-R outperforms the baseline XLM-R on RFEval by the largest margin (+33.5 points), but the improvement is much smaller (+2.8 points) on XNLI. These gains are not an artefact of machine-translated test sets: we observe similar gains on human-translated data (see Fig. 3).

In Tab. 3, we tease apart the sources of improvements. Overall, the impacts of NORM and JOINT-ALIGN are substantial, and their effect is additive and sometimes even superadditive (e.g., m-BERT improves by 10.1 points on RFEval when both NORM and JOINT-ALIGN are applied but only by 1.7 and 7.6 points individually). We note that the improvement from NORM is more consistent across tasks and encoders, despite its simplicity and negligible cost. In contrast, JOINT-ALIGN has a positive effect for m-BERT but it does not help for XLM-R on the XNLI task, notwithstanding the minor difference of two encoders, e.g., much larger training data and a different tokenizer used in XLM-R. We believe the poor discriminative ability of XLM-R, *viz.*, that it cannot distinguish word translations from random word pairs, leads to the inconsistent behavior of JOINT-ALIGN. As a remedy, negative examples such as random pairs could be included in Eq. (3) during training so as to decrease the discriminative gap between m-BERT and XLM-R. This suggests that future research efforts should focus on the robustness of cross-lingual alignments.

Batch vs. Layer Normalization. Unsurprisingly, the choice of batch size greatly influences XNLI performance when applying batch normalization for m-BERT and XLM-R (Fig. 4). We find that (i) the larger the batch size is, the smaller the impacts on XNLI, and (ii) a batch size of 8 performs best. Interestingly, layer normalization does not help for XNLI, even though it yields batch-independent statistics and is effective in stabilizing the training process (Vaswani et al., 2017). We note that per batch sequences with varying time steps (i.e., sentence length) are often padded with zero vectors in practice. This leads to inaccurate batch-independent statistics, as they are computed across all time steps, unlike batch normalization with per batch statistics for individual time steps. In addition to batch and layer normalizations, other nor-

Model	Avg	△	Language Families α(4)	△	β(3)	△	γ(4)	△	δ(4)	△	η(3)	△
Original cross-lingual embeddings												
M-BERT	38.0	-	36.6	-	40.4	-	28.2	-	49.8	-	34.8	-
XLM-R	12.9	-	13.5	-	17.4	-	2.9	-	25.9	-	11.6	-
Modified cross-lingual embeddings												
M-BERT ⊕ JOINT-ALIGN ⊕ NORM	48.1	+10.1	45.9	+9.3	47.5	+7.1	32.4	+4.2	53.4	+3.6	46.0	+11.2
XLM-R ⊕ JOINT-ALIGN ⊕ NORM	46.4	+33.5	46.5	+33.0	48.2	+30.8	37.0	+34.1	53.8	+27.9	47.2	+35.6

(a) Cross-lingual Semantic Text Similarity on the RFEval task

Model	Avg	△	Language Families α(4)	△	β(3)	△	γ(4)	△	δ(4)	△	η(3)	△
Original cross-lingual embeddings												
M-BERT	64.7	-	60.8	-	69.1	-	57.9	-	73.1	-	63.4	-
XLM-R	74.8	-	72.4	-	76.3	-	70.9	-	78.4	-	76.1	-
Modified cross-lingual embeddings												
M-BERT ⊕ JOINT-ALIGN ⊕ NORM	72.3	+7.6	72.3	+11.5	75.8	+6.7	65.2	+7.3	77.4	+4.3	72.0	+8.6
XLM-R ⊕ JOINT-ALIGN ⊕ NORM	77.6	+2.8	74.8	+2.4	79.6	+3.3	73.7	+2.8	80.9	+2.5	78.8	+2.7

(b) Cross-lingual Zero-shot transfer on the XNLI task

Table 2: Overall results of established cross-lingual baselines and our modifications, for RFEval and XNLI. Brackets denote the number of languages per group. Results are averaged per group. △ is the difference between the performance of the original and the modified encoders.

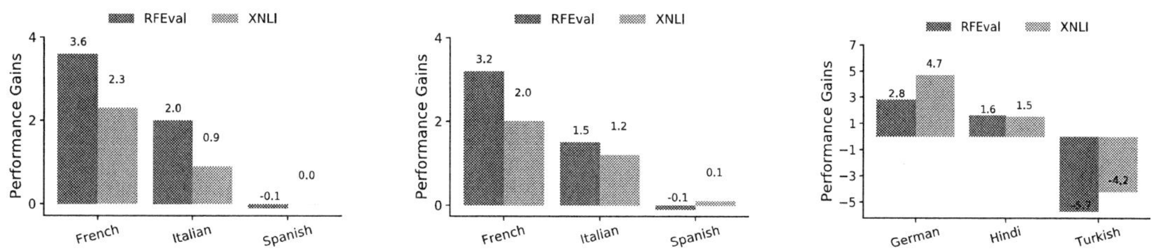

(a) Removing contractions (b) Reversing adjective-noun order (c) Reversing object-verb order

Figure 5: Performance gains on RFEval and XNLI obtained by three types of TEXT operations .

Model	XNLI	RFEval
M-BERT ⊕ NORM	+1.9	+1.7
M-BERT ⊕ JOINT-ALIGN	+5.2	+7.6
M-BERT ⊕ JOINT-ALIGN ⊕ NORM	+7.6	+10.1
XLM-R ⊕ NORM	+2.5	+27.1
XLM-R ⊕ JOINT-ALIGN	−0.2	+11.6
XLM-R ⊕ JOINT-ALIGN ⊕ NORM	+2.8	+33.5

Table 3: Ablation tests of our modified encoders. Performance gains are averaged over all languages.

Model	XNLI	RFEval	Avg
M-BERT	17.4	24.5	21.0
XLM-R	11.1	37.8	24.5
M-BERT ⊕ JOINT-ALIGN ⊕ NORM	9.8	14.4	12.1
XLM-R ⊕ JOINT-ALIGN ⊕ NORM	8.4	4.3	6.3

Table 4: Performance gap (lower is better) for cross-lingual classification transfer, and reference-based and reference-free MT.

malizers such as GroupNorm (Wu and He, 2018) and PowerNorm (Shen et al., 2020) also receive attention in many communities. This raises another concern towards a systematic investigation of normalizers for future work.

Linguistic Manipulation. We apply input modifications to language pairs that contrast in either of three typological features: word contractions, noun-adjective and object-verb orderings. Fig. 5 shows that reducing the linguistic gap between languages by TEXT can sometimes lead to improvements (exemplified by m-BERT). Both French and Italian benefit considerably from both removing contractions (a) and reversing the order of adjectives and nouns (b), with no changes observed for Spanish.

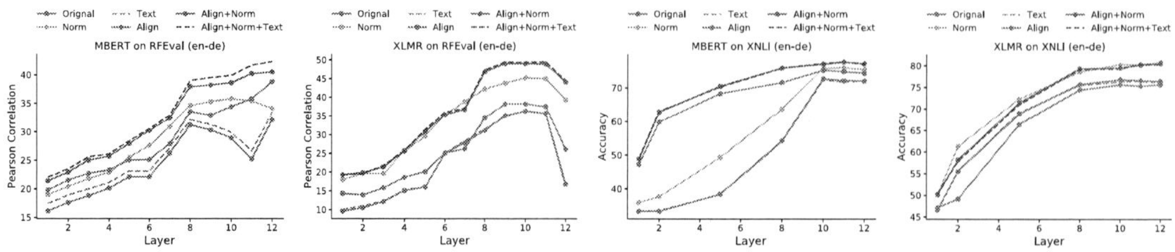

Figure 6: Results of m-BERT and XLM-R and our modifications across layers on the RFEval and XNLI tasks.

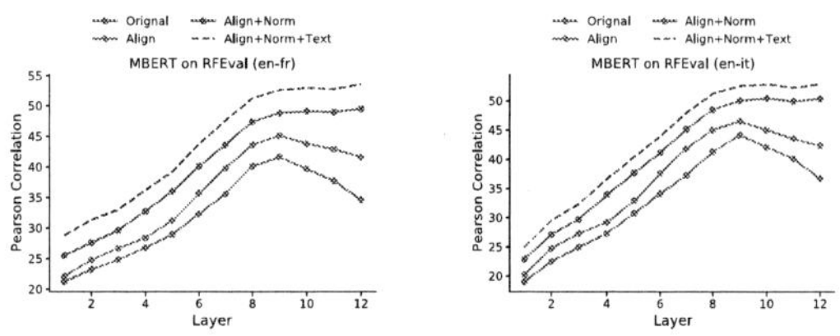

Figure 7: Results of m-BERT across layers on RFEval.

As for reversing object-verb order (c), we again see improvements for 2 out of 3 languages. We hypothesize that the few cases without gains are due to the differing frequencies of occurrences of linguistic phenomena in XNLI and RFEval. Another error source is the automatic analysis from Straka et al. (2016), and improving this pre-processing step may further increase the performance of TEXT.

6 Analysis

(Q1) *How sensitive are normalization and post-hoc re-mapping across layers?*

In Fig. 6, rather than checking results for the last layer only, we investigate improvements of our three modifications on RFEval across all layers of and XLM-R for one high-resource language pair (de-en) and one low-resource pair (jv-en) (see appendix). This reveals that, (1) for XNLI, applying JOINT-ALIGN, NORM and TEXT to the last layer of m-BERT and XLM-R consistently results in the best performance. This indicates that the modifications to the last layer could be sufficient for *supervised* cross-lingual transfer tasks. (2) However, the best results on RFEval are oftentimes obtained from an intermediate layer. Further, (3) we observe that JOINT-ALIGN is not always effective, especially for XLM-R. E.g., it leads to the worst performance across all layers on XNLI for XLM-R, even below the baseline performance. (4) Reporting improvements on only the last layer may sometimes give a false and inflated impression, especially for RFEval. E.g., the improvement (on RFEval) of the three modifications over the original embeddings is almost 30 points for the last layer of XLMR, but it is less than 15 points for the penultimate layer. (5) Normalization and remapping typically stabilize layer-wise variances. (6) The gains of the three modifications are largely complementary across layers. (see also Fig. 7).

(Q2) *To what extent can our modifications decrease the cross-lingual transfer gap, especially in low-resource scenarios and dissimilar languages?*

Tab. 4 shows that applying re-mapping and vector space normalization[5] to the last layer of m-BERT and XLM-R considerably reduces performance gaps *viz.*: a) zero-shot transfer performance on XNLI between the English test set and the average performance on the other 18 languages; b) the difference between mono- and cross-lingual textual similarity on RFEval, i.e., the difference between the average correlations of XMoverScore and human judgments on 19 languages obtained from *reference-based*[6] and *reference-free* MT evaluation setups. Although smaller, the remaining gaps indicates further potential for improvement. Fig. 9 shows the largest gains are on (1) low-resource languages and (2) languages most distant to English.

(Q3) *Are our modifications to contextualized cross-lingual encoders language-agnostic?*

Fig. 8 (a) shows that the centroid vectors[7] of languages within the same language family lie closely in the vector space, further showing that language

[5] We do not apply text normalization in this setup because not all languages are covered in UDPipe.

[6] Reference-based evaluation assigns semantic similarity scores to pairs of system and reference translations in English.

[7] Language centroids are representative (sentence) embeddings of languages averaged over monolingual Wikipedia data, as in Libovický et al. (2019). Although they use language families as a proxy, recent work shows that *structural similarities* of languages are a more likely candidate (Bjerva et al., 2019b).

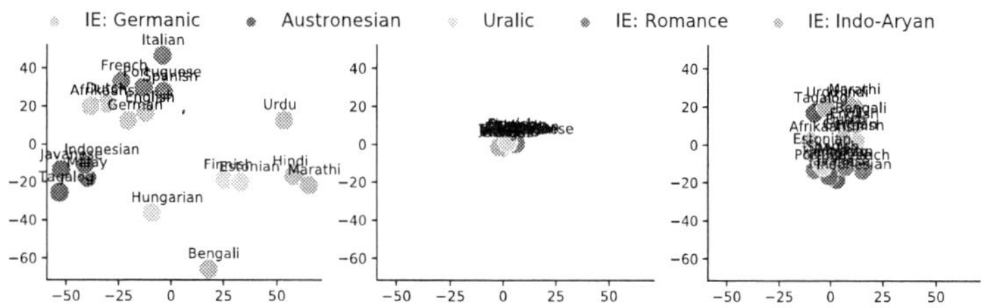

(a) Original Space (b) Re-aligned Space (c) Normalized Space

Figure 8: t-SNE distributions of language centroids based on the last m-BERT layer.

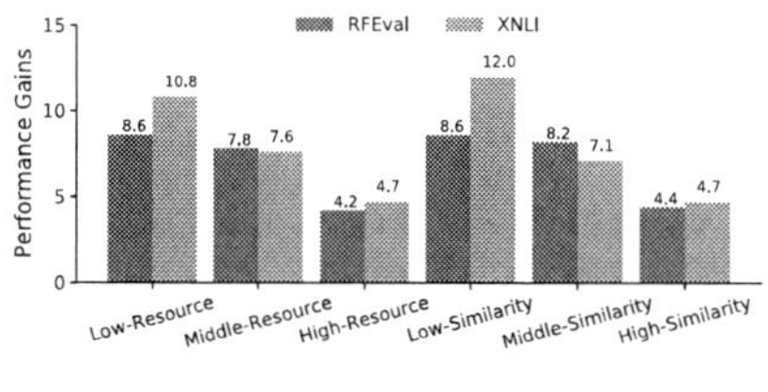

Figure 9: Performance gains across language groups for M-BERT ⊕ JOINT-ALIGN ⊕ NORM.

Model	τ	r	ρ
M-BERT	53.2	74.7	71.8
XLM-R	54.4	70.1	73.5
M-BERT ⊕ JOINT-ALIGN ⊕ NORM	17.5	57.3	21.2
XLM-R ⊕ JOINT-ALIGN ⊕ NORM	15.9	57.7	26.0

Table 5: Correlations (Kendall τ, Pearson r and Spearman ρ) between language similarities induced by m-BERT/XLM-R and WALS for 19 languages.

identity signals are stored in the m-BERT embeddings. Fig. 8 (b)+(c) shows that these signals are diminished in both re-aligned and normalized vector spaces, suggesting that the resulting embeddings in them are more language-agnostic.

(Q4) *To what extent do the typological relations learned from contextualized cross-lingual encoders deviate from those set out by expert typologists?*

Tab. 5 shows that language similarities, between English and other 18 languages, obtained from m-BERT and XLM-R have high correlations with structural language similarities[8] obtained from WALS[9] via the syntactic features listed, indicating that language identifiers stored in the original embeddings are a good proxy for the annotated linguistic features. In contrast, this correlation is smaller in the modified embedding spaces, which we believe is because language identity is a much less prominent signal in them.

7 Conclusion

Cross-lingual systems show striking performance for transfer, but their success crucially relies on two constraints: the similarity between source and target languages and the size of pre-training corpora. We comparatively evaluate three approaches to address these challenges, removing language-specific information from multilingual representations, thus learning language-agnostic representations. Our extensive experiments, based on a typologically broad sample of 19 languages, show that (vector space and input) normalization and re-mapping are oftentimes complementary approaches to improve cross-lingual performance, and that the popular approach of re-mapping leads to less consistent improvements than the much simpler and less costly normalization of vector representations. Input normalization yields benefits across a small sample of languages; further work is required for it to achieve consistent gains across a larger language sample.

Acknowledgments

We thank the anonymous reviewers for their insightful comments and suggestions, which greatly improved the final version of the paper. This work has been supported by the German Research Foundation as part of the Research Training Group Adaptive Preparation of Information from Heterogeneous Sources (AIPHES) at the Technische Universität Darmstadt under grant No. GRK 1994/1, as well as by the Swedish Research Council under grant agreement No 2019-04129.

References

Željko Agić and Ivan Vulić. 2019. JW300: A wide-coverage parallel corpus for low-resource languages. In *Proceedings of the 57th Annual Meeting of the*

[8]The language similarity induced by WALS is the fraction of structural properties that have the same value in two languages among all 192 properties.

[9]WALS covers approximately 200 linguistic features over 2500 languages, annotated by expert typologists.

Association for Computational Linguistics, pages 3204–3210, Florence, Italy. Association for Computational Linguistics.

Hanan Aldarmaki and Mona Diab. 2019. Context-aware cross-lingual mapping. In *Proceedings of the 2019 Conference of the North American Chapter of the Association for Computational Linguistics: Human Language Technologies, Volume 1 (Long and Short Papers)*, pages 3906–3911, Minneapolis, Minnesota. Association for Computational Linguistics.

Mikel Artetxe, Gorka Labaka, and Eneko Agirre. 2017. Learning bilingual word embeddings with (almost) no bilingual data. In *Proceedings of the 55th Annual Meeting of the Association for Computational Linguistics (Volume 1: Long Papers)*, pages 451–462, Vancouver, Canada. Association for Computational Linguistics.

Lei Jimmy Ba, Jamie Ryan Kiros, and Geoffrey E. Hinton. 2016. Layer normalization. *CoRR*, abs/1607.06450.

Johannes Bjerva and Isabelle Augenstein. 2018. From phonology to syntax: Unsupervised linguistic typology at different levels with language embeddings. In *Proceedings of the 2018 Conference of the North American Chapter of the Association for Computational Linguistics: Human Language Technologies, Volume 1 (Long Papers)*, pages 907–916, New Orleans, Louisiana. Association for Computational Linguistics.

Johannes Bjerva and Isabelle Augenstein. 2021. Does typological blinding impede cross-lingual sharing? In *Proceedings of the 16th Conference of the European Chapter of the Association for Computational Linguistics: Main Volume*, pages 480–486, Online. Association for Computational Linguistics.

Johannes Bjerva, Yova Kementchedjhieva, Ryan Cotterell, and Isabelle Augenstein. 2019a. A probabilistic generative model of linguistic typology. In *Proceedings of the 2019 Conference of the North American Chapter of the Association for Computational Linguistics: Human Language Technologies, Volume 1 (Long and Short Papers)*, pages 1529–1540, Minneapolis, Minnesota. Association for Computational Linguistics.

Johannes Bjerva, Robert Östling, Maria Han Veiga, Jörg Tiedemann, and Isabelle Augenstein. 2019b. What Do Language Representations Really Represent? *Computational Linguistics*, 45(2):381–389.

Ondřej Bojar, Yvette Graham, and Amir Kamran. 2017. Results of the WMT17 metrics shared task. In *Proceedings of the Second Conference on Machine Translation*, pages 489–513, Copenhagen, Denmark. Association for Computational Linguistics.

Steven Cao, Nikita Kitaev, and Dan Klein. 2020. Multilingual alignment of contextual word representations. *CoRR*, abs/2002.03518.

Alexis Conneau, Kartikay Khandelwal, Naman Goyal, Vishrav Chaudhary, Guillaume Wenzek, Francisco Guzmán, Edouard Grave, Myle Ott, Luke Zettlemoyer, and Veselin Stoyanov. 2019. Unsupervised cross-lingual representation learning at scale. *CoRR*, abs/1911.02116.

Alexis Conneau, Ruty Rinott, Guillaume Lample, Adina Williams, Samuel Bowman, Holger Schwenk, and Veselin Stoyanov. 2018. XNLI: Evaluating cross-lingual sentence representations. In *Proceedings of the 2018 Conference on Empirical Methods in Natural Language Processing*, pages 2475–2485, Brussels, Belgium. Association for Computational Linguistics.

Jacob Devlin, Ming-Wei Chang, Kenton Lee, and Kristina Toutanova. 2019. BERT: Pre-training of deep bidirectional transformers for language understanding. In *Proceedings of the 2019 Conference of the North American Chapter of the Association for Computational Linguistics: Human Language Technologies, Volume 1 (Long and Short Papers)*, pages 4171–4186, Minneapolis, Minnesota. Association for Computational Linguistics.

Matthew S. Dryer and Martin Haspelmath, editors. 2013. *WALS Online*. Max Planck Institute for Evolutionary Anthropology, Leipzig.

Chris Dyer, Victor Chahuneau, and Noah A. Smith. 2013. A simple, fast, and effective reparameterization of IBM model 2. In *Proceedings of the 2013 Conference of the North American Chapter of the Association for Computational Linguistics: Human Language Technologies*, pages 644–648, Atlanta, Georgia. Association for Computational Linguistics.

Kawin Ethayarajh. 2019. How contextual are contextualized word representations? comparing the geometry of BERT, ELMo, and GPT-2 embeddings. In *Proceedings of the 2019 Conference on Empirical Methods in Natural Language Processing and the 9th International Joint Conference on Natural Language Processing (EMNLP-IJCNLP)*, pages 55–65, Hong Kong, China. Association for Computational Linguistics.

Junjie Hu, Sebastian Ruder, Aditya Siddhant, Graham Neubig, Orhan Firat, and Melvin Johnson. 2020. XTREME: A massively multilingual multi-task benchmark for evaluating cross-lingual generalization. *CoRR*, abs/2003.11080.

Philipp Koehn. 2005. Europarl: A parallel corpus for statistical machine translation. In *MT summit*, volume 5, pages 79–86. Citeseer.

Taku Kudo and John Richardson. 2018. SentencePiece: A simple and language independent subword tokenizer and detokenizer for neural text processing. In *Proceedings of the 2018 Conference on Empirical Methods in Natural Language Processing: System Demonstrations*, pages 66–71, Brussels, Belgium. Association for Computational Linguistics.

Guillaume Lample, Alexis Conneau, Marc'Aurelio Ranzato, Ludovic Denoyer, and Hervé Jégou. 2018. Word translation without parallel data. In *ICLR*.

Anne Lauscher, Vinit Ravishankar, Ivan Vulic, and Goran Glavas. 2020. From zero to hero: On the limitations of zero-shot cross-lingual transfer with multilingual transformers. *CoRR*, abs/2005.00633.

Yann LeCun, Léon Bottou, Genevieve B. Orr, and Klaus-Robert Müller. 1998. Efficient backprop. In *Neural Networks: Tricks of the Trade, This Book is an Outgrowth of a 1996 NIPS Workshop*, page 9–50, Berlin, Heidelberg. Springer-Verlag.

Miryam de Lhoneux, Johannes Bjerva, Isabelle Augenstein, and Anders Søgaard. 2018. Parameter sharing between dependency parsers for related languages. In *Proceedings of the 2018 Conference on Empirical Methods in Natural Language Processing*, pages 4992–4997.

Jindrich Libovický, Rudolf Rosa, and Alexander Fraser. 2019. How language-neutral is multilingual bert? *CoRR*, abs/1911.03310.

Jindrich Libovický, Rudolf Rosa, and Alexander Fraser. 2020. On the language neutrality of pre-trained multilingual representations. *CoRR*, abs/2004.05160.

Joakim Nivre, Marie-Catherine de Marneffe, Filip Ginter, Jan Hajic, Christopher D. Manning, Sampo Pyysalo, Sebastian Schuster, Francis M. Tyers, and Daniel Zeman. 2020. Universal dependencies v2: An evergrowing multilingual treebank collection. *CoRR*, abs/2004.10643.

Helen O'Horan, Yevgeni Berzak, Ivan Vulić, Roi Reichart, and Anna Korhonen. 2016. Survey on the use of typological information in natural language processing. *arXiv preprint arXiv:1610.03349*.

Telmo Pires, Eva Schlinger, and Dan Garrette. 2019. How multilingual is multilingual BERT? In *Proceedings of the 57th Annual Meeting of the Association for Computational Linguistics*, pages 4996–5001, Florence, Italy. Association for Computational Linguistics.

Edoardo Maria Ponti, Helen O'horan, Yevgeni Berzak, Ivan Vulić, Roi Reichart, Thierry Poibeau, Ekaterina Shutova, and Anna Korhonen. 2019. Modeling language variation and universals: A survey on typological linguistics for natural language processing. *Computational Linguistics*, 45(3):559–601.

Andreas Rücklé, Steffen Eger, Maxime Peyrard, and Iryna Gurevych. 2018. Concatenated power mean word embeddings as universal cross-lingual sentence representations. *arXiv*.

Tal Schuster, Ori Ram, Regina Barzilay, and Amir Globerson. 2019. Cross-lingual alignment of contextual word embeddings, with applications to zero-shot dependency parsing. In *Proceedings of the 2019 Conference of the North American Chapter of the Association for Computational Linguistics: Human Language Technologies, Volume 1 (Long and Short Papers)*, pages 1599–1613, Minneapolis, Minnesota. Association for Computational Linguistics.

Sheng Shen, Zhewei Yao, Amir Gholami, Michael Mahoney, and Kurt Keutzer. 2020. PowerNorm: Rethinking batch normalization in transformers. In *Proceedings of the 37th International Conference on Machine Learning*, volume 119 of *Proceedings of Machine Learning Research*, pages 8741–8751. PMLR.

Milan Straka, Jan Hajič, and Jana Straková. 2016. UDPipe: Trainable pipeline for processing CoNLL-u files performing tokenization, morphological analysis, POS tagging and parsing. In *Proceedings of the Tenth International Conference on Language Resources and Evaluation (LREC'16)*, Portorož, Slovenia.

Ashish Vaswani, Noam Shazeer, Niki Parmar, Jakob Uszkoreit, Llion Jones, Aidan N Gomez, Ł ukasz Kaiser, and Illia Polosukhin. 2017. Attention is all you need. In *Advances in Neural Information Processing Systems*, volume 30. Curran Associates, Inc.

Dingquan Wang and Jason Eisner. 2016. The galactic dependencies treebanks: Getting more data by synthesizing new languages. *Transactions of the Association for Computational Linguistics*, 4:491–505.

Adina Williams, Nikita Nangia, and Samuel Bowman. 2018. A broad-coverage challenge corpus for sentence understanding through inference. In *Proceedings of the 2018 Conference of the North American Chapter of the Association for Computational Linguistics: Human Language Technologies, Volume 1 (Long Papers)*, pages 1112–1122, New Orleans, Louisiana. Association for Computational Linguistics.

Shijie Wu, Alexis Conneau, Haoran Li, Luke Zettlemoyer, and Veselin Stoyanov. 2019. Emerging cross-lingual structure in pretrained language models. *CoRR*, abs/1911.01464.

Shijie Wu and Mark Dredze. 2019. Beto, bentz, becas: The surprising cross-lingual effectiveness of BERT. In *Proceedings of the 2019 Conference on Empirical Methods in Natural Language Processing and the 9th International Joint Conference on Natural Language Processing (EMNLP-IJCNLP)*, pages 833–844, Hong Kong, China. Association for Computational Linguistics.

Yuxin Wu and Kaiming He. 2018. Group normalization. In *Computer Vision - ECCV 2018 - 15th European Conference, Munich, Germany, September 8-14, 2018, Proceedings, Part XIII*, volume 11217 of *Lecture Notes in Computer Science*, pages 3–19. Springer.

Wei Zhao, Goran Glavaš, Maxime Peyrard, Yang Gao, Robert West, and Steffen Eger. 2020. On the limitations of cross-lingual encoders as exposed by reference-free machine translation evaluation. In *Proceedings of the 58th Annual Meeting of the Association for Computational Linguistics*, pages 1656–1671, Online. Association for Computational Linguistics.

Wei Zhao, Maxime Peyrard, Fei Liu, Yang Gao, Christian M. Meyer, and Steffen Eger. 2019. MoverScore: Text generation evaluating with contextualized embeddings and earth mover distance. In *Proceedings of the 2019 Conference on Empirical Methods in Natural Language Processing and the 9th International Joint Conference on Natural Language Processing (EMNLP-IJCNLP)*, pages 563–578, Hong Kong, China. Association for Computational Linguistics.

Modeling Sense Structure in Word Usage Graphs with the Weighted Stochastic Block Model

Dominik Schlechtweg, Enrique Castaneda,
Jonas Kuhn, Sabine Schulte im Walde
Institute for Natural Language Processing, University of Stuttgart
{schlecdk,jonas.kuhn,schulte}@ims.uni-stuttgart.de, kicasta@gmail.com

Abstract

We suggest to model human-annotated Word Usage Graphs capturing fine-grained semantic proximity distinctions between word uses with a Bayesian formulation of the Weighted Stochastic Block Model, a generative model for random graphs popular in biology, physics and social sciences. By providing a probabilistic model of graded word meaning we aim to approach the slippery and yet widely used notion of word sense in a novel way. The proposed framework enables us to rigorously compare models of word senses with respect to their fit to the data. We perform extensive experiments and select the empirically most adequate model.

1 Introduction

Word Usage Graphs (WUGs) are a relatively new model of graded word meaning in context (Erk et al., 2013; McCarthy et al., 2016; Schlechtweg et al., 2021). They represent word uses (i.e., words in context) within a weighted undirected graph, with edge weights reflecting the semantic proximity between uses. WUGs may be obtained via human annotation by presenting annotators with pairs of words uses and asking them for proximity judgments. The WUGs may then be clustered into sets of uses exhibiting high semantic proximity, in order to reflect traditional word sense distinctions (McCarthy et al., 2016), and to provide insight into key aspects of word meaning such as polysemy, vagueness, and lexical semantic change (Schlechtweg et al., 2020, 2021).

We suggest to model WUGs with a Bayesian formulation of the Weighted Stochastic Block Model (WSBM), a generative model for random graphs popular in biology, physics and social sciences (Aicher et al., 2014; Peixoto, 2017). The basic assumption of WSBMs is that vertices belong to latent blocks (clusters), and that vertices in the same block are stochastically equivalent (i.e., they have edges drawn from the same distribution). Fitting the model is equivalent to determining the optimal latent block structure providing a **clustering** of word uses.

By using a Bayesian **probabilistic model** of WUG data we aim to approach graded word meaning in a rigorous scientific way: We perform **model selection**, i.e., different models are compared according to their fit to the data, and the model which explains the data best is chosen as most adequate representation of the semantic structure behind human-annotated word uses. If blocks are equated with **word senses**, this allows us to approach this slippery and yet widely used concept in a novel way. We may test long-standing hypotheses such as whether a graded model allowing sense overlap is a better model than a discrete one (Kilgarriff, 1997; Erk et al., 2013; McCarthy et al., 2016).

As a probabilistic model, the WSBM allows to **generate data** from a fitted model, which is useful for simulating realistic WUGs, e.g. when planning annotation studies. A fitted WSBM may also be used to **predict** values of unobserved edge weights, which is helpful for enhancing annotations.

Our contributions can be summarized as follows:

- Introducing a rigorous scientific way to infer the number and the nature of word senses.
- Improving WSBM with marginalizing over edge probabilities.
- Model selection: inferring the most likely number of discrete word senses for words in DWUG DE/EN data sets (Schlechtweg et al., 2021).
- Model checking: validating WSBMs as a reasonable model of WUGs and word senses with respect to external criteria.
- Publication of fitted WSBM models which can be used for simulating realistic data.

Proceedings of the 10th Conference on Lexical and Computational Semantics, pages 241–251
August 5–6, 2021, Bangkok, Thailand (online)

- Analysis: identifying shortcomings of WS-BMs (such as edge probabilities, hub effect).

2 Related Work

Our approach generally falls within the area of Bayesian probabilistic modeling (Koch, 2007). More specifically, it is related to model-based graph clustering techniques, e.g., Latent Space models such as Gaussian Mixture Models (Hoff et al., 2002; Duda and Hart, 1973). These methods are common in the field of *community detection* (Abbe, 2017). Within computational linguistics our approach is most strongly related to generative probabilistic topic models, where words in documents are modeled as being drawn from a latent topic distribution (Steyvers and Griffiths, 2007). Topics are often interpreted as senses (Frermann and Lapata, 2016; Perrone et al., 2019). Another common, yet non-probabilistic, modeling approach for word senses is to group word uses expressing similar meanings into clusters based on contextual features (Schütze, 1998; Biemann, 2006).

As to our knowledge, only a small set of studies is concerned with the modeling of *human-annotated* WUGs (McCarthy et al., 2016; Schlechtweg et al., 2020, 2021). This research line is motivated by insights from lexical semantics that word senses are no discrete objects (Kilgarriff, 1997; Erk et al., 2013). Most important to note is the pioneering work of McCarthy et al. (2016) as the first to represent human-annotated word uses within graphs and then clustering the uses based on heuristics such as connected components and cliques. McCarthy et al. derived edge weights from human lexical substitution judgments for the respective target words and binarized them according to a threshold. This idea was recently modified and extended by Schlechtweg et al. (2020, 2021). Schlechtweg et al. used semantic proximity judgments to annotate edges. They applied correlation clustering (Bansal et al., 2004) in connection with a global threshold to group vertices with high edge weights and developed an efficient iterative sampling strategy for edges to reduce annotation load. However, these approaches are ad-hoc clustering methods which do not provide a probabilistic model for WUGs.

3 Data

A Word Usage Graph $\mathbf{G} = (\mathbf{U}, \mathbf{E}, \mathbf{W})$ is a weighted, undirected graph, where vertices $u \in U$ represent word uses and weights $w \in W$ represent the semantic proximity of a pair of uses $(u_1, u_2) \in E$ (Schlechtweg and Schulte im Walde, submitted). In practice, semantic proximity can be measured by human annotator judgments on a scale of relatedness (Brown, 2008; Schlechtweg et al., 2018) or similarity (Erk et al., 2013). Human-annotated WUGs are often sparsely observed and noisy, i.e., only a small percentage of edges from the full graph are annotated, and annotators often show disagreements, e.g. for ambiguous uses, as can be seen in Figure 1.

↑	
	4: Identical
	3: Closely Related
	2: Distantly Related
	1: Unrelated

Table 1: DURel relatedness scale (Schlechtweg et al., 2018).

Recently, Schlechtweg et al. (2020, 2021) developed a large-scale multi-lingual resource of WUGs. Annotators were asked to judge the semantic relatedness of pairs of word uses (such as the two uses of *grasp* in (1) and (2)) according to the scale in Table 1.[1]

(1) He continued to **grasp**, between forefinger and thumb, the edge of the cloth I had been sewing.

(2) For just a moment he didn't **grasp** the import of what the old man had said.

The uses were sampled from diachronic corpora of four languages (English, German, Latin, Swedish). The data was annotated in four rounds. After each round the accumulated annotations from the previous rounds wer represented in a WUG, which was then clustered with correlation clustering (Bansal et al., 2004), and then further use pairs were chosen according to heuristics aiming to compare uses to clusters to which they had not yet been compared. Annotators showed high agreement, and comparable to previous studies. The final resource consists of WUGs for 168 words with a total of 100,000 judgments including nouns, verbs and adjectives as well as monosemous and polysemous words. In our experiments we use the German and English subparts of the data set comprising 88 WUGs.

While for some WUGs a clustering structure grouping vertices with high edge weights together

[1] https://www.ims.uni-stuttgart.de/data/wugs

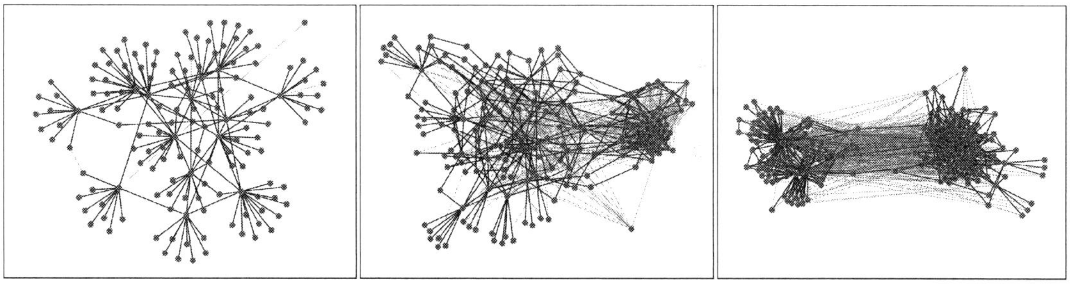

Figure 1: Word Usage Graphs of German *Festspiel* (left), *Abgesang* (middle) and *zersetzen* (right). Vertices represent uses of the respective target word. Edge weights represent the median of relatedness judgments between uses (**black**/gray lines for **high**/low edge weights, i.e., weights $\geq$ 2.5/weights < 2.5).

is obvious, for others this is not the case (cf. McCarthy et al., 2016). For example, see Figure 1 showing the annotated uses for three words from Schlechtweg et al. (2021).

The uses of the word *Festspiel* on the left and *zersetzen* on the right can be clearly partitioned into one/two main clusters, while the uses of *Abgesang* in the middle have a less clearly clusterable structure. Hence, it is unclear how many senses *Abgesang* has and what the assignment of uses to senses should be. We approach these two questions by searching for the model which best explains the data. The block structure inferred by this model will then give us a number of blocks and an assignment of uses to blocks.

4 Stochastic Block Model

The Stochastic Block Model (SBM) (Holland et al., 1983) is a simple generative process of random graphs based on the notion of groups of vertices. It assumes that each vertex of an observed graph G is member of a latent block (group) and that G was generated by first sampling vertices and then sampling edges between these vertices where the probability of observing an edge between two vertices is only determined by the block membership. Once this process is formulated mathematically, the optimal latent block structure can be inferred from G. For this, given the partition $b = \{b_i\}$ of G into B blocks, where $b_i \in [0, B-1]$ is the block membership of vertex i, we define a model that generates a graph A with a probability

$$P(A|\theta, b)$$

where θ are additional model (edge bundle) parameters that govern how the vertex partition affects the placing of edges (Peixoto, 2014a). Therefore, if we observe a graph A, the likelihood that it was generated by a given partition b is given by the Bayesian posterior probability

$$P(b|A) = \frac{\sum_\theta P(A|\theta, b)P(\theta, b)}{P(A)}$$

where $P(\theta, b)$ is the prior probability of the model parameters, and $P(A)$ is called the *evidence*, and corresponds to the total probability of the data summed over all model parameters (Peixoto, 2014a). The standard SBM takes as parameters the partition of the vertices into blocks b and a $B \times B$ matrix of edge counts e, where e_{rs} is the number of edges between groups r and s.

4.1 Edge weights

The Weighted Stochastic Block Model (WSBM) is an extension of the standard SBM to weighted graphs (Aicher et al., 2014; Peixoto, 2017). In the WSBM the inference of the latent block structure is driven by both edge existence and edge weights. This is achieved by treating edge weights as covariates that are sampled from some distribution (e.g. binomial) conditioned on the vertex partition (Peixoto, 2014a), i.e.,

$$P(A, x|\theta, \gamma, b) = P(x|A, \gamma, b)P(A|\theta, b)$$

with the covariates being sampled only on existing edges, and where γ_{rs} is a set of parameters that govern the sampling of the weights between groups r and s. The posterior partition distribution is then

$$P(b|A, x) = \frac{P(x|A, b)P(A|b)P(b)}{P(A, x)},$$

omitting the parameters θ, γ as in the non-parametric WSBM through the use of marginal likelihoods (Peixoto, 2017). In our experiments we use the non-parametric, micro-canonical implementation of the WSBM which avoids explicitly

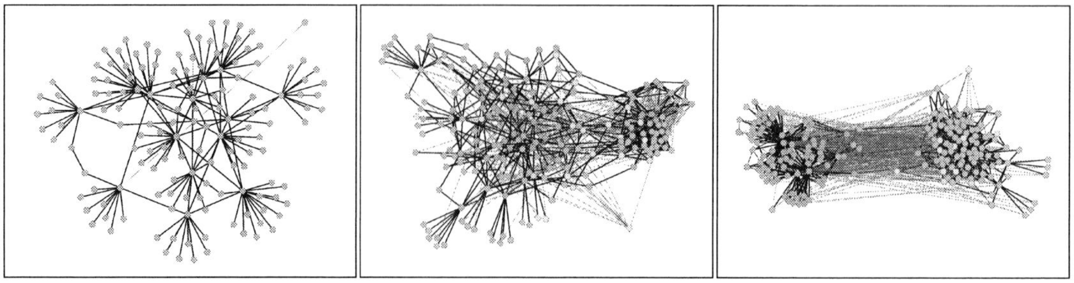

Figure 2: Word Usage Graphs of German *Festspiel* (left), *Abgesang* (middle) and *zersetzen* (right) with inferred block structure.

encoding distribution parameters for edge weights by replacing them with hard quantities (Peixoto, 2014c).[2] The non-parametric model avoids overfitting, and micro-canonical distributions are easier to compute while approaching their canonical counterparts asymptotically (Peixoto, 2017).[3]

4.2 Marginalizing over edge probabilities

The basic assumption of the WSBM is that vertices in the same block are stochastically equivalent. This should hold with respect to edge weights x and edge probabilities A. However, the distribution of edge probabilities in our case is guided exclusively by Schlechtweg et al.'s sampling procedure. Hence, the assumption of stochastic equivalence of edge probabilities does not hold for WUGs. Thus, we aim to make the block structure independent from the observed edge probability distribution between blocks as far as possible.[4] We reach this by marginalizing over edge probabilities, while keeping their number the same between groups. The latter is needed as the edge probabilities build the support of the edge weights. The posterior partition distribution is then

$$P(b|x) = \frac{P(x|b)P(b)}{P(x)}$$

where

$$P(x|b) = \sum_{A \in \Lambda} P(x|A,b)P(A|b)$$

and Λ is the set of all networks A that have the same number of edges between groups as the observed network A' under block assignment b. We sum over all possible edge assignments with the same number of edges between groups. In this way edge probabilities are marginalized and the posterior distribution $P(x|b)$ is mainly driven by edge weights.

4.3 Inference

Finding the maximum of the posterior distribution of the WSBM is NP-hard (Peixoto, 2015). Hence, we infer the optimal partitioning of vertices $P(b|x)$ asymptotically with multilevel agglomerative Markov chain Monte Carlo Peixoto (2014b). The central idea is to sample from $P(b|x)$ by first starting from some initial state and making move proposals depending on the current state such that, ultimately, the Markov Chain converges to $P(b|x)$. In order to alleviate the problem of metastable states the chain is first equilibrated for a larger number of blocks, which are then merged. (Find a discussion of the problem of metastable states in Peixoto (2014b).)

4.4 A Model for Word Senses?

The basic assumption of the WSBM with marginalized edge probabilities is that vertices in the same block are stochastically equivalent with respect to edge weights. We argue that this assumption is reasonable for word senses: From previous work we inherit the insight that graded proximity judgments reflect single-sense judgments (Erk et al., 2013; McCarthy et al., 2016). This is to say that use pairs expressing the same sense receive high values on

[2]We recover the non-microcanonical versions of the distributions by fitting these to the observed edge weights between blocks after fitting the WSBM.

[3]All experiments were done with graph-tool: https://graph-tool.skewed.de/. Additional code is provided at https://github.com/kicasta/Modeling_WUGS_WSBM.

[4]Note that degree-correction relaxes the homogeneity assumption and would thus serve as a first modeling approach (Karrer and Newman, 2011; Peixoto, 2019). However, the degree-corrected model still suffers from the hub effect, i.e., vertices with many edges tend to be assigned to the same block (Peixoto, 2020). This effect could be avoided with Latent Poisson models (Peixoto, 2020). However, we want the inferred block structure to be largely independent from edge probabilities, which neither of the models fully guarantees.

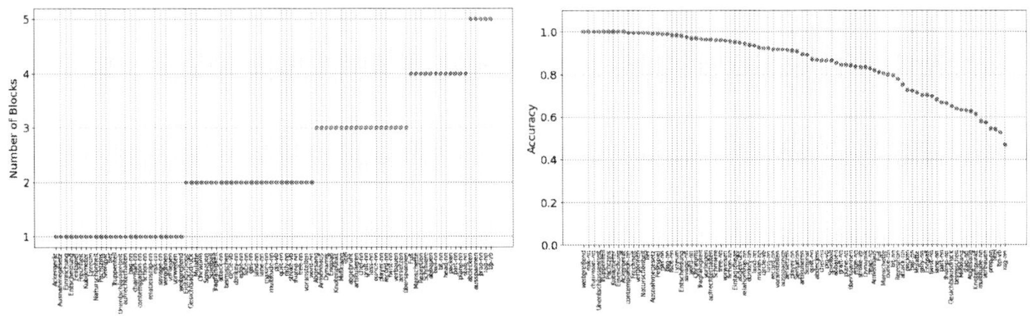

Figure 3: Inferred number of blocks with best-fitting models (left). Correspondence to clustering result from Schlechtweg et al. (2021) (right).

the annotation scale, while use pairs expressing different senses receive low values. This behavior can be modeled by assuming that same-sense pairs receive edge weights chosen from a common distribution with a high mean, while the same holds for different-sense pairs with a distribution with a low mean. The interesting question is, though, how well the WSBM (or any other model) can model the unclear cases, i.e., use pairs receiving intermediate judgments on the annotation scale. The WSBM is a very general model that can learn many different structures. It can handle heterogenous and overlapping edge weight distributions and also allows blocks to be more or less related to each other. In principle, it also allows mixed membership of vertices in blocks (Peixoto, 2015). The advantage of our approach is that we do not have to define senses in any further way. As latent variables, they can be found by themselves, guided by the independent criterion of how well they explain the data.

Note that this approach does not in any way depend on the concept of sense. In principle, any other probabilistically formulated model aiming to explain WUG data can be introduced. Such a model does not have to rely on the idea of stochastically equivalent blocks. If this model were to explain the data better, the WSBM could be neglected.

5 Model Selection[5]

Following Peixoto (2015) we select the best model according to the Minimum Description Length Principle (Grünwald and Grunwald, 2007). The description length of a graph measures the amount of information required to describe the data, if we encode it using a particular parametrization of the model being tested. This approach corresponds to an implementation of Occam's razor, where the simplest model is selected, among all possibilities with the same explanatory power (Peixoto, 2014a).

5.1 Number of blocks

88 WUGs were fitted using three different distributions for edge weights (see below). The optimal number of blocks is found during fitting (Peixoto, 2014b). We start fitting by choosing an initial number of blocks $1 \leq b \leq 30$. Peixoto's algorithm then tries to find a partition of the Graph into $1 \leq b \leq 30$ blocks with minimum description length. It does so by choosing some $b' > b$, finding the best partition of the graph into b' blocks and then greedily merging these b' into b blocks. Then, it repeats this step for a b_1 and b_2, such that $b_1 < b < b_2$ and decides whether it should increase the number of blocks or decrease it depending on whether it results in a decrease in description length. This is done until convergence. Figure 3 (left) shows the optimal number of blocks obtained for each WUG in the above-described way. We see a tendency to favor simpler structures over more complex ones. That is, most WUGs are modeled best with one or two blocks. The highest number of blocks found is 5. The inferred block structure for the three graphs in Figure 1 is displayed in Figure 2 with 1/3/3 blocks respectively.[6]

5.2 Edge Weight Distribution

Each WUG was fitted using three different distributions for edge weights: (micro-canonical versions of) binomial, poisson and geometric. Figure 4 (left) shows the number of graphs for which each dis-

[5]We provide all fitted models as well as our code at `https://github.com/kicasta/Modeling_WUGS_WSBM`.

[6]For further example plots see Figures 7 and 8 in Appendix A.

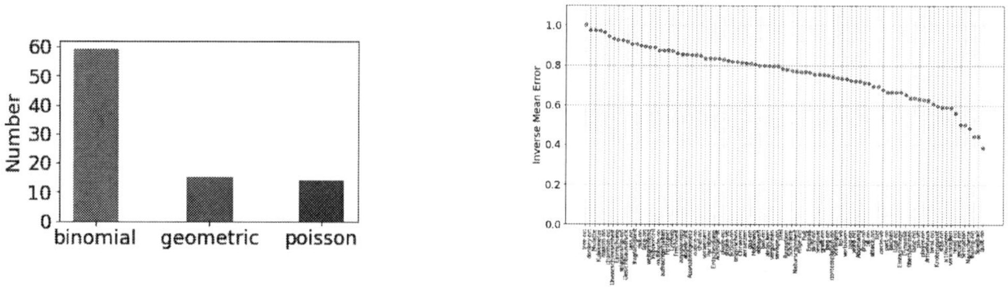

Figure 4: Comparison of model fit wrt. edge weight distributions (left), where Y-axis gives number of graphs for which the respective distribution had minimum description length. Evaluation result of link prediction (right).

tribution type yielded the best fit. The binomial distribution shows the best fits in the large majority of cases. This makes sense, because it is also the most general and flexible of the three distributions. Figure 5 shows the observed edge weight distributions of the graphs between blocks after fitting (red) and within blocks (blue), as well as the respective inferred distributions (curve). Despite the fact that edge weight distributions may be heterogenous (middle), there is a clear tendency for negative edges between blocks and positive edges within blocks. The inferred distributions reflect this pattern.[7]

5.3 Analysis

We now take a closer look at the WUGs from Figures 1 and 2 and their block-related edge weight distributions in Figure 5. For example, the following two use pairs of *Festspiel* homogeneously received high ratings of 3 and 4. The best fit is reached with one block and a binomial distribution.

(3) ...war die DDR bei den Wiener Festwochen, den Salzburger **Festspielen** und...
*'...the GDR was represented at the Wiener Festwochen, the Salzburg **Festival** and...'*

(4) ...im Rahmen der Wettbewerbe und **Festspiele** der Volkskunst...
*'...as part of the competitions and **festivals** of folk art...'*

Abgesang is a different case: It received heterogenous judgments across the scale from 1–4. No clear block structure is visible at first in Figure 1. The best fit is obtained with three blocks and a binomial distribution. The three blocks reflect meaningful fine-grained sense differences as displayed by the following three examples:

(5) In den ersten Strophen der Klage der Ceres findet sich ein [...] 4 zeiliger Aufgesang mit einem 8 zeiligen **Abgesang**.
*'In the first stanzas of Ceres' lament there is a [...] 4-line stance start with an 8-line **stance end**.'*

(6) ...und radelte unter dem **Abgesang** schmutziger Lieder davon.
*'...and cycled off while **singing** dirty songs.'*

(7) ...daß dieser Vorgriff auf den Sommer nicht schon den **Abgesang** des Wintersports bedeutet...
*'...that this anticipation of summer doesn't mean the **swan song** of winter sports...'*

We observe that the sparsity of the annotation has a strong influence: if a word use is richly annotated with several edges, then the model has information on its relation to other blocks and can infer a reasonable block assignment, even if there are annotation errors. If, however, the use is only annotated with e.g. one low-valued edge, the model is likely to assign it to a block with semantically very different uses which also tend to have low judgments with other uses. That is, unrelated uses may appear homogeneous to the model, because they have similar (as sparsely observed) relations to third uses. This effect disappears with richer annotation.

Just as *Abgesang*, *zersetzen* yields the best fit with three blocks and a binomial distribution. As can be seen in Figure 5, the weights also cover the whole scale. However, in this case they are more homogeneously distributed within and between blocks. This is because *zersetzen* has two main and clearly distinguishable senses, as illustrated by (8) and (9):

[7] Note that Figure 5 shows only the combined distributions within and between blocks across all combinations. The per-block distributions are very similar though, as can be seen in Figure 9 in Appendix A for *zersetzen*.

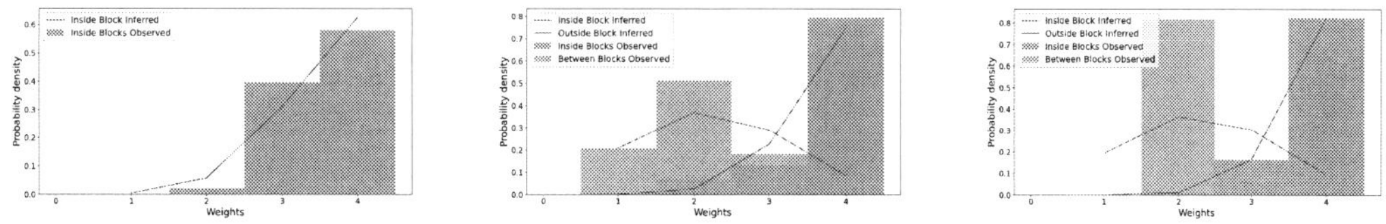

Figure 5: Combined weight distributions of German *Festspiel* (left), *Abgesang* (middle) and *zersetzen* (right). The curves show the inferred distributions.

(8) ...dass die Pflanzen das kohlensaure Gas beym Sonnenlichte **zersetzen**...
'...*that the plants* ***decompose*** *the carbonic acid gas in the sunlight...*'

(9) Das System des Frontstadtsenats hat die westberliner Schule bedrohlich **zersetzt**.
'*The system of the front city senate has* ***destroyed*** *the West Berlin school.*'

There is a third block where uses are mostly variations of the sense in (9), e.g. referring to a rather physical than chemical decomposition, or uses where the meaning is unclear. We made a similar observation for other graphs (e.g. *rag*): There are separate and semantically heterogeneous blocks for unclear and sparsely annotated uses. German *zersetzen* also illustrates an effect that we observe across many graphs: While the inferred binomial distribution within blocks (see Figure 5) can be closely fit, the distribution between blocks has a considerable error. This is mostly because weights of 1 are rare, while weights of 4 are common. The probability mass of weights between blocks is concentrated at 2, not 1. The binomial distribution has considerable problems modeling this behavior. Other distributions are also deficient, however: the geometric distribution cannot model right-skewed distributions at all, and thus has high errors for within-block distributions. Consequently, the cases where it yields the best fits, are the ones with a high number of low edge weights (e.g. *tip*) which lead to strongly left-skewed distributions. The poisson distribution suffers from the problem that it cannot model steep and peeked distributions. An important challenge for future modeling approaches will be to find appropriate distributions to model the behavior of edge weights. We believe that a signed (invertible) geometric distribution will yield good fits in many cases. Another important challenge will be to avoid sparsity of annotation, e.g. by developing efficient and iterative sampling techniques for edges. It also should be examined how much the inferred block structure is influenced by the difference in the way a particular annotator interprets uses, yielding homogeneous judgments for edges annotated exclusively by this annotator. This could be modeled by multi-graph models (Peixoto, 2017) where the information from each annotator can be represented individually.

6 Model Checking

In order to validate the fitted models externally we test whether the inferred clustering corresponds to a clustering obtained with an independent algorithm. Additionally, we use two internal validation criteria which test how well the structural properties of the observed graphs are recoverable from the inferred models. For this we apply two strategies: (i) Posterior Predictive Checking (Gelman et al., 2013) and (ii) Link Prediction (Liben-Nowell and Kleinberg, 2007).

6.1 Correspondence to Independent Clustering Algorithm

Figure 3 (right) shows the correspondence (accuracy) of the inferred block structures to those found by Schlechtweg et al. (2021) with correlation clustering and a global threshold on edge weights. The results often show strong correspondence ($> .9$) to Schlechtweg et al., although they were obtained with a completely different approach. For a number of graphs with one inferred block the structures are exactly the same. However, there are also clear differences: Especially for graphs with complex block structures (e.g. *tip* or *rag*) the correspondence to Schlechtweg et al. is very low. This also holds for some cases with simpler block structure (e.g. *Gesichtsausdruck* or *multitude*). Our three graphs from Figure 1 nicely display this pattern: *Festspiel* has a simple one-block structure and high accuracy (≈ 1.0), while *Abgesang* has a complex structure and low accuracy (< 0.6). *zersetzen* has three blocks (as *Abgesang*), but two main and clearly separated blocks and rather high accuracy.

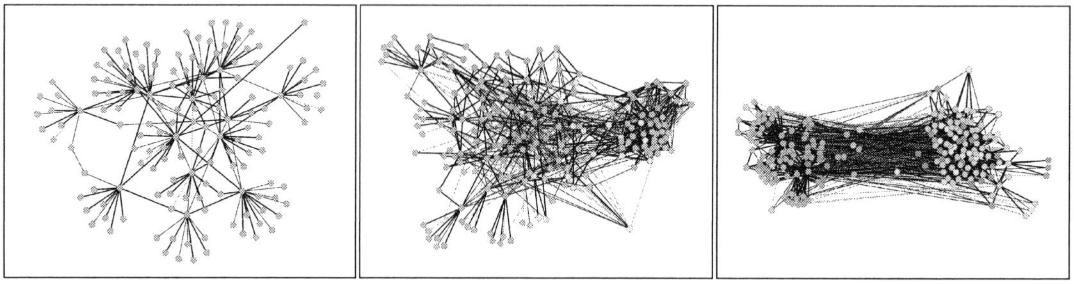

Figure 6: Sampled Word Usage Graphs of German *Festspiel* (left), German *Abgesang* (middle) and *zersetzen* (right).

In summary, the two clustering algorithms often make similar decisions, but different decisions especially where the clustering structure is complex and unclear.

6.2 Posterior Predictive Checking

We now test how well a model $P(b|A,x)$ fitted to a WUG $G = (U, E, W_G)$ retains the structural properties of G. For this we create a new graph $H = (U, E, W_H = \{\})$ with the same vertices and edges as G, but without the weights. This means $U_G = U_H$ and $E_G = E_H$. Then for all edges $e \in E_H$ we sample from the inferred distribution $\mathcal{D}$ with parameters $\mathcal{P}$ that best describes the weight distribution for the respective block combination (b_{e_1}, b_{e_2}) of e. For a model with a very close fit to the data the drawn edge weights will resemble the observed weights. We then visually compare the observed and the sampled graphs (Figures 6 vs. 2).

In Figure 6 we can see that in simple graphs like *Festspiel* the inferred structure coincides completely with the observed one. However, in graphs with a more complex structure like *Abgesang* and *zersetzen* (see Figure 5, middle and right) no distribution is flexible enough to fully describe the observed weight distributions, reflecting the observations from above. This is clearly manifested in the amount of high weights (black edges) inferred between the different blocks which are not present in the observed graph (see Figure 2).

6.3 Link Prediction

With link prediction we test how well a fitted model $P(b|A,x)$ from a WUG $G = (U, E, W_G)$ can predict unobserved annotations, i.e., missing edges in the graph. For this we randomly delete 5% of the edges of G and predict them by drawing from the distribution $\mathcal{D}$ as described above. We then quantify the difference between each predicted w_p and the corresponding observed edge weight w_o and define the Inverse Mean Error

$$\text{IME} = 1 - \frac{|w_o - w_p|}{4-1}$$

as a measure of how well a model structure predicts the observed graph structure (Figure 4, right). For about half of the graphs this score is quite high (IME $>$ .8), i.e., the sampled weights are close to the observed values. Again, simpler block structures are easier to fit and are thus better predictable. For half of the graphs the predictability is lower though, for some even $<$ .5. These results quantitatively confirm our observations from above, i.e., the fitted distributions often do not model the observed graphs sufficiently well.

7 Conclusion

We suggested to model human-annotated Word Usage Graphs with a Bayesian formulation of the Weighted Stochastic Block Model, compared several variations of the model and chose the best-fitting model in a principled way. In addition, we demonstrated how to interpret the inferred model as a model of word senses, but also that this interpretation is in no way necessary. The inferred models provide a stochastically-driven clustering and can be used to simulate realistic WUGs. An analysis of the model fits illustrated that more flexible distributions for edge weights are needed to yield good fits for a range of graphs.

We would like to emphasize that we do *not* claim that the WSBM is the *best* model for WUGs. Rather, we propose WSBMs as a reasonable probabilistic model for our data that can be rigorously compared against competing models in a Bayesian probabilistic framework, and potentially be neglected.

In the future, we aim to test more flexible edge weight distributions and to compare WSBMs to further probabilistic models, such as Gaussian Mixture models (Duda and Hart, 1973) and Latent Space models (Hoff et al., 2002). These models are interesting because they explicitly enforce the triangular property on graphs, which certain types of proximity judgments are known to obey (Erk et al., 2013). We also aim to explore Mixed Membership SBMs (Airoldi et al., 2008; Peixoto, 2015) and multi-graph models (Peixoto, 2017) where the information from each annotator can be represented individually.

Acknowledgments

We thank Tiago de Paula Peixoto for advice and for providing the idea and an implementation of the marginalization over edge probabilities. We further thank the reviewers for their constructive feedback. Dominik Schlechtweg was supported by the Konrad Adenauer Foundation and the CRETA center funded by the German Ministry for Education and Research (BMBF) during the conduct of this study.

References

Emmanuel Abbe. 2017. Community detection and stochastic block models: recent developments.

Christopher Aicher, Abigail Z. Jacobs, and Aaron Clauset. 2014. Learning latent block structure in weighted networks. *Journal of Complex Networks*, 3(2):221—-248.

Edoardo M. Airoldi, David M. Blei, Stephen E. Fienberg, and Eric P. Xing. 2008. Mixed membership stochastic blockmodels. *Journal of Machine Learning Research*, 9:1981–2014.

Nikhil Bansal, Avrim Blum, and Shuchi Chawla. 2004. Correlation clustering. *Machine Learning*, 56(1-3):89–113.

Chris Biemann. 2006. Chinese whispers: An efficient graph clustering algorithm and its application to natural language processing problems. In *Proceedings of the First Workshop on Graph Based Methods for Natural Language Processing*, TextGraphs-1, page 73–80, USA. Association for Computational Linguistics.

Susan Windisch Brown. 2008. Choosing sense distinctions for WSD: Psycholinguistic evidence. In *Proceedings of the 46th Annual Meeting of the Association for Computational Linguistics on Human Language Technologies: Short Papers*, pages 249–252, Stroudsburg, PA, USA.

Richard O. Duda and Peter E. Hart. 1973. *Pattern classification and scene analysis*.

Katrin Erk, Diana McCarthy, and Nicholas Gaylord. 2013. Measuring word meaning in context. *Computational Linguistics*, 39(3):511–554.

Lea Frermann and Mirella Lapata. 2016. A Bayesian model of diachronic meaning change. *Transactions of the Association for Computational Linguistics*, 4:31–45.

A. Gelman, J.B. Carlin, H.S. Stern, D.B. Dunson, A. Vehtari, and D.B. Rubin. 2013. *Bayesian Data Analysis, Third Edition*. Chapman & Hall/CRC Texts in Statistical Science. Taylor & Francis.

Peter D. Grünwald and Abhijit Grunwald. 2007. *The Minimum Description Length Principle*. Adaptive computation and machine learning. MIT Press.

Peter D. Hoff, Adrian E. Raftery, and Mark S. Handcock. 2002. Latent space approaches to social network analysis. *Journal of the American Statistical Association*, 97(460):1090–1098.

Paul W. Holland, Kathryn Blackmond Laskey, and Samuel Leinhardt. 1983. Stochastic blockmodels: First steps. *Social Networks*, 5(2):109 – 137.

Brian Karrer and M. E. J. Newman. 2011. Stochastic blockmodels and community structure in networks. *Physical Review E*, 83:016107.

Adam Kilgarriff. 1997. "I don't believe in word senses". *Computers and the Humanities*, 31(2).

Karl-Rudolf Koch. 2007. *Introduction to Bayesian Statistics*, 2nd edition. Springer Publishing Company, Incorporated.

David Liben-Nowell and Jon Kleinberg. 2007. The link-prediction problem for social networks. *Journal of the American Society for Information Science and Technology*, 58(7):1019–1031.

Diana McCarthy, Marianna Apidianaki, and Katrin Erk. 2016. Word sense clustering and clusterability. *Computational Linguistics*, 42(2):245–275.

Tiago Peixoto. 2017. Nonparametric weighted stochastic block models. *Physical Review E*, 97.

Tiago P. Peixoto. 2014a. Documentation of the graph-tool python library. (last checked july 17, 2020).

Tiago P. Peixoto. 2014b. Efficient monte carlo and greedy heuristic for the inference of stochastic block models. *Physical Review E*, 89(1).

Tiago P. Peixoto. 2014c. The graph-tool python library. *figshare*.

Tiago P. Peixoto. 2015. Model selection and hypothesis testing for large-scale network models with overlapping groups. *Physical Review X*, 5:011033.

Tiago P. Peixoto. 2019. Bayesian stochastic blockmodeling. In *Advances in Network Clustering and Blockmodeling*, chapter 11, pages 289–332. John Wiley & Sons, Ltd.

Tiago P. Peixoto. 2020. Latent poisson models for networks with heterogeneous density. *Physical Review E*, 102:012309.

Valerio Perrone, Marco Palma, Simon Hengchen, Alessandro Vatri, Jim Q. Smith, and Barbara McGillivray. 2019. GASC: Genre-aware semantic change for ancient Greek. In *Proceedings of the 1st International Workshop on Computational Approaches to Historical Language Change*, pages 56–66, Florence, Italy. Association for Computational Linguistics.

Dominik Schlechtweg, Barbara McGillivray, Simon Hengchen, Haim Dubossarsky, and Nina Tahmasebi. 2020. SemEval-2020 Task 1: Unsupervised Lexical Semantic Change Detection. In *Proceedings of the 14th International Workshop on Semantic Evaluation*, Barcelona, Spain. Association for Computational Linguistics.

Dominik Schlechtweg and Sabine Schulte im Walde. submitted. Clustering Word Usage Graphs: A Flexible Framework to Measure Changes in Contextual Word Meaning.

Dominik Schlechtweg, Sabine Schulte im Walde, and Stefanie Eckmann. 2018. Diachronic Usage Relatedness (DURel): A framework for the annotation of lexical semantic change. In *Proceedings of the 2018 Conference of the North American Chapter of the Association for Computational Linguistics: Human Language Technologies*, pages 169–174, New Orleans, Louisiana.

Dominik Schlechtweg, Nina Tahmasebi, Simon Hengchen, Haim Dubossarsky, and Barbara McGillivray. 2021. DWUG: A large Resource of Diachronic Word Usage Graphs in Four Languages. *CoRR*, abs/2104.08540.

Hinrich Schütze. 1998. Automatic word sense discrimination. *Computational Linguistics*, 24(1):97–123.

Mark Steyvers and Tom Griffiths. 2007. *Probabilistic Topic Models*. Lawrence Erlbaum Associates.

A Additional Plots

Find additional plots in Figures 7, 8 and 9.

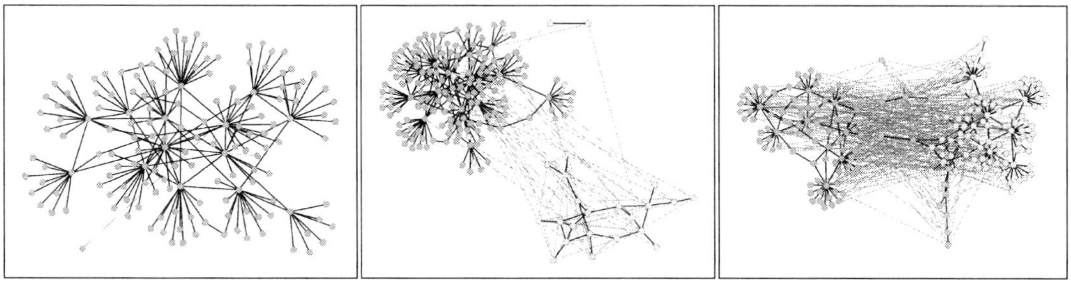

Figure 7: Word Usage Graphs of German *Ausnahmegesetz* (left), *stroke* (middle) and *plane* (right).

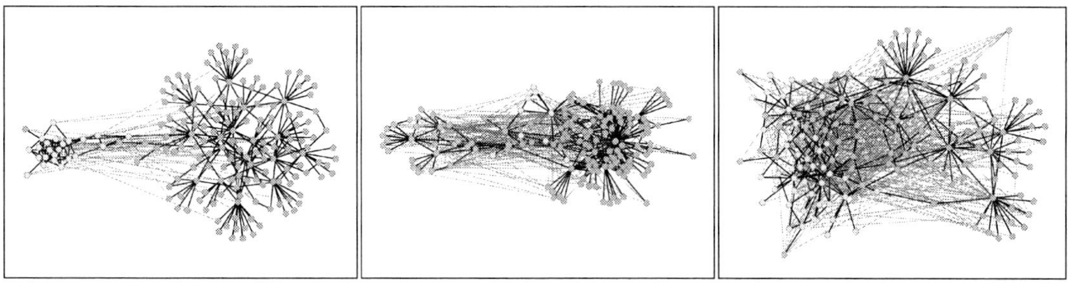

Figure 8: Word Usage Graphs of German *Sensation* (left), German *artikulieren* (middle) and *verbauen* (right).

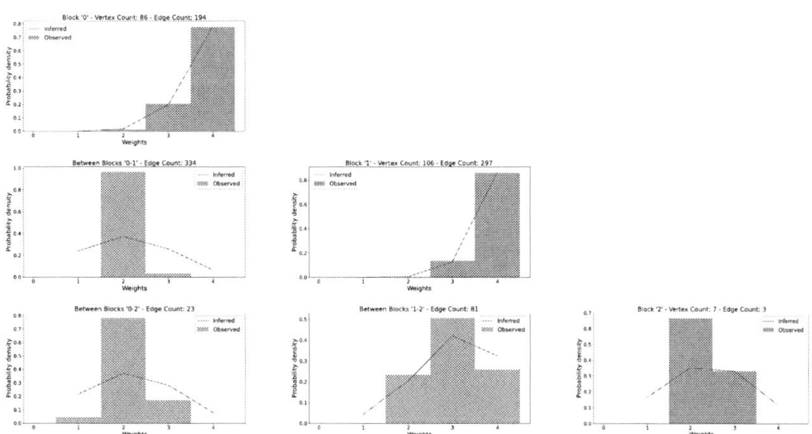

Figure 9: Detailed weight distribution of German *zersetzen*. Distribution within blocks in the diagonal and between blocks outside. Block '0' maps the cyan cluster, Block '1' the green cluster and Block '2' the yellow one in Figure 2. The bars represent the observed values while the curves represent the inferred binomial distribution.

Compound or Term Features? Analyzing Salience in Predicting the Difficulty of German Noun Compounds across Domains

Anna Hätty[1,2], Julia Bettinger[2], Michael Dorna[1], Jonas Kuhn[2], Sabine Schulte im Walde[2]
[1]Robert Bosch GmbH, Corporate Research, Renningen, Germany
[2]Institute for Natural Language Processing, University of Stuttgart, Germany
{anna.haetty, michael.dorna}@de.bosch.com,
{julia.bettinger,jonas.kuhn,schulte}@ims.uni-stuttgart.de

Abstract

Predicting the difficulty of domain-specific vocabulary is an important task towards a better understanding of a domain, and to enhance the communication between lay people and experts. We investigate German closed noun compounds and focus on the interaction of compound-based lexical features (such as frequency and productivity) and terminology-based features (contrasting domain-specific and general language) across word representations and classifiers. Our prediction experiments complement insights from classification using (a) manually designed features to characterise termhood and compound formation and (b) compound and constituent word embeddings. We find that for a broad binary distinction into *easy* vs. *difficult* general-language compound frequency is sufficient, but for a more fine-grained four-class distinction it is crucial to include contrastive termhood features and compound and constituent features.

1 Introduction

In times of a constant growth of domain-specific data, it is more important than ever to analyse characteristics of domain-specific vocabulary. Domains are topically restricted subject fields containing domain-specific vocabulary that encode domain knowledge. The more technical the terminology in the domain vocabulary, the more difficult it is perceived by lay people unfamiliar with the domain. Predicting the difficulty of domain-specific vocabulary is therefore an important task for enhancing the communication between lays and experts. A prominent example in this respect is the medical domain, where the prediction of difficulty of medical terms can enhance the communication between doctors and patients, e.g. by simplifying medical texts (Abrahamsson et al., 2014; Grabar and Hamon, 2014; Wandji Tchami and Grabar, 2014). While the medical domain represents a well-researched focus, the problem of miscommunication appears across domains.

Previous research on automatic term difficulty prediction already explored a large number of parameters, but as to our knowledge there is yet no study that investigated how difficulty can be attributed to complex phrase formation processes (a language phenomenon) in interaction with domain specialization (a domain phenomenon). The current study investigates these aspects, goes beyond domain peculiarities (such as Latin words in the medical domain), and performs analyses across three rather different domains: *Cooking, DIY ('do-it-yourself')* and *Automotive*.

While we choose a diverse set of domains, we otherwise focus on a special phenomenon within domain-specific vocabulary: German closed compounds. Closed compounds are complex expressions that consist of several lexemes and are written in a single string of characters. An example is *Bremsflüssigkeit* 'brake fluid', which is composed of the two simple words *Bremse* 'brake' and *Flüssigkeit* 'fluid'. By focusing on closed compounds, the boundaries of the phrases to pre-extract in text are unambiguous, and feature analysis will not be biased by how the extraction method is designed. Furthermore, closed compounds are a frequent phenomenon in German: Baroni et al. (2002) found that 47% of the word types in a general-language corpus in German are compounds, and according to Clouet and Daille (2014) compounding is even more productive in specialized domains. The interaction of domain features and lexical features can be easily demonstrated at the examples of closed compounds: For example, the compound *Hydraulikleitung* 'hydraulic line' is considered difficult because it contains the rather technical constituent 'hydraulic'. In contrast, the compound *Blaukochen* (lit: 'blue boiling', a special kind of boiling fish by adding acid) only contains con-

Proceedings of the 10th Conference on Lexical and Computational Semantics, pages 252–262
August 5–6, 2021, Bangkok, Thailand (online) ©2021 Association for Computational Linguistics

stituents that are well-known to lay people but is nevertheless difficult for them because the compound is not semantically transparent regarding its constituent 'blue', i.e. it is not obvious what the constituent contributes to the meaning of the compound. In sum, the difficulty of a compound cannot be derived from only compound attributes; in addition, it is influenced by the role and properties of the constituents.

In this study, we want to empirically investigate how phrase formation and domain-specific termhood[1] attributes interact in the automatic prediction of compound difficulty. In order to train predictive models, we use a German compound dataset with a total of 1,030 compounds across the above-mentioned three domains. Based on two settings of the gold standard dataset (a four-class and a binary version) we apply a decision tree classifier using manually designed features to characterize termhood and compound formation, and neural classifiers using word embeddings.

2 Related Work

Term difficulty prediction (also referred to as term familiarity or term technicality prediction) can be seen as a subtask of automatic term extraction. For automatic term extraction, a major strand of methodologies are contrastive techniques, where a term candidate's distribution in a domain-specific text corpus is compared to the distribution in a reference corpus, for example a general-language corpus (Ahmad et al., 1994; Rayson and Garside, 2000; Drouin, 2003; Kit and Liu, 2008; Bonin et al., 2010; Kochetkova, 2015; Lopes et al., 2016; Mykowiecka et al., 2018, i.a.). Many term difficulty prediction studies rely on some variant of contrastive approaches, mostly frequency-based; notable exceptions are Zeng-Treitler et al. (2008), who apply a contextual network, and Bouamor et al. (2016), who use a likelihood ratio test based on two language models. Most studies fall into the medical, biomedical or health domain. They rely on classical readability features such as frequency, term length, syllable count, the Dale-Chall readability formula or affixes (Zeng et al., 2005; Zeng-Treitler et al., 2008; Vydiswaran et al., 2014; Grabar et al., 2014). Some features are tailored to the medical domain, for example relying on neo-classical word components, since medical terminology is considered to be highly influenced by Greek and Latin (Deléger and Zweigenbaum, 2009; Bouamor et al., 2016).

As to our knowledge, there is no previous work that investigated term difficulty prediction for complex phrases. Regarding the more general task of automatic term extraction, a few studies included complex phrases and their constituents. For example, the *C-value* (Frantzi et al., 1998) combines linguistic and statistical information and takes nested terms into account for evaluating termhood. The *FGM score* (Nakagawa and Mori, 2003) relies on the geometric mean of the number of distinct left and right neighboring words for each constituent in a complex term. *Contrastive Selection via Heads (CSvH)* (Basili et al., 2001) is a corpora-comparing measure that computes termhood for a complex term by biasing the termhood score with the general-language frequency of the head. Hätty et al. (2017) combine termhood measures within a random forest classifier to extract single and multiword terms and apply the measures recursively to the components. Hätty and Schulte im Walde (2018) demonstrate that propagating constituent information through neural networks improves the prediction of compound termhood.

3 Data

3.1 German Closed Noun Compounds

Closed compounds are complex expressions that consist of several lexemes and that are written in a single string of characters. The lexemes are called constituents. The constituents of a two-part compound can be divided into *modifier* and *head*, where the latter is word-final in German.

An important empirical compound attribute is the morphological family size (De Jong et al., 2000) of a lexeme, which we refer to as *productivity* henceforth. Morphological family size is defined as the type count of morphological family members, which comprise compounds and derived words that contain the given lexeme as a constituent. We distinguish between two kinds of productivity as a compound attribute: The productivity of a modifier refers to the number of compound types where a certain word type occupies the position of the modifier, and the productivity of a head refers to the number of compound types where a certain word type occupies the position of the head.

[1] Termhood refers to the degree to which a lexical unit can be considered a domain-specific concept (Kageura and Umino, 1996).

3.2 Corpora

As corpus for general language, we rely on the *SdeWaC* (Faaß and Eckart, 2013), a cleaned version of the web-crawled corpus *deWaC* (Baroni et al., 2009), containing $\approx$ 880 million words.

As domain-specific corpora, we use the three domain corpora that are described by Bettinger et al. (2020). The corpora were crawled for the domains of *Cooking, DIY* and *Automotive*. They were selected to include a variety of different domains; for example, the *Automotive* domain was chosen because it was expected to be more technical than the *Cooking* domain. The domain corpora consist of both user-generated and expert content. User-generated content was extracted from Wikipedia, `wikihow.de` and `wikibooks.de`, filtered by domain-related categories. Further, domain-specific homepages such as `kochwiki.org` were crawled. Expert texts include tool manuals and books (e.g. on *Automotive* and on *Handicraft*), as well as redacted text crawled from homepages such as `1-2-do.com`. Finally, all corpora were reduced to the size of the smallest corpus and are equally-sized with 5.6 million tokens. The texts are tokenized, lemmatized and POS-tagged with spaCy[2].

3.3 Gold Standard

We rely on the domain-specific compound difficulty gold standard developed on the basis of the just-described domain-specific corpora (Bettinger et al., 2020). The gold standard contains 1,030 closed compounds from the domains of *Cooking, DIY* and *Automotive*. Compounds were automatically identified in text by applying the Simple Compound Splitter (Weller-Di Marco, 2017). All compounds with a frequency smaller than three were excluded, which resulted in a pool of 12,400 *Cooking* compounds, 16,935 *DIY* compounds and 20,468 *Automotive* compounds, A subset was selected which was balanced for the following features: frequency of the compound, productivity of the head, productivity of the modifier and frequency of the head. The final dataset was rated by 26 annotators on a Likert-like difficulty scale (Likert, 1932) from 1 (easy; the term does not require specialized knowledge to be understood) to 4 (difficult; the term requires specialized knowledge). After the annotation process, the 20 annotations were selected where annotators agreed most. The average pairwise Spearman's ρ correlations of the 20 annotators is 0.61.

We base our models on two specifications of the gold standard:

four-class: For each compound, we calculate the median.[3] In case of being between values, we decide for the upper median (i.e. if the value is .5, it is rounded up).

binary: We simplify the annotation and break down the four graded classes into two broader classes: *easy* and *difficult*. We decide to cluster classes 2, 3 and 4 into a new class 'difficult' and keep class 1 as 'easy' for the following reasons: Annotators agreed most for class 1, so this is by far the biggest class. Our binary grouping balances the class sizes more equally and we believe that annotators can easily recognize when they find a compound to be easy (because they fully understand it, which is why we get such a good agreement), but when it comes to specifying difficulty they have more problems to express to which degree they do not understand the compound (due to the fact that they cannot know how much they do not understand).

Figure 1 presents the binary and four-class distributions across the three gold standards. The graphs show that there are more difficult compounds in *Automotive* than in *Cooking* and *DIY*.

4 Experiments on Predicting Difficulty

Our prediction experiments investigate and complement insights from decision tree classification using manually designed features to characterise termhood and compound formation (section 4.1), and logistic regression (LR) and multilayer perceptron (MLP) classification using compound and constituent word embeddings (section 4.2).

For evaluation, we use 5-fold cross-validation and Micro- and Macro-F1 score. As a comparison to the model results, we apply a majority-class baseline. When testing for significance, we use the McNemar's significance test (McNemar, 1947), a paired non-parametric statistical hypothesis test.

4.1 Classification with Term and Compound Features

A core research question for the classification experiments is to which degree attributes that are

[2]`https://spacy.io/`

[3]Alternatively, one could calculate the mean compound difficulty values, but the means are more sensitive to outliers, and in our dataset therefore less appropriate.

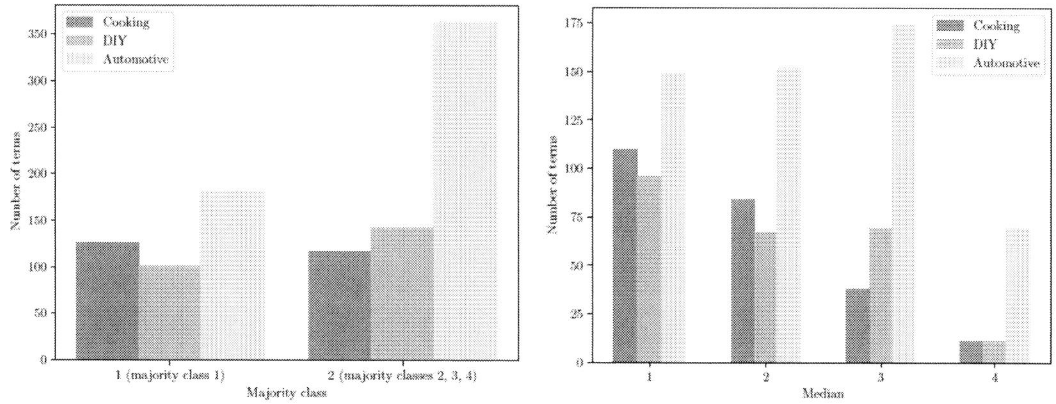

Figure 1: Gold standard: binary and four-class distributions across gold standards (figures taken from Bettinger et al. (2020)).

related to compoundhood influence the prediction, in contrast and in combination with attributes that are related to termhood. The feature types tailored to represent these attributes are the following:

- COMPOUNDHOOD (C) FEATURES[4]:
  frequencies and productivities of compounds, heads and modifiers in the general-language and the domain-specific corpora; cosine distances between compound modifier and compound head embeddings
- TERMHOOD (T) FEATURES:
  contrastive measures *Weirdness Ratio* (Ahmad et al., 1994), *TFITF – Term Frequency Inverse Term Frequency* (Bonin et al., 2010), and *CSvH – Contrastive Selection via Heads* (Basili et al., 2001)
- COMBINED C+T FEATURE:
  FGM-Score, a termhood measure that combines compound and termhood attributes (Nakagawa and Mori, 2003)

Note that we decided against a direct computation of compound–constituent compositionality (Reddy et al., 2011; Schulte im Walde et al., 2013, 2016) as a feature, because the compound dataset was balanced for frequency. It includes infrequent compounds for which word embeddings and compositionality measures would be imprecise.

Method: Decision Trees. Decision tree classifiers (DTs) are supervised machine learning methods that are represented as tree structures. DTs were chosen for this task because they are easy to interpret. We identify the optimal tree depth of our decision trees by constantly growing the trees until results decrease, with relying on Gini impurity as the branch splitting criterium. In this way we found an optimal depth of three for the decision tree in the binary task, and an optimal depth of five for the decision tree in the four-class task.

Overall results. Table 1 shows the results for the decision tree classification using all features. The classification models significantly outperform the respective baselines in the binary classification tasks, but in the four-class distinctions this only applies to the *Automotive* domain and across all domains (non-significant results are in italics). For the binary task, the results for *Automotive* are better than for *Cooking* and *DIY*. We assume that this divergence is due to a higher imbalance of class sizes across the domains, cf. figure 1.

Results by feature group. Having looked at the results when using all features at the same time, we now use coherent groups of features:

1. ***Domain-specific corpus-related features:*** frequencies of compounds, heads and modifiers; productivities of heads and modifiers; FGM-Score
2. ***General-language corpus-related features:*** frequencies of compounds, heads and modifiers; productivity of heads and modifiers; FGM-Score
3. ***Contrastive features:*** weirdness scores and TFITFs of compounds, heads and modifiers; CSvH
4. ***Cosine distance features:*** cosine scores of word2vec and fastText constituent vectors

[4]Note that for all but one of these features we have a balanced set of compounds in the gold standard, see section 3.3.

Baselines and Gold Standards	Binary Micro-F1	Binary Macro-F1	Four-class Micro-F1	Four-class Macro-F1
Baseline *Cooking*	0.519	0.342	0.498	0.166
Baseline *DIY*	0.584	0.369	0.407	0.145
Baseline *Automotive*	0.667	0.400	0.325	0.123
Baseline All	0.604	0.377	0.376	0.137
Cooking	0.646	0.631	*0.543*	*0.312*
DIY	0.712	0.684	*0.519*	*0.406*
Automotive	0.750	0.720	0.471	0.286
All	**0.732**	**0.707**	**0.492**	**0.405**

Table 1: Results for classification using all features. All results but those in italics are significant.

Feature Group	Micro-F1	Macro-F1
Baseline	0.604	0.377
Cosine	0.594*	0.391*
Head	0.608*	0.568*
Domain	0.635*	0.593*
Modifier	0.656	0.627
Constituent	0.661	0.648
Contrastive	0.713	0.690
All	**0.732**	**0.707**
General	0.735	0.703
Compound	0.736	0.713

Table 2: Binary: results by feature groups.

significant improvement

Feature Group	Micro-F1	Macro-F1
Baseline	0.376	0.137
Cosine	0.400*	0.258*
Domain	0.405*	0.300*
Head	0.418	0.287
Constituent	0.455	0.364
Modifier	0.457	0.370
General	0.458	0.359
Compound	0.480	0.342
All	**0.492**	**0.405**
Contrastive	0.510	0.408

Table 3: Four-class: results by feature group.

Feature	Micro-F1	Macro-F1
Baseline	0.604	0.377
comp_TFITF	0.637	0.566
FREQ_head_gen	0.642	0.571
FREQ_mod_gen	0.645	0.619
PROD_mod_gen	0.653	0.616
comp_WEIRD	0.709	0.690
FGM_gen	0.713	0.696
FREQ_gen	0.732	0.706

Table 4: Binary: individual features which significantly outperform the baseline.

Feature	Micro-F1	Macro-F1
Baseline	0.376	0.137
comp_TFITF	0.412	0.238
FREQ_mod_dom	0.415	0.280
Num_comp	0.417	0.248
PROD_head_gen	0.426	0.306
FREQ_head_gen	0.435	0.290
FREQ_mod_gen	0.454	0.322
PROD_mod_gen	0.455	0.298
comp_WEIRD	0.462	0.330
FREQ_gen	0.464	0.343
FGM_gen	0.467	0.339

Table 5: Four-class: individual features which significantly outperform the baseline.

5. ***Compound features:***
   compound frequencies in general-language and domain-specific corpora; numbers of compound constituents; weirdness scores and TFITFs of compounds
6. ***Modifier features:***
   frequencies and productivities of modifiers in general-language and domain-specific corpora; weirdness scores and TFITFs of modifiers; CSvH
7. ***Head features:***
   frequencies and productivities of heads in general-language and domain-specific corpora; weirdness scores and TFITFs of heads; CSvH
8. ***Constituent features:***
   union of modifier and head features

Tables 2 and 3 show the results obtained by feature group, sorted by increase in Micro-F1. We

Chosen Feature	Micro-F1	Macro-F1
+FREQ_gen	0.732	0.706
+PROD_mod_dom	0.739	0.720
+PROD_mod_gen	0.744	0.725
+mod_WEIRD	0.746	0.727
+FREQ_dom	0.746	0.727

Table 6: Binary: feature selection.

Chosen Feature	Micro-F1	Macro-F1
+FGM_gen	0.467	0.339
+head_TFITF	0.487	0.350
+PROD_mod_gen	0.493	0.362
+PROD_head_gen	0.511	0.370
+NUM_comp	0.511	0.370

Table 7: Four-class: feature selection.

can see that most feature groups achieve lower results in comparison to using all features (in bold font), but at the same time 'All' does not achieve the best results. The categories Cosine, Domain and Head perform worst and do in most cases not even significantly improve over the baseline. The modifier features are better than the head features, which is in line with the results in (Hätty et al., 2017) where the modifier features are more important for detecting termhood than head features. For both the binary and the four-class tasks, the groups General, Compound and Contrastive perform best, with Compound as the winner for the binary task and Contrastive as the winner for the four-class task. The arrows in the result tables indicate which group results are significantly different to the winner group result.

Individual features. Tables 4 and 5 show the results for those individual features which perform significantly better than the respective baseline, sorted by increase in F1. For the four-class task, three more features perform significantly better than the baseline in comparison to the binary task; these features are marked in bold. The best individual features are the same for both tasks, with almost the same rankings. The best three individual features address distinct attributes of a compound term: a compound's general-language frequency (FREQ_gen), a termhood measure involving constituents (FGM_gen), and a contrastive termhood measure (comp_WEIRD).

Best feature combination. Tables 6 and 7 analyze how features interact: We perform feature selection by repeatedly adding the best-performing individual feature for each task, based on Micro-F1, until the scores stagnate or decrease. The resulting best feature combinations provide us with the best results for each task, while only comprising five individual feature types in both tables. The optimal combinations address attributes of the whole compounds and attributes of constituents.

Analyzing frequency and productivity. For investigating the influence of frequency and productivity properties of compounds and constituents, we created subsets of the gold standard where we distinguished between tertiles regarding compound frequency and constituent productivity: 'low', 'mid' and 'high'. Each property type is assessed once for the general-language and once for the domain-specific language. The 6×3 tertiles are determined by sorting all elements regarding one property and cutting the data into three equally-sized portions. The resulting ranges are shown in table 8.

We then compare the classifier results for the two extreme tertiles, 'low' and 'high', using all features on these subsets. The results are shown in the right-hand part of table 8. It is obvious that across all properties better results are achieved for the 'low'-category, as indicated by the bold font. The gap between the results for 'low' and 'high' is especially large for the productivities of modifiers and heads. Thus low productivity represents a rather clear indicator for a compound to be either easy or difficult (given that the model achieves better results in the prediction), while high productivity is an attribute of harder to distinguish easy and difficult terms. In order to investigate this effect further, we inspect the gold label distribution in the 'low' and 'high'-categories. We find a dominance of difficult compounds in the 'low'-categories, while there is a higher balance between easy and difficult compounds in the 'high'-categories. This shows that low productivity and frequency are indicators of difficulty, while high productivity and frequency are less distinctive.

4.2 Classification with Word Embeddings

For our second kind of classification experiments, we do not use hand-crafted features anymore but semantic representations of compounds and components for general-language and domain. Two kinds of word embeddings are used in the follow-

Compound and Constituent Properties	Tertiles and Ranges			Micro-F1	
	low	mid	high	low	high
compound frequency (domain)	3–4	4–8	8–444	**0.773**	0.722
compound frequency (general)	0	0–17	17–53,569	**0.779**	0.722
modifier productivity (domain)	1–14	14–55	55–665	**0.863**	0.658
modifier productivity (general)	0–101	103–588	590–4,976	**0.884**	0.661
head productivity (domain)	1–14	14–61	62–1,157	**0.802**	0.652
head productivity (general)	0–119	119–786	786–8,293	**0.812**	0.693

Table 8: Ranges of selected properties across tertiles, and results on binary classification for extreme 'low' and 'high' tertiles when using all features (cf. **All** in Table 2 with Micro-F1=**0.732**).

ing: *word2vec* (Mikolov et al., 2013) and *fastText* (Bojanowski et al., 2017).[5]

We use the word2vec model, because it is a standard model for natural language processing applications. The fastText model works on character n-grams and not on words, and Bojanowski et al. (2017) argues that it performs well on closed compounds. This model is particularly interesting for us because a compound embedding is learned partially from the same n-grams as the embeddings of its constituents. Thus, we implicitly have a representation of the constituents in the compound embedding, which we expect to be beneficial for our classification task. Inspecting some words and their nearest neighbors for the two models confirms our intuition. For the verb *kochen* ("cook") the following six words are the most similar according to word2vec: *sieden* ("to boil"), *garen* ("to refine"), *brutzeln* ("to sizzle"), *braten* ("to fry"), *grillen* ("to barbecue") and *zubereiten* ("to prepare"). According to fastText we find the nearest neighbors *erkochen* ("to reach by cooking"), *garkochen* ("to cook sth. well"), *teekochen*[6] ("to make tea"), *reiskochen* ("to cook rice"), *eierkochen* ("to cook eggs") and *bekochen* ("to cook for someone"). The similarity in word2vec neighbors is more on the semantic level in contrast to fastText, where the words are highly similar on a surface morphological level. The embeddings are trained for each domain individually, by concatenating SdeWaC and the respective domain data as input.

Methods: LR and MLP We use our pre-trained word embeddings for compounds and constituents as features and apply two kinds of classifiers:

- *logistic regression*: simple neural network with only input and output layers but no hidden layer,
- *multilayer perceptron*: neural network with each one input, hidden and output layer.

For the binary classification task, the classifiers use a sigmoid activation in the output layer, for the four-class task the classifiers use softmax activation. For the multilayer perceptron, we also use a sigmoid activation for the hidden layer. Concerning the parameters, the batch size is set to 32, there are 50 epochs and the hidden layer has a dimension of 64.

Results. We compare three different input settings for the classification tasks: The first model only takes the compound word embeddings as input (see 'compound' in table 9). For all settings, we distinguish between two differently trained word embeddings: the word-based word2vec and the character-based fastText word embedding models. The second model ('comp+const') takes the concatenated embeddings of the compound and of its constituents (binary split, i.e. two constituents) as input, to evaluate the impact of the constituents. The third model ('only const') only uses the concatenated constituent vectors, to evaluate if this information is competitive.

The results for the classifications are shown in table 9. For the binary task we reach the best results (marked in bold) with word2vec when using a combination of compound and constituent information, and with fastText when only using the compound embeddings. This tendency was expected: Since fastText embeddings are character-based, the constituents are implicitly encoded as well. Using only constituent information provides lower result scores in comparison to using compound information, which is in line with the results of the previous section.

[5] We do not use state-of-the-art contextualized word embeddings such as BERT (Devlin et al., 2019), because we predict difficulty on a type-based, not context-dependent level.

[6] We cite words in their original lowercased version as used in the model.

The distribution of the results of the four-class task in table 9 is similar to the binary task, except for now also for fastText the combination of compound and constituent information works best. This might be caused by the more difficult task and is also indicated by the fact that for the four-class task MLP with the additional hidden layer produces the best results, while for the binary task the simpler model LR obtains the best results.

Interestingly, word2vec models mostly perform better than fastText models, although fastText implicitly contains constituent information. We argue that because 171 infrequent compound vectors are missing for word2vec (with a minimum frequency threshold for word vectors to be trained), these 171 compounds are assigned to the same random vector. Given that low frequency is a reasonable indicator for difficulty, the model might learn from the missing vectors which compounds are infrequent.

Although models using both compound and constituent information seem to be superior to models using only compound information, these results can only be treated as a tendency. For word2vec and both the binary and the four-class tasks, models using both compound and constituent embeddings are not significantly better than models using only compound embeddings. However, although models using compound embeddings perform significantly better than models using only constituent embeddings (which is intuitive), the latter still perform significantly better than the baseline. This shows that constituent embeddings carry informative characteristics for classifying compounds for difficulty.

4.3 Discussion

Our experiments investigated how compound formation and termhood and domain attributes influence the prediction of compound difficulty.

Compounds and constituents. The binary task, as the presumably simpler task, reached better results with simpler means: General-language frequency of the compound is a good indicator (2% better than the second-best feature for Micro-F1); in addition, there is a 5% gap between compound and constituent features (table 4), which shows that compound features are sufficient for this task. For the four-class task, features differ less; the best results include compound and constituent information (table 5). However for both tasks we can see: a combination of compound and constituent features leads to best results (tables 6 and 7).

The experiments with using neural networks show the same tendency (table 9): While for half of the cases in the binary task the compound vector is sufficient, the improvement over 'comp+const' is not significant, and overall using both compound and constituent vectors ('comp+const') provides the best results. We conclude that constituents influence the degree of difficulty of the compounds.

Termhood. Contrastive features (i.e. termhood features) are more important for the four-class task than for the binary task (tables 2 and 3): For the four-class task, they perform significantly better than the general-language features, while for the binary task 'FREQ_gen' is the best individual feature (table 4). In sum, for a broad difficulty distinction as for the binary task, general-language information might be sufficient, but for the more fine-grained four-class task contrastive termhood features are supportive.

Domains. There are no striking differences in the predictive power of the models across domains (table 1). For all three gold standards, the binary classification models outperform the respective baselines. In the four-class distinction, this is only the case for *Automotive*, which includes more difficult compounds than *Cooking* and *DIY*. Presumably, prediction differences are due to the differently (im)balanced sizes of the classes.

Low versus high productivity and frequency. When contrasting the lower and upper tertile value ranges for compound frequency and constituent productivity, we found that low productivity and low frequency are very salient indicators for the level of difficulty. This seems counterintuitive: e.g. high frequency could be a reliable indicator for simplicity of a compound, while low frequency could indicate difficulty, but low frequency could also indicate that concepts are newly coined (which does not mean that they are difficult), or because of spelling or inflection errors. The dataset was cleaned for the latter, but the former case was not paid attention to. Concerning productivity, the gap between 'high' and 'low' is even more extreme. We hypothesize that this could be due to a compound being judged as difficult because of one difficult constituent, but an easy compound requires all constituents to be easy. This is why single easy constituents might be no good indicators – difficulty depends on the other constituent for the compound to be easy or difficult.

	network	word2vec Mi-F1	word2vec Ma-F1	fastText Mi-F1	fastText Ma-F1	word2vec Mi-F1	word2vec Ma-F1	fastText Mi-F1	fastText Ma-F1
compound	LR	0.760	0.722	**0.746**	**0.724**	0.514	0.385	0.459	0.338
	MLP	0.761	0.729	0.738	0.720	0.518	0.383	0.469	0.341
comp+const	LR	**0.771**	**0.758**	0.734	0.715	0.515	0.429	0.465	0.355
	MLP	0.749	0.735	0.732	0.716	**0.525**	**0.431**	**0.477**	**0.369**
only const	LR	0.701	0.685	0.703	0.679	0.460	0.362	0.447	0.355
	MLP	0.714	0.697	0.713	0.696	0.493	0.389	0.469	0.365

Table 9: LR/MLP Classifiers: Mi(cro)-F1 and Ma(cro)-F1 results for the Binary (left) and Four-Class (right) task.

5 Conclusion

This study investigated the automatic prediction of difficulty for domain-specific German compounds across three domains. We asked to what extent compound formation attributes and domain-specific termhood attributes influence and interact in the prediction. We found that plain general-language compound frequency is a reliable indicator for difficulty in our dataset, which shows that effects of domain-specialization and compound formation are reflected to a large extent by general corpus frequency. However, for a more fine-grained four-class distinction of difficulty going beyond a broad binary distinction into 'easy' and 'difficult', contrastive termhood features and compound and constituent information are crucial.

References

Emil Abrahamsson, Timothy Forni, Maria Skeppstedt, and Maria Kvist. 2014. Medical text simplification using synonym replacement: Adapting assessment of word difficulty to a compounding language. In *Proceedings of the 3rd Workshop on Predicting and Improving Text Readability for Target Reader Populations*, pages 57–65, Gothenburg, Sweden.

Khurshid Ahmad, Andrea Davies, Heather Fulford, and Margaret Rogers. 1994. What is a term? The semi-automatic extraction of terms from text. *Translation Studies: An Interdiscipline. Selected papers from the Translation Studies Congress, Vienna, 1992*, 2:267–-278.

Marco Baroni, Silvia Bernardini, Adriano Ferraresi, and Eros Zanchetta. 2009. The WaCky wide web: A collection of very large linguistically processed web-crawled corpora. *Language Resources and Evaluation*, 43(3):209–226.

Marco Baroni, Johannes Matiasek, and Harald Trost. 2002. Predicting the components of German nominal compounds. In *Proceedings of the 15th European Conference on Artificial Intelligence*, pages 470–474, Lyon, France.

Roberto Basili, Maria T. Pazienza, Alessandro Moschitti, and Fabio M. Zanzotto. 2001. A contrastive approach to term extraction. In *Proceedings of the 4th Terminology and Artificial Intelligence Conference*, Nancy, France.

Julia Bettinger, Anna Hätty, Michael Dorna, and Sabine Schulte im Walde. 2020. A domain-specific dataset of difficulty ratings for German noun compounds in the domains DIY, Cooking and Automotive. In *Proceedings of the 12th International Conference on Language Resources and Evaluation*, pages 4352–4360, Marseille, France.

Piotr Bojanowski, Edouard Grave, Armand Joulin, and Tomas Mikolov. 2017. Enriching word vectors with subword information. *Transactions of the Association for Computational Linguistics*, 5:135–146.

Francesca Bonin, Felice Dell'Orletta, Giulia Venturi, and Simonetta Montemagni. 2010. A contrastive approach to multi-word term extraction from domain corpora. In *Proceedings of the 7th International Conference on Language Resources and Evaluation*, pages 19—21, Valletta, Malta.

Dhouha Bouamor, Leonardo Campillos Llanos, Anne-Laure Ligozat, Sophie Rosset, and Pierre Zweigenbaum. 2016. Transfer-based learning-to-rank assessment of medical term technicality. In *Proceedings of the 10th International Conference on Language Resources and Evaluation*, Portorož, Slovenia.

Elizaveta Loginova Clouet and Béatrice Daille. 2014. Splitting of compound terms in non-prototypical compounding languages. In *Proceedings of the First Workshop on Computational Approaches to Compound Analysis*, pages 11–19, Dublin, Ireland. Association for Computational Linguistics and Dublin City University.

Nivja H. De Jong, Robert Schreuder, and Harald R. Baayen. 2000. The morphological family size effect and morphology. *Language and Cognitive Processes*, 15(4–5):329–365.

Louise Deléger and Pierre Zweigenbaum. 2009. Extracting lay paraphrases of specialized expressions from monolingual comparable medical corpora. In *Proceedings of the 2nd Workshop on Building and Using Comparable Corpora: from Parallel to Non-parallel Corpora*, pages 2–10.

Jacob Devlin, Ming-Wei Chang, Kenton Lee, and Kristina Toutanova. 2019. BERT: Pre-training of

Deep Bidirectional Transformers for Language Understanding. In *Proceedings of the 17th Annual Conference of the North American Chapter of the Association for Computational Linguistics: Human La nguage Technologies*, pages 4171–4186, Minneapolis, Minnesota, USA.

Patrick Drouin. 2003. Term extraction using non-technical corpora as a point of leverage. *Terminology. International Journal of Theoretical and Applied Issues in Specialized Communication*, 9(1):99–115.

Gertrud Faaß and Kerstin Eckart. 2013. SdeWaC – A corpus of parsable sentences from the web. In Iryna Gurevych, Chris Biemann, and Torsten Zesch, editors, *Language Processing and Knowledge in the Web*, volume 8105 of *Lecture Notes in Computer Science*, pages 61–68. Springer, Berlin Heidelberg.

Katerina T. Frantzi, Sophia Ananiadou, and Jun-ichi Tsujii. 1998. The c-value/nc-value method of automatic recognition for multi-word terms. In *Proceedings of the 2nd European Conference on Research and Advanced Technology for Digital Libraries*, pages 585–604, London, UK.

Natalia Grabar and Thierry Hamon. 2014. Unsupervised method for the acquisition of general language paraphrases for medical compounds. In *Proceedings of the 4th International Workshop on Computational Terminology*, pages 94–103, Dublin, Ireland.

Natalia Grabar, Thierry Hamon, and Dany Amiot. 2014. Automatic diagnosis of understanding of medical words. In *Proceedings of the 3rd Workshop on Predicting and Improving Text Readability for Target Reader Populations*, pages 11–20, Gothenburg, Sweden.

Anna Hätty, Michael Dorna, and Sabine Schulte im Walde. 2017. Evaluating the reliability and interaction of recursively used feature classes for terminology extraction. In *Proceedings of the Student Research Workshop at the 15th Conference of the European Chapter of the Association for Computational Linguistics*, pages 113–121, Valencia, Spain.

Anna Hätty and Sabine Schulte im Walde. 2018. Fine-grained Termhood Prediction for German Compound Terms using Neural Networks. In *Proceedings of the COLING Joint Workshop on Linguistic Annotation, Multiword Expressions and Constructions*, pages 62–73, Santa Fe, NM, USA.

Kyo Kageura and Bin Umino. 1996. Methods of automatic term recognition: A review. *Terminology. International Journal of Theoretical and Applied Issues in Specialized Communication*, 3(2):259–289.

Chunyu Kit and Xiaoyue Liu. 2008. Measuring mono-word termhood by rank difference via corpus comparison. *Terminology. International Journal of Theoretical and Applied Issues in Specialized Communication*, 14(2):204–229.

Natalia A. Kochetkova. 2015. A method for extracting technical terms using the modified weirdness measure. *Automatic Documentation and Mathematical Linguistics*, 49(3):89–95.

Rensis Likert. 1932. A technique for the measurement of attitudes. *Archives of psychology*.

Lucelene Lopes, Paulo Fernandes, and Renata Vieira. 2016. Estimating term domain relevance through term frequency, disjoint corpora frequency-tf-dcf. *Knowledge-Based Systems*, 97:237–249.

Quinn McNemar. 1947. Note on the sampling error of the difference between correlated proportions or percentages. *Psychometrika*, 12(2):153–157.

Tomas Mikolov, Kai Chen, Greg Corrado, and Jeffrey Dean. 2013. Efficient estimation of word representations in vector space. *arXiv preprint arXiv:1301.3781*.

Agnieszka Mykowiecka, Małgorzata Marciniak, and Piotr Rychlik. 2018. Recognition of irrelevant phrases in automatically extracted lists of domain terms. *Terminology. International Journal of Theoretical and Applied Issues in Specialized Communication*, 24(1):66–90.

Hirosi Nakagawa and Tatsunori Mori. 2003. Automatic term recognition based on statistics of compound nouns and their components. *Terminology. International Journal of Theoretical and Applied Issues in Specialized Communication*, 9(2):201–219.

Paul Rayson and Roger Garside. 2000. Comparing corpora using frequency profiling. In *Proceedings of the Workshop on Comparing Corpora*, pages 1–6, Hong Kong.

Siva Reddy, Diana McCarthy, and Suresh Manandhar. 2011. An empirical study on compositionality in compound nouns. In *Proceedings of 5th International Joint Conference on Natural Language Processing*, pages 210–218, Chiang Mai, Thailand.

Sabine Schulte im Walde, Anna Hätty, and Stefan Bott. 2016. The role of modifier and head properties in predicting the compositionality of English and German noun-noun compounds: A vector-space perspective. In *Proceedings of the 5th Joint Conference on Lexical and Computational Semantics*, pages 148–158, Berlin, Germany.

Sabine Schulte im Walde, Stefan Müller, and Stefan Roller. 2013. Exploring vector space models to predict the compositionality of German noun-noun compounds. In *Proceedings of the 2nd Joint Conference on Lexical and Computational Semantics*, pages 255–265.

V.G-Vinod Vydiswaran, Qiaozhu Mei, David A Hanauer, and Kai Zheng. 2014. Mining consumer health vocabulary from community-generated text. In *AMIA Annual Symposium Proceedings*, pages 1150–1159.

Ornella Wandji Tchami and Natalia Grabar. 2014. Towards automatic distinction between specialized and non-specialized occurrences of verbs in medical corpora. In *Proceedings of the 4th International Workshop on Computational Terminology*, pages 114–124, Dublin, Ireland.

Marion Weller-Di Marco. 2017. Simple compound splitting for German. In *Proceedings of the 13th Workshop on Multiword Expressions*, pages 161–166, Valencia, Spain.

Qing Zeng, Eunjung Kim, Jon Crowell, and Tony Tse. 2005. A text corpora-based estimation of the familiarity of health terminology. *International Symposium on Biological and Medical Data Analysis*, pages 184–192.

Qing Zeng-Treitler, Sergey Goryachev, Tony Tse, Alla Keselman, and Aziz Boxwala. 2008. Estimating consumer familiarity with health terminology: A context-based approach. *Journal of the American Medical Informatics Association*, 15(3):349–356.

Spurious Correlations in Cross-Topic Argument Mining

Terne Sasha Thorn Jakobsen[1] **Maria Barrett**[2] **Anders Søgaard** [3]

[1]Copenhagen Center for Social Data Science,
University of Copenhagen terne.thorn@sodas.ku.dk
[2]Computer Science Department, IT University of Copenhagen mbarrett@itu.dk
[3]Department of Computer Science, University of Copenhagen soegaard@di.ku.dk

Abstract

Recent work in *cross-topic* argument mining attempts to learn models that generalise across topics rather than merely relying on within-topic spurious correlations. We examine the effectiveness of this approach by analysing the output of single-task and multi-task models for cross-topic argument mining through a combination of linear approximations of their decision boundaries, manual feature grouping, challenge examples, and ablations across the input vocabulary. Surprisingly, we show that cross-topic models *still* rely mostly on spurious correlations and only generalise within closely related topics, e.g., a model trained only on closed-class words and a few common open-class words outperforms a state-of-the-art cross-topic model on distant target topics.

Figure 1: In human interaction, it is evident that relying on topic words for recognizing an argument is nonsensical. It is, nevertheless, what a BERT-based cross-topic argument mining model does.

1 Introduction

When a sentiment analysis model associates the word *Shrek* with positive sentiment (Sindhwani and Melville, 2008), it relies on a spurious correlation. While the movie Shrek was popular at the time the training data was sampled, this is unlikely to transfer across demographics, platforms and years. While there exists a continuum from sentiment words such as *fantastic* to spurious correlations such as *Shrek*, with words such as *Hollywood* or *anticipation* being perhaps in a grey zone, demoting spurious correlations is key to learning robust NLP models (Sutton et al., 2006; Søgaard, 2013; Tu et al., 2020).

This paper studies a similar problem in state-of-the-art cross-topic argument mining systems. The task of argument mining is to recognise the existence of claims and premises in a text span. The standard evaluation protocol is to evaluate argument mining systems *across topics*, i.e., on held-out topics, precisely to avoid over-fitting to a single topic (Daxenberger et al., 2017; Stab et al., 2018; Reimers et al., 2019). This study shows that despite this sensible cross-topic evaluation protocol, state-of-the-art systems nevertheless rely primarily on spurious correlations, e.g., *guns* (Figure 1). These spurious correlations transfer across some topics in popular benchmarks, but only because the topics are closely related.

Contributions We present experiments with an out-of-the-box learning architecture for argument mining, yet with state-of-the-art performance, based on Microsoft's MT-DNN library (Liu et al., 2019). We train models on the UKP Sentential Argument Mining Corpus (Stab et al., 2018), the IBM Debater Argument Search Engine Dataset (Levy et al., 2018), the Argument Extraction corpus (Swanson et al., 2015), and the Vaccination Corpus (Morante et al., 2020). We analyse the models with

All code will be publicly available at https://github.com/terne/spurious_correlations_in_argmin

Proceedings of the 10th Conference on Lexical and Computational Semantics, pages 263–277
August 5–6, 2021, Bangkok, Thailand (online) ©2021 Association for Computational Linguistics

respect to spurious correlations using the post-hoc interpretability tool LIME (Ribeiro et al., 2016) and we find that the models rely heavily on these. This analysis is the paper's main contribution: In §5, we: a) evaluate our best-performing model on a small set of challenge examples, which we make available, and which motivate our subsequent analyses; b) manually analyse how many of the words our models rely the most on are spurious correlations; c) evaluate how much weight our models attribute to open class words and whether multi-task training effectively moves emphasis to closed-class items that likely transfer better across topics; d) evaluate how much weight our models attribute to words in a manually constructed claim indicator list (Morante et al., 2020; Stab and Gurevych, 2017), and whether multi-task training effectively moves emphasis to such claim indicators that likely transfer better across topics; and lastly e) evaluate the performance of models trained only on closed-class words or closed class and open class words that are shared across topics. Surprisingly, we find that models with access to only closed-class words, and a few common (topic-independent) open-class words, perform better across distant topics than our baseline, state-of-the-art models (Table 5).

2 Argument mining

We first describe the task of argument mining, focusing, in particular, on the subtle difference between argument mining ('this is an argument for or against x') and stance detection ('this is an expression of opinion for or against x'). Both tasks are very relevant for social scientists, monitoring the dynamics of public opinion. Still, whereas stance detection can be used to see what fractions of demographic subgroups are in favor of or against some topic, argument mining can be used to identify the arguments made for and against policies in political discussions.

What is an argument? An argument is made up of propositions (claims), which are statements that are either true or false. Traditionally, an argument must consist of at least two claims, with one being the conclusion (major claim) and at least one reason (premise) backing up that claim. Some argument annotation schemes ask annotators to label premises and major claims separately (Lindahl et al., 2019). Others simplify the task to identifying claim or claim-like sentences (Morante et al., 2020) or to whether sentences are claims supporting or opposing a particular idea or topic (Levy et al., 2018; Stab et al., 2018). The resources used in our experiments below are of the latter type: Sentences are labeled as arguments if they present evidence or reasoning in relation to a claim or topic and are refutable.

The resources used in our experiments are annotated with arguments in the context of a particular topic, as well as the argument's polarity, i.e., what is annotated relates to *stance*. The key difference between the current task and stance detection is that arguments require the author to present evidence or reasoning for or against the topic.

Spurious correlations of arguments Arguments for or against a policy typically refer to different concepts. Take, for example, discussions of minimum wage and the terms *living wages* and *jobs*. Since these terms are frequent in arguments for and against minimum wage, they will be predictive of arguments (in discussions of minimum wage). Still, mentions of the terms are not themselves markers of arguments, but simply *spurious correlations* of arguments. We use the same definition of spurious correlations as Wang and Culotta (2020), mainly that a relationship between a term and a label is spurious if one cannot expect the term to be a *determining factor* for assigning the label.[1] Examples of the contrary are terms such as *if* and *because* (and to some degree stance terms), which one can reasonably expect to be determining factors for an argument to exist (and therefore to be stable across topics and time).

3 Datasets

The UKP Sentential Argument Mining Corpus (UKP) (Stab et al., 2018) contains 25,492 sentences spanning eight controversial topics (abortion, cloning, death penalty, gun control, marijuana legalization, school uniforms, minimum wage and nuclear energy), each annotated at the sentence level as one of three classes; NO ARGUMENT, ARGUMENT AGAINST, and ARGUMENT FOR. For example, a sentence about *death penalty* may not be arguing for or against death penalty (NO ARGUMENT), may present an argument against having death penalty as a punishment for a severe crime

[1] Arjovsky et al. (2019) provides the example of a classifier trained to distinguish between images of cows and camels; if prone to spurious correlations, the classifier may be challenged by a picture of a cow on a sandy beach. Bommasani and Cardie (2020) also refer to spurious correlations as *reasoning shortcuts*.

(ARGUMENT AGAINST), or may present an argument in favor of the same (ARGUMENT FOR). The data is annotated such that the evaluation of a sentence (being an argument or not) is not strictly dependent on the topic. However, it should still be unambiguously supportive of or against a topic. Claims will not be annotated as an argument unless they include some evidence or reasoning behind the claim; however, Lin et al. (2019) do find a few wrongly annotated sentences in this regard. The corpus comes with a fixed 70-10-20 split.

The IBM Debater Argument Search Engine Dataset (IBM) is from a larger dataset of argumentative sentences defined through query patterns by Levy et al. (2017, 2018). We use only the 2,500 sentences that are gold labelled — with binary labels, where positive labels were given to statements that directly support or contest a topic. The sentences are from Wikipedia articles and span 50 topics. Since the authors used queries to mine the examples, the data is imbalanced (70% positive). We introduce a random 70-30 split.

The Argument Extraction Corpus (AQ) (Swanson et al., 2015) contains 5,374 sentences annotated with argument quality on a continuous scale between 0 (hard to interpret the argument) and 1 (easy to interpret the argument). Of the corpora included in our study, this differs most from the others; however, the topics included are controversial topics (gun control, gay marriage, evolution, and death penalty), similar to the UKP Corpus. The sentences are partly from the Internet Argument Corpus (Walker et al., 2012) and partly from createdebate.com. We introduce a random 70-30 split.

The Vaccination Corpus (VacC) was presented in Morante et al. (2020) and consists of 294 documents from online debates on vaccination with marked claims. A claim is defined as opinionated statements wrt. vaccination. For our purpose, we split the documents into sentences (23,467). We use binary labels (claim or not) and introduce a random 70-10-20 split.

4 Experimental setup

We now describe our learning architecture, an almost out-of-the-box application of the MT-DNN architecture in Liu et al. (2019). It is a strong model that achieves a better performance than previously reported across the benchmarks.

The MT-DNN model of Liu et al. (2019) combines the pre-trained BERT architecture with multitask learning. The model can be broken up into *shared layers* and *task-specific layers*. The shared layers are initialised with the pre-trained BERT base model (Devlin et al., 2019). We add a task-specific output layer for each task and update all model parameters during training with AdaMax. The task-specific layers are logistic regression classifiers with softmax activation, minimising cross-entropy loss functions for classification tasks or mean squared error for regression tasks. If we only have a single output layer, we refer to the architecture as single-task DNN (ST-DNN) rather than MT-DNN. We train all models over 10 epochs with a batch size of 5 for feasibility and otherwise use default hyperparameters.

Following Stab et al. (2018), we iteratively combine the training and validation data from seven of the eight topics of the UKP Corpus for training and parameter tuning and use the test data of the held-out topic for testing. We firstly treat the task as a single-sentence classification task and train an ST-DNN with the BERT-base model as shared layers. Since Tu et al. (2020) argues multi-task learning effectively reduces sensitivity to spurious correlations, we experiment with MT-DNN models based on different data and task combinations: For each auxiliary dataset (IBM, AQ, and VAcC), we train an MT-DNN model with the UKP Corpus as one task and the auxiliary data as another task. We denote the MT-DNN models as follows: **MT-DNN+IBM** refers to a model trained with the IBM data as an auxiliary claim classification task; **MT-DNN+AQ** is trained with AQ as an auxiliary regression task; **MT-DNN+VacC** is trained with VAcC data as an auxiliary claim classification task; **MT-DNN+AQ+IBM+VacC** is our largest model trained with all auxiliary tasks. **Topic-MT-DNN** provides us with an upper bound: In this setting, all topics are used in training and tuning, including the target topic, as eight separate tasks.

5 Analysis

We evaluate the models on the UKP Corpus using the cross-topic evaluation protocol of (Stab et al., 2018) – training with seven topics and testing on a held-out topic. We report the average macro F_1 across five random seeds. Table 1 shows the average cross-topic results as well as results for each held-out topic for all models. With single-task mod-

Model	Average	abortion	cloning	death penalty	gun control	marijuana legal	school uniforms	minimum wage	nuclear energy
				IN-TOPIC MODELS *(upper bounds)*					
Topic-MT-DNN†	.665	.571	.733	.595	.611	.724	.707	.716	.662
				CROSS-TOPIC MODELS					
ST-DNN	.642±.011	.473±.012	.715±.012	.595±.009	.593±.011	.703±.010	.698±.015	.710±.013	.650±.002
MT-DNN+IBM	.643±.009	.466±.019	**.726**±.010	.595±.006	.582±.004	.704±.010	.703±.010	**.718**±.009	.655±.006
MT-DNN+AQ	.643±.011	**.479**±.015	.716±.006	**.600**±.012	.590±.010	.699±.011	**.710**±.010	.698±.008	.649±.015
MT-DNN+VacC	.641±.010	.472±.016	.716±.008	.589±.009	**.601**±.009	.701±.011	.690±.010	.699±.013	**.660**±.006
MT-DNN+VacC+IBM+AQ	**.644**±.011	.476±.009	.720±.021	.587±.011	.598±.005	**.716**±.011	.696±.003	.701±.018	.655±.006
				CONSTRAINED CROSS-TOPIC MODELS *(lower bounds)*					
CLOSED	.481±.014	.472±.016	.492±.006	.467±.013	.452±.015	.515±.021	.478±.012	.520±.012	.519±.008
CLOSED+SHARED	.501±.010	.426±.012	.508±.016	.475±.009	.469±.006	.552±.004	.490±.005	.565±.017	.519±.008

Table 1: Macro F_1 scores across topics of the three-class UKP data. IN-TOPIC models are (also) trained on the training data of the target topic. CONSTRAINED models only rely on closed-class words and open class words shared across *all* topics. In-topic, cross-topic and constrained models cannot be directly compared. Still, in-topic and constrained models provide upper and lower bounds in the sense that they represent scenarios where models are encouraged, respectively prohibited, to rely on spurious features. We report averages across 5 random seeds except †, which is only one run. The best performances per column within cross-topic models are boldfaced.

els, we achieve an average macro F_1 of .642, which is a big improvement from the .429 reported by Stab et al. (2018). Our ST-DNN model also outperforms the best-reported score in the literature, which, as far as we know, is .633 by Reimers et al. (2019). Reimers et al. (2019) used BERT Large and, unlike us, integrated topic information in the model. Multi-task learning can improve the performance to .644, a 35% error reduction relative to the upper bound of training a model on all eight topics, i.e., including in-topic training data. We see a large variation in the performance across topics for all models, with the abortion topic being hardest to classify and cloning being easiest. With two classes – argument or not – the average macro F_1 is .776, again with large differences across topics; abortion being hardest to classify (.656) and minimum wage being easiest (.828). To analyze our models, we use the popular post-hoc interpretability tool LIME (Ribeiro et al., 2016). By training linear (logistic regression) models on perturbations of each instance, LIME learn interpretable models that locally approximate our models' decision boundaries. The weights of the LIME models tell us which features are locally important.[2]

a) Challenge examples For an initial qualitative error analysis, 19 short text pieces are taken from exercises made by Jon M. Young for his Critical Thinking course at Fayetteville State University.[3][4] Of these, the first six are examples of sentences that comprise an argument or not, and if they do, the conclusions and premises have been annotated by Young. The last 13 examples are from exercises where we annotated the correct answers. We contrast the LIME analyses of the predictions of our best performing model, i.e. MT-DNN+VacC+IBM+AQ, as well as our ST-DNN baseline.[5] An example of the LIME explanations can be seen in Figure 2. The remaining LIME explanations are in the appendix in Figures 4-7.

Out of the 19 examples, seven were incorrectly classified by our best model. Common to these misclassified examples is either a rather uncontroversial, everyday topic (4c, 4g, 5e) or a very informative language (4h, 5g, 5h). Since the model was mainly trained on controversial topics, it is not surprising that these uncontroversial cases make the model misstep. While this is a tiny sample, these incorrect classifications do suggest that our models do not transfer well to *any* topic, possibly indicating they rely more on topic words than on

[2]LIME has several weaknesses: LIME is linear (Bramhall et al., 2020), unstable (Elshawi et al., 2019) and very sensitive to the width of the kernel used to assign weights to input example perturbations (Vlassopoulos, 2019; Kopper, 2019), an increasing number of features also increases weight instability (Gruber, 2019), and Vlassopoulos (2019) argues that with sparse data, sampling is insufficient. Laugel et al. (2018) argues the specific sampling technique is suboptimal. Since we use aggregate LIME statistics across hundreds of data points, these weaknesses should have limited impact on our results; LIME remains a *de facto* standard, and most alternatives suffer from similar weaknesses or are prohibitively costly to run.

[3]`https://tinyurl.com/y6ldjtvh`

[4]`https://tinyurl.com/yyw5uhtm`

[5]For LIME, we use a neighbourhood of size 500 both here and in the following experiments. We use models trained with random seed 2018 for the current and following LIME experiments, and for the current analysis, we use models trained with the cloning topic as our held-out topic.

Topic	Argument words	Topic words	Stance words	Other
abortion	if, that, for	abortion, life, women, woman, human, pregnancy, unborn	right, legal, hates	the , is, to, in, it, be
cloning	would, will, if, could, potential	cloning, clone, cloned, genetic	not, no, abnormalities	the , to, is, it, have, be, do
death penalty	would, if	death, penalty, punishment, killing, crime	not, murder, murderers	the , to, in, is, of, are, people, it
gun control		gun, guns, criminals, background, checks, disarm, arms, armed	no, safer, right, more, not, abiding	a , the, are, and, in, is
marijuana legalization	would	marijuana, use, effects, legalizing, legalization, drug, prohibition, drugs	no, not, more, abuse, costs	is , the, are, it
school uniforms	if, but	uniforms, uniform, school, students, clothing, wears	not, less, improve, decreased, uncomfortable, costs	to , can, it, without
minimum wage	would, that, if	wage, minimum, workers, wages, living, jobs, hour	cost, more, no, many	the , it, is, are, can
nuclear energy	that, if, for	nuclear, power, energy, reactors, plants, waste, chernobyl, fuel	safety, less	is , the, to, has, can, it

Table 2: Top 20 words for each topic based on accumulated LIME weights towards the predicted label of each sentence. Divided into word categories.

All of this talk about banning guns makes me sick! Isn't it obvioius that if we ban guns, law-abiding citizens will not own them, while only the criminals will have them?

(a)

All of this talk about banning guns makes me sick! Isn't it obvioius that if we ban guns, law-abiding citizens will not own them, while only the criminals will have them?

(b)

Figure 2: Non-argumentative example sentence (because it is question rather than argument) explained with LIME. The orange highlights indicate words weighted positively towards the ARGUMENT AGAINST class. The darker the colour, the larger the weight. a) using MT-DNN+AQ+IBM+VacC as the predictor. b) using ST-DNN as the predictor. Both models used were trained with the cloning topic held out.

argument markers. This is supported by the observation that open-class words – rather than argumentative language patterns – are given most of the weight towards the argument classes. Open-class words are defined as nouns, verbs and adjectives, and closed-class words are the remains. For example, we see "guns" as an argument indicator rather than "if" in 2a and 2b; we see "people" and "needs" emphasized more than "if" in 5f; and in 5i, the stance indicator "disastrous" and the open-class word "television" have large weights, while "seems" and "caused" are not emphasized at all. Overall, this suggests our models learn what *arguments are about* but not what *constitutes an argument*. The single-task model exhibits similar patterns. In fact, there seems to be little difference between what the two models attend to.

This initial evaluation raises two questions: To what extent do our models rely on topic-specific spurious correlations with limited ability to transfer across (distant) topics instead of relying on more generic argument markers? And to what extent do simple regularization techniques like multi-task learning, as suggested in Tu et al. (2020), prevent our models from over-fitting in this way?

b) How many of the words we rely on are spurious? We generate and accumulate LIME explanations for our single-task models over the corresponding held-out topics' development sets to evaluate how much our models rely on spurious correlations. We accumulate LIME weights for words towards the predicted class. Words are sorted by accumulated weights, and we manually annotate the top k words for whether they are spurious.

Specifically, and to better understand the distribution of word types, we divide the top 20 words into four categories: *argument words*, *topic words*, *stance words*, and *other*. We define argument words as words that likely appear when presenting claims, independent on the topic, including markers of evidence and reasons such as "if", "that" and "because" and similar lexical indicators based on (Stab and Gurevych, 2017). Contrary to argument words, we define topic words as words that have no relation to the act of presenting an argument but are clearly related to the specific topic, e.g., nouns or verbs frequently used when debating or merely describing the topic. Lastly, we define stance words as opinionated words that express a stance toward a topic (but is not only used in the context of arguments, i.e., presenting evidence). Examples include describing death penalty as "murder" or school uniforms as "uncomfortable". Three annotators agreed on the classification. Words that did not fit our scheme were categorised as *other*. Table 2 shows the top 20 words, categorised, for all development sets.[6]

Our first observation is that 62.5% of the top 20 words are topic words, and for the GUN CONTROL topic, none of the words are argument words. Instead, topic words such as "criminals", "background" and "checks" receive high weights. These words are neither indicative of an argument or stance – hence, they are spurious correlations. Interestingly, the only topic where *argument words* is the majority category is cloning – the held-out topic where all our models perform best. This suggests reducing our models' reliance on topic words can improve the cross-topic performance of argument mining models, which we will investigate in the following experiments. Of course, our models, nevertheless, show relatively good performance across topics, suggesting that some topic words transfer across topics in the UKP corpus. We will discuss recommendations for experimental protocols and the importance of evaluating across *distant* topics below.

Note that we do not normalize the accumulated LIME weights by word frequency, which favors frequent words. When normalising the weights, our models also rely heavily on low-frequency stance words and for all topics, except cloning, there are many topic words among the top 20. High-frequency words (as well as most argument words) are naturally ranked much lower after normalisation. Stance words are, of course, not spurious for our three-way classification problem, but a near disappearance of argument words in the normalized top 20 suggests our models are unlikely to capture low-frequency argument markers.

c) How much weight do our models attribute to open class words, and does multi-task learning move emphasis to closed-class items? Multi-task learning is a regularization technique (Søgaard and Goldberg, 2016; Liu et al., 2019) and may, as suggested by Tu et al. (2020), reduce the extent to which our models rely on spurious correlations, which tend to be open class words. To compare the weight attributed to open-class words, across single-task and multi-task models, we define a score reflecting the weight put on open class words in a sentence: For each word in the sentence, we consider the maximum LIME weight of the two weights towards the argument classes ARGUMENT AGAINST and ARGUMENT FOR. We then take the sum of LIME weights put on open class words, normalised by the total sum of weights, and divide the normalised weight by the sentence fraction of open-class words. Table 3 shows the average sentence scores for each topic and model. We observe that the weights are very similar across single-task and multi-task models (and topics), and a Wilcoxon signed-rank test confirms that there is no significant difference between single-task and multi-task open class sentence scores. We also performed the test with sentence scores defined for each class separately (rather than taking the maximum weight) and again found no significant differences.

Topic	ST	MT
abortion	1.447	1.408
cloning	1.404	1.416
death penalty	1.441	1.421
gun control	1.436	1.381
marijuana legalization	1.387	1.414
school uniforms	1.461	1.402
minmum wage	1.398	1.412
nuclear energy	1.379	1.366
mean	1.419	1.402

Table 3: The sentence scores reflecting the weight put on open class words across domains and model types. There is no significant difference between mean sentence scores of ST and MT models.

d) How much weight do our models attribute to claim indicators, and does multi-task learning move emphasis to such indicators? As a set of

[6]Top 20 words along with their frequency and LIME weights are provided at `github.com/terne/spurious_correlations_in_argmin/top_words`

Claim indicators	*indicates, because, proves, however, shows, result, opinion, conclusion, given, accordingly, since, clearly, mean, truth, consequently, must, would, points, therefore, whereas, obvious, demonstrates, thus, fact, if, that, hence, i, could, should, for, contrary, potential, may, believe, suggests, probable, conclude, clear, point, sum, entails, think, implies, explanation, follows, reason*
Shared open	*political, single, debate, had, asked, made, policy, last, legal, cause, long, few, said, want, person, issue, say, group, possible, use, people, believe, good, have, fact, point, society, time, such, going, put, used, come, based, question, think, example, part, other, are, year, including, argument, only, way, effects, go, many, support, more, several, end, has, day, see, need, make, get, means, public, is, high, help, money, find, found, same*

Table 4: Claim indicators (see text) and shared open class words across the UKP topics.

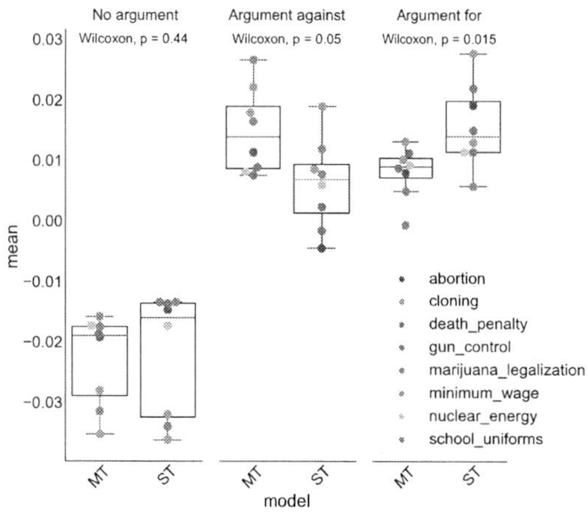

Figure 3: Boxplot of argument word LIME weights with each point representing the topic mean of the argument word weights. We find significant differences between the weights resulting from a single-task and multi-task model towards the two argument classes ARGUMENT AGAINST and ARGUMENT FOR at the 5 and 1 percent significance level, respectively. Furthermore, argument words are weighted significantly higher in the two argument classes than in the NO ARGUMENT class, at the 0.01 significance level.

words indicative of arguments, we use the claim indicator list provided in the appendix for the Vaccination Corpus' annotation guideline (Morante et al., 2020), which is in turn based on (Stab and Gurevych, 2017). We simplify the indicators to unigrams and combine the set with a few additions from Young's Critical Thinking course website; see Table 4. For each held-out topic, we compute the average LIME weight of each claim indicator. Figure 3 shows a boxplot with these averages across single-task and multi-task models. We test for significance using the Wilcoxon signed-rank test. Argument words are weighted significantly higher in the two argument classes compared to NO ARGUMENT, at the 0.01 significance level, as would be expected. With ARGUMENT AGAINST, we find significantly higher weights attributed to argument words by the multi-task models. However, with ARGUMENT FOR, the opposite scenario is observed. Hence, multi-task learning does not robustly move emphasis to claim indicators. Moreover, when normalising the weights by frequency before averaging, the significant difference between single-task and multi-task in ARGUMENT FOR disappears.

e) Removing spurious features We have seen how our models rely on spurious features such as *gun* and *marijuana*. What happens if we remove this? Obviously, removing *only* such words would require expensive manual annotation (like we did for the top-20 LIME words), but we can do something more aggressive (with high recall), namely to remove all open class words. If a model that relies only on closed-class words exhibits better performance across distant topics than state-of-the-art models, this is strong evidence that this model overfits to spurious features.

To this end, we train single-task models (ST-DNN) with all open class words replaced by unknown tokens. We call this model CLOSED. We report macro F_1 on UKP for each held-out topic, as well as an average across topics, in Table 1. We also train a model with closed-class words *and* the open class words that are shared across *all* eight topics. This amounts to 67 open class words, in total; see Table 4.[7] We include these 67 open class words in CLOSED+SHARED (in Table 1) – and find that this small set of words increase the average macro F_1 with 2 percentage points over CLOSED. Another effect of training CLOSED and CLOSED+SHARED models is that the large *variance in performance across topics largely disappears.*

To explore whether removing open class words may improve generalization to more distant topics, we test the constrained models on the test sets of VacC and IBM. While the UKP dataset has three classes, the evaluation datasets have two. We, there-

[7]It is worth noting that the set of 67 common open class words above reflects that *some* words common across topics are in fact of an argumentative nature, with verbs such as "said", "find" and "found" that are often used for referencing sources when providing reasons for claims. We inspected common words among the highest-ranking open class words. We found that very few highly weighted words transfer across more than a few topics, e.g. even at the top 200 level, only one word, namely *cost*, transfer across four, i.e. half, of the topics.

Model	IBM	VacC
ST-DNN	.656	.504
CLOSED+SHARED	**.670**	**.569**
Supervised *(upper bound)*		
MT-DNN+VacC+IBM+AQ	.813	.856

Table 5: ST-DNN and CLOSED+SHARED models are trained solely on the UKP corpus, and we here report these model's performance (macro F1) on the binary, out-of-domain corpora (IBM and VacC). The supervised upper bound is (multi-task) trained on the training data of all four datasets.

fore, merge the two argument classes in UKP when evaluating test performance on VacC and IBM. We report the average test score of the eight models (holding out different UKP topics). Results are found in Table 5 along with a single-task model baseline, i.e., the standard ST-DNN model trained on the UKP corpus, as well as the upper bound on performance provided by an MT-DNN model trained on all four datasets, including the two target datasets. The CLOSED+SHARED model – somewhat surprisingly and very encouragingly – performs *better* than the unconstrained ST-DNN for both test sets (by some margin). This indicates that state-of-the-art argument mining systems overfit to spurious correlations, as well as the need for evaluation on more distant topics.

6 Related Work

Feature analysis in argument mining Daxenberger et al. (2017) underline, like us, the challenge of cross-domain generalization in argument mining, finding that models performing best in-domain may not be the ones performing best out-of-domain, which they argue may in part be due to different notions of claims in the dataset development. Through experiments with different feature groups, such as embeddings, syntax or lexical features, they find lexical clues to be the "essence" of claims and that simple rules are important for cross-domain performance. Simple lexical clues are also found to be effective for argument mining in Levy et al. (2018), who create a claim lexicon, as well as in Lin et al. (2019) who investigate the effectiveness of integrating lexica (a claim lexicon, a sentiment lexicon, an emotion lexicon and the Princeton WordNet[8]) in the attention mechanism of a BiLSTM, but evaluate this only in the context of in-domain argument mining.

[8]https://wordnet.princeton.edu/

Feature analysis in deep neural networks Feature analysis in deep neural networks is not straightforward but, by now, several approaches to attribute importance in deep neural networks to features or input tokens are available. One advantage of LIME is that it can be applied to any model post-hoc. Other approaches for interpreting transformers, specifically, focus on inspections of the attention weights (Abnar and Zuidema, 2020; Vig, 2019) and vector norms (Kobayashi et al., 2020).

Spurious correlations in text classification Landeiro and Culotta (2018) provide a thorough description of spurious correlations deriving from confounding factors in text classification and outline methods from social science of controlling for confounds. However, these methods require the confounding factors to be known, which is often not the case. This problem is tackled by Wang and Culotta (2020) who, in contrast, develop a computational method for distinguishing spurious from genuine correlations in text classification to adjust for the identified spurious features to improve model robustness. They consider spurious correlations in sentiment classification and toxicity detection. McHardy et al. (2019) identified similar problems in sarcasm detection and suggested adversarial training to reduce sensitivity to spurious correlations. Kumar et al. (2019) present a similar method to avoid "topical confounds" in native language identification.

MTL to regularize spurious correlations Tu et al. (2020) suggest multi-task learning increase robustness to spurious correlations. Multi-task learning has previously been shown to be an effective regularizer (Søgaard and Goldberg, 2016; Sener and Koltun, 2018), leading to better generalization to new domains (Cheng et al., 2015; Peng and Dredze, 2017). Jabbour et al. (2020), though, presents experiments in automated diagnosis of disease based on chest X-rays suggesting that multi-task learning is not always robust to spurious correlations. In our study, we expected multi-task learning to move emphasis to closed-class items and claim indicators and away from the spurious correlations that do not hold as general markers of claims and arguments across topics and domains. Still, our analysis of feature weights does not indicate that multi-task learning is effective to this end.

7 Conclusion

We have shown that cross-topic evaluation of argument mining is insufficient to prevent models from relying on spurious features. Many of the spurious correlations that our models rely on are shared across some pairs of UKP topics but fail to generalise to distant topics (IBM and VacC). This shows cross-topic evaluation *can* encourage learning from signals, rather than spurious features; the problem with the protocol in Stab et al. (2018) is using *multiple* source topics. When using multiple source topics for training (and if the annotation relies on arguments being related to these topics), the models may overly rely on features that are frequent in debates of these topics but are not related to the forming of an argument and hence do not generalise well to unseen topics. The variance in cross-topic performance may be explained by some topic words transferring across a few topics, since the large variance disappears when removing open-class words. We propose evaluating on more distant held-out topics or simply considering the worst-case performance across all pairs of topics to estimate real-world out-of-topic performance.[9]

Acknowledgements

Maria Barrett is supported by a research grant (34437) from VILLUM FONDEN.

References

Samira Abnar and Willem Zuidema. 2020. Quantifying attention flow in transformers. In *Proceedings of the 58th Annual Meeting of the Association for Computational Linguistics*, pages 4190–4197, Online. Association for Computational Linguistics.

Martin Arjovsky, Léon Bottou, Ishaan Gulrajani, and David Lopez-Paz. 2019. Invariant risk minimization. Cite arxiv:1907.02893.

Rishi Bommasani and Claire Cardie. 2020. Intrinsic evaluation of summarization datasets. In *Proceedings of the 2020 Conference on Empirical Methods in Natural Language Processing (EMNLP)*, pages 8075–8096, Online. Association for Computational Linguistics.

Steven Bramhall, Hayley Horn, Michael Tieu, and Nibhrat Lohia. 2020. Qlime-a quadratic local interpretable model-agnostic explanation approach. *SMU Data Science Review*, 3.

[9]See Rüd et al. (2011) or Sultan et al. (2016), for example, for similar arguments in cross-domain NLP.

Hao Cheng, Hao Fang, and Mari Ostendorf. 2015. Open-domain name error detection using a multi-task RNN. In *Proceedings of the 2015 Conference on Empirical Methods in Natural Language Processing*, pages 737–746, Lisbon, Portugal. Association for Computational Linguistics.

Johannes Daxenberger, Steffen Eger, Ivan Habernal, Christian Stab, and Iryna Gurevych. 2017. What is the essence of a claim? cross-domain claim identification. In *Proceedings of the 2017 Conference on Empirical Methods in Natural Language Processing*, pages 2055–2066, Copenhagen, Denmark. Association for Computational Linguistics.

Jacob Devlin, Ming-Wei Chang, Kenton Lee, and Kristina Toutanova. 2019. BERT: Pre-training of deep bidirectional transformers for language understanding. In *Proceedings of the 2019 Conference of the North American Chapter of the Association for Computational Linguistics: Human Language Technologies, Volume 1 (Long and Short Papers)*, pages 4171–4186, Minneapolis, Minnesota. Association for Computational Linguistics.

Radwa Elshawi, Mouaz Al-Mallah, and Sherif Sakr. 2019. On the interpretability of machine learning-based model for predicting hypertension. *BMC Med Inform Decis Mak.*, 19.

Sebastian Gruber. 2019. LIME and sampling. In Christoph Molnar, editor, *Limitations of Interpretable Machine Learning Methods*, chapter 13.

Sarah Jabbour, David Fouhey, Ella Kazerooni, Michael W. Sjoding, and Jenna Wiens. 2020. Deep learning applied to chest x-rays: Exploiting and preventing shortcuts.

Goro Kobayashi, Tatsuki Kuribayashi, Sho Yokoi, and Kentaro Inui. 2020. Attention is not only a weight: Analyzing transformers with vector norms. In *Proceedings of the 2020 Conference on Empirical Methods in Natural Language Processing (EMNLP)*, pages 7057–7075, Online. Association for Computational Linguistics.

Philipp Kopper. 2019. Lime and neighborhood. In Christoph Molnar, editor, *Limitations of Interpretable Machine Learning Methods*, chapter 13.

Sachin Kumar, Shuly Wintner, Noah A. Smith, and Yulia Tsvetkov. 2019. Topics to avoid: Demoting latent confounds in text classification. In *Proceedings of the 2019 Conference on Empirical Methods in Natural Language Processing and the 9th International Joint Conference on Natural Language Processing (EMNLP-IJCNLP)*, pages 4153–4163, Hong Kong, China. Association for Computational Linguistics.

Virgile Landeiro and Aron Culotta. 2018. Robust text classification under confounding shift. *Journal of Artificial Intelligence Research*, 63:391–419.

Thibault Laugel, Xavier Renard, Marie-Jeanne Lesot, Christophe Marsala, and Marcin Detyniecki. 2018. Defining locality for surrogates in post-hoc interpretablity. *arXiv preprint arXiv:1806.07498*.

Ran Levy, Ben Bogin, Shai Gretz, Ranit Aharonov, and Noam Slonim. 2018. Towards an argumentative content search engine using weak supervision. In *Proceedings of the 27th International Conference on Computational Linguistics*, pages 2066–2081, Santa Fe, New Mexico, USA. Association for Computational Linguistics.

Ran Levy, Shai Gretz, Benjamin Sznajder, Shay Hummel, Ranit Aharonov, and Noam Slonim. 2017. Unsupervised corpus–wide claim detection. In *Proceedings of the 4th Workshop on Argument Mining*, pages 79–84, Copenhagen, Denmark. Association for Computational Linguistics.

Jian-Fu Lin, Kuo Yu Huang, Hen-Hsen Huang, and Hsin-Hsi Chen. 2019. Lexicon guided attentive neural network model for argument mining. In *Proceedings of the 6th Workshop on Argument Mining*, pages 67–73, Florence, Italy. Association for Computational Linguistics.

Anna Lindahl, Lars Borin, and Jacobo Rouces. 2019. Towards assessing argumentation annotation - a first step. In *Proceedings of the 6th Workshop on Argument Mining*, pages 177–186, Florence, Italy. Association for Computational Linguistics.

Xiaodong Liu, Pengcheng He, Weizhu Chen, and Jianfeng Gao. 2019. Multi-task deep neural networks for natural language understanding. In *Proceedings of the 57th Annual Meeting of the Association for Computational Linguistics*, pages 4487–4496, Florence, Italy. Association for Computational Linguistics.

Robert McHardy, Heike Adel, and Roman Klinger. 2019. Adversarial training for satire detection: Controlling for confounding variables. In *Proceedings of the 2019 Conference of the North American Chapter of the Association for Computational Linguistics: Human Language Technologies, Volume 1 (Long and Short Papers)*, pages 660–665, Minneapolis, Minnesota. Association for Computational Linguistics.

Roser Morante, Chantal van Son, Isa Maks, and Piek Vossen. 2020. Annotating perspectives on vaccination. In *Proceedings of The 12th Language Resources and Evaluation Conference*, pages 4964–4973, Marseille, France. European Language Resources Association.

Nanyun Peng and Mark Dredze. 2017. Multi-task domain adaptation for sequence tagging. In *Proceedings of the 2nd Workshop on Representation Learning for NLP*, pages 91–100, Vancouver, Canada. Association for Computational Linguistics.

Nils Reimers, Benjamin Schiller, Tilman Beck, Johannes Daxenberger, Christian Stab, and Iryna Gurevych. 2019. Classification and clustering of arguments with contextualized word embeddings. *arXiv*, page 1906.09821v1.

Marco Tulio Ribeiro, Sameer Singh, and Carlos Guestrin. 2016. "why should I trust you?": Explaining the predictions of any classifier. In *Proceedings of the 22nd ACM SIGKDD International Conference on Knowledge Discovery and Data Mining, San Francisco, CA, USA, August 13-17, 2016*, pages 1135–1144.

Stefan Rüd, Massimiliano Ciaramita, Jens Müller, and Hinrich Schütze. 2011. Piggyback: Using search engines for robust cross-domain named entity recognition. In *Proceedings of the 49th Annual Meeting of the Association for Computational Linguistics: Human Language Technologies*, pages 965–975, Portland, Oregon, USA. Association for Computational Linguistics.

Ozan Sener and Vladlen Koltun. 2018. Multi-task learning as multi-objective optimization. In *Advances in Neural Information Processing Systems*, volume 31, pages 527–538. Curran Associates, Inc.

Vikas Sindhwani and Prem Melville. 2008. Document-word co-regularization for semi-supervised sentiment analysis. In *ICDM*.

Anders Søgaard. 2013. Part-of-speech tagging with antagonistic adversaries. In *Proceedings of the 51st Annual Meeting of the Association for Computational Linguistics (Volume 2: Short Papers)*, pages 640–644, Sofia, Bulgaria. Association for Computational Linguistics.

Anders Søgaard and Yoav Goldberg. 2016. Deep multi-task learning with low level tasks supervised at lower layers. In *Proceedings of the 54th Annual Meeting of the Association for Computational Linguistics (Volume 2: Short Papers)*, pages 231–235, Berlin, Germany. Association for Computational Linguistics.

Christian Stab and Iryna Gurevych. 2017. Parsing argumentation structures in persuasive essays. *Computational Linguistics*, 43:619–659.

Christian Stab, Tristan Miller, Benjamin Schiller, Pranav Rai, and Iryna Gurevych. 2018. Cross-topic argument mining from heterogeneous sources. In *Proceedings of the 2018 Conference on Empirical Methods in Natural Language Processing*, pages 3664–3674.

Md Arafat Sultan, Jordan Boyd-Graber, and Tamara Sumner. 2016. Bayesian supervised domain adaptation for short text similarity. In *Proceedings of the 2016 Conference of the North American Chapter of the Association for Computational Linguistics: Human Language Technologies*, pages 927–936, San Diego, California. Association for Computational Linguistics.

Charles Sutton, Michael Sindelar, and Andrew McCallum. 2006. Reducing weight undertraining in structured discriminative learning. In *Proceedings of the Human Language Technology Conference of the NAACL, Main Conference*, pages 89–95, New York City, USA. Association for Computational Linguistics.

Reid Swanson, Brian Ecker, and Marilyn Walker. 2015. Argument mining: Extracting arguments from online dialogue. In *Proceedings of the 16th annual meeting of the special interest group on discourse and dialogue*, pages 217–226.

Lifu Tu, Garima Lalwani, Spandana Gella, and He He. 2020. An empirical study on robustness to spurious correlations using pre-trained language models. *Transactions of the Association for Computational Linguistics*, 8:621–633.

Jesse Vig. 2019. A multiscale visualization of attention in the transformer model. In *Proceedings of the 57th Annual Meeting of the Association for Computational Linguistics: System Demonstrations*, pages 37–42, Florence, Italy. Association for Computational Linguistics.

Georgios Vlassopoulos. 2019. Decision boundary approximation: A new method for locally explaining predictions of complex classification models. Technical report, University of Leiden.

Marilyn A Walker, Jean E Fox Tree, Pranav Anand, Rob Abbott, and Joseph King. 2012. A corpus for research on deliberation and debate. In *LREC*, volume 12, pages 812–817. Istanbul.

Zhao Wang and Aron Culotta. 2020. Identifying spurious correlations for robust text classification. In *Findings of the Association for Computational Linguistics: EMNLP 2020*, pages 3431–3440, Online. Association for Computational Linguistics.

Appendix

We must resist all effort to allow the government to censor entertainment. Freedom of speech and expressions are essential to a democratic form of government. As soon as we allow some censorship, it won't be long before censorship will be used to silence the opinions critical of the government. The next thing we know, we will have no more freedom than the Germans did under Hitler.

(a) This is an argument with the claim as the first sentence. The model has predicted ARGUMENT AGAINST. This makes sense because it is an argument against censorship, with this being the focus of the conclusion.

To install the program, you must first put the CD in the player. Open up the File Manager, click on 'Run' and type in 'D: Install.'. After the program is loaded, you will need to restart the computer to use the program.

(b) The model has rightly predicted the example as not being an argument.

Roger Maris' record of 61 homeruns in a single season stood from 1961 until 1998. He should be admitted into the Baseball Hall of Fame.

(c) This is an argument with the last sentence as the conclusion. The model incorrectly predicts it as not being an argument.

All of this talk about banning guns makes me sick! Isn't it obvioius that if we ban guns, law-abiding citizens will not own them, while only the criminals will have them?

(d) This is not an argument. The model incorrectly predicts it as being an argument against something. This example is not formally an argument because it is formulated as a question. We note that Stab et al. (2018) likewise found questions among false positives in their error analysis.

Two teenagers saw the movie, Natural Born Killers, and went out on a killing spree. A number of teenagers who have committed violence at schools have spent many hours playing video games filled with murder and violence. We must have some stricter controls on the content of entertainment that is viewed by teenagers.

(e) This is an argument with the conclusion as the last sentence. The model correctly predicts it as an argument for something (for stricter controls on the content of entertainment).

Research has shown that people who do at least 30 minutes a day of vigorous exercise reduce their risk of heart disease and some forms of cancer. It would be wise for you to begin a daily program of exercise.

(f) This is an argument with the conclusion as the last sentence. The model correctly predicts it as an argument for something (for exercise).

Carlos must be sick today. He did not show up for work. And he has never missed work unless he was sick.

(g) This is an example is an argument with the confusion as the first sentence. The model incorrectly predicts it as not being an argument.

Fayetteville, North Carolina is a great place to live. The city has many great restaurants and movie theaters, the schools are good, and the weather is never terribly bad

(h) This is an argument with the conclusion as the first sentence. The model incorrectly predicts it as not being an argument.

Figure 4: LIME explanations of the first eight challenge examples predicted by the best MT model, MT-DNN+AQ+IBM+VacC. Highlight colours represents weight towards a class; blue: NO ARGUMENT; orange: ARGUMENT AGAINST; green: ARGUMENT FOR. Darker colours mean larger weights.

Many U.S. cities have the name of Fayetteville. Fayetteville, North Carolina has the distinction of being the first to be named after the Marquis de Lafayette, the French general who supported the American Revolution, and the only Fayetteville that the famous Marquis visited.

(a) This example is not an argument. The model correctly predicts it so.

The United States, as the most powerful nation in the world, has a moral obligation to give assistance to people who are subjected to inhumane treatment. The ethnic Albanians were being persecuted in Kosovo. It was proper for the U.S. to become involved in the air campaign against Kosovo.

(b) This example is an argument with the conclusion as the last sentence. The model correctly predicts it as an argument, although as an argument against something rather than for (U.S. involvement).

The United States government is organized into three branches, the executive, legislative, and the judicial. This structure is designed to ensure checks and balances in the powers of the different branches.

(c) This example is not an argument, and the model correctly predicts it so.

Students should attend class regularly and punctually. Our research shows that there is a director correlation between good grades and regular class attendance.

(d) This example is an argument with the conclusion as the first sentence. The model correctly predicts it as an argument for something (for student class attendance).

The last person we hired from Bayview Tech turned out to be a bad employee. I'm not willing to hire anybody else from that school again.

(e) This is an argument with the conclusion as the last sentence. The model incorrectly predicts is as not being an argument.

A people needs land for its activities, land for its nourishment. No people needs it as much as the German people which is increasing so rapidly and whose old boundaries have become dangerously narrow. If we do not soon acquire new territories, we are moving toward a frightful catastrophe.

(f) This example is an argument with the conclusion as the last sentence. The model correctly predicts it as an argument against something (against an upcoming catastrophe caused by not acquiring new territories).

Marriage has always been a very different thing for man and for woman. The two sexes are necessary to each other, but this necessity has never brought about a condition of reciprocity between them. Women have never constituted a caste making exchanges and contracts with the male caste upon a footing of equality. A man is socially an independent and complete individual. He is regarded first of all as a producer whose existence is justified by the work he does for the group. The reproductive and domestic role to which woman is confined has not guaranteed her an equal dignity.

(g) This example is an argument with the conclusion as the first sentence. The model incorrectly predicts it as not being an argument.

Paul Kennedy's The Rise and Fall of the Great Powers has had a remarkable impact in the United States since its publication late last year. It has been widely and almost universally favorably reviewed. Its arguments have been discussed in editorials and opinion columns. One major national magazine ran excerpts as its cover story, while another called it the 'book of the year'.

(h) This example is an argument with the conclusion as the first sentence. The model incorrectly predicts it as not being an argument.

Television has a disastrous impact on children. It appears to be shortening the attention span of the young. It also seems to be eroding their linguistic powers and ability to handle mathematical symbolism. Television also caused them to be increasingly impatient with deferred gratification. Even more serious, television is opening all of society's secrets and taboos, thus erasing the dividing line between childhood and adulthood....

(i) This example is an argument with the conclusion as the first sentence. The model correctly predicts it as an argument against something (against children watching television).

In one half of all traffic deaths in the United States, the driver has been drinking. One third of pedestrians struck and killed by cars were drunk. Driving while intoxicated, or DWI, is illegal in every state. In most states, it is illegal to drive a car if the Blood Alcohol Content is 0.1 percent or greater. In most states, it is illegal to drink alcohol while driving. In some, it is against the law to have an open container of any alcoholic drink inthe car.

(j) This example is not an argument and the model correctly predicts it so.

Studies show that even one drink harms vision and reactions. A driver with a Blood Alcohol Content (BAC) of 0.05 percent, even though he or she is within the legal limit, is twice as likely to have an accident as a non drinking driver. A BAC of 0.1 percent increases the risk of being in an accident by seven times. At BAC 0.15, the risk is ten times greater. You should never drink and drive.

(k) This example is an argument with the conclusion as last sentence. The model correctly predicts it as an argument against something (against drinking and driving).

Figure 5: LIME explanations of the last 11 challenge examples predicted by the best model MT model, MT-DNN+AQ+IBM+VacC. Highlight colours represents weight towards a class; blue: NO ARGUMENT; orange: ARGUMENT AGAINST; green: ARGUMENT FOR. Darker colours mean larger weights.

We must resist all effort to allow the government to censor entertainment. Freedom of speech and expressions are essential to a democratic form of government. As soon as we allow some censorship, it won't be long before censorship will be used to silence the opinions critical of the government. The next thing we know, we will have no more freedom than the Germans did under Hitler.

(a)

To install the program, you must first put the CD in the player. Open up the File Manager, click on 'Run' and type in 'D: Install.'. After the program is loaded, you will need to restart the computer to use the program.

(b)

Roger Maris' record of 61 homeruns in a single season stood from 1961 until 1998. He should be admitted into the Baseball Hall of Fame.

(c)

All of this talk about banning guns makes me sick! Isn't it obvioius that if we ban guns, law-abiding citizens will not own them, while only the criminals will have them?

(d)

Two teenagers saw the movie, Natural Born Killers, and went out on a killing spree. A number of teenagers who have committed violence at schools have spent many hours playing video games filled with murder and violence. We must have some stricter controls on the content of entertainment that is viewed by teenagers.

(e)

Research has shown that people who do at least 30 minutes a day of vigorous exercise reduce their risk of heart disease and some forms of cancer. It would be wise for you to begin a daily program of exercise.

(f)

Carlos must be sick today. He did not show up for work. And he has never missed work unless he was sick.

(g)

Fayetteville, North Carolina is a great place to live. The city has many great restaurants and movie theaters, the schools are good, and the weather is never terribly bad

(h)

Many U.S. cities have the name of Fayetteville. Fayetteville, North Carolina has the distinction of being the first to be named after the Marquis de Lafayette, the French general who supported the American Revolution, and the only Fayetteville that the famous Marquis visited.

(i)

The United States, as the most powerful nation in the world, has a moral obligation to give assistance to people who are subjected to inhumane treatment. The ethnic Albanians were being persecuted in Kosovo. It was proper for the U.S. to become involved in the air campaign against Kosovo.

(j)

The United States government is organized into three branches, the executive, legislative, and the judicial. This structure is designed to ensure checks and balances in the powers of the different branches.

(k)

Students should attend class regularly and punctually. Our research shows that there is a director correlation between good grades and regular class attendance.

(l)

Figure 6: LIME explanations of the first 12 challenge examples predicted the single-task model. Highlight colours represents weight towards a class; blue: NO ARGUMENT; orange: ARGUMENT AGAINST; green: ARGUMENT FOR. Darker colours means larger weights.

The last person we hired from Bayview Tech turned out to be a bad employee. I'm not willing to hire anybody else from that school again.

(a)

A people needs land for its activities, land for its nourishment. No people needs it as much as the German people which is increasing so rapidly and whose old boundaries have become dangerously narrow. If we do not soon acquire new territories, we are moving toward a frightful catastrophe.

(b)

Marriage has always been a very different thing for man and for woman. The two sexes are necessary to each other, but this necessity has never brought about a condition of reciprocity between them. Women have never constituted a caste making exchanges and contracts with the male caste upon a footing of equality. A man is socially an independent and complete individual. He is regarded first of all as a producer whose existence is justified by the work he does for the group. The reproductive and domestic role to which woman is confined has not guaranteed her an equal dignity.

(c)

Paul Kennedy's The Rise and Fall of the Great Powers has had a remarkable impact in the United States since its publication late last year. It has been widely and almost universally favorably reviewed. Its arguments have been discussed in editorials and opinion columns. One major national magazine ran excerpts as its cover story, while another called it the 'book of the year'.

(d)

Television has a disastrous impact on children. It appears to be shortening the attention span of the young. It also seems to be eroding their linguistic powers and ability to handle mathematical symbolism. Television also caused them to be increasingly impatient with deferred gratification. Even more serious, television is opening all of society's secrets and taboos, thus erasing the dividing line between childhood and adulthood....

(e)

In one half of all traffic deaths in the United States, the driver has been drinking. One third of pedestrians struck and killed by cars were drunk. Driving while intoxicated, or DWI, is illegal in every state. In most states, it is illegal to drive a car if the Blood Alcohol Content is 0.1 percent or greater. In most states, it is illegal to drink alcohol while driving. In some, it is against the law to have an open container of any alcoholic drink inthe car.

(f)

Studies show that even one drink harms vision and reactions. A driver with a Blood Alcohol Content (BAC) of 0.05 percent, even though he or she is within the legal limit, is twice as likely to have an accident as a non drinking driver. A BAC of 0.1 percent increases the risk of being in an accident by seven times. At BAC 0.15, the risk is ten times greater. You should never drink and drive.

(g)

Figure 7: LIME explanations of the last seven challenge examples predicted by the single-task model. Highlight colours represents weight towards a class; blue: NO ARGUMENT; orange: ARGUMENT AGAINST; green: ARGUMENT FOR. Darker colours means larger weights.

Learning Embeddings for Rare Words Leveraging Internet Search Engine and Spatial Location Relationships

Xiaotao Li, Shujuan You, Yawen Niu, Wai Chen
China Mobile Research Institute, Beijing, China
{lixiaotao, youshujuan, niuyawen}@chinamobile.com
wai.w.chen@gmail.com

Abstract

Word embedding techniques depend heavily on the frequencies of words in the corpus, and are negatively impacted by failures in providing reliable representations for low-frequency words or unseen words during training. To address this problem, we propose an algorithm to learn embeddings for rare words based on an Internet search engine and the spatial location relationships. Our algorithm proceeds in two steps. We firstly retrieve webpages corresponding to the rare word through the search engine and parse the returned results to extract a set of most related words. We average the vectors of the related words as the initial vector of the rare word. Then, the location of the rare word in the vector space is iteratively fine-tuned according to the order of its relevances to the related words. Compared to other approaches, our algorithm can learn more accurate representations for a wider range of vocabulary. We evaluate our learned rare-word embeddings on the word relatedness task, and the experimental results show that our algorithm achieves state-of-the-art performance.

1 Introduction

Since Bengio et al. (2003) introduced the idea of learning continuous vectors for words using network-based language models, many word embedding techniques have been proposed such as Word2vec (Mikolov et al., 2013a,b), GloVe (Pennington et al., 2014), etc. However, nearly all existing word embedding approaches need words that have a high frequency in the corpus and cannot learn good representations for rare words (including low-frequency words and unseen words). As words in a corpus follow a Zipfian distribution, only a small proportion of the total tokens are frequent words, while most of them are rare words. Therefore, how to learn qualified embeddings for rare words is an essential issue to be solved.

From the human perspective, when encountering a new word, it is an instinct to take a look at its structure or to look up its definition in a dictionary. The essence of both behaviours is to transform a rare word to a set of familiar words expressing the same meaning to it. Based on the above ideas, some proposed techniques have attempted to exploit subword information or lexical resources to predict the rare word representation.

In the area of subword-based approaches, FastText (Bojanowski et al., 2017) learns representations for character n-grams and represents words as the sum of the n-gram vectors. Ngram2vec (Zhao et al., 2017) learns n-gram representations from n-gram co-occurrence statistics and incorporates this information into the word representations. Pinter et al. (2017) proposed the Mimick model to predict vectors for out-of-vocabulary words by learning a function from spellings to distributional embeddings. The attentive mimicking model (AM) (Schick and Schütze, 2019a) and the form context model (FCM) (Schick and Schütze, 2019b) jointly use surface form and context information to improve representations of rare words.

In another way, lexical resources are used to infer the representation for a rare word from the vectors of the words having a semantic association with it. SemLand (Pilehvar and Collier., 2017) infers the representations for rare words by exploiting the definitions and relationships in an external lexicon WordNet (Miller, 1995). Faruqui et al. (2015) proposed to use word relation knowledge found in semantic lexicons to retrofit word vectors. Bahdanau et al. (2018) proposed to train a Long Short-Term Memory (LSTM) network to predict the representations of rare words based on auxiliary data (e.g., a dictionary definition) from knowledge bases. Prokhorov et al. (2019) embedded a knowledge base into a vector space by the node2vec (Grover and Leskovec, 2016) graph embedding algorithm and then mapped the embedded words from this space to a corpus-based space. However, the performance of these approaches

Proceedings of the 10th Conference on Lexical and Computational Semantics, pages 278–287
August 5–6, 2021, Bangkok, Thailand (online) ©2021 Association for Computational Linguistics

heavily depends on the coverage of external data sources. If a rare word is uncovered by the lexicon, the rare-word embedding will not be available.

In addition to the approaches outlined above, a great concern has been raised over the pre-trained language models for their outstanding performance in various natural language processing (NLP) tasks. Among the pre-trained models, ELMo (Peters et al., 2018) and BERT (Devlin et al., 2019) are two most typical ones. Based on the pre-trained language model, we can use a function of the internal layers as the vector of a word. The pre-trained language models have strong coverage ability and can predict vectors for nearly all rare words. However, based on our experimental results (section 3.4), we found the semantics of rare words are not learned well when the context information is not provided or the rare words come from specific domains.

As the largest source of information in the world, the Internet consists of billions of pages of data in all fields. To figure out the meaning of a rare word, almost everyone's first priority has changed to retrieve it on the Internet and extract the useful information from the associated webpages. Inspired by this, we propose a two-step algorithm to learn rare-word embeddings using the Internet search engine and the spatial location relationships. We firstly find the top-n most relevant words to a rare word from the webpages returned by the Internet search engine and compute the initial embedding of the rare word by averaging the vectors of these extracted words. According to the order of the top-n most relevant words, we further iteratively fine-tune the location of the rare word in the vector space to make it satisfy the constraints of spatial location relationships. The constraints are that if a rare word is more relevant to a word than other words, the distance between the rare word and this word is closer than the distances between the rare word to others in the vector space. Compared to the existing approaches, there are three advantages of our approach: (i) we can obtain a powerful coverage for rare words; (ii) we can provide more accurate vector representations for rare words; (iii) we can support representing multilingual rare words.

This paper is organized as follows: Section 2 describes our methodology in detail. Section 3 presents the experimental results. The paper is concluded in Section 4.

2 Methodology

In this section, we will begin by introducing our motivation, then describe how we define the relevance metric and obtain the top-n related words to a rare word using the Internet search engine, and finally present the fine-tuning process toward achieving the more precise embedding learning.

2.1 Motivation

To solve the rare word representation problem, as mentioned above, the most direct way is to find a series of familiar tokens expressing the same meaning to the rare word. Further, the embedding of a rare word can be induced by the embedding of its semantically related tokens in the word embedding model. Based on the above analysis, there are two main challenges in the task of the rare word representation: (i) how to obtain the semantically related words for more rare words? and (ii) how to ensure the quality of the learned rare-word embeddings? To address these issues, we propose an algorithm to learn embeddings for rare words, as shown in Figure 1, which consists of two processes: a coarse-tuning one and a fine-tuning one. The coarse-tuning process is to obtain the semantically related words for a rare word and to predict its approximate location in the vector space (i.e., the coarse-grained representation). The fine-tuning process is to adjust the coarse-grained vector of the rare word intensively to optimize its meaning representation accuracy; and the final learned-vector is the fine-grained representation.

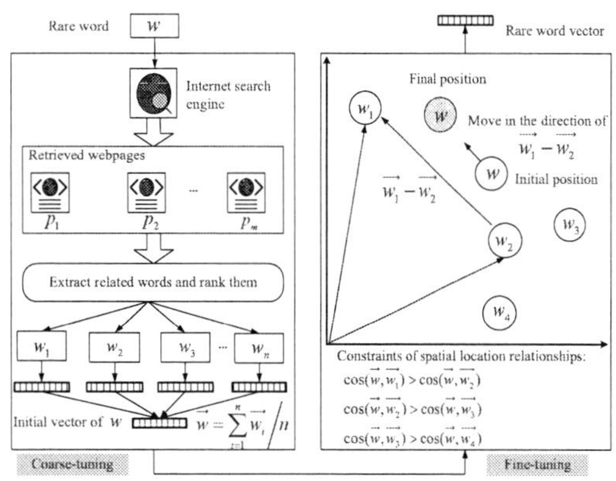

Figure 1: Procedure of learning rare-word embeddings.

To extend the coverage for rare words in the coarse-tuning process, we use information on the Internet as the data source and utilize the Internet search engine to achieve fast acquisition of the topic-related webpages to the rare word. With the help of the large-scale data on the Internet, we can find the semantically related information for nearly all of the words in different fields, which brings better coverage capacity than the existing lexicon-based approaches. As the webpage documents vary widely in their internal structure and contain a lot of interference information such as advertisements, navigation texts, etc, we use only the titles from the retrieved documents to extract the semantically related words of the rare word.

For a rare word w, we firstly use a search engine to search for w and capture the first m relevant records: $P = \{p_1, p_2, p_3, ..., p_m\}$. Then, a set of n most related words $W = \{w_1, w_2, w_3, ..., w_n\}$ to the rare word are extracted from the titles of these m relevant webpages and these n words are ranked by relevance from high to low. The vectors of these n related words is averaged as the initial vector of the rare word (see Equation (1)), which is the coarse-grained representation of w.

$$\vec{w} = \frac{\sum_{i=1}^{n} \vec{w_i}}{n}, \tag{1}$$

where $\vec{w_i}$ is the vector representation of the related word $w_i \in W$. To further ascertain the location of the rare word in the vector space, we consider the constraints of spatial location relationships among the rare word and its n semantically related words. As the related words have been ranked by the relevance to the rare word w, the semantic relatedness between the rare word and a high-ranking word in W is higher than that between the rare word and a low-ranking word in W, i.e.:

$$\begin{aligned} &rel(w, w_i) > rel(w, w_j), \\ &\forall i, j \in [1, n], w_i \in W, w_j \in W, i < j, \end{aligned} \tag{2}$$

where rel is a metric function of the semantic relatedness. In the word embedding model, the semantic relatedness between two words can be represented as the cosine distance of their vectors in the vector space. Therefore, the constraints can be expressed as follows:

$$\begin{aligned} &\cos(\vec{w}, \vec{w_i}) > \cos(\vec{w}, \vec{w_j}), \\ &\forall i, j \in [1, n], w_i \in W, w_j \in W, i < j. \end{aligned} \tag{3}$$

To satisfy the constraints of the spatial location relationships, the vector of the rare word is iteratively fine-tuned as follows:

$$\begin{aligned} &\vec{w} = \vec{w} + (\vec{w_i} - \vec{w_j}) \times \Delta, \\ &if : (\cos(\vec{w}, \vec{w_i}) < \cos(\vec{w}, \vec{w_j})) and (i < j), \end{aligned} \tag{4}$$

where $\vec{w_i} - \vec{w_j}$ is the movement direction of w, and Δ is the step length. As shown in Figure 1, the location of the rare word w is the center of its four semantically related words after the coarse-tuning process, where the hyper-parameter n is set to 4 as an example. However, the current coarse-grained vector of w does not satisfy the constraint: $\cos(\vec{w}, \vec{w_1}) > \cos(\vec{w}, \vec{w_2})$. In the fine-tuning process, the location of w gradually heads toward w_1 in the direction of $\vec{w_1} - \vec{w_2}$, and the final location of w is closer to its real location.

2.2 Coarse-grained Rare Word Representation

The specific procedure of the coarse-tuning process is described in Algorithm 1. We define a dictionary of key-value pairs to store the relevance scores among the rare word and its semantic related words (Line 3). Given a rare word w, the search engine S is invoked to query the related webpages P (Line 4). For each page, the `lxml` module of Python is exploited to extract its title. We decompose it into a set of distinct words and delete the stop words from the segmentation result (Lines 8-11). Based on our tests, there is a list of titles lacking of discrimination and interfering the acquisition of related words. Take the English word "self-discipline" for example, the title of one of its related webpages is "*what is self-discipline - definitions*". The word "definitions" is not exclusively related to "self-discipline" in meaning, because this word also appears in the titles of the retrieved webpages for numerous other search words. To address this issue, we define a noise word set Γ which currently includes 10 words: {"**definition**", "**wiktionary**", "**synonyms**", "**antonyms**", "**dictionary**", "**blog**", "**html**", "**www**", " **encyclopedia**", " **journal**"}. If a title contains a word of Γ, it will be abandoned in our algorithm (Line 13).

At this point, the keys of map (i.e., semantic related words) are assigned with the words included in the filtered webpage titles. To measure the relevance score between two words, we take the co-occurrence information and the number of word meanings into account. The co-occurrence frequency is defined by the number of titles that contain the related word. Since the vector of a polyseme is actually a compromise of all its meanings, the polyseme is likely to locate far from the rare word in the vector space. According to this con-

Algorithm 1 Coarse-tuning.

Input: The word embedding model, M; the rare word, $w \notin M$; the max number of related words, n; the Internet search engine, S; the semantic lexicon L; the noise word set Γ;

Output: The semantically related word set of w, W; the coarse-grained embedding of w, $\vec{w_c}$;

1: **Initialize** $\vec{w_c} \leftarrow \vec{0}$;
2: // key is a semantically related word to w, and $value$ is the relevance score
3: $map \leftarrow dict(key, value)$;
4: $P \leftarrow Search(S, w)$;
5: **for** each $p \in P$ **do**
6:     // Extract the title of the webpage p
7:     $S \leftarrow GetTitle(p)$;
8:     // Decompose S into some distinct tokens
9:     $T \leftarrow Decompose(S)$;
10:     // Remove the stop words
11:     $T \leftarrow RemoveStopWords(T)$;
12:     // Exclude the titles including noise words
13:     **if** $T \cap \Gamma = \varnothing$ **then**
14:         **for** each $t \in T$ **do**
15:             **if** $t \in M$ **and** $t \in L$ **then**
16:                 // Update the relevance score
17:                 $s = 1/GetSenseNum(L, t)$;
18:                 $map[t] \leftarrow map[t] + s$;
19:             **end if**
20:         **end for**
21:     **end if**
22: **end for**
23: // Rank the semantic words by the relevance score from high to low
24: $map.Sort()$;
25: **for** each $key \in map.keys$ **do**
26:     // Get the first n words out of map as the semantically related word set W
27:     **if** $|W| < n$ **then**
28:         $W.append(key)$;
29:         $\vec{w_c} \leftarrow \vec{w_c} + M[key]$;
30:     **end if**
31: **end for**
32: **if** $|W| > 0$ **then**
33:     $\vec{w_c} \leftarrow \vec{w_c}/|W|$;
34: **end if**
35: **return** $\vec{w_c}$, W;

sideration, we put more emphasis on the univocal words than the polysemes to infer the rare word embeddings. The relevance score is proportional to the co-occurrence frequency and inversely proportional to the number of word meanings, i.e.:

$$Score(w, v) = \frac{m_v}{GetSenseNum(L, v)}, \quad (5)$$

where v is a word related to the rare word w; m_v is the number of webpage titles that include the word v; $GetSenseNum$ is an abstract function to obtain the number of meanings of v, and the parameter L is a semantic lexicon used as a sense inventory. For example, if WordNet (Miller, 1995) is used as the lexicon, the function $GetSenseNum$ is to find the number of synsets that a word belongs to. To provide the candidate meanings and the vector representation for each related word, it requires the semantically related words to be covered by the lexicon and the pre-trained word embedding model (Line 12). It should be noted that there is a clear difference between our algorithm and the lexicon-based approaches. We do not need the rare word to be covered by the lexicon but seek to find a list of related words in the lexicon to learn the rare word vector representation. Therefore, our algorithm is not susceptible to the coverage of the semantic lexicon. Uniformly, for each rare word, we use the top-n most related words and average their embeddings as the coarse-grained representation (Lines 24-34). The parameter n is used to limit the number of semantically related words when the size of map is greater than n.

2.3 Fine-grained Rare Word Representation

The fine-tuning process builds on the coarse-tuning process to optimize the rare word vectors. The main idea of the fine-tuning process is that the more related the two words are, the closer their word embeddings locate in the vector space. Based on this, the specific procedure of this process is described in Algorithm 2. On account of the semantically related words in the order of relevance and the coarse-grained embedding of w, the vector $\vec{w_f}$ is iteratively fine-tuned to fulfill the constraints of the spatial location relationships. The hyper-parameter K is used to control the total number of fine-tuning epochs (Line 5). During a fine-tuning epoch, if the relevance score between the rare word w and each semantically related word $w_i \in W$ is less than the relevance score between the rare word w and each semantically related word $w_j \in W$ with lower order than i, as declared by Equation (4), the rare word w will move one step (Δ) to get closer to w_i (Lines 14-15). Finally, the vector of w will be updated to a new position in the vector space, where the meaning of w can be more accurately represented.

Algorithm 2 Fine-tuning.

Input: The word embedding model, M; the rare word, $w \notin M$; the semantically related word set of w, W; the coarse-grained embedding of w, $\vec{w_c}$; the number of epochs, K; the step size, Δ.

Output: The fine-grained embedding of w, $\vec{w_f}$;

```
Initialize w_f ← w_c;
// The number of the semantically related words
n = |W|;
if n > 1 then
    for k = 1 to K do
        for i = 1 to n − 1 do
            w_i ← W[i − 1];
            w⃗_i ← M[w_i];
            rel_i = cos(w⃗_f, w⃗_i);
            for j = i + 1 to n do
                w_j ← W[j − 1];
                w⃗_j ← M[w_j];
                rel_j = cos(w⃗_f, w⃗_j);
                if rel_i < rel_j then
                    // w moves one step in the direction of w⃗_i − w⃗_j
                    w⃗_f ← w⃗_f + (w⃗_i − w⃗_j) × Δ;
                end if
            end for
        end for
    end for
end if
return w⃗_f;
```

3 Experiments

In this section, we present our experimental settings and results. We take the word relatedness task as the evaluation framework, and the Spearman correlation coefficient ($\rho \times 100$) is adopted to assess the quality of the learned embeddings. Also, the percentage of missed pairs (PMP) is used to evaluate the vocabulary coverage of our model. `Baidu`[1] search engine is used to retrieve the relevant webpages in our coarse-tuning process. All experiments use the same fine-tuning settings: $K = 50$, $\Delta = 0.1$.

We first report the performance of our algorithm in different hyper-parameters. Then, we compare the quality of the rare-word embeddings before and after the fine-tuning process to verify the effectiveness of our two-step approach. Next, we compare our algorithm with the `CBOW` algorithm and six state-of-the-art English rare-word embedding learning algorithms. Finally, we evaluate our algorithm on two Chinese word datasets to investigate the scalability of our approach for a language other than English.

3.1 Experimental Settings

Training corpus: We select the English Wikipedia[2] dump on April 1, 2015, as the training corpus.

Benchmark datasets: We use four benchmark datasets to perform evaluations and comparisons for different rare word representation techniques, including the Stanford Rare Word (RW) dataset (Luong et al., 2013), the Cambridge Rare Word (Card-660) dataset (Pilehvar et al., 2018), the UMNSRS dataset (Pakhomov et al., 2010) and the MayoSRS dataset (Pakhomov et al., 2011). Among them, RW (2,034 pairs) and Card-660 (660 pairs) are two general domain datasets, while UMNSRS (566 pairs) and MayoSRS (101 pairs) are two datasets in the biomedical field.

Baseline algorithms: We compare our algorithm with the `CBOW` algorithm (Mikolov et al., 2013a) and six rare-word learning algorithms: (i) `FastText` (Bojanowski et al., 2017), (ii) `FCM` (Schick and Schütze, 2019b), (iii) `SemLand` (Pilehvar and Collier., 2017), (iv) `Align` (Prokhorov et al., 2019), (v) `ELMo` (Peters et al., 2018) and (vi) `BERT` (Devlin et al., 2019). Among these approaches, `FastText` and `FCM` are two subword-based approaches, `SemLand` and `Align` are two lexicon-based approaches, `ELMo` and `BERT` are two pre-trained language models. The lexion WordNet (Miller, 1995) is selected as the word meaning inventory, and we use the `CBOW` word embedding model as the pre-trained model to induce the vectors of rare words.

3.2 Influences of Hyper-parameters

In this experiment, we investigate the influences of the two hyper-parameters in the coarse-tuning process for the quality of the learned rare-word embeddings including the number of relevant records (m) and the number of semantically related words (n), and seek the optimal range of the two hyper-

[1]http://www.baidu.com

[2]https://dumps.wikimedia.org/enwiki/20150401

parameters. We randomly select a third of records from the four benchmark datasets respectively and form four sub-datasets to evaluate the performance of our algorithm in different hyper-parameters. We first set m to 100 and change n from 1 to 10, then record the Spearman coefficients on the four sub-datasets. The dimension of all the vectors is 300, and the results are presented in Figure 2. We can see that the Spearman coefficients of our algorithm on the four sub-datasets all increase at the early stage and then decrease with the parameter n. When the parameter n is between 4 and 8, the quality of the learned rare-word embeddings is optimal. To analyze the reason, when $n < 4$, the semantic information of the related words is limited for its lower quantity, which is insufficient to predict the accurate vectors of rare words. At one extreme (when $n = 1$), the vector of a rare word directly equals to that of the only one related word without the fine-tuning process. Unless the rare word and its related word are synonymous, the rare word will obtain a wrong representation. When $n > 8$, it increases the likelihood of introducing noise words that are actually not related to the rare word into the semantic word set, which will also produce a negative effect on the right place of the rare word in the vector space.

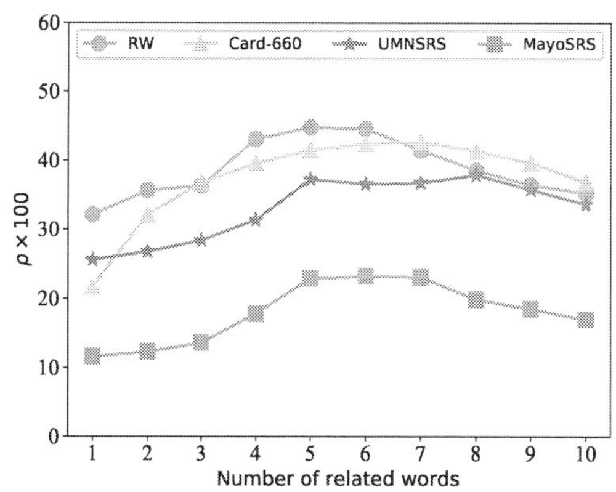

Figure 2: Spearman performance in different number of semantically related words

In the next experiment, the parameter n is set to 5, and the other parameter m is changed from 20 to 200. We record the Spearman coefficients on the four sub-datasets as well. We can see from Figure 3 that the performance reaches the peak values on the two general domain sub-datasets when the parameter m are set to 140 and 160 respectively. On the other side, the Spearman coefficients on the two biomedical field sub-datasets increase with the parameter m, then show some small fluctuations when $m > 100$. The results indicates that more retrieved records are required for general-domain rare words to obtain high-quality word representations. One reason is that the titles of the retrieved records for general-domain rare words are more likely to contain the words in the defined noise word set, and these records will be abandoned in the coarse-tuning process. Moreover, it may be unnecessary to use too many records as well because the lower-ranking records have declined in the relevance with the rare word. Based on the above results, we set m and n to 100 and 5 respectively to learn better rare-word embeddings in the follow-up experiments.

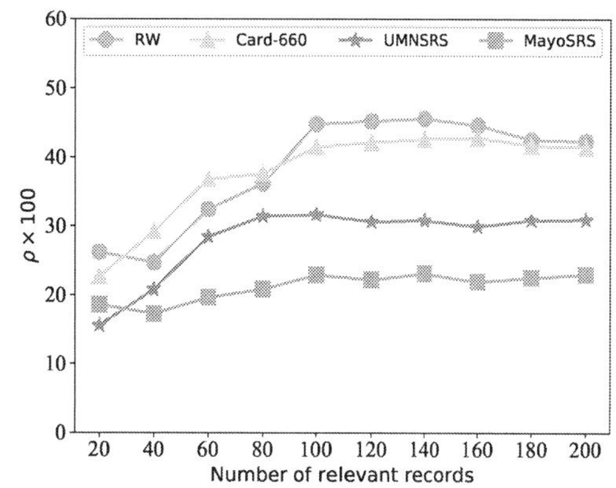

Figure 3: Spearman performance in different number of relevant records

3.3 Performance Comparison between Coarse-tuning and Fine-tuning

The coarse-tuning operation in our algorithm provides a coarse-grained vector representation from scratch for each rare word by averaging the vectors of the semantically related words, while the fine-tuning process constantly adjusts the coarse-grained embedding of the rare word to a fine-grained vector with a more suitable position in the vector space. In this experiment, we compare the Spearman correlations of the learned coarse-grained embeddings with that of the fine-grained embeddings to verify the effectiveness of the fine-tuning operation. To have a fair comparison, we report the performance of the learned rare-word embeddings on the multiple datasets in four different dimensions: 100, 200, 300 and 400.

We can see from Figure 4 that the Spearman correlations of the fine-grained embeddings outperform that of the coarse-grained embeddings on the four datasets regardless of the vector dimensions. It demonstrates that the quality of the coarse-grained embeddings can be further enhanced by the fine-tuning process with consideration of the constraints of spatial location relationships. The order information of the relevances between the rare word to its semantically related words is fully utilized to correct the vector of the rare word. Owing to the fine-tuning process, the relevance score is not required to precisely measure the relatedness between two words, but only needs to compare the relatednesses among the rare word and its semantic words relatively, which has effectively reduced the difficulty of the relevance metric design in the coarse-tuning process.

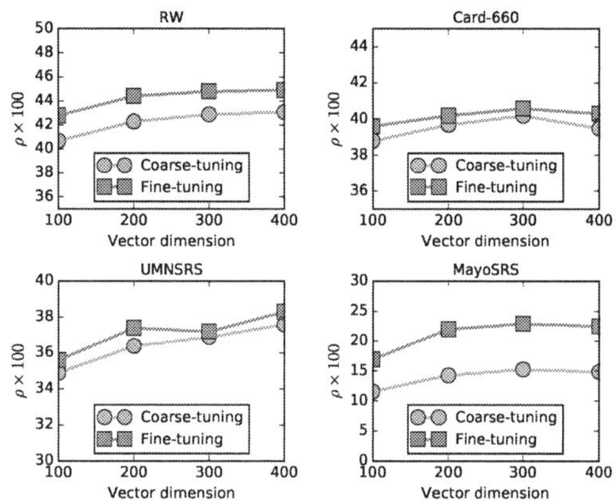

Figure 4: Performance comparison between coarse-tuning and fine-tuning over vector dimensions.

3.4 Performance Comparison with Previous Work

In this experiment, the dimension of all vectors is set to 300. Table 1 shows the comparison results, in which the best result is shown in bold. Among the baseline approaches, `ELMo` and `BERT` have the best coverage ability due to their character-based representation. Even so, we still achieve almost the same coverage performance as these two pre-trained language models except for failing to cover a tiny part (0.75%) of the word pairs in Card-660. Compared to the PMP values on domain-general datasets, the coverage performance of `FastText` and `FCM` on domain-specific datasets decline significantly. The reason is that the domain-specific terms and their subwords both rarely appear in the training corpus, which causes the vectors of many subwords in the biomedical field to be unavailable in these two models. `SemLand` and `Align` opt for WordNet as the general domain lexical resource and use the Medical Subject Headings (MeSH)[3] as the medical lexical resources. However limited by the coverage of the lexical resources, the PMP performance of these two approaches is unsteady on different datasets. We use all the information resources on the Internet to find the semantically related words of a rare word, which is far beyond the scopes of any lexical resource. Whether for domain-general rare terms or domain-specific rare terms, nearly all the vectors can be learned by our algorithm with their semantically related words.

With respect to the quality of rare word representations, our algorithm outperforms the other approaches on the four benchmark datasets. Let us go further to identify the reasons for the superiority of our algorithm. Although `ELMo` and `BERT` have the powerful coverage ability for rare words, the learned rare-word embeddings do not have high quality, especially for the domain-specific rare terms. Compared to `FastText`, the vector of a rare word in our algorithm is represented by its semantically related words instead of the inner subwords, which can provide more explicit semantic meanings than the subwords. `FCM` leverages the context information in addition to the n-gram information and learns higher-quality embeddings than `FastText` for the domain-general words, but fails to achieve the same performance on the domain-specific datasets. The reason is that most of the domain-specific terms are unseen in the Wikipedia corpus, so the context information is insufficient to learn the `FCM` word embeddings. In contrast to `SemLand` and `Align`, our algorithm is independent of specific lexical resources and has stable coverage for rare words in different fields. Therefore, our algorithm can induce eligible embeddings for more words and eventually achieve better Spearman correlations on the datasets.

3.5 Performance on Chinese rare words

To investigate the scalability of our approach for multilingual words, we evaluate our algorithm on Chinese rare words in this section. We select the Chinese Wikipedia[4] dump on November 20, 2016, as the corpus and use two Chinese benchmark datasets to perform evaluations, including the wordsim-240 (Chen et al., 2015) word

[3]https://www.nlm.nih.gov/mesh/

[4]https://dumps.wikimedia.org/zhwiki/20161120/

Table 1: The Performance of Spearman correlation and coverage on four English datasets.

Approach	RW		Card-660		UMNSRS		MayoSRS	
	PMP	$\rho \times 100$	PMP	$\rho \times 100$	PMP	$\rho \times 100$	PMP	$\rho \times 100$
CBOW	14%	35.5	54%	2.2	19%	15.9	64%	11.9
FastText	3%	38.8	5%	20.4	14%	17.6	34%	14.4
FCM	3%	39.5	5%	24.2	14%	18.8	34%	13.7
SemLand	**0%**	40.0	39%	33.2	15%	20.1	29%	10.9
Align	**0%**	42.0	39%	32.5	15%	22.4	29%	14.5
ELMo	**0%**	**44.8**	**0%**	20.2	**0%**	17.2	**0%**	7.8
BERT	**0%**	20.7	**0%**	16.2	**0%**	8.8	**0%**	7.7
Ours	**0%**	**44.8**	0.75%	**41.5**	**0%**	**37.3**	**0%**	**22.9**

pairs and the wordsim-296 (Jin and Wu, 2012). We compare our algorithm with the CBOW algorithm and four rare-word learning algorithms: (i) CWE (Chen et al., 2015), (ii) cw2vec (Cao et al., 2018), (iii) ELMo and (iv) BERT. The lexicon Tongyici Cilin (Tian and Zhao, 2010) is selected as the Chinese sense inventory.

We can see from Table 2 that our algorithm and the four baseline approaches all have outstanding coverage ability for the Chinese rare words. The character-based approach CWE and the stroke-based approach cw2vec fail to deduce the embedding of an outlier word "OPEC" in the wordsim-296, which brings a little loss for their performance. However, it is not a problem for our algorithm because we can extract the related words from the Internet to infer its vector including "石油 (fossil fuel)", "组织 (organization)", etc. Compared to the coverage results, our algorithm has more significant advantages over the other baseline approaches in terms of the quality and achieves the highest Spearman correlations on the two datasets. To analyze the reason, we note the extracted related words in our algorithm are more helpful to induce the embedding of a rare word than the characters in CWE and the strokes in cw2vec. Take the rare word "马拉多纳 (Maradona)" for example, it is actually not related with the character "马 (horse in Chinese)". Conversely, we can extract the semantically related words like "足球 (soccer)", "阿根廷 (Argentina)", etc, to represent this word, which can more accurately reflect its meaning, i.e., name of an athlete. Moreover, the fine-tuning operation can promote the quality of the rare-word embeddings as well.

Table 2: Evaluation results on the wordsim-240 dataset and the wordsim-296 dataset.

Approach	wordsim-240		wordsim-296	
	PMP	$\rho \times 100$	PMP	$\rho \times 100$
CBOW	4%	34.5	11%	26.1
CWE	**0%**	35.5	0.3%	38.2
cw2vec	**0%**	42.5	0.3%	43.4
ELMo	**0%**	6.0	**0%**	14.6
BERT	**0%**	15.9	**0%**	29.7
Ours	**0%**	**44.0**	**0%**	**47.2**

4 Conclusions

In this paper, we have proposed a novel algorithm to learn embeddings for rare words, which consists of a coarse-tuning process and a fine-tuning process. In the coarse-tuning process, we use an Internet search engine to retrieve webpages relevant to the rare word on Internet and extract n most related words from their titles to infer the rare word's initial vector. In the fine-tuning process, we iteratively adjust the position of the rare word in the vector space to satisfy the constraints of the spatial location relationships and get close to its semantic meaning. We evaluated our approach on multiple datasets and compared the performance with other state-of-the-art approaches. The experimental results demonstrate that our algorithm is superior to existing approaches in both the accuracy of semantic expression and the coverage for rare words.

In future, we plan to extend our algorithm to learn contextualized representations for rare words. At present, existing work on contextualized rare word representation concentrates on the improved versions of attentive mimicking (AM) architecture such as the adapted AM model (Schick and Schütze, 2020b) and the BERTRAM model (Schick and Schütze, 2020a). We consider combining our algorithm with the AM architecture, and utilize the semantically relevant information together with the surface-form information and context information to learn higher-quality context-dependent representations for rare words.

Other future work involves evaluating our algorithm leveraging other search engines (e.g., Google, Bing, etc) on multiple languages. On this basis, we seek to bring further improvements on our algorithm by selecting the most suitable search engine for a specific language to induce the embeddings of the rare words of this language.

References

D. Bahdanau, T. Bosc, S. Jastrzebski, E. Grefenstette, P. Vincent, and Y. Bengio. 2018. Learning to compute word embeddings on the fly. *arxiv:1706.00286*.

Y. Bengio, R. Ducharme, and P. Vincent. 2003. A neural probabilistic language model. *Journal of Machine Learning Research*, 3:1137–1155.

P. Bojanowski, E. Grave, A. Joulin, and T. Mikolov. 2017. Enriching word vectors with subword information. *Transactions of the Association for Computational Linguistics*, 5:135–146.

S. S. Cao, W. Lu, J. Zhou, and X. L Li. 2018. cw2vec: Learning chineseword embeddings with stroke n-gram information. In *Proceedings of the 32nd AAAI Conference on Artificial Intelligence (AAAI)*, New Orleans, Louisiana, USA.

X. X. Chen, Z. Y. Liu1 L. Xu, M. S. Sun, and H. B. Luan. 2015. Joint learning of character and word embeddings. In *Proceedings of the International Joint Conference on Artificial Intelligence (IJCAI)*, pages 1236–1242, Buenos Aires, Argentina.

J. Devlin, M. W. Chang, K. Lee, and K. Toutanova. 2019. Bert: Pre-training of deep bidirectional transformers for language understanding. In *Proceedings of the Annual Conference of the North American Chapter of the Association for Computational Linguistics (NAACL-HLT)*, Minneapolis, USA.

M. Faruqui, J. Dodge, S. K. Jauhar, C. Dyer, E. Hovy, and N. A. Smith. 2015. Retrofitting word vectors to semantic lexicons. In *Proceedings of the Annual Conference of the North American Chapter of the Association for Computational Linguistics (NAACL-HLT)*, pages 1606–1615, Denver, Colorado, USA.

A. Grover and J. Leskovec. 2016. node2vec: Scalable feature learning for networks. In *Proceedings of the 22nd ACM SIGKDD International Conference on Knowledge Discovery and Data Mining*, pages 3393–3399, San Francisco, CA, USA.

T. H. Haveliwala. 2002. Topic-sensitive pagerank. In *Proceedings of 11th International Conference on World Wide Web*, pages 5053–5061, Honolulu, Hawaii, USA.

P. Jin and Y. F. Wu. 2012. Semeval-2012 task 4: Evaluating chinese word similarity. In *Proceedings of First Joint Conference on Lexical and Computational Semantics*, pages 373–374, Montreal, Canada.

M. T. Luong, R. Socher, and C. D. Manning. 2013. Better word representations with recursive neural networks for morphology. In *Proceedings of the Computational Natural Language Learning (CoNLL)*, pages 104–113, Sofia, Bulgaria.

T. Mikolov, K. Chen, G. Corrado, and J. Dean. 2013a. Efficient estimation of word representations in vector space. In *Proceedings of International Conference on Learning Representations*, Scottsdale, Arizona, USA.

T. Mikolov, I. Sutskever, K. Chen, G. Corrado, and J. Dean. 2013b. Distributed representations of words and phrases and their compositionality. In *Proceedings of International Conference on Neural Information Processing Systems (NIPS)*, pages 3111–31119, Lake Tahoe, Nevada, USA.

George A Miller. 1995. Wordnet: a lexical database for english. *Communications of the ACM*, 38(11):39–41.

S. Pakhomov, B. McInnes, T. Adam, and Y. Liu. 2010. Semantic similarity and relatedness between clinical terms: An experimental study. In *Proceedings of the Annual Symposium of the American Medical Informatics Association*, pages 572–576, Washington, D.C, USA.

S. Pakhomov, T. Pedersen, B. McInnes, G. B. Melton, A. Ruggieri, and C. G. Chute. 2011. Towards a framework for developing semantic relatedness reference standards. *Journal of Biomedical Informatics*, 4:251–265.

J. Pennington, R. Socher, and C. D. Manning. 2014. Glove: Global vectors for word representation. In *Proceedings of the 19th Conference on Empirical Methods in Natural Language Processing (EMNLP)*, pages 1532–1543, Doha, Qatar.

M. E. Peters, M. Neumann, M. Iyyer, and M. Gardner. 2018. Deep contextualized word representations. In *Proceedings of the Annual Conference of the North American Chapter of the Association for Computational Linguistics (NAACL-HLT)*, pages 2227–2237, New Orleans, Louisiana, USA.

M. T. Pilehvar and N. Collier. 2017. Inducing embeddings for rare and unseen words by leveraging lexical resources. In *Proceedings of the 15th Conference of the European Chapter of the Association for Computational Linguistics*, pages 388–393, Valencia, Spain.

M. T. Pilehvar, D. Kartsaklis, V. Prokhorov, and N. Collier. 2018. Card-660: Cambridge rare word dataset - a reliable benchmark for infrequentword representation models. In *Proceedings of the 23rd Conference on EmpiricalMethods in Natural Language Processing (EMNLP)*, Brussels, Belgium.

Y. Pinter, R. Guthrie, and J. Eisenstein. 2017. Mimicking word embeddings using subword rnns. In *Proceedings of the 22nd Conference on Empirical Methods in Natural Language Processing (EMNLP)*, pages 102–112, Copenhagen, Denmark.

V. Prokhorov, M. T. Pilehvar, D. Kartsaklis, P. Lio, and N. Collier. 2019. Unseen word representation by aligning heterogeneous lexical semantic spaces. In *Proceedings of the 33rd AAAI Conference on Artificial Intelligence (AAAI)*, pages 6900–6907, Copenhagen, Denmark.

T. Schick and H. Schütze. 2019a. Attentive mimicking: Betterword embeddings by attending to informative contexts. In *Proceedings of the Annual Conference of the North American Chapter of the Association for Computational Linguistics (NAACL-HLT)*, pages 489–494, Minneapolis, USA.

T. Schick and H. Schütze. 2019b. Learning semantic representations for novel words: Leveraging both form and context. In *Proceedings of the 33rd AAAI Conference on Artificial Intelligence (AAAI)*, pages 6965–6973, Copenhagen, Denmark.

T. Schick and H. Schütze. 2020a. Bertram: Improved word embeddings have big impact on contextualized model performance. In *Proceedings of the 58th Annual Meeting of the Association for Computational Linguistics*, pages 3996–4007, Tokyo, Japan.

T. Schick and H. Schütze. 2020b. Rare words: A major problem for contextualized embeddings and how to fix it by attentive mimicking. In *Proceedings of the 34th AAAI Conference on Artificial Intelligence (AAAI)*, New York, NY, USA.

J. L. Tian and W. Zhao. 2010. Words similarity algorithm based on tongyici cilin in semantic web adaptive learning system. *Journal of Jilin University*, 28(6):602–608.

Z. Zhao, T. Liu, S. Li, B. F. Li, and X. Y. DU. 2017. Ngram2vec: Learning improvedword representations from ngram co-occurrence statistics. In *Proceedings of the 22nd Conference on Empirical Methods in Natural Language Processing (EMNLP)*, pages 244–253, Copenhagen, Denmark.

Overcoming Poor Word Embeddings with Word Definitions

Christopher Malon
NEC Laboratories America
Princeton, NJ 08540
malon@nec-labs.com

Abstract

Modern natural language understanding models depend on pretrained subword embeddings, but applications may need to reason about words that were never or rarely seen during pretraining. We show that examples that depend critically on a rarer word are more challenging for natural language inference models. Then we explore how a model could learn to use definitions, provided in natural text, to overcome this handicap. Our model's understanding of a definition is usually weaker than a well-modeled word embedding, but it recovers most of the performance gap from using a completely untrained word.

1 Introduction

The reliance of natural language understanding models on the information in pre-trained word embeddings limits these models from being applied reliably to rare words or technical vocabulary. To overcome this vulnerability, a model must be able to compensate for a poorly modeled word embedding with background knowledge to complete the required task.

For example, a natural language inference (NLI) model based on pre-2020 word embeddings may not be able to deduce from "Jack has COVID" that "Jack is sick." By providing the definition, "COVID is a respiratory disease," we want to assist this classification.

We describe a general procedure for enhancing a classification model such as natural language inference (NLI) or sentiment classification, to perform the same task on sequences including poorly modeled words using definitions of those words. From the training set $\mathcal{T}$ of the original model, we construct an augmented training set $\mathcal{T}'$ for a model that may accept the same token sequence optionally concatenated with a word definition. In the case of NLI, where there are two token sequences, the definition is concatenated to the premise sequence. Because $\mathcal{T}'$ has the same form as $\mathcal{T}$, a model accepting the augmented information may be trained in the same way as the original model.

Because there are not enough truly untrained words like "COVID" in natural examples, we probe performance by scrambling real words so that their word embedding becomes useless, and supplying definitions. Our method recovers most of the performance lost by scrambling. Moreover, the proposed technique removes biases in more *ad hoc* solutions like adding definitions to examples without special training.

2 Related Work

We focus on NLI because it depends more deeply on word meaning than sentiment or topic classification tasks. Chen et al. (2018) pioneered the addition of background information to an NLI model's classification on a per-example basis, augmenting a sequence of token embeddings with features encoding WordNet relations between pairs of words, to achieve a 0.6% improvement on the SNLI (Bowman et al., 2015) task. Besides this explicit reasoning approach, implicit reasoning over background knowledge can be achieved if one updates the base model itself with background information. Lauscher et al. (2020) follows this approach to add information from ConceptNet (Speer et al., 2018) and the Open Mind Common Sense corpus (Singh et al., 2002) through a fine-tuned adapter added to a pretrained language model, achieving better performance on subsets of NLI examples that are known to require world knowledge. Talmor et al. (2020) explore the interplay between explicitly added knowledge and implicitly stored knowledge on artificially constructed NLI problems that require counting or relations from a taxonomy.

In the above works, explicit background infor-

Proceedings of the 10th Conference on Lexical and Computational Semantics, pages 288–293
August 5–6, 2021, Bangkok, Thailand (online) ©2021 Association for Computational Linguistics

mation comes from a taxonomy or knowledge base. Only a few studies have worked with definition text directly, and not in the context of NLI. Tissier et al. (2017) used definitions to create embeddings for better performance on word similarity tasks, compared to word2vec (Mikolov et al., 2013) and fastText (Bojanowski et al., 2017) while maintaining performance on text classification. Their work pushes together embeddings of words that co-occur in each other's definitions. Recently, Kaneko and Bollegala (2021) used definitions to remove biases from pretrained word embeddings while maintaining coreference resolution accuracy. In contrast, our work reasons with natural language definitions without forming a new embedding, allowing attention between a definition and the rest of an example.

Alternatively, Schick and Schütze (2020) improved classification using rare words by collecting and attending to all of the contexts in which they occur in BookCorpus (Zhu et al., 2015) combined with Westbury Wikipedia Corpus.[1] Like the methods above that use definitions, this method constructs a substitute or supplementary embedding for a rare word.

3 Methods

3.1 Critical words

The enhanced training set $\mathcal{T}'$ will be built by providing definitions for words in existing examples, while obfuscating the existing embeddings of those words. If a random word of the original text is obfuscated, the classification still may be determined or strongly biased by the remaining words. To ensure the definitions matter, we select carefully.

To explain which words of a text are important for classification, Kim et al. (2020) introduced the idea of input marginalization. Given a sequence of tokens $\mathbf{x}$, let $\mathbf{x}_{-i}$ represent the sequence without the ith token x_i. They marginalize the probability of predicting a class y_c over possible replacement words $\tilde{x_i}$ in the vocabulary $\mathcal{V}$ as

$$p(y_c|\mathbf{x}_{-i}) = \sum_{\tilde{x_i} \in \mathcal{V}} p(y_c|\tilde{x_i}, \mathbf{x}_{-i}) p(\tilde{x_i}|\mathbf{x}_{-i}) \quad (1)$$

and then compare $p(y_c|\mathbf{x}_{-i})$ to $p(y_c|\mathbf{x})$ to quantify the importance of x_i. The probabilities $p(\tilde{x_i}|\mathbf{x}_{-i})$ are computed by a language model.

[1] `http://www.psych.ualberta.ca/~westburylab/downloads/westburylab.wikicorp.download.html`

We simplify by looking only at the classification and not the probability. Like Kim et al. (2020), we truncate the computation of $p(y_c|\tilde{x_i}, \mathbf{x}_{-i})$ to words such that $p(\tilde{x_i}|\mathbf{x}_{-i})$ exceeds a threshold, here .05. Ultimately we mark a word x_i as a *critical word* if there exists a replacement $\tilde{x_i}$ such that

$$\text{argmax}_y p(y|\tilde{x_i}, \mathbf{x}_{-i}) \neq \text{argmax}_y p(y|\mathbf{x}) \quad (2)$$

and

$$p(\tilde{x_i}|x_{-i}) > .05. \quad (3)$$

Additionally we require that the word not appear more than once in the example, because the meaning of repeated words usually impacts the classification less than the fact that they all match. Table 1 shows an example.

Premise	A young man sits, looking out of a *train* [side → Neutral, small → Neutral] window.
Hypothesis	The man is in his room.
Label	Contradiction

Table 1: An SNLI example, with critical words shown in italics and replacements shown in brackets.

A technicality remains because our classification models use subwords as tokens, whereas we consider replacements of whole words returned by `pattern.en`. We remove all subwords of x_i when forming $\mathbf{x}_{-i}$, but we consider only replacements $\tilde{x_i}$ that are a single subword long.

3.2 Definitions

We use definitions from Simple English Wiktionary when available, or English Wiktionary otherwise.[2] Tissier et al. (2017) downloaded definitions from four commercial online dictionaries, but these are no longer freely available online as of January 2021.

To define a word, first we find its part of speech in the original context and lemmatize the word using the `pattern.en` library (Smedt and Daelemans, 2012). Then we look for a section labeled "English" in the retrieved Wiktionary article, and for a subsection for the part of speech we identified. We extract the first numbered definition in this subsection. In practice, we find that this method usually gives us short, simple definitions that match the usage in the original text.

[2] We use the 2018-02-01 dumps.

When defining a word, we always write its definition as "*word* means: *definition*." This common format ensures that the definitions and the word being defined can be recognized easily by the classifier.

3.3 Enhancing a model

Consider an example $(\mathbf{x}, y_c) \in \mathcal{T}$. If the example has a critical word $x_i \in \mathbf{x}$ that appears only once in the example, and $\tilde{x}_i$ is the most likely replacement word that changes the classification, we let $\mathbf{x}'$ denote the sequence where x_i is replaced by $\tilde{x}_i$, and let $y'_c = \text{argmax}_y p(y|\mathbf{x}')$. If definitions $\mathbf{h}_i$ and $\mathbf{h}'_i$ for x_i and $\tilde{x}_i$ are found by the method described above, we add $(\mathbf{x}, \mathbf{h}_i, y_c)$ and $(\mathbf{x}', \mathbf{h}'_i, y'_c)$ to the enhanced training set $\mathcal{T}'$.

In some training protocols, we scramble x_i and $\tilde{x}_i$ in the examples and definitions added to $\mathcal{T}'$, replacing them with random strings of between four and twelve letters. This prevents the model from relying on the original word embeddings. Table 2 shows an NLI example and the corresponding examples generated for the enhanced training set.

Original	A blond man is drinking from a public fountain. / The man is drinking water. / Entailment
Scrambled word	a blond man is drinking from a public yfcqudqqg. yfcqudqqg means: a natural source of water; a spring. / the man is drinking water. / Entailment
Scrambled alternate	a blond man is drinking from a public lxuehdeig. lxuehdeig means: lxuehdeig is a transparent solid and is usually clear. windows and eyeglasses are made from it, as well as drinking glasses. / the man is drinking water. / Neutral

Table 2: Adding background information to examples from SNLI

4 Experiments

4.1 Setup

We consider the SNLI task (Bowman et al., 2015). We fine-tune an XLNet (base, cased) model (Yang et al., 2019), because it achieves near state-of-the-art performance on SNLI and outperforms Roberta (Liu et al., 2019) and BERT (Devlin et al., 2019) on later rounds of adversarial annotation for ANLI (Nie et al., 2020). For the language model probabilities $p(\tilde{x}_i|\mathbf{x}_{-i})$, pretrained BERT (base, uncased) is used rather than XLNet because the XLNet probabilities have been observed to be very noisy on short sequences.[3]

One test set $SNLI_{crit}^{full}$ is constructed in the same way as the augmented training set, but our main test set $SNLI_{crit}^{true}$ is additionally constrained to use only examples of the form $(\mathbf{x}, \mathbf{h}_i, y_c)$ where y_c is the original label, because labels for the examples $(\mathbf{x}', \mathbf{h}'_i, y'_c)$ might be incorrect. All of our derived datasets are available for download.[4]

In each experiment, training is run for three epochs distributed across 4 GPU's, with a batch size of 10 on each, a learning rate of 5×10^{-5}, 120 warmup steps, a single gradient accumulation step, and a maximum sequence length of 384.

4.2 Results

Table 3 compares the accuracy of various training protocols.

Protocol	$SNLI_{crit}^{true}$
Original	85.1%
No scrambling, no defs	84.6%
No scrambling, defs	85.2%
Scrambling, no defs	36.9%
Scrambling, defs	81.2%
Scrambling, subs	84.7%
Train on normal SNLI, test on scrambled no defs	54.1%
Train on normal SNLI, test on scrambled defs	63.8%
Train on unscrambled defs, test on scrambled defs	51.4%

Table 3: Accuracy of enhancement protocols

Our task cannot be solved well without reading definitions. When words are scrambled but no definitions are provided, an SNLI model without special training achieves 54.1% on $SNLI_{crit}^{true}$. If trained on $\mathcal{T}'$ with scrambled words but no definitions, performance drops to 36.9%, reflecting that $\mathcal{T}'$ is constructed to prevent a model from utilizing the contextual bias.

With definitions and scrambled words, performance is slightly below that of using the original words. Our method using definitions applied

[3]https://github.com/huggingface/transformers/issues/4343
[4]https://figshare.com/s/edd5dc26b78817098b72

to the scrambled words yields 81.2%, compared to 84.6% if words are left unscrambled but no definitions are provided. Most of the accuracy lost by obfuscating the words is recovered, but evidently there is slightly more information accessible in the original word embeddings.

If alternatives to the critical words are not included, the classifier learns biases that do not depend on the definition. We explore restricting the training set to verified examples $\mathcal{T}'_{true} \subset \mathcal{T}'$ in the same way as the $SNLI^{true}_{crit}$, still scrambling the critical or replaced words in the training and testing sets. Using this subset, a model that is not given the definitions can be trained to achieve 69.9% performance on $SNLI^{true}_{crit}$, showing a heavy contextual bias. A model trained on this subset that uses the definitions achieves marginally higher performance (82.3%) than the one trained on all of $\mathcal{T}'$. On the other hand, testing on $SNLI^{full}_{crit}$ yields only 72.3% compared to 80.3% using the full $\mathcal{T}'$, showing that the classifier is less sensitive to the definition.

Noisy labels from replacements do not hurt accuracy much. The only difference between the "original" training protocol and "no scrambling, no defs" is that the original trains on $\mathcal{T}$ and does not include examples with replaced words and unverified labels. Training including the replacements reduces accuracy by 0.5% on $SNLI^{true}_{crit}$, which includes only verified labels. For comparison, training and testing on all of SNLI with the original protocol achieves 90.4%, so a much larger effect on accuracy must be due to harder examples in $SNLI^{true}_{crit}$.

Definitions are not well utilized without special training. The original SNLI model, if provided definitions of scrambled words at test time as part of the premise, achieves only 63.8%, compared to 81.2% for our specially trained model.

If the defined words are not scrambled, the classifier uses the original embedding and ignores the definitions. Training with definitions but no scrambling, 85.2% accuracy is achieved, but this trained model is unable to use the definitions when words are scrambled: it achieves 51.4%.

We have not discovered a way to combine the benefit of the definitions with the knowledge in the original word embedding. To force the model to use both techniques, we prepare a version of the training set which is half scrambled and half unscrambled. This model achieves 83.5% on the unscrambled test set, worse than no definitions.

Definitions are not simply being memorized. We selected the subset $SNLI^{new}_{crit}$ of $SNLI^{true}_{crit}$ consisting of the 44 examples in which the defined word was not defined in a training example. The definition scrambled model achieves 68.2% on this set, well above 45.5% for the original SNLI model reading the scrambled words and definitions but without special training. Remembering a definition from training is thus an advantage ($SNLI^{true}_{crit}$ accuracy was 81.2%), but not the whole capability.

Definition reasoning is harder than simple substitutions. When definitions are given as one-word substitutions, in the form "*scrambled* means: *original*" instead of "*scrambled* means: *definition*", the model achieves 84.7% on $SNLI^{true}_{crit}$ compared to 81.2% using the definition text. Of course this is not a possibility for rare words that are not synonyms of a word that has been well trained, but it suggests that the kind of multi-hop reasoning in which words just have to be matched in sequence is easier than understanding a text definition.

4.3 A hard subset of SNLI

By construction of the SentencePiece dictionary (Kudo and Richardson, 2018), only the most frequent words in the training data of the XLNet language model are represented as single tokens. Other words are tokenized by multiple subwords. Sometimes the subwords reflect a morphological change to a well-modeled word, such as a change in tense or plurality. The language model probably understands these changes well and the subwords give important hints. The lemma form of a word strips many morphological features, so when the lemma form of a word has multiple subwords, the basic concept may be less frequently encountered in training. We hypothesize that such words are less well understood by the language model.

To test this hypothesis, we construct a subset $SNLI^{true}_{multi}$ of the test set, consisting of examples where a critical word exists whose lemma form spans multiple subwords. This set consists of 332 test examples. The critical word used may be different from the one chosen for $SNLI^{true}_{crit}$. This subset is indeed harder: the XLNet model trained on all of SNLI attains only 77.7% on this subset using no definitions, compared to 90.4% on the original test set.

In Table 4 we apply various models constructed in the previous subsection to this hard test set. Ideally, a model leveraging definitions could compen-

Protocol	$SNLI^{true}_{multi}$
Normal SNLI on unscrambled	77.7%
Defs & unscrambled on defs & unscrambled	77.1%
Defs & some scrambling on defs & unscrambled	73.8%
Defs & scrambled on defs & scrambled	69.9%
Defs & scrambled on defs & unscrambled	62.7%

Table 4: Accuracy on the hard SNLI subset

sate for these weaker word embeddings, but the method here does not do so.

5 Conclusion

This work shows how a model's training may be enhanced to support reasoning with definitions in natural text, to handle cases where word embeddings are not useful. Our method forces the definitions to be considered and avoids the application of biases independent of the definition. Using the approach, entailment examples like "Jack has COVID / Jack is sick" that are misclassified by an XLNet trained on normal SNLI are correctly recognized as entailment when a definition "COVID is a respiratory disease" is added. Methods that can leverage definitions without losing the advantage of partially useful word embeddings are still needed. In an application, it also will be necessary to select the words that would benefit from definitions, and to make a model that can accept multiple definitions.

References

Piotr Bojanowski, Edouard Grave, Armand Joulin, and Tomas Mikolov. 2017. Enriching word vectors with subword information. *arXiv preprint*, 1607.04606.

Samuel R. Bowman, Gabor Angeli, Christopher Potts, and Christopher D. Manning. 2015. A large annotated corpus for learning natural language inference. In *Proceedings of the 2015 Conference on Empirical Methods in Natural Language Processing*, pages 632–642, Lisbon, Portugal. Association for Computational Linguistics.

Qian Chen, Xiaodan Zhu, Zhen-Hua Ling, Diana Inkpen, and Si Wei. 2018. Neural natural language inference models enhanced with external knowledge. In *Proceedings of the 56th Annual Meeting of the Association for Computational Linguistics (Volume 1: Long Papers)*, pages 2406–2417, Melbourne, Australia. Association for Computational Linguistics.

Jacob Devlin, Ming-Wei Chang, Kenton Lee, and Kristina Toutanova. 2019. Bert: Pre-training of deep bidirectional transformers for language understanding. *arXiv preprint*, 1810.04805.

Masahiro Kaneko and Danushka Bollegala. 2021. Dictionary-based debiasing of pre-trained word embeddings. *arXiv preprint*, 2101.09525.

Siwon Kim, Jihun Yi, Eunji Kim, and Sungroh Yoon. 2020. Interpretation of NLP models through input marginalization. In *Proceedings of the 2020 Conference on Empirical Methods in Natural Language Processing (EMNLP)*, pages 3154–3167, Online. Association for Computational Linguistics.

Taku Kudo and John Richardson. 2018. SentencePiece: A simple and language independent subword tokenizer and detokenizer for neural text processing. In *Proceedings of the 2018 Conference on Empirical Methods in Natural Language Processing: System Demonstrations*, pages 66–71, Brussels, Belgium. Association for Computational Linguistics.

Anne Lauscher, Olga Majewska, Leonardo F. R. Ribeiro, Iryna Gurevych, Nikolai Rozanov, and Goran Glavaš. 2020. Common sense or world knowledge? investigating adapter-based knowledge injection into pretrained transformers. In *Proceedings of Deep Learning Inside Out (DeeLIO): The First Workshop on Knowledge Extraction and Integration for Deep Learning Architectures*, pages 43–49, Online. Association for Computational Linguistics.

Yinhan Liu, Myle Ott, Naman Goyal, Jingfei Du, Mandar Joshi, Danqi Chen, Omer Levy, Mike Lewis, Luke Zettlemoyer, and Veselin Stoyanov. 2019. Roberta: A robustly optimized bert pretraining approach. *arXiv preprint*, 1907.11692.

Tomas Mikolov, Kai Chen, Greg Corrado, and Jeffrey Dean. 2013. Efficient estimation of word representations in vector space. *arXiv preprint*, 1301.3781.

Yixin Nie, Adina Williams, Emily Dinan, Mohit Bansal, Jason Weston, and Douwe Kiela. 2020. Adversarial NLI: A new benchmark for natural language understanding. In *Proceedings of the 58th Annual Meeting of the Association for Computational Linguistics*, pages 4885–4901, Online. Association for Computational Linguistics.

Timo Schick and Hinrich Schütze. 2020. BERTRAM: Improved word embeddings have big impact on contextualized model performance. In *Proceedings of the 58th Annual Meeting of the Association for Computational Linguistics*, pages 3996–4007, Online. Association for Computational Linguistics.

Push Singh, Thomas Lin, Erik T. Mueller, Grace Lim, Travell Perkins, and Wan Li Zhu. 2002. Open mind common sense: Knowledge acquisition from the general public. In *On the Move to Meaningful Internet Systems 2002: CoopIS, DOA, and*

ODBASE, pages 1223–1237, Berlin, Heidelberg. Springer Berlin Heidelberg.

Tom De Smedt and Walter Daelemans. 2012. Pattern for python. *Journal of Machine Learning Research*, 13(66):2063–2067.

Robyn Speer, Joshua Chin, and Catherine Havasi. 2018. Conceptnet 5.5: An open multilingual graph of general knowledge. *arXiv preprint*, 1612.03975.

Alon Talmor, Oyvind Tafjord, Peter Clark, Yoav Goldberg, and Jonathan Berant. 2020. Leap-of-thought: Teaching pre-trained models to systematically reason over implicit knowledge. In *Advances in Neural Information Processing Systems 33: Annual Conference on Neural Information Processing Systems 2020, NeurIPS 2020, December 6-12, 2020, virtual.*

Julien Tissier, Christophe Gravier, and Amaury Habrard. 2017. Dict2vec : Learning word embeddings using lexical dictionaries. In *Proceedings of the 2017 Conference on Empirical Methods in Natural Language Processing*, pages 254–263, Copenhagen, Denmark. Association for Computational Linguistics.

Zhilin Yang, Zihang Dai, Yiming Yang, Jaime Carbonell, Russ R Salakhutdinov, and Quoc V Le. 2019. Xlnet: Generalized autoregressive pretraining for language understanding. In *Advances in Neural Information Processing Systems*, volume 32, pages 5753–5763. Curran Associates, Inc.

Yukun Zhu, Ryan Kiros, Rich Zemel, Ruslan Salakhutdinov, Raquel Urtasun, Antonio Torralba, and Sanja Fidler. 2015. Aligning books and movies: Towards story-like visual explanations by watching movies and reading books. In *2015 IEEE International Conference on Computer Vision (ICCV)*, pages 19–27.

Denoising Word Embeddings by Averaging in a Shared Space

Avi Caciularu[1] **Ido Dagan**[1] **Jacob Goldberger**[2]
[1]Computer Science Department, Bar-Ilan University
[2]Faculty of Engineering, Bar-Ilan University
avi.c33@gmail.com, dagan@cs.biu.ac.il, jacob.goldberger@biu.ac.il

Abstract

We introduce a new approach for smoothing and improving the quality of word embeddings. We consider a method of fusing word embeddings that were trained on the same corpus but with different initializations. We project all the models to a shared vector space using an efficient implementation of the Generalized Procrustes Analysis (GPA) procedure, previously used in multilingual word translation. Our word representation demonstrates consistent improvements over the raw models as well as their simplistic average, on a range of tasks. As the new representations are more stable and reliable, there is a noticeable improvement in rare word evaluations.

1 Introduction

Continuous (non-contextualized) word embeddings have been introduced several years ago as a standard building block for NLP tasks. These models provide efficient ways to learn word representations in a fully self-supervised manner from text corpora, solely based on word co-occurrence statistics. A wide variety of methods now exist for generating word embeddings, with prominent methods including word2vec (Mikolov et al., 2013a), GloVe (Pennington et al., 2014), and FastText (Bojanowski et al., 2017). Recently, contextualized embeddings (Peters et al., 2018; Devlin et al., 2019), replaced the use of non-contextualized embeddings in many settings. Yet, the latter remain the standard choice for typical lexical-semantic tasks, e.g., semantic similarity (Hill et al., 2015), word analogy (Jurgens et al., 2012), relation classification (Barkan et al., 2020a), and paraphrase identification (Meged et al., 2020). These tasks consider the generic meanings of lexical items, given out of context, hence the use of non-contextualized embeddings is appropriate. Notably, FastText was shown to yield state-of-the-art results in most of these tasks (Bojanowski et al., 2017).

While word embedding methods proved to be powerful, they suffer from a certain level of noise, introduced by quite a few randomized steps in the embedding generation process, including embedding initialization, negative sampling, subsampling and mini-batch ordering. Consequently, different runs would yield different embedding geometries, of varying quality. This random noise might harm most severely the representation of rare words, for which the actual data signal is rather weak (Barkan et al., 2020b).

In this paper, we propose denoising word embedding models through generating multiple model versions, each created with different random seeds. Then, the resulting representations for each word should be fused effectively, in order to obtain a model with a reduced level of noise. Note, however, that simple averaging of the original word vectors is problematic, since each training session of the algorithm produces embeddings in a different space. In fact, the objective scores of both word2vec, Glove and FastText are invariant to multiplying all the word embeddings by an orthogonal matrix, hence, the algorithm output involves an arbitrary rotation of the embedding space.

For addressing this issue, we were inspired by recent approaches originally proposed for aligning multi-lingual embeddings (Chen and Cardie, 2018; Kementchedjhieva et al., 2018; Alaux et al., 2019; Jawanpuria et al., 2019; Taitelbaum et al., 2019). To obtain such alignments, these methods simultaneously project the original language-specific embeddings into a shared space, while enforcing (or at least encouraging) transitive orthogonal transformations. In our (monolingual) setting, we propose a related technique to project the different embedding versions into a shared space, while optimizing the projection towards obtaining an improved fused representation. We show that this results in im-

Proceedings of the 10th Conference on Lexical and Computational Semantics, pages 294–301
August 5–6, 2021, Bangkok, Thailand (online) ©2021 Association for Computational Linguistics

proved performance on a range of lexical-semantic tasks, with notable improvements for rare words, as well as on several sentence-level downstream tasks.

2 Word Averaging in a Shared Space

Assume we are given an ensemble of k pre-trained word embedding sets, of the same word vocabulary of size n and the same dimensionality d. In our setting, these sets are obtained by training the same embedding model using different random parameter initializations. Our goal is to fuse the k embedding sets into a single "average" embedding that is hopefully more robust and would yield better performance on various tasks. Since each embedding set has its own space, we project the k embedding spaces into a shared space, in which we induce averaged embeddings based on a mean squared error minimization objective.

Let $x_{i,t} \in \mathbb{R}^d$ be the dense representation of the t-th word in the i-th embedding set. We model the mapping from the i-th set to the shared space by an orthogonal matrix denoted by T_i. Denote the sought shared space representation of the t-th word by $y_t \in \mathbb{R}^d$. Our goal is to find a set of transformations $T = \{T_1, ..., T_k\}$ and target word embeddings $y = \{y_1, ..., y_n\}$ in the shared space that minimize the following mean-squared error:

$$S(T, y) = \sum_{i=1}^{k} \sum_{t=1}^{n} \|T_i x_{i,t} - y_t\|^2. \quad (1)$$

For this objective, it is easy to show that for a set of transformations $T_1, ..., T_k$, the optimal shared space representation is:

$$y_t = \frac{1}{k} \sum_{i=1}^{k} T_i x_{i,t}.$$

Hence, solving the optimization problem pertains to finding the k optimal transformations.

In the case where $k = 2$, the optimal T can be obtained in a closed form using the Procrustes Analysis (PA) procedure (Schönemann, 1966), which has been employed in recent bilingual word translation methods (Xing et al., 2015; Artetxe et al., 2016; Hamilton et al., 2016; Artetxe et al., 2017a,b; Conneau et al., 2017; Artetxe et al., 2018a,b; Ruder et al., 2018). In our setting, to obtain an improved embedding, we wish to average more than two embedding sets.

However, if $k > 2$ there is no closed form solution to (1) and thus, we need to find a solution using an iterative optimization process. To that end, we follow several works that suggested employing the General Procrustes Analysis (GPA) procedure, which is an extension of PA to multi-set alignment (Gower, 1975; Kementchedjhieva et al., 2018). Generally, the GPA consists of an alternate minimization procedure where we iterate between finding the orthogonal transformations and computing the shared space. The optimal transformation from each embedding space to the shared space is found by minimizing the following score,

$$S(T_i) = \sum_{t=1}^{n} \|T_i x_{i,t} - y_t\|^2, \qquad i = 1, ..., k.$$

The minimum of $S(T_i)$ can then be found by the closed form PA procedure. The updated transformation is $T_i = U_i V_i^\top$, where $U_i \Sigma_i V_i^\top$ is the singular value decomposition (SVD) of the $d \times d$ matrix $\sum_{t=1}^{n} y_t x_{i,t}^\top$. At each step in the iterative GPA algorithm, the score (1) is monotonically decreased until it converges to a local minimum point.

Algorithm 1 Shared Space Embedding Averaging

```
Input: Ensemble of k word embedding sets.
Task: Find the optimal average embedding.
Preprocessing:
Compute the cross-correlation matrices:
C_ij = C_ji^T = Σ_{t=1}^n x_{j,t} x_{i,t}^T    1 ≤ i < j ≤ k
Initialization: T_1 = ··· = T_{k-1} = 0, T_k = I
while not converged do
    for i = 1, ..., k do
        UΣV^T = SVD(Σ_{j≠i} T_j C_ij)
        T_i ← UV^T
    end for
end while
Compute the average embedding:
y_t ← (1/k) Σ_{i=1}^k T_i x_{i,t}        t = 1, ..., n
```

For large vocabularies, GPA is not efficient, because, in each iteration, when computing the SVD we need to sum over all the vocabulary words. To circumvent this computational cost, we adopt the optimization procedure from Taitelbaum et al. (2019), which we apply within each iteration. Instead of summing over the whole vocabulary, the following extension is proposed. Let $C_{ij} = \sum_t x_{j,t} x_{i,t}^\top$ be the cross-correlation matrix

	original	denoised
word2vec	0.40 ± 0.005	0.059 ± 0.003
GloVe	0.38 ± 0.006	0.058 ± 0.003
FastText	0.35 ± 0.003	0.054 ± 0.001

Table 1: Average MSE scores of the embedding models with and without applying the SSEA algorithm.

for a pair (i, j) of two original embedding spaces, which can be computed once, for all pairs of spaces, in a pre-processing step. Given the matrices C_{ij} the computational complexity of the iterative averaging algorithm is independent of the vocabulary size, allowing us to compute efficiently the SVD. The resulting algorithm termed Shared Space Embedding Averaging (SSEA) is presented in Algorithm 1.[1]

3 Experimental Setup and Results

This section presents our evaluation protocol, datasets, data preparation, hyperparameter configuration and results.

3.1 Implementation Details and Data

We trained word2vec (Mikolov et al., 2013a), FastText (Bojanowski et al., 2017) and GloVe (Pennington et al., 2014) embeddings. For word2vec we used the skip-gram model with negative sampling, which was shown advantageous on the evaluated tasks (Levy et al., 2015). We trained each of the models on the November 2019 dump of Wikipedia articles[2] for $k = 30$ times, with different random seeds, and used the default reported hyperparameters; we set the embedding dimension to $d = 200$, and considered each word within the maximal window $c_{max} = 5$, subsampling[3] threshold of $\rho = 10^{-5}$ and used 5 negative examples for every positive example. In order to keep a large amount of rare words in the corpus, no preprocessing was applied on the data, yielding a vocabulary size of $1.5 \cdot 10^6$. We then applied the SSEA algorithm to the embedding sets to obtain the average embedding. The original embedding sets and averaged embeddings were centered around the 0 vector and normalized to unit vectors.

3.2 Improved Embedding Stability

We next analyze how our method improves embedding quality and consistency, notably for rare words. To that end, for any two embedding sets, u and v, we can find the optimal mapping Q between them using the PA algorithm and compute its mean square error (MSE), $\frac{1}{n}\sum_{t=1} \|Qu_t - v_t\|^2$. We define the stability of an embedding algorithm by the average MSE (over 10 random pairs of samples) between two instances of it. This score measures the similarity between the geometries of random instances generated by a particular embedding method , and thus reflects the consistency and stability of that method. The scores of the different models are depicted in Table 1. As observed, after applying SSEA the Average MSE drops by an order of magnitude, indicating much better stability of the obtained embeddings.

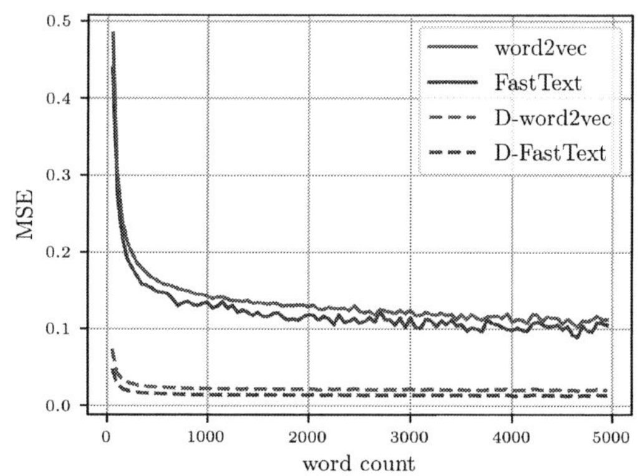

Figure 1: Average MSE for word embeddings vs their corpus occurrence count (binned with resolution of 50).

We can perform a similar analysis for each word separately. A consistent embedding of the t-th word in both sets u and v should result in a small mapping discrepancy $\|Qu_t - v_t\|^2$. Figure 1 depicts MSE for the models and their computed SSEA, as a function of the word's frequency in the corpus. The denoised version of the models is marked with a 'D-' prefix. For clarity of presentation, we did not include the results for GloVe (which are similar to word2vec). As expected, embedding stability always increases (MSE decreases) with word frequency. SSEA is notably more stable across the frequency range, with the error minimized early on and reduced most drastically for low frequencies.

3.3 Comparison of methods

We next compare our denoised model, denoted with a 'D-' prefix, with the original embedding models. As an additional baseline, we considered also the naïve averaged embedding model, denoted with a 'A-' prefix, where for every word we computed the simplistic mean embedding across all origi-

[1]The algorithm demonstration code is available at github.com/aviclu/SSEA. In practice, we utilized an efficient PyTorch implementation based on Taitelbaum et al. (2019).

[2]dumps.wikimedia.org/enwiki/latest/

[3]To speed up the training.

Method	SimLex999	MEN	WS353	AP	Google	MSR	SemEval2012(2)	BLESS	RW
word2vec	33.7	72.4	60.7	62.2	69.5	51.3	19.2	79	42
A-word2vec	33.1	72.3	**60.8**	61.9	69.2	51.2	19	78.1	41.7
D-word2vec	**33.9**	**73.2**	**60.8**	**63.1**	**70.3**	**51.9**	**20**	**79.6**	**43.4**
GloVe	34.4	73.4	62.3	63.3	75.1	54.5	19.7	79.2	47.2
A-GloVe	34.2	73.1	61.9	62.8	74.7	54.2	19.6	79	47.1
D-GloVe	**34.8**	**75.1**	**62.7**	**64.3**	**75.9**	**55.2**	**20.1**	**79.9**	**48.5**
FastText	41.2	78.6	70.7	72.2	75.7	63.4	19.8	81.5	47.1
A-FastText	41	78.1	69.7	72.1	74.1	62.8	19.4	80.8	46.6
D-FastText	**42.2**	**79.3**	**71.8**	**72.9**	**77.4**	**63.8**	**20.2**	**82.7**	**50.3**

Table 2: Results for lexical-semantic benchmarks. Best performance is bolded.

nal spaces. Note that we did not compare other proposed embeddings or meta-embedding learning methods, but rather restricted our analysis to empirically verifying our embedding aggregation method and validating the assumptions behind the empirical analysis we performed.

3.4 Evaluations on Lexical Semantic Tasks

We evaluated the performance of our method over lexical-semantic tasks, including word similarity, analogy solving, and concept categorization: **SimLex999** (Hill et al., 2015), **MEN** (Bruni et al., 2014), **WS353** (Finkelstein et al., 2002), **AP** (Almuhareb and Poesio, 2004), **Google** (Mikolov et al., 2013b), **MSR** (Mikolov et al., 2013c), **SemEval-2012** (Jurgens et al., 2012), **BLESS** (Baroni and Lenci, 2011) and **RW** (Luong et al., 2013), (focusing on rare words). For the analogy task, we reported the accuracy. For the remaining tasks, we computed Spearman's correlation between the cosine similarity of the embeddings and the human judgments.

Results The results of the lexical-semantic tasks are depicted in Table 2, averaged over 30 runs for each method. Our method obtained better performance than the other methods, substantially for FastText embeddings. As shown, the naïve averaging performed poorly, which highlights the fact that simply averaging different embedding spaces does not improve word representation quality. The most notable performance gain was in the rare-words task, in line with the analysis in Fig. 1, suggesting that on rare words the raw embedding vectors fit the data less accurately.

3.5 Evaluations On Downstream Tasks

For completeness, we next show the relative advantage of our denoising method also when applied to several sentence-level downstream benchmarks. While contextualized embeddings dominate a wide range of sentence- and document- level NLP tasks (Peters et al., 2018; Devlin et al., 2019; Caciularu et al., 2021), we assessed the relative advantage of our denoising method when utilizing (non-contextualized) word embeddings in sentence- an document- level settings. We applied the exact procedure proposed in Li et al. (2017) and Rogers et al. (2018), as an effective benchmark for the quality of static embedding models. We first used sequence labeling tasks. The morphological and syntactic performance was evaluated using part-of-speech tagging, **POS**, and chunking, **CHK**. Both named entity recognition, **NER**, and multiway classification of semantic relation classes, **RE**, tasks were used for evaluating semantic information at the word level. For the above POS, NER and CHK sequence labeling tasks, we used the CoNLL 2003 dataset (Sang and Meulder, 2003) and for the RE task, we used the SemEval 2010 task 8 dataset (Hendrickx et al., 2010). The neural network models employed for these downstream tasks are fully described in (Rogers et al., 2018). Next, we evaluated the following semantic level tasks: document-level polarity classification, **PC**, using the Stanford IMDB movie review dataset (Maas et al., 2011), sentence level sentiment polarity classification, **SEN**, using the MR dataset of short movie reviews (Pang and Lee, 2005), and classification of subjectivity and objectivity task, **SUB**, that uses the Rotten Tomatoes user review snippets against official movie plot summaries (Pang and Lee, 2004). Similarly to the performance results in Table 2, the current results show that the suggested denoised embeddings obtained better overall performance than the other methods, substantially for FastText embeddings.

4 Related Work

A similar situation of aligning different word embeddings into a shared space occurs in multi-lingual

Method	POS	CHK	NER	RE	PC	SEN	SUB
word2vec	81.5	80.1	93.3	71.4	89.2	73.9	76.4
A-word2vec	78	77.5	90.9	67.4	86.4	64.3	75.6
D-word2vec	**81.6**	**80.2**	**93.6**	**73.1**	**89.7**	**74**	**77.4**
GloVe	77.5	70.4	85.2	66.7	80.2	70.2	72.7
A-GloVe	77.1	70.2	84.9	62.3	77.7	62.2	71.8
D-GloVe	**77.8**	**71.1**	**86.6**	**68.2**	**80.8**	**71.3**	**73.9**
FastText	80.6	79.1	92.2	74	88.9	74.9	73.9
A-FastText	78.4	78.8	90.2	73.6	89	74.1	73.3
D-FastText	**82.4**	**81.2**	**94.9**	**75.2**	**90.5**	**77.3**	**76.7**

Table 3: Results for downstream task. Best performance is bolded.

word translation tasks which are based on distinct monolingual word embeddings. Word translation is performed by transforming each language word embeddings into a shared space by an orthogonal matrix, for creating a "universal language", which is useful for the word translation process. Our setting may be considered by viewing each embedding set as a different language, where our goal is to find the shared space where embedding averaging is meaningful.

The main challenge in multilingual word translation is to obtain a reliable multi-way word correspondence in either a supervised or unsupervised manner. One problem is that standard dictionaries contain multiple senses for words, which is problematic for bilingual translation, and further amplified in a multilingual setting. In our case of embedding averaging, the mapping problem vanishes since we are addressing a single language and the word correspondences hold trivially among different embeddings of the same word. Thus, in our setting, there are no problems of wrong word correspondences, neither the issue of having different word translations due to multiple word senses. Studies have shown that for the multi-lingual translation problem, enforcing the transformation to be strictly orthogonal is too restrictive and performance can be improved by using the orthogonalization as a regularization (Chen and Cardie, 2018) that yields matrices that are close to be orthogonal. In our much simpler setting of a single language, with a trivial identity word correspondence, enforcing the orthogonalization constraint is reasonable.

Another related problem is *meta-embedding* (Yin and Schütze, 2016), which aims to fuse information from different embedding models. Various methods have been proposed for embedding fusion, such as concatenation, simple averaging, weighted averaging (Coates and Bollegala, 2018; Kiela et al., 2018) and autoencoding (Bollegala and Bao, 2018). Some of these methods (concatenation and autoencoding) are not scalable when the goal is to fuse many sets, while others (simple averaging) yield inferior results, as described in the above works. Note that our method is not intended to be a competitor of meta-embedding, but rather a complementary method.

An additional related work is the recent method from (Muromägi et al., 2017). Similarly to our work, they proposed a method based on the Procrustes Analysis procedure for aligning and averaging sets of word embedding models. However, the mapping algorithm they used is much more computationally demanding, as it requires to go over all the dictionary words in every iteration. Instead, we propose an efficient optimization algorithm, which requires just one such computation during each iteration, and is theoretically guaranteed to converge to a local minimum point. While their work focuses on improving over the Estonian language, we suggest evaluating this approach on English data and on a range of different downstream tasks. We show that our method significantly improves upon rare words, which is beneficial for small sized / domain-specific corpora.

5 Conclusions

We presented a novel technique for creating better word representations by training an embedding model several times, from which we derive an averaged representation. The resulting word representations proved to be more stable and reliable than the raw embeddings. Our method exhibits performance gains in lexical-semantic tasks, notably over rare words, confirming our analytical assumptions. This suggests that our method may be particularly useful for training embedding models in low-resource settings. Appealing future research may extend our approach to improving sentence-level representations, by fusing several contextualized embedding models.

Acknowledgments

The authors would like to thank the anonymous reviewers for their comments and suggestions. The work described herein was supported in part by grants from Intel Labs, Facebook, the Israel Science Foundation grant 1951/17 and the German Research Foundation through the German-Israeli Project Cooperation (DIP, grant DA 1600/1-1).

References

Jean Alaux, Edouard Grave, Marco Cuturi, and Armand Joulin. 2019. Unsupervised hyperalignment for multilingual word embeddings. In *International Conference on Learning Representations (ICLR)*.

Abdulrahman Almuhareb and Massimo Poesio. 2004. Attribute-based and value-based clustering: An evaluation. In *Proceedings of the conference on empirical methods in natural language processing (EMNLP)*.

Mikel Artetxe, Gorka Labaka, and Eneko Agirre. 2016. Learning principled bilingual mappings of word embeddings while preserving monolingual invariance. In *Proceedings of the Conference on Empirical Methods in Natural Language Processing (EMNLP)*.

Mikel Artetxe, Gorka Labaka, and Eneko Agirre. 2017a. Learning bilingual word embeddings with (almost) no bilingual data. In *Annual Meeting of the Association for Computational Linguistics (ACL)*.

Mikel Artetxe, Gorka Labaka, and Eneko Agirre. 2018a. Generalizing and improving bilingual word embedding mappings with a multi-step framework of linear transformations. In *Proceedings of the AAAI Conference on Artificial Intelligence (AAAI)*.

Mikel Artetxe, Gorka Labaka, and Eneko Agirre. 2018b. A robust self-learning method for fully unsupervised cross-lingual mappings of word embeddings. *arXiv preprint arXiv:1805.06297*.

Mikel Artetxe, Gorka Labaka, Eneko Agirre, and Kyunghyun Cho. 2017b. Unsupervised neural machine translation. *arXiv preprint arXiv:1710.11041*.

Oren Barkan, Avi Caciularu, and Ido Dagan. 2020a. Within-between lexical relation classification. In *Proceedings of the 2020 Conference on Empirical Methods in Natural Language Processing (EMNLP)*, pages 3521–3527, Online. Association for Computational Linguistics.

Oren Barkan, Idan Rejwan, Avi Caciularu, and Noam Koenigstein. 2020b. Bayesian hierarchical words representation learning. In *Proceedings of the 58th Annual Meeting of the Association for Computational Linguistics*, pages 3871–3877, Online. Association for Computational Linguistics.

Marco Baroni and Alessandro Lenci. 2011. How we blessed distributional semantic evaluation. In *Proceedings of the GEMS 2011 Workshop on GEometrical Models of Natural Language Semantics*.

Piotr Bojanowski, Edouard Grave, Armand Joulin, and Tomas Mikolov. 2017. Enriching word vectors with subword information. *Transactions of the Association for Computational Linguistics (TACL)*.

Danushka Bollegala and Cong Bao. 2018. Learning word meta-embeddings by autoencoding. In *International Conference on Computational Linguistics, (COLING)*.

Elia Bruni, Nam-Khanh Tran, and Marco Baroni. 2014. Multimodal distributional semantics. *Journal of Artificial Intelligence Research*.

Avi Caciularu, Arman Cohan, Iz Beltagy, Matthew E Peters, Arie Cattan, and Ido Dagan. 2021. Cross-document language modeling. *arXiv e-prints*, pages arXiv–2101.

Xilun Chen and Claire Cardie. 2018. Unsupervised multilingual word embeddings. In *Conference on Empirical Methods in Natural Language Processing (EMNLP)*.

Joshua Coates and Danushka Bollegala. 2018. Frustratingly easy meta-embedding – computing metaembeddings by averaging source word embeddings. In *North American Chapter of the Association for Computational Linguistics (NAACL)*.

Alexis Conneau, Guillaume Lample, Marc'Aurelio Ranzato, Ludovic Denoyer, and Hervé Jégou. 2017. Word translation without parallel data. *arXiv preprint arXiv:1710.04087*.

Jacob Devlin, Ming-Wei Chang, Kenton Lee, and Kristina Toutanova. 2019. BERT: Pre-training of deep bidirectional transformers for language understanding. In *Proceedings of the 2019 Conference of the North American Chapter of the Association for Computational Linguistics: Human Language Technologies, Volume 1 (Long and Short Papers)*, pages 4171–4186, Minneapolis, Minnesota. Association for Computational Linguistics.

Lev Finkelstein, Evgeniy Gabrilovich, Yossi Matias, Ehud Rivlin, Zach Solan, Gadi Wolfman, and Eytan Ruppin. 2002. Placing search in context: The concept revisited. *ACM Transactions on information systems*.

John C Gower. 1975. Generalized procrustes analysis. *Psychometrika*.

William L Hamilton, Jure Leskovec, and Dan Jurafsky. 2016. Diachronic word embeddings reveal statistical laws of semantic change. *arXiv preprint arXiv:1605.09096*.

Iris Hendrickx, Su Nam Kim, Zornitsa Kozareva, Preslav Nakov, Diarmuid Ó Séaghdha, Sebastian Padó, Marco Pennacchiotti, Lorenza Romano, and Stan Szpakowicz. 2010. SemEval-2010 task 8: Multi-way classification of semantic relations between pairs of nominals. In *Proceedings of the 5th International Workshop on Semantic Evaluation*, pages 33–38, Uppsala, Sweden. Association for Computational Linguistics.

Felix Hill, Roi Reichart, and Anna Korhonen. 2015. Simlex-999: Evaluating semantic models with (genuine) similarity estimation. *Computational Linguistics*.

Pratik Jawanpuria, Arjun Balgovind, Anoop Kunchukuttan, and Bamdev Mishra. 2019. Learning multilingual word embeddings in latent metric space: a geometric approach. *Transactions of the Association for Computational Linguistics (TACL).*

David A Jurgens, Peter D Turney, Saif M Mohammad, and Keith J Holyoak. 2012. Semeval-2012 task 2: Measuring degrees of relational similarity. In *Proceedings of the First Joint Conference on Lexical and Computational Semantics-Volume 1: Proceedings of the main conference and the shared task, and Volume 2: Proceedings of the Sixth International Workshop on Semantic Evaluation.*

Yova Kementchedjhieva, Sebastian Ruder, Ryan Cotterell, and Anders Søgaard. 2018. Generalizing procrustes analysis for better bilingual dictionary induction. In *The SIGNLL Conference on Computational Natural Language Learning (CoNLL).*

Douwe Kiela, Changhan Wang, and Kyunghyun Cho. 2018. Dynamic meta-embeddings for improved sentence representations. In *Proceedings of thr Conference on Empirical Methods in Natural Language Processing (EMNLP).*

Omer Levy, Yoav Goldberg, and Ido Dagan. 2015. Improving distributional similarity with lessons learned from word embeddings. *Transactions of the Association for Computational Linguistics (TACL).*

Bofang Li, Tao Liu, Zhe Zhao, Buzhou Tang, Aleksandr Drozd, Anna Rogers, and Xiaoyong Du. 2017. Investigating different syntactic context types and context representations for learning word embeddings. In *Proceedings of the 2017 Conference on Empirical Methods in Natural Language Processing*, pages 2421–2431, Copenhagen, Denmark. Association for Computational Linguistics.

Thang Luong, Richard Socher, and Christopher Manning. 2013. Better word representations with recursive neural networks for morphology. In *Proceedings of Conference on Computational Natural Language Learning.*

Andrew L. Maas, Raymond E. Daly, Peter T. Pham, Dan Huang, Andrew Y. Ng, and Christopher Potts. 2011. Learning word vectors for sentiment analysis. In *Proceedings of the 49th Annual Meeting of the Association for Computational Linguistics: Human Language Technologies*, pages 142–150, Portland, Oregon, USA. Association for Computational Linguistics.

Yehudit Meged, Avi Caciularu, Vered Shwartz, and Ido Dagan. 2020. Paraphrasing vs coreferring: Two sides of the same coin. In *Findings of the Association for Computational Linguistics: EMNLP 2020*, pages 4897–4907, Online. Association for Computational Linguistics.

Tomas Mikolov, Ilya Sutskever, Kai Chen, Greg S Corrado, and Jeff Dean. 2013a. Distributed representations of words and phrases and their compositionality. In *Advances in Neural Information Processing Systems (NIPS).*

Tomas Mikolov, Ilya Sutskever, Kai Chen, Greg S Corrado, and Jeff Dean. 2013b. Distributed representations of words and phrases and their compositionality. In *Advances in Neural Information Processing Systems (NIPS).*

Tomas Mikolov, Wen-tau Yih, and Geoffrey Zweig. 2013c. Linguistic regularities in continuous space word representations. In *Proceedings of the Conference of the North American Chapter of the Association for Computational Linguistics (NAACL).*

Avo Muromägi, Kairit Sirts, and Sven Laur. 2017. Linear ensembles of word embedding models. In *Proceedings of the 21st Nordic Conference on Computational Linguistics*, pages 96–104, Gothenburg, Sweden. Association for Computational Linguistics.

Bo Pang and Lillian Lee. 2004. A sentimental education: Sentiment analysis using subjectivity summarization based on minimum cuts. In *Proceedings of the 42nd Annual Meeting of the Association for Computational Linguistics (ACL-04)*, pages 271–278, Barcelona, Spain.

Bo Pang and Lillian Lee. 2005. Seeing stars: Exploiting class relationships for sentiment categorization with respect to rating scales. In *Proceedings of the 43rd Annual Meeting of the Association for Computational Linguistics (ACL'05)*, pages 115–124, Ann Arbor, Michigan. Association for Computational Linguistics.

Jeffrey Pennington, Richard Socher, and Christopher D. Manning. 2014. GloVe: global vectors for word representation. In *Empirical Methods in Natural Language Processing (EMNLP).*

Matthew Peters, Mark Neumann, Mohit Iyyer, Matt Gardner, Christopher Clark, Kenton Lee, and Luke Zettlemoyer. 2018. Deep contextualized word representations. In *Proceedings of the 2018 Conference of the North American Chapter of the Association for Computational Linguistics: Human Language Technologies, Volume 1 (Long Papers)*, pages 2227–2237, New Orleans, Louisiana. Association for Computational Linguistics.

Anna Rogers, Shashwath Hosur Ananthakrishna, and Anna Rumshisky. 2018. What's in your embedding, and how it predicts task performance. In *Proceedings of the 27th International Conference on Computational Linguistics*, pages 2690–2703, Santa Fe, New Mexico, USA. Association for Computational Linguistics.

Sebastian Ruder, Ryan Cotterell, Yova Kementchedjhieva, and Anders Søgaard. 2018. A discriminative latent-variable model for bilingual lexicon induction. *arXiv preprint arXiv:1808.09334.*

Erik F. Tjong Kim Sang and Fien De Meulder. 2003. Introduction to the CoNLL-2003 shared task: Language-independent named entity recognition. In *Proceedings of the Conference on Natural Language Learning (CoNLL)*.

Peter Schönemann. 1966. A generalized solution of the orthogonal procrustes problem. *Psychometrika*.

Hagai Taitelbaum, Gal Chechik, and Jacob Goldberger. 2019. A multi-pairwise extension of procrustes analysis for multilingual word translation. In *Conference on Empirical Methods in Natural Language Processing (EMNLP)*.

Chao Xing, Dong Wang, Chao Liu, and Yiye Lin. 2015. Normalized word embedding and orthogonal transform for bilingual word translation. In *Conference of the North American Chapter of the Association for Computational Linguistics: Human Language Technologies (NAACL)*.

Wenpeng Yin and Hinrich Schütze. 2016. Learning word meta-embeddings. In *Annual Meeting of the Association for Computational Linguistics (ACL)*.

Evaluating a Joint Training Approach for Learning Cross-lingual Embeddings with Sub-word Information without Parallel Corpora on Lower-resource Languages

Ali Hakimi Parizi and **Paul Cook**
Faculty of Computer Science, University of New Brunswick
Fredericton, NB E3B 5A3 Canada
{ahakimi,paul.cook}@unb.ca

Abstract

Cross-lingual word embeddings provide a way for information to be transferred between languages. In this paper we evaluate an extension of a joint training approach to learning cross-lingual embeddings that incorporates sub-word information during training. This method could be particularly well-suited to lower-resource and morphologically-rich languages because it can be trained on modest size monolingual corpora, and is able to represent out-of-vocabulary words (OOVs). We consider bilingual lexicon induction, including an evaluation focused on OOVs. We find that this method achieves improvements over previous approaches, particularly for OOVs.

1 Introduction

Word embeddings are an essential component in systems for many natural language processing tasks such as part-of-speech tagging (Al-Rfou' et al., 2013), dependency parsing (Chen and Manning, 2014) and named entity recognition (Pennington et al., 2014). Cross-lingual word representations provide a shared space for word embeddings of two languages, and make it possible to transfer information between languages (Ruder et al., 2019). A common approach to learn cross-lingual embeddings is to learn a matrix to map the embeddings of one language to another using supervised (e.g., Mikolov et al., 2013b), semi-supervised (Artetxe et al., 2017), or unsupervised (e.g., Lample et al., 2018) methods. These methods rely on the assumption that the geometric arrangement of embeddings in different languages is the same. However, it has been shown that this assumption does not always hold, and that methods which instead jointly train embeddings for two languages produce embeddings that are more isomorphic and achieve stronger results for bilingual lexicon induction (BLI, Ormazabal et al., 2019), a well-known intrinsic evaluation for cross-lingual word representations (Ruder et al., 2019; Anastasopoulos and Neubig, 2020). The approach of Ormazabal et al. uses a parallel corpus as a cross-lingual signal. Parallel corpora are, however, unavailable for many language pairs, particularly low-resource languages.

Duong et al. (2016) introduce a joint training approach that extends CBOW (Mikolov et al., 2013a) to learn cross-lingual word embeddings from modest size monolingual corpora, using a bilingual dictionary as the cross-lingual signal. Bilingual dictionaries are available for many language pairs, e.g., Panlex (Baldwin et al., 2010) provides translations for roughly 5700 languages. These training resource requirements suggest this method could be well-suited to lower-resource languages. However, this word-level approach is unable to form representations for out-of-vocabulary (OOV) words, which could be particularly common in the case of low-resource, and morphologically-rich, languages.

Hakimi Parizi and Cook (2020b) propose an extension of Duong et al. (2016) that incorporates sub-word information during training and therefore can generate representations for OOVs in the shared cross-lingual space. This method also does not require parallel corpora for training, and could therefore be particularly well-suited to lower-resource, and morphologically-rich, languages. However, Hakimi Parizi and Cook only evaluate on synthetic low-resource languages. We refer to the methods of Duong et al. and Hakimi Parizi and Cook as DUONG2016 and HAKIMI2020, respectively.

Most prior work on BLI focuses on in-vocabulary (IV) words and well-resourced languages (e.g., Artetxe et al., 2017; Ormazabal et al., 2019; Zhang et al., 2020), although there has been some work on OOVs (Hakimi Parizi and Cook, 2020a) and low-resource languages (Anastasopoulos and Neubig, 2020). In this paper, we evaluate HAKIMI2020 on BLI for twelve lower-resource

Proceedings of the 10th Conference on Lexical and Computational Semantics, pages 302–307
August 5–6, 2021, Bangkok, Thailand (online) ©2021 Association for Computational Linguistics

languages, and also consider an evaluation focused on OOVs. Our results indicate that HAKIMI2020 gives improvements over DUONG2016 and several strong baselines, particularly for OOVs.

2 Joint Training Incorporating Sub-word Information

Equation 1 shows the cost function for DUONG2016, which jointly learns embeddings for a word w_i and its translation $\bar{w}_i$, where h_i is a vector encoding the context, α is a weight parameter, and D_s and D_t are the source and target language vocabularies, respectively.

$$O = \sum_{i \in D_s \cup D_t} \Big(\alpha \log \sigma(u_{w_i}^T h_i) + (1-\alpha) \log \sigma(u_{\bar{w}_i}^T h_i) + \sum_{j=1}^{p} \mathbb{E}_{w_j \sim P_n(w)} \log \sigma(-u_{w_j}^T h_i)\Big) \quad (1)$$

Following Bojanowski et al. (2017), HAKIMI2020 modifies Equation 1 by including sub-word information during the joint training process as follows:

$$O = \sum_{i \in D_s \cup D_t} \Big(\alpha \log S(w_i, h_i) + (1-\alpha) \log S(\bar{w}_i, h_i) + \sum_{j=1}^{p} \mathbb{E}_{w_j \sim P_n(w)} \log -S(w_j, h_i)\Big) \quad (2)$$

$$S(w, h) = \frac{1}{|G_w|} \sum_{g \in G_w} z_g^T h \quad (3)$$

where G_w is the set of sub-words appearing in w and z_g is the sub-word embedding for g. h is calculated by averaging the representations for each word appearing in the context, where each word is itself represented by the average of its sub-word embeddings.

HAKIMI2020 use character n-grams as sub-words. Specifically, each word is augmented with special beginning and end of word markers, and then represented as a bag of character n-grams, using n-grams of length 3–6 characters. The entire word itself (with beginning and end of word markers) is also included among the sub-words.

Language	Family	# Tokens	# Dict. entries
Afrikaans	Germanic	25M	70k
Albanian	Albanian	21M	17k
Azerbaijani	Turkic	36M	25k
Bengali	Indic	26M	114k
Bosnian	Slavic	18M	23k
Croatian	Slavic	54M	388k
Estonian	Uralic	38M	201k
Greek	Greek	78M	253k
Hebrew	Semitic	143M	79k
Hindi	Indic	34M	296k
Hungarian	Uralic	133M	460k
Turkish	Turkic	79M	319k

Table 1: The language family, size of corpus, and size of Panlex dictionary, for each source language.

3 Experimental Setup

We consider BLI from twelve lower-resource source languages to English. The languages (shown in Table 1) were selected to cover a variety of language families, while having small to medium size Wikipedias and BLI evaluation datasets available. We compare HAKIMI2020 with DUONG2016, VECMAP (Artetxe et al., 2018), and MEEMI (Doval et al., 2018). In each case, we use cosine similarity to find the closest target language translations for a source language word. We evaluate using precision@N (Ruder et al., 2019) for $N = 1, 5, 10$.

3.1 Training Corpora and Dictionaries

The corpus for each language is a Wikipedia dump from 27 July 2020, cleaned using tools from Bojanowski et al. (2017), and tokenized using EuropalExtract (Ustaszewski, 2019), except for Bengali and Hindi, which are tokenized using NLTK (Bird et al., 2009). Because DUONG2016 and HAKIMI2020 can learn high quality cross-lingual embeddings from monolingual corpora of only 5M sentences each, we down-sample the English corpus for these two methods to 5M sentences.

DUONG2016 benefits from a relatively large training dictionary (Duong et al., 2016), therefore, for DUONG2016 and HAKIMI2020 we follow Duong et al. to create large training dictionaries by extracting translation pairs from Panlex. Details of the training corpora and Panlex dictionaries are shown in Table 1.

3.2 Baselines

We compare against two baselines: VECMAP (Artetxe et al., 2018), a supervised mapping-based method, and MEEMI (Doval et al., 2018), a post processing method. We consider various training corpora and dictionaries to create strong baselines.

Supervised mapping-based approaches tend to see a reduction in performance with seed lexicons larger than roughly 5k pairs (Vulić and Korhonen, 2016). Training translation pairs from MUSE (Lample et al., 2018) are therefore used, except for Azerbaijani, which is not included in MUSE, where training pairs from Anastasopoulos and Neubig (2020) are used. We first train VECMAP using these MUSE pairs, and embeddings learned from the full English corpus, to give this baseline access to as much training data as is available. We then consider this approach, but using the down-sampled English corpus. We found that the smaller English corpus gave higher precision@N (for $N = 1$, 5, and 10) for both the IV and OOV evaluations in Section 4. This could be due to the smaller corpus having a smaller vocabulary. We then also consider VECMAP trained using Panlex training pairs and embeddings learned from the down-sampled English corpus.

We next consider MEEMI applied to each of the three sets of cross-lingual embeddings obtained from VECMAP. In each case we train MEEMI using the same training pairs (MUSE or Panlex) that were used to train VECMAP. In Section 4 we report results for the baseline that performs best.

3.3 Hyper-Parameter Settings

Hakimi Parizi and Cook (2020b) show that DUONG2016 performs best using its default parameters, i.e., an embedding size of 200 and window size of 48, but that HAKIMI2020 performs better using an embedding size of 300 and window size of 20. We use these parameter settings here.

fastText is used to train monolingual embeddings for VECMAP and MEEMI. We use skipgram with its default settings, except the dimension of the embeddings is set to 300 (Bojanowski et al., 2017).

4 Experimental Results

In this section, we present results for BLI for IV words, and then OOV source language words.

4.1 BLI for In-Vocabulary Words

For these experiments we use MUSE test data for all languages except Azerbaijani, where we use test data from Anastasopoulos and Neubig (2020). Because our focus here is on IV words, we only consider translation pairs that are IV with respect to the embedding matrices learned from our corpora. We compare HAKIMI2020 with DUONG2016 and MEEMI trained using the down-sampled English corpus and MUSE training pairs, which performed best of the baselines considered for each evaluation measure. Results are shown in Table 2.[1]

Method	% Precision		
	@1	@5	@10
MEEMI	**38.64**	55.42	60.45
DUONG2016	22.12	45.71	52.08
HAKIMI2020	30.91	**56.00**	**62.24**

Table 2: Precision@N for BLI for IV words, averaged over the twelve languages. The best precision for each evaluation measure is shown in boldface.

HAKIMI2020 improves over DUONG2016, indicating that DUONG2016 can indeed be improved by incorporating sub-word information during training. Comparing HAKIMI2020 and MEEMI, the results are more mixed. In terms of precision@1, MEEMI substantially outperforms HAKIMI2020, although for precision@10 HAKIMI2020 outperforms MEEMI.

4.2 BLI for OOVs

Following Hakimi Parizi and Cook (2020a) we use Panlex to construct a test dataset of translation pairs in which the source language words are OOV and the target language words are IV. However, Hakimi Parizi and Cook observe that some translations in Panlex are noise. To avoid noisy translations, we use all translation pairs for which the source language word is OOV with respect to the embedding matrix, i.e., the embedding models have no direct knowledge of these words, but is attested in the source language corpus, i.e., there is evidence that this is indeed a word in the source language.[2] The resulting test datasets consist of between 806 translation pairs in the case of Azerbaijani to roughly 11k pairs for Hungarian.

Here we compare against the VECMAP baseline using the down-sampled English corpus and Panlex training pairs, which performed best of the baselines considered for each evaluation measure. For VECMAP, we follow Hakimi Parizi and Cook (2020a) by forming a representation

[1] Results for each of the twelve languages are available in the appendix.

[2] For each embedding method, we set the minimum frequency for words in the embedding matrix to 5; as such, all methods have the same source language vocabulary.

Language	Method	% Precision @1	@5	@10
Afrikaans	VECMAP	5.65	11.84	14.89
	COPY	10.68	-	-
	HAKIMI2020	9.42	21.80	27.41
	HAKIMI2020+COPY	**19.16**	**30.15**	**35.17**
Albanian	VECMAP	6.28	12.00	15.75
	COPY	5.62	-	-
	HAKIMI2020	7.93	15.20	18.61
	HAKIMI2020+COPY	**13.11**	**19.49**	**22.58**
Azerbaijani	VECMAP	3.60	8.93	11.41
	COPY	5.96	-	-
	HAKIMI2020	10.17	16.00	17.25
	HAKIMI2020+COPY	**10.92**	**19.35**	**21.96**
Bengali	VECMAP	1.60	4.50	6.00
	COPY	0.27	-	-
	HAKIMI2020	**5.31**	**10.95**	**13.85**
	HAKIMI2020+COPY	5.28	10.86	13.76
Bosnian	VECMAP	3.82	8.28	10.83
	COPY	21.23	-	-
	HAKIMI2020	8.17	15.71	18.58
	HAKIMI2020+COPY	**29.19**	**35.88**	**38.11**
Croatian	VECMAP	6.41	13.29	17.03
	COPY	4.35	-	-
	HAKIMI2020	11.86	24.70	30.13
	HAKIMI2020+COPY	**15.65**	**28.02**	**33.21**
Estonian	VECMAP	5.29	10.61	13.79
	COPY	7.56	-	-
	HAKIMI2020	8.15	18.79	23.66
	HAKIMI2020+COPY	**14.93**	**24.65**	**29.15**
Greek	VECMAP	6.66	14.30	17.91
	COPY	1.90	-	-
	HAKIMI2020	11.65	23.55	28.05
	HAKIMI2020+COPY	**13.50**	**25.15**	**29.58**
Hebrew	VECMAP	3.07	8.38	10.53
	COPY	11.15	-	-
	HAKIMI2020	8.18	17.08	20.55
	HAKIMI2020+COPY	**19.02**	**26.89**	**29.75**
Hindi	VECMAP	2.09	5.16	6.98
	COPY	0.06	-	-
	HAKIMI2020	4.57	11.64	15.39
	HAKIMI2020+COPY	**4.60**	**11.66**	**15.41**
Hungarian	VECMAP	4.30	9.49	12.50
	COPY	4.60	-	-
	HAKIMI2020	7.82	17.42	21.66
	HAKIMI2020+COPY	**11.62**	**20.56**	**24.53**
Turkish	VECMAP	3.39	7.23	9.62
	COPY	8.15	-	-
	HAKIMI2020	7.13	15.43	19.38
	HAKIMI2020+COPY	**14.27**	**21.31**	**24.77**
Average	VECMAP	4.35	9.50	12.27
	COPY	6.70	-	-
	HAKIMI2020	8.36	17.36	21.21
	HAKIMI2020+COPY	**14.27**	**22.83**	**26.50**

Table 3: Precision@N for BLI for OOV source language words. The best precision for each dataset and evaluation measure is shown in boldface.

for the OOV source language word from its subword embeddings, and then mapping it into the shared space. We cannot, however, compare directly against DUONG2016 because it is a word-level approach that cannot represent OOVs. We therefore instead compare against a baseline in which the OOV source language word is copied into the target language. This approach, referred to as COPY, could work well in the case of borrowings and named entities.[3]

Table 3 shows the results. HAKIMI2020 outperforms VECMAP for all languages and evaluation measures. This finding suggests that sub-word information can be more effectively transferred in a cross-lingual setting when sub-words are incorporated into the training process — as is the case for HAKIMI2020 — than when they are not — as for VECMAP here. Comparing HAKIMI2020 to COPY, although there are several languages for which COPY outperforms HAKIMI2020, on average, HAKIMI2020 performs better. In the cases that COPY outperforms HAKIMI2020, it appears to be largely related to the presence of English abbreviations in the source language Wikipedia dump.

Because of the relatively strong performance of COPY on several languages, we propose an approach that combines COPY and HAKIMI2020, referred to as HAKIMI2020+COPY. Given a source language word, we first check whether it is in the target language embedding matrix. If so, we assume it is a word that does not require translation (e.g., a named entity) and copy it into the target language.[4] If the source language word is not in the target language embedding matrix, we apply HAKIMI2020 to find the target language translation under this model. This approach improves over both COPY and HAKIMI2020 for all languages, except Bengali, and gives substantial improvements on average.[5] Although COPY is a very simple approach, it is complementary to HAKIMI2020, and the two approaches can be effectively combined to improve BLI for OOVs.

5 Conclusions

We evaluated an extension of a joint training approach to learning cross-lingual embeddings that incorporates sub-word information during training, which could be well-suited to lower-resource and morphologically-rich languages because it can be

[3]COPY only produces one target language candidate for a given source word, and as such we only compute precision@1 for this method.

[4]This assumption can be incorrect, e.g., Afrikaans *kits* is IV for English, but translates to English *moment*.

[5]We also observe that there is little improvement for HAKIMI2020+COPY over HAKIMI2020 on Hindi. For both Hindi and Bengali COPY achieves very low precision, and so little or no improvement can be obtained over HAKIMI2020 by combining COPY with HAKIMI2020.

trained on modest amounts of monolingual data and can represent OOVs. In two BLI tasks for twelve lower-resource languages focused on IV words and OOVs, we found that this method improved over previous approaches, particularly for OOVs. Evaluation data and code for learning the cross-lingual embeddings is available.[6]

In future work we plan to explore the impact of the target language on the quality of the cross-lingual embeddings, and in particular consider source and target languages from the same family. We further intend to evaluate these cross-lingual embeddings in down-stream tasks for low-resource languages, such as language modelling (Adams et al., 2017) and part-of-speech tagging (Fang and Cohn, 2017), and to compare against approaches based on contextualized language models.

References

Oliver Adams, Adam Makarucha, Graham Neubig, Steven Bird, and Trevor Cohn. 2017. Cross-lingual word embeddings for low-resource language modeling. In *Proceedings of the 15th Conference of the European Chapter of the Association for Computational Linguistics: Volume 1, Long Papers*, pages 937–947, Valencia, Spain. Association for Computational Linguistics.

Rami Al-Rfou', Bryan Perozzi, and Steven Skiena. 2013. Polyglot: Distributed word representations for multilingual NLP. In *Proceedings of the Seventeenth Conference on Computational Natural Language Learning*, pages 183–192, Sofia, Bulgaria. Association for Computational Linguistics.

Antonios Anastasopoulos and Graham Neubig. 2020. Should all cross-lingual embeddings speak English? In *Proceedings of the 58th Annual Meeting of the Association for Computational Linguistics*, pages 8658–8679, Online. Association for Computational Linguistics.

Mikel Artetxe, Gorka Labaka, and Eneko Agirre. 2017. Learning bilingual word embeddings with (almost) no bilingual data. In *Proceedings of the 55th Annual Meeting of the Association for Computational Linguistics (Volume 1: Long Papers)*, pages 451–462, Vancouver, Canada. Association for Computational Linguistics.

Mikel Artetxe, Gorka Labaka, and Eneko Agirre. 2018. Generalizing and improving bilingual word embedding mappings with a multi-step framework of linear transformations. In *Proceedings of the Thirty-Second AAAI Conference on Artificial Intelligence*, pages 5012–5019.

[6]`https://github.com/Cons13411/XLing_Subword`

Timothy Baldwin, Jonathan Pool, and Susan Colowick. 2010. PanLex and LEXTRACT: Translating all words of all languages of the world. In *Coling 2010: Demonstrations*, pages 37–40, Beijing, China. Coling 2010 Organizing Committee.

Steven Bird, Edward Loper, and Ewan Klein. 2009. *Natural Language Processing with Python*. O'Reilly Media Inc.

Piotr Bojanowski, Edouard Grave, Armand Joulin, and Tomas Mikolov. 2017. Enriching word vectors with subword information. *Transactions of the Association for Computational Linguistics*, 5:135–146.

Danqi Chen and Christopher Manning. 2014. A fast and accurate dependency parser using neural networks. In *Proceedings of the 2014 Conference on Empirical Methods in Natural Language Processing (EMNLP)*, pages 740–750, Doha, Qatar. Association for Computational Linguistics.

Yerai Doval, Jose Camacho-Collados, Luis Espinosa-Anke, and Steven Schockaert. 2018. Improving cross-lingual word embeddings by meeting in the middle. In *Proceedings of the 2018 Conference on Empirical Methods in Natural Language Processing*, pages 294–304, Brussels, Belgium. Association for Computational Linguistics.

Long Duong, Hiroshi Kanayama, Tengfei Ma, Steven Bird, and Trevor Cohn. 2016. Learning crosslingual word embeddings without bilingual corpora. In *Proceedings of the 2016 Conference on Empirical Methods in Natural Language Processing*, pages 1285–1295, Austin, Texas. Association for Computational Linguistics.

Meng Fang and Trevor Cohn. 2017. Model transfer for tagging low-resource languages using a bilingual dictionary. In *Proceedings of the 55th Annual Meeting of the Association for Computational Linguistics (Volume 2: Short Papers)*, pages 587–593, Vancouver, Canada. Association for Computational Linguistics.

Ali Hakimi Parizi and Paul Cook. 2020a. Evaluating sub-word embeddings in cross-lingual models. In *Proceedings of The 12th Language Resources and Evaluation Conference*, pages 2712–2719, Marseille, France. European Language Resources Association.

Ali Hakimi Parizi and Paul Cook. 2020b. Joint training for learning cross-lingual embeddings with subword information without parallel corpora. In *Proceedings of the Ninth Joint Conference on Lexical and Computational Semantics*, pages 39–49, Barcelona, Spain (Online). Association for Computational Linguistics.

Guillaume Lample, Alexis Conneau, Marc'Aurelio Ranzato, Ludovic Denoyer, and Hervé Jégou. 2018. Word translation without parallel data. In *6th International Conference on Learning Representations,*

ICLR 2018, Vancouver, BC, Canada, April 30 - May 3, 2018, Conference Track Proceedings. OpenReview.net.

Tomas Mikolov, Kai Chen, Greg Corrado, and Jeffrey Dean. 2013a. Efficient estimation of word representations in vector space. In *Proceedings of Workshop at the International Conference on Learning Representations, 2013*, Scottsdale, USA.

Tomas Mikolov, Quoc V. Le, and Ilya Sutskever. 2013b. Exploiting similarities among languages for machine translation. *CoRR*, abs/1309.4168.

Aitor Ormazabal, Mikel Artetxe, Gorka Labaka, Aitor Soroa, and Eneko Agirre. 2019. Analyzing the limitations of cross-lingual word embedding mappings. In *Proceedings of the 57th Annual Meeting of the Association for Computational Linguistics*, pages 4990–4995, Florence, Italy. Association for Computational Linguistics.

Jeffrey Pennington, Richard Socher, and Christopher Manning. 2014. Glove: Global vectors for word representation. In *Proceedings of the 2014 Conference on Empirical Methods in Natural Language Processing (EMNLP)*, pages 1532–1543, Doha, Qatar. Association for Computational Linguistics.

Sebastian Ruder, Ivan Vuliundefined, and Anders Søgaard. 2019. A survey of cross-lingual word embedding models. *Journal of Artificial Intelligence Research*, 65(1):569–630.

Michael Ustaszewski. 2019. Optimising the europarl corpus for translation studies with the europarlextract toolkit. *Perspectives*, 27(1):107–123.

Ivan Vulić and Anna Korhonen. 2016. On the role of seed lexicons in learning bilingual word embeddings. In *Proceedings of the 54th Annual Meeting of the Association for Computational Linguistics (Volume 1: Long Papers)*, pages 247–257, Berlin, Germany. Association for Computational Linguistics.

Mozhi Zhang, Yoshinari Fujinuma, Michael J. Paul, and Jordan Boyd-Graber. 2020. Why overfitting isn't always bad: Retrofitting cross-lingual word embeddings to dictionaries. In *Proceedings of the 58th Annual Meeting of the Association for Computational Linguistics*, pages 2214–2220, Online. Association for Computational Linguistics.

Adversarial Training for Machine Reading Comprehension with Virtual Embeddings

Ziqing Yang[1†], Yiming Cui[2,1†], Chenglei Si[3], Wanxiang Che[2], Ting Liu[2], Shijin Wang[1], Guoping Hu[1]

[1]State Key Laboratory of Cognitive Intelligence, iFLYTEK Research, China
[2] Research Center for SCIR, Harbin Institute of Technology, Harbin, China
[3] University of Maryland, College Park MD, USA
†{zqyang5,ymcui}@iflytek.com

Abstract

Adversarial training (AT) as a regularization method has proved its effectiveness on various tasks. Though there are successful applications of AT on some NLP tasks, the distinguishing characteristics of NLP tasks have not been exploited. In this paper, we aim to apply AT on machine reading comprehension (MRC) tasks. Furthermore, we adapt AT for MRC tasks by proposing a novel adversarial training method called PQAT that perturbs the embedding matrix instead of word vectors. To differentiate the roles of passages and questions, PQAT uses additional virtual P/Q-embedding matrices to gather the global perturbations of words from passages and questions separately. We test the method on a wide range of MRC tasks, including span-based extractive RC and multiple-choice RC. The results show that adversarial training is effective universally, and PQAT further improves the performance.

Passage: ... *The rock cycle is an important concept in geology which illustrates the relationships between these three types of rock, and magma. When a rock crystallizes from melt (magma and/or lava), it is an igneous rock. ...*
Question: *An igneous* ***rock*** *is a* ***rock*** *that crystallizes from what?*

Table 1: An example from the SQuAD dataset. We highlight two words *rock* and *igneous* for better demonstration. The words with the same color are injected with the same perturbation by PQAT. The different occurrences of the same word (for example, *rock* in passage and question) are perturbed differently depending on their roles.

1 Introduction

Neural networks have achieved superior performance on many tasks, but they are vulnerable to *adversarial examples* (Szegedy et al., 2014) – examples that have been mixed with certain perturbations. *Adversarial training* (AT) (Goodfellow et al., 2015) uses both clean and adversarial examples to improve the robustness of the model for image classification.

In the field of NLP, Miyato et al. (2017) have applied adversarial training on text classification tasks and improved the model performance. From then on, many AT methods has been proposed (Wu et al., 2017; Yasunaga et al., 2018; Bekoulis et al., 2018; Zhu et al., 2020; Jiang et al., 2019; Pereira et al., 2020; Liu et al., 2020). They mostly adopt a general AT strategy, but focus less on the adaptation of AT to NLP tasks. To explore this adaptation, in this work, we aim to apply adversarial training on machine reading comprehension (MRC) tasks, which exhibit complex NLP characteristics.

The objective of MRC is to let a machine read the given passages and ask it to answer the related questions. There are several types of MRC tasks. In this work we focus on span-based extractive RC (Rajpurkar et al., 2016, 2018; Yang et al., 2018) and multiple-choice RC (Lai et al., 2017). To apply adversarial training on MRC tasks, we notice that there are several salient characteristics of MRC compared to other tasks such as image classification: (1) The inputs are discrete. Unlike pixels, which can take continuous values, words are discrete tokens. (2) The tokens in the input sequences are not independent. A word may occur in an input sequence several times. After the embedding layer, these occurrences are represented by the word vectors with the same value and hold the same semantic meaning (although the word may be polysemous). (3) The roles of passages and questions are different. Given a question as the query, the model needs to look up the correct answer in the passage.

People have utilized the first characteristic to apply adversarial training by perturbing input word vectors instead of tokens. However, the second and third characteristics have been largely ignored. For

Proceedings of the 10th Conference on Lexical and Computational Semantics, pages 308–313
August 5–6, 2021, Bangkok, Thailand (online)

example, in Table 1, which is a passage-question pair from the SQuAD dataset, the word *rock* has appeared multiple times. In the standard adversarial training, the perturbations added to each occurrence of *rock* are different, ignoring the fact that they share the same meaning. On the other hand, the multiple occurrences of the same word in the passage and question play different roles, such as the *rock* in the passage and question. It is appropriate to treat them differently.

To take the second and the third characteristics into consideration, we propose a novel adversarial training method called **PQAT**. The core of PQAT is the virtual P/Q-embeddings, which are two independent embedding spaces for passages and questions. Each time we calculate perturbations, P/Q-embeddings gather the perturbations from passages and questions for each word, then generate a global and role-aware perturbation for each word from passages and questions separately. For example, in Table 1, the perturbations on all the occurrences of *rock* in the passage and question will be gathered into two matrices separately, forming global and role-aware perturbations of *rock*. PQAT is as efficient as the standard AT with nearly no extra time cost. Also, The virtual P/Q-embeddings are only used during training. They are discarded once the training is finished. Thus PQAT does not increase the model size and inference time for predictions.

We have applied adversarial training on several MRC tasks, including span-based extractive RC and multiple-choice RC. Results show that adversarial training improves the MRC model performance universally and consistently, even over the strong pre-trained model baseline. Furthermore, the PQAT method outperforms the standard AT on both normal datasets and adversarial datasets. Lastly, our results verify the usefulness of incorporating information of task form into the design of the adversarial training method.

2 Standard Adversarial Training

Adversarial training first constructs adversarial examples by generating worst-case perturbations that maximize the current loss, then minimize the loss on those adversarial examples. In NLP tasks, a popular approach to generate perturbations is to perturb word vectors from the embedding layer (Miyato et al., 2017). We denote the input token sequence as X and the operation of looking up in an embedding layer $\boldsymbol{E}$ as $emb(\boldsymbol{E}, \cdot)$. The objective

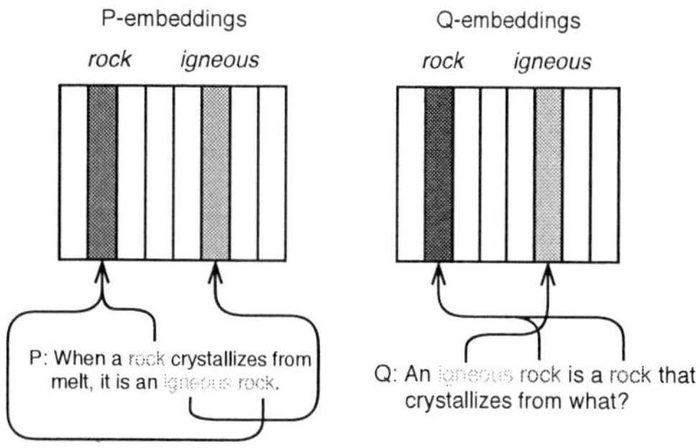

Figure 1: P/Q-emebddings collect the perturbations on each word from passages and questions separately.

of AT is

$$\min_{\theta,E} \mathbb{E}_{(X,y)\sim\mathcal{D}} \left[\max_{\|\delta\|<\epsilon} \mathcal{L}(f_\theta(X_{vec} + \delta), y) \right] \quad (1)$$

where $f_\theta(\cdot)$ is the model parametrized by θ excluding word embedding layer; $X_{vec} = emb(\boldsymbol{E}, X)$ is the word vectors of input sequence. $\mathcal{L}$ is the loss function. We perturb the word vectors with the adversarial perturbations δ.

δ can be estimated by linearizing $\mathcal{L}(f_\theta(X_{vec} + \delta), y)$ around X and perform the multiple-step projected gradient descent (PGD) (Madry et al., 2018):

$$\delta_{t+1} = \Pi_{\|\delta\|\leq\epsilon}(\delta_t + \alpha g_t / \|g_t\|) \quad (2)$$

$$g_t = \nabla_\delta \mathcal{L}(f_\theta(X_{vec} + \delta), y)|_{\delta=\delta_t} \quad (3)$$

where t is the gradient descent step, $\Pi_{\|\delta\|\leq\epsilon}$ denotes projection δ back onto the ϵ-ball. g_t is the gradient of the loss with respect to perturbation δ. The more gradient descent steps, the better approximation of δ, but also more expensive in computation.

3 Adversarial Training for MRC

In the above algorithm, when generating the perturbations on X_{vec} through backward propagation, each word vector X^i_{vec} is perturbed independently, like the pixels in an image. It ignores the semantic relationship among the word vectors of a word's different occurrences. To make the perturbation on each occurrence aware of other occurrences of the same word, we adapt AT by gathering not only the perturbations on each word vector, but also the perturbations on the embedding matrix. The latter can be seen as the global perturbations, which provide context-insensitive semantic information.

The global perturbations are rather coarse-grained, since all the occurrences of the same word receive the same global perturbation. Note that in MRC tasks, words in passages and questions play different roles. Thus, to keep this information, we distinguish the words in passages and questions by creating two *virtual* embedding matrices $\boldsymbol{P}$ and $\boldsymbol{Q}$: P-embedding matrix $\boldsymbol{P}$ collects the perturbations of all the words from the passages; Q-embedding matrix $\boldsymbol{Q}$ for the questions. We give an illustration in Figure 1. P/Q-embedding matrices are *virtual* since they only provide perturbations, no the real word vectors. During training, perturbations from virtual embeddings and word vectors are summed up to form the adversarial input Z_{vec}. The final objective is

$$\min_{\theta,E} \mathbb{E}_{(X,y)\sim\mathcal{D}} \left[\max_{\|\delta\|<\epsilon} \mathcal{L}(f_\theta(Z_{vec}), y) \right] \quad (4)$$

$$Z_{vec} = [X^P_{vec} + P_{vec}; X^Q_{vec} + Q_{vec}] + \delta \quad (5)$$

$P_{vec} = emb(\boldsymbol{P}, X^P)$, $Q_{vec} = emb(\boldsymbol{Q}, X^Q)$ are the perturbations from the virtual embeddings. X^P and X^Q stand for the passage and question sections in X. $[\cdot;\cdot]$ denotes concatenation. In this way, we have generated fine-grained local perturbations δ by standard AT, and global role-aware perturbations P_{vec} and Q_{vec} by the virtual P/Q-embeddings. We call the later process as **PQAT**, which is the main adaptation of adversarial training for MRC.

We list the overall algorithm of adversarial training for MRC in Algorithm 1. We initialize $\boldsymbol{P}$ and $\boldsymbol{Q}$ with the gaussian distribution. For each batch, we perform K-step gradient descent (line 9–22): we look up the original word vectors and P/Q-embedding vectors from the embedding layer $\boldsymbol{E}$ and the P/Q-embedding matrices. The adversarial inputs are constructed by summing them with local perturbations δ. Then we compute the gradients of model parameters $\boldsymbol{g_t}$, local perturbations $\boldsymbol{g_\delta}$ and P/Q-embedding matrices $\boldsymbol{g_P}$ and $\boldsymbol{g_Q}$. These gradients can be calculated in a single backward pass. Lastly, we update the virtual embeddings and local perturbations (line 18–21).

Note that P/Q-embedding matrices serve as the containers for perturbations. When the training is finished, P/Q-embedding matrices are no longer needed and can be discarded.

ϵ_δ, ϵ_P and ϵ_Q control the strengths of standard AT and PQAT. If $\epsilon_\delta = 0$, we have a pure P/Q-embeddings based adversarial training, i.e., PQAT; while if $\epsilon_P = \epsilon_Q = 0$, we recover the standard AT.

Algorithm 1: Adversarial Training for Machine Reading Comprehension

Notation: V is the vocabulary size; D is the embedding dimension.
Input: Training samples $\mathcal{D} = \{(X, y)\}$, P/Q-embedding matrices $\boldsymbol{P}, \boldsymbol{Q} \in \mathbb{R}^{V\times D}$, initialization variance σ, perturbation strength $\{\epsilon_\delta, \epsilon_P, \epsilon_Q\}$, adversarial steps K.

1 *Initialize P/Q-embedding matrices*
2 $\boldsymbol{P} \leftarrow \mathcal{N}(0, \sigma^2 I)$, $\boldsymbol{Q} \leftarrow \mathcal{N}(0, \sigma^2 I)$
3 **for** *batch* $B \subset \mathcal{D}$ **do**
4   *Normalize P/Q-embedding matrices*
5     $\boldsymbol{P} \leftarrow (\boldsymbol{P} - mean(\boldsymbol{P})/std(\boldsymbol{P}) \cdot \sigma$
6     $\boldsymbol{Q} \leftarrow (\boldsymbol{Q} - mean(\boldsymbol{Q}))/std(\boldsymbol{Q}) \cdot \sigma$
7   *Initialize perturbation and gradient*
8     $\delta \leftarrow \frac{1}{\sqrt{D}} U(-\sigma, \sigma)$, $\boldsymbol{g_0} \leftarrow 0$
9   **for** $t = 1, \ldots, K$ **do**
10         $X_{vec} = emb(\boldsymbol{E}, X)$
11         $P_{vec} = emb(\boldsymbol{P}, X^P)$
12         $Q_{vec} = emb(\boldsymbol{Q}, X^Q)$
13         $Z_{vec} = X_{vec} + P_{vec} + Q_{vec} + \delta$
14         $\boldsymbol{g_t} = \boldsymbol{g_{t-1}} + \mathbb{E}[\nabla_{\theta,\boldsymbol{E}} \mathcal{L}(f_\theta(Z_{vec}), y)]$
15         $\boldsymbol{g_\delta} = \mathbb{E}[\nabla_\delta \mathcal{L}(f_\theta(Z_{vec}), y)]$
16         $\boldsymbol{g_P} = \mathbb{E}[\nabla_{\boldsymbol{P}} \mathcal{L}(f_\theta(Z_{vec}), y)]$
17         $\boldsymbol{g_Q} = \mathbb{E}[\nabla_{\boldsymbol{Q}} \mathcal{L}(f_\theta(Z_{vec}), y)]$
18         $\delta \leftarrow \delta + \boldsymbol{g_\delta} / \|\boldsymbol{g_\delta}\|_2 \cdot \|X_{vec}\|_2 \, \epsilon_\delta$
19   *Update with token-wise normalization*
20         $P^i \leftarrow P^i + \boldsymbol{g^i_P} / \|\boldsymbol{g^i_P}\|_2 \cdot \|X^i_{vec}\|_2 \, \epsilon_P$
21         $Q^i \leftarrow Q^i + \boldsymbol{g^i_Q} / \|\boldsymbol{g^i_Q}\|_2 \cdot \|X^i_{vec}\|_2 \, \epsilon_Q$
22   **end**
23     $\{\theta, \boldsymbol{E}\} \leftarrow$ AdamUpdate($\{\theta, \boldsymbol{E}\}, \boldsymbol{g_K}$)
24 **end**

4 Experiments Setup

Datasets. We perform experiments on several English MRC tasks, including span-based extractive MRC tasks – SQuAD 1.1 (Rajpurkar et al., 2016), SQuAD 2.0 (Rajpurkar et al., 2018), HotpotQA (Yang et al., 2018), and multiple-choice MRC task RACE (Lai et al., 2017). We also test model robustness on the adversarial datasets AddSent andAddOneSent (Jia and Liang, 2017).

Model Settings. We build the MRC model with RoBERTa (Liu et al., 2019), following the standard model structure for SQuAD and RACE (Devlin et al., 2018). For HotpotQA, we follow the model in Shao et al. (2020). It uses RoBERTa as the encoder followed by a multi-task prediction layer. We denote the passage as P and the question as Q. To construct the inputs, for span-based extractive RC, we concatenate each P and Q with model-dependent special tokens; for multiple-choice RC with m options for each example, we append each option to the concatenation of P and Q, and construct m input sequences from each example.

When applying AT or PQAT, we only perturb

Model	SQuAD 1.1 EM	SQuAD 1.1 F1	SQuAD 2.0 EM	SQuAD 2.0 F1	HotpotQA joint EM	HotpotQA joint F1	RACE Acc
BASE setting							
RoBERTa	84.72	91.54	79.77	83.18	41.70	69.30	74.75
PQAT	**85.87**	**92.33**	**81.66**	**84.79**	**43.03**	**70.40**	**76.32**
LARGE setting							
RoBERTa	87.76	93.90	85.67	88.86	45.91†	73.93†	84.66
PQAT	**88.32**	**94.34**	**86.35**	**89.49**	**46.79**	**74.63**	**86.02**

Table 2: Results on the development sets of SQuAD 1.1, SQuAD 2.0 and HotpotQA, and results on the test set of RACE. †: the results are taken from Shao et al. (2020).

Model	SQuAD 1.1 EM	SQuAD 2.0 EM	RACE Acc
BASE setting			
PQAT	85.87 (0.08)	**81.66** (0.21)	76.32 (0.32)
PQAT + AT	**85.96** (0.10)	81.11 ↓ (0.14)	**76.50** (0.35)
AT	85.64 ↓ (0.15)	81.23 ↓ (0.30)	75.94 ↓ (0.37)

Table 3: Comparison of PQAT, standard AT and the combination. AT is short for Standard AT. Arrows indicate the drops relative to the PQAT. Numbers in the parentheses are the standard deviations.

Model	AddSent	AddOneSent	Dev
R.M-Reader†	58.5	67.0	86.6
KAR‡	60.1	72.3	83.5
ALUM$_{\text{BERT-BASE}}$§	60.4	69.8	90.8
RoBERTa$_{\text{BASE}}$	59.7	68.8	91.5
PQAT	**64.7**	**73.6**	**92.3**
AT	63.2	72.6	92.1

Table 4: Model performance (F1) on AddSent, AddOneSent and SQuAD 1.1 dev set. AT is short for Standard AT. †:Wang and Jiang (2018). ‡: Hu et al. (2018), §: Liu et al. (2020).

the word embeddings and leave the position embeddings unchanged. For PQAT on RACE, we let the Q-embedding matrix collect perturbations from both questions and options.

Training Settings and Hyperparameters. All the models are implemented with Transformers (Wolf et al., 2019) and trained on a single Nvidia V100 GPU. To improve the stability and reduce the uncertainty of the results, we run each experiment four times with different seeds and report the mean value of performance. We use AdamW as our optimizer with batch size 24 and learning rate 3e-5 for RoBERTa$_{\text{BASE}}$ and 2e-5 or 1e-5 for RoBERTa$_{\text{LARGE}}$. The maximum number of epochs is set to 3 for SQuAD and 5 for RACE and HotpotQA. A linear learning rate decay schedule with warmup ratio 0.1 was used. For PQAT, ϵ_δ is set to 0, ϵ_P and ϵ_Q is set to 4e-2 for RACE and 2e-2 for other tasks. The variance σ is 1e-2. We set the number of gradient descent steps $K = 2$ to balance speed and performance.

5 Results

5.1 Overall Results

The overall results are summarized in Table 2, where we compare PQAT with the baseline. PQAT is able to boost model performance across all MRC tasks and outperforms the RoBERTa baseline significantly. On HotpotQA, which is a complicated MRC task that features multi-hop questions and asks for multiple kinds of predictions, PQAT still outperforms the baseline by 1.3/1.1 on Joint EM/Joint F1. On RACE, PQAT improves the performance significantly by 1.5% in accuracy. The universal improvements on various kinds of MRC tasks prove the wide applicability of PQAT.

5.2 Comparison

We compare different adversarial training methods and their combinations by tuning the strengths of perturbations $\{\epsilon_\delta, \epsilon_P, \epsilon_Q\}$. The results are in Table 3. The underlined scores are the ones reported in Table 2. Firstly, to test the effectiveness of standard AT, we disable PQAT with $\epsilon_P = \epsilon_Q = 0$ and enable standard AT with ϵ_δ =2e-3 for RACE and 1e-2 for other tasks [1]. Other settings are unchanged, and we still follow Algorithm 1. PQAT consistently outperforms standard AT on the three tasks. Then we enable both PQAT and standard AT by setting all the strengths $\{\epsilon_\delta, \epsilon_P, \epsilon_Q\}$ to non-zero values. The performance gets slightly better on SQuAD 1.1 and RACE, but gets worse on SQuAD 2.0.

[1]We have searched from 1e-3 to 1e-1 and taken the best value.

Compared with the standard AT, PQAT achieves higher performance by itself. Therefore PQAT could be a better alternative to applying adversarial training on MRC tasks.

5.3 Robustness on Adversarial Datasets

We assess the robustness of MRC models with AddSent and AddOneSent. AddSent and AddOneSent are two adversarial datasets built on SQuAD 1.1. In both datasets, passages are appended with distracting sentences. MRC models that heavily rely on text matching may be easily fooled to predict wrong answers from the distracting sentences.

The results are shown in Table 4. With the standard adversarial training (AT), the MRC model improves its robustness by about 5% over RoBERTa$_{\mathrm{BASE}}$ in F1. PQAT further improves the performance over AT by about 1% on both AddSent and AddOneSent.

6 Conclusion

We have applied adversarial training on a wide range of MRC tasks, including span-based extractive RC and multiple-choice RC. Especially, we have proposed a novel adversarial training method PQAT, which uses virtual P/Q-embedding matrices to generate global and role-aware perturbations that consider the characteristics of MRC tasks. Our experiments demonstrate that adversarial training improves the MRC model performance universally and consistently, even over the strong pre-trained model baseline. The PQAT method further improves the model performance over the standard AT on both normal datasets and adversarial datasets.

Acknowledgments

We would like to thank all anonymous reviewers for their valuable comments on our work. This work is funded by National Key R&D Program of China (No.2018YFC0831601).

References

Giannis Bekoulis, Johannes Deleu, Thomas Demeester, and Chris Develder. 2018. Adversarial training for multi-context joint entity and relation extraction. In *Proceedings of the 2018 Conference on Empirical Methods in Natural Language Processing*, pages 2830–2836, Brussels, Belgium. Association for Computational Linguistics.

Jacob Devlin, Ming-Wei Chang, Kenton Lee, and Kristina Toutanova. 2018. Bert: Pre-training of deep bidirectional transformers for language understanding. *arXiv preprint arXiv:1810.04805*.

Ian Goodfellow, Jonathon Shlens, and Christian Szegedy. 2015. Explaining and harnessing adversarial examples. In *International Conference on Learning Representations*.

Minghao Hu, Yuxing Peng, Zhen Huang, Xipeng Qiu, Furu Wei, and Ming Zhou. 2018. Reinforced mnemonic reader for machine reading comprehension. In *Proceedings of the Twenty-Seventh International Joint Conference on Artificial Intelligence, IJCAI 2018, July 13-19, 2018, Stockholm, Sweden.*, pages 4099–4106.

Robin Jia and Percy Liang. 2017. Adversarial examples for evaluating reading comprehension systems. In *Proceedings of the 2017 Conference on Empirical Methods in Natural Language Processing*, pages 2021–2031, Copenhagen, Denmark. Association for Computational Linguistics.

Haoming Jiang, Pengcheng He, Weizhu Chen, Xiaodong Liu, Jianfeng Gao, and Tuo Zhao. 2019. SMART: robust and efficient fine-tuning for pretrained natural language models through principled regularized optimization. *CoRR*, abs/1911.03437.

Guokun Lai, Qizhe Xie, Hanxiao Liu, Yiming Yang, and Eduard Hovy. 2017. RACE: Large-scale ReAding comprehension dataset from examinations. In *Proceedings of the 2017 Conference on Empirical Methods in Natural Language Processing*, pages 785–794, Copenhagen, Denmark. Association for Computational Linguistics.

Xiaodong Liu, Hao Cheng, Pengcheng He, Weizhu Chen, Yu Wang, Hoifung Poon, and Jianfeng Gao. 2020. Adversarial training for large neural language models. *CoRR*, abs/2004.08994.

Yinhan Liu, Myle Ott, Naman Goyal, Jingfei Du, Mandar Joshi, Danqi Chen, Omer Levy, Mike Lewis, Luke Zettlemoyer, and Veselin Stoyanov. 2019. Roberta: A robustly optimized BERT pretraining approach. *CoRR*, abs/1907.11692.

Aleksander Madry, Aleksandar Makelov, Ludwig Schmidt, Dimitris Tsipras, and Adrian Vladu. 2018. Towards deep learning models resistant to adversarial attacks. In *6th International Conference on Learning Representations, ICLR 2018, Vancouver, BC, Canada, April 30 - May 3, 2018, Conference Track Proceedings*. OpenReview.net.

Takeru Miyato, Andrew M. Dai, and Ian J. Goodfellow. 2017. Adversarial training methods for semi-supervised text classification. In *5th International Conference on Learning Representations, ICLR 2017, Toulon, France, April 24-26, 2017, Conference Track Proceedings*.

Lis Pereira, Xiaodong Liu, Fei Cheng, Masayuki Asahara, and Ichiro Kobayashi. 2020. Adversarial training for commonsense inference. *CoRR*, abs/2005.08156.

Pranav Rajpurkar, Robin Jia, and Percy Liang. 2018. Know what you don't know: Unanswerable questions for SQuAD. In *Proceedings of the 56th Annual Meeting of the Association for Computational Linguistics (Volume 2: Short Papers)*, pages 784–789, Melbourne, Australia. Association for Computational Linguistics.

Pranav Rajpurkar, Jian Zhang, Konstantin Lopyrev, and Percy Liang. 2016. SQuAD: 100,000+ questions for machine comprehension of text. In *Proceedings of the 2016 Conference on Empirical Methods in Natural Language Processing*, pages 2383–2392, Austin, Texas. Association for Computational Linguistics.

Nan Shao, Yiming Cui, Ting Liu, Shijin Wang, and Guoping Hu. 2020. Is Graph Structure Necessary for Multi-hop Question Answering? In *Proceedings of the 2020 Conference on Empirical Methods in Natural Language Processing (EMNLP)*, pages 7187–7192, Online. Association for Computational Linguistics.

Christian Szegedy, Wojciech Zaremba, Ilya Sutskever, Joan Bruna, Dumitru Erhan, Ian J. Goodfellow, and Rob Fergus. 2014. Intriguing properties of neural networks. In *2nd International Conference on Learning Representations, ICLR 2014, Banff, AB, Canada, April 14-16, 2014, Conference Track Proceedings*.

Chao Wang and Hui Jiang. 2018. Exploring machine reading comprehension with explicit knowledge. *CoRR*, abs/1809.03449.

Thomas Wolf, Lysandre Debut, Victor Sanh, Julien Chaumond, Clement Delangue, Anthony Moi, Pierric Cistac, Tim Rault, R'emi Louf, Morgan Funtowicz, and Jamie Brew. 2019. Huggingface's transformers: State-of-the-art natural language processing. *ArXiv*, abs/1910.03771.

Yi Wu, David Bamman, and Stuart Russell. 2017. Adversarial training for relation extraction. In *Proceedings of the 2017 Conference on Empirical Methods in Natural Language Processing*, pages 1778–1783, Copenhagen, Denmark. Association for Computational Linguistics.

Zhilin Yang, Peng Qi, Saizheng Zhang, Yoshua Bengio, William W. Cohen, Ruslan Salakhutdinov, and Christopher D. Manning. 2018. Hotpotqa: A dataset for diverse, explainable multi-hop question answering. In *Proceedings of the 2018 Conference on Empirical Methods in Natural Language Processing, Brussels, Belgium, October 31 - November 4, 2018*, pages 2369–2380.

Michihiro Yasunaga, Jungo Kasai, and Dragomir Radev. 2018. Robust multilingual part-of-speech tagging via adversarial training. In *Proceedings of the 2018 Conference of the North American Chapter of the Association for Computational Linguistics: Human Language Technologies, Volume 1 (Long Papers)*, pages 976–986, New Orleans, Louisiana. Association for Computational Linguistics.

Chen Zhu, Yu Cheng, Zhe Gan, Siqi Sun, Tom Goldstein, and Jingjing Liu. 2020. Freelb: Enhanced adversarial training for natural language understanding. In *8th International Conference on Learning Representations, ICLR 2020, Addis Ababa, Ethiopia, April 26-30, 2020*. OpenReview.net.

Author Index

Association for Computational Linguistics
209 N. Eighth Street
Stroudsburg, Pennsylvania 18360

ISBN 978-1-7138-3388-8

CURRAN ASSOCIATES INC.
proceedings
.com